Emma J

CONSUMER BEHAVIOUR

MARGARET CRAIG-LEES • SALLY JOY • BEVERLY BROWNE

JOHN WILEY & SONS
BRISBANE • NEW YORK • CHICHESTER • TORONTO • SINGAPORE

First published 1995 by
JOHN WILEY & SONS
33 Park Road, Milton, Qld 4064

Offices also in Sydney and Melbourne

Typeset in 10/11.5 New Baskerville

© Jacaranda Wiley Ltd 1995

National Library of Australia
Cataloguing-in-Publication data

Craig-Lees, Margaret.
    Consumer behaviour.

    Includes index.
    ISBN 0 471 33518 5.

    1. Consumer behaviour. I. Joy, Sally. II. Browne,
    Beverly. III. Title.

658.8342

Cover image: The Image Bank/Geoffrey Gove

Printed in Singapore
10 9 8 7 6 5 4 3 2 1

Contents

PART 2: EXTERNAL INFLUENCES

7. SOCIAL INFLUENCE: SOCIAL GROUPS AND CONSUMERS   170

8. ATTITUDES   198

9. ATTITUDE CHANGE AND COMMUNICATION   218

10. FAMILIES AND HOUSEHOLDS   242

11. SOCIAL STRATIFICATION   267

Preface

This book was designed as an introductory consumer behaviour text for marketing students. Consumer behaviour has been taught as a distinct subject for over twenty-five years in Australia, yet there has been a marked absence of original texts published here for our unique market. This text was written in response to a strong demand, from students and teaching colleagues alike, for a textbook that was in tune with the study needs of future marketers in Australia and New Zealand.

Many consumer behaviour students come to the subject without any prior knowledge of the behavioural and social sciences. Concepts from these disciplines form the basis of consumer research and directly influence marketing decisions, so every effort has been made to present these concepts and research clearly. The text aims to provide readers with a broad understanding of the accumulated knowledge and how it can be applied in developing marketing strategies and tactics. Advertisements and news items are used extensively to illustrate the topics under discussion.

During the evolution of consumer behaviour as a specific discipline, two major themes have influenced researchers: how we as consumers acquire products and how the 'owning' of products influences our lives. The first theme has dominated consumer behaviour studies and there is an abundance of research and knowledge on the purchasing process. This is given detailed coverage in the text. Studies into the aspects of owning products are fewer but are growing in number so the theme of consumption as sociopsychological behaviour is incorporated throughout the text.

As well as gaining a sound grasp of concepts and theories, it is equally important to see how they are applied in and relate to the marketplace. The ideas of media commentators and marketing practitioners are therefore presented as case studies to give students insights into the real-life applications of consumer behaviour theories in an Australasian context. Discussion and essay questions are also provided at the end of each chapter to stimulate debate and encourage further research.

Acknowledgements

The authors are indebted to a number of people who read the manuscript at various stages of completion: Constance Hill, colleagues at the University of New South Wales, Mary Caldwell, Paul Henry and the many students who gave their time as 'product-testers' and provided useful input. Thanks also to Neil Shoebridge and *Business Review Weekly* for allowing the use of articles as case studies.

The authors and publisher would like to thank the following individuals and organisations for permission to use their material:

Medical Benefits Fund of Australia: fig. 1.1; Whitehall Laboratories Pty Ltd: fig. 1.5; United Media: fig. 2.3; Peter Robinson, Fairfax Photo Library: p. 36 (*top*); *Good Weekend*: p. 36 (*bottom*); Telecom: figs 2.6, 2.7 (*right*), 13.4 and 16.6; Pizza Haven: fig. 2.8; Christina Siciliano and Kraft Foods Ltd: fig. 3.6; Werner Langer: figs 3.5, 3.13, 10.4, 15.5 and 17.1; Seiko Australia Pty Ltd: figs 3.12 and 16.5; Dunlop & Olympic Tyres: figs 3.14 and 9.8; Fisher & Paykel: fig. 3.15; Robert Bosch (Australia) Pty Ltd: fig. 3.16; Wander (Australia) Pty Ltd: fig. 3.18; James Kemsley, Jimera Pty Ltd: fig. 3.19; The Roy Morgan Research Centre: fig. 4.2; Reckitt & Colman: figs 4.3, 4.8 and p. 454 (*bottom*); Angove's Winemakers and Distillers: fig. 4.4; Pizza Hut Australia: fig. 4.5; Traders Ltd (Aeroplane Jelly): p. 87; SMH Australia Ltd: fig. 4.6; S. Smith & Son: fig. 4.7; Black and Decker: fig. 4.10; Coca-Cola South Pacific: figs 4.11, 19.2; Coo-ee Picture Library: fig. 5.1; Telstra Corporation: fig. 5.5; North America Features Syndicate: p. 114; Nerada Teas: fig. 5.8; Loyalty Pacific: fig. 5.9; Eric Taylor: figs 5.10(a) and 14.3; Geoff Potter: fig. 5.10(b); Pulsar Australia Pty Ltd: fig. 6.2; Swift & Moore: fig. 6.6; Bausch & Lomb: fig. 6.8; Tooheys: fig. 7.1; National Australia Bank: figs 7.2 and 13.5; Bill Bass Optical: fig. 7.3; Country Road Australia: fig. 7.4; Apple: fig. 7.6; Bega Cheese: fig. 8.1(a); Lever & Kitchen: fig. 8.1(b); Wella Australia: fig. 8.1(c); James Hardie: fig. 8.1(d); Colgate-Palmolive Pty Ltd: fig. 8.3; Uncle Toby's and L'Oreal: fig. 8.4; Australian Made Campaign, Advance Australia Foundation: p. 222 and fig. 9.2; Food Delicacies, a division of Nestlé Australia Ltd: figs 9.3 and 16.4; Life. Be in it: fig. 9.4; Ampol: fig. 9.6; Transport Accident Commission: fig. 9.7; Greg Gaul/Australian Consumers Association: fig. 10.2; Australian Consumers Association: figs 10.3 and 18.1; Mars Confectionery of Australia: fig. 10.5; Bedarra Island and Adams Bernard Amici Pty Ltd: fig. 11.1; *The Australian*: fig. 11.2; Mount Broughton, Golf and Country Club: fig. 11.3; Toyota: fig. 12.4; Universal Press Syndicate: figs 13.3, 14.2 and 19.1; *Australian Country Style*: fig. 13.6; TeleItalia: fig. 13.7; SABCO Australia Ltd: fig. 14.1; Richard Collins: fig. 14.5; Hot Spring Spas Australasia: fig. 14.6; Sunbeam: fig. 15.2 (*left*); General Motors Holden's Automotive Ltd: fig. 15.2 (*right*); Canon Australia: fig. 15.3; Driza-Bone: fig. 16.2; Myer Grace Bros: fig. 16.3; Bärbel Bredeck: fig. 16.7; Swamp Productions: p. 428 (*bottom*); Hallas Trading Co.: fig. 17.2; Horizon/IFA: fig. 17.3; SBS: fig. 17.4; *HQ* magazine, courtesy of ACP Publishing Pty Ltd: fig. 17.6; Andrew Perrin, *Sydney Morning Herald*: fig. 17.8; Consumer Affairs, NSW: fig. 18.2; Trade Practices Commission: fig. 18.3; Office of the Chief Electrical Inspector: fig. 18.4; Federal Bureau of Consumers Affairs: fig. 18.5; Nuttelex Food Products: fig. 18.6; Australian Marketing Institute: fig. 18.7.

Every effort has been made to trace the ownership of copyright material. Information that will enable the publisher to rectify any error or omission in future editions will be welcome.

CHAPTER 1

The study of consumer behaviour

OBJECTIVES

This chapter should help you to:

• understand the relationship between consumer behaviour and marketing
• understand why it is important for marketers to study consumer behaviour
• understand what the study of consumer behaviour entails
• know what factors influence behaviour.

 MARKETING AND CONSUMER BEHAVIOUR

WHAT IS MARKETING?

Marketing is generally thought of as a purely commercial activity, and concerned with advertising and selling. It is in fact much more. Although there has been some debate in recent years as to how the term 'marketing' should be defined, the following definition is popular:[1]

&&Marketing is the process of planning and executing the conception, pricing, promotion and distribution of ideas, goods, and services to create exchanges that satisfy individual and organisational objectives.&&

This definition has recently been extended to describe how an organisation can efficiently achieve its goals:[2]

&&The marketing concept states that an entity achieves its own exchange determined goals most efficiently through a thorough understanding of potential exchange partners and their needs and wants, through a thorough understanding of the costs associated with satisfying those needs and wants, and then designing, producing and offering products in the light of this understanding.&&

In other words, an organisation's objectives can be reached by anticipating consumer (customer or client) demands and directing a flow of demand-satisfying goods and services to consumers. Essentially, this requires effective exchanges and necessitates managing the organisation in such a way that the right products (goods or services) in the right quantity are available to consumers (users) at the right place and at the right time. Obviously, if it is a commercial organisation it should make a profit out of the transaction.

Historically, strategic marketing planning has focused on the elements of the marketing mix — product, price, distribution and communication. But there is a growing acknowledgement that marketing planning should incorporate such factors as the relevant aspects of the political environment and focus more on managing the actual relationship between the buyer and the seller.[3]

THE EXCHANGE PROCESS

Marketing is an exchange process that links an organisation and the consumer.[4] When individuals buy particular products they are in fact entering an exchange relationship with the producer and/or the seller of that product. The following conditions should exist for an exchange to take place:
- there must be two or more parties
- each party must have something of value to exchange
- each party must be able to communicate and execute the transaction
- the exchange must be voluntary.

Although the aim of the individual transactions is to exchange goods, services, money or other resources, it may well be that an important aspect of the exchange is the creation of future transactions. If this is an aim, then it is important that each transaction be beneficial to both parties. To create brand loyalty, repeat purchases and a positive attitude, consumers need to have a degree of trust in the seller.

TRUST AND ETHICAL BEHAVIOUR

Trust can be defined in many ways, but it can often mean confidence in an outcome. An expression of such confidence might be: 'I know that this CD player will be well made as all of this company's products are of excellent quality; if there is anything wrong with it they will fix it or replace it without a fuss.'

In long-term relationships, the level of trust between buyer and seller is extremely important. A key factor in the creation and maintenance of trust is open and honest communication and the overall ethical conduct of both parties.[5]

Ethics are normative judgements concerned with what is right or wrong. Ethical problems often arise in situations where there is a conflict between self- (or organisational) interests and a society's perceived standard of conduct. For example, when a well known brand of baby milk formula was sold in Africa, mothers were encouraged to use the formula instead of breast milk. Unfortunately many of the mothers could not read the instructions and did not give the babies enough formula. It was expensive so the mothers tried to obtain as many feeds as possible from one can. Also, most mothers had no access to sterilisation facilities for the bottles. As a result, many babies died.[6]

With the growth of consumer activism and an increased tendency for governments to regulate in Australia and New Zealand, many industries have found it expedient to engage in self-regulation. They set and maintain ethical principles and behaviour for their own industries. For some time now the advertising industry has been concerned with self-regulation. The industry has a number of 'watchdogs', such as the Advertising Standards Council (ASC) and the Federation of Australian Commercial Television Stations (FACTS). Their task is to monitor advertisements in terms of set standards. For the ASC, these standards are set out in their code of ethics as follows.

ADVERTISING STANDARDS COUNCIL — CODE OF ETHICS

1. The conformity of an advertisement with this Code will be assessed in terms of its probable impact, taking into account its content as a whole, upon a reasonable person within the class of those to whom the advertisement is directed and also taking into account its probable impact on those persons within other classes to whom it is likely to communicate.
2. Advertisements shall comply with Commonwealth law and the law of the relevant State or Territory.
3. Advertising shall not encourage breaches of Commonwealth law of the relevant State or Territory.
4. Advertising shall not encourage dangerous behaviour and shall not encourage illegal or unsafe road usage procedures.
5. Advertising shall not engage in unlawful discrimination and shall not demean the dignity of men, women or children.
6. Advertisements shall not contain anything which, in the light of generally prevailing community standards, is likely to cause a serious offence to the community or a significant segment of the community.
7. Advertisements shall be truthful and not misleading or deceptive.
8. Advertisements shall be clearly distinguishable as such.
9. Advertisements of a controversial nature shall disclose their source.
10. Advertisements shall not exploit superstition nor unduly play on fear.
11. Advertisements shall not disparage identifiable products, services or competitors in an unfair or misleading way.
12. Advertisements for any product which is meant to be used or purchased by children shall not contain anything, including dangerous practices, which would result in their physical, mental or moral harm. Advertisements shall not directly urge children to put pressure on their parents to purchase the product advertised.
13. Scientific, statistical or other research data quoted in advertisements shall be neither misleading nor irrelevant.
14. Testimonials used in advertisements shall honestly reflect the sentiments of the individuals represented. Claims in testimonials are subject to the same rules as other advertising.
15. All guarantees or warranties referred to in an advertisement shall comply with the provisions laid down by Commonwealth law and the law relevant to the State or Territory.

(*Source*: The Media Council of Australia, *Advertising Code of Ethics*, 30 April 1993)

The Commercials Acceptance Division (CAD) of FACTS provides the television industry with a checklist for commercials so that the advertiser knows how to comply with the regulations set out in the Trade Practices Act and those established by the Australian Broadcasting Authority. Suggestions from other authorities are also used. For example, a directive linked to children and bicycles states:[7]

66 Road safety authorities suggest that when children are depicted in advertisements as bicycle riders, such advertisements should:
1. not show a child who appears to be less than nine years old riding on any road;
2. show children who appear to be between the ages of nine and thirteen riding only on quiet streets;
3. show all children wearing safety helmets, closed-in footwear and bright clothing. 99

SUCCESSFUL COMPANIES SATISFY CONSUMER NEEDS

Since producers and consumers form the key parties in the exchange process, successful businesses pay close attention to how their consumers (potential and actual) behave in the marketplace. The most successful companies are consumer oriented. Peters and Waterman Jr[8] have suggested that being customer oriented differentiates excellent companies from other companies, and that:

66 being customer oriented doesn't mean that excellent companies are slouches when it comes to technological or cost performance. But they do seem to us more driven by their direct orientation to their customers than by technology or by a desire to be the low-cost producer. 99

This implies that consumer sovereignty is the pivot of marketing decisions. The consumer should be at the centre of the marketing effort and successful companies produce good quality products that consumers want. They also try to understand all aspects of the behaviour that consumers display in the purchasing and use of products. The term 'product' is a generic term used in marketing to denote not only goods and services but also people and ideas, such as in the marketing of politicians and political parties.

Commercial organisations that focus on understanding their consumers usually carry out the following activities:
• identification of consumer needs, wants and preferences
• identification of market segments and target markets
• design and implementation of their marketing mix
• environmental scanning/analysis
• marketing research
• product audits.

If these activities are carried out effectively, management is better able to develop and implement successful marketing strategies. A marketing strategy is a mechanism through which management establishes a match between a target market and a product, and designs the marketing mix so as to create a viable exchange. For example, environmental scanning shows that children are becoming taller earlier and that, nowadays, people in general have larger feet. This means that traditional sizes in the clothing and footwear industry need to change. Children's clothes will need to be produced in larger sizes and shoe manufacturers will need to produce more shoes in the larger size ranges.

Market research is central to effective marketing management. A major feature in effective product management is knowing whether the members of your target market know about your products, what they think about them and why they do or do not buy them.

SUCCESSFUL PUBLIC ORGANISATIONS UNDERSTAND CONSUMERS

Historically, consumer research has been driven by the managerial needs of commercial firms, but it is also important to the public sector. Public organisations such as art galleries, museums, schools and hospitals must raise funds, manage taxpayers' money and deliver goods and services to the public that use them. They must also maintain themselves as efficient and effective entities.

For some organisations, much of their activity is directed at persuading consumers to behave in such a way that some of the services provided by the organisation will not need to be used. Examples are the anti-smoking campaigns run by health services encouraging behaviour that reduces the risk of cancer, and the preventive or early detection programs established by the Medical Benefits Fund of Australia (see figure 1.1 and below).

The 'MBF Know Your Heart' campaign

Heart disease is the largest killer of Australian men, and a heart check-up is the best protection against it. The 'MBF Know Your Heart' test was introduced to provide men with the resources to address heart disease. It needed to be about prevention, not cure, and provide a solution, not a problem.

The 'MBF Know Your Heart' test provides individual medical and lifestyle assessments which are designed to determine a person's risk of cardiovascular or heart disease. Through a combination of medical tests and questions about lifestyle and diet, a team of doctors and health professionals can determine a person's 'Coronary Risk Profile' and provide the appropriate advice and information to improve your heart health.

The communication of this campaign had to convince men that the 'MBF Know Your Heart' check would assist longevity. The campaign also needed to defuse the fear, and provide information and education on heart disease — to show that finding out isn't 'the end of the road' but a great opportunity to do something about it.

Through the use of a unique 'documentary' style of advertising, three episodes were developed for television, each representing a phase of the test and portraying the feelings with which men could empathise when deciding to have a heart test.

(*Source*: Medical Benefits Fund of Australia, 1994)

YOU WILL NEVER forget this masterpiece. It tells the story of Bathsheba and King David. It was painted by REMBRANDT in 1654. A fateful detail is the letter being read by Bathsheba. It is from King David. ※∗∗∗∗∗∗∗∗※ ※ It asks that she meet him in secret. The consequences for Bathsheba – already wed – can only be tragic. But there is an even more fateful detail, discovered only recently. It gives new meaning to the brooding poignancy of "BATHSHEBA." ※ Look closely at the model's left breast. Can you see the dimpling? This detail, recorded unknowingly by Rembrandt, is advanced breast cancer. ※∗∗※ ※ The consequences for the model? Well, she died several years later. ※∗∗∗∗∗∗∗∗※ ※ She was *Hendrickje Stoffels.* She was also Rembrandt's common-law wife and, within a year of the painting, mother of his daughter. (Was she pregnant as she posed?) ※ In those days, neither model nor artist, nor anyone, had heard of breast cancer. Expert medical opinion now is that, almost certainly, she died of breast cancer. ※∗∗∗∗∗∗∗∗※

"Bathsheba with King David's Letter," 1654.

TO AN ART LOVER,
THIS IS A CLASSIC REMBRANDT.

TO A DOCTOR,
IT'S CLASSIC BREAST CANCER.

A WOMAN'S BEST *PROTECTION* IS EARLY *DETECTION.*

Breast cancer is the most common cancer in women. ※∗ ※ These days, doctors can detect breast cancer long before it becomes even an unseen, unfelt lump. And long, long before it becomes the classic *"orange peel dimpling"* recorded by Rembrandt. For many women early detection can mean a complete cure. ※∗ ※ Early DETECTION is your best PROTECTION from the consequences of breast cancer. It can save your life, often without the need for a mastectomy.

THE ONLY EARLY DETECTION THAT WORKS IS REGULAR *SCREENING MAMMOGRAMS.*

Regular screening mammograms are recommended for women over 40 and for younger women where there is a family history of breast cancer. ※∗∗∗∗∗∗∗∗∗∗※ ※ *Screening mammograms* are not covered by Medicare unless symptoms are present or unless there is that family history. ※ If you are under 40, with no family history of breast cancer, your doctor is the best person to talk to about breast health and a detection regimen most appropriate for you. ※∗∗※

THE MBF SYDNEY SQUARE BREAST CLINIC.

MBF is determined to provide for its members what Medicare does not. For this reason, MBF recently acquired the respected Sydney Square Diagnostic Breast Clinic, now the MBF SYDNEY SQUARE BREAST CLINIC. Subsidised screening mammograms for MBF members, according to the medical guidelines above, are now available. ※∗∗∗∗∗∗∗∗※ ※ The fee is JUST $20. (Screening mammograms are available to non-members for the standard $60 fee.) ※∗∗∗∗∗∗※

ADVANCE BOOKING ESSENTIAL. CALL (02) 285 9999.

There is a limit to the number of screening mammograms that can be carried out. ※∗∗∗∗∗※ ※ Not because of the equipment – MBF can always buy more equipment to meet the demand of its members. The limiting factor is the *highly-skilled personnel* essential to perform and interpret the X-rays. ※∗∗∗∗∗∗∗∗※ ※ MBF acquired the Clinic for its members because it is run by some of Australia's most skilled and experienced breast

health experts and *specialist radiologists.* ※∗∗∗∗∗∗∗∗∗∗※ ※ The Clinic views more than 10,000 X-rays each year. The MBF Sydney Square Breast Clinic can currently handle 100 screening mammograms a week, so naturally, advance booking is essential. For more information, call the Clinic on (02) 285 9999. ※∗∗∗∗∗∗∗∗※ ※ If you are an MBF member, please have your membership number handy.

MBF

Figure 1.1: This advertisement is low-key in that it does not show the outcome of breast cancer in horrific terms but uses, instead, a work of art. Its message is received in a way that is less threatening to women.

When undertaking these campaigns, an organisation must understand consumers well enough to create effective communication messages. Many of the messages are directed at people who are at risk so it is important to understand that people who are at risk sometimes block out information they see as threatening. Messages should be designed in such a way that those who are at risk are not threatened by the message content. Humour is a useful technique or a low-key approach as in figure 1.1.

Governments of countries like Australia and New Zealand are responsible to the public and they must respond to issues that the public considers important. Members of the public, in their role as consumers, can and do put pressure on governments to regulate aspects of the marketplace, such as:

- cigarette smoking controls
- television advertising
- safety caps/tops on dangerous substances
- content disclosures on packaging
- shopping hours.

There are many consumer organisations in Australia and New Zealand. The majority of the Australian organisations are affiliated with the Australian Federation of Consumer Organisations in Canberra. The largest of these, the Australian Consumers Association, publishes information on a wide range of products. Its magazine, *Choice*, is a key information source for consumers. Other organisations are concerned with advertising issues, particularly the impact of advertising on children.[9] These groups have been able to force governments to regulate not only on the content of advertisements but also on the time and place of delivery.

SUCCESSFUL CONSUMERS UNDERSTAND THEIR OWN BEHAVIOUR

Consumers who understand their own behaviour when purchasing and using products maximise their position. They become better consumers. For example, it is useful to know that you need not be afraid of subliminal advertising. It is also useful to know that supermarkets and stores have been specifically designed to encourage you to buy products. Next time you go into a department store you should know that the colours on the floor and walls and the meandering layout are all designed to slow you down and keep you in the store. Research shows that the longer a customer is in a store the more she or he is likely to buy.[10]

 ## WHAT IS CONSUMER BEHAVIOUR?

When attempting to understand consumer behaviour there is a tendency to rely on intuitive decision making. Intuitive decisions based solely on personal experience are dangerous because they essentially rely on guesswork and assume that all consumers react to marketing stimuli in the same way that you do. Consumers differ in terms of the money they have to spend, the time they have to make decisions, the kinds of products that are viewed as important, and how they select products. The following two cases demonstrate the ways in which consumers can differ.

Case A

It is the 25th wedding anniversary of Tom and Mary, the parents of Karen and Craig who are twins. In their culture, it is customary to give a gift of silver on the 25th wedding anniversary. Karen is a final year medical student and Craig has been working for one year as a high school teacher. Since money is scarce, they have decided to combine resources and buy a joint present.

They know that various members of the family will give silver as gifts. However, Mary has continually mentioned that she and Tom would love a CD player — one that would complement their fairly expensive hi-fi system. After weighing up the situation, Karen and Craig decide that they will buy a CD player and, to match the tone of the occasion, they will have a small silver plaque engraved and attached to the gift. The key factors influencing their choice are the input from Mary and the fact that it will solve future gift problems, as CDs could be purchased.

In choosing the model and brand, Craig and Mary have two key factors to consider. One is that it must complement the existing hi-fi system, the second is price. Information search reveals more than a dozen suitable models, but only three within their price range, produced by Technics, JVC and Sanyo. After an extensive price comparison search and some 'bargaining' behaviour, Karen and Craig buy the JVC model.

Case B

James is a busy executive who has been tied up with meetings for the past two weeks, meetings that he hopes will lead to a successful merger with another company. On his way to yet another meeting, his secretary reminds him that it is his mother's birthday tomorrow. James has forgotten. His schedule for the next two days has no room for shopping time. He asks his secretary to help him out by buying his mother a present.

'What shall I buy her? How much should I spend?' she asks.

'I don't know. Get her something that your mother would like. Up to $100,' James replies.

Marketers need reliable information about their consumers and the skills to analyse and interpret the information. This need has led to the development of consumer behaviour as a specific area of study within marketing. Consumer behaviour, as the term suggests, is the behaviour that individuals display in purchasing and using goods and services. It is commonly defined as '... the activities of individuals in the discovery, evaluation, acquisition, consumption and disposal of goods and services'. Marketers have studied consumers carefully and consistently since the 1950s in order to develop a systematic method of studying their activities.

The current trend is to study consumer behaviour as part of the broader area loosely labelled 'human behaviour'. As such it falls within the parameters of the humanities and behavioural sciences. This has resulted in an interdisciplinary approach to the subject. Much of our understanding of consumers comes from disciplines such as anthropology, economics, psychology, social psychology and sociology. These disciplines are quite distinct, although the aim of each is to provide insights into human behaviour.

- **Anthropology** is the study of human societies. Its particular focus is on the evolution of humans and the communities they develop. It is generally studied through participation in field work and naturalistic observation. The information provided is usually historical and descriptive rather than analytical and predictive.
- **Economics** is the study of the flow of goods and services in a society. It is based on the presumption that all societies establish an economic system or a way of organising the use of its resources, i.e. the production of goods and services, their distribution and their consumption by various individuals and groups in the society.
- **Psychology** is the study of the individual and individual differences in behaviour. It includes emotional and mental health and motivation, how individuals perceive and make sense of their world, how they develop and how they adjust to their environment.
- **Social psychology** is the study of interpersonal behaviour. It focuses on how individuals interact with each other in groups and how other people influence a person's behaviour.
- **Sociology** is closely related to anthropology and social psychology. It is essentially the study of how different groups of people interact in a society. It does not focus on the relationships within a group but on the relationship between groups in a society.

 ## INFLUENCES ON BEHAVIOUR

According to most behavioural scientists, two factors determine a person's behaviour. One is a person's psychological set and the other is the context in which the behaviour occurs. According to Kurt Lewin,[11] behaviour is a function of the person in combination with the situation:

$$B = f(P \times S)$$

where: B = behaviour
         P = psychological set of the person
         S = the situation.

PSYCHOLOGICAL SET

Lewin used the term 'person', but in recent years 'person' has become synonymous with the term 'psychological set'. A psychological set is defined as 'an individual's predisposition or potential to behave in a particular way at a particular time'. To understand a consumer's psychological set we need to identify and understand the factors that influence the set. It is commonly accepted that the interaction of the factors shown in figure 1.2 determines an individual's psychological set.

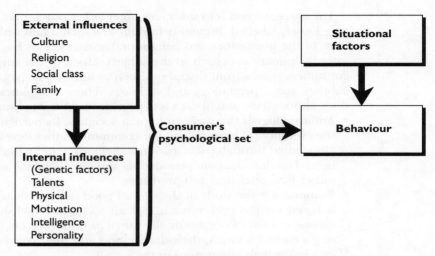

Figure 1.2: The relationship of the psychological set, the situation and behaviour

The diagram suggests that our psychological set is derived from two influences — internal and external. Internal influences are mainly genetic. These include physical characteristics, innate talents and personality disposition. External influences are factors in the environment which shape our thoughts and actions. Every living organism must develop the ability to survive in its physical environment. Survival depends on learning the correct responses and possessing an ability to adapt to change. Humans survive best in groups and this means that our behaviour is shaped and modified by other people in our society.

People are highly developed animals in terms of communication and memory skills and they can learn effectively from direct experience or from others. All societies socialise (train) their young in the acceptable ways of thinking and behaving within the society, usually in the context of a family structure. Families interact with many groups in society, for example, cultural groups which may be based on class, religion or ethnicity.

Since no two individuals share the same gene pattern (apart from identical twins), and each person interacts with others uniquely, people develop into distinct individuals, each with their own psychological set. They bring this psychological set to every situation, including purchase and consumption situations. It determines their needs, wants, attitudes, how they evaluate information and their choices.

THE SITUATION

An understanding of the consumer's psychological set helps to intepret and possibly predict consumer behaviour. But there are also situational factors to be taken into account, such as the context of the purchase, the availability of products, social norms, point of purchase promotions and store atmosphere. These all have a direct influence on buyer behaviour.

External influences on behaviour include culture, family, friends and marketing stimuli, and their impact can be difficult to assess precisely. One way to think of these influences is in terms of their scope, strength and immediacy (see figure 1.3). It is easier to assess the impact on consumer behaviour of marketing activities such as sales promotions, stock-out situations and store atmosphere than the impact of culture.

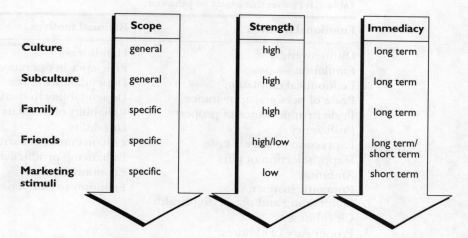

	Scope	Strength	Immediacy
Culture	general	high	long term
Subculture	general	high	long term
Family	specific	high	long term
Friends	specific	high/low	long term/ short term
Marketing stimuli	specific	low	short term

Scope: The sweep or reach of the impact

Strength: The power to impact on behaviour

Immediacy: Direct impact on behaviour, i.e. there are no intervening factors

Figure 1.3: The impact of external influences on behaviour (*Source*: Adapted from W. L. Wilkie, *Consumer Behaviour*, 2nd edn, John Wiley and Sons, 1990)

 # HISTORY OF CONSUMER BEHAVIOUR CONCEPTS

Many current concepts used to study consumer behaviour are derived from the behavioural sciences. At the turn of the century, it was thought that marketplace behaviour could be best understood by adopting an economic model of behaviour. The economic model or 'rational man' concept was concerned with examining and understanding how a 'rational' consumer decides what and how much to buy. The view was that consumers obtain satisfaction from goods, and that satisfaction is a function of the utility of the product, i.e., how useful a product is in relation to its cost and performance. This means that a rational consumer would always seek to maximise and match the utility of products with time and money costs. This view does explain some consumer behaviour but does not hold for all purchase situations. For example, it does not explain the role of aesthetics nor the fact that some products are purchased to display status and competition. Nor does it explain behaviour that seeks to maximise pleasure at a cost, for example, in the purchase of French perfume, entertainment, cosmetics, wine or other luxuries.

In an attempt to extend the economic approach, Copeland allowed that consumers did have 'emotional' reasons for purchasing products.[12] In 1925, he listed both rational and emotional motives that impact on behaviour (see table 1.1). It is interesting to note that cleanliness, fun and security from danger are emotional motives.

Table 1.1: Motives that impact on behaviour

Emotional motives	Rational motives
Distinctiveness	Handiness
Emulation	Efficiency in operation or use
Economical emulation	Dependability in use
Pride of personal appearance	Dependability in quality
Pride in appearance of property	Reliability of auxiliary service
Proficiency	Durability
Expression of artistic taste	Enhancement of earnings
Happy selection of gifts	Enhancing productivity of property
Ambition	Economy in use
Romantic instinct	Economy in purchase
Maintaining and preserving health	
Cleanliness	
Proper care of children	
Satisfaction of the appetite	
Pleasing sense of taste	
Securing personal comfort	
Alleviation of laborious tasks	
Security from danger	
Pleasure of recreation	
Entertainment	
Obtaining opportunity for greater leisure	
Securing home comfort	

(*Source*: Adapted from Melvin Thomas Copeland, *Principles of Merchandising*, A. W. Shaw Company, Chicago, 1925)

The aim of the economic model was to develop an understanding of how consumers make choices and not why consumers need or want particular products in the first instance. To understand the 'why', researchers applied motivation theories to consumer behaviour. An important outcome of motivation research was the recognition that consumers may not be consciously aware of some of the reasons for their behaviour. Consumer motivation research in conjunction with the economic models did expand the knowledge base of consumer behaviour. But it did not provide knowledge as to how consumers obtain information about products, or what they do with that information. It failed to show how emotional states affect the processing of information and how situational factors influence choice. For this reason, during the latter half of the 1960s there was a gradual shift towards more comprehensive models of the consumption process.

At this time the notion emerged that consumer purchasing behaviour should be studied as a process. This resulted in the development of a number of models by which this process could be formalised.[13] The model that has been most accepted and adapted is the Engel, Kollat and Blackwell model. It assumes that consumer behaviour is a problem-solving activity made up of the following key phases:

- the **pre-purchase phase** or acquisition phase which occurs when consumers recognise that they need a product and engage in information search and evaluation behaviour
- the **purchase phase** which occurs when consumers select a product and ownership is transferred to the consumers
- the **post-purchase phase**, sometimes referred to as the post-acquisition stage, which occurs when consumers use the product. If the product does not perform to the consumers' expectation then dissatisfaction will occur.

An advantage of the decision process approach is that it can incorporate all consumer activities, from the need (problem recognition) task through to use (outcomes) of the purchase. It can even be extended to incorporate the disposal of products — an asset in the current climate of recycling. Another important advantage is that the approach can accommodate the influence of emotions on product choice.[14]

The decision process and the factors influencing each phase of the process are described in the model shown in figure 1.4. The elements that can influence behaviour at each phase are shown. The psychological set, the consumer's lifestyle and mood state have an impact on their need for the product in the first place; how and when they receive information about the products available and situational factors influence their choice.

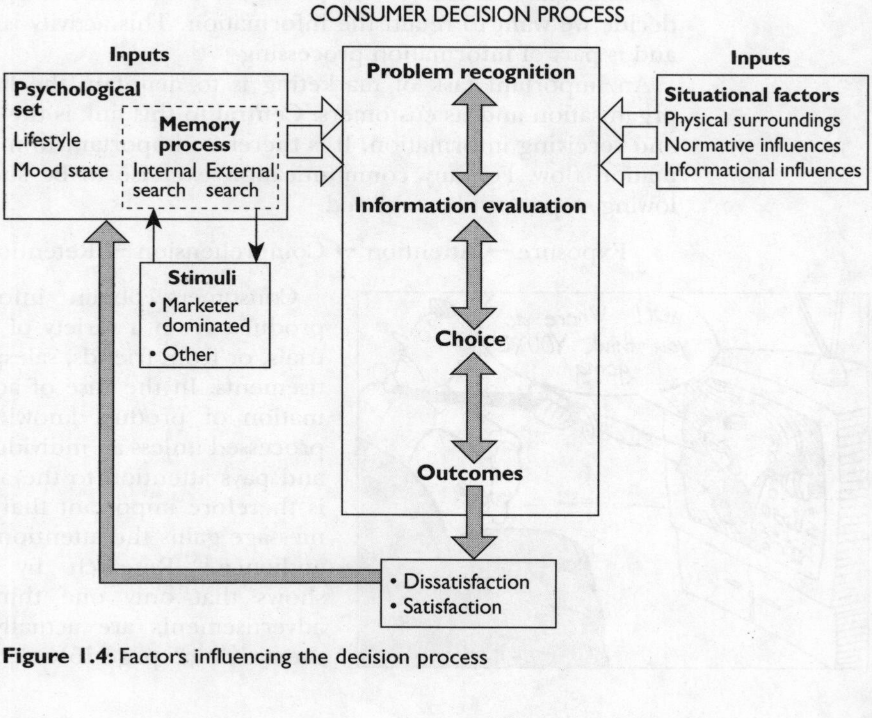

CONSUMER DECISION PROCESS

Figure 1.4: Factors influencing the decision process

A factor not included is time, that is, the time spent in the actual consumption process. This is difficult to assess. Time spent in the process is a function of an individual consumer's knowledge, situational factors such as the availability of the product, and/or how important the purchase is to the consumer. Consumers can take months, even years to purchase some products, but products such as an ice-cream can take only a few minutes to buy and consume.

CONSUMERS AS PROBLEM SOLVERS

The decision process suggests that purchase behaviour is essentially a problem-solving activity. According to Punj and Stewart,[15] consumer problem solving is a process of multiple, reciprocal interactions among consumers' cognitive processes, emotional state behaviours, and aspects of their physical and social environment. A key feature of problem solving is cognitive activity. Understanding the mental activities by which external information in the environment is transformed into meaning or thoughts, and how this in conjunction with the consumer's mood state affects the consumer's decision has become an important area of research.

INFORMATION PROCESSING

Information processing is the mental processes by which consumers interpret and integrate information from the environment. Raw information is obtained via our senses and given meaning. Information that is consciously analysed can be stored in our conscious memory systems if we decide we want to retain the information. This activity is called *perception* and is part of information processing.

An important task of marketing is to maintain the link between the organisation and its customers. Central to this link is the act of providing and receiving information. It is therefore important to manage the information flow. For any communication exercise to be successful the following steps must be achieved.

Exposure → Attention → Comprehension → Retention → Action

Consumers obtain information about products from a variety of sources such as trials, or from friends, salespeople or advertisements. In the case of advertising, information or product knowledge cannot be processed unless an individual is exposed to and pays attention to the advertisement. It is therefore important that any advertising message gains the attention of its intended audience.[16] Research by News Limited shows that only one third of television advertisements are actually watched (see the article on page 15).

The commercial break

— NEIL SHOEBRIDGE —

News Limited is distributing an interesting piece of research to advertisers and advertising agencies. The research claims that only a third of television commercials are actually watched by viewers. Obviously, News Limited, which is Australia's biggest newspaper publisher, has a vested interest in denigrating television advertising. But the research highlights a big problem for television advertisers.

News Limited's research claims that only 34.3% of viewers watch commercials. During a commercial break, 24.5% of viewers read or talk, 18.3% cook or eat meals, 13.8% leave the room and 9.1% hop between channels. The research was conducted in 1990, but there is no reason to believe viewers' habits during commercial breaks would have changed significantly during the past two years.

Every media advertising campaign contains an element of waste. Some of the people who notice a television commercial or a newspaper ad for a product will not fall into the product's target market, and some of the people in the target market will not see the ad. Critics of television contend that it contains the highest wastage factor. It is true that no other medium can reach as many people in one hit, but television's opponents argue that many of those people are not paying attention.

Capturing the attention of consumers is half the battle for all advertisers in every medium. The special challenge for television advertisers is to find a way to capture the attention of the 65.7% of viewers who do not watch commercials. If viewers do not notice a commercial, they will not hear the selling message. If the message is not heard, the commercial is a waste of time and money.

Remember that most television advertisers have only 30 to 60 seconds to grab a viewer's attention and communicate a message. Remember also that an hour-long program is cluttered with dozens of commercials, plus promotions for the station's programs. People can take their time consuming ads in newspapers or magazines, but when a television commercial is gone, it's gone. Constant repetition of a television commercial can improve the chances of it rising above the clutter and being noticed. But repetition does not guarantee that a viewer will stop eating or talking to watch the ad. It is the idea contained in a commercial, not the frequency of exposure, that captures the viewer's attention.

The past year has produced only a handful of attention-grabbing television commercials, ads that forced viewers to listen to the sales pitch. John Singleton Advertising's "I like it like that" campaign for Kentucky Fried Chicken produced startling sales spikes for the fast-food retailer. Clemenger Sydney used the comedian Jean Kittson in her Veronica Glenhuntly guise in a series of stunning ads for PepsiCo's 7UP lemonade (it's difficult to believe the same agency is responsible for the fatuous Strongbow White cider ad).

The ads produced by the Campaign Palace for various Edgell–Birds Eye brands are among the best commercials this year. BAM-SSB employed two sick whales in a striking ad for Aspro Clear, and Republic Advertising found an eye-catching way to sell underpants in its work for Jockey Australia. DDB Needham pushed the boundaries of fast-food advertising with its ad for McDonald's that featured a James Dean lookalike.

Many of the new television commercials this year were like wallpaper: consumers knew they were there, but paid them scant attention. The year produced more than its fair share of unclear television commercials. The ad agency Young & Rubicam's use of the American actor Peter Falk in a current series of ads for the Mitsubishi Lancer car seem irrelevant and irritating. George Patterson produced an expensive, elaborate commercial to sell the Optus long-distance telephone service. Set in a courtroom, the ad looks good but its meaning is opaque. Some viewers might have noticed it. Few would have been able to extract a message from the ad.

Business Review Weekly,
18 December 1992

Designers of advertisements use many techniques to attract attention and a favourite tool is the use of music. Another is to expose consumers to something surprising, novel, threatening or unexpected. Such stimuli result in an automatic response, i.e. involuntary attention. The advertisement in figure 1.5, for example, attempts to gain involuntary attention by the use of humour.

There's an easier way to avoid swimmer's ear.

OFFICIAL SUPPLIER • AUSTRALIAN INSTITUTE OF SPORT

Swimmer's ear is that painful ear infection which attacks when water is trapped in your ear canals. But it needn't be painful avoiding it.
A few drops of Aquaear after every swim help dry out the ears and curb the growth of bacteria.
So before you get wet this summer, get Aquaear.

aqua ear SOLUTION
35ml

Figure 1.5: This advertisement for Aquaear uses humour to capture the attention of consumers.

Gaining exposure and attention are only the first steps. It is also necessary to ensure that the audience understands the message and transfers it to their long-term memory systems. To do this marketers need to understand:
• how the perceptual system operates
• how the memory systems work
• how learning occurs.
They also need to understand how these relate to each other.

EMOTIONS

There have been considerable advances in our knowledge about how consumers process information cognitively but research into the role played by the emotions in information gathering, product evaluation and choice is relatively new. There is evidence to show that people who are in a positive frame of mind are more receptive to information.[17] But there is also some confusion over emotion in the context of mood states and emotion in the context of rational decision making — for example, buying something because it makes you 'feel good'.

Some writers distinguish between the experiential approach and the information processing approach. They do this on the grounds that the information processing approach requires 'rational' reasons for product choice, whereas the experiential approach acknowledges that people buy products because they provide fun, excitement and variety.[18] The implication is that hedonic reasons are somehow irrational. Since this implies some form of value judgement along the lines of rational versus irrational, it may be more practical to talk of 'legitimate' reasons for purchase, legitimacy being determined by the consumer. Viewed in this way, experiential purchases do not negate the decision processes and the information processing approach. The only aspect to change is the recognition that expressive/experiential reasons for purchase are legitimate evaluative criteria.

This text takes the view that people buy products for functional, experiential and expressive reasons and that these reasons are legitimate. It also takes the view that the parameters of the information processing paradigm are broad enough to encompass hedonic purchases and mood states.

 ## MULTIPLE ROLES

Many consumption situations involve more than one player so there could be more than one psychological set involved in the decision process. Family purchases often involve multiple players whose roles in the process differ. Daughter may ask for muesli, son may ask for cornflakes, a parent goes shopping, selects and pays for one or both cereals which are then consumed by the son and daughter. In gift-giving situations the process will always involve at least two people. One is the initiator, information gatherer, evaluator and/or decider, the other is the user. We can classify buying roles into seven categories:

- **Initiator**: recognises that a problem situation exists and that a purchase must be made
- **Information gatherer**: brings together the information
- **Gatekeeper**: person who is able to control the information given to the evaluator and/or the decider, such as a parent giving limited information to children
- **Evaluator**: sets the criteria for choice and examines the information about the product
- **Decider**: makes the final choice as to what, where and how the purchase is made
- **Purchaser**: carries out the actual transaction
- **User**: consumes or uses the product.

These roles may all be played by one individual. Or there may be more than one player, in which case it is useful to know what their particular roles are. For example, in the purchase of mechanical garden equipment the males in the family may be the key gatherers and evaluators of information. It would therefore be sensible if the message content reflected this.

The purchase roles in family and organisational buying decisions are similar; different influences shape how each task is handled. In organisations, individuals think that they place more emphasis on economic and utility factors. A sale is often influenced by the relationship quality between the buyer and seller. Also, power structures and expertise levels are different in organisations.[19]

In general, this means that different marketing messages should be directed to different parts of the buying process. For example, products such as cereals are often purchased on a 'collective' basis. Often, the child is the initiator and user of the product while the parent is the evaluator, decider and the purchaser. Information about the taste, shape, colour and product gifts (competitions, collectables, and so on) is best directed at the child, while information about nutrition and price is best directed at the parent.

 ## CONSUMERS AS AGGREGATES

Because actual behaviour is a function of many forces it is difficult to study with precision. Attempts to predict how consumers will behave in a given situation are made more difficult because most organisations interact with consumers as an aggregate and at a distance. (Some companies do interact with their customers on an individual basis. This is labelled 'custom marketing' or 'customised marketing' and is more frequent in services and industrial exchanges.)

Although each consumer has a psychological set that makes that person unique, marketers operating in mass consumer markets cannot possibly know and interact with each consumer as a unique entity. They must deal with consumers en masse and focus on aspects of consumers' psychological sets that are common to all or to specific groups or clusters.

Consumers share many basic characteristics, which are a function of being human. For example, if you were asked to stop reading and to hold up three fingers on your left hand, there is a seventy per cent chance that you would hold up your three middle fingers. It has been shown that if individuals are exposed to colours from the warm end of the spectrum, an increase in brain activity can be observed, with the right equipment. Research has shown that, at the conscious processing level, humans can only process seven, plus or minus two, bits of information at a time. If you were to show someone the following mix of numbers for approximately sixteen seconds, it is likely that they will remember a minimum of five and a maximum of nine items:

1 7 M 0 I 8 C
2 S 3 X 9 4 K
V W 6 Z G F D
Y L T 5 U B E

This is called Miller's Law and has a considerable effect on how consumers receive and process information.[20]

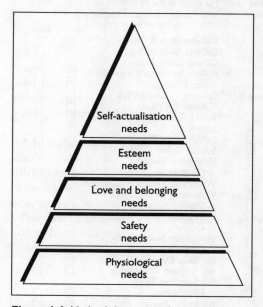

Figure 1.6: Maslow's hierarchy of universal human needs

Humans share basic emotions such as anxiety, happiness and fear. They also share some basic needs. Abraham Maslow suggested that all humans have basic needs, shown in figure 1.6, that must be satisfied if they are to be considered as fully functioning individuals.[21] There has been much discussion about whether these needs are in fact hierarchical. It may well be that we behave in such a way as to ensure that all or as many as possible of the basic needs are being met.

Although we may share the basic needs, the activities we engage in to satisfy them may be different. Factors such as customs, rules and regulations dictate acceptable behaviours and these often differ between cultures. We are all members of a number of social groups which can be based on ethnicity, social class and age groups. A group's dynamics result in the formation of values and norms that are specific to that particular group and are accepted by its members. As a result, the members tend to develop similar characteristics and behaviours.

The premise is that the members of these sub-markets will have similar values and/or other backgrounds that will cause them to act similarly towards a marketing mix. This behaviour makes market segmentation, targeting and niche selection possible. Market segmentation is the dividing of a heterogeneous market into a number of homogeneous sub-markets that a company can then target. It may also identify specific groups or niches within these markets that are not being serviced. If profitable, the company could develop a marketing mix for one or more niches.

 # CONSUMER BEHAVIOUR RESEARCH

When considering the sources of knowledge about consumer behaviour, a distinction is often made between *marketing* research and *market* research. *Market research* can be thought of as applied research and is usually carried out to facilitate managerial decisions. The most common tool in market research is the survey. Survey types vary, but the most common approaches are mail surveys, telephone calls and personal interviews. The subject matter of the surveys commonly includes attitude measurement, brand awareness and perception, consumer satisfaction levels, advertising recall and recognition, and consumer lifestyles. The questionnaire in figure 1.7 is an example of a product awareness and purchase behaviour survey. The attraction of the survey is that consumer responses can be quantified, making analysis easier.

MAGAZINES

Which of these statements best describes your household's readership of magazines?

- ☐ Never read
- ☐ Read from time to time
- ☐ Used to read but no longer read
- ☐ Currently read

If you read magazines, which magazines do you currently read, have seen or have heard of?

	Currently Read	Have Seen	Heard Of
Women's Weekly	☐	☐	☐
Woman's Day	☐	☐	☐
New Idea	☐	☐	☐
Who Weekly	☐	☐	☐
Choice	☐	☐	☐
Family Circle	☐	☐	☐
Vogue	☐	☐	☐
Mode	☐	☐	☐
Elle	☐	☐	☐
New Woman	☐	☐	☐
Cosmopolitan	☐	☐	☐
Cleo	☐	☐	☐
Ita	☐	☐	☐
Interiors	☐	☐	☐
Belle	☐	☐	☐
Country Style	☐	☐	☐
HQ	☐	☐	☐
TV Week	☐	☐	☐
Home Beautiful	☐	☐	☐
Your Garden	☐	☐	☐
Better Homes & Garden	☐	☐	☐
Australasian Post	☐	☐	☐
Other	☐	☐	☐

MOUTHWASH

Which of the following statements best describes your household's use of mouthwash?

- ☐ Never bought/Never tried
- ☐ Never purchased but would like to try a sample
- ☐ Have purchased in the past but no longer purchase
- ☐ Occasionally purchase
- ☐ Regularly purchase

Ever bought in past 12 months
Regularly buy

	Ever bought	Regularly buy
Listerine	☐	☐
Colgate Acti-Brush	☐	☐
Faulding Anti-Plaque	☐	☐
Ultrafresh	☐	☐
Plax	☐	☐
Cepacol	☐	☐
Listermint	☐	☐
Reach Antiplaque	☐	☐
Other	☐	☐

SHAVING

For those in the household who shave, which is the main razor that you/they use?

	Females	Males
Gillette Blue II	☐	☐
Gillette Blue II Plus	☐	☐
Gillete Daisy Plus	☐	☐
Gillete Sensor for Women	☐	☐
Gillette Sensor	☐	☐
Gillette Contour/Plus	☐	☐
Gillette GII/Plus	☐	☐
Schick Extra II Disposable	☐	☐
Schick FX	☐	☐
Schick Ultra/Plus	☐	☐
Schick Other	☐	☐
Wilkinson Sword Disposable	☐	☐
Wilkinson Sword Aquaglide	☐	☐
Wilkinson Sword Pivot Shava	☐	☐
Wilkinson Sword Retractor Colours	☐	☐
Wilkinson Sword Lady Glide	☐	☐
Bic Twin Disposable	☐	☐
Bic Regular Disposable	☐	☐
Bic Sensitive Skin Disposable	☐	☐
Bic Lady Shaver	☐	☐
Bic Pastel Disposable	☐	☐
Home Brand Disposable (e.g. No Name)	☐	☐
Home Brand Replacement Blades (e.g. No Frills)	☐	☐

SHOPPING

From the following list of stores, where do you do MOST of your shopping?

- ☐ Coles
- ☐ Safeway
- ☐ Franklins
- ☐ Woolworths
- ☐ Bi-Lo
- ☐ Campbells Cash 'n Carry
- ☐ 7-Eleven
- ☐ Jewels
- ☐ Food Plus
- ☐ Big W
- ☐ SSW
- ☐ MFC
- ☐ Payless
- ☐ Riteway
- ☐ Tuckerbag
- ☐ Other

MICROWAVE OVENS

Do you own a microwave oven?

☐ Yes   ☐ No

Do you buy the following Microwave Snacks?

- ☐ Edgell Quick Shots
- ☐ Kraft Microwave Meals
- ☐ Uncle Toby's Microwave Popcorn
- ☐ Green's Microwave Popcorn
- ☐ Generic/Home Brand Meals

Figure 1.7: Extracts from a survey sheet of the Promotional Sampling Company. Used with permission.

New pack adds value

SYDNEY: Promotional Sampling has launched a direct sampling program to Australian households called "Value Pack", which allows consumers to test products away from television advertising and supermarket "clutter". In turn the company claims marketers have the opportunity to create trial and brand awareness among audiences targeted by age, geo-demographically or on the basis of being users of competitor products.

By completing a survey form consumers receive a bag of groceries valued at more than $25 for a postage and handling cost of $8.95. The Value Pack program accesses one million households and contains products from companies which include Kellogg, L&K: Rexona, Colgate, Unifoods and Gillette.

Marketing, February 1994

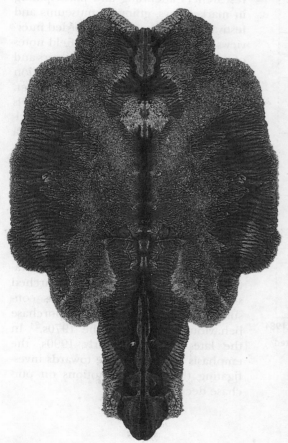

Figure I.8: The inkblot test. What do you see?

It is difficult to devise a survey that will measure consumer motivations, the role of emotion in decisions and the experiential aspects of consumption. In most instances, people are unable to label or describe accurately their reasons for buying products, so market researchers also use focus groups, consumer panels and thematic testing of individual consumers. In thematic testing, individual consumers are shown a picture or sets of words and asked to describe what it represents to them. Trained researchers interpret the descriptions and try to identify any underlying motives and influences on consumption behaviour (see figure 1.8).

Marketing research, on the other hand, refers to research studies that are carried out in order to expand or improve the quality of marketing knowledge. It tends to be exploratory rather than problem-solving oriented. This research is not normally driven by managerial necessity.

In essence, however, it is not the techniques that differ in each case but the subject matter and the purpose of the research. Similar techniques for collecting and analysing data are used in both. These techniques can be broadly grouped into two categories:

- quantifiable, generalisable data
- qualitative, interpretive data.[22]

Quantifiable, generalisable data are used to predict the average behaviour of a group of people who share similar characteristics. As such they are not designed to predict the behaviour of a single individual. The most common techniques are survey or census, but controlled experiments, structured unobtrusive and participant observation can be used.

Qualitative, interpretive approaches to data collection are used when in-depth knowledge of consumers is required. To carry out quantifiable and/or generalisable research, it is necessary to know what kinds of questions one should ask or what kinds of behaviour to observe. Often, to understand unconscious motives and the impact of emotions on behaviour it is necessary to carry out in-depth studies of a few people. The techniques used in these instances can vary from thematic testing, or content analysis of interviews and media (such as advertisements or literature) to observation. Recent research that used an ethnographic approach (the researcher joins the group and examines its behaviour in terms of social rules and beliefs) was the Odyssey. The Odyssey project involved a group of researchers attending and participating in market days, going to museums and festivals. The researchers recorded interviews, took photos and made field notes of the observed behaviours of buyers and sellers.[23] This type of data collection requires interpretation by the researcher. Since the interpretation of the data is influenced by the researcher's acknowledged beliefs and experiences, the data generated are considered to be subjective. This type of research, although it does yield valuable information, is still in its infancy and the techniques for collecting data are still being developed.

Figure 1.9 indicates the topics in the consumer research area that have been studied over time. Consumer preferences, attitude formation and motivation have been continuously researched since the 1950s. Topics such as consumer involvement and post-purchase behaviour emerged in the 1970s.[24] In the late 1980s and early 1990s, the emphasis has been more towards investigating the role of emotions on purchase decisions.

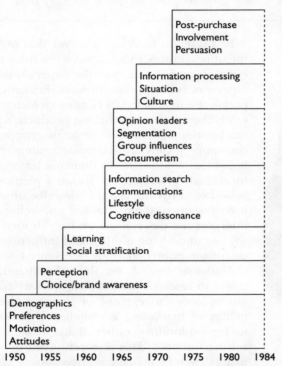

Figure 1.9: Major topics of consumer research reported in marketing journals over time (*Source*: Adapted from J. G. Hegelson et al., 'Trends in Consumer Behaviour Literature: A Content Analysis', *Journal of Consumer Research*, Vol. 10, 1984)

SUMMARY

This chapter introduces the field of knowledge known as consumer behaviour. An understanding of consumer behaviour means that marketers can improve their strategies and tactics, especially those relating to market segmentation and target market selection decisions. Knowing how consumers perceive products and what factors affect their preferences improves product and price decisions. Understanding how consumers process information allows marketers to make better media selections and devise better messages.

Consumer behaviour has been conceptualised as a process which encompasses the activities of individuals (singly or in groups) in the discovery, evaluation, acquisition, use and disposal of goods and services. To understand the dynamics of this process, marketers need to understand the factors that influence these activities. Essentially this means understanding the mind of the consumer and the socio-environmental factors that influence marketplace behaviour.

Although each of us has our own unique psychological set, we have many characteristics in common with other people. For example, we make the same physical responses to colour, music and temperature, our memory systems are the same and we learn in similar ways. As members of social groups we learn to think and behave within the rules of the group. By focusing on these shared characteristics we are able to study consumers as collectives. A number of conceptual frameworks have been used to study consumer behaviour. The most widely known and the ones discussed in this chapter are the decision process and information processing frameworks. The frameworks describe the behaviour and the influences that drive the behaviour of individuals during the decision process. The framework presumes that consumer behaviour is a problem-solving activity, and consumers take in and act on information from the marketplace (and society in general). This information, in conjunction with pre-set preferences, emotional influences and situational factors, triggers behaviour. In order to use this framework it is important to understand the consumers' psychological sets and the influence of the environment on their behaviour.

We have presented and described some approaches used to understand consumers' psychological sets, such as the economic, the emotion and the motivation based approaches and the most recent, the information processing paradigm. Although it has its critics, the information processing approach has growing support, primarily because it has the potential to include within its parameters the full range of influences (conscious and unconscious) on consumer behaviour.

A complicating feature of consumer decisions is that many involve more than one person. In addition to understanding the psychological sets and the situational influences impacting on individuals, we must also understand how people interact with each other. For this we need to know about the various buying roles that exist and make judgements about who is more likely to play each role. In this chapter we have labelled the roles as initiator, information gatherer, gatekeeper, evaluator, decider, purchaser and user.

At the base of any field of knowledge are the techniques used to collect that knowledge. In terms of knowledge gathering and testing, consumer research is both pure and applied. The research techniques, however, are similar. A range of techniques can be used to collect knowledge about consumers. They are varied and serve different functions. In general, quantifiable, generalisable techniques are more frequent in applied research, but the use of qualitative research techniques is increasing.

PLAN OF THE BOOK

Part One of this text concentrates on internal factors — how consumers perceive their world, process and store information, how they learn, and what factors direct their behaviour. In this respect Australian and New Zealand consumers are similar to consumers in other countries. In Part Two, we examine the external factors that influence behaviour. These are the social forces that shape consumer attitudes, values and behaviour. We examine the forces that make Australian and New Zealand consumers different from consumers in other countries. Part Two introduces the concept of social influence and describes how social and kin groups are formed and how they influence our ideas, attitudes and behaviour. In chapters 8 and 9 we look at attitudes in detail — how they are formed and how they shape our preferences and ultimately our product choices. Chapters 11, 12 and 13 describe the relationship of social stratification, lifestyles and culture to marketplace behaviour, such as consumer decision making and market segmentation. Part Three looks at the consumption process of individuals, households and organisations. Part Four examines social change, public policy, consumer activism and concludes with a chapter on current issues and future direction of the discipline.

 ## *Questions*

1. What is meant by 'consumer sovereignty'? Can you identify an organisation that you think directs its business from the consumer sovereignty perspective? What aspects of its behaviour lead you to this conclusion?

2. Select three television commercials and three print advertisements that have 'grabbed' your attention. Describe how each of them achieves this.

3. In September 1991 the food manufacturer Plumrose launched its new dairy dessert for children, Petit Miam. Develop an advertisement for this product recognising that there will be multiple players and multiple roles involved in the consumption process.

4. What factors do you think have the most important influence on consumers' product choice? Would you describe these factors as functional or emotional?

5. Define market segmentation, target markets and niche markets. In what ways can consumer markets be segmented?

6. Situational factors have an impact on our consumption behaviour but so far it has been difficult to show what these factors are and how they have an impact. What reasons can you give for this? Can you suggest a means by which some or all of the difficulties may be overcome?

7. Marketers suggest that it is important to isolate and classify rational and non-rational reasons for product choice. Why do you think they take this view? Do you think the distinction is necessary? Why?

8. By understanding their consumers, organisations can design and implement a more efficient and effective marketing mix. Take each element of the marketing mix and describe how an understanding of the consumer could influence strategic and tactical decisions.

9. Outline the benefits of studying consumer behaviour as a consumption process.

10. Consumers are individuals and unique. How, therefore, can we identify 'clusters' with the potential to respond in a similar way to marketing stimuli?

Case study

The marketing and advertising industry is facing another tough year. Fifteen days into 1993, marketers and advertisers know that persuading consumers to spend will not be any easier than it was last year. The new year has not brought a new mood among Australian shoppers and the challenges marketers faced in 1992 have returned.

The Melbourne advertising agency Badjar recently held a meeting of its clients to discuss Australia's economic and marketing future. The picture that emerged was not pretty. Consumer spending will remain flat, growing 2.5% this year, 1.8% in 1994 and 1.4% in 1995. Consumer attitudes formed over the past three years will not disappear when the economy improves.

The recession has created a vulnerable consumer. It is evident in many areas. Take credit. Consumers are working hard to reduce their debts. They feel vulnerable, particularly about job security, and believe their exposure to risk is too high. They are in no mood to take risks, so low interest rates, for example, are not encouraging them to take on debt.

Consumers this year are informed, anxious, sceptical, conservative and stressed. They want marketers to provide them with information, facts and tangible reasons to buy a product or service. Chastened by the recession and the excesses of the now discredited 1980s, consumers have become tougher, noisier, more demanding and more discerning. They have higher expectations and greater freedom of choice. They are ready to complain if treated badly by a company or a product. They are increasingly aware of their rights as consumers and increasingly willing to exercise those rights. They will shift their brand loyalties in an instant if they are offended or short-changed.

Australians have experienced enormous social, cultural, political and technological change during the past 20 years. With 60% of all Australian mothers with dependent children working full-time or part-time, the role of women — and, by extension, men — has changed and will continue to change. Families and households are being redefined. Half of Australian households contain only one or two people.

The rapid change has produced a conservative, family-oriented consumer. Wealth, greed and conspicuous consumption are out. The "in" list includes attitudes such as: save before you spend; buy more for less; spend more time with the family; and provide for your future.

In theory, the emergence of a conservative, family-oriented consumer should be good news for the marketers of big, established brands. But the big brands are under constant scrutiny and reappraisal by the informed, sceptical, stressed consumer of 1993. Consumers are smarter about brands and more willing to demand what they want from a product or service. While a brand's heritage might give it a selling edge, it does not guarantee customer loyalty or sales. Heritage must be matched by quality, service, convenience and, above all, value for money.

Value marketing was one of the key marketing trends during the first two years of the 1990s. It's back this year. All manufacturers, marketers and retailers are being assessed in terms of the value-for-money they offer. If consumers perceive them as offering poor value, they will be swiftly rejected. Then it will take the manufacturer or retailer a long time to win back customers. But if a company can establish and maintain a value-for-money image, it will attract a loyal group of customers.

Meeting the marketing challenges of this year will not be easy. Consumers are highly sceptical about advertising. They want advertising campaigns that are based on content rather than style. Any marketer that forgets it is dealing with an informed, demanding consumer will fail. You have been warned.

Neil Shoebridge,
Business Review Weekly,
15 January 1993

 ## Case study questions

1. In this 1993 article, Neil Shoebridge described consumers as 'informed, anxious, sceptical, conservative and stressed'. In 1994 he argued that, even though consumers were more confident, marketing to consumers would still be difficult (*Business Review Weekly*, 7 March 1994, p. 82). Is this true of current consumers?

2. What general guidelines would you suggest managers adopt to maximise their position in the current climate?

SUGGESTED READING

M. Walker, D. Burnham and R. Borland, *Psychology*, 2nd edn, John Wiley and Sons, Brisbane, 1994.

T. Levitt, *The Marketing Imagination*, The Free Press, New York, 1986.

F. S. Houston and J. B. Gassenheimer, 'Marketing and Exchange', *Journal of Marketing*, Oct. 1987, pp. 3–18.

N. Sheth, *Contemporary Views on Marketing Practice*, Lexington Books, Mass., 1987.

T. Robertson and H. Kassarjian (eds), *Handbook of Consumer Theory and Research*, Prentice-Hall, Englewood Cliffs, NJ, 1991.

ENDNOTES

1. This definition was developed by the American Marketing Association Committee. It appeared in *Marketing News*, 1 March 1965.

2. Frank Houston, 'The Marketing Concept: What it is and what it is not', *Journal of Marketing*, April 1986, pp. 81–87. For a broader understanding of the marketing concept see Theodore Levitt, 1960, 'Marketing Myopia', *Harvard Business Review*, July/August. 'What is the Marketing Management Concept?', *Frontiers of Marketing Thought and Action*, AMA, Chicago, pp. 71–82. Shelby Hunt, 'General Theories and the Fundamental Explanada of Marketing', *Journal of Marketing*, Fall 1983, pp. 9–17. Frederick E. Webster, 'The Rediscovery of the Marketing Concept', *Business Horizons*, Vol. 31, May/June 1988. Theodore Levitt, *Marketing Imagination*, Free Press, New York, 1983. Frederick E. Webster, 'The Changing Roles of Marketing in The Corporation', *Journal of Marketing*, Vol. 56, Oct. 1992, pp. 1–17. W. V. Watershoot and Van den Bulte, '4P Classification of the Marketing Mix Revisited', *Journal of Marketing*, Vol. 56, 1992.

3. Regis McKenna, *Relationship Marketing: Successful Strategies for the Age of the Customer*, Addison-Wesley, Reading, Mass., 1991. Jagdish Sheth, *Relationship Marketing: An Emerging School of Marketing Thought*, Sheth & Associates, Atlanta, Georgia, 1993. Clive Porter, 'Relationships: How Good Are You?', *Marketing Magazine*, JMB Group, Sydney, Oct. 1991. Philip Kotler, 'Marketing's New Paradigm: What's Really Happening Out There', *Planning Review*, Sept./Oct. 1992, pp. 50–52. Christopher Martin, Adrian Payne and David Ballantyne, *Relationship Marketing: Bringing Quality Customer Service and Marketing Together*, Butterworth Heineman, Oxford, 1991. Jonathan R. Corpulsky and Michael Wolf, 'Relationship Marketing: Positioning for the Future', *Journal of Business Strategy*, July/Aug. 1990. Christian Gronroos, *Service Management and Marketing*, Maxwell McMillan International Editions, Singapore, 1990. Christian Gronroos, 'Relationship Approach to Marketing in Service Contexts: The Marketing and Organisational Interface', *Journal of Business Research*, 20, 1990, pp. 3–11. Christian Gronroos, 'Quo Vadis Marketing? Towards a Paradigm Shift in Marketing?', Paper presented at the European Marketing Academy Annual Conference in Barcelona, 25–28 May 1993. Evert Gummesson, 'The New Marketing — Developing Long-term Interactive Relationships', *Long Range Planning*, Vol. 20, No. 4, 1987, pp. 10–20. B. Collins, 'When the Supplier Becomes the Customer', *Australian Professional Marketing*, 32, Nov. 1992.

4. Richard P. Bagozzi, 'Marketing as Exchange', *Journal of Marketing*, 39, Oct. 1975, pp. 32–39. F. S. Houston and J. B. Gassenheimer, 'Marketing and Exchange', *Journal of Marketing*, Oct. 1987, pp. 3–18.

5. Syed Saad Andaleeb, 'Trust and Dependence in Channel Relationships: Implications for Satisfaction and Perceived Stability', *American Marketing Association*, Summer Educators Conference, Summer 1991, pp. 249–50. Greg S. Martin, 'The Concept of Trust in Marketing Channel Relationships: A Review and Synthesis', *American Marketing Association*, Summer 1991. Mary C. Martin and Ravipreet Sohi, 'Maintaining Relationships with Customers: Some Critical Factors', *American Marketing Association Conference Paper*, 1993.

6. J. Post, 'International Consumerism in the Aftermath of the Infant Formula Controversy', in P. Bloom and R. Smith, *The Future of Consumerism*, Lexington Books, 1986. J. Post, 'Assessing the Nestlé Boycott: Corporate Accountability and Human Rights', *Californian Management Review*, Vol. 27, No. 2, 1985. L. P. Gerlach, 'The Flea and The Elephant: Infant Formula Controversy', *Society*, Sept./ Oct. 1980, pp. 10–14.

7. *Commercial Television Industry Code of Practice*, published by FACTS, Aug. 1993. The Media Council of Australia, *Advertising Code of Ethics*, 30 April 1993.

8. T. J. Peters and R. H. Waterman Jr, *In Search of Excellence*, Harper and Row, New York, 1982.

9. Australian Consumers Association — see 'Into the Mouth of Babes: TV ads give junk food the wrong message', *Choice*, Oct. 1990. The ACA also provides a resource training kit, 'I know what Ads are'. Various organisations voice concern about children and television, such as the Australian Institute for Family Studies.

10. P. Kotler, 'Atmospherics as a Marketing Tool', *Journal of Retailing*, 49, Winter 1973. R. Donovan and J. Rossiter, 'Store Atmosphere: An Environmental Psychology Approach', *Journal of Retailing*, 58, Spring 1982, pp. 34–57.

11. Kurt Lewin, *A Dynamic Theory of Personality*, McGraw-Hill, New York, 1936.

12. M. T. Copeland, *Principles of Merchandising*, A. W. Shaw Co., Chicago, 1925.

13. There has been a range of consumer behaviour models developed since the 1960s. These include:
    1. *Andreason Model.* A. R. Andreason, *Attitudes and Customer Behaviour: A Decision Model in New Research in Marketing*, Institute of Business and Economic Research, University of California, 1965.
    2. *Nicosia Model.* F. M. Nicosia, *Consumer Decision Process*, Prentice-Hall, Englewood Cliffs, NJ, 1966.
    3. *Howard-Sheth Model.* J. Howard and J. Sheth, *The Theory of Buyer Behaviour*, John Wiley and Sons, New York, 1969.
    4. *Engel, Kollat and Blackwell Model* of consumer behaviour for high involvement situations, in *Consumer Behaviour*, 4th edn, by J. F. Engel, R. D. Blackwell, CBS College Publishing, Holt, Reinhart and Winston, 1982.

14. R. B. Zajonic and H. Markus, 'Affective and Cognitive Factors in Preferences', *Journal of Consumer Research*, 9, Sept. 1982, pp. 123–31. D. J. MacInnis and B. J. Jaworski, 'Information Processing from Advertisements: Towards an Integrative Framework', *Journal of Marketing*, Vol. 53, 1989, pp. 1–23.

15. G. N. Punj and D. W. Stewart, 'An Interaction Framework of Consumer Decision Making', *Journal of Consumer Research*, Sept. 1983, pp. 181–86.

16. J. Franz, '$95 Billion for What?: Ads Remembered as Forgettable in 1985', *Advertising Age*, Vol. 57, 3 March 1984, p. 4.

17. R. E. Burnkrant, 'A Motivational Model of Information Processing Intensity', in M. Wallendorf and G. Zaltman, *Readings in Consumer Behaviour*, John Wiley and Sons, New York, 1984.

18. M. B. Holbrook, 'Emotion in the Consumption Experience: Toward a New Model of the Human Consumer', in *The Role of Affect in Consumer Behaviour*, Lexington Books, USA, 1986. M. B. Holbrook and E. Hirschman, 'The Experiential Aspects of Consumption: Consumer Fantasies, Feeling and Fun. M. B. Holbrook, J. O'Shaughnessy and S. Bell, 'Action and Reaction in the Consumer Experience', *Research in Consumer Behaviour*, Vol. 4, pp. 131–63. E. Hirschman, 'Innovativeness, Novelty Seeking and Consumer Creativity', *Journal of Consumer Research*, Vol. 9, Dec. 1980. D. Kahneman and A. Tversky, 'The Psychology of Preferences', *Scientific American*, No. 46, 1982. R. W. Olushavsky and D. H. Granbois, 'Consumer Decision Making: Fact or Fiction?, *Journal of Consumer Research*, 6, Sept. 1979, pp. 93–100.

19. E. F. Fern and J. R. Brown, 'The Industrial/Consumer Marketing Dichotomy: A Case of Insufficient Justification', *Journal of Marketing*, Vol. 48, 1984. B. C. Ames and J. D. Hlaracek, *Managerial Marketing for Industrial Firms*, Random House, New York, 1984.

20. G. Miller, 'The Magical Number Seven, Plus or Minus Two: Some Limits on Our Capacity to Process Information', *Psychological Review*, 76, 1967, pp. 81–97.

21. A. Maslow, 'A Theory of Human Motivation', *Psychological Review*, 50, 1943, pp. 370–96.

22. L. A. Hudson and J. L. Ozanne, 'Alternative Ways of Seeking Knowledge in Consumer Research', *Journal of Consumer Research*, Vol. 14, 1988, pp. 508–21.

23. R. W. Belk, F. Sherry Jr and M. Wallendorf, 'A Naturalistic Inquiry into Buyer and Seller Behaviour at a Swap Meet', *Journal of Consumer Research*, 14, 1988, pp. 449–69. R. W. Belk, M. Wallendorf and J. F. Sherry Jr, 'The Sacred and the Profane in Consumer Behaviour: Theodicy on the Odyssey', *Journal of Consumer Research*, Vol. 16, June 1989, pp. 1–38.

24. J. Mowen, 'Beyond Consumer Decision Making', *Journal of Consumer Marketing*, 5, Winter 1988, pp. 15–25. J. G. Helgeson, E. A. Kluge, J. Mager and C. Taylor, 'Trends in Consumer Behaviour Literature: A Content Analysis', *Journal of Consumer Research*, Vol. 10, 1984, pp. 449–54.

PART 1

1

INTERNAL INFLUENCES

CHAPTER 2

Information processing

This chapter should help you to:

- understand the relationship between consumer behaviour research and psychology
- know the various influences on the study of consumers' internal processes
- have a good working knowledge of consumers' information processing systems.

 ## PREDICTING BEHAVIOUR

As you saw in the previous chapter, behaviour is a function of the interaction between an individual's psychological mindset and the situation. To understand and possibly predict behaviour, it is important to know what elements of the psychological processes or the situation are likely to influence behaviour.

For centuries, humans have been preoccupied with understanding and predicting behaviour. Up until the latter half of this century, most behavioural scientists thought it was the personality type of individuals that directed their behaviour. So they concentrated on developing ways to identify and classify personality types. One method was to use astrology charts, another was to observe a person's physical characteristics or body form. The latter practice probably began in Ancient Greece and continued well into the twentieth century with the work of Harvard scientist

W. H. Sheldon in 1940. He believed that there are three major mor-
phologies, or body types, that correspond with specific personality traits.
These are:

- **endomorphs**, with soft, rounded bodies and big stomachs. These people
  are inclined to be sociable, enjoy relaxing and lazing about, talk a great
  deal, and seek physical comfort.
- **mesomorphs**, with hard, square, bony bodies and over-developed muscles. These people are energetic, assertive, courageous and sanguine.
  Their preferences will be for sport and power.
- **ectomorphs**, with tall, thin bodies and over-developed heads. These
  people are introverted, inhibited, intellectual and prefer being alone to
  being in a crowd.

There are a number of problems with Sheldon's theory, so there is little
current support for his ideas. The main criticisms are that:

- he did not consider the environment in which people develop. Some
  cultures value the endomorph shape. This means that the majority of
  the population would have soft rounded bodies and big stomachs, but
  not all would be sociable or talk a great deal.
- he offered no reason as to why or how body shape influences thoughts,
  feelings and behaviours
- he made his own subjective assessment of which characteristics match
  the body types.

Another theory for predicting behaviour was phrenology, or the art of
reading the bumps on the head. This was popular in the late nineteenth
century and, although discredited now, it can be an intriguing icebreaker
at a party (see figure 2.1).

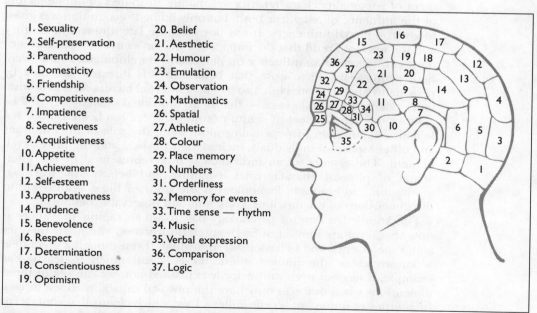

1. Sexuality
2. Self-preservation
3. Parenthood
4. Domesticity
5. Friendship
6. Competitiveness
7. Impatience
8. Secretiveness
9. Acquisitiveness
10. Appetite
11. Achievement
12. Self-esteem
13. Approbativeness
14. Prudence
15. Benevolence
16. Respect
17. Determination
18. Conscientiousness
19. Optimism
20. Belief
21. Aesthetic
22. Humour
23. Emulation
24. Observation
25. Mathematics
26. Spatial
27. Athletic
28. Colour
29. Place memory
30. Numbers
31. Orderliness
32. Memory for events
33. Time sense — rhythm
34. Music
35. Verbal expression
36. Comparison
37. Logic

Figure 2.1: Segments of the skull according to phrenology, and the meaning attached to each bump. The size of
the bump indicates the strength of a quality.

Phrenology

Phrenology was founded by a German doctor named Gall. He concluded that the brain was the controlling organ of the body and that different parts had special functions. Gall argued that the bumps on the head revealed the development (or lack of it) of that part of the brain that lay immediately underneath the bump. If one knew what faculties corresponded to those areas of the brain one would be able to evaluate character by examining the bumps. Gall's key disciple, a Scotsman named George Combe, identified 37 significant areas of the brain — each defining a specific characteristic. Since the brain has two lobes, each characteristic is represented by two bumps, one on each side of the head. For example bumps one and two represent sexuality and self-preservation. If bump one, representing sexuality, is too small it means a lack of energy, perhaps even of balance. If it is too large this indicates a great interest in the opposite sex, so much so that it could prove a handicap — unless it is suppressed and turned towards religious or charitable works. If the self-preservation bump (bump two) is too small it indicates possible suicidal tendencies. A relatively small bump suggests a disregard for personal safety. A large bump indicates someone who does not take risks and is perhaps a coward.

There were many attempts to explain the existence and development of 'personality'. Until the nineteenth century, the existence and development of personality characteristics was mainly attributed to innate factors or the influence of a deity or both, but only limited recognition was given to environmental influences. It was not until the late nineteenth century and the work of Freud that the impact of a person's environment was seriously considered as an influence on personality development. In the twentieth century, the idea arose that behaviour was directed not only by personality characteristics but also by other internal factors such as motivations, talents and intelligence — that is, an individual's psychological set.

From the late nineteenth century onwards, there has been a more systematic examination of personality, motivation, the role of the emotions and other aspects of individuals, such as their physical and cognitive development. The essence of an individual is now represented by the interaction of physical characteristics, cognitive and behavioural learning, motivation and emotion. Psychology is the study of these strands within the dimensions of unconscious, conscious and observable behaviour.

The knowledge base of psychology has grown so rapidly that there is now an enormous amount of fragmented information and many theories about the essence and behaviour of individuals. Even though a great deal is known about the human mind, there is still much to learn. For example, it has not been satisfactorily explained how we can see in three dimensions when our eyes only have the physical capability to see in two. In another example, we accept Miller's Law[1] which claims that short-term memory can only process between five and nine 'bits' of information at a time, but we still do not know why the limitation exists.

PSYCHOLOGY AND CONSUMER BEHAVIOUR

As with all new areas of knowledge, many theories were and are still being developed to describe and explain aspects of the individual. Until the 1960s, research activity in psychology was directed at understanding abnormal versus normal behaviour, personality, human motivation, learning, cognitive development and intelligence. During this period the psychoanalytic and behavourist perspectives dominated research activity.

Historically, consumer researchers have used knowledge from psychology to understand the mind of the consumer. The practice has been to adopt and apply new developments in psychology as they emerge. These developments have had an influence on how the consumption process is understood. In particular, the unconscious dimension has dominated the study of consumer motivation and the identification of consumer needs and wants. However, the strongest and most consistent influence has been the behavioural dimension, particularly in relation to shaping consumers' behaviour. Recently, an interest also has developed in the area of cognitive learning and emotions and their role in understanding consumption activity.

THE BEHAVIOUR DIMENSION AND THE BEHAVIOURISTS

According to behaviourists, the development of cognitive processes, personality and all behaviour is a function of training or learning. The learning occurs when the individual is exposed to rewards or punishment, and is based on the idea of response to a stimulus. The idea is that behaviour can be manipulated by external inputs. This implies that consumer behaviour is learned behaviour — for example, brand preference is trained behaviour whereby consumers are trained through reinforcement (rewards) to be brand loyal.[2]

Perhaps the most useful application of behaviourist theories in marketing is the notion of applied behavioural analysis. Applied behavioural analysis is the process of manipulating environmental variables in order to alter behaviour. In a marketing situation, this process is most commonly used in the area of sales promotion. The correct choice and management of incentives can have considerable impact on the sales performance of a product. Although it is not easy to identify the most effective rewards, there are a number of guidelines that narrow the choice. William Gaidis and James Cross[3] identified six steps in developing a behaviour modification program for effective use of sales promotion variables.

1. Identify the specific behaviour change required.
2. Measure the frequency of the behaviour.
3. Develop environmental reinforcers/punishers that would shape the behaviour.
4. Develop procedures to use the reinforcers/punishers.
5. Test whether behaviour has changed.
6. Evaluate the costs and benefits of the exercise.

For example, a garden maintenance service might receive few orders on Saturday afternoons, Sundays, Mondays and Tuesdays, but be over-booked on the other days. To even out its bookings, the service could try behaviour modification. For example, a discount could be offered on the slow trade days as an incentive (reinforcer) for more bookings. Obviously, the discount would have to be cost effective.

Under the influence of the behaviourists, the traditional approach to studying consumer behaviour was the 'black box approach' (see figure 2.2).

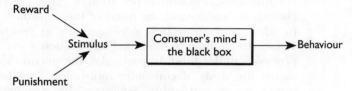

Figure 2.2: The 'black box' approach to consumer behaviour

This approach looked at external inputs and the outputs that seem to result from them, but it did not examine the mental processes involved in the consumer's behaviour. For example, if shopper A purchased Berri Orange Juice after its price was reduced by 20 per cent, then the extrinsic reward (the 20 per cent discount) would be said to have worked because the desired behaviour occurred. If shopper B saw the same offer but did not purchase the orange juice, behaviourists would say that another type of reward was necessary to obtain the same behaviour as from shopper A. However, choosing the right incentive is difficult. We would need to assume that shopper B knows what incentive would be attractive, that we could ask him or her what that incentive is, and that shopper B knows how to retrieve the information to answer us. Behaviourists have not adequately developed techniques for identifying the source of the information, why shopper B would retain it, and how it would influence his or her behaviour. This is the key weakness of the behavourist approach. The theory does not attempt to get into the mind of the consumer, and therefore does not satisfactorily explain memory, judgement and perceptual processes, or the impact of emotions on behaviour.[4]

COGNITIVE PSYCHOLOGY

Technological advances and sophisticated research techniques have facilitated the development of cognitive psychology. The main contribution of cognitive psychology is the notion of individuals as processors of information. The advantage of the cognitive approach is that it allows for some understanding of how humans obtain, process, act on and store information. In short, it allows for cognitive knowledge and emphasises the role of internal learning. Behavioural learning is essentially learning by experience, by doing something and being rewarded or punished for the behaviour. In cognitive learning, the perceptual and memory systems of individuals play a key role.[5] The cognitive approach is not a substitute for behavourist ideas on the influence of reinforcement on behaviour. Rather, it is both supplementary and complementary to behavourist and other approaches.

THE INFLUENCE OF EMOTIONS

The most difficult and the least studied strand in consumer research is the role of emotion, particularly its influence on our cognitive processing and behaviour. Emotion has always been accepted as having an impact on behaviour.

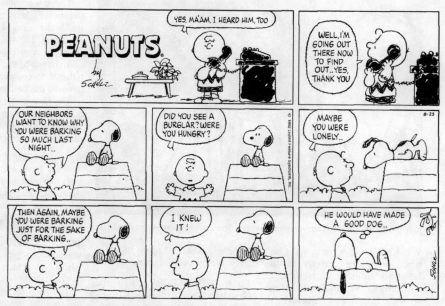

Figure 2.3: Just as Snoopy barks for the sheer enjoyment, many people shop and buy products for the pleasure.[6] (Reprinted with permission.)

Emotions are difficult to measure and there is only limited research into how emotions affect behaviour. The research that has been done shows that mood states (transitory emotions) influence shopping behaviour and our perceptions of products and brands.[7] For example, people who are in a happy, contented mood state are more receptive to marketing stimuli such as advertising and salespeople. This means that a key function of retail staff is to create positive, warm and empathetic relationships with customers. According to Barry Urquhart, a recent Australian survey shows that companies lose customers not because of product defects but because of poor sales techniques.[8]

We consume many products and services because we enjoy the experience of the associated emotions — for example, we revel in the 'fright state' aroused by horror movies such as *Silence of the Lambs*. This is called experiential consumption behaviour and it covers all non-functional and expressive benefits associated with products. Many products are bought for such benefits, and the major benefit sought is hedonistic experience.[9] Hedonism is commonly defined as the gaining of pleasure through the senses. In hedonic consumption situations, such as in the purchase of entertainment, a massage or perfume, emotional needs dominate utilitarian reasons. Some consumers engage in activities that are dangerous and exciting, such as skydiving, rock climbing and bungy-jumping. Fun parks have flourished for many decades by providing similar thrills for users (see page 36).

It's just a gut feeling

JEFF ALLAN and ANDREW MASTERSON

Just when you hope it's over, the Demon does it all again — backwards.

WE KNEW we were in for a bad time when we arrived at the latest $5 million installation at Australia's Wonderland. Huge wrought-iron gates opened to reveal the crumbling remains of the House of Usher set in the entrance of the new Transylvania-land, where weather-beaten headstones mark the demise of Dracula and Vlad the Impaler (1656–?). And looming above us, the cold, black, twisted metal of the **Demon**, billed as the "largest, meanest and fastest steel roller-coaster in the southern hemisphere".

After wolfing down half a bucket of greasy chips and a Coke (a prerequisite for any fright ride), we were strapped in snugly. Two seconds later, as the carriage was dragged agonisingly slowly up a 45-degree incline, I began having doubts about the chips. So did the people behind me.

Then, kapow, we were rocketed through a series of heart-stopping loops, twists and turns until we barrelled up another 45 degree hill — and proceeded to do it all again, backwards and faster. A truly breathtaking ride. Warning: if the incredible rush lures you,

like me, to do it all again immediately, reconsider the chips.

THE OPERATORS of the **Gravitron** at Melbourne's Luna Park like to leave prospective clients in no doubt about the nature of the ride.

"People with heart complaints or any other medical disorder ride at own risk," reads the sign. Any clear-headed, sensible person would heed the warnings and head for the nearest coffee shop.

Those who don't, however, find themselves leaning against a wall inside the windowless cabin of the machine. The whole contraption starts to spin at sickening speed and, thanks to the wonders of centrifugal force, propels one firmly towards the ceiling.

The Gravitron is a descendant of a NASA invention for testing astronauts. The only difference is that the astronauts were paid to ride in it.

AT FIRST sight the **Enterprise**, again at Luna Park, looks benign: a sort of ground-level, aluminium carousel, glinting in the weak winter sun. Do not be fooled. It is the merry-go-round from hell.

At first you simply sit in your cubicle and go round in circles. But you suddenly pick up speed and the whole structure simultaneously lurches upwards and sideways.

The next thing you know, you are looping the loop at enormous speed. This means you spend much time zooming upside down, the G-forces banging your bum into the seat and forcing your nose to investigate your ears.

This is called fun?

Good Weekend,
12 September 1992

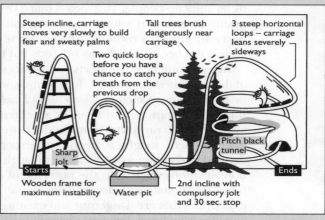

A monster of the mind: will anyone dare build this suicide machine?

It is easier to understand behaviour that is designed to satisfy hunger or thirst or to gain social acceptance, than behaviour that actually threatens life. However, the latter is common behaviour, because the adrenalin produced by the stress of these activities stimulates chemicals in the brain that produce pleasure sensations and release tensions.

On a less dangerous level there are many aesthetic, curiosity and 'ownership' experiences that produce good feelings. These also are thought to be a central influence on the choice of products, particularly when function, performance and price factors are relatively equal. Morris B. Holbrook is one researcher who has actively studied the impact of emotion on purchase behaviour. Holbrook and O'Shaughnessy developed a model (see figure 2.4) which incorporates emotions and reasons into the consumer's decision-making process.[10] This acknowledges that, alongside utilitarian reasons, emotions impact on the purchase of utilitarian products such as cars and household white goods.

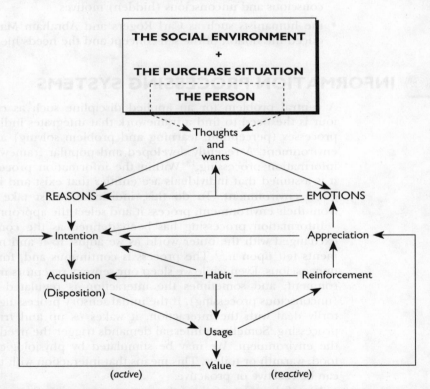

Figure 2.4: Decision-making model which incorporates emotions (*Source*: Adapted from M. B. Holbrook, J. O'Shaughnessy and S. Bell, 'Action and Reaction in the Consumer Experience', *Research in Consumer Behaviour*, 4, 1990)

Some writers have suggested that impulse purchasing is irrational, emotional behaviour.[11] Others have defined it as a 'buying action undertaken without a prior consciously recognised problem or a buying intention formed prior to entering the store'.[12] These definitions suggest that impulse buying and unplanned purchases are the same behaviour, and that such behaviour is not necessarily irrational. Point-of-sale displays and promotions certainly contribute to impulse purchases, of which the Australian Retailers Association estimates as constituting at least 60 per cent of supermarket buying.

UNDERSTANDING CONSUMERS

Each of these strands in psychology contributes to an understanding of individuals and their behaviour. Behaviourist theories show that individuals react to environmental stimuli, while cognitive theories explain how individuals interpret stimuli and then store the memory of the experience.

Other dimensions of psychology have also helped our understanding of consumers, including:

- the psychoanalytic theories of Freud, who introduced the notion of conscious and unconscious (hidden) motives
- the humanists such as Carl Rogers and Abraham Maslow, who introduced the notion of the self-concept and the needs hierarchy.

 ## INFORMATION PROCESSING SYSTEMS

A central problem for an applied discipline such as consumer behaviour is the need to find a framework that integrates individuals' internal processes (perception, learning and problem solving) and the external environment. A recently developed and popular framework is known as information processing.[13] Within the information processing approach, it is assumed that individuals are entities that exist and interact within a given environment. To do this, individuals must take in information from their environment, process it and select the appropriate responses.

Information processing has been defined as the content of what is exchanged with the outer world as we adjust to it and make our adjustments felt upon it.[14] The process is continuous and, for the most part, unconscious. Even while we sleep our sensory receptors monitor the environment, and sometimes the interaction is regulated while we sleep (unconscious processing). If the initial sensory processing cannot satisfactorily deal with the interaction, it wakes us up and triggers conscious processing. Sometimes internal demands trigger the need to interact with the environment. We may be stimulated by physiological demands for food, warmth or toilets. This means that interaction with the environment can be reactive or proactive.

A useful aspect of the information processing framework is that it is integrated, and thus allows for the influence on our actions of the unconscious and conscious dimensions, mood states, motivation, perception, memory and thinking. Essentially, however, it is based on three assumptions:

- that there is an external environment
- that the organism has the capacity to take in the information
- that it has the capacity to process the information.

Knowledge about the workings of the human mind and body is still in the embryonic stage. Cognitive scientists are unable to describe fully the workings of the mind and its relationship to physical processes. Therefore, the diagram in figure 2.5 is a simplistic description of how information processing occurs.

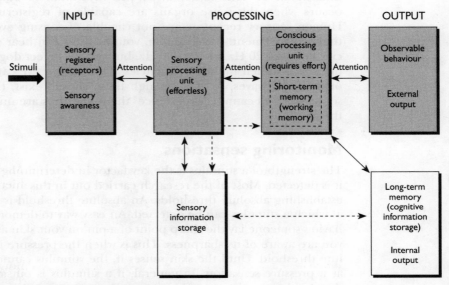

Figure 2.5: Information processing

Currently, information processing is viewed as two interacting systems — the sensory and the conceptual. The sensory system refers to the operation of the five senses — sight, smell, touch, taste and hearing. These senses enable individuals to be in contact with their external world. The conceptual system is the capacity to think, which requires the operation of memory, judgement, imagination and problem solving.

Information processing also takes place at both the conscious and unconscious levels and depends on the functioning of the brain's perceptual mechanisms and memory systems. The necessary requirements for the process are:

• **exposure** to stimuli
• **attention** to the stimuli
• **interpretation** of the stimuli.

Unless an individual is exposed to a stimulus, processing cannot begin. Also, if the strength of the stimulus is too weak or too strong, then the sensory receptors will not respond. Part of responding is paying attention to the stimulus, that is, focusing the physical senses and thoughts on the stimulus in order to receive information. Interpretation, or encoding as it is sometimes labelled, is the process of taking information in the environment and converting it to knowledge.

A popular way of viewing the process is in terms of input, processing and output, which we will now look at in more detail. The application of this process to consumer decisions is discussed more fully in chapters 14 and 15.

THE INPUT STAGE

The diagram in figure 2.5 shows that information processing is initiated when stimuli (raw data) are sensed by the sensory receptors (the nerves in our eyes, nose, ears, and skin). Firstly, there must be exposure, either intentional or unintentional, of the individual to stimuli. Sensation occurs when the sense organs are capable of registering the stimuli. Human sensory receptors are not capable of sensing every stimulus in their environment. For example, young adults can hear sound frequencies between 20 Hz and 20 000 Hz, but cannot detect dog whistles which operate at much higher frequencies. The human eye cannot see X-rays or infra-red waves, so even though these stimuli exist, the human sensory receptors cannot 'experience' them and thus are unable to process them.

Monitoring sensations

The strength of a stimulus is the key factor in determining whether or not it is detected. Most of the research carried out in this area has focused on establishing absolute thresholds. An absolute threshold is the lowest level at which a stimulus can be detected. An easy way to demonstrate this is by having someone lay the sharp point of a pin on your skin and press it until you are aware of its sharpness. This is when the pressure is on your absolute threshold. Until the skin senses it, the stimulus cannot be processed as a pressure sensation. In general, if a stimulus is outside the absolute threshold range, it cannot be processed.

Related to the notion of an absolute threshold is the concept of subliminal messages. The term 'subliminal' means 'below the threshold of awareness' (from Latin *limen*, meaning 'threshold'), in other words, something that is too weak to be received and processed by an individual's sensory receptors. On the other hand, a supraliminal stimulus is too strong to be received and processed by our sensory receptors, as is the case with sounds above 20 000 Hz. The term 'supraliminal' is rarely used, and the term 'subliminal' has come to refer to any stimulus that is outside the capacity of human sensory receptors, such as the sound of a feather hitting the ground. Although this is the strict definition of the term 'subliminal', usage has caused it to have a different meaning. Now, a subliminal stimulus is considered to be one that is within the capacity of human sensory receptors and able to be processed by the sensory processing unit, but too weak for conscious processing. Note that subliminal messages may be stored in our sensory memory and processed unconsciously.[15]

SENSORY PROCESSING

Once a sensation is detected, it obtains the attention of the sensory processing unit and perception begins. The initial processing of raw stimuli is fast, continuous and unconscious. Most of the stimuli to which we are exposed do not make strong enough impressions for us to be conscious of them.

The brain contains many more cells for processing visual data than for sound, smell and touch. Over 70 per cent of the information from the external environment comes via our visual receptors. However, just to consciously analyse all the visual information to which we are constantly exposed would require a brain one cubic light year in volume.[16]

A key factor in processing information is the holistic performance of the brain. Research into the physiology of the brain indicates that each hemisphere of the brain is specialised for particular functions. The left side contains the main language centre and the mechanism for carrying out mathematical calculations. We use the right side of the brain for spatial construction, visual imagery, musical ability, simple language comprehension and non-verbal idea development. It also seems that the right side of the brain specialises in the control of the emotions. If the right side is damaged, a person may be unable to produce or interpret emotional expressions, or even act out feelings of joy, sadness or anger. Some people are able to integrate and use both hemispheres more effectively than other people. The research in this area is fragmented and its usefulness in understanding consumer behaviour is yet to be determined.

Sensory processing and perception

The task of processing sensory information from the environment is the work of the perceptual systems. The perceptual systems extract and interpret information about the objects sensed by our sensory receptors. This allows us to create order out of the complex array of sensations reported by our sense organs, and to sort out the stimuli which require conscious processing. It is impossible to separate perception from sensation completely. Traditionally, the term 'sensation' refers to the physiological processes by which our nervous system registers stimuli. By contrast, 'perception' refers to the processes by which our brains arrive at a meaningful interpretation of basic sensations. Therefore, perception is a key element in understanding how our internal processes function. Chapter 3 describes the function and dynamics of perception, and its role in understanding consumer behaviour.

Sensory processing and sensory memory

There is much speculation about the sensory memory systems.[17] One school of thought suggests that they can retain an almost unlimited amount of uncoded information — in other words, all sensations accumulate in and are retained by the sensory memory systems. Other theorists think that sensations decay, although they cannot agree on the rate of decay. Since the content of the sensory memory cannot easily be brought into conscious awareness, it is difficult to test for decay. It is agreed, however, that most of the countless impressions received by the sensory memory never even reach the level of conscious awareness.

CONSCIOUS PROCESSING

Once the sensory receptors for each sense register a stimulus, the sensory processing unit determines whether it requires conscious processing. This initial processing is unconscious and effortless.

Attention to the raw stimuli by the sensory level of the processing unit is governed by at least four factors.

- **A strong stimulus which forces attention**. A loud noise will be processed — for example, loud television or radio commercials are more likely to be attended to; large print in advertisements attracts attention; and we are more likely to be attracted to strong smells, bright light and saturated (strong) colours.
- **Variations in the intensity of stimuli**. Varying the intensity of a stimulus means that we are more likely to attend to it. For example, is it true that the sound levels of television commercials are greater than those of the programs? (See the box below.)
- **Familiarity with stimuli**. A stimulus that stands out from other stimuli by virtue of contrast, novelty or surprise will draw our attention.
- **Consciously focused interest**. This forces all our information-processing capacity on a particular stimuli. For example, if we are searching for particular products in a supermarket, such as stock cubes or particular brands of soap powder, our sensory receptors are forced to process all the stimuli in the area to identify these products.

Are TV ads louder than the programs?

Advertisers use a number of tricks to make sure television commercials gain our attention — for example, not varying the sound, but maintaining the sound at peak levels permitted. During normal programs, the sound levels vary, so sound increases are processed as part of the program. Also loud parts in programs do not last long, so we do not notice them. However, we do notice 30 or 60 seconds at maximum sound level. Another tactic used by advertisers is to start their commercials with sounds that are different from the program sounds — for example, music or jingles. The break in continuity focuses our attention, so the commercial will seem louder.

Figure 2.6: This advertisement appeals to the conscious processing unit

Combining the four factors in a message increases our attention at the sensory processing level, which can lead to further processing by the conscious processing unit (CPU). At this point, the brain decides whether a reflexive action is required. If not, the attention of the CPU is activated. This attention at the conscious level requires mental effort (concentration). Once the CPU is activated, it is possible that the stimulus, if it is a message, will ultimately be transferred to the consumer's long-term memory storage.

Often the impetus to pay attention to a stimulus is generated by the long-term memory through the CPU. For example, a customer who is in the market for a mobile phone will seek out and pay attention to advertisements such as the one shown in figure 2.6, which is not a message that would grab your attention unless you were seeking such information.

The 'telegram' in figure 2.7 is an attempt to gain attention and thus save the message from the garbage bin. In the OTC advertisement, the attention of our sensory processing unit is attracted by the large print (strong stimuli). As well, the message is novel, thus activating conscious processing so that it is highly likely to gain sensory and mental attention.

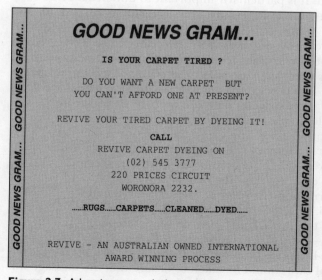

Figure 2.7: Advertisements which attract the attention of both our sensory and conscious processing units

Short-term memory

More is known about the mechanisms of the conscious processing unit than is known about the sensory memory systems, but our knowledge is still limited. It is clear that to successfully store and retrieve information it has to be given meaning so that it can be linked to our store of knowledge. This means that it must go through the conscious processing unit (CPU) to have meaning attached. The CPU has a number of labels, the most well-known one being the 'short-term memory system'. It can also be called the working memory.

Since the CPU can only hold information for approximately eighteen seconds before it decays, information needs to be organised so as to cope with this potential blockage.[18] To alleviate the limitation, people use chunking strategies. Chunking is the organisation of incoming information into the largest possible familiar clusters. The short-term memory then deals with each cluster as if it were a single unit. For example, looking at the rows of numbers below, it is easier to hold the second line in the working memory than the first. Presented with the first line, an individual probably would break the information down into the chunks of the second line, enabling easier transference to the long-term memory.

20331985204617341642001

2033 1985 2046 1734 1642 2001

Speed reading is a form of sophisticated chunking. When learning to read, the first stage is learning to read single alphabet letters. Then we learn to chunk these codes into words. Reading single words is slow, but chunking them into sentences and reading sentences is faster. Chunking words and sentences into paragraphs and reading those is even faster.

For effective communication of messages such as advertisements, it is crucial to understand the processes by which the information enters the CPU and is processed. It is particularly important to understand how messages should be presented, to ensure that consumers attend to and process the message.

The limited capacity of the short-term memory (the CPU) has a number of important implications for message design and delivery. If an electronic medium is used, such as radio or television, then the primacy/recency rule applies. This is because commercials in these media are delivered in an extremely short space of time (on average 15–30 seconds). The primacy/recency rule states that the important aspects of a message should be given at both the beginning and the end of the message. This is because the short-term memory will take in the first bits of information and then become overloaded.[19] Then, because we can recognise and do not want to miss the end, we 'skip' the details in the middle and focus on the last bits of information we receive. Messages designed for the electronic media should be kept simple, repeated, and pre-chunked if possible. Examples are the Pizza Hut home delivery telephone number in Sydney — 481 11 11 — and Pizza Haven's 131 241, which ties in with their frequent two-for-one-low-price promotions. If the target market is children or the elderly, special care should be taken to ensure that the message will be processed. Children have difficulty with abstract concepts so it is better to demonstrate the benefits of a product to them, rather than telling them. The elderly often have hearing or sight problems, so messages aimed at them must be delivered at a slower pace.

Figure 2.8: In this Pizza Haven advertisement, the telephone number 131 241 is an effective use of chunking. It also links the number to the sales promotion — two for one low price.

Long-term memory

It is vitally important to understand the mechanisms that transfer information from the working memory (short-term memory) to the long-term memory. For the most part, unless consumers are able to store information about products, it is unlikely that they will buy or use the product advertised. Considering the cost of advertisements, advertising messages should be designed to effectively overcome this problem. For this reason there has been substantial research focusing on the transfer of information from working memory to long-term memory. This research and its application to consumer decision making is described in chapter 4.

It has proved difficult to research the links between sensory information storage, the conscious processing unit and the long-term memory. It is thought that there are links, but how they work is virtually unknown. The links between these components in figure 2.5 (page 39) are shown as broken lines, indicating their equivocal nature.

Stimuli that are processed at the preconscious level would come from the sensory memory systems, so subliminal messages could affect conscious memory.[20] Research by William Kilbourne and others[21] found some support for the role of sexual embeds (information in a message that is below conscious awareness but above the threshold of awareness) in messages. Groups of students were used to test reactions to advertisements for cigarettes and Scotch whisky. A nude female form was embedded in the whisky advertisement and male genitals were embedded in the cigarette advertisement. Comparisons of responses to non-embedded and embedded advertisements showed differences in message processing. More attention was given to the advertisements with the embeds. In another example, Hawkins[22] found that by presenting words associated with thirst, respondents reported increased thirst ratings. Possibly, for reactions to the embeds to occur, the message must have been flashed at the absolute thresholds or just above but still too weak to be processed by conscious activity.[23] Such research did not explain why and how these weak messages are transferred to the long-term memory. Research findings related to the impact of embeds are contradictory and there is some debate as to the effectiveness of embeds in brand choice.[24]

Information processing and emotion

Because emotions impact on our thinking and judgement, feelings have an impact on all aspects of our information processing. To date, the majority of research has focused on the impact of emotional appeals and images (symbols) in advertising. Research by Meryl Gardner[25] shows that individuals who are feeling happy or good (positive mood state) respond more favourably to emotional appeals, while those who are in a negative mood state respond more to functional appeals.[26] Robert Zajonic and Hazel Markus have suggested that it is possible to create positive attitudes towards a brand by simply exposing consumers to it often enough. Their rationale was that familiarity will lead consumers to like the brand, thus affecting their judgement.[27]

Deborah MacInnis and Bernard Jaworski[28] have attempted to tie in consumer information processing and affective responses by developing a framework that incorporates both cognitive and emotional factors into the processing of advertising messages. Their proposed model (see figure 2.9) links cognitive and emotional responses to brand attitude formation. Although their work is rudimentary, it is important because it addresses and attempts to conceptualise the relationship between feeling and judgement, and how the two ultimately impact on consumer attitudes to brands.

THE OUTPUT STAGE

The output of processing can be an action such as an enquiry or a purchase. The output can also be the storage of information in the long-term memory system without any observable behaviour. This may act as the impetus for purchasing behaviour at a later date. The fact that an advertisement does not immediately generate the expected sales does not mean that the advertisement has been unsuccessful. It may be that the message has been received and stored by the target audience, and that other factors are inhibiting purchases. Similarly, window shopping is a popular way of obtaining information for future purchases.[29] In a recession, consumers are generally unwilling to purchase. They may register the message about a product, and resolve that they will purchase the item as soon as they have the money or the economy improves.

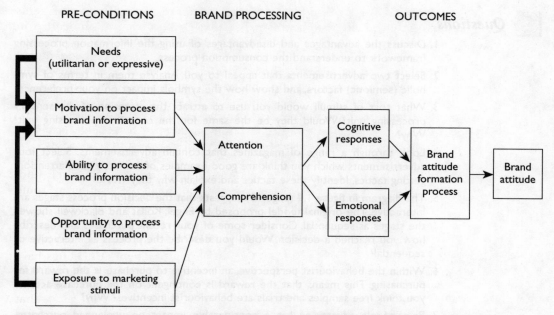

PRE-CONDITIONS   BRAND PROCESSING   OUTCOMES

Figure 2.9: The role of emotion in brand attitude formation (*Source*: Adapted from D. J. MacInnis and B. J. Jaworski, 'Information Processing from Advertisements: Towards an Integrative Framework', *Journal of Marketing*, 53, 1989)

SUMMARY

Information processing has been defined as the content of what is exchanged with the outer world as we adjust to it and make our adjustments felt upon it. It has been conceptualised as having two key processing units, the sensory and the conscious processing units. The conventional approach has been to analyse the process in terms of input, processing and outputs. To understand the process fully, we must have a good working knowledge of how our perceptual process interprets incoming data and how our memory systems function.

Applying the information processing framework in consumer research is a recent addition to the various conceptual frameworks we use to understand the consumption process. The main advantage of the information processing approach is that it allows marketers to understand how consumers acquire, integrate and store knowledge. Understanding how consumers process information is a crucial factor in the design of effective communication strategies. It can provide insights into how messages should be presented so as to ensure consumer attention and processing.

Information processing also has the potential to help us understand the impact of emotion on judgement and behaviour. By studying how consumers process information, we may even be able to develop a deeper understanding of the roles played by subliminal messages, symbols and atmosphere in influencing consumers' judgement and behaviour.

 *Questions*

1. Discuss the advantages and disadvantages of using the information processing framework to understand the consumption process.

2. Select two advertisements that appeal to you. Analyse them in terms of symbolic (semiotic) factors, and show how the symbols impact on your preference.

3. What sort of stimuli would you use to attract the attention of the sensory processing unit? Would they be the same for the conscious processing unit? Why?

4. Look through a range of magazines that contain advertisements. Select four advertisements which you think are good examples of correctly used attention-getting tactics. Identify these tactics and explain why they work.

5. The diagram in figure 1.4 (page 13) suggests that the decision process stages are interactive. The original model proposed by Engel, Kollat and Blackwell showed the stages as sequential. Consider some of your recent purchases and describe how you reached a decision. Would you describe the process as interactive or sequential?

6. Within the behaviourist perspective, an incentive to purchase is the reward for purchasing. This means that the reward is contingent on the purchase act. Do you think free samples and trials are behaviourist incentives? Why?

7. Point-of-sale advertising has a considerable impact on unplanned purchases. Select three occasions when you were influenced to purchase a product at the point of sale. What was the point-of-sale strategy? Why did it work on you?

8. Watch a local 'sitcom' or 'soapie' and try to identify as many products as you can that are used in the show. Discuss how, if you were not specifically searching for the products, you would be influenced by the products shown in this way.

9. Figure 1.4 (page 13) depicts the factors which we need to know to understand the influences and activities involved in purchase decisions. Examine the factors and their relationship that featured in at least two of your recent purchases. How would you draw your decision process? How different is it from the diagram shown in figure 1.4?

10. Because of our limited capacity to process information quickly, information overload is a problem for any communication exercise. What media are likely to have the most problems? Why? What tactics could you use to reduce information overload? Would they be different for print and electronic media?

 Case study questions

Read the article on page 49 then answer the following questions.

1. Do you think that because the 1990s are emerging as a 'warm, fuzzy decade of kinder, gentler people', that the role of emotions in purchase decisions will change?

2. Identify a product that you have bought recently and which you did not consider to have any functional benefits. Why were functional benefits not relevant to you?

3. List four of your recent purchases which you would describe as hedonic purchases. Discuss what, if any, utilitarian (functional) factors influenced your choice.

4. Explain why advertisements which combine emotional and functional benefits could be more effective than those that don't. Do you think this is true for all products?

Case study

Fast-food king McDonald's is running an unusual television commercial. Created by ad agency DDB Needham, it features a young boy and his very pregnant mother in a McDonald's restaurant. The boy is worried about how his life will change when the baby arrives. The mother reassures him that he won't have to share everything with the new baby, certainly not his McDonald's meals. She asks him what the new baby should be named and he answers "Pickles".

The ad is a good example of emotional advertising. It offers no functional reasons why people should eat at McDonald's. There is no mention of the food or the experience of eating at the fast-food chain. In attempting to link McDonald's to motherhood, kids and "special times", the ad is aimed directly at the heart.

McDonald's is not the only company employing emotional, as opposed to functional advertising. More companies are abandoning unique selling propositions — a stalwart of marketing and advertising strategies since the 1950s — in favor of emotional selling propositions. With little differentiation between most products, marketers figure the use of an emotion-based sales pitch will give them an edge over their rivals. But is emotion relevant in the 1990s?

After the glitz and greed of the 1980s, the 1990s are emerging as a warm, fuzzy decade of kinder, gentler people. But market researchers say this is also a decade of hard-headed, tough consumers who want solid reasons for buying a product or service. Selling the feeling of using a product, rather than its utilitarian aspects, may not work with the consumer of the 1990s.

But emotion is a proven seller. Successful ad campaigns such as the sugar industry's "Sugar. A natural part of life" promotion and OTC's "Memories" ads rely heavily on emotion. They offer no functional reasons for people to use sugar or phone their relatives overseas. The ads convey how people will feel if they buy the product.

Every product and service has a function that can be communicated through advertising. But some companies choose to ignore the function and concentrate on the emotion. Nestle and its ad agency, McCann-Erickson, are running a TV campaign for Nescafe coffee called "Now you're talking". Previous Nescafe ads focused on the product's taste, aroma or origins. The new campaign's premise is that a cup of coffee can draw people together. The ads pull on the heartstrings, particularly the ad in which the frosty relationship between a father and son is thawed over a cup of coffee.

The TV commercial to launch Mitsubishi Australia's new Magna is all emotion. Created by Young & Rubicam, it features billowing white curtains and a car gliding along a wet road, with a soft voice-over extolling the benefits of the car. At the end, a Japanese man delivers the campaign's theme line, "Please consider". Consider what? It is a nice-looking ad, but it offers no compelling reason for people to buy a Magna. It is warm and bewildering.

Compare the Magna ad to the new commercial for Streets Ice-Cream's Cornetto brand, made by the Lintas agency. For most of the 1980s, Streets used emotion to sell Cornetto, with scenes of young people lying around, munching Cornettos. The new ad focuses on what is inside the Cornetto — Streets Blue Ribbon icecream — and uses the theme "It's what's inside that really matters". The ad uses an emotional trigger in the form of two young lovers, but the function benefit of the icecream inside the cone is the hook.

The most effective ads are those that combine emotional and functional benefits, such as Coca-Cola's, which sell the refreshment benefits of drinking Coke and the "good times" it brings, and Chiat/Day/Mojo's "You oughta be congratulated" campaign for Meadow Lea margarine.

Neil Shoebridge,
Business Review Weekly, 3 May 1991

SUGGESTED READING

R. A. Peterson, W. D. Hoyer and W. R. Wilson, *The Role of Affect in Consumer Behaviour: Emerging Theories and Applications*, Lexington Books, USA, 1986.

M. Walker, D. Burnham and R. Borland, *Psychology*, 2nd edn, John Wiley and Sons, Brisbane, 1994, pp. 250–77.

J. R. Bettman, *An Information Processing Theory of Consumer Choice*, Addison-Wesley, Reading, Mass., 1979.

ENDNOTES

1. G. Miller, 'The Magical Number Seven. Plus or Minus Two: Some Limits on our Capacity to Process Information', *Psychological Review*, 76, 1967, pp. 81–97.

2. W. R. Nord and P. J. Peter, 'A Behaviour Modification Perspective on Marketing', *Journal of Marketing*, 44, 1980. M. L. Rothschild and W. C. Gaidis, 'Behavioural Learning Theory: Its Relevance to Marketing and Promotions', *Journal of Marketing*, 45, No. 2, Spring 1981, pp. 70–78.

3. W. C. Gaidis and J. Cross, 'Behavioural Modification as a Framework for Sales Promotion Management', *Journal of Consumer Marketing*, 4, Spring 1987, pp. 65–74.

4. M. Walker, D. Burnham and R. Borland, *Psychology*, 2nd edn, John Wiley and Sons, Brisbane, 1994, pp. 218–46. A. Dickinson, *Contemporary Animal Learning Theory*, Cambridge University Press, 1980. E. R. Hilgard and G. H. Bower, *Theories of Learning*, 4th edn, Appleton-Century-Crofts, New York, 1974. G. E. Zuriff, *Behavourism: A Conceptual Reconstruction*, Columbia University Press, New York, 1985. C. Janiszewski and L. Warlop, 'The Influence of Classical Conditioning Procedures on Subsequent Attention to the Conditioned Brand', *Journal of Consumer Research*, Vol. 20, No. 2, Sept. 1992, pp. 171–89.

5. P. N. Johnson-Lairs, *The Computer and the Mind: An Introduction to Cognitive Science*, Fontana Masters Guide, 1989. H. Gardner, *The Mind's New Science: A History of the Cognitive Revolution*, Basic Books, New York, 1985. R. S. Siegler, 'Mechanisms of Cognitive Development', in M. R. Rosenzweig and L. W. Porter (eds), *Annual Review of Psychology*, 40, 1989, pp. 353–79.

6. E. M. Tauber, 'Why Do People Shop?', *Journal of Marketing*, 47, Oct. 1972, pp. 46–59.

7. Marvin Zukerman, *Sensation and Seeking: Beyond the Optimum Level of Arousal*, Lawrence Erlbaum, Hillsdale, NJ, 1979. P. S. Raju, 'Optimum Stimulation Level: Its Relationship to Personality, Demographics and Exploratory Behaviour', *Journal of Consumer Research*, 7 Dec. 1980, pp. 272–82. M. Holbrook and E. Hirschman, 'The Experiential Aspects of Consumption: Consumer Fantasies, Feelings and Fun', *Journal of Consumer Research*, 9 Sept. 1982, pp. 132–40. W. R. Swinyard, 'The Effects of Mood, Involvement and Quality of Store Experience on Shopping Intentions', *Journal of Consumer Research*, Vol. 20, No. 2, Sept. 1993, pp. 271–80.

8. B. Urquhart, 'It's War Between Staff and Customers', *Marketing*, Sept. 1993, p. 4.

9. E. Hirschman and M. Holbrook, 'Hedonic Consumption: Emerging Concepts, Methods and Propositions', *Journal of Marketing*, 46, Summer 1982, pp. 92–101. E. Hirschman, 'Innovativeness, Novelty Seeking and Consumer Creativity, *Journal of Consumer Research*, Dec. 1980, pp. 283–95. R. L. Celsi, R. L. Rose and T. W. Leigh, 'An Exploration of High-Risk Leisure Consumption through Skydiving', *Journal of Consumer Research*, Vol. 20, No. 1, June 1993, pp. 1–23.

10. M. B. Holbrook, J. O'Shaughnessy and S. Bell, 'Action and Reaction in the Consumer Experience', *Research in Consumer Behaviour*, Vol. 4, 1990, pp. 131–63. M. B. Holbrook, 'Emotion in the Consumption Experience: Toward a New Model of the Human Consumer', in Hoyer et al., *The Role of Affect in Consumer Behaviour*, Lexington Books, USA, 1986. M. B. Holbrook and E. Hirschman, 'The Experiential Aspects of Consumption: Consumer Fantasies, Feeling and Fun', *Journal of Consumer Research*, 9, Sept. 1982, pp. 272–82. O. T. Ahtola, 'Hedonic and Utilitarian Aspects of Consumer Behaviours: An Attitudinal Perspective', in E. C. Hirschman and M. Holbrook (eds), *Advances in Consumer Research*, Ann Arbor, Mich., Association for Consumer Research, Vol. 12, 1985, pp. 7–10.

11. D. Rook, 'The Buying Impulse', *Journal of Consumer Research*, 14, Sept. 1987, pp. 189–99.

12. J. Engel and R. D. Blackwell, *Consumer Behaviour*, 4th edn, The Dryden Press, Chicago, 1982.

13. P. Lindsay and D. Norman, *Human Information Processing*, 2nd edn, Academic Press, New York, 1977. R. C. Schank and R. P. Abelson, *Scripts, Plans, Goals and Understanding: An Enquiry into Human Knowledge*, Lawrence Erlbaum, NJ, 1977.

14. N. Weiner, 'Cybernetics in History', in W. Buckley (ed.), *Modern Systems: Research for the Behavioural Scientist*, Aldine Publishing Company, Chicago, 1968, pp. 31–36.

15. W. R. Kunst-Wilson and R. B. Zajonic, 'Affective Discrimination of Stimuli that Cannot be Recognized', *Science*, 207, 1980, pp. 557–58. C. A. Fowler, G. Wolford, R. Slade and L. Tassinary, 'Lexical Access With and Without Awareness', *Journal of Experimental Psychology: General*, 110, 1981, pp. 341–62. A. Marcel, 'Conscious and Unconscious Perception: Experiments in Visual Masking and Word Perception, *Cognitive Psychology*, 15, 1983, pp. 197–238. A. Marcel, 'Conscious and Unconscious Perception: An Approach to the Relations Between Phenomenal Experience and Perceptual Processes', *Cognitive Psychology*, 15, 1983, pp. 238–300. H. Krugman, 'The Impact of Television in Advertising: Learning Without Involvement', *Public Opinion Quarterly*, Vol. 29, 1965, pp. 349–56. N. Dixon, *Subliminal Perception: The Nature of a Controversy*, McGraw-Hill, London, 1971. S. A. Hawkins and S. J. Hoch, 'Low-Involvement Learning: Memory Without Evaluation', *Journal of Consumer Research*, Vol. 19, No. 2, Sept. 1992, pp. 212–25.

16. W. J. McKeachie and C. L. Doyle, *Psychology*, Addison-Wesley, Reading, Mass., 1966. R. R. Bootzin et al., *Psychology Today: An Introduction*, 6th edn, Random House, New York, 1986.

17. J. Leask, R. N. Haber and R. B. Haber, 'Eidetic Imagery in Children: 11 Longitudinal and Experimental Results', *Psychonomic Monograph Supplements*, 35, 1969. S. M. Kosslyn, *Image and Mind*, Harvard University Press, Cambridge, Mass., 1980. S. M. Josslyn, *Ghosts in the Mind's Machine*, Norton, New York, 1984.

18. D. E. Broadbent, *Perception and Communication*, Pergamon Press, London, 1958. N. C. Waugh and D. A. Norman, 'Primary Memory', *Psychological Review*, 72, 1965, pp. 89–104. R. C. Atkinson and R. M. Shiffrin, 'Human Memory: A Proposed System and its Control', in K. W. Spence and J. T. Spence (eds), *The Psychology of Learning and Motivation*, Vol. 2, Academic Press, New York, 1968.

19. H. Gleitman, *Basic Psychology*, 3rd edn, Norton, New York, 1992. N. Miller and D. Campbell, 'Recency and Primacy in Persuasion as a Function of the Timing of Speeches and Measurement', *Journal of Abnormal and Social Psychology*, 59, 1959, pp. 1–9.

20. H. E. Krugman, 'Memory Without Recall, Exposure Without Recognition', *Journal of Advertising*, 17, 1977, pp. 36–48.

21. W. Kilbourne, S. Painton and D. Ridley, 'The Effect of Sexual Embedding on Responses to Magazine Advertisements', *Journal of Advertising*, Vol. 14, No. 2, 1985, pp. 48–56.

22. D. Hawkins, 'The Effects of Subliminal Stimulation on Drive Level and Brand Preference', *Journal of Marketing Research*, Vol. 7, No. 3, 1970, pp. 322–26.

23. R. B. Zajonic, 'Attitudinal Effect of Mere Exposure', *Journal of Personality and Social Psychology: Monograph Supplement*, 1968. A. J. Marcel, 'Conscious and Unconscious Perception: An Approach to the Relations Between Phenomenal Experience and Perceptual Processes', *Cognitive Psychology*, 15, 1983, pp. 238–300.

24. S. H. Hart and S. McDaniel, 'Subliminal Stimulation: Marketing Applications', in J. U. McNeal and S. W. Daniel (eds), *Consumers' Behaviour: Classical and Contemporary Dimensions*, Little Brown, Boston, 1982, pp. 165–75. J. Saegert, 'Why Marketing Should Quit Giving Subliminal Advertising the Benefit of the Doubt', *Psychology and Marketing*, Summer 1987, pp. 107–120. R. Cuperfain and T. K. Clarke, 'A New Perspective on Subliminal Perception', *Journal of Advertising*, 14, 1, 1985.

25. M. P. Gardner, 'Mood States and Consumer Behaviour: A Critical Review', *Journal of Consumer Research*, Vol. 12, Dec. 1985, pp. 281–300.

26. T. Srull, 'Memory, Mood and Consumer Judgement', *Advances in Consumer Research*, Vol. 14, 1987.

27. R. B. Zajonic and H. Markus, 'Affective and Cognitive Factors in Preference', *Journal of Consumer Research*, Vol. 9, 1982, pp. 123–31.

28. D. J. Macinnis and B. J. Jaworski, 'Information Processing from Advertisements: Towards an Integrative Framework', *Journal of Marketing*, Vol. 53, Oct. 1989, pp. 1–23.

29. P. Bloch and M. Richins, 'Shopping Without Purchase: An Investigation of Consumer Browsing Behaviour', in R. Bagozzi and A. Tybout (eds), *Advances in Consumer Research*, 10, Association for Consumer Research, Ann Arbor, Mich., 1983, pp. 389–93.

C H A P T E R

3

Perception

O B J E C T I V E S

This chapter should help you to:

*   understand the role of perception in marketing activity
*   have an overview of how the brain turns sensations into meaning
*   understand some of the factors that contribute to the positioning of products.

 ## WHAT IS PERCEPTION?

Perception plays an important part in marketing activity. An understanding of the way consumers perceive their world and of how products are perceived and positioned in the minds of consumers allows marketers to develop more efficient marketing strategies, and make effective decisions on packaging and pricing.

If you look up from this book and observe the room you are in, you could easily describe the room to someone else. But have you ever stopped to consider that what you see and describe may be different from what other people might see and describe? If you have ever listened to two friends describe the same film to you, you may notice that they have different opinions about the film and may even relate the story differently. Is one of them lying to you? Probably not. The differences that they express are based on differences in perception.

Perception can be described as the act of taking in information from the world around us through our sensory receptors and interpreting it. It is a crucial step in information processing.

THE ROLE OF THE SENSES

We are linked to the external world through our senses of touch, smell, taste, sight and hearing. Each of our sense organs contains special receptor cells that transmit messages via the central nervous system to the brain. Sensation occurs when the senses are stimulated and information is collected. Perception is the act of interpreting or giving meaning to the sensed information. We sense through our senses but we perceive the world with our brain.

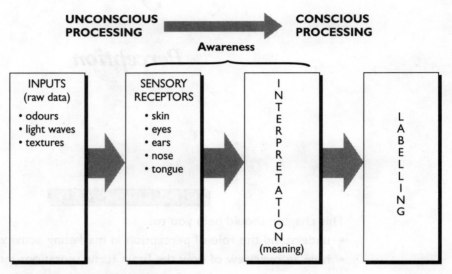

Figure 3.1: Sensory processing

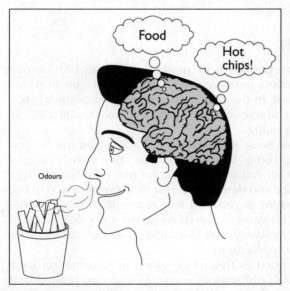

Figure 3.2: Identifying and labelling odours

The brain organises raw data from the senses into meaningful patterns and then, if it can, labels the experiences. Labelling is dependent on the information that is already stored in our memory systems.[1] For example, receptor cells in the nose register different odours, the brain groups similar odours together and attaches a meaning to them. If the brain has had prior experience of, say, food odours and perfume odours it can differentiate between the two. If the particular food smell is familiar, the brain might label the odour 'hot chips'. If the perfume is unfamiliar, then the smell will be stored in the sensory memory, unlabelled, until the smell is later identified as, say, Giorgio perfume. Future experiences of that smell will then be given the label 'Giorgio'.

Reading starts with our eyes registering a pattern of shapes on a page. We are taught that the shapes are letters and that groups of letters are words, so the brain interprets the shapes as 'text'. Whether you comprehend the actual meaning of the words depends on your capacity to decode the text. For example, your brain would classify the following pattern (from 'Jabberwocky' by Lewis Carroll) as text:

> 66Twas brillig, and the slithy toves
> Did gyre and gimble in the wabe:
> All mimsy were the borogoves,
> And the mome raths outgrabe.99

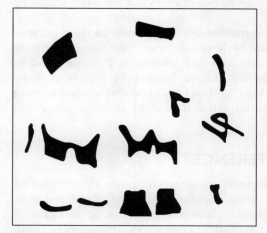

Figure 3.3: How do you interpret this pattern? (Does a hint such as 'a huge animal found in India and Africa' affect your interpretation?)

Because it rhymes, your memory system would classify it as a poem and because you have learned the code for some words you can extract meaning from them. Because you do not know the code for the others, you cannot.

How you respond to different stimuli will depend on your previous experience and expectations. Look at the illustration in figure 3.3 and consciously examine your thought processes as you try to interpret the pattern.

If new information is inconsistent with what you already know, you are likely to either discount the new information or alter your existing knowledge. So if you believe that all cats have green eyes and you are confronted with a blue-eyed cat, then you will either discount the information as 'an exception to the rule' or change what you believe.

Different individuals derive different meanings from the same sensory information and they also have differences in their sensory receptors. A blind person may have a better sense of touch or smell than a sighted person. Other individual differences may be less pronounced but may also have an effect on individuals' perceptual differences. For example, research has shown that nearly 10 per cent of men have some degree of red/green colour-blindness, yet advertisers rarely take this factor into account when designing advertising that is specifically directed towards men.[2] Many elderly people have difficulty reading small print, but few marketers have increased the sizes of their labels or product information to increase the probability that older people will be able to see their information easily.

DETECTING SENSATIONS

The initial processing of raw data from the senses is fast and continuous. The three main tasks of the brain at this stage are:
- registering sensations
- assessing their strength
- organising them into meaningful patterns.

Every individual has an absolute threshold below or above which sensory information cannot be sensed. During the processing of stimuli that are strong enough to be sensed, the sensory receptors adapt to the strength of the stimuli. At this point, focused, even conscious, awareness stops. Conscious awareness of sensory input depends on the 'background' to the input as well as on the abilities of the receptors. In a noisy room, you may not notice the sound of a clock ticking or a refrigerator switching off and on. But if you are studying quietly you may be very conscious of such noises. Each of our sensory receptors has a level at which it will detect a change. For example, our sensors that detect the temperature around us may not notice a change of two degrees but are likely to notice a change of ten degrees.

How our receptors 'sense' the outside world depends on their current state. You can demonstrate this by a simple test. Take three bowls of water, one very cold, one very hot and one lukewarm. Put one hand in the cold water, the other in the hot. Leave them there for about three minutes, then put both hands into the bowl of lukewarm water and note your sensations. One hand should sense it as cold and the other will sense it as hot.

JUST NOTICEABLE DIFFERENCE

While marketers must be concerned about a consumer's awareness of their product or service, they must also be concerned about the consumer's ability to detect differences between products or services, as changes in price and packaging can affect consumers' responses to products. This means that marketers need to establish at what point consumers become aware of differences. This is often difficult to judge, but one tool that has been applied to this aspect of marketing is Weber's Law. In the late nineteenth century, Ernst Weber developed a formula to measure the just noticeable difference (jnd). The just noticeable difference is the point at which any changes in the strength of a stimulus are noticed. These changes in stimuli can occur without our conscious awareness. If we are interested in the stimuli, we will notice any changes, no matter how slight, so long as they are above (or below) our threshold of awareness. When we are not so interested, the jnd factor will have to be high for us to notice a change.

Weber's Law states that the smallest difference in intensity that can be detected is directly proportional to the background intensity.[3] The formula for calculating the jnd is:

$$\text{jnd} \, \frac{\Delta I}{I} = K$$

where I = the original intensity of a stimulus

ΔI = the difference in stimulation required to make the two intensities just noticeably different

K = a constant.

Weber discovered that for each sense there was a fixed ratio that could be used to calculate the jnd (see table 3.1).

Table 3.1: Weber's fixed ratios for calculating the jnd for selected sensations

Sensation	Weber fraction	Per cent change needed to notice a difference
Pitch	$\frac{1}{333}$	0.3
Deep pressure	$\frac{1}{77}$	1.3
Brightness of a light (vision)	$\frac{1}{62}$	1.6
Lifted weight	$\frac{1}{53}$	1.9
Held weight	$\frac{1}{30}$	3.3
Loudness of a tone	$\frac{1}{11}$	9.1
Smell — amount of rubber smell	$\frac{1}{10}$	10.0
Pressure on the skin surface	$\frac{1}{7}$	14.2
Taste — amount of salty taste	$\frac{1}{5}$	20.0

If marketers want to alter the price or the packaging of a product, they can calculate the degree of change permissible according to whether or not they want consumers to notice the change. If a price reduction is being offered, it is necessary to ensure that the price change is greater than the just noticeable difference, especially if the reduction is being used to attract attention. For example, in a busy supermarket, the reduction will have to be enough for consumers to react. Reducing the price of a fifty-cent chocolate bar so that a difference will be noticed, using Weber's Law, you need to reduce it by at least 9 cents (18 per cent), and make sure that the original price is displayed.

$$\text{jnd } \frac{\Delta I}{.50} = \frac{1}{62}$$
$$\Delta I = 9c$$

A common practice of retailers is to reduce items by approximately 20 per cent which is close to the 1/62 value of K for sight (or 'brightness', as in the table above).[4] It is important to remember that there is a range of factors that determine whether the price reduction will translate into purchase, such as product relevance and affordability, even with the reduction.

Figure 3.4: Are these reductions enough to be above the just noticeable difference?

Marketers may need to update packaging to conform to changes in legislative requirements or simply to update the product image. To do this without losing the brand-loyal consumers who readily recognise the packaging, marketers can make a number of small changes. An example of a package that has undergone subtle or unnoticeable changes is the Vegemite jar (see figure 3.6). Vegemite has been a popular item in the pantries of Australian households since the 1920s and its distinctive label is part of its charm. Therefore, any changes to it have been planned so as not to affect its ability to be recognised.

Figure 3.5: Manufacturers make an assortment of claims so that their products appear different from and superior to the competing brands.

Sometimes, alterations to the product itself are necessary due to changing consumer demands or regulations. If the change is to be perceived as an improvement, marketers need to determine the amount of difference required for the product to be perceived by the consumer as 'improved'. If a detergent is to be advertised as 'new — thicker and richer', then research should be conducted with users to assess how much 'thicker and richer' the product must be in order to meet these criteria. The product claim will only be perceived as realistic if the difference is above the jnd.[5]

Recent changes in our attitude to salt have led manufacturers of products such as Vegemite to gradually reduce the salt content. If the manufacturer does not want the changes in taste to be noticeable, alterations must be below the jnd.

The decision to alter a product and tell consumers about the alteration must be handled with care. After 99 years the Coca-Cola Company decided to abandon its original formula in favour of a sweeter variation, named 'New Coke'. The reason for altering the taste was the Pepsi Challenge and Coca-Cola's own research that showed people preferred the taste of Pepsi — it was sweeter.[6] In general, a sweeter flavour tends to be preferred in blind taste tests. The outcry from loyal Coke drinkers to bring back 'their coke' was loud. If Coca-Cola had increased the level of sugar slowly (below the jnd) and had not gone public, the declining growth rate (13 per cent to 2 per cent) could have been averted.

As costs increase, a producer may be faced with the decision whether to increase prices or to reduce product size or quality. In cases where the product has a low price and the market is price-sensitive, it may be very difficult to increase prices. Reducing the size or quality of the product and maintaining the same price may have less impact on sales.[7] For example, Pizza Hut adopted the strategy of reducing the size of their pizzas to bring them into line with those of competitors and consumers did not complain about the reduction (see the article on page 60).

THE VEGEMITE LABEL

Since its introduction in 1923 the ▶ Vegemite jar has passed through many different phases of packaging and labelling. Its first label was orange and red and described it as 'Pure Vegetable Extract'. By 1940 (*right*) the label was red and yellow, it was a pad label rather than 'wrap-around', and was described more accurately as 'Concentrated Yeast Extract'.

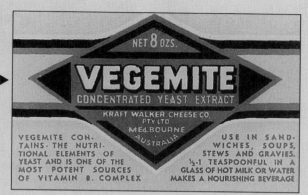

1950s — Success was now being pursued abroad and differing requirements and standards in various countries saw minor label changes over time. The first of these was reversion to the wrap-around label for the USA market and included on this was a vitamin statement indicating daily requirements. In 1952 Kraft's association with Vegemite became clear on the label for the first time.

◀ **1960s** — In 1961 and 1963 respectively the label reverted to a two panel design and the horizontal lines were removed. A major change in the Kraft logo occurred in 1964 when the single 'K' was replaced with the full word 'Kraft' surrounded by an elongated hexagon.

1970s — 1970 saw the introduction into Australia ▶ and New Zealand of rounded corners on the diamond. Kraft's logo, too, was moved to become part of the lower end of the diamond. By 1975 Australians required only metric information on labels.

1980s–present — The present label was introduced in 1989, with the added words 'All Natural' in line with consumer requirements.

Figure 3.6: Changes to the Vegemite label (*Source*: Christina Siciliano and Kraft Foods Ltd)

Revealed: secret of the shrinking pizza

RICHARD MACEY

Cowabunga! Pizza Hut, the fast food giant, has secretly shrunk its pizzas.

In an operation launched three weeks ago, Pizza Hut reduced the diameter of its two biggest pizzas, the medium and the large (sometimes known as the family) by about two centimetres.

The company's Australian Marketing Director, Mr Jim Collier, confirmed that the size of the pizzas had been trimmed. But, he added, the move was designed to increase sales rather than save dough.

Mr Collier claimed that for many years, Pizza Hut pizzas had been about four centimetres wider than those produced by many competitors. As a result, Pizza Hut had also become more expensive.

"Our competitors were heaps smaller, but they were also heaps cheaper and that was putting us at a disadvantage," he said. "We were giving the competition too much of a free kick."

Mr Collier said the company had been absorbing price increases for two years. Changing to smaller pizzas meant the company would be able to continue holding down costs for at least another year, reducing price differences between Pizza Hut and the opposition.

He said that in real terms, "you now get about 10 to 15 per cent better value in mouthful for money".

He admitted that, although introducing smaller boxes and pans into the 325 stores across Australia had been "a major logistics operation", there had been no announcement.

The company had "not crowed" about absorbing price increases over the past two years and did not have to advertise the size trim.

Mr Collier declined to detail how much dough the company would save with the smaller pizzas. He said Pizza Hut sells nine million pizzas a year in Australia — half the market.

He said the pizza industry was almost recession-proof.

"Last year was our best year ever," he said, adding that in hard economic times, many people abandoned expensive restaurants in favour of cheaper fast food chains.

Mr Charlie Bell, vice-president of McDonald's, said his sales also were ahead of last year's. "We are not reducing the size of our burgers,' he added.

Kentucky Fried Chicken said sales were keeping pace with the previous year's.

Sydney Morning Herald,
8 March 1991

INFLUENCES ON PERCEPTION

SUBLIMINAL INFLUENCES

As we saw in chapter 2, subliminal perception refers to 'weak' sensations, sensations of which we are not consciously aware.[8] The use of subliminal influences in marketing started in 1957 when James Vicary, an executive with the Coca-Cola Company, set up an experiment in an American movie theatre to test the influence of subliminal messages on the audience. He arranged for messages to be flashed onto the screen while the movie was running. The messages were the words 'Eat Popcorn' and 'Drink Coca-Cola' and they were each flashed for 1/300 of a second, at approximately five second intervals. He claimed that sales of popcorn went up by 57 per cent and Coke by 17 per cent. Vicary did not supply any written reports on how he conducted the survey and various replications did not produce positive results.[9]

At the time, these findings raised great fears that unscrupulous advertisers would be able to influence the behaviour of consumers without consumers being aware of these influences. Vance Packard's *The Hidden Persuaders* pursued this interest in subliminal perception. Another major surge of interest occurred in the mid-1970s with allegations that advertisers were using 'embedded images' in print advertising. Wilson Key, in *Subliminal Seduction*,[10] argued that emotionally loaded words and pictures were being inserted in most advertising in North America. The most well-known claim was that Ritz crackers had the word 'sex' etched in the surface of each biscuit, below absolute threshold. According to Key, 'sex' is the word most frequently used to trigger a subliminal response.

There are contrary views on the effectiveness of subliminal techniques[11] but there is evidence that physiological drives, such as hunger, thirst, sex and emotions, may be aroused by messages just on the threshold. However, there is no evidence that brand information and message recall can be created subliminally.[12] One study exposed individuals to the word 'beef' and concluded that, although this group reported being more hungry than a control group, they did not choose beef from a menu more often than the control group.[13]

It may be that exposure to the brand name and some brand attributes at the subliminal level can influence our feelings towards the brand, even if it cannot create conscious knowledge.[14] Two possible explanations for this effect are:[15]

• that constant exposure (repetition) transfers the brand name to the long-term memory. Some research suggests that the greater the number of exposures, the more positive the individual's response.

• that the message is associated with an unconscious wish.

Other individual factors may influence the processing of subliminal information. Some research suggests that differences in personality, anxiety, current mood and level of arousal may have an impact on perceptual performance.[16] High arousal may narrow an individual's attention to dominant information suggesting that anxious subjects are likely to have different threshold levels.[17]

INFLUENCE OF COLOUR

Even when colours are well above the threshold of awareness, we are not often aware of their impact. But colours do have a direct impact on the way we act and feel.[18] Not all colours affect all people the same way, but most do produce distinctive responses. Colours from the warm end of the spectrum, such as bright red, cause the pituitary gland to produce adrenalin. Exposure to red therefore can cause us to become physically active and could explain why we should not wave a red flag at a bull.[19] Exposure to colours from the cool end of the spectrum, such as blue and green, has the opposite effect — it reduces adrenalin flows. Use of colour in advertisements, packaging and store design to influence our mood states should be carefully managed to produce the desired results. Some guidelines for using colour are listed on pages 62–63.[20]

Selling with colour

The following is an extract from John Miner's *Complete Colour Reference Manual*, a guide to using colour in display and for creating moods.

COLOUR FOR DISPLAY

Bright colours:	Recommended for impulse attraction.
Light colours:	Good impulse attraction, depending on the colour.
Dark colours:	Little attraction value.
Neutrals:	Some neutrals have impulse attraction.
Violet:	Little value from an attraction standpoint.
Blue:	Essentially a background colour, passive, little impact.
Blue/green:	Has more impact than pure blue, particularly turquoise, which has good impulse value.
Green:	Luminous shades of green have good attraction value especially those having a good proportion of yellow. Other variations are best used for background.
Yellow:	Excellent attention getter but avoid very pale yellows and harsh acidic variations.
Orange:	Red/orange has by far the strongest impulse value. It is almost impossible to ignore. (Preferred to brilliant orange.)
Brown:	Not recommended. Fawn does have some attraction value but is not as good as orange.
Red:	Excellent attention getter but use reds on the yellow side. Vermilion is particularly recommended and appeals universally. Flame red is also good but avoid blue-type reds. Do not use red for background except in special circumstances.
Pink:	Luminous tones of pink have excellent attraction value but avoid pale pinks. Coral pink is recommended.
White:	Background only.
Off/white:	Not recommended for impulse applications.
Grey:	Background only, not recommended for impulse applications.
Black:	May be useful in special circumstances.
Grey tints:	Not recommended.

CREATING MOODS WITH COLOUR

Hard colours:	Generally create an exciting mood and express vitality. They are inviting to the viewer.
Soft colours:	Subduing — generally create a quiet mood but can also suggest the sea.
Bright colours:	Pale green and yellow will suggest the spring and turn people's thoughts to new clothes and furnishings.
Muted colours:	Subduing — can suggest luxury and sophistication.
Light colours:	Help to direct attention outwards.
Dark colours:	Tend to create a sombre, serious mood.
Neutrals:	Create a mood of dignity and safety.
Violet:	Purple is enigmatic and dramatic; royal purple creates an influential atmosphere. Evokes conflicting emotions — people either like it or hate it. It indicates depth of feeling, sensuality and richness but used the wrong way it can cause confusion and can be unsettling.

Blue: The perfect colour to release highly strung, overworked people because it calms their emotions. It is a peace maker. It denotes quietness because it retards automatic responses. It is also a colour of softness, coolness, freshness, cleanliness, and the great outdoors generally. Blue is fresh and translucent but may also be subduing and depressing if not used with care. Large areas of blue are cold.

Blue/green: Less subduing than blue. Infers coolness, freshness, cleanliness. It is also flattering to the complexion.

Green: Represents stability and security, soothing, refreshing, abates excitement, non-aggressive and tranquil. Denotes freshness, restfulness, the outdoors. Although classed as a cool colour, green is neither inviting or uninviting to the viewer and in this context is neutral. It creates a feeling of spring in the country, fresh and translucent. Pastel greens can be a little subduing, grey/green creates an influential image.

Yellow: Friendly and cheerful, it provides inspiration and a sunny disposition. It is the happiest of colours and brings out the cold. It is energising and conducive to vitality. Pale yellow produces a quieter note.

Orange: Gives a feeling of solidity and warmth, serenity and assurance. Cheerful and stimulating it can also be tiring and slightly irritating over large areas. Compels interest and indicates excitement.

Brown: Evokes a deep restful feeling and tranquility. Earthy browns are intimate; yellow/browns create an intense mood (but tan is soft and warm). Shades such as tan and sandstone are influential, while fawns and beiges are sophisticated.

Red: Makes for passion, warmth and excitement, because it increases autonomic response. Can be welcoming and cosy but also an irritant, especially over large areas. Many people quarrel when they are in a bright red room. People react more quickly to red than to any other colour. Rich reds and terracotta are intimate.

Pink: Creates a gentler mood than red. Peach is a warm colour associated with happiness.

White: Neutral in character. Creates a stark atmosphere but is associated with weddings and joyous occasions.

Off-white: Gives a distinctive tone to an otherwise white world. Creates a mood of dignity and safety.

Black: Creates a "deep tone". Can be dramatic but may also suggest mourning and in the wrong context can be depressing.

Grey: Creates a mood of dignity and safety and denotes common sense and influence, but in the wrong context may be depressing and suggest old age. A conservative colour which reduces emotional response and is non-commital.

Grey tints: Tend to be subduing, but effect depends on the base colour.

(Reprinted in *Marketing* magazine, Dec./Jan. 1992)

TASTE AND SMELL

Taste is our most limited sense and its main task is to keep poisons out and let foodstuffs in. Humans can only differentiate sweet, sour, salt and bitter. The average person has about 10 000 tastebuds on the tongue but as we age our sense of taste diminishes.

We 'experience' food mainly with our nose and eyes. Colour can be a key influence on taste. One study showed that colouring a chocolate dessert light brown, medium brown or dark brown resulted in different ratings of flavour, although the colour used had no flavouring. The dessert that was coloured darkest was rated by 62 per cent of consumers as having the best chocolate flavour, whereas the light-coloured dessert was rated as the most creamy.[21]

In contrast to taste, our sense of smell is quite well developed. Odours can have a profound effect on our mood states and judgement. Grocery stores that put baking smells through their air-conditioners report higher sales.[22] A classic study conducted over sixty years ago demonstrated the impact of smell on product quality judgement. A light spray of perfume over one pair of stockings caused women to evaluate them higher than two other identical pairs on attributes such as durability, shine and denier.[23]

According to Neil Shoebridge, the influence of music in advertising is also an important one (see page 87).

> **66** Music. It is overused. Sometimes it is abused. But it remains one of the most powerful tools in advertising. Many advertisers and ad agencies rely on it to capture the consumer's attention, make an otherwise dull ad stand out, and etch a product or service's brand name into the consumer's mind. **99**

PERCEPTUAL PROCESSING

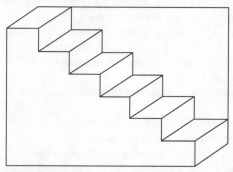

Figure 3.7: Inverted staircase

How do we give meaning to sensory inputs? How do we turn light and sound waves, odours and taste into cars, trees, music, perfume and so on? Why do we perceive in three dimensions when our eyes can only record two-dimensional images? How do we know something is moving when the eye records static pictures? We know that we sense with our sensory receptors and perceive with our brain. That we 'see' with our brain can be demonstrated by looking at the staircase in figure 3.7. Tell your eyes to 'see' it upside down. It may take a few attempts but eventually you will be able to invert the staircase. When you have successfully inverted the staircase, you have trained yourself to 'see' in a particular way.

The main problem for psychologists has been to work out how we do this. One plausible and well accepted explanation was proposed by Gestalt psychologists early this century. They stated that our brain organises the incoming raw data into forms (patterns). To do this, the brain uses three main mechanisms:

• grouping
• constancy
• figure and ground.

GROUPING

What determines whether the brain will group, or will not group, a set of stimuli? The brain has three rules that it follows — proximity, similarity and closure. These three rules apply to all our senses (see figure 3.8).

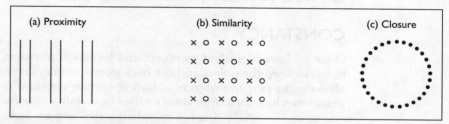

Figure 3.8: The mechanisms involved in grouping

Proximity

If images are arranged in a way that positions some of them close together and others further apart, those closer together will be seen to be related. In figure 3.8(a), you are likely to see three 'sets' of lines, rather than six individual lines. We also use this rule every time we hear music as we automatically group notes according to their proximity in time.

Similarity

The principle of similarity leads us to group together information that is similar. So the crosses and circles in figure 3.8(b) are seen as alternating columns rather than a jumble of shapes. In marketing, this principle suggests that products with the same brand name will be more similar on attributes such as quality or value for money, than products of different brands. If a company is perceived to be a producer of high quality goods, it may decide to adopt a family brand name strategy. A family brand is a brand that is used for several products, as in Kellogg's Cornflakes, Kellogg's Rice Bubbles and so on. In this way, Kellogg's products benefit from each other and any new product introduced will be presumed to be of similar quality.

Closure

Individuals tend to see images as complete. They add the 'missing' pieces, so that the picture in figure 3.8(c) is seen as a circle rather than a series of unrelated dots. You used the same technique when you 'filled in' the gaps in figure 3.3 (page 55) to see the elephant.

A marketing example of this principle is the use of slogans which invite the consumer to finish them off, such as 'Which Bank ...?' and 'Anyhow ...', and Toyota's 'Oooh what a feeling ... !' Since closure requires interaction with stored information, it forces the conscious processing of a brand name which increases its chances of being stored in long-term memory.

While closure can be made to work for a message it can also work against it. If you do not provide enough information for your target audience to complete the message in the way you intend, they are likely to misunderstand your message. The principles of grouping have a direct bearing on product positioning and differentiation. Products that are perceived to share similar attributes will be 'grouped' together. If you do not provide enough information about your product, then principles of closure can operate and consumers will 'fill in' their product knowledge gaps — perhaps incorrectly.

CONSTANCY

Once we have identified an object and located it in space, the brain then needs to keep the object and the background stable. Perceptual constancy allows us to perceive objects as having certain constant or stable properties, even when their appearance varies in certain contexts. It relies on the

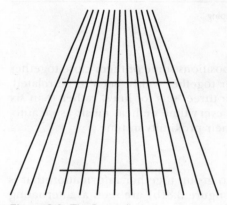

brain's knowledge that objects maintain their size, shape, colour and location no matter how our eyes 'see' them. For example, when we look at a closed door straight on, a rectangular shape hits our eyes. When we look at a half-opened door, a trapezium shape hits our eyes, but we 'see' and still know that the door is rectangular (see figure 3.10).

The Ponzo or railway lines illusion also demonstrates constancy. In figure 3.9, the line at the top appears longer because we are used to interpreting perspective in this way. We assume that the lines on the side are suggesting a sense of distance and therefore an object in the distance, of the same size, should appear smaller. Where this does not occur, we assume that the distant line must be longer.

Figure 3.9: The Ponzo illusion

Figure 3.10: Demonstration of constancy

FIGURE AND GROUND

Figure and ground is a mechanism by which the brain separates patterns into (1) the dominant object and (2) the context or ground in which the object appears. This task requires the grouping mechanism to function effectively. If the grouping mechanism does not have clear guidelines as to how the data should be grouped, no clear figure–ground pattern can be identified. The illustrations in figure 3.11 are classic examples of two patterns that are equally capable of being the figure. As a result, the brain is confused as to what should be the figure and what should be the ground. Once you have identified the saxophone player and the woman's face (figure 3.11(a)), they will continue to interchange, as will the two faces and the vase in figure 3.11(b).

(a)   **(b)**

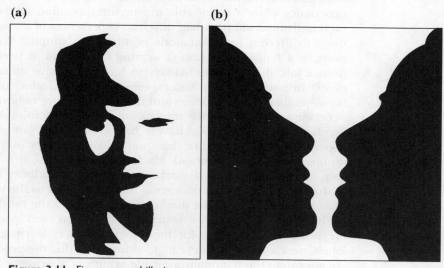

Figure 3.11: Figure–ground illusions

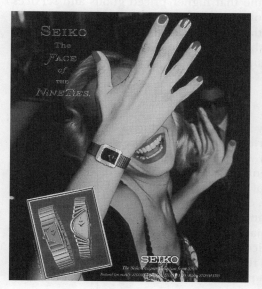

When designing messages, marketers need to be aware of figure–ground. It is essential that the product is clearly the figure. For example, the advertisement in figure 3.12 leaves no doubt as to what the product is. If your product is a supermarket item, designing a package that will stand out from the others is difficult but necessary. So that consumers can easily identify supermarket items, advertisements should show the product clearly. This allows a potential customer to more easily recognise it from other products, thus giving it a chance to be identified and selected.

Figure 3.12: The position of the arm and watch in the foreground of this advertisement ensures that the product is clearly recognised as the 'figure'.

PERCEPTUAL INTERPRETATION

Because many of the stimuli that a consumer receives have some element of ambiguity, consumers rely on their past experiences to help them understand the world. Ambiguity may arise because of short exposure, lack of concentration, high levels of interference (from other visual images or noise), or due to the different physical attributes of consumers, such as variations in hearing or eyesight.

How consumers interpret a particular stimulus will depend on their own perceptual set. The perceptual set is the readiness to perceive or act in a particular way to a situation. It is determined by beliefs, motives, interests, past experience and how clearly the stimulus is perceived. Past experience plays a major role in our interpretation of the world. Since each individual will have had different experiences of the world, this gives rise to different interpretations of the same stimuli. According to Le Roux, if a female boss who is wearing Chanel No. 5 perfume fires you from a job, the perfume is likely to have a negative impact on you forever.[24] In a similar way, a bad experience with a product or company will be remembered by customers and direct their future behaviour towards it.

Because past experience teaches consumers how to evaluate products, familiar brands are likely to have a 'halo effect'. For example, a favourable experience with a brand of shampoo is likely to carry over to a hair conditioner with the same brand. Marketers can also use this 'halo effect' to gain market share from a market leader. When Cadbury launched their Moro bar, they did so in packaging that was similar to the well established Mars Bar, thus gaining the market perception that the product was similar to the market leader. This strategy has also been used by generics, which are positioned as 'value for money'. Consumers learn to interpret the labels, over a large product range, as implying that the products will all be cheaper than the nationally available brands of alternative products.

Consumers are likely to assume that higher priced goods and services are of higher quality. They will often use price as a determinant of quality when they are unfamiliar with the product category. For example, a consumer who is unfamiliar with bottles of wine is more likely to buy an expensive bottle to take to an important dinner party than a cheap bottle.

ATTENTION

Information overload is a reality for today's consumer. Consider a trip to a local supermarket to buy groceries. The range of products, signals, special offers and other promotions make for a large number of stimuli attempting to attract your attention. Even if we consider only one purchase such as milk, the range of options is daunting — low fat, high calcium, skim, soybean, full cream, extra cream, long life, and so on. There is also a range of container sizes and types — cardboard, glass and plastic.

In order to deal with information overload, consumers adopt specific strategies that make their choices easier.[25] Firstly they select only those inputs which are important to them. The selection can be unconscious, such as when we 'tune-out' advertisements.

Then, consumers use their previous experience to recall products that they have used before and were satisfied with. They develop an evoked set of products. An evoked set consists of those brands and products recalled from long-term memory that are acceptable for further comparison because they meet certain criteria. Other products may not even be noticed and they are effectively screened out of the buying decision. This leaves the consumer with a smaller, and more manageable group of products from which to select an alternative. In cases of high brand loyalty or strong habitual purchasing, the evoked set may contain only one product so that, as long as that product is available, no alternatives will be considered.[26]

Figure 3.13: With the range of similar products available on supermarket shelves, marketers must make their product stand out from the crowd if it is to be noticed.

SELECTIVE ATTENTION BARRIER

66 Advertising will always remain the key marketing weapon for some product categories. But a growing number of marketing directors are questioning the tradition of selling mass-produced goods to a mass market through mass media. High on the list of factors is advertising overkill. Australians are bombarded with thousands of advertising messages every day fired at them from TV screens, magazines, newspapers, taxis, billboards. As the number of advertising messages increases, the impact decreases. Advertising clutter creates confusion and leads to consumer resistance. **99**

Neil Shoebridge, *Business Review Weekly*, 15 February 1991

Breaking through the selective attention barrier and encouraging consumers to consider a different product is one of the most difficult tasks for a marketer. In the case of a new product, providing consumers with additional information may encourage them to re-evaluate their decision.

To return to our milk example, how could a marketer encourage a consumer to change from low fat to high calcium milk? Advertising that highlights the need for people to increase their level of calcium intake as they age and their bones become more brittle may encourage some consumers to try the product. Others may be concerned about taste, so they may be more influenced by advertising that portrays the product as tasting the same as other milk products. In order to assess what will be the most effective strategy, a marketer needs to know what information is important, what needs are being met by the product and how this information can be communicated in a way that will be attended to by the consumer.

Since individuals are all different, they will have different requirements. This means that consumers will be more likely to pay attention to marketing stimuli that meet their needs. A consumer interested in buying a new stereo is more likely to notice promotional activity related to this need. A consumer interested in managing a household budget is more likely to notice advertisements for supermarket specials than a consumer without the same budgetary constraints. Of course, those on a small income may not be the only consumers interested in economical supermarket purchases. People on a high income but with motives to save money or to spend it in other areas may be equally concerned shoppers. This is one reason why income based segmentation studies do not always explain why consumers behave in the way that they do. Sometimes a lifestyle segmentation will yield a fuller picture of the needs, wants and motives that affect purchase behaviour.

PERCEPTUAL DEFENCES

Not only will consumers pay more attention to marketing stimuli that meet their needs, but they are also likely to avoid advertising and other marketing stimuli that do not fit with their view of themselves and their world. Thus individuals may 'tune out' from advertising that is inconsistent with their views. Smokers, for example, commonly 'switch off' from anti-smoking advertisements that they find frightening or inconsistent with their views on smoking. This reaction is termed 'perceptual defence'.

The problem of perceptual defences is one that marketers have attempted to overcome using a variety of means. Using more neutral stimuli is one successful approach. A famous 'Life. Be in it' campaign is a good example. A realistic portrayal of an overweight and inactive individual may have turned people away from the idea of doing more exercise, whereas the use of a cartoon character, 'Norm', was less likely to be offensive and more likely to be seen as humorous.

Encouraging consumers to buy a particular insurance policy can be difficult, as many people do not want to be reminded of unpleasant events. Useful tactics are to use humour or to distance the event. The advertisement in figure 3.14 does this by focusing on the danger to others of buying cheap car tyres.

You could make a killing buying cheaper overseas tyres.

Your tyres are one of the most important safety features of your car.
So it's essential that you buy quality tyres that are made in Australia for Australian conditions.
They may cost a little more, but you might discover one day that it's a very small price to pay.
To find out more, ask your Olympic dealer, Dunlop Super Dealer or Beaurepaires for tyres.

OlympicTyres.

Figure 3.14: This advertisement implies that poor tyres are a danger to children, not only to the driver.

PRODUCT POSITIONING

In order to simplify their decisions, consumers develop clusters of information about products which enable them to compare products and to group like products together. From a marketing perspective, products and services are 'positioned' in the mind of the consumer. Packaging, advertising messages, brand names and the consumer's experience interact to create a product 'idea'. The perceived characteristics of a product (which may not be the reality of the characteristics) will determine how a product is perceived by the consumer.

To position products effectively involves knowing how consumers perceive the marketer's product. Marketers aim to position products and services on 'unique' characteristics so as to reduce competition. For example, in the whitegoods market Fisher and Paykel encourage consumers to re-evaluate the appearance of refrigerators. In the advertisement in figure 3.15, they suggest that refrigerators with 'rounded corners' are more attractive than those with square corners. They are attempting to position their product as unique in the refrigerator market.

In a different way, the advertisement in figure 3.16 attempts to position the Bosch dishwasher as 'value for money'. Even though it is among the more expensive dishwashers, it uses 'German precision engineering' so consumers are told their money will be well spent and that servicing costs will be reduced.

Figure 3.15: The message in this advertisement is 'style and quality'.

Figure 3.16: The message here is 'quality and value for money'.

PERCEPTUAL MAPPING

One technique that is used by marketers to position products is perceptual mapping. This technique enables marketers to develop a diagrammatic view of consumers' perceptions of products within a specific area, for example, the breakfast cereal market. It shows how consumers position products in a product category in relation to one another. A perceptual map for a brand of muesli, for example, could show that people thought that muesli was good for you, but that it was less tasty than other cereal alternatives. Consumers might evaluate breakfast cereals on two criteria — those that taste good and those that are nutritionally good for you (see figure 3.17).

	Tastes good	
Kellogg's Komplete		*Froot Loops*
		Coco Pops
High on nutrition	*Kellogg's Just Right*	**Low on nutrition value**
Uncle Toby's Natural Muesli	**Does not taste good**	

Figure 3.17: Perceptual map for breakfast cereal

Figure 3.18: This advertisement repositions the product as adult, particularly female, oriented, low in fat and still with the chocolate taste.

Data could be collected from consumers to rate a range of products against these criteria. In this way, marketers may discover how their products are perceived and discover 'gaps' in the market for a new product. This information could then be used to develop an advertising strategy. The introduction of Copper Kettle by Cottees was the result of a gap in the instant coffee market (see page 116). Market research showed that there was a need for a mild coffee and the need was not being met.

The results of perceptual mapping can also be used to uncover perceived faults with the product. The Ovaltine Light Break advertisement in figure 3.18, for example, shows an attempt to position Ovaltine as a 'delicious, chocolaty drink that's light in weight but not in taste'. This suggests that the original Ovaltine could be perceived as being high in calories, but that the chocolate taste is enjoyed by consumers. This may have led to the development of the new product that retains the 'chocolate' image but repositions the product as a female oriented product which is 'light'.

SEMIOTICS

As much of our reactions to stimuli are unconscious, an area of perception that is growing in importance is semiotics. Semiotics is the study of the way in which individuals interpret symbols. These symbols may be gestures, pictures, logos and even products themselves. Semiotics or semiosis analysis is concerned with understanding how people react emotionally to influences from symbolic aspects of their environment. Technically the term derives from *semi* meaning 'half', and *octic* or *osis* meaning 'sound' and 'shape'. It is based on the assumption that shapes and sounds (symbols) in our environment influence our thoughts and behaviour without our full awareness.[27]

The success of symbols in marketing lies in their ability to convey a consistent meaning. Their meaning must be understood by both the marketer and the consumer. Some symbols, such as the use of red to mean 'stop', as in traffic lights, are internationally recognised. Others, such as the colours of a football team, may only have local meaning, and even they may be meaningless to people who do not follow football.

Many marketing activities rely on the meaning of easily and widely recognised symbols. Symbols recognised in many parts of the world include those belonging to McDonalds, Coca-Cola and Mercedes Benz. They convey the generally understood meanings of fast food, soft drink and prestige motoring. Other symbols, such as those used by banks, may not be recognised outside their country of origin, but may be widely recognised within their own country.[28]

Semiotics has a key role in influencing how an individual will respond to a message and indeed a product. In the main, the response to symbols is emotional and is often unconscious. Subtle factors, such as the shape of containers and external packaging or the use of objects, people and words in messages, all have an important impact on a consumer's emotional response to the product.

Figure 3.19: Ginger Meggs cartoon © Jimera Pty Ltd

◎ SUMMARY

This chapter examined the role of sensation and perception in marketing activity. Perception is defined as the act of taking information from the world around us through our sensory receptors and interpreting it. We looked at how consumers' sensory processes function and how sensory inputs can be influenced. Applications of the just noticeable difference to marketing have been described, as well as the notion of subliminal influences.

Consumers' perceptual processes translate raw stimuli and this demonstrates how dependent we are on our brains to understand our world. Our brains also have a controlling influence on the way we interpret all marketing stimuli and on selecting which stimuli we pay attention to and subsequently process at a conscious level. From an understanding of how perceptual selection works, we can understand why some information is selected and other information is given less attention. This understanding can help marketers to increase the probability that their promotional activities will be noticed.

Perceptual experience has a crucial impact on the way we look at products and make judgements about them. Another important facet of perception is the role of the unconscious process — information that is taken in at a preconscious level that can impact on our perceptions and choice of products.

Questions

1. Collect three marketing examples of Weber's Law and show how marketers have used the concept of just noticeable difference to reduce price, change packaging or improve the product.

2. Find two advertisements that demonstrate the concepts of 'proximity' and 'similarity'. Show how these advertisements have been used to imply product or service characteristics.

3. Discuss how you have developed the set of criteria that you use to assess products. Select one product category, such as coffee, and discuss the role that your friends and family have played in your assessment of the product.

4. Discuss whether or not subliminal techniques should be used in advertisements.

5. Consider the Traffic Accident Commission advertisements directed at young people who drink and drive. How effective have they been in altering your behaviour? What other factors have contributed to a change in your behaviour (if it has changed)?

6. Conduct research in your class and compile a product positioning map for brands or types of drinks. Does this suggest any gaps in the market? What new product could you develop for your classmates?

7. Select four advertisements that you like and four you dislike. Using the guidelines on pages 62–63, analyse the colours in each advertisement. What role have the colours played in shaping your feelings?

8. Select some advertisements that you think are rich in symbols. Identify the symbols and comment on how effective they are in relation to the product and the target market.

9. Many films and television programs use identifiable products in their shows. Since we do not always note these products at the level of conscious awareness, what impact, if any, do you think this might have on our buying behaviour?

10. Examine the principle of figure–ground in relation to:
    (a) displaying products on a supermarket shelf
    (b) designing advertisements
    (c) promoting a dress shop that is next to five other dress shops.

Case study

What cannot be found on supermarket shelves but was one of the fastest-growing products in the Australian food industry last year? Shoppers can't buy it directly, but they consumed $400 million worth of food and beverages containing it last year. Almost all Australians are aware of it, but only a handful have seen it.

Give up? It is aspartame, a powdery artificial sweetener known in Australia as Nutra-Sweet. Since it arrived here seven years ago as the main ingredient in a sugar substitute called Equal, NutraSweet has pushed its way into the soft-drink, yoghurt, flavored milk, chewing gum and jelly markets. Last year, retail sales of products containing NutraSweet hit $400 million, up from $100 million in 1987. Sales are expected to top $500 million by the end of this year.

This year's projected growth will be driven by increased sales of products that already use NutraSweet, such as Diet Coke and Diet Pepsi softdrinks and Extra chewing gum, plus the use of NutraSweet in new product categories. Aspartame-laden chocolate and sugar confectionery products will appear during the next six months. Government health authorities are expected to approve the use of NutraSweet in icecream products by March. Discussions about introducing NutraSweet to other product categories are taking place between food manufacturers and government officials.

NutraSweet's owner, the US-based NutraSweet Company, plans to launch another artificial food ingredient in Australia. In December, local health authorities ruled that a fat substitute called Simplesse could be marketed here as a foodstuff. NutraSweet's Australian executives are now devising ways to make and market Simplesse, which contains 1.3 calories per gram compared with normal fat's nine calories count.

Simplesse was launched in the US last February and is now used in products made by several food companies, including the NutraSweet Company itself, which launched an icecream called Simple Pleasures to demonstrate how Simplesse can be used. The fat substitute is made with the protein from milk and egg whites, which is heated and whipped into tiny globules. The small, flavorless spheres — 50 billion to the teaspoon — mimic the texture of fat particles.

The main drawback of Simplesse is that it cannot be used in frying or baking; intense heat distorts the shape of the globules. But the NutraSweet Company is confident Simplesse will be a hit with the manufacturers of salad dressing, mayonnaise, margarine, icecream, yoghurt and butter. A Simplesse-based icecream product is expected to hit the Australian market by late this year.

Simplesse was developed to give the NutraSweet Company a second product line. The patents set in place when NutraSweet was launched around the world during the 1980s have expired in all countries except the US, where they expire in 1992, and Australia (1993). But Peter Maher, sales and marketing manager at the NutraSweet Company's Australian arm, claims the expiry of NutraSweet's patents in markets such as Britain and Canada has not affected sales of the artificial sweetener. "Nutra-Sweet is more than just a food ingredient," he says. "It is a strong brand name in its own right."

NutraSweet is an unusual food product. Maher claims the sweetener, which is shipped to Australia from the US and Japan as a powder and sold to local food and beverage companies in 25-kilogram drums, is the only branded food ingredient in the world.

"It is a food and beverage ingredient that can be marketed in its own right to consumers, rather than simply sold to manufacturers as an additive for their products," Maher says. "It is different from other ingredients such as yeast and starch or rival artificial sweeteners such as saccharin and cyclamates in that it is not positioned as a commodity. It is positioned as a brand."

The development of Nutra-Sweet started in 1965, when James Schlatter, a chemist at the US chemical and consumer products maker G. D. Searle & Co, was working on an ulcer remedy. Schlatter mixed two protein components, aspartic acid and phenylalanine, and created a sweet mixture. During the following 16 years, Searle chemists turned that sweet mixture into aspartame, which was launched in the US as Nutra-Sweet in 1981 (aspartame is 200 times sweeter than sugar). Searle set up the NutraSweet Company in 1982 to make and market its sweetener worldwide. In 1985, the NutraSweet Company was acquired by the Monsanto chemical group.

The National Health & Medical Research Council granted permission for the use of NutraSweet in foodstuffs in Australia in 1982. Two years later, Searle's Australian subsidiary launched Equal tabletop sweetener. In 1986, PepsiCo Inc's then Australian bottler, Cadbury Schweppes, launched a version of Diet Pepsi containing NutraSweet.

(continued)

Eleven months later, Coca-Cola South Pacific introduced a NutraSweet-based version of Diet Coke and the Wrigley Company unveiled Extra chewing gum with NutraSweet. In 1989, NutraSweet appeared in yoghurt, dessert mixes and skim milk.

The selling and marketing of NutraSweet in Australia is handled by the NutraSweet Company's four local executives, plus a battery of consultants covering areas such as public relations, advertising, telemarketing and government lobbying. Their job is to convince food and beverage manufacturers to switch to aspartame, which is 700–1000% more expensive than rival artificial sweeteners, and to sell the NutraSweet name, logo and image to consumers.

"Yes, NutraSweet is more expensive than other sweeteners," says Tracey Jannusch, marketing services manager at the NutraSweet Company's Australian division, "but it is more than an anonymous food ingredient. The use of the NutraSweet name instantly flags to consumers that the product carrying it is low-calorie and tastes good. People know what the use of the NutraSweet name and logo on a food or beverage product means."

A key part of the NutraSweet Company's job is to promote the NutraSweet brand. It has spent $10 million on media advertising for NutraSweet since 1987, running television advertising every year to promote the low-calorie and taste benefits of products sweetened with aspartame. Its $1.9-million 1990 TV ad campaign was the first to feature products that contain NutraSweet.

The NutraSweet Company spends about $2 million a year on its own media advertising, but its customers shell out an estimated $25 million a year on

their own advertising for products such as Diet Coke, Extra, Danone Diet Lite yoghurt and Diet Pepsi. NutraSweet and its customers pay separately for their advertising, but Jannusch says the NutraSweet Company runs some "cooperative" marketing programs with its buyers, including public relations campaigns, direct mailing to consumers and a telephone marketing program.

The combination of the NutraSweet Company's marketing efforts and NutraSweet buyers' individual advertising campaigns pushed awareness of the NutraSweet brand among Australians to 97% last year, up from 86% in 1989. The percentage of Australians who have tried products containing NutraSweet climbed from 46% in 1989 to 55% last year.

The $27 million spent on advertising for NutraSweet and its products last year dwarfed the $5 million spent on media advertising by CSR Limited and other sugar marketers. Maher claims most consumers now see NutraSweet as a viable, natural, good-tasting alternative to sugar. But research conducted by CSR late in 1989 found that only 5% of Australians think NutraSweet is as natural as sugar. Only a quarter of the people polled for CSR said aspartame tasted as good as sugar, while 78% described NutraSweet as a chemical product and 45% said it had an "awful" aftertaste.

Despite these negative perceptions, six new products containing NutraSweet were launched in 1990, including Silhouette yoghurt from Plumrose Australia, Go Lite flavored milk from QUF Industries and two low-calorie softdrinks from Cadbury Schweppes. Maher claims that all products containing the artificial sweetener now rank first or second in their

categories. Wrigley's Extra brand, for example, has grabbed 25% of chewing gum sales and the number one spot in its market since it was launched in 1987. Sales of Diet Pepsi have rocketed 630% (albeit from a low base) since it switched from saccharin to NutraSweet in December 1986.

Maher points to Sportlife, a chewing gum relaunched by Stimorol Australia last year, as proof of the power of the NutraSweet brand. Stimorol added the NutraSweet name and logo to the Sportlife pack and ran a brief media advertising campaign in Victoria. Sales doubled last year.

Softdrinks accounted for 70% of the $400-million worth of retail sales generated by products containing NutraSweet last year. Maher says Coca-Cola's decision to switch to NutraSweet for Diet Coke (a move that increased the cost of making the product by an estimated $8 million a year) was the biggest boost for awareness and sales of NutraSweet in Australia.

The NutraSweet Company has sold 200 tonnes of NutraSweet in Australia since 1984. Its turnover is not available, but Maher claims the local company is profitable. "Obviously our growth mirrors the growth in retail sales of NutraSweet-based products," he says.

Sales of products containing NutraSweet are expected to grow 20–25% this year. Confectionery makers will release a clutch of NutraSweet-based products in the next six months (Maher will not reveal which confectionery companies are joining the NutraSweet bandwagon), and icecream makers expect to receive permission to use NutraSweet in their products by March.

Neil Shoebridge,
Business Review Weekly,
18 January 1991

Case study questions

Read the article on pages 75–76 then answer the following questions.
1. Discuss the relevance of the 'taste' of NutraSweet to consumers.
2. Evaluate NutraSweet's brand name and brand management strategies.

SUGGESTED READING

M. Walker, D. Burnham and R. Borland, *Psychology*, 2nd edn, John Wiley and Sons, Brisbane, 1994, pp. 187–216.

A. A. Berger, *Signs in Contemporary Culture: An Introduction to Semiotics*, Longman, New York, 1984.

W. B. Key, *Media Sexploitation*, Prentice-Hall: Englewood Cliffs, NJ, 1976; and *The Clamplate Orgy*, Prentice-Hall, Englewood Cliffs, NJ, 1980.

ENDNOTES

1. H. Gleitman, *Basic Psychology*, 3rd edn, W. W. Norton & Co., New York, 1992, chapter 4.

2. R. L. Gregory, *Eye and Brain — the Physiology of Seeing*, World University Library, 1966, p. 126.

3. For a basic introduction to Weber's Fraction and Fechner's Law see M. Walker et al., *Psychology*, 2nd edn, John Wiley and Sons, Brisbane, 1994, pp. 40, 181–82. S. H. Britt, 'How Weber's Law Can be Applied to Marketing', *Business Horizons*, Feb. 1975.

4. R. L. Miller, 'Dr Weber and the Consumer', *Journal of Marketing*, Jan. 1962. E. J. Wilson, 'Using the Dollarmetric Scale to Estimate the Just Meaningful Difference in Price', *AMA Summer Educators Proceedings*, 1987.

5. A. Adam, A. DiBenedetto and R. Chandran, 'Can you Reduce Your Package Size without Damaging Sales?', *Long Range Planning*, Vol. 24, Aug. 1991.

6. B. Buchanan, M. Givon and A. Goldman, 'Measurement of Discrimination Ability in Taste Tests: An Empirical Investigation', *Journal of Marketing Research*, May 1987, pp. 154–63. R. I. Allison and K. P. Uhl, 'Influences of Beer Brand Identification on Taste Perception', *Journal of Marketing Research*, Vol. 2, No. 3, 1964, pp. 36–39. G. A. Mauser, 'Allison and Uhl Revisited: The Effect of Taste and Brand Name on Perception and Preferences', *Advances in Consumer Research*, Vol. 6, 1979, pp. 161–65.

7. R. F. Hartley, *Marketing Mistakes*, 5th edn, John Wiley and Sons, New York, 1993.

8. D. Kiley, 'Shrinking the Brand to Fit Hard Times', *Marketing Week*, Nov. 1990, p. 6.

9. H. Brean, 'What Hidden Sell is all About', *Life*, 31 March 1958.

10. W. B. Keys, *Subliminal Seduction*, Prentice Hall, Englewood Cliffs, NJ, 1973. V. Packard, *Hidden Persuaders*, Penguin Books, 1957.

11. S. J. Kelly, 'Subliminal Imbeds in Printing Advertising: A Challenge to Advertising Ethics', *Journal of Advertising*, No. 8, 1979. J. Saegert, 'Why Marketing Should Quit Giving Subliminal Advertising the Benefit of the Doubt', *Psychology and Marketing*, Summer 1987, pp. 107–20. P. M. Merikle and J. Cheesman, 'Current Status of Research on Subliminal Perception', in M. Wallendorf and P. Anderson

(eds), *Advances in Consumer Research*, No. 45, Association for Consumer Research, Provo, Utah, 1987, pp. 298–302. W. Kilbourne, S. Painton and D. Ridley, 'The Effect of Sexual Embedding on Responses to Magazine Advertisments', *Journal of Advertising*, 1985, pp. 48–56. J. V. McConnell, R L. Cutter and E. McNeil, 'Subliminal Stimulation: An Overview', *American Psychologist*, 13 May 1958. T. Moore, 'Subliminal Advertising: What You See Is What You Get', *Journal of Marketing*, 46, 1982, pp. 38–47.

12. D. Hawkins, 'The Effects of Subliminal Stimulation on Drive Level and Brand Preferences', *Journal of Marketing Research*, No. 7, 1970, pp. 322–26.

13. J. A. Natale, 'Are You Open to Suggestion?', *Psychology Today*, Sept. 1988, pp. 28–30.

14. R. Cuperfain and T. K. Clarke, 'A New Perspective on Subliminal Perception', *Journal of Advertising*, Vol. 14, No. 1, 1985, pp. 36–41.

15. R. Bornstein et al., 'The Generalizability of Subliminal Mere Exposure Effects: Influence of Stimuli Perceived Without Awareness on Social Behaviour', *Journal of Personality and Social Psychology*, Vol. 53, No. 6, 1987.

16. J. C. Gilchrist, J. F. Ludeman and W. Lysak, *Journal of Abnormal and Social Psychology*, Vol. 49, 1954. N. F. Dixon, *Quarterly Journal of Experimental Psychology*, Vol. 10, 1958.

17. G. R. Hardy and D. Legg, *Quarterly Journal of Experimental Psychology*, Vol. 20, 1968.

18. R. Alsop, 'Colour Grows More Important in Catching Consumers' Eyes', *The Wall Street Journal*, 29 Nov. 1984, p. 18.

19. J. A. Bellizzi, Ayn E. Crowley and R. Hasty, 'The Effects of Color in Store Design', *Journal of Retailing*, Vol. 59, No. 1, 1983, pp. 21–45.

20. J. Miner, *Complete Colour Reference Manual*, Carina, Queensland, 1992. F. and R. Mahnke, *Colour and Light in Man-made Environments*, Van Nostron, Rhineholt, 1993.

21. T. G. Barnett, W. Lew and J. Selmants, 'Cueing the Consumer: The Role of Salient Cues In Consumer Perception', *Journal of Consumer Marketing*, 4, Spring 1987, pp. 23–27.

22. P. J. Black, 'No-one's Sniffing at Aroma Research', *Business Week*, 23 Dec. 1991, pp. 82–83. C. Miller, 'Research Reveals How Marketers Can Win by a Nose', *Marketing News*, 25 Feb. 1991, p. 2.

23. D. A. Laird, 'How the Consumer Estimates Quality by Subconscious Sensory Impressions — With Special Reference to the Role of Smell', *Journal of Applied Psychology*, Vol. 16, June 1932, pp. 241–46.

24. M. Le Roux, 'What Lies Behind the Sweet Smell of Success', *Business Week*, Feb. 1984, p. 10.

25. K. Lewin, 'Getting Around Commercial Avoidance', *Marketing and Media Decisions*, 4 Dec. 1988, p. 116.

26. R. Alsop, 'Advertisers See Big Gains in Odd Layouts', *Wall Street Journal*, June 1988. R. B. Schindler, M. Berbaum and D. R. Weinzimer, 'How an Attention Getting Device Can Affect Choice Among Similar Alternatives', *Advances in Consumer Research*, 1987, pp. 505–509.

27. K. Boulding, *The Image*, University of Michigan Press, Ann Arbor, Mich., 1956. A. A. Berger, *Signs in Contemporary Culture: An Introduction to Semiotics*, Longman, New York, 1984.

28. D. Mick, 'Consumer Research and Semiotics: Exploring the Morphology of Signs, Symbols and Significance', *Journal of Consumer Research*, 13 Sept. 1986, pp. 196–213.

C H A P T E R

4

Memory

OBJECTIVES

This chapter should help you to:
- understand the different types of memory
- understand how these different systems interrelate
- know how to ensure product knowledge is retained by consumers
- know what factors are likely to promote recall and recognition.

 ## THEORY AND RESEARCH

Without memory, there would only be the present. We would not be able to remember names, faces or products. We would not be able to use skills we learned one day on the next. We would not 'know' who we are. Memory is fundamental to our existence and, therefore, fundamental to marketing. If consumers were not able to be aware of, store and retrieve information about products, the marketplace would not exist.[1]

Memory is a process consisting of three phases. The first phase is the acquisition phase, where we take in information. The second phase is storage (memory traces) and the third phase is retrieval. Much of the research on memory has focused on understanding the storage phase in the process. The Ancient Greeks were first to liken memory to a large storehouse of filed information.

Another approach, the stage theory of memory, which emerged out of the information processing approach, provided a useful framework for understanding memory and formed the basis of the organisation approach to memory. The stage theory of memory suggests that there are at least three interactive memory systems: short term, long term and sensory.[2] These have been conceived as 'storage' areas, which people fill with information and knowledge. The duration of the storage (minutes for short term, years for long term) and the type of information stored varies in each stage. Basic to the stage theory of memory is the view that for information to reach the long-term memory system, it must first pass through the short-term memory system. Until recently, very little was known about the sensory memory system except that it is the storehouse of all our sensory experiences.[3] The sensory memory operates as the first system of processing information. It receives and categorises information on the basis of colour, taste, smell, feel or sound. As we saw in the previous chapter (page 54), the scent of a perfume will be remembered in the sensory memory system, but the label 'Giorgio' requires a semantic label and therefore needs to be processed by the short-term memory and then stored in the long-term memory system. However, the label will be linked to the smell stored in the sensory memory.

Consumers receive an enormous amount of sensory information but will choose to consciously process only a small fraction. Marketers try to encourage consumers to consciously process information by using attention-gaining tactics, some of which are described later (pages 84–85).

Constant exposure to or repetition of messages can influence the degree of brand 'liking' experienced by the consumer, but only to a point. Research also shows that long-term storage of labelling information, including brand names, can occur with constant repetitions (visual or sound) and without conscious processing through the short-term memory system.[4]

MEMORY AS ORGANISATION

Since the 1980s, there has been an increasing tendency towards viewing short-term and long-term memory not as separate storage systems but as active and passive memory. Active memory is said to be an area of the brain where various items of experience are held while they are sorted, manipulated and organised. The passive memory is said to hold the information traces that are 'dormant' until prompted. The implication of the organisation approach is that the task of the active (short-term) memory is to process incoming data by using information already stored in the passive memory. The emphasis is on the way new and old information is processed rather than on understanding how information is stored.[5]

The memory traces in the active memory are of short duration and the memory traces in the passive memory of long duration. Therefore, many researchers prefer to use the terms 'short-term' and 'long-term' to describe these memory systems. For this reason and because they are familiar labels, short-term and long-term have been used in figure 4.1 as alternative terms for active and passive memory. The diagram, however, is based on the organisational approach to memory.

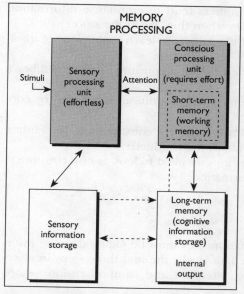

MEMORY PROCESSING

Figure 4.1: Memory component of information processing (see figure 2.5, page 39, for complete diagram)

Viewing the short-term (active) memory as a processing unit alters how we understand the limited capacity factor.[6] It implies that the limited capacity of the short-term memory described by Miller is not due to limited memory-storage capabilities but to *limited processing capacity*. There is only so much mental effort that the active memory can engage in at any one time.[7] This creates the primacy and recency effects found in information processing. The primacy effect describes the enhanced recall of items at the beginning of messages. The recency effect designates the greater recall for those at the end.[8] The explanation for the primacy effect is that consumers recognise that initially they have time to retrieve information from the passive memory. As the processing continues they realise that the end of the message is coming and so as not to 'lose' the information, they focus on the last bits of information. The importance of these effects for message construction is that important information should be at the beginning and at the end of messages.

Another important factor for marketers is information overload, which occurs when consumers are given more information than they can cope with in the time available. Consumers have up to 60 seconds to process information from a television or radio commercial. In order for the message to be understood and stored, the message must be simple and the commercial must be repeated many times.

There has been considerable research into how much product information consumers can manage during the search process. Even though consumers are actively seeking product information, some researchers have argued that there are limits to how much information consumers can gather and examine. If consumers were given too much information, it was thought that they would make confused and inadequate decisions. More recent research seems to discount this, although consumers do have 'cut-off' points beyond which it is not cost effective to gather more information.[9]

 # PRODUCT KNOWLEDGE

An important factor in product choice and ultimate purchase is product knowledge. Marketers need to ensure that consumers acquire and store information about products and companies. They also need to ensure that product knowledge can be retrieved when consumers recognise that they require products. To do this effectively, management of communication messages and situation cues is essential. According to James Bettman, marketers need to address such questions as:

• What is remembered from an advertisement or a product-related conversation?

- Under what conditions do consumers tend to emphasise information on packages or stored in memory when they are in the store?
- How much time is necessary for consumers to learn some piece of information from an advertisement?
- How many repetitions are needed before a consumer can remember a piece of information?
- What can be done to facilitate in-store recognition of a brand by consumers?
- What types of new information are easier for consumers to remember, given their current knowledge about the product?[10]

To address these and other questions we need to look at how consumers acquire, store and remember information.

 # ACQUISITION

For consumers to acquire information they must be exposed to the information and be able to process it. This is why the first three steps in effective communication — exposure, attention and comprehension — are intrinsically linked to memory.

EXPOSURE

For any message to be processed, the consumer must see or hear it. This means that it is necessary to carry out research to find out where consumers get information about products. If messages are to be delivered through the mass media, the marketer needs to know whether consumers read magazines and newspapers and if they do, which ones. Likewise, the marketers must discover whether they watch television and if so, which stations. For example, if your target audience is professional and highly educated with incomes over $50 000, then using commercial television stations is not a good idea, as the statistics in figure 4.2 show.

Product knowledge is often obtained from informal sources, such as one consumer talking to another and asking the other's opinion of a product. For some products, information will always be delivered to the consumer through 'gatekeepers' or through other consumers. A gatekeeper is a person who is able to control the flow of information. Doctors, for example, are the gatekeepers of prescription medicines, so drug companies need to target doctors, even though they are not the end user.

Exposure to messages can also be improved by the adoption of an integrated marketing communication (IMC) program. The main feature of IMC programs is that consumers are exposed to product information from a variety of sources. To be successful these programs should be:

- **comprehensive**, in that all personal selling, advertising, media and promotional events, sales promotion, public relations programs and all other communication activities are coordinated and complement each other
- **unified**, in that the messages delivered by all media, including packaging, in-store promotions and atmospherics, have the same theme and are directed at the same target market.[11]

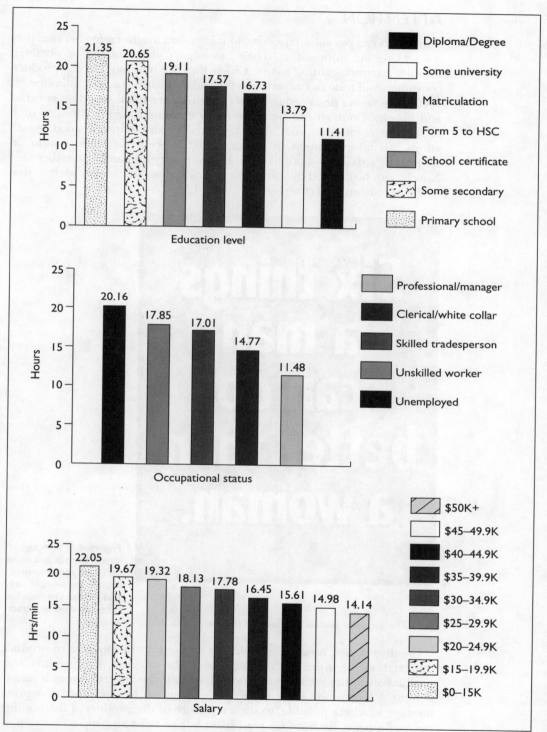

Figure 4.2: Weekly commercial television viewing hours, Australia (*Source*: Roy Morgan Research, Sept. 1988)

ATTENTION

Consumers can pay voluntary, conscious attention to advertising because they are seeking out information. Their involuntary attention can be obtained through attention-gaining tactics. Unless they are interested in the product, consumers will tune out advertisements and it is hard to attract attention.[12]

Creative tactics designed to attract attention are often based on contrast and novelty. Contrast can be achieved by creating a strong stimulus such as intense colour, unusual shapes (symbols) and unusual word associations. An advertisement or package that is seen, for some reason, as unusual or striking is more likely to be given attention and remembered.[13] Novelty can be created by using new or unexpected messages, such as that of the Mr Sheen advertisement in figure 4.3.

Figure 4.3: Although shown in black and white here, this advertisement actually has a bright red background. The message is constructed to attract attention.

Creative tactics, however, should not be used at the expense of product information. In order for the message to be effective, the product and product attributes must be mentioned, even if the advertisement is entertaining.[14] A common tactic for drawing attention to a product in a print message is, where possible, to show a picture of the product at the bottom right of a page. Because we read from left to right and top to bottom, a picture of the product in this position brings the recency effect into play.

COMPREHENSION

Unless the consumer understands what the message is about, then all the effort to gain attention will be wasted. To ensure comprehension, it is necessary to talk to the audience in a language they understand. It is also necessary to know how much information consumers can handle, so that overload can be avoided.[15]

How well new information is processed is a function of the 'networks' of information that consumers have previously developed and how easily they can incorporate this new information into old networks.[16] For example, to appreciate the advertisement in figure 4.4, you need to be familiar with the Kenny Rogers song 'You picked a fine time to leave me, Lucille'. If you did not know this song, the words in the message would not necessarily link into other stored information.

Research shows, in fact, that messages are often misunderstood. A study that showed 60 thirty-second commercials to consumers found that less than four per cent totally understood the messages and that the overall miscomprehension rate was 30 per cent. Education was not a factor, as consumers with tertiary education showed only a 25 per cent comprehension factor.[17]

Figure 4.4: Some advertisements rely on the consumer's previous 'network' of information. Interestingly, this particular advertisement has been very popular, which indicates that the Kenny Rogers song *is* part of many people's information networks.

 **STORAGE**

The aim of most marketing communications is for product information to be remembered and easily retrieved. In general, product information will be remembered and more easily understood if:

- it has pictures (images), music and words (semantics)
- it states and repeats important product attributes
- it presents information in useful chunks, as in the 'double-one, double-one' of the Pizza Hut home delivery number
- the content of the commercial is linked to the actual product or the claims repeated at point of sale.

Figure 4.5: Pizza Hut's telephone number is made up of easily remembered segments.

Research shows that our visual memory is particularly strong and interacts with the words stored in our 'semantic networks'.[18] Semantics is concerned with the meaning of words and concepts and many psychologists take the view that our entire vocabulary is stored in our long-term memory. Because pictures are said to be 'concrete' and words 'abstract', it seems that a message can be more easily understood and remembered if both pictures and words are used.[19] It may also be easier to remember diagrams than text, so you may remember the diagram in figure 4.1 (page 81) that summarises the functions of memory more easily than you could remember the text that describes memory.

Moreover, when the theme music from a television show is used for radio promotions, consumers 'see' the pictures that they have previously associated with the music.[20] The influence of a catchy jingle cannot be underrated. Even though the 1940s commercial for Aeroplane Jelly was not played commercially for over twenty years, people, including children who had never been exposed to the commercial, could still sing it. The 'Aeroplane Jelly' and 'Happy Little Vegemite' songs became so popular that they are now part of Australian popular culture.

I like Aeroplane Jelly
Aeroplane Jelly for Me
I like it for dinner
I like it for tea
A little each day is a good recipe
The quality's high as the name will imply
And it's made from pure fruits, one more good reason why
I like Aeroplane Jelly
Aeroplane Jelly for Me.

Music in advertising

NEIL SHOEBRIDGE

MUSIC. It is overused. Sometimes it is abused. But it remains one of the most powerful tools in advertising. Many advertisers and ad agencies rely on it to capture the consumer's attention, make an otherwise dull ad stand out, and etch a product or service's brand name into the consumer's mind.

Critics of music in advertising, particularly sing-a-long jingles, claim that its use hides the lack of a strong creative idea and that the agency's creative directors cannot think of a way to speak about the benefit of the product or service, so they sing it. But that argument ignores the fact that music is a proven product-seller.

Most people respond well to music and many of the most successful campaigns in Australian advertising history have been based on catchy tunes. Music is a key ingredient in memorable campaigns for Coca-Cola, St George Building Society and Toyota. Jingle kings Alan Morris and Allan Johnston have made a fortune from singing the praises of products such as Tooheys Draught, Meadow Lea and World Series Cricket.

Sometimes the music used in an ad takes on a life of its own. The British advertising industry is witnessing a strange phenomenon at present, with several old pop songs used in television commercials re-entering the pop music charts. Advertising's ability to give old songs a new lease of life proves the power of music in advertising.

Jeans maker Levi Strauss has been featuring old songs in its British and Australian advertising for four years. Earlier this year, it launched a new ad in Britain featuring *Should I Stay or Should I Go*, a song by British group the Clash. When the Clash first released the song in 1982, it limped to number 17. Five weeks after the Levi ad made its debut, the song was number one in Britain.

The transformation of jingles into hits has been going on for more than 30 years. US group the Monotones had a hit in 1958 with *Book of Love*, which was based on an ad for Pepsodent toothpaste. In 1965, two jingles appeared on the pop charts: the Kingsmen's *Jolly Green Giant*, which was based on a US ad for vegetables, and the T-Bones' *No Matter What Shape (Your Stomach's In)*, which used the soundtrack from an Alka-Seltzer TV commercial. In 1971, British group the New Seekers scored a number one hit with a reworking of Coca-Cola's *I'd Like to Teach the World to Sing* jingle.

Business Review Weekly,
21 June 1991

However, whilst music and pictures can have a powerful positive effect, it is possible for the effect to be negative. For this reason, music and pictures need to be tested before they are used, as individual consumers may have different interpretations of sensory data.[21]

Constant repetition of information is another way of creating memory traces, so, provided consumers are paying attention, repeating advertisements can lay down information about products.[22] It is also possible that a liking for the product (or the advertisement) will develop, but only to a point, as the consumer may also become bored with the repetition. To avoid boredom, theme or serial content can be used. These are exemplified by the 'Significant Moments' theme used by Omega watches, displayed in figure 4.6.

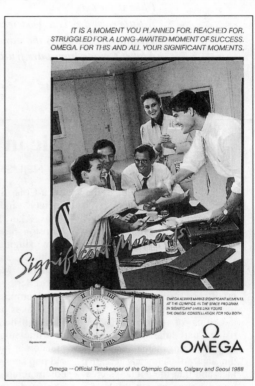

Figure 4.6: Omega advertisements use the same message theme, 'Significant Moments', in different settings for different styles of watches. By showing the advertisements on consecutive pages, the message is more likely to be read and remembered.

Another tactic that can be used with frequent exposure is the use of messages that force the repetition of key words or product attributes. See, for example, the advertisement for Pewsey Vale wine in figure 4.7.

It has also been found that information is more easily transferred to long-term memory systems if it is associated with information already stored. If you want to remember the phone number of a friend, it is necessary to repeat the information a number of times and then link the stored number pattern to the friend's name.

Figure 4.7: This advertisement encourages interest by using a crossword. The questions focus on the quality of the wine in comparison with other unnamed wines. The one answer to all the thirteen questions is the word 'medal'.

Advertisements that refer consumers to previously stored information about products can be quite successful. A useful tactic is recycling old advertisements. The producers of Mortein fly spray, Reckitt and Colman, capitalised on the fact that in the early 1980s children aged under 7 could sing the jingle for Mortein's 'Louie the Fly' advertisements of the 1960s. The company resurrected the character of Louie the Fly in their subsequent television commercials (see figure 4.8). By maintaining advertising, the consumer is reminded of the product, which increases the likelihood of the product remaining in the consumer's evoked set (see page 91).

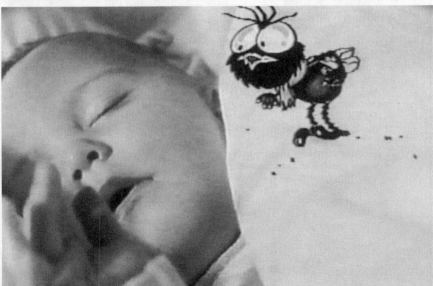

Figure 4.8: Louie the Fly was a memorable character in the 1960s (*above*), particularly with children. Adults in the 1990s remember Louie and his message, and the more recent advertisements (*below*) capitalise on this memory.

SEMANTIC NETWORKS

Because most information is delivered to consumers through words, it is important to understand semantic networks.[23] The notion of a network is important as it implies that all the words stored in our memory are connected. It is important to note that the information within networks does not necessarily relate only to product categories, as, for example, in figure 4.9 where the link with 'trees' sets up a link with 'woodchips' which could extend to environmental protection.

The creation of semantic maps allows words (bits of information) that consumers associate with products to be identified. These can then be used in messages to encourage information storage and as the basis for product differentiation. Using the semantic map in figure 4.9, it is possible to identify a consumer's preferred orange juice brands and a group of alternative products that would be considered when the favourite brand was not available. This group of products that is easily recalled is termed the 'evoked set'. Messages about a new product or new information about an existing product should be categorised into the evoked set by using some of the key linking words.

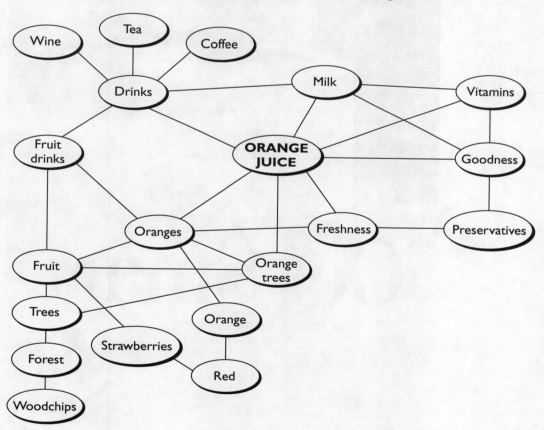

Figure 4.9: This example of a semantic map shows the various links that could emerge when a consumer thinks of orange juice.

However, information already stored in the memory may interfere with new information coming into long-term storage. For example, if the name Black and Decker is associated with power tools and the consumer sees an advertisement for a Black and Decker toaster (figure 4.10), this information may be stored with 'power tools', so when the consumer tries to search for names of toasters, the name Black and Decker is not there. However, advertising can effectively reduce the likelihood of this occurring by strongly linking the brand with a well-known person associated with the category. Thus, Black and Decker's use of Maggie Tabberer, who is strongly associated with housewares and not power tools, is likely to strengthen the relationship between Black and Decker and domestic appliances.

Figure 4.10: The association of Black and Decker products and Maggie Tabberer helps to adjust consumers' thinking about the brand name.

RETRIEVAL

Retrieval from long-term memory occurs through recognition and recall. Recognition is used when consumers match the image of the product that is in front of them with an image stored in their memory. In recall, the consumer brings product information into active memory by thinking about the product or by responding to an external cue. This activation may be caused by cues related to the product, such as the smell of a hot-bread shop. This smell may 'remind' consumers that they are hungry or that they have run out of bread. Trademarks and corporate logos can also act as reminders of specific products. Thus, in a computer showroom the Apple logo may be noticed because it is familiar.

Recognition can also be aided by ensuring that the product is displayed clearly in any message. It can also be aided by creating links between advertisements, point-of-sale displays and product packaging. One successful interlinking of advertising messages was the 'This goes with that at Sussan's' campaign conducted by the Sussan clothing chain. This slogan appeared on television commercials and was repeated on signs in the stores. The clothes shown in the commercials and in the magazine advertisements also featured in window displays.

Most people think in pictures, not words. Because pictures may be more clearly remembered than product information, using 'pack shots' is important in advertising as this will provide a visual cue that consumers can recognise when shopping. Kellogg's, for example, reprinted stills from its television commercial for 'Just Right' on the back of the cereal packet, reinforcing the central message 'not too heavy, not too light'.

Figure 4.11: On passing this billboard, consumers would immediately recall the highly successful television commercial which captured the excitement and novelty of skydiving on a surfboard. ('Coca-Cola' and 'Coke' are trademarks of the Coca-Cola Company.)

The retrieval process is also aided by the initial 'placement' of the information in the long-term memory. Information about a brand would be clustered not only with information about related brands but also with the attributes the consumer associates with the product category. If a product can be clearly differentiated from the competition, choice factors are clear and the competition product will not be bought 'by mistake'.

Moreover, the way that information is placed in the mind of the consumer will affect the way a brand is selected. If information is stored on the basis of product attributes then consumers are likely to compare brands. But if information is stored on the basis of brands then consumers are more likely to compare attributes.

Retailers commonly use both approaches. If you decide to buy a new pair of socks, you may visit one store that has socks arranged by colour (encouraging you to compare the same colour socks by different manufacturers). Another store may have the same range of socks grouped by manufacturer. The second store is likely to be encouraging you to make an initial selection of manufacturer and then decide on the colour. These different store displays may mean that while you are encouraged to see the attribute of colour as the most important variable in the first store, the second store encourages you to see the brand of the sock as the most important variable.

FORGETTING

We use the word 'forgetting' to describe memory failure. Memory failures are usually the result of decay, interference (faulty storage procedures) or mood states. According to decay theory, the strength of the memory trace will fade over time.[24] Interference, such as distraction and poor information, can cause faulty storage, the result of which is that incoming information is not clearly linked to relevant stored material; or, if it is, the link has somehow been 'misplaced'.[25]

Forgetting can also be the result of conditions at the moment of recall.[26] Emotional factors such as anxiety can inhibit recall. Information is most likely to be recalled when the mood at the time of learning the information is the same as that operating when recall is needed. This concept of 'mood congruence' has important implications for advertising because a consumer is more likely to recall a product if the level of arousal during an advertisement is the same as that experienced in the purchase environment. For example, an advertisement depicting people having fun at the beach and drinking Coke is most likely to be recalled when the person feels thirsty at the beach.

Marketers also use the emotional aspects of nostalgia as product clues, so seeing an old advertisement for Vegemite may remind consumers of happy childhood days, and they would then associate these memories with Vegemite. This may encourage parents of today to buy Vegemite for their own children or for themselves.

Continued exposure to a product will also prevent messages from being mislaid. However, mere repetition of the same advertising may have some negative effects. Consumers are less likely to take notice of an advertisement that offers little new information.[27] To maximise memory, a message should, ideally, make links with previous messages and add new information.

TESTING MESSAGE EFFECTIVENESS

Two measures that are commonly used for testing whether messages have been remembered are recall and recognition of advertisements. Testing recall of advertising involves asking consumers which advertisements they can remember without prompting. For example, a researcher may ask a consumer to try to recall advertising seen during the previous night's television watching. If the researcher were to ask, for example, which margarine advertisements the consumer could recall, the researcher would be using the technique of prompted recall.

In unprompted recall, the consumer must search, in an undirected fashion, his or her memory for advertising, whereas prompted recall provides the consumer with some cues for the search.

A third method may involve showing a frame from a television commercial, or a picture from a print advertisement, and asking whether the consumer has seen the advertisement. Research has shown that consumers generally do better on recognition than on recall measures because there are more clues provided to aid the search process, making recognition a simpler process for consumers.[28]

However, it is important to remember that testing will indicate product awareness levels only. Product purchases are a function of how well the marketing mix has been managed and of consumer preferences. Consumers may remember the advertising for a particular brand of coffee because they liked the music, or found the advertisement amusing, but may still continue to buy the same brand because it is the brand they have always bought, or the price suits their budget.

SUMMARY

Memory is the label used to describe the storage and retrieval of information. It consists of three phases:

- the acquisition phase, during which information is taken in
- the storage phase, during which information (memory) traces are laid down
- the retrieval phase, during which the stored information is brought into active memory.

A popular conception of memory is that it consists of three interacting systems: the sensory, short-term and long-term. While these terms are still used, our understanding of them has changed. Initially, these were considered to be three separate storage areas; now they are considered to be different interactive levels of processing. The short-term memory is now considered to be active or working memory that interacts with dormant information in the long-term or the passive memory.

Regardless of the way we analyse memory, it is important that any message delivery to consumers will reach, be understood and be retained by consumers. To ensure this, marketers need to manage the delivery of messages effectively. This chapter has described the problems of gaining attention and has described some attention-gaining tactics.

Once you have consumers' attention, it is crucial that they understand the message and that they are able to store salient information. Tactics such as the use of music, pictures and key words have been described. Of key importance is the idea of semantic networks. Creating semantic networks for a target audience allows key words, associations and ideas, which can then be incorporated into messages that the target audience can relate to.

After the consumer has comprehended and stored a message, it must then be retrieved. A number of different factors affect retrieval. One factor, described as 'mood congruence' suggests that information is most likely to be recalled when the mood at the time of learning is replicated at the time of retrieval. Familiarity also aids recall, as does novelty and the use of images. It has also been found that text combined with images will be more easily retrieved than text alone.

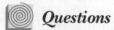

Questions

1. Define each of the three phases of memory and show how advertisers apply these concepts in the development of an advertising campaign.

2. Explain how information already stored in your long-term memory has 'interfered' with new information (for example, learning to type with two fingers may make it more difficult to learn to type the 'correct' way).

3. Explain the way in which your 'evoked set' of cars is constructed. Think about the similarities and differences between the products within this category.

4. Consider how you, as a marketer, could use the concept of the evoked set to launch a new product (try different product types such as soft drinks, margarine, magazines, pasta or garden hoses) and a new service (try things such as an airline, hotel or restaurant).

5. Think of your earliest memories. What sort of things do you remember? How have these memories been influenced by photos taken when you were young or stories that you have been told about your childhood?

6. Given what you have read about retrieval and the factors that affect retrieval, list five things that you could do to improve your exam performance.

7. Ask a friend to browse through a magazine. Ask them what advertisements they recall from the magazine. Get them to describe those advertisements in as much detail as possible. When they have completed that task, show them a series of advertisements taken from the magazine as well as some from earlier issues of the same magazine that are not in this edition, and ask them to identify those from the current edition. (You will need two copies of the magazine so that you can remove advertisements to show them in the second part of the research).

   Repeat the experiment with a different person (preferably a demographically different person, that is, different age, sex, socioeconomic status).

   What conclusions could you draw about the way in which advertising material is recalled by your two subjects? What differences existed in the recall versus the recognition processes? How can you explain these? If one of your subjects 'remembered' advertisements that were not there, consider why this may have happened.

Case study

In the world of consumer products marketing, a company's most valuable assets are its brand names. Factories become dilapidated. Machines wear out. Distribution systems become outdated. But brand names — those nebulous properties that turn commodities into products and engender loyalty among customers — can survive indefinitely.

But brand names need constant nurturing to remain relevant and successful. Even strong names wither without attention in the form of new products, advertising and promotion. To stay dominant, a brand's image must remain consistent. But even the most consistently marketed brand must adapt to prosper.

Take the Continental brand name. In the 35 years since it appeared in supermarkets on a range of packet dehydrated soups, Continental has become one of Australia's big food brands. Unlike many old brand names in the food industry, Continental continues to grow and push into new product categories. Sales of Continental products have jumped 28–30% during the past five years and the brand's retail sales are about $70 million a year.

Continental's owner, Unilever Australia, believes the recent addition of two new products will push retail sales above $80 million by the end of this year. The two newcomers — Rices of the World and MicroChef — bring to 10 the number of product categories the Continental name spans. Within those categories, which range from packet and instant soups to stock cubes, a dehydrated potato mixture, meal bases and pasta-and-sauce products, Unilever sells 130 different Continental products.

Continental is the top-selling brand in most of the markets in which it competes. In the packet soup market, it captures 65% of sales. In the instant soup category, its market share is 76%. Four of every 10 stock cubes used by Australians are Continental. The brand's packet soups are found in 75% of Australian homes. The Continental Pasta & Sauce product, which was introduced less than four years ago, is in 52% of homes.

Unilever executives are constantly searching for new markets for Continental and new ways to extend the brand name in its existing markets. Using recognition value and reputation to enter a new product category is an old marketing trick. Leveraging a brand name by adding new products often provides a fast and inexpensive way of invading a new market: because the name and image of the parent brand are already established, introducing a spin-off costs about 30% less than launching a new brand.

But stretching a brand name into new areas can undermine the credibility and core product attributes of the parent brand. Shoppers may not believe the new product shares any of the appeal or characteristics of the original product and reject the newcomer.

"You can take a brand such as Continental into new areas as long as you continually check with consumers," says Kim Nicholson, marketing manager (soups and meals) at Unifoods, the Unilever division responsible for Continental. "We want to exploit market opportunities, but we also have to protect the brand. So we look for product categories Continental can credibly enter. Every move we make is carefully planned, researched and checked."

According to Nicholson, Unifoods' research shows that people expect "strong, Australianised, family" flavors from Continental products. "If we introduce mild flavors or new lines that are based on product benefits other than flavor delivery, they are rejected," she says.

Nicholson says Unifoods has maintained a high share of pasta side-dish sales through "absolute bloody-mindedness". She says: "There has been no magic formula, just a lot of hard work in terms of advertising, promotions, introducing new products and pack sizes, and investing in the brand. Retaining the number-one spot has been expensive at times, but we are determined to hang on to what we've got."

Neil Shoebridge,
Business Review Weekly,
30 August 1991

Case study questions

According to the article on page 97, the Continental brand has high brand awareness and consumers have a preference for products with the Continental label. Carry out a survey of shoppers to:
(a) identify those who are aware of Continental products
(b) identify the products consumers associate with the Continental label
(c) identify, by using a semantic-network approach, the evoked set for each of these products.

SUGGESTED READING

M. Walker, D. Burnham and R. Borland, *Psychology*, 2nd edn, John Wiley and Sons, Brisbane, 1994, pp. 249–86.

E. Tulving, 'Remembering and Knowing the Past', *American Scientist*, 77, July 1989.

S. M. Kosslyn, *Ghosts in the Mind's Machine*, Norton, New York, 1984.

ENDNOTES

1. E. Tulving, 'Remembering and Knowing the Past', *American Scientist*, 77, July 1989, pp. 10–13.

2. D. E. Broadbent, *Perception and Communication*, Pergamon Press, London, 1958. N. C. Waugh and D. A. Norman, 'Primary Memory', *Psychological Review*, 72, 1965, pp. 89–104. R. C. Atkinson and R. M. Shiffrin, 'Human Memory: A Proposed System and its Central Processes', in *The Psychology of Learning and Motivation: Advances in Research and Theory*, Academic Press, New York, 1968, pp. 89–195.

3. J. Leask, R. Haber and R. B. Haber, 'Eidetic Imagery in Children: 11 Longitudinal and Experimental Results', *Psychonomic Monograph Supplement*, 3, Whole No. 35, 1969, pp. 25–48. S. M. Kosslyn, *Image and Mind*, Harvard University Press, Cambridge, Mass., 1980. S. M. Kosslyn, *Ghosts in the Mind's Machine*, Norton, New York, 1984. S. M. Kosslyn, T. M. Ball and B. J. Reiser, 'Visual Images Preserve Metric Spatial Information: Evidence from Studies of Image Scanning', *Journal of Experimental Psychology, Human Perception and Performance*, 4, 1978, pp. 1–20.

4. H. Krugman, 'The Impact of Television Advertising: Learning Without Involvement', *Public Opinion Quarterly*, 26, 1965, pp. 349–56. P. Anand and M. B. Holbrook, 'Reinterpretation of Mere Exposure or Exposure of Mere Reinterpretations', *Journal of Consumer Research*, 17, 1990, pp. 242–44. T. Heath, 'The Logic of Mere Exposure: A Reinterpretation of Anand, Holbrook and Stephens', *Journal of Consumer Research*, 17, 1990, pp. 237–41. C. Janiszewski, 'Preconscious Processing Effects: The Independence of Attitude Formation and Conscious Thought', *Journal of Consumer Research*, 15, 1988, pp. 199–209. C. Obermiller, 'Varieties of Mere Exposure: The Effects of Processing Style and Repetition on Affective Response', *Journal of Consumer Research*, 12, 1985, pp. 17–30.

5. R. G. Crowder, 'The Demise of Short-Term Memory', *Acta Psychologica*, 50, 1982, pp. 291–323. W. A. Henry, 'The Effect of Information Processing Ability on Processing Accuracy', *Journal of Consumer Research*, 7, June 1980, pp. 42–48.

6. J. N. MacGregor, 'Short-term Memory Capacity: Limitation or Optimization?', *Psychological Review*, 94, 1987, pp. 107–8. G. Miller, 'The Magical Number Seven, Plus or Minus Two: Some Limits on our Capacity to Process Information', *Psychological Review*, 63, 1956, pp. 81–97. H. A. Simon, 'How Big is a Chunk?', *Science*, 183, Feb. 1974, pp. 482–88. See chapter 2 for more details on 'chunking' strategies.

7. A. D. Baddeley, *The Psychology of Human Memory*, Basic Books, New York, 1976. A. D. Baddeley, 'The Trouble with Levels: A Reexamination of Craik and Lockhart's Framework for Memory Research', *Psychological Review*, 85, 1978, pp. 139–52. A. D. Baddeley, *Working Memory*, Clarendon Press, Oxford, 1986.

8. B. Murdock, 'The Serial Position Effect of Free Recall', *Journal of Experimental Psychology*, 64, 1962, pp. 482–88.

9. K. L. Keller and R. Staelin, 'Effects of Quality and Quantity of Information on Decision Effectiveness', *Journal of Consumer Research*, 14, Sept. 1987, pp. 200–13. J. Jacoby, 'Perspectives on Information Overload', *Journal of Consumer Research*, 10, March 1984, pp. 432–35. N. K. Malhotra, A. K. Jain and S. W. Lagakos, 'The Information Overload Controversy: An Alternative Viewpoint', *Journal of Marketing*, No. 46, 1982, pp. 27–37.

10. J. Bettman, 'Memory Factors in Consumer Choice: A Review', *Journal of Marketing*, Vol. 43, No. 2, 1979, pp. 37–53.

11. R. D. Blackwell, 'Integrated Marketing Communications', in G. L. Frazier and J. N. Sheth (eds), *Contemporary Views on Marketing Practice*, Lexington Books, Mass., 1987.

12. B. J. Calder and B. Sternthal, 'Television Commercial Wearout: An Information Processing View', *Journal of Marketing Research*, 17, 1980, pp. 173–86. A. Abernethy, H. Rotfeld and C. J. Cobb-Walgren, 'Tuning In and Tuning Off: Trends in Television Viewing Habits', in C. Haugtvedt and D. Rosen (eds), *Proceedings of the Society for Consumer Psychology*, Knoxville, 1991. A. Abernethy and H. Rotfeld, 'Zipping Through TV Ads is Old Tradition — But Viewers Are Getting Better At It', *Marketing News*, 7 Jan. 1991, p. 6. P. A. Stout and B. L. Burda, 'Zipped Commercials: Are They Effective?', *Journal of Advertising*, Vol. 18, No. 4, 1989, pp. 23–32.

13. J. W. Alba and A. Chattopadhyay, 'Salience Effects in Brand Recall', *Journal of Marketing Research*, 23, Nov. 1986, pp. 363–70.

14. E. J. Soares, *Promotional Feats*, Quorum Press, 1991, pp. 124–25.

15. J. Jacoby, D. Speller and C. K. Berning, 'Brand Choice Behaviour as a Function of Information Load', *Journal of Marketing Research*, 11, 1974. W. L. Wilkie, 'Analysis of Effects of Information Load', *Journal of Marketing Research*, 11, Nov. 1974, pp. 462–66.

16. R. C. Atkinson and R. M. Shiffrin, 'Human Memory: A Proposed System and Its Central Processes', in K. W. Spence (ed.), *The Psychology of Learning and Motivation: Advances in Research and Theory*, Academic Press, New York, 1968, pp. 89–195.

17. J. Jacoby and W. D. Hoyer, 'Viewer Miscomprehension of Televised Communication: Selected Findings, *Journal of Marketing*, 46, 1982, pp. 12–26.

18. A. Paivo, *Imagery and Verbal Processes*, Holt, Rinehart and Winston, New York, 1971. L. Percy, *Ways in Which the People, Words and Pictures in Advertising Influence its Effectiveness*, Financial Institutions Marketing Association, Chicago, 1984.

19. S. J. McKelvie, C. Daprat, P. Monfette and D. Cooper, 'Effects of Pictorial Interaction on Recall of Brand Names and Lower Imagery Nous', *Australian Journal of Psychology*, Vol. 45, No. 1, 1993. K. Robertson, 'Recall and Recognition Effects of Brand Name Imagery', *Psychology and Marketing*, Spring 1987, pp. 3–13. M. B. Holbrook and W. L. Moore, 'Feature Interactions in Consumer Judgements of Verbal Versus Pictorial Presentations', *Journal of Consumer Research*, No. 8, 1981, pp. 36–44.

20. G. Tom, 'Marketing with Music', *Journal of Consumer Marketing*, Vol. 7, No. 2, 1990, pp. 49–53. J. I. Alpert and M. I. Alpert, 'Music Influences on Mood and Purchase Intentions', *Psychology and Marketing*, Vol. 7, 1990, pp. 109–33. W. T. Wallace, 'Jingles in Advertisements: Can They Improve Recall?', *Advances in Consumer Research*, Vol. 18, 1991.

21. Tulving, ibid. (see note 1), p. 361.

22. E. J. Johnson and J. E. Russo, 'Product Familiarity and Learning New Information', in K. Munroe (ed.), *Advances in Consumer Research*, 8, Association for Consumer Research, Ann Arbor, Mich., 1981, pp. 151–55.

23. A. M. Collins and E. Loftus, 'A Spreading Activation Theory of Semantic Processing', *Psychological Revew*, 82, 1975, pp. 407–28. R. C. Atkinson and R. M. Shiffrin, ibid. (see note 16).

24. H. Gleitman, *Basic Psychology*, 3rd edn, W. W. Norton, New York, 1992, pp. 190–93. There is only limited evidence that the decay notion is valid. For interference, see R. Burke and T. Srull, 'Competitive Interference and Consumer Memory for Advertising', *Journal of Consumer Research*, 15, 1988, pp. 55–68.

25. A. Chattopadhyay and J. W. Alba, 'The Situational Importance of Recall and Interference in Consumer Decision Making', *Journal of Consumer Research*, 15, 1988.

26. T. Srull, 'Memory, Mood and Consumer Judgement', in M. Wallendorf and P. Anderson (eds), *Advances in Consumer Research*, XIV, Association for Consumer Research, Provo, Utah, 1986, pp. 404–7. M. Gardner, 'Mood States and Consumer Behaviour: A Critical Review', *Journal of Consumer Research*, 12, 1985, pp. 281–300. G. H. Bower, 'Mood and Memory', *American Psychologist*, 36, 1981.

27. Chattopadhyay and Alba, ibid. (see note 25). J. Bettman, ibid. (see note 10). B. Walker, R. Celsi and J. Olson, 'Exploring the Structural Characteristics of Consumers' Knowledge', in M. Wallendorf and P. Anderson (eds), *Advances in Consumer Research*, XIV, Association for Consumer Research, Provo, Utah, 1986, p. 134.

28. A. Finn, 'Print Ad Recognition Readership Scores: An Information Processing Perspective', *Journal of Market Research*, 25, May 1988, pp. 168–77.

C H A P T E R

5

Learning

Understanding how you learn is important to you. When you plan to learn to choose is important to plan. Understanding the memory attained theory-shift functions of the joint term to your attention priorities expressed with analysis ... to part of ... plan ... to find assess but all might effective which is learned. Remembering A ... an all-learning. There may ... may remembering to ... to this particular. Once other ... that experiment ... are natural behaviours. So too are behaviours such and to the

This chapter should help you to:
- understand the principles of learning
- become familiar with the various learning theories and how they affect consumer behaviour
- understand the relationship between sales incentives and consumer learning
- understand the relationship between learning and repeat purchase behaviour.

WHAT IS LEARNING?

Learning, or the ability to learn, is fundamental to the survival of many species, including humans. Some organisms do not need to learn survival skills as they have preprogrammed gene patterns that allow them to respond to influences from their environment. However, their range of responses is limited and their flexibility to adapt to changing environments is minimal. Some species have the ability to learn new behaviours although their capacity for learning varies.

In humans, a relatively small proportion of behaviour is preprogrammed or instinctual. Humans have a large cerebral cortex that allows them to analyse and store information, so they are well equipped to learn new ways of adapting to a changing world. In addition, once the new behaviour is learned, it may be passed on to others and to future generations.

Understanding how consumers learn to be consumers and how they learn to choose is important to marketers. Contrary to the message adorning many t-shirts, humans were not 'born to shop'. We are certainly preprogrammed with some survival responses, such as reacting to loud noises, but all marketplace behaviour is learned behaviour. Responding to an advertisement for a department store sale and responding to a 'two for the price of one' offer at the supermarket are learned behaviours. So too are behaviours such as brand loyalty.

Figure 5.1: From an early age, children absorb information from the marketplace and learn how to be consumers.

Most marketing strategies and tactics are based on the assumption that consumers are continually accumulating information about products, and that people can be *taught* to prefer different products and/or brands. In other words, they learn about products and learn how to choose between them.

But what is learning? Initially, learning was defined by researchers as 'a relatively permanent change in behaviour which occurs as a result of experience or practice'. Implicit in this definition is the notion that the individual is capable of learning and the exclusion of any behaviour that is a function of fatigue, drugs or other short-term influences. The focus on observed behaviour is due to the influence of behavioural psychologists who, as their name suggests, are interested in understanding behaviour. Behavioural psychologists have dominated the area of learning and the above definition reflects their perspective. A key advantage of the behavioural definition is that learning is easy to measure; once someone is observed performing a task, then learning can be said to have taken place (see figure 5.2).

The behavioural definition does have a fundamental problem as it presumes that, unless there is some observable evidence (overt behaviour), then learning has not occurred. Thus efforts to change a consumer's attitude to a product can only be said to be successful, in other words, the consumer has learned a new attitude, if:

(a) the consumer is interviewed and her/his attitude is verbally stated (overt behaviour)

or

(b) the consumer actually purchases the product (overt behaviour).

For this reason, a number of psychologists — cognitive psychologists in particular, who are interested not only in behaviour but also in mental processes — found this definition unsatisfactory as they are more concerned with cognitive learning. Cognitive learning psychologists define learning as 'changes in an organism's knowledge about the world that occur as a result of experience'.

Figure 5.2: Behavioural psychologists believe that learning has occurred when some observable behaviour has been performed.

Bower and Hilgard[1] combined these perspectives and said that learning is

> 66 a change in a behavioural disposition that is caused by experience and is not explained on the basis of reflexes, maturation or temporary states. 99

They suggest that it can take place in three ways:

- We can learn by direct experience: acting and seeing the consequences of our actions, i.e. buying a product and being satisfied or dissatisfied with the purchase.
- We can learn vicariously: by observing how other people experience different events, i.e. someone buys a product and tells you about their experience.
- We can learn through language: by being told about or reading about products.

WHAT DO WE LEARN?

To survive, humans must learn a great deal. Some of the first things an infant must learn and do are physical activities that require skill and precision, such as speaking, walking and, later, riding a bicycle. The child must know about the objects in its world, learn what they are and how to categorise them. If the object is harmless, the infant will become accustomed to it and may even be bored by it. In technical terms, the infant has

become 'habituated' to the object. Habituation simply means that an organism has become familiar with a particular stimulus. Consider, for example, how often you went shopping with a parent before you could walk and talk. Children in our society may not have been born to shop, but they are exposed to and learn about shopping, often within weeks of birth. By the time children are able to walk, they are most certainly habituated to the act of shopping. It is important to remember that even if we become habituated to an object or activity we still monitor it, as habituation does not generalise over different stimuli.[2] So if some important feature changes to any great degree, we will once again react fully to the changed object.

The ability to detect changes in a familiar stimulus implies that your brain does not ignore habituated stimuli — it continues to monitor all stimuli even though they are no longer the focus of attention. This means that our sensory receptors and perceptual mechanisms are important elements in our capacity to learn. For this reason, changing the packaging and/or the brand name of a consumer product that has become familiar is risky and perhaps costly, as consumers will have to be retrained to recognise the product.

As we grow, not only must we become familiar with objects in our world, but we also need to learn and remember where objects are located. In other words, we must acquire spatial knowledge. We learn where our house is, where certain types of shops are, how long it takes us to reach them and the best — usually the shortest — route to get there. Once we are in a shop we become familiar with the layout and we 'know' where certain products are. We make a cognitive map or internal representation of the way objects and landmarks are arranged in our environment.[3] When we form cognitive maps, we form mental images of our surroundings based on various landmarks. This is why it is a good idea for supermarket chains to ensure that the layout of the store is consistent in each location. Customers prefer familiar environments as it saves them time and confusion. As we grow older, we move about more and we are exposed to more aspects of our environment, so our cognitive maps become more complicated.

We must also learn about time and causal sequences — the concept that events follow one another — either because they are in a temporal (time) series, like the seasons of the year or the days of the week, or because they are in a causal sequence, for example, lightning precedes thunder. Without this sort of knowledge we cannot plan for or arrange conditions to make certain things happen, which means that we are unable to act effectively.[4]

HOW DO WE LEARN?

RATS, CATS, DOGS AND CONDITIONING

The earliest notions of how we learn were provided by the behaviourists. For them, learning is the acquisition of new behaviours and can be measured by observing behaviour. The underlying premise of the behavioural perspective of learning is that learning occurs because we associate specific actions with specific outcomes. If we do something and we gain a positive or negative result from the behaviour, we will 'learn' to repeat or not repeat the behaviour. At the centre of these theories is the notion of *contiguity*. Contiguity is the situation where a stimuli and a response occur close together, so that we learn to associate one with the other. This means that we learn by association, i.e. we associate good or bad events with specific behaviours, the ultimate goal being to maximise the 'good' events and minimise the 'bad' ones.[5]

There are two basic types of association learning, *classical conditioning* and *instrumental conditioning*. In classical conditioning, behaviours that are already programmed can be produced from stimuli that do not normally produce the response. For example, if you brush an object close to someone's face they will blink their eyes. If you continue to do this and play 'Waltzing Matilda', eventually the person will blink on hearing the tune played. Instrumental conditioning is used to train new behaviours, such as teaching a rat to press a lever. Pressing levers in order to obtain food is not normal 'rat-like' behaviour. In classical conditioning the learner is passive, whereas in instrumental conditioning the learner is active. Also in classical conditioning the stimulus comes before the response, whereas in instrumental conditioning the reinforcements come after the responses. The extensive knowledge we have about this type of learning has come from the rat, cat and dog trials carried out by Pavlov, Thorndike and Skinner.

CLASSICAL CONDITIONING

The first insight into how learning occurs was provided by the now famous experiments of Ivan Pavlov, a Russian physiologist, who was researching salivation responses in dogs. During his experiments he noticed that the dogs in the laboratory salivated when the laboratory lights were switched on by the assistants. As this was before he gave the dogs the meat, the normal trigger of the salivatory response, Pavlov became interested and decided to investigate this phenomenon. He discovered that the regular pairing over time of food that would naturally stimulate salivation with, say, a bell ringing which normally would not, gradually caused the animal to associate the bell with food. Once the association was made, the sound of the bell would trigger the salivary glands of the dogs. Pavlov believed that the process in the animal's brain that corresponded to the bell became linked to another brain process corresponding to the animal's normal response to food, causing the animal to salivate. Pavlov referred to the process as conditioning and it is still referred to as Pavlovian or more commonly, classical conditioning.

In essence, classical conditioning is learning by association. The specific mechanics of this type of learning are that a neutral stimulus, the bell in the case of Pavlov's dog, is repeatedly presented as a signal. It is given just before the stimulus that normally evokes a reflexive response (the food). Eventually the organism learns to expect the second stimulus when the first one is presented. The pattern is described in figure 5.3.

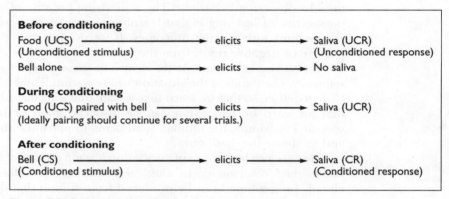

Before conditioning

Food (UCS) ——————→ elicits ——————→ Saliva (UCR)
(Unconditioned stimulus)   (Unconditioned response)

Bell alone ——————————→ elicits ——————→ No saliva

During conditioning

Food (UCS) paired with bell ——→ elicits ——————→ Saliva (UCR)
(Ideally pairing should continue for several trials.)

After conditioning

Bell (CS) ———————————→ elicits ——————→ Saliva (CR)
(Conditioned stimulus)   (Conditioned response)

Figure 5.3: Pavlovian (classical) conditioning

After Pavlov conducted these first experiments, researchers tested all varieties of organisms and tried out a wide variety of stimuli based on visual patterns, sounds and touch. These resulted in the discovery that it was possible to introduce a second neutral stimulus. For example, where the initial neutral stimulus, such as a bell, is paired with the food and becomes the conditioned stimulus (CS), it is possible to replace the bell with a light by the same process, i.e. association. Although the dog gets no meat when it sees the light, it will respond by producing saliva. This phenomenon is known as second order conditioning. The most famous of these later experiments involved the use of a young baby, Albert. Loud noises elicit a fear response in young babies and by associating a loud noise with 'furry' things, Albert was taught to give a fear response when exposed to fur, including men with beards (see figure 5.4).

The optimum conditions for learning via classical conditioning are when:
- the conditioned stimulus is intense
- the unconditioned stimulus follows immediately after the conditioned stimulus
- the unconditioned stimulus is of high magnitude, e.g. shock or fear
- the organism is genetically prepared to connect to the particular kind of stimulus (sound, taste, odour).

(a) Little Albert is given a white rat to play with and neither shows any fear.

(b) The rat is presented contiguously with a loud noise. As children have an innate fear response to loud noises, the child is scared.

(c) Continual pairing of the rat and the noise cause the child to scream each time the rat is presented. After conditioning, the rat alone is capable of eliciting the fear response.

(d) Because humans are capable of stimulus generalisation, Little Albert becomes afraid when shown stuffed toys and men with beards.

Figure 5.4: The 'Little Albert' experiment

Classical conditioning and marketing

A number of studies have used the principles of classical conditioning to understand certain aspects of consumer behaviour. For example, they have been used to explain why made-up brand names, such as Coca-Cola, Vegemite, Aeroplane Jelly and the Marlboro man, still evoke strong responses.

In one study, music was played at different tempos over a nine-week period in a grocery store. The slow tempo music averaged 60 beats per minute while the fast tempo music averaged 108 beats per minute.

Comparisons of sales figures during the different trials showed that sales increased by at least 38 per cent in slow tempo conditions. Sales decreased in both fast tempo and no music situations.[6] In another study, slow and fast tempo music was played in a restaurant. When the music was slow, patrons stayed longer and purchased more from the bar.[7]

Gorn found that when consumers were shown slides of pens of different colours (light-blue and beige) paired with either pleasant or unpleasant music they were more likely to purchase the pen associated with the pleasant music.[8] In a similar study by Stuart et al., consumers were exposed to pictures of beautiful landscapes that were associated with a fictitious brand of toothpaste. The outcome was that consumers showed a positive attitude to the brand of toothpaste over other brands.[9] Other studies have examined the role of colour in eliciting specific responses.[10] Research by Feinberg[11] suggests that the presence (or absence) of a Mastercard influences consumer behaviour. In the study, one group of customers in a buying situation was exposed to a replica of a Mastercard and another group was not. Feinberg found that, when exposed to the replica, customers:

• made the decision to buy more quickly
• spent more on clothing
• gave more to charity.

His explanation for the behaviour of customers was that the Mastercard was associated (had become paired) with the buying act. Because credit cards are strongly associated with purchasing, they have become a conditioned stimulus that elicits a conditioned response — the purchasing of products.

While some researchers have used the principles of classical conditioning to explain some aspects of consumer behaviour, a number of writers suggest that their claims should be viewed with a degree of caution.[12] An example is the supermarket music study. Because we are pre-programmed to respond to rhythmic beats, we slow down when exposed to a slow rhythm and speed up when exposed to a fast one. It may well be that because we are moving slower, we take time to observe the products and are thus more inclined to notice items we need or can use. It also allows us time to observe instore promotions. The principles of classical conditioning state that learning is based on an already existing stimulus–response (S–R) relationship. The music in this instance is the unconditioned stimulus (UCS) and the slow or fast response by consumers is the unconditioned response (UCR). For classical conditioning to have occurred, the fast or slow music would have to be associated with another stimulus, and one that would not normally produce this response, such as the intensity of a light. For example, if the fast tempo music was paired with a bright or even a flashing light for a series of trials, then shoppers could be conditioned to walk faster when exposed to a bright (or flashing) light and still buy more products. Since their unconditioned state produces the same result, conditioning in this instance is not necessary.

Whether increased purchases or specific product choices can be attributed to classical conditioning is also questionable. What may have occurred, for example in the pen study, is that the music creates a positive emotion, makes us feel good and can cause us to view objects differently. So when exposed to music we like, we become emotionally responsive to liking any stimulus, such as a beige pen, that we have been exposed to. Strictly speaking this is not an example of classical conditioning, as pleasant music is the UCS and the 'good feeling' is the UCR. In Gorn's supermarket study it was found that the customers were not consciously aware of the music so perhaps we should look at the role of subliminal influences. The essence of subliminal influences is that products and messages should be presented in such a way, or in association with a stimulus, that will elicit a positive emotion, such as happiness, security and self-worth. The assumption is that if consumers are in a positive mood, they will be more receptive to retaining positive thoughts about the product

and are more likely to retain messages from advertisements that make them feel good. Advertisements such as that for Moove in the 1980s which showed scantily clad people frolicking to sensual music, or the OTC 'Memories' advertisement shown in figure 5.5, may have elicited a strong, positive emotional response, but they are not examples of classical conditioning. It is, after all, standard advertising practice to place brands (or products) close to stimuli that are known to produce a favourable emotional response from consumers in the target audience.

Figure 5.5: This was one of several television commercials by OTC that showed migrants remembering their families back home, featuring the emotive tune and lyric, 'Memories'.

Although there have been many studies claiming the use of classical conditioning in marketing, there is a lack of clear-cut evidence linking behaviours to classical conditioning. For this reason, managers and researchers should treat with caution the notion that consumers can be classically conditioned. Certainly the claims that advertisements are using classical conditioning techniques and that these techniques cause consumers to respond positively to the product are controversial.[13]

INSTRUMENTAL CONDITIONING

Instrumental conditioning, or operant conditioning, is also learning by association, and is triggered by a sequence of events. It is different from classical conditioning basically because there is a relationship between our own behaviour and a particular outcome. Other differences are described more fully on page 111. The term 'instrumental' is used because the appropriate behaviour is viewed as an instrument by which we can achieve our goals. For example, if a small child touches the front of an oven and it is hot, the child soon learns to be careful to avoid being burnt. Thus instrumental conditioning is not reliant on innate responses but on trained responses.

At the turn of the century, when Pavlov was investigating what we now know as classical conditioning, Edward Thorndike was experimenting with cats. He started by confining a cat inside a wooden box. The box had a lever mechanism that if pressed would open the box. Thorndike observed that once the cat, usually by accident, pressed the lever, the next time it was confined it associated the lever with the consequence of escape. Thorndike labelled this 'trial and error learning' and concluded that the cat's escape from confinement served as a reward to strengthen or 'stamp in' the response. From these experiments Thorndike formed his Law of Effect, which is that:[14]

> **"**responses that bring about satisfaction strengthen the stimulus/response association, while responses that produce discomfort tend to weaken the association.**"**

Another major advance in instrumental conditioning occurred in the 1930s when B. F. Skinner, a professor at Harvard, experimented with animals using what has become known as the Skinner box (see figure 5.6). It was used in the following way:

1. An animal, typically a hungry rat, is placed in the box. It explores the box and, when it looks at the lever it is rewarded by a pellet of food. This is the first stage of conditioning and it is usually known as 'shaping'.
2. Shaping is continued until the rat moves towards the lever. From then on it is rewarded only if it moves towards the lever.
3. Once the rat is close enough and, usually by accident, it touches the lever, it is rewarded with a pellet of food. Once this occurs the shaping process is complete and the food is only delivered if the rat presses the lever. The 'abnormal' rat behaviour, i.e. pressing a lever for food, has been conditioned by a reward that was a consequence of the action of pressing the lever.

Figure 5.6: The Skinner box

Instrumental and classical conditioning compared

Instrumental and classical conditioning involve similar phenomena and follow similar rules. Both instrumentally and classically conditioned responses show acquisition, extinction, spontaneous recovery, reconditioning, generalisation, and discrimination. This resemblance is not surprising; after all, in both types of conditioning, the brain is simply learning the correlation between two events in the environment. In classical conditioning the events are the occurrence of the conditioned stimulus (CS) and the unconditioned stimulus (UCS); in instrumental conditioning, they are the response and the rewarding consequence.

As these similarities suggest, most factors that influence one kind of conditioning also influence the other. For example, classical conditioning is usually weak or non-existent unless the interval between the conditioned (bell) and unconditioned (food) stimulus is brief (with the exception of taste aversions). In instrumental conditioning, the longer the delay between response (lever press) and reward (food), the more slowly conditioning progresses. In either case, a long delay makes it difficult for the organism to connect the first event with the second.

But despite great similarities between classical and instrumental conditioning, there are distinct differences in the two procedures.

Classical conditioning	Instrumental conditioning
• UCS follows the CS whether or not subject responds to the CS.	• Reward occurs only if subject makes the critical response.
• Subject's response is generally involuntary — it is a reflex elicited by the UCS.	• Subject's response is voluntary and not elicited by some UCS (i.e. lever does not elicit 'lever-pressing' as if 'lever-pressing' were a reflex).
• Conditioned response usually resembles the unconditioned response, e.g. in Pavlov's experiments both CR and UCR were salivation.	• Conditioned response, e.g. pressing a lever, is usually different from the customary response to the reward, e.g. eating a food pellet. The experimenter can arrange for almost any operant response to bring about almost any reinforcing consequence.
• Response generally involves the autonomic nervous system or internal organs. Most experiments train reactions that are normally involuntary, such as changes in salivation or heart rate.*	• Response generally involves the somatic nervous system. Most experiments involve the modifying of voluntary responses, such as pressing or pecking.*

*This distinction is not perfect, however. Some responses — such as an eyeblink — can be either voluntary or involuntary, and they can be conditioned by either procedure. Autonomic responses such as heart rate apparently can be modified biofeedback, a technique that is a form of instrumental conditioning.

According to Skinner, people and animals behave in a 'purposive' way all the time — from the way we clean our teeth to prevent tooth decay to the way we buy products that will satisfy our needs. We invariably behave in ways that will maximise pleasure and minimise pain. In this way our behaviour is a function of the reinforcers we have been exposed to in the past. Skinner even thought our personalities were shaped in this way. If you are an optimist, honest, reliable and trustworthy, then according to Skinner's ideas someone or something has rewarded you for adopting these characteristics.[15]

The essence of instrumental conditioning is that the researchers arrange the conditioning situation so that the animal's (or person's) instrumental response causes it to encounter a pleasant or an unpleasant event. But they can also arrange the opposite relationship, so that the animal's instrumental response causes the removal or withdrawal of something — whether a pleasant consequence or an unpleasant one. Removing something that is unpleasant provides satisfying relief, so any response that leads to escape from an unpleasant state of affairs will be strengthened. Similarly, removing a pleasant stimulus, such as taking lollies away from a child, causes frustration and dissatisfaction, so the removal acts as punishment. Pleasant consequences are usually classified as 'positive'; examples include rewards, such as a payoff or money bonus for a job well done, or relief from the distress of parental nagging after you clean up your room. Unpleasant consequences are usually classified as 'negative'. They include punishment and the removal of some pleasant situation. A punishment for a child might be a spanking from a parent who thought the youngster had misbehaved. An example of the removal of something pleasant might be a speeding fine or the loss of your driver's licence.

The key principles of instrumental learning are shaping, reinforcement schedules (see page 113), generalisation and discrimination. Generalisation and discrimination occur in instrumental learning just as they do in classical conditioning. If you train a pigeon to peck at a picture of Paul Hogan it will generalise its behaviour and also peck at a picture of Paul Keating as both are pictures of people. The pigeon can also be trained to discriminate, so that it will only peck at the picture of Paul Hogan. The steps one would take to train a pigeon to discriminate between Paul Hogan and Paul Keating are not much different from the steps you would take in order to train consumers to discriminate between competing brands of similar products.

How rewards (usually extrinsic) are administered will determine how fast learning takes place and how long the behaviour will continue once the rewards are removed. So training needs to be carefully controlled to maximise learning and minimise forgetting. For example, learning occurs faster if rewards are given in full and immediately after the response. Partial, variable and delayed reinforcement will result in slower learning but helps to guard against extinction of the trained behaviour. This means that a proficient training program would start with full and immediate rewards followed by a variable pattern of full and/or partial rewards. So that, if you were a shop owner and you were to set up a program that would get and keep new consumers, a reinforcement schedule described in figure 5.7 could work.

Basic instrumental conditioning terms

Positive reinforcers: These are rewards designed to increase the person's tendency to repeat behaviours that result in the rewards.

Negative reinforcers: Includes punishment or the removal of a pleasant situation.

Shaping: A process through which new behaviour is created by reinforcing only responses that are in the desired direction. Shaping deals with a sequence of different responses, not the recurrence of the same response.

Immediate reinforcement: The reward is delivered immediately after the behaviour occurs. Most effective in the initial training stage of new behaviour acquisition.

Delayed reinforcement: The reward is delivered after a period of time has elapsed. Most effective in maintaining the trained behaviour.

Schedules of reinforcement: The basis on which a subject is rewarded for a behaviour. These vary according to the type of training required. The types of schedules are:

- continuous reinforcement schedule — a person is given a reward each time the desired behaviour is performed
- partial reinforcement schedules — these are varied and include:
  - fixed ratio schedules, where rewards come after a specific number of behaviours
  - variable ratio schedules, where rewards are delivered after a variable (unpredictable) number of responses
  - fixed interval schedules, where rewards are delivered after a specific lapse of time since the previous reward
  - variable interval schedules, where rewards are delivered at various (unpredictable) time intervals.

Figure 5.7 demonstrates each type of partial reinforcement schedule.

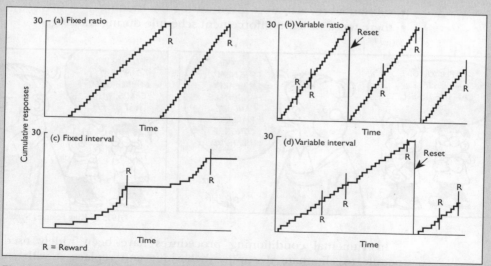

Figure 5.7: Hypothetical, but fairly typical, cumulative response curves under the four schedules of reinforcement

(*continued*)

Points to note about instrumental conditioning:

1. Changes in the magnitude of the reward produce very rapid changes in the level of performance.
2. In general, the more times someone has purchased a product the more likely the person is to purchase it in the future.
3. The level of satisfaction expected from a product determines whether or not it will be purchased.
4. The stronger the stimulus, the stronger the response.
5. Stimulus strength is relative not absolute. The intensity of an object as a stimulus depends on other stimuli and the experience of the shopper.

In any training program it is important to ensure that the person continues with the trained behaviour after the extrinsic rewards are removed. Once an instrumental response has been conditioned, it will continue if it is occasionally rewarded. If the behaviour is not occasionally rewarded it will cease. The technical label given to this is 'extinction'. In some cases, once the rewards are removed, the trained behaviours will increase. These observations have been noted in lower order animals (cats and rats) and in a laboratory setting. So whether the same behaviour occurs in adult humans is debatable. If the extrinsic rewards are removed and intrinsic rewards have not developed there is a good chance that forgetting and/or extinction of the behaviour will occur. Resistance to extinction develops if:

- there is a strong motive/need to perform the act
- there have been many training sessions
- substantial rewards were given during the training
- there was a varied reinforcement schedule during training.

©1975 by King Features Syndicate, Inc.

Instrumental conditioning procedures have been widely used with people to eliminate disruptive behaviour and replace it with sociable behaviour. For example, a schoolteacher may systematically use praise and attention to reinforce peaceful and socially appropriate classroom behaviour in problem children.[16]

Instrumental conditioning and marketing

Unlike the unconscious associations we make during classical conditioning, learning via instrumental conditioning is conscious and obvious. While we may not think of sales promotions such as 'two for the price of one' as a reinforcer (a reward) that causes us to buy the product (the trained behaviour), it is an excellent example of instrumental conditioning. In situations where we buy a product and are happy with it (a reward situation), we are more likely to purchase the product again, in other words, continue the behaviour. For brand loyalty to occur, consumers must receive continual reinforcements, ideally by being satisfied in all respects with the brand. According to Rothschild and Gaidis,[17] behavioural learning theory is an example of the principles that underlie the marketing concept. They point out that:

> 66 Appropriate long-run behaviour only takes place when the reinforcer meets some need. A reinforcer can't be positive if it does not meet needs. 99

This also means that if a product does not meet the needs of the consumer, the extrinsic rewards to encourage purchase won't work.

The challenge for marketers is to control the environment so that consumers will purchase and continue to purchase their products. At the initiating stage, for reinforcement principles to be fully effective, consumers need to be informed or made aware that the product or service is available. At this point, careful target market selection and analysis is important. This should enable information to be delivered in the best message format via the media channels used by members of the target audience and target market. In some instances where consumers have a learned need, i.e. a strong motive for purchasing the product, and there is little or no competition, there may be no need to use extrinsic reinforcers to initiate purchase. In these cases, the intrinsic rewards associated with the product itself and/or its allied benefits serve to produce the desired behaviours. If this is not the case, then a 'consumer learning program' using extrinsic rewards may be useful.

Figure 5.8: The offer displayed on this package of $2 off the next purchase of Nerada tea is an example of a delayed partial reward incentive.

What extrinsic rewards (incentives) should be used and how they should be delivered depends very much on the type of product and the type of behaviours you want from the consumer. Two methods that marketers often use are 'trial incentives', in the case of products that are new to the market or new to the consumer, and 'loading incentives' to encourage repeat purchasing behaviour. Examples of these are given in table 5.1.

Table 5.1: Examples of incentive (sales promotion) objectives

Trial incentives (*to initiate purchase*)	Loading incentives (*to maintain and/or increase purchases*)
Two for the price of one	Coupons
Cash discounts (immediate reward)	Trading stamps
Cash rebates (delayed reward)	Prices
Banded sample	Cents-off deal
Delayed payment	Attached gifts
Free sample	Attached collectables
Product trial	
Associated gifts	

Proper selection of incentives coupled with carefully planned reinforcement schedules can have considerable impact on a product's performance in the market. An example was the well designed launch strategy for Copper Kettle coffee, which involved the use of carefully selected and implemented incentives (described below).

The coffee launch

In the 1970s, Cottees General Foods were producing a number of brands of instant coffee, including Maxwell House. They also produced cheaper brands, but these were facing strong competition from generic and housebrand labels. Market research showed that there was a gap in the market, at the middle range, for a mild coffee. The target market for this coffee was the housewives segment. Analysis of the media habits of this segment showed that they were heavy magazine readers and radio listeners.

Careful product development, branding and pricing strategies coupled with an effective product launch ensured the success of the new Copper Kettle brand (6 per cent market share; expected share 3–4 per cent). Copper Kettle was introduced to the market via radio and magazine advertisements. Apart from ensuring that their distribution and a range of other marketing tactics were effective, Cottees also used an extremely efficient reinforcement schedule during the first year of launch.

The product was launched with a 'two for the price of one' promotions tactic. This was an immediate full reward reinforcement — an effective shaping tactic. After a fixed interval of time, a full but delayed reinforcer was used. This took the form of a coupon that could be redeemed for one dollar — close to half the cost of the coffee. After another time interval, a partial reward tactic was introduced (a 'cents off' deal.). This was followed, again after a time interval, with a free extra amount of coffee. By continually reinforcing the purchase with extrinsic rewards, customers were encouraged to buy the product. Obviously, for the total acceptance of the product, consumers need to develop intrinsic rewards, such as total satisfaction with the product, so that the reward is using the product iself.

Getting it right

What a good sales promotion really sets out to achieve is to push a product or service through the clutter and get it noticed, get it tried.

Traditionally the job of the ad campaign, the proliferation of brands and advertising has seen sales promotion becoming more and more important.

"What I can see is below the line is turning into above the line," says Brian Levy, joint managing director, Australian Slatwell Industries.

"Sales promotion is depended on more and more for success but it has to be planned for.

"While there is (normally) time allocated to produce the ad campaign, quite often the sales promotion seems to be an afterthought.

"While most people could walk into their advertising agency and have a good understanding of what is going on — few marketers understand sales promotion," says Brian.

"And yet it is an area that must be planned to ensure maximum returns for the investment.

"The big thing with sales promotion and product display is to find a company that can get it right, and get it right quickly," says Brian.

When venturing into sales promotion it is important to "Step back from the trees so you can see the whole forest," says Phillip Lyons, managing director, Promotional Thinking.

All too often the detail of day-to-day brand marketing can cloud the real issue of why any brand/product exists — to make a profit for the company! "Today's business environment cannot afford the luxuries of pouring money into products which do not sell or make a profit," says Phillip.

"This scenario often leads to the decision to implement a Sales Promotion.

"It's important to remember, the objective is to increase sales, not to advertise the brand ... this is a side benefit, sales promotions are generally short term, tactical methods of providing Added Value to a brand ... thus encouraging a sale!

"Whilst it is an integral part of every sales promotion to extend and enhance a brand's imagery, it is not the role of a promotion to create or establish this positioning. This is the realm of advertising, and it is a longer term function.

"Many sales promotions can be highly effective in increasing sales, without having a direct link to a brand image's platform. This is because the Added Value element has created a sufficiently attractive inducement to purchase — over and above the benefits of the product itself.

"The moral of this story is ... don't bugger up a good sales promotion, by turning it into a bad ad," says Phillip.

The promotional product industry is an extremely competitive market. The consumer very easily becomes boggled by the options available.

Jenny Conomos, of Conomos and Church, says it's vital that sales promotion companies strive to offer a range of quality products, not only at an affordable price, but with the service to back it up.

"When it comes to separating yourself from the many companies out there offering promotional products, we endeavour to concentrate on points that will make our product just that little extra better," Jenny says.

"A point of difference is extremely important to us. In these severe recessionary times, budgets are lean and the consumer simply can not afford to be spending their valued dollars on just anything that will hopefully get some kind of message across to the end user.

"So many companies spend enormous amounts of money on building an image to attract potential clientele and to keep banging the drum to their existing clientele.

"Yet when it comes to their promotional items, price immediately becomes the governing factor. However much a company has to spend on promotional merchandise, it will be wasted if those 100 polo shirts, for example, shrink, fall apart and then get used to wash the car! Is that item worth the valued promotional dollar?

"There is nothing better than hearing how successful some baseball jackets went and how the end users are wearing them constantly. That's what sales promotion is all about, making an impact on the consumer!" says Jenny.

The selection of a particular incentive is determined by the product, company resources, lead time (the length of time to put the incentive into the marketplace) and consumer characteristics. For example, some products, such as hair colouring and tinting products, preclude the free sample option. An example of an effective loading incentive was the coupon system used by the producers of LanChu tea. A coupon was printed on each packet of LanChu tea and the coupons could be collected then exchanged for gifts. The more coupons collected, the better the quality of the gifts. Catalogues were distributed describing the gifts and the number of coupons required. Centres at which the coupons could be exchanged were set up in all Australian capital cities. A number of companies use similar systems. The Frequent Flyer benefits promoted by the major airlines are an example of loading incentives. The Fly Buys.™ program is another example (see figure 5.9).

Figure 5.9: Fly Buys.™ — the first 'frequent buyer' program in Australia — is based on everyday shopping behaviour.

It has been argued that instrumental conditioning principles are only useful for low involvement consumer decisions.[18] Researchers Peters and Nord reject this notion however, suggesting that there is no reason why incentives to purchase should not work in high involvement situations. They describe a hypothetical situation in which car dealers could, if they wanted, shape an automobile purchase. They could start off by giving free coffee and donuts to anyone who came into the sales yard. They could offer a $5 reinforcer to anyone who was prepared to test drive a car and finally a $500 rebate on a car purchase. In this way, instrumental conditioning principles could be applied to purchasing in a high involvement decision situation.[19] Whether this example of Peter and Nord would work is debatable. However, choosing an airline is a high involvement decision and the Frequent Flyer incentives of the major airlines seem to operate effectively.

Although the careful use of incentives can be of benefit to a company, they can have a negative effect if misused or overused. Consider the jewellery store that is forever announcing another 'once-only sale', and the carpet importer who is 'closing down' at least three times per year — eventually this will devalue the store and the products in the eyes of the consumer, who may ultimately prefer to shop elsewhere.

66 The days of simply adding a premium to a product as an adjunct or afterthought are fast disappearing. Consumers do not wish to be insulted with tacky, cheap and nasty offers that have no relevance to the product they are buying, or to their own interest and expectation with regard to the brand they are considering to associate themselves with. Nor should they. 99

Marketing, October 1993

COGNITIVE LEARNING

Until recently, behaviourist theories have dominated the area of human learning. However, the work of cognitive theorists has succeeded in adding another dimension to the subject of learning — the internal dimension. The outcome is that the acquisition and storage of knowledge is also viewed as learning. Even so, the only way that we can be sure that learning has taken place is by performance. The critical role that cognitive learning plays is that it does help to explain how we learn to perform certain behaviours without being put through a direct stimulus–reward training process.

According to the cognitive theorists, humans and other higher order animals, such as monkeys and apes, are information-storing, problem-solving beings.[20] Humans with their well developed cerebral cortex carry out these processes very efficiently. We observe, either directly or by reading or hearing, what happens if we carry out certain behaviours. Thus, learning is not just a matter of responding to a stimulus; instead, people apply cognitive (thinking) processes to the stimulus. This means that the stimulus becomes information. The shaping stage in instrumental conditioning is therefore unnecessary and we go on to make a decision about whether or not we want to perform Behaviour A to obtain Response B. People can regulate their own behaviour by setting goals to motivate and reward themselves, so they have more control over their response to the environment than the behavioural school of learning suggests. This means that, as Rothschild and Gaidis suggest, if a product does not meet the needs of the consumer, extrinsic rewards to encourage purchase will not work.

Much of our social learning occurs through observing others. Often the learning occurs without us being consciously aware that we are learning. As indicated earlier, we are not 'born to shop' — everything we know about our culture, our traditions and the rules of our social group is learned. A great deal of this knowledge comes from watching others.

According to Bandura, observational learning consists of four processes: attention, retention, motor reproduction and motivation.[21] How much attention we pay to a model depends on the model's attractiveness and importance to us. Attention itself may not be enough. Unless the observer is able to represent, cognitively, the action of the model, the idea of the behaviour will not be retained and there will be no learning. So the easier it is for the observer to create a mental image, the more likely that learning will occur. Unless the observer is able to reproduce — at least approximately — the model's behaviour, there will be no learning.

Finally, there must be motivation to imitate any act. We are more likely to imitate a model's behaviour if the model is seen to be rewarded rather than punished, or if we realise that by imitating a model we will receive a reward, as in the child who imitates mum or dad so that he or she will be given approval and love.

Figure 5.10(a): Children learn by observing adults and imitating their behaviour.

Figure 5.10(b): Skin cancer warning campaigns have resulted in a transformation in the clothing style of Australian surf lifesavers. They are worthy models for other sun-loving Australians to imitate.

These principles have a fundamental message for any advertisement that seeks to influence via modelling. Any message needs to be presented in such a way as to ensure that the observed behaviours are clear, that the target audience is able to emulate the behaviours and that the benefits of doing so are desirable. Charles Manz and Henry Sims[22] claim that source effects are a crucial ingredient in vicarious learning (see also pages 228–29) and that the effectiveness of a model in an advertisement has been shown to increase if:

- the model is physically attractive
- the model is credible
- the model is successful
- the model is similar to the observer
- the model is shown as overcoming difficulties and then succeeding.

Vicarious (observational) learning can be used in marketing to create new behaviours or change existing behaviour. In Australia, because of the increase in skin cancers, a range of advertisements was designed to encourage people to 'slip, slop, slap' — slip on a t-shirt, slop on some sunblock and slap on a hat — which was essentially a new behaviour pattern for Australians. Such advertisements tend to use attractive models.

Vicarious learning, advertising and children

Early learning is through both instrumental learning and largely unconscious, vicarious (observational) learning. Observational learning occurs when people watch the action of others and note the reinforcements they receive for their behaviour. There is a great deal of published research dealing with how children react to and process information. In marketing, most of this deals with television advertisements as, for the majority of children under the age of nine, this is their main source of marketplace information.[23]

Very young children are not capable of abstract thought. According to research carried out last century by Piaget, abstract thought does not develop until about ten years of age (see figure 5.11).[24] For this reason, they are highly vulnerable to advertising messages. Most countries, Australia and New Zealand included, have strict controls on the content and timing of television advertising for children. (Specific regulations are described more fully in chapters 10 and 18.) Researchers have identified the important role that 'live' models, such as parents, teachers and peer groups, have on how advertisements are understood by children. Moschis and Churchill found that 'live' models had a considerable influence on how advertising messages were interpreted, right up until late adolescence.[25]

Sensorimotor stage (0–2 years)	Preoperational thought stage (3–7 years)	Concrete operational stage (8–11 years)	Formal operational stage (11–adulthood)
The child is not capable of abstract thought but language is beginning to develop. Development is mainly physical, driven by external stimuli.	The child begins to use symbols — pictures and other graphics. Can only pay attention to one thing at a time. Most action is still driven by external stimuli.	Child can think about objects and the potential for abstract thought develops.	The individual is capable of abstract thought. Ideas and logical thinking develop. Moves away from single to multiple dimension thinking.

Figure 5.11: Piaget's four stages of child development

INTEGRATED LEARNING

The development of the cognitive ideas on how we learn has forced theorists to look more closely at the learning process. It is now clear that, for humans, both association learning and cognitive learning operate in conjunction with each other. This is particularly so for consumption behaviour as it involves a conscious, controlled act by the consumer and is therefore a much more complicated process than the simple stimulus–response model in association learning. Invariably a purchaser is aware of the potential outcome of a purchase (behaviour) and of any extrinsic and intrinsic incentives or rewards that are offered prior to the purchase of a product (see figure 5.12).

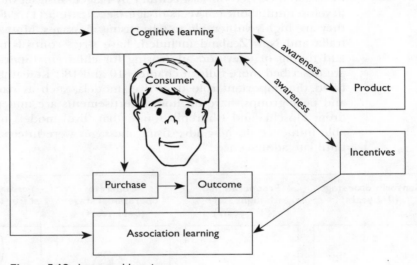

Figure 5.12: Integrated learning

When offering products to the market, a range of factors need to be taken into consideration. During the 1960s, Campbell[26] adapted the earlier work of Hull and Spence to develop a formula for integrated learning,

$$R = f(S \times D \times K \times H)$$

where:

   f = function

   R = response tendency — the intention to purchase or the actual purchase of a product

   S = stimulus — the product or communication about the product

   D = drive — the need state, i.e. problem recognition

   K = incentive motivation — the magnitude of the expected outcome

   H = habit strength — previous purchase patterns in relation to the product category.

Because this perspective of learning incorporates a range of other 'non-learning' inputs, further developments of the integrated learning approach in consumer behaviour have been incorporated in consumer decision making. The realisation that a consumer's response to marketing stimuli is the result of a range of factors has led to a review of how we understand the mechanisms of repeat purchase behaviour and the role of incentives.

LEARNING AND REPEAT PURCHASE BEHAVIOUR

The aim of a company's marketing strategy and planning is to ensure that consumers will purchase and continue to purchase the company's products. In short, the aim is to create a repeat purchase situation. Repeat purchase situations can occur for at least two reasons, habit and brand loyalty. If you always buy the same brand of soap simply because it is familiar, and you do not want to expend mental effort, then the repeat purchase is a function of habit, sometimes labelled 'inertia'. For consumers, habit buying offers savings in time and decision making effort. If, on the other hand, you purchase the soap because you think that in terms of quality, price and performance it is the best brand, then the repeat purchase is an example of brand-loyal behaviour. Brand loyalty is the purchase of a particular brand by an individual in light of alternative brands and is made via an evaluated decision.[27] To be wholly effective the behaviour should persist over time. It is, for marketers, the most desirable repeat purchase behaviour as, unlike habit purchases, it is less susceptible to the marketing activities of competitors. It is also less affected by stock-out situations in stores.

The problem for marketers is that, as both behaviours have the same outcome, you can only distinguish between them by undertaking market research to ascertain why consumers make repeat purchases of the product. Many market research agencies use product consumer panel data — consumers record the products purchased and the reasons for the purchase. Even so, verbal reports by consumers that they are brand loyal need to be evaluated with care, as consumers often seek to justify or rationalise their purchases. This means that they could still be susceptible to the marketing activities of competitors. One outcome of this type of research is the discovery that there are different patterns to brand-loyal behaviour. The three most common patterns are:

- **undivided loyalty** — the purchase of a single brand and the willingness to forgo purchase if the brand is not available
- **divided brand loyalty** — the consistent purchase of two or more brands
- **unstable loyalty** — the purchase of a brand for a period of time, followed by a switch, which is then followed by a period of loyalty.

The ideal situation for a company is to have repeat purchases that result from undivided brand loyalty. The key problem is how to train consumers to be brand loyal. Unfortunately, there is little evidence to suggest that a brand-loyal type of consumer exists. Loyalty, as the diagram in figure 5.13 indicates, seems to be product category specific. Products such as cigarettes and toothpaste seem to produce the most loyal behaviour, and garbage bags and canned vegetables the least. When generics were introduced into the Australian market, the first products to be adopted were garbage bags and paper products. An interesting factor is that, although brand loyalty is seen as risk reduction strategy by consumers, high involvement products such as cars and television sets do not have high loyalty. Only 47 per cent of cars and 35 per cent of television purchases are brand-loyal purchases.[28]

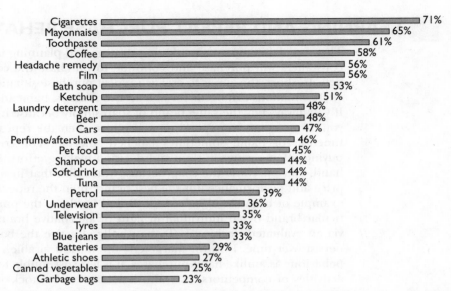

Figure 5.13: Brand loyalty across product categories (*Source*: Adapted from R. Alsop, 'Brand Loyalty is Rarely Blind Loyalty', *The Wall Street Journal*, 19 October 1989)

Another problem that must be faced is the growing trend towards brand parity (brand similarity) and the possible end of brand loyalty. Brand parity is a function of a number of factors, including:

• vast number of new products entering the market
• liberal and short-term sales promotion activities
• rapid technological change
• information and choice overload
• lack of accurate evaluation by consumers
• an inability to discriminate between products.

Also, certain conditions are necessary for brand loyalty, such as:

• customers must be aware of particular brands
• they must be able to differentiate between brands of similar products
• there must be motivation for repeat purchase.

Taking this combination of factors into account, and even with careful product positioning, it is becoming harder for companies to differentiate their products. Because of this, many companies have maintained market share by offering incentives, such as the Fly Buys™ program described in figure 5.9. If carefully managed, this can result in repeat purchases and market share can be maintained.[29] However, in the longer term this may not be a viable strategy, as competing on the basis of incentives can be costly and identifying the right incentives can be difficult. Furthermore it may not create brand-loyal consumers. Alsop notes that loyalty based repeat purchases generally occur with strong brands, 'total quality brands', brands where the purchaser has developed an intrinsic reward mechanism, in other words, using the brand is the reward.[30] Since brand loyalty results from a comparative evaluation of similar products, extrinsic incentives to encourage brand loyalty may even detract from the value of the brand. Unless consumers can differentiate between brands, their purchase decision could well be made on the quality and type of extrinsic incentives offered. For example, the Frequent Flyer participant could assess the quality of the 'gifts' rather than the actual product being purchased.

Unless a company wishes to enter into a continual sales-incentive war, more effort must be made to improve differentiation and the accuracy of product positioning. If brand loyalty cannot be assumed, marketers (product category and/or brand managers) will need to focus more on accurate target market selection, obtaining and improving their knowledge of consumer motivations and both the cognitive and behavioural learning processes.

For mature products, an important activity will be to ascertain how the repeat purchase pattern, if any, developed.

- Did the consumer start off by making a conscious choice about the product in terms of price, quality and performance?
- Did the consumer then develop a preference and continue to buy the product?

After a period of time, conscious awareness of the initial reward situation may have dissipated so now the purchase has become habitual. If this is the case, the purchasers need to be reminded of the initial benefits, and additional benefits if any. They should also be praised for continuing to use the product. Depending on the product, it may be useful to introduce some form of extrinsic reward. But the reward should not be for a single purchase act, it should reward the 'continuing purchase' act. The idea is to guard against consumers forgetting why they purchased the product in the first place. Ideally the incentive should reinforce the evaluation activity associated with brand loyalty and not necessarily the purchase itself. Although there is evidence that sales promotion devices may cause even brand-loyal consumers to switch brand, they may not become brand loyal to the new product unless the brand itself becomes valuable to them.

In conditions of excessive brand parity, an ongoing reinforcement program is necessary to keep loyal consumers from brand switching. Unless the product can be modified in such a way that it can be easily and positively distinguished from its competitors, consumers need to be rewarded in other ways for loyal behaviour. Otherwise they may reward themselves by adopting variety seeking behaviour to reduce the boredom associated with sameness. The reinforcement may not necessarily be extrinsic, such as free gifts; praise for selecting the product, particularly from other consumers, is a fairly strong reward. It may also be given via the mass media. The enduring Meadow Lea margarine slogan — 'you oughta be congratulated' — is an attempt to make purchasers feel good about the product and feel good about themselves. There is a key role for after-sales service, the aim being to establish an ongoing relationship with the consumer.[31] This is much easier in the industrial market. Establishing such a relationship in the consumer market is more difficult. It is, however, becoming more viable with the development of more direct communication systems, such as direct mail, telephone, videotext, computer linking and specialty print media.

Whether or not customers are 'repeat purchasers' is most often a function of the marketer — it is up to the marketer to create the optimum conditions. A basis for the creation of these optimum conditions may be the acceptance that the learning process is more than a simple stimulus–response process. Cognitive factors play a crucial role in determining our final behaviour. The integrated approach to understanding how consumers learn is, therefore, of more use than the behavioural approach alone. Not only must the consumer's needs be met, but careful attention must also be paid to the message strategy used. Ideally messages should be structured so that the information is clear, easily understood and easily transferred into the long-term memory systems. The message should also contain information that would allow consumers to differentiate the brand.

If extrinsic rewards are to be used, they also must 'fit' the consumer's needs — in other words, the consumer must want the gift. It should be clearly understood that, if the objective is to create brand loyalty, relying on extrinsic incentives is foolhardy.

SUMMARY

In this chapter we examined theories and ideas about learning and how they have contributed to our understanding of consumer behaviour. Although the principles of behavioural learning have had a considerable influence on our understanding of the consumer's learning process, in recent years a more holistic perspective has been developing. Learning theories have come from two perspectives — the behavioural and the cognitive. The behavioural school of thought views learning as 'a relatively permanent change in behaviour which occurs as a result of experience or practice', and focuses on actual performance as a measure of learning.

There are two basic types of association learning, classical conditioning and instrumental conditioning. In classical conditioning, behaviours that are already programmed can be produced from stimuli that do not normally produce the response. Instrumental conditioning is used to train new behaviours, such as teaching a dog to fetch the paper. In classical conditioning the learner is passive, whereas in instrumental conditioning the learner is active. Although there have been many attempts to link classical learning principles with specific consumer behaviours, the practical applications seem dubious. Many of the behaviours researched can be more easily explained by theories on the role of sensory inputs and their impact on emotions.

In instrumental conditioning behaviour is influenced by the reinforcers and punishments given after the behaviour is performed. There is a strong body of evidence to show that the rewards or reinforcers that consumers receive during and after the purchase of goods play a significant role in future purchases.

Cognitive learning theories focus on understanding how people take in and store information and how they solve problems. For cognitive theorists, learning is not just a change in observable behaviour. They define learning as 'changes in an organism's knowledge about the world that occur as a result of experience'. The critical role of cognitive learning is in helping to explain how we learn to perform certain behaviours without being put through a direct stimulus–reward training scheme, such as learning by observation or vicarious experiences.

For humans, both associative and cognitive learning operate in conjunction with each other. This applies particularly to consumption behaviour as it involves a conscious, controlled act by the consumer and is therefore a much more complicated process than the simple S–R model in association learning. In instrumental conditioning the reward comes after the behaviour. In the marketing situation, purchasers are certainly aware of the potential outcome of a purchase (behaviour). This means that they are aware of any extrinsic and intrinsic incentives (rewards) that are offered prior to their purchase of any product. So although the reward is contingent on the behaviour, the consumer has 'free choice' of whether or not to respond. Marketers need to consider carefully whether or not behavioural learning can be applied directly to consumer behaviour.

It may be more practical for marketers to view learning as more holistic and integrated. This does not diminish the value of reinforcers in stimulating and maintaining repeat purchase behaviour, but incorporates them into a more comprehensive training program.

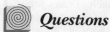

Questions

1. Observational learning is a key influence on how children are socialised. What factors influence the observational learning process? Choose three advertisements (television or print) that are directed towards children and discuss how well these factors are utilised.

2. You are the product manager of a brand washing detergent that has been a consistent but moderate performer since 1948. For the past two years purchases have declined. You recognise that brand parity in the detergent market is a growing problem, so what can you do to maintain market share for your product?

3. It has been suggested that purchase incentives work best at the point of purchase. As a manufacturer of conserves distributed through the major supermarkets, what tactics could you use to stimulate purchase? Explain the specific factors that influence your choice of tactics.

4. You have just purchased a business — Sparters, a well known supplier of automobile parts. How can you ensure that both new and old customers will use and continue to use your service?

5. Discuss how classical (Pavlovian) conditioning principles can be used to maintain and perhaps stimulate purchases.

6. What role do stimulus discrimination and stimulus generalisation play in an integrated learning approach?

7. Collect recent advertisements (print) for cars, perfume and coffee. What reinforcement (rewards), if any, are contained in the messages?

8. What differences are there between brand loyalty that is cognitively learned and that which is habitually learned? From a marketer's point of view, which is more desirable? Why?

9. If it is accepted that the integrative approach to learning is the most useful way to understand consumer learning, how would you measure each of the elements involved?

10. By developing a good relationship with customers, marketers are offering a special type of reward. What is this reward and is it relevant to consumer markets?

Case study

MARKETERS have been talking about integrated marketing for years. The theory of marrying various elements of the marketing mix — such as media advertising, sales promotion and public relations — to produce a tight, connected marketing program is great. But converting the theory to practice is not an easy task.

Integrated marketing is the most logical and smartest way for a company to sell its goods or services. In an age of fragmented media and demographics, customers are becoming increasingly difficult to reach. Grabbing every available weapon and welding them together to form a package that covers several marketing techniques and reaches several levels of consumers makes perfect sense. So why is it not happening?

The creation of integrated marketing programs is being held back by the division, and often antagonism, that exists between advertising agencies — the custodians of media advertising — and the companies that offer services such as sales promotion or direct marketing. Each party is suspicious of the other, jealously guarding its own patch (and income) from predatory moves. Each party delights in undermining the work of the other.

In the past 15 years there has been a gradual shift of dollars away from above-the-line marketing (media advertising) towards below-the-line marketing (sales promotion, public relations, direct mail, sponsorships and so on). Spot-ting the trend, many ad agencies set up below-the-line divisions, but their hearts have rarely been in it. Most agencies complain that revenue from below-the-line projects is too erratic and too difficult to earn. But they argue that farming out below-the-line work to other companies creates disjointed marketing programs.

The critics of below-the-line marketing maintain that techniques such as direct mail and product giveaways are short-term, quick-fix devices that destroy a brand's image and franchise with consumers. Its exponents argue that it offers something media advertising rarely delivers: fast, accountable results.

Both parties are partly right, but their arguments obscure the key point of the debate: is there a way to effectively marry above-the-line and below-the-line marketing to produce an integrated marketing program? The answer is yes.

A handful of companies have managed to produce effective integrated marketing programs. Every year, soft-drink king Coca-Cola supports its multi-million-dollar media advertising program with a battery of below-the-line promotions, such as product giveaways, consumer competitions and rock concert sponsorships. Breakfast cereal and muesli bar maker Uncle Tobys has found a way to blend its $15 million-a-year media ad budget with a range of below-the-line activities, including its sponsorship of an annual iron-man competition.

The integrated marketing programs run by Coke and Uncle Tobys succeed because the brand image — fun, excitement and good times in the case of Coke and good-tasting, good-for-you in the case of Uncle Tobys — remains king. If the below-the-line program matches the brand's image and works with, rather than detracts from, the brand-building efforts of the media advertising campaign, below-the-line devices such as sales promotion and direct marketing can add to both a brand's sales and image.

For an integrated marketing program to work, the offer made by a sales promotion or direct mail must match the picture of the brand. If the offer is inappropriate, it will damage the brand's image and consumer franchise.

A recent commercial break on a Sydney television station contained five ads in a row promoting consumer competitions. The use of such below-the-line techniques is not simply a kneejerk reaction to the recession and flat consumer spending. It is part of a new mood in the Australian marketing community. As the 1990s roll on, more companies will want integrated marketing programs. Ad agencies and marketing consultants must realise that above-the-line and below-the-line marketing tools are not mutually exclusive and that it is time to tear down the barriers and start working together.

Neil Shoebridge,
Business Review Weekly

Case study questions

1. Identify and evaluate two low risk products and two high risk products that have used sales incentives (below-the-line) and brand advertising. Do you think that the sales incentives used 'match' the product? Does the message content of each commercial recognise and complement the type of sales incentives used?
2. Discuss whether or not the decision to use sales incentives was appropriate for the product.

SUGGESTED READING

M. Walker, D. Burnham and R. Borland, *Psychology*, 2nd edn, John Wiley and Sons, Brisbane, 1994, pp. 218–48.

A. Bandura, *Social Foundations of Thought and Action: A Social Cognitive View*, Prentice-Hall, Englewood Cliffs, NJ, 1986.

T. Robertson and H. Kassarjian (eds), *Handbook of Consumer Theory and Research*, Prentice-Hall, Englewood Cliffs, NJ, 1991.

ENDNOTES

1. E. R. Hilgard and G. H. Bower, *Theories of Learning*, 3rd edn, Appleton-Century-Crofts, New York, 1966.
2. M. Figler, 'The Relation Between Eliciting Stimulus Strength and Habituation of the Threat Display in Male Siamese Fighting Fish', *Betta Splendens*, *Behaviour*, 42, 1972, pp. 63–96. H. V. S. Peeke, 'Habituation and the Maintenance of Territorial Boundaries', in H. V. S. Peeke and L. Pettinovich (eds), *Habituation, Sensitization and Behaviour*, Academic Press, New York, 1984.
3. H. Gleitman, *Basic Psychology*, 3rd edn, W. W. Norton and Co., New York, 1992, pp. 102–3.
4. H. Gleitman, 1992, ibid., pp. 70–103.
5. J. P. Houston, *Fundamentals of Learning and Memory*, Academic Press, New York, 1981. R. R. Bootzin, G. H. Bower, R. B. Zajonic and E. Hall, *Psychology Today*, Random House, New York, 1986.
6. R. E. Milliman, 'Using Background Music to Affect the Behaviour of Supermarket Shoppers', *Journal of Marketing*, 42, Summer 1982, pp. 86–91.
7. R. E. Milliman, 'The Influence of Background Music on the Behaviour of Restaurant Patrons', *Journal of Consumer Research*, 13, Sept. 1986, pp. 286–89.
8. G. J. Gorn, 'The Effects of Music in Advertising on Choice Behaviour: A Classical Conditioning Approach', *Journal of Marketing*, 46, 1982, pp. 94–101. C. Bierley, F. McSweeny and R. Vannieuwkerk, 'Classical Conditioning of Preferences for Stimuli', *Journal of Consumer Research*, 12, Dec. 1985, pp. 316–23 (replication of Gorn's study).
9. E. W. Stuart, T. A. Shimp and R. W. Engle, 'Classical Conditioning of Consumer Attitudes: Four Experiments in an Advertising Context', *Journal of Consumer Research*, Vol. 14, Dec. 1987, pp. 334–49.
10. J. A. Bellizzi, A. E. Crowley and R. W. Hasty, 'The Effect of Colour in Store Design', *Journal of Retailing*, Vol. 59, No. 1, Spring 1983, pp. 21–45.

11. R. A. Feinberg, 'Credit Cards as Spending Facilitating Stimuli: A Conditioning Perspective', *Journal of Consumer Research*, 13, Dec. 1986, pp. 348–56.

12. R. A. Rescorla, 'Pavlovian Conditioning: It's Not What You Think It Is', *American Psychologist*, Vol. 43, 1988, pp. 151–60. F. K. McSweeny and C. Bierley, 'Recent Developments in Classical Conditioning', *Journal of Consumer Research*, Vol. 11, Sept. 1984, pp. 619–31. G. J. Gorn, W. J. Jacobs and M. J. Mana, 'Observations on Awareness and Conditioning', *Advances in Consumer Research*, Vol. 14, 1987, pp. 415–16.

13. C. T. Allen and T. Madden, 'A Closer Look at Classical Conditioning', *Journal of Consumer Research*, 12, Dec. 1985, pp. 303–15. C. A. Insko and W. F. Oakes, 'Awareness and the Conditioning of Attitudes', *Journal of Personality and Social Psychology*, Vol. 4, Nov. 1966, pp. 621–23. L. R. Kahle, S. E. Beatty and P. Kennedy, 'Comments on Classical Conditioning Human Consumers', *Advances in Consumer Research*, Vol. 14, 1987, pp. 411–13. J. P. Peter and W. R. Nord, 'A Behaviour Modification Perspective on Marketing', *Journal of Marketing*, Vol. 44, Spring 1980, pp. 36–47. G. Foxall, 'Radical Behaviourism and Consumer Research: Theoretical Promise and Empirical Problems', *International Journal of Research in Marketing*, 4, 1987, pp. 111–29. C. Janiszewski and L. Warlop, 'The Influence of Classical Conditioning Procedures on Subsequent Attention to the Conditioned Brand', *Journal of Consumer Research*, Vol. 20, No. 2, 1993, pp. 171–89.

14. E. L. Thorndike, *Animal Intelligence: Experimental Studies*, MacMillan, New York, 1911.

15. E. R. Hilgard and G. H. Bower, *Theories of Learning*, 3rd edn, Appleton-Century-Crofts, New York, 1966.

16. A. E. Kazdin, *History of Behaviour Modification: Experimental Foundations of Contemporary Research*, University Park Press, Baltimore, 1978.

17. M. L. Rothschild and W. C. Gaidis, 'Behavioural Learning Theory: Its Relevance to Marketing and Promotions', *Journal of Marketing*, Vol. 45, Spring 1981, pp. 70–78.

18. M. L. Rothschild and W. C. Gaidis, ibid.

19. J. P. Peter and W. R. Nord, 'A Clarification and Extension of Operant Conditioning Principles in Marketing', *Journal of Marketing*, Vol. 46, Summer 1982, pp. 102–107. Current unresolved legal and tax issues have created some concerns about the operation of the Frequent Flyer system in Australia. See R. Rose and F. Brown, 'Frequent Flyer Plans Create a Major Mess for Airlines, Travellers', *Wall Street Journal*, 12 Feb. 1988.

20. A. Dickinson, 'Animal Conditioning and Learning Theory', in H. J. Eysenck and I. Martin (eds), *Theoretical Foundations of Behaviour Theory*, Plenum, New York, 1987.

21. A. Bandura, *Social Learning Theory*, Prentice-Hall, Englewood Cliffs, NJ, 1977.

22. C. Manz and H. Sims, 'Vicarious Learning: The Influence of Modeling on Organizational Behaviour', *Academy of Management Journal*, 6, 1981, pp. 105–13.

23. H. E. Krugman, 'The Impact of Television Advertising: Learning Without Involvement', *Public Opinion Quarterly*, 30, 1965, pp. 583–96. D. L. Roedder, 'Age Differences in Children's Responses to Television Advertising: An Information Processing Approach', *Journal of Consumer Research*, Vol. 6, 1981, pp. 144–53.

24. See R. I. Evans (ed.), *Jean Piaget: The Man and his Ideas*, E. P. Dutton, New York, 1973.

25. G. P. Moschis and G. A. Churchill Jr, 'Consumer Socialization: A Theoretical and Empirical Analysis', *Journal of Marketing Research*, Vol. 15, 1978, pp. 101–12. S. L. Ward, 'Consumer Socialization', *Journal of Consumer Research*, Vol. 1, 1974, pp. 1–13.

26. D. Campbell, in W. E. Hill, *Learning: A Survey of Psychological Interpretations*, Chandler, San Francisco, 1963.

27. C. A. Scott, 'The Effect of Trial and Incentives on Repeat Purchase Behaviour', *Journal of Marketing Research*, Aug. 1976, pp. 263–69. F. W. Massy, and T. Lodahl, 'Purchasing Behaviour and Personal Attributes', *Journal of Marketing Research*, Vol. 7, Feb. 1969. J. Jacoby and D. Kyner, 'Brand Loyalty Versus Repeat Purchasing Behaviour', *Journal of Marketing Research*, Vol. 10, Feb. 1973. J. Carmen, 'Correlates of Brand Loyalty: Some Positive Results', *Journal of Marketing Research*, Vol. 7, Feb. 1970. J. Jacoby and R. Chestnut, *Brand Loyalty Measurement and Management*, John Wiley and Sons, New York, 1978.

28. R. Alsop, 'Brand Loyalty is Rarely Blind Loyalty', *The Wall Street Journal*, Oct. 1989, p. 23.

29. R. Alsop, 'Enduring Brands Hold Their Allure by Sticking Close to Their Roots', *The Wall Street Journal*, Centennial Edition, 1989, p. 24.

30. M. Rothschild, 'A Behavioural View of Promotions Effects on Brand Loyalty', in M. Wallendorf and P. Anderson (eds), *Advances in Consumer Research*, Association for Consumer Research, 1987.

31. Regis McKenna, *Relationship Marketing: Successful Strategies for the Age of the Customer*, Addison-Wesley, Reading, Mass., 1991. Jagdish Sheth, 'Relationship Marketing: An Emerging School of Marketing Thought', Sheth & Associates, Atlanta, Georgia, 1993. Clive Porter, 'Relationships, How Good are You?', *Marketing Magazine*, JMB Group, Sydney, Oct. 1991, pp. 10–12. Jonathan R. Corpulsky and Michael Wolf, 'Relationship Marketing: Positioning for the Future', *Journal of Business Strategy*, July/Aug. 1990, pp. 16–23. 'When the Supplier Becomes the Customer', *Australian Professional Marketing*, 32, Nov. 1992, p. 10.

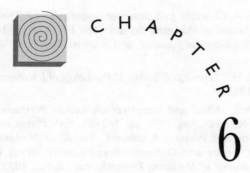

C H A P T E R
6
Personality and motivation

OBJECTIVES

This chapter should help you to:

- understand personality and self-concept
- understand why personality has not been an effective segmentation variable
- describe the motivation process and the role of needs
- understand the nature of needs and how they differ from wants
- know how needs and wants are satisfied through product purchases
- understand the relationship between motivation and product choice.

PERSONALITY, MOTIVATION AND MARKETING

It could be argued that, of all the concepts used to understand consumption behaviour, personality and motivation are the most important:

- motivation, because it is the driving force of behaviour, particularly our consumption behaviour — there must be a reason, a motive for purchasing and using products
- personality, because who we are and who we think we are, in a given situation, are key influences on our behaviour.

A popular definition of personality is: 'an enduring predisposition to respond in a consistent way to similar situations'.[1]

Although this definition appears straightforward, understanding the mechanics of personality is difficult. In essence, an individual's personality is made up of moods, values, attitudes, motives and habitual responses to situations — it is the mental map of the person's 'self' in relation to any situation. In consumer research, attempts have been made to use personality to account for consumers' basic orientation to product categories, brands, store choice, media usage and reaction to messages.

Motivation has been defined as 'the dynamic property of behaviour that directs and defines the end state (the goal)'.[2] It is the driving force behind all human activity including marketplace behaviour. For this reason, understanding what motivates people to purchase and use products is considered central to the understanding of consumer behaviour.

The exact relationship between personality and motivation is obscure but we shall see that there is much overlap between the two. Our motives shape and are shaped by our personalities, and both personality and motivation are influenced by our emotions. Personality theorists such as Sigmund Freud and Abraham Maslow have produced influential motivation theories.

Our personality and motives are central to our behaviour and thus our consumption behaviour. Consumer researchers, therefore, continue to work towards a fuller understanding of both concepts in the hope that they can be of practical use to marketers. It is important for students of consumer behaviour to understand both concepts and the related difficulties that researchers have encountered.

WHAT IS PERSONALITY?

Personality is regarded by many behavioural scientists as the most complex of all human features. The word 'personality' evolved from the Latin term *persona*, which translates literally as 'an actor's face mask', a reflection of early times when it was common for play-actors to change characters by donning different face masks. In one sense our personality is the aspect of our self that we consistently present to the world. In another, our personality represents our 'self' — who and what we are or even who and what we would like to be. If you think of your 'self' as funny, honest, hardworking, respected, dependable or that you would like to have this 'self', then you will be motivated to maintain or develop these characteristics — to be that person.

Differences between individuals and the stability of each individual's behaviour over a long time period are the essence of personality. So the two key questions that personality theorists address are:

1. When exposed to the same situation why do individuals behave differently from each other?
2. What makes an individual's behaviour more or less consistent from one situation to the next?

To answer these questions other issues need to be resolved such as: what aspects of the 'self' can be shaped? what aspects are fixed? why are we motivated to be and/or become 'someone'? Why indeed are we motivated to survive and to do so in a certain way? Many different theories have been, and are still being, developed to explain these questions. We will look at the main theories in turn — Freudian, behaviourist, trait and humanistic.

THEORIES OF PERSONALITY

In order to answer the questions posed in the previous paragraph, the first step is to know the *how* and *why* of personality. Early explanations of why each of us has a particular personality usually revolved around either the influence of a deity, an astrological pattern or, in some Eastern cultures, the year of our birth. There is also a theory — although the idea is almost obsolete — that it is an individual's physical shape that determines personality. Sheldon's morphology theory, described briefly in chapter 2, page 31, is an interesting but doubtful explanation of personality. The more recent ideas about body types conceived by French psychologist Sanones in the 1950s — the carbonic (solid, reliable, rigid), the phosphoric (thin, lean, athletic) and the fluoric (intelligent, impulsive) — are equally doubtful.

In Western cultures, the notion that there are personality types started with the early Greeks. But it was not until Freud published his ideas on personality development that it became a serious area of study.

SIGMUND FREUD

Sigmund Freud (1856–1939) developed the first comprehensive theory of personality and his ideas, described on pages 135–36, still influence modern theorists. Freud's ideas on personality were based on the assumption that the unconscious, which includes instincts, drives, infantile goals and hopes, shapes personality. He and his followers linked personality — its formation and development — to needs, albeit unconscious needs, and so to motivation. The outcome has been the development of a strong link between personality and motivation theories.

Freud's ideas were extremely original and he attracted many followers. The main attraction was his psychoanalytic theory. According to Freud the contents of the conscious mind are only a small part of personality. People's conscious thoughts resemble the small visible tip of an iceberg. The major force on our personality, our unconscious thoughts, lie beneath the surface. Freud thought that our unconscious desires and conflicts had a powerful impact on our conscious thoughts and behaviour. The only way that unconscious thoughts could be ascertained was through hypnosis or by dream interpretation. Because we do not want to, or cannot, 'know' these unconscious thoughts, the unconscious communicates the message to the conscious part of our brain through dreams. Some of the common interpretations of symbols used by therapists (see figure 6.1) are based on the work of Carl Jung.

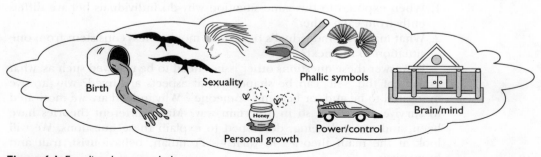

Figure 6.1: Freudian dream symbols

Personality according to Freud

According to Freud, the self is synonymous with personality. An individual's 'self' consists of three major interacting systems, the Id, the Ego and the Super Ego. Each of these systems has its own function, components and operation. Because they interact so closely, it is difficult to ascertain the precise contribution of each system to an individual's personality. Personality is nearly always the result of the interaction of the three systems.

The Id

This is the basic or original system of the personality. It contains everything psychological that is present at birth, including instincts. It is the source of the biological drives. Freud termed it the true psychic reality because it represents the inner world of subjective reality and has no knowledge of the outside world. Where the life instinct is dominant it operates on the pleasure principle, as its aim is to avoid pain and to maximise pleasure. The Id has two action components, reflex and the primary process. Reflexes are automatic responses to stimuli such as blinking and sneezing. The primary process manages the more complicated psychological activity of imagery — usually of objects or events that will remove tension. Because the Id knows only the subjective reality of the individual it does not have facilities for interacting with the external world. Therefore it does not have the means physically to satisfy its needs; for this it needs the Ego.

The Ego

This system is the link between the Id and objective reality — the outside world. The Ego translates the images of the Id into substance. For example the Id imagines the food and the Ego turns the images into action, i.e., causes behaviour to be performed. The Ego is said to be the executive of the personality because it controls the action, i.e., it selects the things in the environment to which it will respond. Although the Ego exists to obtain the aims of the Id and decides what instincts will be satisfied and how, its main function is to satisfy the demands of the Id, not to frustrate them. Tension occurs when the Ego is in a situation where it cannot satisfy the aims of the Id, which often occurs when it has to respond to the controls of the Super-Ego.

The Super-Ego

This is the system in which the traditional values and ideals of the environment (i.e. society) are held. It is the part of the personality that functions as the conscience and/or moral control. The values and ideals are instilled in the Super-Ego during early childhood via the process of socialisation. The main concern of the Super-Ego is to decide whether something is right or wrong by the society's standards so that it can act in accordance with the rules and the moral standards of the society.

(continued)

The Super-Ego functions by the use of ego-ideals. These are the ideal moral values and accepted behaviours that are given to the child, usually placed there by introjection, a system of rewards and punishments that are used to train the child to internalise the values. Once established, parental control is substituted for self-control. The main functions of the Super-Ego are:

- to inhibit the impulses of the Id, particularly those of a sexual or aggressive nature
- to persuade the Ego to substitute moralistic goals for realistic ones
- to strive for perfection.

The Id responds to the controls of the Super-Ego, as often survival of the individual is involved.

Much of Freud's theory of personality centres around instincts. His argument is complex and fraught with difficulties and many of his ideas have been criticised. Freud believed, as did many 19th century philosophers, that energy is never lost. Freud defined energy in terms of the work it performs. Energy may be transferred, i.e. the body consumes food which creates energy which is expended in breathing, exercise, work and eating food to create more energy and so on. Freud did not differentiate between energy used for breathing and digestion and that used for thinking and remembering, which he labelled psychic energy. The point of contact, or 'bridge', between the energy and the body and that of personality is the Id and its instincts.

Freud defined instincts as an inborn psychological representation of the inner somatic source of excitation. The psychological representation is called a wish, and the bodily excitation from which it stems is called a need. The wish acts as a motive for behaviour. The need for the hungry person is food; the wish or want is for specific types of food.

Instincts are considered to be the propelling factor of personality and behaviour. Not only do they drive behaviour, but also determine the direction that behaviour will take. Freud divided instinct into the Life and the Death Instinct. The Life Instinct accounts for individual survival and social propagation. The Death Instinct accounts for self-destruction turned outwards towards substitute objects.

According to Freud, the final organisation of personality (the self) is often manifested by types. The personality types develop through frustrations and tensions that may or may not develop during the following key developmental stages of childhood:

- oral • anal • phallic • latency • genital.

Although the stages and interpretations are now considered doubtful and certainly simplistic, most psychologists agree that the frustrations, tensions and anxiety that can develop during these stages are retained in our unconscious. Early childhood influences can impact on our thoughts and behaviour for our entire lives.

NEO-FREUDIANS

Some of Freud's followers did not wholly agree with all of his ideas, particularly with regard to the factors that, according to Freud, shaped personality. Freud assumed that instinctive, inborn needs were the major influence on personality development. If these needs were frustrated, specific personality traits developed. Those who deviated from Freud's views believed that social influences on the individual were more important. This group became known as the Neo-Freudians and included such thinkers as Alfred Adler, Eric Fromm and Karen Horney. According to Adler, people strive to overcome feelings of inferiority and insecurity and try to obtain a unique lifestyle. Fromm argued that love and companionship are the main factors that influence the development of personality. Karen Horney proposed that an individual's personality develops in accordance with the levels of anxiety and hostility experienced during childhood. These levels can produce three modes of behaviour:

1. **Compliant behaviour** — moving towards others. This involves a high degree of social awareness and an avoidance of social conflict.

2. **Aggressive behaviour** — moving against people. This often involves a desire for power, competition and achievement.

3. **Detached behaviour** — involves moving away from people. Such individuals are highly independent and avoid close relationships.

In the normal healthy personality, the three modes of behaviour are integrated and each should be used in appropriate situations. Neurosis develops when one of these three ways of relating to others becomes the only framework for an individual's social relationships. Although the Freudians and Neo-Freudians did identify and describe various personality traits, they were mainly concerned with identifying and creating healthy, well adjusted personalities.[3]

Pulsar. W_ _ _ _ the birdie.

Pulsar Dress Collection from $99.50 to $395. Left: PPG504 $260. Right: PRY296 $260.

Figure 6.2: Some advertisements could be interpreted as using Freudian symbolism. This advertisement for Pulsar watches, for example, could be said to suggest female sexuality through the image of the bird in flight. The dove has also become an accepted symbol for peace.

BEHAVIOURISTS

Although behaviourism is not an explicit theory of personality, its underlying assumptions have had a considerable impact on personality theory. Behaviourists treat people as empty boxes waiting to be filled up with habits and behaviours. Behaviourists assume that all behaviour, including personality characteristics, is learned, so they reject concepts such as drives — particularly inherent drives — as determinants of personality. The best known behaviourists were B. F. Skinner and J. B. Watson. According to B. F. Skinner, internal events such as thoughts and feelings can be ignored because they are by-products of external observable events, particularly of the consequences that follow a response.[4] This does not mean that behaviourists deny the existence of internal events. They argue that, because any behaviour can be explained by reinforcing events in a person's past, internal events can be safely ignored. This means that characteristics or traits that we develop are a function of learning through a series of rewards and punishments. The problem with the behaviourists' view of personality acquisition is that, if personality is learned, then the degree of uniqueness that is characteristic of personality would not occur. Because there exists a limited number of external rewards or punishments and situations, this would mean that more of us would respond to the same situation in the same way.

Strongly linked to behaviourism is the notion of social learning.[5] Proponents of this view maintain that most behaviours are acquired through observational learning, as we watch the actions of models and vicariously experience their rewards and punishments. Once a personality has been learned, it is maintained and regulated by three kinds of controls:

1. **Stimulus control.** How other people respond to us in a particular situation will determine whether we are friendly or withdrawn or even hostile. We take our response cues from the facial expressions and gestures of others.

2. **Reinforcement control.** As personality characteristics only develop in response to an external stimulus, if a person is continually rewarded for aggressive, competitive behaviour, that person will tend to behave aggressively in most situations. Our parents' behaviour, and in particular how they interact with us when we are children, will determine many of our characteristics.

3. **Cognitive control.** Both the stimulus and reinforcement controls are regulated by our constant cognitive appraisal and self-reinforcement guide. So how we interpret a stimulus will ultimately affect how we respond to it.

In these views, personality characteristics (traits) are considered to be trained, acquired behaviours. The assumption is that personality characteristics can be changed. In general, behaviourists are not concerned with identifying personality characteristics or indeed personality types. In this sense they are not at odds with the trait theorists, who focus on identifying and classifying personality characteristics.

TRAIT THEORIES

A trait is a predisposition to react to related situations in the same way. If, for example, you are employing a receptionist, you would probably prefer someone who is organised, outgoing, sociable, tolerant and even-tempered, rather than someone who preferred their own company and was short-tempered. These characteristics are what psychologists call traits.

Trait theories are based on two main assumptions:
- that individuals have traits
- that the traits can be identified and measured (quantified).

We can only presume, from observed behaviour, that traits exist. Traits can be identified through a series of questions that are scaled to show if a person has a particular trait and how strong the trait is. For example, on a question or range of questions designed to measure sociability, someone who scored ten on a one-to-ten scale would be highly sociable, and someone who scored one would not.

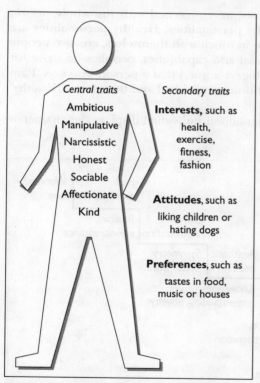

Figure 6.3: Allport's central and secondary traits. According to Gordon Allport, central traits are habitual ways of responding to the world. Secondary traits are characteristic modes of behaviour but they are seen in fewer situations and are subject to change. Measuring central traits is feasible as they are potentially finite. Measuring secondary traits is difficult as they are potentially limitless.

While there are many possible ways to classify traits, there is a general preference for two of these methods. The first, proposed by Gordon Allport, classifies traits into central, secondary and common traits. If a person's habitual response to the world is irritable, short-tempered and sardonic then these traits are *central* to the person's personality. *Secondary* traits are behaviours that are seen less often and are more likely to change, such as a person's taste in clothes and food (see figure 6.3). *Common* traits are traits that all people have. For example, everyone has to some degree a level of aggression. The exact combination of traits that go to make up an individual's personality accounts for the uniqueness of each individual. Allport labelled this a 'personal disposition'. This personal disposition cannot be measured in the same way as individual traits as it can only be discerned after a careful study of the individual.[6]

Raymond Catell, on the other hand, identified two trait categories, *surface* and *source traits*. Surface traits describe clusters of behaviour that tend to go together. For example, 'integrity' would cover behaviours from telling the truth to keeping secrets. Other surface traits are altruism, curiosity, foolishness and honesty. Source traits are the underlying causes of these behaviour clusters.

Although the identification of traits is a popular method of assessing an individual's personality, it does have a number of problems. The main problem is that there is very little evidence that traits do in fact persist across situations. Another is that, by focusing on traits, we tend to obscure individual differences. Finally, trait theory only provides a label, it does not provide any explanations as to why the behaviours exist. For this reason, trait theories as personality theories cannot stand alone. They must be linked to either Freudian, behaviourist or humanistic theories of personality to explain why they occur.[7]

HUMANISTS

Humanistic psychologists think that human beings have the potential for growth, creativity and spontaneity. They emphasise the uniqueness of individuals and their freedom to make choices. The most significant theorists in this area of personality were Carl Rogers and Abraham Maslow.

Essentially, humanistic theorists are concerned with the whole person and stress the notion of healthy personalities. Healthy personalities are characterised by people who are in touch with themselves, creative people who use all their talents, potential and capabilities, people who strive for and achieve self-actualisation. Rogers argued that a person who says 'I am the best I can be' is a fully functioning individual and therefore a 'healthy' personality.[8]

According to Maslow, a self-actualised individual displays the characteristics shown in figure 6.4.

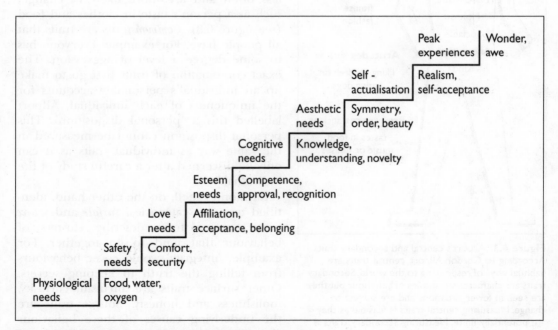

Figure 6.4: Maslow's ideas on the development of needs

Once the basic needs are satisfied, higher order needs emerge and demand satisfaction. Maslow called these *meta needs* and included among them justice, beauty, goodness, order and unity. In most instances, 'deficiency needs' take priority over the meta needs and one meta need can be pursued instead of another, depending on a person's circumstances. When meta needs are not met, alienation, anguish, apathy and cynicism can develop. Maslow's ideas, although criticised, are very popular and have led to companies and other organisations employing psychologists to seek ways of promoting the growth and self-actualisation of workers.[9]

Self-concept

The key aspect of humanistic psychology is the focus on the development of the 'self'. We all have a self. William James, a contemporary of Freud, suggested that the self was made up of two basic components — the 'I' and the 'me'. The 'I' is the whole individual, the active conscious part, the part of us that knows all our experiences. The 'me' represents our view of who and what we are.[10] Rogers labels the 'me' component of James' theory as the self and suggests that it consists of those aspects of individuals that they recognise and accept. Because the self is not a preprogrammed entity and there is the underlying premise of growth, then change occurs and a variety of 'selves' are allowed to form. There have been many suggestions as to what the variety of selves could be. James thought that there were at least three aspects to the self:[11]

- the **material** self: the physical presentation which includes our possessions and our physical status
- the **spiritual** self: our personal belief system and view of the world and knowledge of how we fit into it
- the **social** self: knowledge of the person your friends know, your family knows and the world knows.

Rogers' classification is somewhat similar:[12]

- the **actual** self is how people really perceive themselves
- the **ideal** self is a person's idea of how he or she would like to be
- the **social** self is how people think other people see them.

Underlying the concept of the self is the belief that a complete sense of self develops when the three 'selves' are very similar. According to the humanistic psychologists, the individual and the self (or the 'I' and the 'me') should be identical — 'I am my self and others recognise this'. People need to behave consistently with their self-concept so that other people's experience of that 'self' can confirm it. A healthy personality develops when the individual's idea of their self is more or less in line with other people's idea of the person's self. People with healthy personalities are fully functioning individuals who are open to experience, not defensive, have unconditional self-regard and generally have good relationships with others.

Essentially this means that our emotional and mental health depend on whether or not we can manage to close the gap between our ideal, social and actual selves. To do this our behaviour must consistently reflect who we think we are. This consistency helps us maintain our self-esteem and allows us, and others, to predict our behaviour, thus helping us interact more effectively with others.

There is a growing tendency towards the idea that the three perspectives of personality are not mutually exclusive and ideas as to how they interact are still developing. Most people accept that personality is best studied from a holistic perspective: while it may be possible to identify some characteristics (traits) these do *not* describe an individual's personality as a whole. There is also, however, a growing awareness that while personality does affect an individual's behaviour, establishing the means by which specific behaviour patterns can be predicted may not be feasible. The main reason for this is the now accepted idea that situational factors have a considerable impact on behaviour and thus on marketplace behaviour.[13]

APPLYING THE THEORIES TO MARKETING

We perceive personality as integral to all of our actions, so it is understandable that consumer researchers have continued to focus on it as a key to understanding consumer decisions. The earliest applications of personality theory to marketing were based on trait and psychoanalytic theories. The focus on traits developed from the need to find viable ways to identify market segments. It was thought that by understanding the deep-seated, unconscious needs of consumers through psychoanalysis, products and messages could be designed to obtain the optimum response from the marketplace.

IDENTIFYING CONSUMER SEGMENTS

The use of traits to identify consumer segments was based on the assumption that consumers with similar traits would display similar purchase behaviour. Since the 1960s, there has been a considerable amount of empirical research attempting to link personality traits with consumers' product and brand preferences and to other aspects, such as innovative purchase behaviour.[14]

Two early American studies attempted to link ownership of cars with specific personality traits. Franklin Evans examined consumers' preference for Ford or Chevrolet cars.[15] One study used the Edwards Personal Preference Scale (EPPS). The EPPS is a personality test designed to ascertain whether or not, and to what degree, people have the characteristics associated with Murray's list of personal needs (described on pages 144–45). Some of the choices posed in the EPPS are listed on page 146. There was some association between Ford owners and the needs for dominance and exhibitionism, whereas Chevrolet owners had needs for affiliation and autonomy. However, the correlation was extremely low, as is shown in table 6.1.

This work was replicated by Ralph Westfall but instead of the EPPS he used the Thurstone Temperament Schedule. Westfall also failed to obtain a solid relationship, although he did detect a marginal difference between convertible and non-convertible owners.[16]

Table 6.1: Personality traits and product usage*

Product/Behaviour	Associated trait(s)	Correlation coefficient
Headache remedies	Ascendancy	− 0.46
	Emotional stability	− 0.32
Acceptance of new fashions	Ascendancy	− 0.33
	Sociability	− 0.56
Vitamins	Ascendancy	− 0.33
	Responsibility	− 0.30
	Emotional stability	− 0.09
	Sociability	− 0.27
Cigarettes	None of the four	
Mouthwash	Responsibility	− 0.22
Alcoholic drinks	Responsibility	− 0.36
Deodorant	None of the four	
Cars	Responsibility	0.28
Chewing gum	Responsibility	0.30
	Emotional stability	0.33

(*Source*: Derived from W. T. Tucker and J. J. Painter, 'Personality and Product Use', *Journal of Applied Psychology*, 45, 1961)

* Other research showing no relationship with product choice includes:
  - F. Evans, 'Psychological and Objective Factors in the Prediction of Brand Choice', *Journal of Business*, 1959. Murray's list of personal needs showed 13 per cent more buyers' choices than chance alone in the purchase of Fords/Chevrolets.
  - R. Westfall, 'Psychological Factors in Predicting Brand Choice', *Journal of Marketing*, 1962. The traits of activeness, dominance, sociability and reflectiveness were the same for Ford/Chevrolet purchasers.
  - A. Koponen, 'Personality Characteristics of Purchaser', *Journal of Advertising Research*, 1960. The traits of dominance, achievement, aggression and autonomy were not significant in the purchase of magazines or cigarettes.

In the mid-1960s, Joel Cohen developed the CAD scale, a personality test based on Karen Horney's compliant, aggressive and detached behaviours. Although the differences were not great, he did find a relationship between products such as mouthwash and razors. Compliant people were more likely to use mouthwash and aggressive types more likely to use razors than electric shavers, while detached types were less likely to be aware of the range of brands available.[17] In general, the studies have not produced significant results. Cohen only presented selected data and no statistically significant relationships were found for products such as toothpaste, beer, cigarettes and painkillers. Research using the CAD scale is continuing.[18] Since the original scales were designed to identify extremes or abnormal levels of the characteristics, it is doubtful that future research will be any more successful.

Murray's list of personal needs

1. **Achievement:** To do one's best, to be successful, to accomplish tasks requiring skill and effort, to be a recognised authority, to accomplish something of great significance, to do a difficult job well, to solve difficult problems and puzzles, to be able to do things better than others, to write a great novel or play.

2. **Deference:** To get suggestions from others, to find out what others think, to follow instructions and do what is expected, to praise others, to tell others that they have done a good job, to accept the leadership of others, to read about great men, to conform to custom and avoid the unconventional, to let others make decisions.

3. **Order:** To have written work neat and organised, to make plans before starting on a difficult task, to have things organised, to keep things neat and orderly, to make advance plans when taking a trip, to organise details of work, to keep letters and files according to some system, to have meals organised and a definite time for eating, to have things arranged so that they run smoothly without change.

4. **Exhibition:** To say witty and clever things, to tell amusing jokes and stories, to talk about personal adventures and experiences, to have others notice and comment upon one's appearance, to say things just to see what effect it will have on others, to talk about personal achievements, to be the centre of attention, to use words that others do not know the meaning of, to ask questions others cannot answer.

5. **Autonomy:** To be able to come and go as desired, to say what one thinks about things, to be independent of others in making decisions, to feel free to do what one wants, to do things that are unconventional, to avoid situations where one is expected to conform, to do things without regard to what others may think, to criticise those in positions of authority, to avoid responsibilities and obligations.

6. **Affiliation:** To be loyal to friends, to participate in friendly groups, to do things for friends, to form new friendships, to make as many friends as possible, to share things with friends, to do things with friends rather than alone, to form strong attachments, to write letters to friends.

7. **Intraception:** To analyse one's motives and feelings, to observe others, to understand how others feel about problems, to put one's self in another's place, to judge people by why they do things rather than by what they do, to analyse the behaviour of others, to analyse the motives of others, to predict how others will act.

8. **Succourance:** To have others provide help when in trouble, to seek encouragement from others, to have others be kindly, to have others be sympathetic and understanding about personal problems, to receive a great deal of affection from others, to have others do favours cheerfully, to be helped by others when depresssed, to have others feel sorry when one is sick, to have a fuss made over one when hurt.

9. **Dominance:** To argue for one's point of view, to be a leader in groups to which one belongs, to be regarded by others as a leader, to be elected or appointed chairman of committees, to make group decisions, to settle arguments and disputes between others, to persuade and influence others to do what one wants, to supervise and direct the actions of others, to tell others how to do their jobs.

10. **Abasement:** To feel guilty when one does something wrong, to accept blame when things do not go right, to feel that personal pain and misery suffered does more good than harm, to feel the need for punishment for wrong doing, to feel better when giving in and avoiding a fight than when having one's own way, to feel the need for confession of errors, to feel depressed by inability to handle situations, to feel timid in the presence of superiors, to feel inferior to others in most respects.

11. **Nurturance:** To help friends when they are in trouble, to assist others less fortunate, to treat others with kindness and sympathy, to forgive others, to do small favours for others, to be generous with others, to sympathise with others who are hurt or sick, to show a great deal of affection towards others, to have others confide in one about personal problems.

12. **Change:** To do new and different things, to travel, to meet new people, to experience novelty and change in daily routine, to experiment and try new things, to eat in new and different places, to try new and different jobs, to move about the country and live in different places, to participate in new fads and fashions.

13. **Endurance:** To keep at a job until it is finished, to complete any job undertaken, to work hard at a task, to keep at a puzzle or problem until it is solved, to work at a single job before taking on others, to stay up late working in order to get a job done, to put in long hours of work without distraction, to stick at a problem even though it may seem as if no progress is being made, to avoid being interrupted while at work.

14. **Heterosexuality:** To go out with members of the opposite sex, to engage in social activities with the opposite sex, to be in love with someone of the opposite sex, to kiss those of the opposite sex, to be regarded as physically attractive by those of the opposite sex, to participate in discussions about sex, to read books and plays involving sex, to listen to or to tell jokes involving sex, to become sexually excited.

15. **Aggression:** To attack contrary points of view, to tell others what one thinks about them, to criticise others publicly, to make fun of others, to tell others off when disagreeing with them, to get revenge for insults, to become angry, to blame others when things go wrong, to read newspaper accounts of violence.

(*Source*: Personality needs developed by C. D. Morgan and H. A. Murray, A Method for Investigating Fantasies: The Thematic Apperception Test. *Archives of Neurological Psychiatry*, 34, 1935)

Sample of choices presented to subjects in the Edwards Personal Preference Schedule

A I like people to notice and to comment upon my appearance when I am out in public.
B I like to read about the lives of great men and women.

A I like to avoid situations where I am expected to do things in a conventional way.
B I like to read about the lives of great men and women.

A I would like to be a recognised authority in some job, profession, or field of specialisation.
B I like to have my work organised and planned before beginning it.

A I like to find out what great men and women have thought about various problems in which I am interested.
B If I have to take a trip, I like to have things planned in advance.

A I like to finish any job or task that I begin.
B I like to keep my things neat and orderly on my desk or workspace.

A I like to tell other people about adventures and strange things that have happened to me.
B I like to have my meals organised and a definite time for eating.

A I like to be independent of others in deciding what I want to do.
B I like to keep my things neat and orderly on my desk or workspace.

A I like to be able to do things better than other people can.
B I like to tell amusing stories and jokes at parties.

A I get so angry that I feel like throwing and breaking things.
B I like to avoid responsibilities and obligations.

A I like to be successful in things undertaken.
B I like to form new friendships.

A I like to follow instructions and to do what is expected of me.
B I like to have strong attachments with my friends.

A I like written work that I do to be precise, neat, and well organised.
B I like to make as many friends as I can.

A I like to tell amusing stories and jokes at parties.
B I like to write letters to my friends.

A I like to be able to come and go as I want to.
B I like to share things with my friends.

A I like to solve puzzles and problems that other people have difficulty with.
B I like to judge people by why they do something — not by what they actually do.

A I like to accept the leadership of people I admire.
B I like to understand how my friends feel about various problems they have to face.

A I like to have my meals organised and a definite time for eating.
B I like to study and to analyse the behaviour of others.

(*Source*: A. L. Edwards, *Edwards Personal Preference Schedule*, The Psychological Corp., New York, 1959)

In the 1970s, a number of researchers thought that it should be possible to identify innovators. Innovativeness in the purchase situation is the tendency to buy new or different products as soon as they are exposed to the marketplace. Innovators are thought to be largely responsible for the overall adoption rate of new products so early targeting of them is desirable. Initially it was thought there could be a link between innovativeness and dogmatism. People who are dogmatic tend to think rigidly and to be intolerant of new ideas, i.e., they are 'close-minded'. So it could be presumed that they would not be the first to buy new products. The researchers used Milton Rokeach's Dogmatism Scale which measures the degree to which an individual is open- or close-minded, identified dogmatic individuals and measured their innovative behaviour.[19] To date, a positive association between dogmatism and innovativeness has not been demonstrated.[20] As Rokeach designed his scale to identify abnormal levels of both open- and close-mindedness, there should only be a small group of people who are either wholly close-minded or open-minded. It is therefore not surprising that their results were inconclusive.

A commonsense explanation for this lack of association is that, more often than not, innovative behaviour is a function of interest in the product category, which overrides specific trait factors. A study that focused on gift-giving did, however, identify a relationship. Individuals who scored high on the dogmatism scale displayed more innovative behaviour in their product choice than individuals who scored low on the same scale when buying gifts. One explanation for this is that individuals who are 'dogmatic' are more likely to lack confidence and thus choose goods that are novel.[21]

A recent study attempted to identify people who were predisposed to using coupons in the purchase situation. The study attempted to link people who were value-conscious (people for whom getting value for money in the purchase situation is important) to the level of coupon usage.[22] The results showed that coupon proneness was strongly related to value-consciousness — which from a commonsense point of view is hardly surprising. Whether this study can be considered to be an application of trait theory is somewhat debatable, as value-consciousness is a function of beliefs and attitudes and coupon-proneness is a behaviour, not a trait.

▼IABILITY OF TRAIT THEORIES

Since the late 1960s, there has been considerable concern with the viability of trait theory. Although many researchers have moved away and focused on other perceptions of personality, such as self-concept, many others are still attempting to find a way to establish links between traits and marketplace behaviour. The results of past research suggest that they are likely to be unsuccessful.[23] Even in the most conclusive studies, traits have failed to explain more than about 10 per cent of variance in behaviour. Since it is now accepted that personality is multi-faceted and that many factors influence behaviour, the reliance on a single characteristic or even a cluster of characteristics is impractical.

In 1971, Harold Kassarjian reviewed over 200 studies that used personality traits as segmentation variables. He found that a few studies showed a
strong relationship between personality and brand choice; a few showed
no relationship; and the great majority showed correlations so weak as to
be questionable and perhaps meaningless.[24] He also pointed out how surprising it was that any studies showed any relationship, considering the
many factors that can and do influence behaviour. Factors such as age,
income, education, occupation and the situation all influence purchase
behaviour. An examination of studies shows a variety of reasons for the
failure to find relationships between traits and marketplace behaviour.[25]
The main reasons can be summarised as follows.

- **The nature of the personality scales.** Personality scales are designed to
  identify extremes. For example Rokeach's test for dogmatism is
  designed to identify individuals who are exceedingly close-minded (or
  open-minded), with a view to 'treating' them. As such, both groups
  would only represent a fraction of the population. Even if a correlation
  had been found between innovativeness and dogmatism, the resulting
  segments would be too small to be viable.
- **The applicability of the tests.** It is highly unlikely that a specific personality trait (or even a cluster) would, by itself, have an impact on purchase behaviour, especially when other factors such as age, income and
  sex have a crucial impact on behaviour. For example, John and Harry
  may both be serious, self-assured and aggressive, but John may be
  eighteen and Harry sixty-five and a grandfather. Also situational factors,
  such as feasibility of purchase, play an important role.
- **The validity of the scales.** There are some doubts as to whether many of
  the personality trait scales actually measure what they purport to measure
  and whether the scales (and the traits) are stable over time. There is a
  current view that our personality (including traits) can and does alter.
- **Situational factors.** It is now accepted that, even if traits are identified, it
  is difficult to predict behaviour as situational factors can and do impact
  on behaviour.

THE SELF-CONCEPT APPROACH TO MARKETING

Although some researchers do use traits as a basis for understanding some
aspects of consumer behaviour,[26] the poor results from the applications of
trait theory have caused researchers to 'shift focus'. Although previously
neglected by marketers, the self-concept approach to personality and how
it relates to the consumption pattern of consumers is now being given
considerable attention. The reason for this recent focus stems from the
notion that we use products to express to others who and what we are.
This is not a new idea by any means. In the late nineteenth century, Theodore Veblen introduced the idea that many of the products we purchase
are expressions or statements of our social status, or *status symbols.*[27] Since
the material self, as described by James, includes things we own and our
bodies, then it is reasonable to assume that products can be used to
enhance and make statements about our self. In essence, this means that
apart from having a functional use, products are also used to make statements to the world about who and what we are.[28]

Our possessions can be used (often unconsciously) to create, maintain and reinforce our identities, particularly in unfamiliar or neutral settings, such as the workplace. Go into any office and you will see that most people attempt to personalise their immediate surroundings with pictures, pot plants, ornaments or anything they think communicates their identity. Research has found that people view their possessions as extensions of themselves — 'I am what I own'. Objects that are significant for us and treasured can become so much a part of our 'self' that we treat them as we treat ourselves. This can include many things, such as a lucky coin, a piece of jewellery handed down, or a car. A frequent comment by people who have been burgled indicates the extent to which we do this — they say that they feel 'violated' by a stranger being familiar with and taking their possessions.

Self-image and product choice

According to humanistic theorists such as Carl Rogers and Abraham Maslow, individuals are constantly working towards keeping the gap between the actual, ideal and social selves at a minimum. Products may be purchased because they help to close the gap. Consumer researchers have found that there is a congruous relationship between certain products and self-image which they have labelled 'self-image congruity'. Underpinning this concept is the notion that people will choose products that match some attribute(s) of their self-image. To do this effectively requires both self-evaluation and product evaluation. This means that when consumers choose products, they do not base their choice on the product alone. Instead they construct a mental image of themselves using the product, then decide if they like that image.

Obviously some products are more likely than others to be used as expressions of self. For example, in one study where the subjects were shown pictures of lounge rooms, they were able to describe with surprising accuracy the type of people who lived in them.[29] In another study, subjects were given a list of products and asked to rate them according to how important they were in the role of self-expression. Products that required a high level of psychological (mental and emotional) input during the purchase phase tended to be highly rated. Products such as toothpaste, soap, tissues and shampoo were given a low rating.[30] Other studies show that clothes, cars, personal grooming and hygiene products, home decorations, magazines and some household cleaning items have a high level of congruence with self-image.[31] An examination of these studies shows that the product categories most often used to reflect a consumer's self-image are:

- those with high visibility, i.e., their use (consumption) must be readily apparent to others
- those that are known in the marketplace and where other people know what factors to associate with the product, for example, the money to buy it, status and/or specific values such as concern for the environment.

This means that for people to use products as statements about themselves the products need to take on an image — an identity that is recognisable. It also means that the notion of products as symbols becomes significant. Symbols are 'things which stand for or express something else'. Because the relationships we have with others play a significant role in forming our self-concept, there must be a common understanding of the meanings associated with objects (and actions). So when teenagers buy Billabong and Quicksilver shorts and Doc Marten shoes they are using the products to communicate to other teenagers (and adults) aspects of their self-concept. The use of products to define the self is more prevalent when identity is yet to be formed. Adolescents and the 'nouveau riche' are more prone to using products in this way.

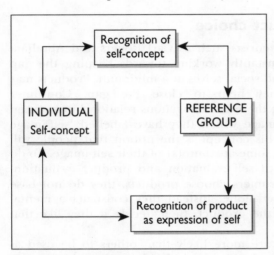

Figure 6.5: The role of reference groups in the acceptance of a product as a symbolic representation of the self

Symbolic self-completion theory suggests that people who have an incomplete self-definition will strive to complete this identity by acquiring symbols that will make a positive statement about their identity. This can be effective only if the symbolic meaning of the product(s) is correctly interpreted by others. Since there must be a collection of individuals who understand the symbolic meaning of the products, an essential ingredient is the existence of reference groups. The resulting relationship pattern (see figure 6.5) means that communication about the product must be addressed to a specific target market and not a specific individual. The task for marketers therefore is to communicate to their target market the self-image aspects with which their products connect.

Measuring a self-concept

Using self-concept to identify a target market means identifying individuals with similar self-concepts. It also means ascertaining whether or not the product is perceived as having the appropriate image. There must be some measurement so that the self-concept characteristics of the reference group can be identified. It is at this point that application difficulties with the concept emerge.

In 1981, Naresh Malhotra developed a scale using a semantic differential format to measure both product image and self-concept[32] (see table 6.2). Consumers in the target market were asked to rate their self-image on the scale. Then they were asked to rate various brands of products on the same scale. Where a pattern of responses for a particular brand corresponds with the consumer's self-image, the brand is expected to be preferred by the consumer. An important point to note is that consumer researchers such as Malhotra are using scales that identify and group traits, which may indeed form a part of an individual's self-concept but do not reflect the whole person.

Table 6.2: A scale to measure product images and self-images

1. Rugged	1 2 3 4 5 6 7	Delicate
2. Excited	1 2 3 4 5 6 7	Calm
3. Uncomfortable	1 2 3 4 5 6 7	Comfortable
4. Dominating	1 2 3 4 5 6 7	Submissive
5. Thrifty	1 2 3 4 5 6 7	Indulgent
6. Pleasant	1 2 3 4 5 6 7	Unpleasant
7. Contemporary	1 2 3 4 5 6 7	Uncontemporary
8. Organised	1 2 3 4 5 6 7	Unorganised
9. Rational	1 2 3 4 5 6 7	Emotional
10. Youthful	1 2 3 4 5 6 7	Mature
11. Formal	1 2 3 4 5 6 7	Informal
12. Orthodox	1 2 3 4 5 6 7	Liberal
13. Complex	1 2 3 4 5 6 7	Simple
14. Colourless	1 2 3 4 5 6 7	Colourful
15. Modest	1 2 3 4 5 6 7	Vain

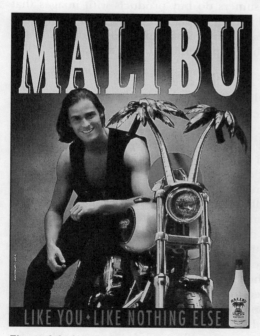

Figure 6.6: A general yet personalised message

A year after Malhotra's study, Joseph Sirgy commented that measurement was still in its infancy stage, as he observed many inconsistencies and areas of confusion.[33] Unfortunately, over a decade later and in spite of many attempts, the situation has not altered. There are still no effective means to measure self-concept.[34] The fundamental problem is that there is no agreement as to what is meant by 'self'. Also, the concept as conceived by humanistic theorists was not designed for classification — they consider that an individual's self-concept is unique. While we may all have actual, ideal and social 'selves', how they are constituted is unique across individuals. One way that advertisers side-step the complexity of matching self-concepts and product characteristics and retain the individuality of the 'self' is by keeping their advertising statements general (see the Malibu advertisement in figure 6.6 — 'Like you. Like nothing else.').

Materialism and product choice

In the late 1980s, self-concept research took a slightly different focus under the influence of Belk's research into the ownership of goods. Russell Belk sought to ascertain what possessions consumers value and focused on people who were concerned with their material self, assuming that these people would have a tendency to materialism. Materialism is a trait which affects the importance a consumer attaches to worldly possessions. At the highest level, possessions have a central place and provide the greatest source of satisfaction (and dissatisfaction). Belk's scale identified degrees of materialism in individuals[35] and showed that highly materialistic individuals were:

* less willing to donate body organs
* more approving of spending large amounts on houses and cars
* less likely to eat in expensive restaurants
* more likely to view Christmas as a time for shopping
* less likely to believe that others will appreciate their help.

People who are more focused on their material self and physical well-being are more likely to be high-volume consumers of goods and services. It may well be that specific clusters of associated behaviours could be identified, so as to refine product characteristics and communication strategies.

Self-concept and brand image

Although there have been difficulties in the application of the self-concept to marketplace activity, it may be premature to dismiss it entirely. There are indications that consumers do buy products with images that are compatible with their actual and ideal self-concepts.[36] This has positive implications for the notion of brand image or brand personality. A brand personality is the profile of a brand presented to the marketplace. The profile is a combination of:

* **functional attributes**, or what a product does
* **physical attributes**, i.e. the colour, price and ingredients
* **characterisation** of the product, which in essence is the image communicated to the marketplace.

Products may be positioned and perceived as serious, frivolous, old-fashioned, trendy, sophisticated or as any other characteristic. Individuals who may, for example, have seriousness and sophistication as part of their self-image may lean towards products projecting these characteristics. If the functional and physical attributes are similar across a range of product choices, then characterisation may be the only differentiation factor. The main restriction on the kind of characteristics that can be given to a product is in the type of product it is. Obviously products such as pacemakers and aspirin cannot be given a humorous image as these are 'serious' products, whereas other products such as toilet rolls may have humorous characteristics applied to them.

So far attempts to use personality theories to predict consumer behaviour have not been successful. It is likely that they will remain so, as prediction usually requires measurement. The underlying problem for personality is that it is a difficult concept to define. If something cannot be clearly defined, its characteristics cannot be identified nor parameters set. Unless this can be done, measurement is not feasible.

Even if it were possible to measure personality, there would still be problems. In order to predict consumer behaviour, personality differences must reflect clear-cut variations in consumer activity. To be able to attribute variations in behaviour to personality, individuals must be similar in terms of age, income, education or any other factor that could have an impact on choice and ability to purchase. Even if it was possible to achieve this, it is likely that the resulting segments would be too small to be actionable.

PSYCHOANALYTIC THEORIES

Concurrent with the attempts to apply personality theory to market segmentation were studies concerned with understanding the mind and motives of consumers. From the 1950s onwards, motivation researchers were at work on psychoanalytic theories of personality — particularly the ideas of Freud and Jung — which had a substantial influence on marketing thought. The basis of Freudian thought (see pages 135–36) is that the unconscious part of the mind influences behaviour. Unless explored through hypnosis or dream analysis, we remain unaware of these unconscious forces.

Our dreams have both *manifest* and *latent content*. The manifest content is the events in a dream that the dreamer remembers. But these are only symbols — the events remembered are coded, disguised messages. They are presented this way because a function of the unconscious is to protect the mind. If a forgotten memory becomes a conscious thought before we are ready to deal with it, we can have a traumatic reaction. To avoid this, we dream in symbols which can be interpreted by trained therapists through hypnotherapy.

The best known symbols and their interpretation are the phallic and ovarian symbols. Phallic symbols are long and cylindrical while ovarian symbols are fan- or wedge-shaped, and female sexual activity is often denoted by birds in flight (see the advertisement in figure 6.2). According to Freud the two main instincts that drive our behaviour are the life and the death instincts. Freud argued that the death wish is just as powerful as the life instinct. A Freudian psychologist would argue that heavy smokers and spirit drinkers have a death wish that, subconsciously, they want satisfied.

Since the 1950s, the role of Freudian theory in marketing has been controversial. One issue was the alleged use of 'embeds'. Embeds are hidden or disguised figures inserted into print advertisements by the use of air-brushing, high speed photography. Not strong enough for conscious processing, the figures, usually sexual in nature, are thought to act as a strong but unconscious influence on behaviour. Vance Packard and Wilson Keys[37] claimed that Freudian symbols were being used as 'embeds' in advertisements and to design product packaging. One of their claims was that spirit manufacturers had death masks embedded in ice-cubes in their advertisements.

Official enquiries have shown that agencies say they do not use phallic symbols to trigger unconscious reactions from an audience.[38] The choice of the bird in flight in the Pulsar watch advertisement (see page 137) may have been inspired by aesthetic considerations, or may symbolise peace, and it could also be seen as a Freudian symbol for female sexuality.

As the discussion of subliminal messages in chapters 2 and 3 suggests, the use of 'hidden' messages must be viewed with caution. There is evidence that subliminal 'embeds' may influence the emotional state of consumers but their role in the cognitive processing of information is unclear.

CONSUMER MOTIVATION

There are a number of definitions of motivation, most of which contain two main elements:
• a mechanism to arouse bodily energy
• a force (drive) that provides direction to that bodily energy.

The mechanism that serves to arouse the energy is the tension that results when a discrepancy between an actual and a desired state is felt, either consciously or unconsciously. People experience wishes, desires and needs. These can originate from unmet physical needs or from a fantasy or imagery. This means that they can be triggered by both internal and external prompts. Once the individual recognises that a physical demand or the satisfaction of a fantasy must be met, the individual will begin to feel uncomfortable and a state of tension is generated. The diagram in figure 6.7 shows that once the tension state occurs the individual will be activated or energised to reduce the tension. This activated state is often labelled the 'drive'. The intensity of the drive is influenced by a range of factors. These factors include physical and emotional states, the intensity of the needs, wishes and desires, and external situational factors.

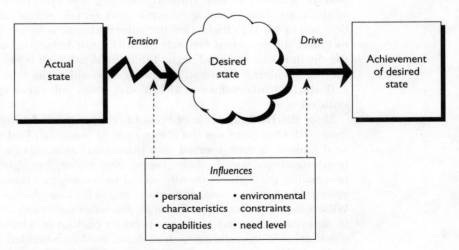

Figure 6.7: The motivation process

Changes in an individual's physical state, such as hunger, thirst or physical danger, will cause the individual to feel tense and to engage in behaviours that will reduce the tension. Humans also like to engage in cognitive activity — thinking, problem solving, daydreaming, and so on. Daydreaming about how you look can initiate the purchase of a year's subscription to the local gym. External events, such as running out of coffee or smashing the car, can be the motivating factors for coffee purchases and car repairs.

There are many factors that can trigger motivation and motivation researchers try to identify and understand these factors. The tendency has been to focus on needs and a popular approach has been to assume that people do not act arbitrarily. Freud, even though he introduced the notion that our behaviour was often influenced by unconscious needs, thought that all behaviours had a purpose. Reasons for making a purchase can, therefore, be conscious or unconscious. Unconscious reasons, such as the need to satisfy feelings of insecurity, loneliness and separateness, can lead to the purchase of products that could permit group membership (see, for example, the Ray-Ban sunglasses advertisement, figure 6.8). Conscious reasons for such purchases may be a liking for the gear and because it is fashionable. On the surface, a teenager may purchase a Torana SLX, Doc Marten shoes and Jag jeans because it is the right car and the right gear. Hidden reasons for such purchases may be the need to identify with a social group other than the family, a need to belong to a group and the need to develop one's own identity.

Figure 6.8: Ray-Ban sunglasses are identified here with a specific group, bikers.

In the 1950s, Ernest Dichter conducted in-depth interviews designed to identify the deep-seated needs that consumers were attempting to satisfy. He investigated over 250 products. One outcome of his research was the famous slogan of the 1950s, 'Put a Tiger in Your Tank', used to advertise Esso petrol. His explanation for the success of the campaign was that cars satisfy an unconscious need for power and control and tigers are associated with power.[39] Interestingly, while this slogan worked in the United States, it did not have the same impact on purchasing behaviour in Europe. The explanation was that the petrol in America had different price and quality ranges whereas in Europe both price and quality were regulated, which meant that consumers could not easily differentiate between types of petrol on the basis of its functional attributes.[40]

CONSUMER NEEDS

Motivation theorists have focused on needs in terms of the innate and the acquired. Freud thought that there were only two basic drives — the life and the death instincts. Other theorists have classified needs into two basic groups, *biogenic* needs and *psychogenic* needs. However, the most widely known classification of basic needs is Maslow's hierarchy. Maslow's work was described earlier in this chapter (pages 140–41) and also in chapter 1 (see page 19). Although there is a suggestion of a hierarchy, for most people the main task is to maintain satisfaction of the basic needs. While Maslow's hierarchy is popular, it has been criticised for, among other things, not taking into account heroic and altruistic behaviour.

Jeffrey Durgee identified a number of motives that are similar to Maslow's and gave examples of the types of products that could be used to satisfy them (see table 6.3).

Table 6.3: Durgee's examples of motives and appropriate products

Motives	Products
Security	Ice-cream, ironed shirts, plaster walls, home baking and hospital care
Status	Scotch, carpets
Social acceptance	• Companionship: ice-cream, coffee • Affection: toys, sugar, honey • Acceptance: soap, beauty products
Femininity	Cakes, cookies, dolls, silk, tea, household ornaments
Masculinity	Sugary products, large breakfasts, power tools, coffee, red meat

(*Source*: Adapted from 'Interpreting Dichter's Interpretations: An Analysis of Consumption Symbolism', in *The Handbook of Consumer Motivations*, Marketing and Semiotics Conference, Copenhagen School of Economics. J. F. Durgee, 'Self-Esteem Advertising', *Journal of Advertising*, Vol. 14, 1986)

William McGuire classified needs into internal needs and external needs (see table 6.4). According to McGuire, internal needs can be satisfied by the individual alone while external needs require social interaction.[41]

An area that has caused some confusion in motivation theory is the role of Murray's list of personal needs (see pages 144–45). These needs have been commonly tested using a thematic apperception test or the Edwards Personal Preference Schedule, a popular personality test in the 1960s. For this reason, it is not clear whether Murray's personal needs are in fact 'needs' as, described in this way, they bear a strong relationship to personality traits.

Table 6.4: McGuire's list of motives

	Internal, non-social motives or needs
Consistency	The need for equilibrium or balance in thoughts and attitudes
Causation	The need to determine who or what causes things to happen to us
Categorisation	The need to establish categories or mental partitions which provide frames of reference
Cues	The need for observable symbols which enable us to infer what we feel or know
Independence	The need for feeling of self-governance or self-control
Curiosity	The need for variety and novelty
	External, social motives or needs
Self-expression	The need to impress, identify ourself to others
Ego-defence	The need to protect our identities
Assertion	The need to increase self-esteem
Reinforcement	The need to act in such a way that others will reward us
Affiliation	The need to develop mutually satisfying relationships with others
Modelling	The need to base behaviours on those of others

(*Source*: Adapted from W. J. McGuire, 'Psychological Motives and Communication Gratification', in J. G. Blumler and C. Katz (eds), *The Uses of Mass Communications: Current Perspectives on Gratification Research*, Sage Publications, 1974, pp. 167–96)

AROUSAL AND INVOLVEMENT

For the most part, purchases will not be made unless the consumer experiences a need and is activated to satisfy it. Unsatisfied needs create a state of tension. There is agreement that most individuals are tension avoiders. If tension cannot be avoided, most people would wish to resolve tension as quickly as possible.

Some writers have assumed that risk-taking activity is undertaken by individuals who actually enjoy tension states. Risky activities, such as sky-diving, bungy-jumping and rock-climbing, do create a 'fear state' but do not create the tension associated with unsatisfied needs. Risky activities are a means to satisfy needs. They may satisfy the need for a 'high' that such achievements give, and they can also satisfy self-esteem and social acceptance needs.[42]

When a need is unsatisfied, varying degrees of tension can be experienced and this will affect the subsequent type of behaviour. The amount of energy a person is willing to expend in the purchase of a product is a function of both the level of tension the unsatisfied need state creates and the degree to which the consumer thinks the product will satisfy the need. Motivation levels, therefore, can range from inertia to passion. This in turn affects the level of *involvement* consumers display in the purchase situation.

The notion of consumer involvement was introduced by Herbert Krugman in 1965 and is an important concept in consumer behaviour. John Antil defined it as 'the level of perceived personal importance and/ or interest evoked by a stimulus (or stimuli) within a specific situation'. In the purchase situation, involvement refers to the importance or value placed on the acquisition of the product. How important a purchase is to a consumer is a function of the underlying needs being met. For a consumer to display high involvement there must be a strong motivation to acquire and/or experience a product. Other factors, such as conflicting needs and wants, the level of perceived risk and the context of the purchase, also affect the level of involvement. The level of involvement in a purchase has considerable impact on how consumers select and buy products.

MOTIVATING CONSUMERS

Much of marketing activity is directed at motivating consumers to buy and use products. This can range from providing information to interested consumers to the use of attention-getting devices for disinterested ones. Because consumers have an innate sense of curiosity , stimuli with properties such as novelty, surprise, ambiguity and uncertainty have the potential to draw people.[43] Curiosity is linked to survival — we need to pay attention to and investigate the unusual as it could be dangerous. Once you have gained attention, then the product or service should relate to a need that the consumer can satisfy by purchasing the product.

So far, much of motivation research in marketing has concentrated on identifying consumers' deep-seated needs. The methods have included in-depth interviews, the use of focus groups, personal interviews, projective tests and scaled questionnaires. Although a costly exercise, the information gained has provided considerable insight into how consumers use products to satisfy needs. More research is required into why consumers choose a particular product, what influences their choice, or what factors cause consumers to develop specific wants.

CONSUMER WANTS

An important issue in understanding consumer motivation is the relationship between needs and wants. There has been some debate as to whether marketers are capable of *creating* needs. Since there does seem to be some agreement among motivation theorists that basic needs are innate, this means that needs are finite and cannot be created, only satisfied. Needs are few and basic, whereas wants are alternative ways of satisfying a need and are therefore many and can be substituted. For example, the biogenic need 'thirst' may be satisfied in many ways: 'I am thirsty, I need a drink, I want a Tooheys'.

Manipulating consumers means plumbing motivational depths

GEORGE KELLY

One of the earliest forms of market research was provided by economists who identified themselves as Statists. These people grouped and classified economic and consumer behavioural facts into usable and understandable groupings.

The demands of modern marketers then created the need for Motivation Research to understand why consumers actually behave in the ways that force them into these groupings.

This motivational research has in recent years largely degenerated into the simple behavioural classification of the early Statists. These behaviour observations and classifications are of little use to marketers trying to position products in categories where the positioning is as important as, or sometimes more important than, the intrinsic attributes of the product.

The concepts and methods of the Statists have inhibited brand positioning.

Much of the current research is derived from consumers' conscious thought processes based on group discussion or questionnaire data. BUT! Decision making for many consumer products is 80–90% unconscious.

Positioning tends to be product-focused: How to make the product different just to be unique. BUT! Differences have to make a difference to be different. Making a difference is a function of the consumer's personality and emotional approval to the product.

Positioning to categories with observed different behavioural Statist types of segments results in diluted messages to cover all objectives. BUT! The motivation to buy may be the same despite the apparent segmental differences. (Sports cars are desired by the young and bought by the old. The motivation then has persisted. Only the capacity to purchase has formed the segmentation.)

Trying to position on rational grounds as a result of consumer-conscious (socially acceptable) responses to research questions only works if the rational issues are true motivators. BUT! Consumers are human, and humans are irrational much of the time. (Many purchase decisions are not important enough to require the effort of rational thought.)

"Can we reliably measure the underlying unconscious motivations?"

The answer to this question is YES, but only if appropriate techniques are used. Current conventional research methods are just not adequate.

The so-called extra perception of the group moderators is largely suspect since, first, very few moderators have had the experience of assessing people's unconscious motivations in a clinical sense.

Further, there is insufficient time available with respondents and the numbers present in group discussion make it very difficult to get behind "the information babble".

The analysis of the temperament or personality of the category of consumers is the only sure method of positioning, and communicating that positioning.

Emotional needs determine how people think. These needs in turn determine which "facts" will be accepted, ignored or discounted. Our personality thus determines the information which we allow into our decision-making system. The equation is not reversible so we cannot guess from behaviour clusters just how this complex decision process will work for a new or revised product.

The ways to measure these unconscious motivations are available to very few research practitioners but if you have access to the appropriate measures, the marketers are two steps ahead of the game of brand positioning.

Personality-based segmentation is the real way to understand the "Australian Ethos".

George Kelly has been a prominent motivational psychologist and researcher for over 25 years. He has used personality "Motivative" techniques with great success for Meadow Lea margarine, Toohey's beer, Tetley tea, Bushells coffee, Taubmans paints, and Rothmans cigarettes.

Marketing, March 1990

Most of the successful products in the marketplace satisfy basic needs, but the choice of a specific product or brand depends upon the individual's unique history, learning experiences and cultural environment. For example, consider a common, frequently purchased item such as toothpaste. The underlying needs that cleaning one's teeth satisfy are:

- survival — preservation of teeth and gums
- belonging — social acceptance, affiliation
- self-esteem — feeling good about oneself.

All individuals (including animals) engage in behaviours to maintain their teeth. So cleaners must satisfy this need. Consumers may prefer to brush, rinse or indeed soak their teeth. They may 'want' a cleansing agent that is pleasant tasting, gives them whiter teeth, and controls breath odour. For consumers, having healthy functioning teeth is a need. Marketers can convince consumers that they need white teeth and fresh breath. Durgee's list of motives (table 6.3) may be used to direct the types of products that could satisfy the need but not the flavour, style, colour or brand. Since needs are finite, it would seem that the focus of motivation research in consumer behaviour should be at the 'want' level.

Wants and desires develop in and are therefore influenced by the social environment in which we live. We may *need* food, but we *want* it in the form of fettucine boscaiola, damper, tomato soup and so on. We may need to drink, but we want Coca-Cola or a milk shake. Wants and desires direct our interest in a product category, and our preference for specific product forms and brands. As such, wants and desires are: learned; substitutable; many; mutable.

The product form and the brands we choose to satisfy these wants and desires will depend on such factors as their availability in the marketplace, their affordability to the consumer, the consumer's lifestyle and the consumer's preferences.

These factors will also determine whether we consider the product to be a necessity or a luxury. Necessities are product categories that are basic or essential to a lifestyle. Luxuries are product categories that consumers want but they consider indulgences. Whether a product is classified as a necessity or a luxury really depends on the consumer's perceptions. Products such as chocolates, perfume, liqueurs and silk ties are more likely to be viewed as indulgences than washing machines, shampoo or milk.

Consumers also require products to fulfil many functions, of which there are three main types:

1. **Utilitarian function** — the product's capacity to perform in terms of practical, physical attributes, measured on a profile of choice attributes
2. **Hedonistic/experiential function** — the product's capacity to satisfy novelty, knowledge, creativity and to create emotional arousal, such as fun, excitement, joy and fear
3. **Expressive function** — the product's capacity to communicate aspects of the self (social image) and group membership.

Many researchers acknowledge that consumers need to maximise both the utility and the symbolic benefits of a purchase decision.[44] Most products fulfil these functions in varying degrees. Furniture polish primarily serves a utilitarian function, but as the polishing of furniture 'says' something about a person it also, to a lesser degree, serves the expressive function. Some products provide experiences such as fun, excitement and sensual satisfaction, but they also allow us to say something about ourselves. Although consumers are buying excitement when they ride the roller-coaster, the roller-coaster must be 'safe'. So an integral part of the product is the functional benefit of well built and maintained machinery.

SUMMARY

Personality and motivation are important concepts in the study of consumer behaviour. Motivation is important because it is the driving force of behaviour. There must be a reason, a motive, for purchasing and using products and it is important for marketers to identify and understand those reasons. Our motives also affect our perception, what and how we learn, and our personality as often we are 'motivated' to change ourselves in some way. Personality is an important concept because who we are and who we think we are influences our choice of products and how we use them.

While motivation and personality are important concepts, their use as strategic marketing tools is limited. There have been many attempts to use personality as a segmentation variable, so far without success. This is mainly because personality is a complex concept and difficult to measure. Without measurement, it is impossible to group individuals into segments. Although research is now focusing on the notion of self-concept and its impact on product choice, similar problems have been encountered. To use self-concept as a strategic tool requires the grouping of similar self-concepts. This requires measurement and researchers have had difficulties in labelling self-concepts and measuring the concept. The difficulties with personality and self-concept have resulted in a shift away from the direct matching of personality-based segments with brand images. Instead the 'individual' aspects of products are being emphasised.

For us to be motivated to purchase a product, the product should satisfy basic needs and wants. These needs and wants can originate in unmet physical needs, through fantasy, daydreams, thoughts and situational factors. It is important to understand the difference between needs and wants. Needs are considered to be innate, few, fixed and non-substitutable, whereas wants are learned, many, substitutable and mutable.

Questions

1. Discuss the use of self-concept in product positioning.

2. Select four advertisements that you think contain messages that reflect manifest and latent motives. Which advertisement has the stronger impact? Why?

3. The article on page 159 is an example of the confusion and overlap between personality and motivation. Discuss the following:
   (a) the difference between personality and motivation
   (b) the difference between rational and irrational decisions. Are consumers irrational for much of the time?

4. Identify four or five people who you think are highly materialistic and four or five who are not. Do they show any common behaviours that could be used to direct advertising messages?

5. Interview four people who are 'collectors'. Try to ascertain how:
   • the art of 'collecting'
   • the objects that are collected
   • the method of collecting the objects
   relate to the person's self-concept.

6. Discuss the relationship between needs, wants, desires and involvement.

7. How do needs and wants relate to the product functions, that is:
   • the utilitarian function
   • the expressive function
   • the experiential function?

8. Compare and contrast psychoanalytic and trait theories of personality. What are the major problems with the application of these theories to marketing strategies?

9. Discuss the role of symbolism in product choice.

10. Recall a purchase situation in which you had conflicting needs and/or wants. How did you resolve the conflict? What effect, if any, did your resolution approach have on other purchases?

 Case study

When the US rock band Guns N' Roses staged its outdoor concerts in Sydney and Melbourne earlier this year, Tony Blain was delighted. The 37-year-old New Zealander owns Acme Merchandising, a Sydney-based company that sells products plastered with rock bands' names and logos. Sixty Acme employees worked the crowd at the Guns N' Roses concert at Sydney's Eastern Creek raceway, selling a raft of merchandise, while 70 staff worked the band's Calder Park concert in Melbourne.

The Guns N' Roses concerts provided a healthy sales boost for Acme. The 13-year-old company will finish 1992–93 with sales of $15 million, up 10% from $13.6 million in 1991–92. Most of this year's growth has been generated by the sale of products linked to concert tours. At the same time,

Acme has steadily increased its presence in retail stores and broadened its product range.

Acme's Sydney factory makes and prints a million T-shirts a year. At any given time, Acme has about 400 designs on the market. It sells its wares through more than 2000 retail outlets, ranging from Myer and K mart to jeans shops and record stores. Music-related products account for 60% of its annual sales; the remainder is generated by products based on properties owned by companies such as Walt Disney Company, Warner Bros, PepsiCo and Harley-Davidson.

Although the core target market for Acme's products is, according to Blain, "the black T-shirt brigade" — teenage boys obsessed with heavy-metal bands such as Metallica, AC/DC, Megadeth and Iron Maiden — the company's range

covers hundreds of different brands, singers and band names. Acme is making T-shirts, sweatshirts, key rings, badges and so on for two very different concert tours: Paul McCartney this month and Metallica in March–April. For the McCartney concerts, Acme is producing six T-shirt designs. For Metallica, which has been one of its top-selling properties since 1987, it is making five designs ...

The first Australian bands that agreed to let Blain use their names and images on products were Midnight Oil and INXS. Acme still works with Midnight Oil, and INXS recently returned to Blain after using another merchandising company for a few years. Acme signed its first international act in 1982, striking a deal with the managers of Irish rock music band U2 ...

The contracts that cover the merchandising of products based on a band or singer are similar to the deals struck by music publishers and record companies. Acme signs a contract with a band's management company, agreeing to pay royalties on the sale of products based on the band. It also pays an advance against royalties and guarantees to sell a certain number of products. With products sold through retail stores, Acme pays 15% of wholesale sales to the band. In the case of products sold at concerts, the band receives between 20% and 40% of gross sales. Big crowd-pullers such as Metallica and Guns N' Roses get 40%, and less popular bands get 20–30%.

Blain says that Australians spend $60–100 million a year on products based on bands and singers. Unauthorised designs produced by bootleggers in Australia and overseas are said to take up 10–40% of the market. At Melbourne airport recently, Customs agents seized 6000 Guns N' Roses products from two British tourists, and some people at the band's Sydney concert were wearing bootleg T-shirts bought at Newcastle railway station.

Acme spent $100 000 on legal fees to protect its designs and copyrights last year and will spend a similar amount this year. It recently spent $20 000 to prevent the Auckland retailer Rock Shop from selling unauthorised Harley-Davidson T-shirts, and

received a $5000 settlement. "Our aim is to put the bootleggers out of business," Blain says. "I don't care how much it costs." Acme employs security people to find bootleg products at concerts and private investigators to check retail stores.

"Beating the counterfeiters is difficult," Blain says. "It's easy to set up a backyard operation screen-printing T-shirts. It is relatively easy to convince a T-shirt printer to run up 10 000 bootleg T-shirts late at night for a cash payment. If we don't fight the counterfeit products, the problem will only get worse."

The design of Acme's products is controlled by the bands and singers or, in the case of non-music properties, the owner of the property. The smallest print run of a new T-shirt design is 1000 copies, and new designs that are expected to sell strongly are produced in batches of 10 000.

Blain and Acme's promotions manager, Jimmy Hendricks, track new album releases and trends in popular music to determine the style and quantity of products to make. "If a band goes out of vogue, products carrying its name or image are as popular as last year's calendar," Blain says. "We have to keep in touch with what is popular on the streets, what is hot among rock 'n' roll fans."

Making its own clothing products gives Acme tight control over inventory levels. T-shirts, sweatshirts, shorts and

other items of clothing account for 95% of its sales and are made by the company (80% of the T-shirts it sells are black). Other products such as belt buckles and badges are commissioned from contract manufacturers.

Acme signed its first non-music client in 1986, when it bought the rights to sell T-shirts based on Disney characters in gift shops and small fashion boutiques. Since then, it has acquired licences to Warner Bros' Looney Tunes characters, Pepsi-Cola, Chevrolet and Harley-Davidson (Blain owns five Harley motorcycles). This year it signed a deal with the video-game distributor Sega-Ozisoft to create products based on Sega characters such as Sonic the Hedgehog.

Blain returned to the New Zealand market in 1988, opening an Acme sales office in Auckland. A two-year-old office in Singapore is selling products based on Australian bands, Warner Bros cartoon characters and Harley-Davidson in local retail stores. Blain is keen to launch concert-based products in Asia. Metallica will perform in Singapore in April, with Acme handling product sales at the concert, and several Australian bands that are signed to Acme are also considering regional tours.

Neil Shoebridge,
Business Review Weekly,
5 March 1993

 Case study questions

1. The article mentions a major problem for 'labelled' products such as Gucci, Dior, LaCoste — the imitation. Fighting imitations is a costly business. Could you design a 'pull' advertising strategy to encourage the purchase of the legitimate product using consumers' self-concept?

2. What role would owning an original label play in a teenager's search for self-identity? Do you think Acme could use this search to its advantage? If so, how?

SUGGESTED READING

M. Walker, D. Burnham and R. Borland, *Psychology*, 2nd edn, John Wiley and Sons, Brisbane, 1994, pp. 357–92 and 584–618.

C. S. Hall and L. Gardner, *Theories of Personality*, John Wiley and Sons, New York, 1987.

H. J. Kassarjian and M. J. Sheffett, *Personality and Consumer Behaviour: One More Time*, Proceedings Series No. 37, American Marketing Association, 1988.

B. Winer, *Theories of Motivation: From Mechanism to Cognition*, Markham Press, Chicago, 1972.

M. Rosenberg, *Conceiving the Self*, Basic Books, New York, 1979.

ENDNOTES

1. C. S. Hall and L. Gardner, *Theories of Personality*, John Wiley and Sons, New York, 1987. R. R. Bootzin, *Psychology Today*, 6th edn, Random House, New York, 1986.
2. R. R. Bootzin, ibid.
3. C. S. Hall and G. Lindzey, *Theories of Personality*, 3rd edn, John Wiley and Sons, New York, 1978. R. R. Bootzin, ibid.
4. C. S. Hall and G. Lindzey, ibid. R. R. Bootzin, ibid. B. F. Skinner, *Science and Human Behaviour*, Macmillan, New York, 1953.
5. A. Bandura, *Principles of Behaviour Modification*, Holt, Rinehart and Winston, New York, 1969. A. Bandura, *Social Learning Theory*, Prentice-Hall, Englewood Cliffs, NJ, 1977.
6. C. S. Hall and G. Lindzey, ibid. R. R. Bootzin, ibid. B. F. Skinner, ibid. A. Bandura, *Social Learning Theory*, Prentice-Hall, Englewood Cliffs, NJ, 1977.
7. C. S. Hall and G. Lindzey, ibid. R. R. Bootzin, ibid. G. W. Allport, *Personality: A Psychological Interpretation*, Henry Holt, New York, 1937. R. B. Cattell, *The Scientific Analysis of Personality*, Aldine, Chicago, 1966.
8. C. S. Hall and G. Lindzey, ibid. R. R. Bootzin, ibid. C. Rogers, *On Becoming a Person: A Therapist's View of Psychotherapy*, Houghton Mifflin, Boston, 1961.
9. A. Maslow, *Motivation and Personality*, Harper and Row, New York, 1954. A. Maslow, *Toward a Psychology of Being*, 2nd edn, Van Nostrand, Princeton, NJ, 1968.
10. W. James, *The Principles of Psychology*, Henry Holt, New York, 1890.
11. W. James, ibid.
12. M. Rosenberg, *Conceiving the Self*, Basic Books, New York, 1979.
13. K. Lewin, *A Dynamic Theory of Personality*, McGraw-Hill, New York, 1935.
14. J. Kaponin, 'Personality Characteristics of Purchasers', *Journal of Advertising Research*, Vol. 1, Jan. 1960, pp. 6–12. S. Budner, 'Intolerance for Ambiguity as a Personality Variable', *Journal of Personality*, Vol. 30, 1962, pp. 29–50. J. Kernan, 'Choice Criteria, Decision Behaviour and Personality', *Journal of Marketing Research*, Vol. 5, 1968, pp. 155-64. R. Brody and S. Cunningham, 'Personality Variables and the Consumer Decision Process', *Journal of Marketing Science Research*, Vol. 5, 1968, pp. 50–57. A. Marcus, 'Obtaining Group Measures from Personality Test Scores: Auto Brand Choice Predicted from the Edwards Personal Preference Schedule', *Psychological Reports*, Vol. 17, 1965, pp. 523–31. C. Winick, 'The Relationship Among Personality Needs, Objective Factors and Brand Choice: A Re-Examination', *Journal of Business*, Vol. 34, 1961, pp. 61–66. J. B. Cohen, 'Toward an Interpersonal Theory of Consumer Behaviour', *Californian Management Review*, Vol. 10, 1968. J. B. Cohen, 'An Interpersonal Orientation to the Study of Consumer Behaviour', *Journal of Marketing Research*, Vol. 4,

1967, pp. 270–78. J. B. Cohen and E. Golden, 'Informational Social Influence and Product Evaluation', *Journal of Applied Psychology*, Vol. 50, 1972, pp. 54–59. J. Kernan, 'Choice Criteria, Decision Behaviour and Personality', *Journal of Marketing Research*, Vol. 5, 1968, pp. 155–64. L. I. Price and N. Ridgway, 'Development of a Scale to Measure Innovativeness', in R. P. Bagozzi and A. M. Tybout (ed.), *Advances in Consumer Research*, Association for Consumer Research, Ann Arbor, Mich., 1983. S. Bither and I. Dolich, 'Personality as a Determinant Factor in Store Choice', in M. Venkatesan (ed.), Proceedings of the Third Annual Conference, Association for Consumer Research, College Park M.D., 1972.

15. F. B. Evans, 'Psychological and Objective Factors in the Prediction of Brand Choice', *Journal of Business*, Vol. 32, Oct. 1959, pp. 340–69. F. Evans and H. Roberts, 'Fords and Chevrolets and the Problem of Discrimination', *Journal of Business*, Vol. 36, 1961, pp. 67–73. F. Evans, 'Reply: You Still Can't Tell a Ford Owner from a Chevrolet Owner?', *Journal of Business*, Vol. 34, 1963, pp. 242–49.

16. R. Westfall, 'Psychological Factors in Predicting Brand Choice', *Journal of Marketing*, 26, 1962, pp. 34–40.

17. J. B. Cohen, 'An Interpersonal Orientation to the Study of Consumer Behaviour', *Journal of Marketing Research*, Vol. 4, No. 6, pp. 270–78.

18. J. P. Noerager, 'An Assessment of CAD, a Personality Instrument Developed Specifically for Marketing Research', *Journal of Marketing Research*, Vol. 16, 1979, pp. 53–59. A. Woodside and R. Andress, 'CAD Eight Years Later', *Journal of the Academy of Marketing Science*, Vol. 3, 1975, pp. 309–13. P. F. Tyagi, 'Validation of the CAD Instrument: A Replication', *Advances in Consumer Research*, Vol. 10, 1983, pp. 112–18. M. E. Slama, T. G. Williams and A. Tashchian, 'Compliant, Aggressive and Detached Types Differ in Generalised Purchasing Involvement', *Advances in Consumer Research*, Vol. 15, 1988, pp. 158–62.

19. T. Robertson, *Innovation and the Consumer*, Holt, New York, 1971. L. E. Boone, 'The Search for the Consumer Innovator', *Journal of Business*, Vol. 43, 1979, pp. 20–23.

20. B. Blake, R. Perlof and R. Heslin, 'Dogmatism and the Acceptance of New Products', *Journal of Marketing Research*, Vol. 7, 1970, pp. 483–86.

21. K. A. Coney and B. Harmon, 'Dogmatism and Innovation: A Situational Perspective', in W. Wilkie (ed.), *Advances in Consumer Research*, Vol. 6, Association for Consumer Research, Ann Arbor, Mich., 1975, pp. 118–21.

22. D. R. Lichtenstein, R. G. Netemeyer and S. Burton, 'Distinguishing Coupon Proneness from Value Consciousness: An Acquisition Transaction Utility Theory Perspective', *Journal of Marketing*, Vol. 54, July 1990, pp. 54–67.

23. J. Murphy, 'Questionable Correlates of Automobile Shopping Behaviour', *Journal of Marketing*, Vol. 27, Oct. 1963, pp. 71–72. W. T. Tucker and J. Painter, 'Personality and Product Use', *Journal of Applied Psychology*, Vol. 45, Oct. 1961, pp. 325–29. W. D. Wells, 'Personality as a Determinant of Buyer Behaviour: What's Wrong? What Can Be Done About It?', in David Sparks (ed.), *Broadening the Concept of Marketing*, American Marketing Association, Chicago, 1970. W. Wells, 'General Personality Tests and Consumer Behaviour', in J. W. Newman (ed.), *On Knowing the Consumer*, John Wiley and Sons, New York, 1966.

24. H. Kassarjian, 'Personality and Consumer Behaviour: A Review,' *Journal of Marketing Research*, Vol. 8, 1971, pp. 409–18.

25. W. Mischel, 'On the Future of Personality Measurement', *American Psychologist*, 32, April 1977, p. 2. W. D. Wells and J. Beard, 'Personality in Consumer Behaviour', in Scott Ward and T. Robertson (eds), *Consumer Behaviour: Theoretical Sources*, Prentice-Hall, Englewood Cliffs, NJ, 1973. L. A. Crosby and S. L. Grossbart, 'A Blueprint for Consumer Behaviour: Research on Personality', *Advances in*

Consumer Research, Vol. 11, 1984, pp. 447–52. P. Albanese, 'A Paradox of Personality in Marketing: A New Approach to the Problem', AMA Educators Proceedings, 1989. G. R. Foxall and R. E. Goldsmith, 'Personality and Consumer Research: Another Look', *Journal of the Marketing Research Society,* Vol. 30, No. 2, 1988, pp. 111–25. K. Villani and Y. Wind, 'On the Usage of "Modified" Personality Trait Measures', *Journal of Consumer Research,* Vol. 5, 1978, pp. 223–28. G. Brooker, 'Representativeness of Shortened Personality Measures', *Journal of Consumer Research,* Vol. 5, 1978, pp. 143–44. H. J. Kassarjian and M. J. Sheffett, 'Personality and Consumer Behaviour: One More Time', *Proceedings Series No. 37,* American Marketing Association, 1988. J. Lastovicka and E. A. Joachimsthaler, 'Improving the Detection of Personality–Behaviour Relationships in Consumer Research', *Journal of Consumer Research,* 14, March 1988, pp. 583–87. R. Hill, 'The Impact of Interpersonal Anxiety on Consumer Information Processing', *Psychology and Marketing,* Vol. 4, 1987, pp. 93–105. E. Gutman, 'The Role of Individual Differences and Multiple Senses in Consumer Imagery Processing: Theoretical Perspectives', in M. Houston (ed.), *Advances in Consumer Research,* Vol. 15, Association for Consumer Research, Provo, Utah, 1988, pp. 191–96. D. MacInnis, 'Constructs and Measures of Individual Differences in Imagery Processing: A Review', in M. Wallendorf and P. Anderson (eds), *Advances in Consumer Research,* Association for Consumer Research, Vol. 16, Provo, Utah, 1987, pp. 88–92. J. T. Plummer, 'How Personality Makes a Difference', *Journal of Advertising Research,* Vol. 24, No. 6, Jan. 1985. R. Horton, 'Some Relationships Between Personality and Consumer Decision Making', *Journal of Marketing Research,* Vol. 16, May 1979, pp. 27–31. C. Schaninger and D. Sciglimpaglia, 'The Influences of Cognitive Personality Traits and Demographics on Consumer Information and Acquisition', *Journal of Consumer Research,* Vol. 8, 1981, pp. 208–15. R. C. Lewis and D. M. Klein, 'Personal Constructs: Their Use in the Marketing of Intangible Services', *Psychology and Marketing,* Vol. 2, Fall 1975. H. Cetola and K. Prinkey, 'Intraversion–Extraversion and Loud Commercials', *Psychology and Marketing,* Vol. 3, 1986, p. 123.

26. S. Epstein, 'Traits are Alive and Well', in D. Magnusson and N. Endler (eds), *Personality at the Crossroads: Current Issues in Interactional Psychology,* Lawrence Erlbaum Associates, Hillsdale, NJ, 1977. B. Josephy and S. J. Vyas, 'Concurrent Validity of a Measure of Innovative Cognitive Style', *Journal of the Academy of Marketing Science,* Vol. 12, 1984, pp. 159–75.

27. T. Veblen, *The Theory of the Leisure Class,* Mentor Books, New York, 1958 (a reprint of *The Theory of the Leisure Class,* MacMillan, New York, 1899).

28. M. Rosenberg, *Conceiving the Self,* Basic Books, New York, 1979. J. F. Hair Jr, 'The Self-Image/Store-Image Matching Process: An Empirical Test', *Journal of Business,* Vol. 50, 1977, pp. 63–69. S. Epstein, 'The Self-Concept: A Review and the Proposal of an Integrated Theory of Personality', in Ervin Staub (ed.), *Personality: Basic Issues and Current Research,* Prentice-Hall, Englewood Cliffs, NJ, 1974. S. Onkvist and J. Shaw, 'Self-Concept and Image Congruence: Some Research and Managerial Issues', *Journal of Consumer Marketing,* Vol. 4, Winter 1987, pp. 13–23. S. J. Levy, 'Symbols for Sale', *Harvard Business Review,* Vol. 37, 1959. E. Goffman, *Presentation of the Self in Everyday Life,* Doubleday, Garden City, NY, 1959. R. Belk, K. D. Bahn and R. N. Mayer, 'Development Recognition of Consumption Symbolism', *Journal of Consumer Research,* Vol. 9, June 1982, pp. 4–17. R. Belk, M. Wallendorf, F. Sherry, M. Holbrook and S. Roberts, 'Collectors and Collecting', in M. Houston (ed.), *Advances in Consumer Research,* Vol. 15, Association for Consumer Research, Provo, Utah, 1987, pp. 548–53. R. Belk, 'My Possessions Myself', *Psychology Today,* July/Aug. 1988, pp. 50–52. E. L. Grubb and H. Grathwohl, 'Consumer Self-Concept, Symbolism and Market Behaviour: A Theoretical Approach', *Journal of Marketing,* 31, Oct. 1967, pp. 22–27. H. C. Triandis, 'The Self and Social Behaviour in Differing Cultural Contexts', *Psychological Review,* Vol. 96, 1989, pp. 506–20. E. Yoffe, 'You

Are What You Buy', *Newsweek*, 4 June 1990. M. R. Solomon, 'The Role of Products as Social Stimuli: A Symbolic Interactionism Perspective', *Journal of Consumer Research*, Vol. 10, Dec. 1983, pp. 319–29. R. A. Wicklund and P. M. Gollwitzer, *Symbolic Self-Completion*, Lawrence Erlbaum, Hillsdale, NJ, 1982. D. A. Prentice, 'Psychological Correspondence of Possessions, Attitudes and Values', *Journal of Personality and Social Psychology*, Vol. 53, 1987, pp. 993–1002. M. Csikszentmihalyi and E. Rochberg-Halton, *The Meaning of Things: Domestic Symbols and the Self*, Cambridge University Press, Cambridge, Mass., 1981. R. Belk, 'Possessions and the Extended Self', *Journal of Consumer Research*, Vol. 15, 1988, pp. 139–68.

29. S. B. Verschure and J. Burroughs, 'Identity Symbolism in Housing', *Environment and Behaviour*, Vol. 19, 1987, pp. 579–87. M. R. Solomon and H. Assel, 'The Forest or the Trees? A Gestalt Approach to Symbolic Consumption', in J. Umiker-Sebeok (ed.), *Marketing and Semiotics: New Directions in the Study of Signs for Sale*, Mouton de Gruyter, Berlin, 1987. J. L. Nasar, 'Symbolic Meanings of House Styles', *Environment and Behaviour*, Vol. 21, May 1989, pp. 235–57.

30. R. Holman, 'Product as Communication: A Fresh Appraisal of a Venerable Topic', in Ben M. Enis and K. J. Roering (eds), *Review of Marketing*, American Marketing Association, Chicago, 1981.

31. H. Markus, 'Self Schemata and Processing Information about Self', *Journal of Personality and Social Psychology*, Vol. 35, 1977, pp. 63–68. J. G. Hull and A. S. Levy, 'The Organisational Function of the Self: An Alternative to the Duvval and Wicklund Model of Self Awareness', *Journal of Personality and Social Psychology*, Vol. 37, 1979, pp. 756–68. I. Ross, 'Self-Concept and Brand Preference', *Journal of Business*, Vol. 44, 1971, pp. 38–50. L. Landon, 'Self-Concept, Ideal Self-Concept and Consumer Purchase Intentions', *Journal of Consumer Research*, Vol. 1, 1974, pp. 41–51. T. O'Brien, T. Humberto and T. Sanchez, 'Consumer Motivation: A Developmental Self-Concept Approach', *Journal of the Academy of Marketing Science*, Vol. 4, No. 3, 1976, pp. 608–16. G. Belch, 'Belief Systems and the Differential Role of the Self-Concept', *Advances in Consumer Research*, Vol. 5, 1978, p. 320. C. B. Hamm and E. W. Cundiff, 'Self Actualisation and Product Perception', *Journal of Marketing Research*, Vol. 6, 1969, pp. 470–72. C. Miller and C. Leigh-Cox, 'Public Self-Consciousness and Make-up', *Personality and Social Psychology Bulletin*, Vol. 4, 1982, pp. 748–51. M. R. Solomon and J. Schopler, 'Self Consciousness and Clothing', *Personality and Social Psychology Bulletin*, Vol. 8, 1982, pp. 508–14. A. E. Birdwell, 'A Study of Influence of Image Congruence on Consumer Choice', *Journal of Business*, Vol. 41, Jan. 1964, pp. 76–88. E. L. Grubb and G. Hupp, 'Perception of Self, Generalized Stereotypes and Brand Selection', *Journal of Marketing Research*, Vol. 5, 1986, pp. 58–63. I. J. Dolich, 'Congruence Relationship Between Self-Image and Product Brands', *Journal of Marketing Research*, Vol. 6, 1969, pp. 80–84. D. N. Bellenger, E. Steinberg and W. Stanton, 'The Congruence of Store Image and Self Image as It Relates to Store Loyalty', *Journal of Retailing*, Vol. 52, 1976, pp. 17–32. B. L. Stern, R. F. Bush and J. F. Hair Jr, 'The Self-Image/Store-Image Matching Process: An Empirical Test', *Journal of Business*, Vol. 50, 1977, pp. 63–69. W. DeLozier and R. Tillman, 'Self Image Concepts — Can They Be Used to Design Marketing Programs?', *The Southern Journal of Business*, Vol. 7, 1972, p. 11. J. B. Manson and M. L. Mayer, 'The Problem of the Self Concept in Store Image Studies', *Journal of Marketing*, Vol. 34, April 1970. I. J. Dolich and N. Shilling, 'A Critical Evaluation of the Problem of Self-Concept in Store Image Studies', *Journal of Marketing*, Vol. 25, 1971, pp. 71–73. B. B. Brown and M. Lohr, 'Peer Group Affiliation and Adolescent Self-Esteem: An Integration of Ego-Identity and Symbolic Interaction Theories', *Journal of Personality and Social Psychology*, Vol. 1, No. 52, 1987, pp. 47–55. E. L. Grubb and B. Stern, 'Self Concept and Significant Others', *Journal of Marketing Research*, Vol. 8, 1971, pp. 382–85.

32. N. K. Malhotra, 'A Scale to Measure Self-Concept, Person Concepts and Product Concepts', *Journal of Marketing Research*, Vol. 18, Nov. 1981, pp. 456–64.

33. J. Sirgy, 'Self-Concept in Consumer Behaviour: A Critical Review', *Journal of Consumer Research*, Vol. 9, Dec. 1982, pp. 287–300.

34. J. M. Munson and W. A. Spivey, 'Assessing Self-Concept', *Advances in Consumer Research*, Vol. 7, 1980, pp. 598–603. J. Sirgy, 'Using Self Congruity and Ideal Congruity to Predict Purchase Motivation', *Journal of Business Research*, Vol. 13, 1985, pp. 195–206. M. B. Holbrook, M. R. Solomon and S. Bell, 'A Re-examination of Self-Monitoring and Judgement of Furniture Designs', *Home Economics Research Journal*, Vol. 19, Sept. 1990, pp. 6–16. M. Snyder and S. Gangestad, 'On the Nature of Self Monitoring: Matters of Assessment, Matters of Validity', *Journal of Personality and Social Psychology*, Vol. 51, 1986, pp. 125–39. G. E. Belch and E. L. Landon Jr, 'Discriminant Validity of a Product-Anchored Self-Concept Measure', *Journal of Marketing Research*, Vol. 14, May 1977, pp. 252–56.

35. R. W. Belk, 'Three Scales to Measure Constructs Related to Materialism; Reliability, Validity and Relationships to Measure of Happiness', in T. Kinnear (ed.), *Advances in Consumer Research*, Association for Consumer Research, Ann Arbor, Mich., 1984, p. 291. R. W. Belk, 'Materialism: Trait Aspects of Living in the Material World', *Journal of Consumer Research*, 37, Dec. 1985, pp. 265–80.

36. A. G. Greenwald and Banaji, 'The Self as a Memory System: Powerful But Ordinary', *Journal of Personality and Social Psychology*, 57, 1989, pp. 41–54. J. M. Sirgy, 'Self-Concept in Relation to Product Preference and Purchase Intention', in V. Bellur (ed.), *Developments in Marketing Science*, Vol. 3, Academy of Marketing Science, Marquette, Mich., 1980, pp. 1–10. R. F. Baumeister, D. M. Tice and D. Hutton, 'Self Presentation Motivations and Personality Differences in Self-Esteem', *Journal of Personality*, Vol. 57, 1989, pp. 547–75. C. T. Schenk and R. Holman, 'A Sociological Approach to Brand Choice: The Concept of Situational Self Image', in J. C. Olsen (ed.), *Advances in Consumer Research*, Vol. 7, Association for Consumer Research, Ann Arbor, Mich., 1980, pp. 610–14.

37. V. Packard, *The Hidden Persuaders*, Penguin Press, New York, 1957. W. B. Keys, *Subliminal Seduction*, Signet Books, Englewood Cliffs, NJ, 1976. W. B. Keys, *Subliminal Seduction: Ad Media's Manipulation of a Not So Innocent America*, Prentice-Hall, Englewood Cliffs, NJ, 1973.

38. J. Haberstroh, 'Can't Ignore Subliminal Ad Charges', *Advertising Age*, Vol. 55, Sept. 1984, p. 34. J. Caccaval, T. Wanty and J. Edell, 'Subliminal Implants in Advertisements: An Experiment', in A. Mitchell (ed.), *Advances in Consumer Research*, Vol. 9, Association for Consumer Research, Ann Arbor, Mich., 1982, pp. 418–23.

39. E. Dichter, 'How Word of Mouth Advertising Works', *Harvard Business Review*, 44, Nov. 1966, p. 148.

40. J. Cerha, *Selective Mass Communications*, P. A. Norstedt and Sonder, Stockholm, Sweden, 1967.

41. W. J. Mcguire, 'Psychological Motives and Communication Gratification', in J. G. Blumler and C. Katz (eds), *Users of Mass Communications: Current Perspectives on Gratification Research*, Sage Publications, 1974.

42. J. H. Antil, 'Conceptualization and Operationalisation of Involvement', in T. C. Kinnear (ed.), *Advances in Consumer Research*, 11, Association for Consumer Research, Provo, Utah, 1984, p. 204. R. L. Celsi, L. R. Randall and T. Leigh, 'An Exploration of High Risk Leisure Consumption through Skydiving', *Journal of Consumer Research*, Vol. 20, No. 1, 1993, pp. 1–23.

43. D. E. Berlyne, 'Novelty, Complexity and Hedonic Value', *Perception and Psychophysics*, 8, Nov. 1970, pp. 279–86.

44. Holbrook and O'Shaughnessy, ibid. Zajonic and Markus, ibid.

P A R T

2

EXTERNAL
INFLUENCES

C H A P T E R

7

Social influence: social groups and consumers

OBJECTIVES

This chapter should help you to:

- understand social groups and how they function
- understand how groups influence consumer behaviour
- understand the marketing implications of social groups
- understand what opinion leadership is
- understand how new products diffuse into the population.

 INTRODUCTION

Australians have always adored their sports stars, which is why the corporate world is eager to have sports personalities endorse their products. Recent product endorsements have included Olympic swimmer Kieren Perkins for Sizzler, ironman Guy Leech for Saucony, and rugby league star Andrew Ettinghausen for Cebe sportsglasses.[1] Sports sponsorship is a major source of income for golfer Greg Norman and motorcyclist Michael Doohan. Australians identify strongly with sports personalities who, except for their athletic talent, are seen as a nice bunch of ordinary people. As such, they have mass appeal and serve as referents for large numbers of Australians.

It is important for marketers to understand the influence of other people on consumers if they are to formulate successful marketing strategies. In this chapter, we examine the basis of the influence exerted by reference groups on consumer behaviour. First, we will examine the way in which groups can be classified. Second, we will consider the mechanisms by which groups exert influence. Finally, we will examine the implications of group influence on marketing strategy. The role of opinion leaders in facilitating product acceptance and diffusion is also discussed.

 # SOCIAL GROUPS

A 'group' can be defined as two or more individuals who have implicitly or explicitly defined relationships with one another. The members of a group feel related because of their interactions with each other.[2] Throughout life, each person will belong to a variety of groups that exert a strong influence on consumption behaviour. One reason for the strength of this group influence is that most consumer behaviour takes place in group settings. Nevertheless, group influence is important even when we make solitary purchases of goods intended for our own use, because more purchases are motivated by our desire to identify ourselves with desirable persons and to meet expectations of others who are important to us.

Groups have three definitive features. First, individual members of a group share common needs, norms, values and beliefs. Second, group members interact with each other through social networks and perceive every other member as part of the group. Third, members of a group interact with each other over a period of time.

In a lifetime, a person will belong to a variety of groups that will include the immediate and extended family, peers and groups organised around specific activities. In all groups, members are expected to conform to the group's beliefs, values and norms and to behave in certain ways. The individuals in the group serve as agents of consumer socialisation, and may actively teach other group members about appropriate consumption behaviours. For example, parents teach children what products are acceptable — such as limiting the purchase of lollies and soft drink. Furthermore, most people keep in mind groups to which they would like to be admitted. These groups can also serve as reference groups and direct behaviour. A 'reference' group is any social grouping that individuals use to guide their ideas and behaviour. The behaviour and ideas of group members act as a frame of reference for the consumer. Whether a social group is a reference group for the consumer is determined by the consumer.

A categorisation of groups appears in table 7.1.[3] Groups can be classified by membership, type and frequency of contact, degree of attraction, and degree of organisation.

Membership

'Membership' is a dichotomous variable, that is, groups can be classified as those that we belong to and those that we do not. Within the membership category, however, there are degrees of belonging. Membership in some groups will be more tenuous than in others. This and other personal factors will affect the degree of influence the group has on the individual. For example, Bearden and Rose found that people differ in their use of social comparison information, some people being less likely to use others as comparison standards.[4]

Table 7.1: Categorisation of groups

Category	Criteria	Group	Example
Membership	Yes	Member	Admitted student
	No	Non-member	Applicant
Contact	Frequent, personal	Primary	Family, peers
	Less frequent, distant	Secondary	Religious and ethnic subcultures
Attraction	Positive contact, non-member	Aspiration	Management levels/ social class
	Positive non-contact, non-member	Symbolic	Sporting and 'pop' stars
	Negative, non-member	Dissociative	School leaver
	Mixed, member	Disclaimant	Political party
Organisation	Extensive, specified	Formal	Church, clubs
	Weak	Informal	Family, peers

Contact

'Type and frequency of contact' refers to how much interpersonal contact the members of the group have. For example, 'primary groups' are characterised by regular face-to-face interaction and members of such a group tend to have relationships that are spontaneous, free and often emotional. Discussion topics are boundless, with members interacting with one another on any topic that interests them. Examples of primary groups are the immediate family, relatives and friends. Groups whose members have indirect contact with one another are called 'secondary groups'. These include religious, class, subcultural and national groups. The group shapes the behaviour and ways of thinking of the members. Relationships within secondary groups are distant.

Among primary groups, the members of one's immediate family usually have the greatest influence on consumer behaviour. Family members have a high degree of face-to-face interaction and actively socialise with one another. The members of a family will sometimes acquiesce to other family members' preferences in a purchase decision and, at other times, attempt to influence the purchase decisions of others in the family. Children, for example, are likely to consult parents about the purchase of toys, clothing and other expensive items, but they also influence the parents' product and brand choices.[5] In addition, many consumption decisions are made jointly with family members taking on different roles depending on the choice to be made.

Peers, especially close friends, also exert strong influence on consumer behaviour. Friends fulfil a wide range of needs including companionship, security and information; they are also likely to have common values, beliefs and attitudes, and to participate in similar activities. Since they meet frequently, friends have opportunities to discuss products, services and store patronage. Moreover, members of a friendship group may tend to imitate the consumption behaviour of other members whom they admire.[6] Friends often wear similar clothing, read the same books, own the same type of car, and even carry the same credit cards. When making difficult personal-purchase decisions, consumers rely more on friends than on other sources of information because friends are approachable and reliable.

Advertising often attempts to simulate primary-group influence. In response to research that showed a growing demand for mid-strength beers in the New South Wales market, Tooheys Limited launched Tooheys Gold Bitter. The 1993 campaign for Tooheys Gold featured the 'music men', a group of rugby-playing mates who sang silly songs in pubs. The ads showed the men sneaking away from their coach to have a night out on the town, when they were supposed to be resting for the big match. Rugby teams, such as the one portrayed in the advertisement, are formally organised groups, but the relationships between the team members are frequent and often intense. Thus, the members of the team form a primary group. Most rugby enthusiasts in the major target market of Tooheys would identify with the idea of the sporting culture, the comradeship of the figures in the advertisement and with the situation portrayed (figure 7.1). Tooheys believed they would also associate those feelings with the consumption of Tooheys Gold, a beer that allows beer drinkers to enjoy the taste and flavour of regular beer without the full strength.

Figure 7.1: A scene from the Tooheys Gold advertisement

Attraction

'Attraction' refers to the degree of desirability that membership in a given group has for the individual. Attraction ranges from positive to negative. Groups that the individual admires and wants to be a member of are said to have positive attraction. Those that the individual wishes to avoid are said to have negative attraction. These groups are also known as 'dissociative groups'. Groups with negative attraction can influence consumer behaviour just as much as groups with positive attraction, because consumers will avoid products that may cause them to resemble the negative group. For example, a conservative National Party politician would avoid wearing clothing that would make him or her appear similar to a member of a Green party.

Sometimes an individual will agree with only some of the values and norms of a group. Such groups are known as 'disclaimant groups'. Membership in a disclaimant group is likely to be nominal rather than committed. The individual may join the group to gain access to certain rights and benefits, without having entirely positive attitudes towards all aspects of the group. For example, major airlines have travellers' clubs that offer members personalised services and travel advantages, such as free drinks in the club lounge and priority baggage handling. Individuals may join the travellers' club for the benefits but may not favour the airline's overall policies or agree with their practices.

'Aspiration groups' are those that the consumer would like to join (an identified member). These groups have a positive attraction for a person. As such they exert an influence on consumer behaviour. Consumers may purchase products and services that are used by the aspiration group in order to gain, symbolically, a degree of membership. An aspiration group is 'anticipatory' if actual membership is likely to occur in the future. A good example of an anticipatory aspiration group is the upper management in the company that employs an individual. The upwardly mobile employee may observe the behaviour of upper management, imitate their dress and manners, and read the same magazines and newspapers. These activities allow the employee to practise upper management behaviour and become, symbolically, more closely related to upper management.

Individuals have many aspiration groups throughout life. An example of the use of aspiration group figures appears in figure 7.2.

"It's ours."

"Now we can save years and thousands with a National Tailored Home Loan."

If you think Cathy and Cameron look happy in their new home, you're right.

'It certainly hasn't been as difficult as I would have thought. They tailored the loan to suit our lifestyle . . . I think the National has got the competitive edge by way of service,' said Cameron.

If you think it's time you asked the National how much a National Tailored Home Loan could do for you, just call into your local branch of the National or phone **008 630 600.**

©National Australia Bank Limited 1994. 330004

National
Australia Bank

Tailoring banking to your needs.

Figure 7.2: A young couple aspiring to own a home would identify with the couple in this advertisement.

ORIGINALS

Kirstie Marshall – World Champion Freestyle Skier wears Originals 496.

Figure 7.3: This Bollé advertisement appeals to those consumers who aspire to be like Kirstie Marshall.

The advertisement, targeted at couples buying their first home, shows a young couple who has been able to purchase a home with a National Australia Bank loan, tailored to meet their lifestyle. Couples who also anticipate being in the position of owning their own home are likely to identify with the young couple in the advertisement.

In contrast, 'symbolic aspiration groups' with positive attraction are groups whose values, attitudes and behaviour are accepted by a consumer, despite the small likelihood of attaining membership. Celebrities who endorse products belong to this particular category. An example appears in figure 7.3. Melbourne's Bill Bass Optical is the distributor for Bollé brand sunglasses in Australia, New Zealand and most of Asia.[7] In order to stem the recession-based slump at the top-end of the sunglasses market, they have employed sports stars in fashion layouts. The consumer is encouraged to become more like these famous athletes by wearing Bollé sunglasses. (See also the discussion on pages 228–29.)

Organisation

'Organisation' refers to the degree of formal structure of the group. A formal group is one in which the structure of the group and its functions are specified and members in the group have designated roles and authority levels. Examples of formal groups are a labour union, a business organisation and a religious organisation. Formal groups are very different from informal groups in that the buyer behaviour of formal groups is explicitly defined. In formal groups there are usually written specifications for products, specific purchase procedures to follow and purchase departments to do the buying.

Informal groups, on the other hand, are loosely organised and lack specified, written rules and roles. When friends shop together, they form an informal group. Other examples of informal groups include neighbours, work associates and sports groups. Despite lack of organisation, however, informal groups are often more influential than formal ones in consumer purchase decisions. In order to understand the influence of informal groups on purchase behaviour, consider the last time you made an important purchase. You may have sought information from various marketing channels such as advertisements, salespeople and point-of-purchase displays. Nevertheless, it is likely that you also turned to group members for advice and information and that you considered carefully the advice these individuals provided.

THE NATURE OF GROUPS

Groups have several characteristics which have an impact on consumers. Members of the group act according to norms, take on roles, have status, and learn appropriate behaviour through socialisation processes.[8] In addition, groups exert power and influence over their members.

Norms

Norms are rules and standards of conduct established by groups. Each group has its own norms, which relate to all aspects of group functioning, including personal appearance and behaviour. For example, a young manager may believe he should wear a Ralph Lauren shirt and an expensive but conservative tie in order to fulfil the requirements of his position. These dress norms would be quite different from those of a group of teenagers who favour plaid flannel shirts and baggy pants. Violations of norms within a group can result in sanctions or punishments that may include exclusion from the group. A teenager who shows up at a party dressed in a business suit is in for some teasing; a manager who comes to work dressed like the teenager may be reprimanded.

Roles

Roles are patterns of behaviour that are expected of individuals because of their position in a given situation. Individuals typically take on a number of roles in their lives. For any single role there will be a range of behaviours, or 'role parameters', that will be acceptable. This range will vary depending on the role and the group within which it is performed. More formal groups tend to have narrower role parameters so that individuals have less flexibility in their role performance. In order to function appropriately in a group, the members must learn the roles that they are expected to enact. These roles may change as the group changes or the individual changes.

When individuals take on too many roles or role demands are not compatible, 'role overload' and 'role conflict' occur.[9] For example, working mothers often experience both conditions because the roles of mother and worker are often demanding and in conflict with one another. The notion of role acquisition and transition is important to marketers because it presents opportunities for positioning products and brands. Marketers of pre-prepared foods, microwaves, and other convenience items have used the concept of role conflict and overload to position their products for busy women.

When people make group purchases, they also take on roles. In group purchasing behaviour, the following roles can be identified.

- The influencer is the consumer who makes initial suggestions about the best available product or brand to be purchased.
- The gatekeeper is the consumer who has the most control over the flow of information into the group.
- The decision maker is the consumer who makes the final decision.
- The purchasing agent is the organisation or individual who purchases the product or brand.
- The consumer is the one who uses the product or brand.

Typically, individuals within a group assume different roles in different purchase situations.[10] For example, in family decision making, children may make the decision about the choice of an item of personal clothing for themselves, but will assume an influencer role in the choice of pet. Teenagers may influence the purchase of a family car, but the decision makers are likely to be the parents.

Products are frequently used as adjuncts to role play. A 'role-related product cluster' is a set of products that is considered necessary to fulfil the requirements of a role.[11] Products may be functionally necessary for role play (for example, the tennis player's racquet and shoes) or symbolically necessary. An example of a symbolically necessary product might be a four-wheel drive vehicle owned by a suburban business manager. Originally, the four-wheel drive was intended to allow the car to operate off the road in rough terrain but many suburban owners of such vehicles never leave the city. Thus, the car has no functional value as a rough-terrain vehicle but it symbolises a connection with the rural past. People who feel nostalgic about the past or adhere to certain traditional values may buy the car for its symbolic value.

Status

Status refers to the position of the consumer within the group. High status implies greater power and authority.[12] In a formal organisation, those at the highest level of management generally have the highest status within the organisation. They also occupy the largest office, drive the best company car and have the largest expense account. Informal reference groups also have status hierarchies in that leaders have more influence than other members. High-status people tend to be more assertive, active, and provide more information to other group members than those with less status. The kinds of products and services an individual acquires are often related to that person's position in the status hierarchy. For example, elegant dress and expensive cars are symbols of wealth and may be purchased in order to show group membership.

Socialisation

The process by which a consumer learns the group's norms and role expectations is called socialisation. Consumer socialisation is the process by which a consumer acquires the necessary knowledge and skills needed to adapt successfully to the marketplace. Examples of socialisation abound because most human behaviour is affected by socialisation. Children learn appropriate market-related behaviour from parents, peers and market sources as they grow up.[13] Similarly, immigrants to Australia and New Zealand learn different consumer behaviour as part of adapting to the culture of their new countries. In order to function in Australasian society, they must learn to use different forms of retailing, become aware of pricing structures, learn about new products and brands, and discover new media-related sources of information.

Power and influence

Social power refers to the capacity to change the actions of others. The influence of a group depends very much on the group's social power and on the nature of the group. A typology of consumer influence appears in table 7.2.

Table 7.2: Typology of group influence

Type of influence	Consumer objectives	Perceived source characteristics	Type of power	Behaviour
Informational	Knowledge	Credibility Believability Trustworthiness	Expert	Acceptance
Comparative	Confirmation Enrichment	Similarity Attractiveness	Referent	Identification
Normative	Reward	Power Ability	Coercive	Conformity

(*Source*: Adapted from Robert E. Burnkrant and Alain Cousineau, 'Informational and Normative Social Influence in Buyer Behaviour', *Journal of Consumer Research*, 2 Dec. 1975, p. 207. A similar adaptation appears in Henry Assael, *Consumer Behaviour and Marketing Action*, p. 409.)

Groups do not always influence members in the same way. Deutsch and Gerard classified group influence into three categories: informational, comparative and normative.[14] 'Informational influence' occurs when an individual accepts opinions or uses the behaviour of others as evidence of reality. People who have informational influence exert 'expert power'. To have expert power, an individual must have experience, knowledge and skills in the relevant product area. For example, a friend's recommendation to purchase certain shares may be accepted if the friend is knowledgeable about the stock market. The same friend may not have equal influence in the purchase of another item about which he or she has less information.

'Normative influence', sometimes referred to as 'utilitarian influence', occurs when an individual conforms to group norms in order to gain rewards or escape sanctions. Normative influence is based on 'reward power', which is the ability of the group to provide rewards or punishments. For example, business organisations have the power to reward employees with promotions and salary increases. Peer groups can punish group members who violate clothing or behaviour norms with verbal taunting or shunning. The power of the group to give and withhold rewards is sometimes called 'coercive power'.

'Comparative influence', also known as 'identification influence' or 'value expressive influence', operates by comparing the consumer's beliefs, attitudes and behaviour to those of the group. Referents serve as a basis for the evaluation of the consumer's image. Thus, the basis of comparative influence is 'referent power'. Referent power depends on the consumer's identification with members of the group. The greater the similarity between the individual's beliefs and attitudes and those of group members, the greater the degree of referent power asserted by the group. Referent power is particularly important to the development of marketing strategy, as consumers voluntarily change their behaviour to identify with their referents. For example, the 'You oughta be congratulated' commercials for Meadow Lea margarine offered a referent in the Meadow Lea mother.[15] The Meadow Lea mother figure is young, perky but never glamorous, always heroic, and has a happy, healthy family. Although frequently criticised, the long-running campaign has continued to sell margarine for its sponsors, partly because mothers identify with the character of the Meadow Lea mother.

FACTORS AFFECTING GROUP INFLUENCE

The earlier section described three types of influence that groups exert on consumers. Now we focus on some of the factors that affect group influence. These factors are product knowledge and experience, reference-group characteristics, and commitment to group norms.

The use of group members as reference points depends largely on how much product knowledge and experience a consumer has. A consumer who feels confident of his or her knowledge about a product will be less likely to consult or be influenced by reference-group opinions than an inexperienced consumer. For example, research indicates that young and first-time buyers of new cars search for information from personal sources; but experienced new-car buyers are likely to rely on their previous knowledge and skills.[16] Furthermore, the influence of group members tends to be higher for new products when consumers are considering the adoption of a market innovation and their product knowledge is minimal.

Two important characteristics that affect the power of a referent are the credibility and attractiveness of group members when giving advice on a particular product or brand. Credibility of group members is related to knowledge, trustworthiness, and believability. Group members are likely to possess these characteristics for some product categories but not others. Similarly, celebrities may be good spokespersons for some products and utter failures for others because they lack credibility. Weight Watchers, a division of Heinz Australia, knew this when, in 1991, they hired Lynn Redgrave to promote Weight Watchers products.[17] Consumers know that Lynn Redgrave has not always been slender and, as an actor, must watch her weight. Therefore, she has credibility based on presumed knowledge of weight gain and on success at combating it.

A third factor is the degree to which the individual is committed to group norms. The more strongly the individual identifies with the group, the more he or she will accept the norms and values of the group. Under such conditions, the group member would find any deviation from group norms and values to be threatening. Therefore, the opinions of group members are likely to be more important. For example, a young person who is deeply submerged in heavy metal subculture is likely to be more influenced by changes in the symbols of group membership than a person whose membership is tangential.

DETERMINANTS OF GROUP CONFORMITY

Groups exert strong pressure to conform. In an experiment conducted by Asch,[18] eight subjects (one naive subject and seven confederates of the experimenter) were told they were participating in an experiment on perception. They were asked to judge which of three unequal lines was closest in length to a fourth, 'standard' line. The judgement order was arranged so that the naive respondent reported last, after the confederates. The confederates, who knew the true purpose of the experiment, unanimously chose the wrong line. In the group of 50 naive subjects, 37 conformed to the judgement of the group, making a total of 194 errors. In contrast, a control group that was not subjected to group influence produced only 3 errors. The Asch experiment shows that even strangers can cause people to alter their behaviour and even their perceptions of reality. Other conditions, such as being with reference-group members, having an ill-defined task, or having high needs for affiliation, can increase this effect.

A second set of experiments by Milgram illustrates the effect that authority figures have on compliance and obedience.[19] Milgram designed a series of experiments in which subjects were told to administer an electric shock to another person, called the 'learner', when that individual failed to answer questions correctly. The 'shock' was non-existent, but the subject was not told this. After each incorrect answer the subject was directed to increase the level of the shock. None of the subjects delivering the shock knew that the 'learner' was not really present and that the answers and pleas to stop that they heard were pre-recorded. Milgram found that people would continue to administer shocks at increasingly high levels if they were instructed to do so by a person in authority, in this case an experimenter in a white lab coat. Although the 'teachers' delivering the shock protested to the experimenter and said they wanted to stop, an astonishing 65 per cent of subjects delivered the bogus shock up to a maximum, dangerous level.

The Asch experiment explains the successfulness of group selling situations. Tupperware and other firms that use 'party' sales formats are relying on group influence to increase their sales. Tupperware products are used in the home, are rarely seen by others, and are low-risk, relatively necessary products. Therefore, they are not products for which there would normally be a high level of group influence. However, when the sale takes place in the party atmosphere, the product becomes a visible focus of attention. The purchases made by others in the group put pressure on non-purchasing group members to conform. In addition, the salesperson acts as an authority when explaining the benefits of the product to the potential customers and asking for orders.

DETERMINANTS OF GROUP INFLUENCE ON PRODUCT AND BRAND CHOICE

The amount of influence a reference group can exert varies across products and brands. Several studies have found that variation in influence is related to two dimensions: firstly, a visibility or public/private dimension; and secondly, an exclusivity or luxury/necessity dimension. A product is exclusive if it connotes luxury and is consumed by only a few people. A product is visible if others can observe its consumption.

In the late 1940s, Bourne classified products according to visibility and exclusiveness.[20] He hypothesised that group influence would be greatest for products that were exclusive, because owning the product makes a statement about the owner. He also believed that group influence on brand choice would be great for products that are visible, because the fact of ownership is apparent for a visible product. Bearden and Etzel updated and confirmed Bourne's typology in a 1983 study.[21] They found that groups could have an influence on both product category or class and brand, on the product alone, or on the brand alone. Products classified according to this typology appear in table 7.3.

Table 7.3: Dimensions of group influence on product and brand choice

	Necessity	Luxury
Public	Influence on product: weak Influence on brand: strong Examples: wristwatches, cars, suits, laser disc players	Influence on product: strong Influence on brand: strong Examples: sailboats, golf clubs, snow skis, compact discs
Private	Influence on product: weak Influence on brand: weak Examples: mattress, refrigerator, television	Influence on product: strong Influence on brand: weak Examples: trash compactor, ice maker

(*Source*: Adapted from William O. Bearden and Michael J. Etzel, 'Reference Group Influence on Product and Brand Purchase Decisions', *Journal of Consumer Research*, 9, Sept. 1982, p. 185)

Groups have an influence on both product and brand if the product is both visible and a luxury (exclusive). Examples of products in this category are golf clubs, skis, yachts, cars and some fashion items. It is critical that the item be distinctive. Once the item gains general acceptance, i.e. becomes less expensive, the group is unlikely to influence the product category although they may still influence the brand choice.

Groups have an influence on the purchase of brands when the product is visible but not exclusive. The strongest influence on the purchase of brands is when the item is a luxury item, fashion items being a good example. Hats, boots and other clothing items are not exclusive, but certain brands are. R. M. Williams boots, Akubra hats and Country

Road clothing are highly visible products that make a statement about the owner. Figure 7.4 shows an advertisement for Country Road which features new fashions for autumn. Country Road products are recognised as quality goods in Australia and are highly visible. Therefore, they are likely to be purchased with the opinion of the reference group in mind.

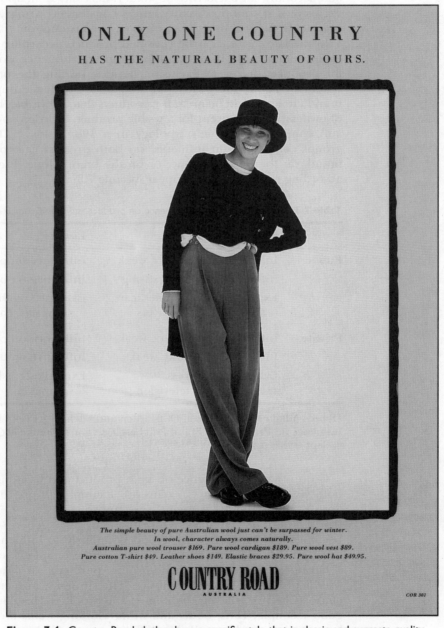

ONLY ONE COUNTRY

HAS THE NATURAL BEAUTY OF OURS.

The simple beauty of pure Australian wool just can't be surpassed for winter.
In wool, character always comes naturally.
Australian pure wool trouser $169. Pure wool cardigan $189. Pure wool vest $89.
Pure cotton T-shirt $49. Leather shoes $149. Elastic braces $29.95. Pure wool hat $49.95.

C OUNTRY ROAD
AUSTRALIA

COR 381

Figure 7.4: Country Road clothes have a specific style that is classic and suggests quality.

When products are exclusive enough to represent specific group norms even though they are not visible, product choice alone is influenced by the reference group. A home-maker may purchase certain household equipment, such as an expensive coffee-maker in order to be similar to a certain group. The actual brand may be less important, as long as it is a respected one.

When a product is neither visible nor exclusive, groups tend to have very little influence on its purchase. Items falling in this category are frequently low-cost consumables. Examples of products on which there exists little group influence are dog food, junk food and items for personal consumption such as pencils and notepads.

MARKETING STRATEGIES BASED ON GROUP INFLUENCE

Knowledge of group influence is used by marketers in the areas of segmentation, advertising strategy, and personal sales strategies. Some examples of the use of group principles are presented below.

SEGMENTATION AND SOCIAL GROUPS

Groups often serve as the basis of segmentation. Marketers try to identify target groups within their target markets because they know that these groups exert a strong influence. Furthermore, members of a group are likely to be quite similar with respect to benefits sought, media habits and activity participation, and thus form a segment for a product or service.

Role transitions often involve moving from one group to another. Thus, they provide marketers with opportunities to demonstrate how their product will facilitate the role change. For example, when a university student completes a degree course and enters the workplace, the change in status will be accompanied by a change in groups and a change in needs. In the United States, Brooks Brothers and other marketers of clothing for the working person attempt to reduce the insecurity of the individual entering a new role by suggesting that their product is purchased by many successful members of the new referent group.

ADVERTISING STRATEGY

Advertisers consistently portray group images in advertising. In doing so, they try to manipulate all three forms of social influence. Advertising that shows knowledgeable, credible spokespersons for the product attempt to exert informational influence on the receiver of the advertising message. For example, advertisements for pharmaceutical products frequently contain endorsements by 'medical' personnel. Because these spokespersons are portrayed as experts, the risks of purchase are assumed to be substantially reduced for the purchaser. In recent years, Kellogg's Australia, the Australian Dairy Association and the Milk Marketing Board have launched advertising campaigns to promote the nutritional value of their products to doctors. They provide information about products and brands just as the pharmaceutical industry provides information about drugs to doctors. Doctors are particularly credible sources when they convey drug-related information to patients.[22]

The use of celebrities to extol the virtues of a product is an attempt to evoke comparative influence. 'Fantasy' advertising, which weaves a fantasy around the product or its use, is also designed to exert comparative influence. An example of such advertising is Coca-Cola's recent advertising that features a dreadlocked teenager with a skateboard shooting rapidly from frame to frame, dropping in and out of fantastic adventures. The advertisement creates a sense of excitement that will be associated with Coke.

'Slice-of-life' and 'lifestyle' advertising attempts to evoke normative influence. The former type of advertising shows people using the product in a normal setting, one that might be similar to the consumer's own home. Lifestyle advertising tries to relate the product to the consumer's lifestyle and how the product would help the consumer play particular roles. Often images of the 'common person' are used to encourage the consumer to conjure up similar referents from his or her past. A recent television commercial for Weiss bars uses two traditional Australian blokes to extol the goodness of Weiss bars. In another advertisement for Telecom, a boy asks his mother to pick him up as he has lost his money wrestling on the oval and suffered other tragedies. These images do not remind us of glamorous celebrities, but rather of people we know well and to whom we can relate.

SELLING STRATEGIES

Both primary group and secondary group influence can be used to facilitate sales. Groups provide an excellent climate for the acceptance of certain products and services which are approved by group members.

Many companies have utilised primary groups as a component of selling. Tupperware and Avon were among the first companies to adopt this approach. Avon has traditionally assigned women to a specified number of homes in their neighbourhood as an exclusive sales territory. The representatives are knowledgeable about cosmetics and fashion, and thus act as opinion leaders for their customers. In response to the increased numbers of women in the workforce, Avon women are now also selling their products in offices and factories. One reason for Avon's success may be found in research conducted by Avon on their representatives, which shows that their opinions and attitudes are very similar to those of customers, a condition that facilitates group influence.

When consumers shop together, their shopping patterns deviate from those when they shop alone.[23] In group shopping, consumers tend to make more unplanned purchases, as a result of both normative and informational influence. The normative influence is in force when consumers purchase something to gain the approval of other group members. For example, when the majority of one's friends decide to have lunch at a particular restaurant, there is strong pressure for all members of the group to comply with the group decision. Consumers will often change their shopping patterns simply because they are exposed to more products and stores through information from other group members. This reflects the informational influence on shopping patterns. For these reasons, retailers would be advised to develop strategies to encourage more group-shopping activities by providing incentives for group purchase.

When firms use group formats to sell products they recognise that several forces encourage purchase behaviour. Being a member of a group implies certain role responsibilities. For example, if consumers accept an invitation to a Tupperware party, the acceptance implies that they will be willing to purchase Tupperware products. 'Cognitive dissonance' also produces pressure to purchase in such group situations. A person may agree to attend the party, sometimes reluctantly, under pressure from a neighbour, and a degree of psychological unrest or dissonance is likely. To reduce dissonance, individuals can either refuse to participate or change their attitude towards the purchase situation. People are unlikely to create conflict in a group situation, so there is a tendency for them to view the situation as positive and engage in purchasing. A third group influence is based on 'modelling'. Seeing others positively evaluating the product and placing orders 'teaches' the individual to purchase the product also.

OPINION LEADERSHIP

Opinion leaders are people whose product-specific opinions are sought by less knowledgeable consumers, often at community or neighbourhood levels. They are very influential people in terms of the pace and direction that product opinions are disseminated. Examples of opinion leaders are merchants selling sports shoes, salespeople in a retail store selling cosmetics and perfumes, computer consultants, doctors, pharmacists, fashion designers and research consultants of marketing research houses. Where their opinions are valued because of trained expertise, such as doctors, the term 'gatekeeper' is often used. For example, a doctor prescribes drugs and a computer consultant recommends software programs.

Community opinion leaders are consumers with specific characteristics.[24] They are better informed about particular product categories and are consequently more fashion conscious, more prone to new ideas and innovations and more socially active. Chan and Misra, in a recent investigation of opinion leadership, found that risk preference, open-mindedness and mass media exposure all correlated with opinion leadership. However, the strongest predictor of opinion leadership was a personality trait known as 'public individuation'. People who are high in public individuation feel differentiated from other people and able to act differently from them. In other words, opinion leaders tend to be independent in thought and action.

Many studies show that the most important characteristic of opinion leaders is 'enduring involvement' with a product category. Because opinion leaders seek information about the product and become extremely knowledgeable, opinion leadership tends to be product specific. However, there are individuals who have knowledge about many product and market conditions. These opinion leader generalists are known as 'market mavens'.[25] Market mavens initiate discussions about products and provide information to less knowledgeable consumers. Market mavens do not have specific demographic characteristics but they are extensive users of all forms of mass media, including television and radio.

Opinion leaders are particularly useful for marketers who are launching new products or services, because they create awareness of the product. However, getting a list of opinion leaders for marketing purposes is not easy as there are few demographic factors reliably related to opinion leadership. Obtaining mailing lists of product information users and of people who request free samples of new products is one way of identifying opinion leaders.

Celebrities, movie stars, sport players, musicians, racing-car drivers and the like act as public opinion leaders. They differ from community opinion leaders in that we don't directly have any contact or formal relationship with them. As we tend to emulate their behaviour, opinions and attitudes, they strongly influence how we think, what we buy, watch, use, eat, drink, listen to and indulge in. The effect of such celebrity endorsements can be dramatic. The appearance of Mark Jackson in the Energizer batteries advertisements helped to lift consumer awareness of this brand five-fold.

Hiring celebrities can be expensive and dangerous if they do not succeed in creating a positive brand image, so companies sometimes try to create their own celebrities. The well-known Mrs Marsh was one such 'made-up' personality. Mrs Marsh first appeared in her familiar trench-coat, carrying a tube of Colgate Fluoriguard toothpaste in 1976. In 20 different commercials over a 13-year run, Mrs Marsh burned the name of Colgate Fluoriguard into the minds of Australian families by lecturing young children on tooth decay. People either loved or hated Mrs Marsh, but she raised sales of Colgate Fluoriguard from 27 to 40 per cent of market share.[26]

There has been substantial investigation of exactly how opinion leaders have their effect. Lazarsfeld and colleagues have proposed that information about new products and ideas comes to opinion leaders through the media.[27] Opinion leaders are particularly alert to media information about products in their interest area and they pass that information on to others through word-of-mouth. This process has come to be known as a two-step flow. Other investigations of the process of opinion leadership have shown that it is much more complicated than originally thought. The media influences both the opinion leader and the follower, and it may cause a follower to seek information from more influential and knowledgeable members of his or her reference group. This information seeking may trigger information seeking on the part of the opinion leader. Thus, opinion leaders both give information to and obtain information from other group members.

GROUP INFLUENCE AND THE DIFFUSION OF PRODUCTS

The acceptance of innovation is primarily a group process in which opinion leadership plays a large role. An innovation is any idea, practice or product that is perceived to be new by a target market. However, innovations vary in the degree of newness and in the amount of behavioural change required of the user: some innovations require the user to learn entirely new behaviour and to radically alter attitudes and beliefs; other innovations require only small changes on the part of the user.

New products can be classified according to how innovative they are.[28] 'Continuous innovations' require relatively minor changes in behaviour. For example, light beer is different from regular beer as it contains less alcohol. However, consuming it requires little behavioural change. 'Dynamically continuous innovations' require a major change in user behaviour but only in a way that is unimportant to the consumer. The development of the compact-disc player, for example, involved substantial technological innovation, and buyers have had to alter their entire music systems to incorporate compact discs. However, the process of using the disc is relatively similar to pre-existing technology. 'Discontinuous innovations', on the other hand, require the user to make a major change in behaviour. When computers first appeared on the market, for example, they represented an entirely new technology that required consumers to learn quite different behaviour.

Most new product introductions involve little change in consumer behaviour. However, truly new products are characterised by an 'adoption process', with distinct stages of diffusion during which the acceptance of the product spreads through the marketplace. According to Rogers, this process is embedded in time, and different groups of consumers accept the product at different times in its life cycle.[29] Research has identified five groups of consumers that differ in their acceptance of new products (see figure 7.5).[30]

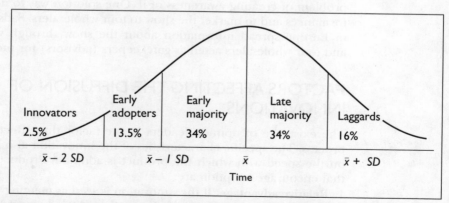

Figure 7.5: Consumer groups and the adoption process (*Source:* Everett M. Rogers, *Diffusion of Innovations*, Free Press, New York, 1983)

'Adopter categories' are based on the relative time it takes a consumer to adopt a product. The 'innovator' group comprises the first 2.5 per cent to adopt an innovation. Innovators tend to be venturesome risk-takers who may be product enthusiasts. Innovators tend to look to other innovators within a product category for reference-group information. People in this adopter category are likely to be younger, better educated, more socially mobile, and more media aware than other groups.

'Early adopters' comprise the next 13.5 per cent of the market. Early adopters are also successful, well educated, and younger. They use commercial media, professional sources, sales personnel, and peer group communications to learn about products. Early adopters are important to marketers because they are often opinion leaders for their peer groups. The 'early majority' are the next 34 per cent of the market to adopt the product. They are somewhat more cautious than the first two adopter groups and tend to wait until the product is well-established and prices have begun to drop. Adopters in this category are relatively social but rely upon information from friends, neighbours, and colleagues for product information. Demographically, they tend to be older, less educated, and less socially mobile.

The last adopter groups are the 'late majority' (34 per cent of the market) and the 'laggards' (16 per cent of the market). The late majority tend to be hesitant and sceptical about adopting new products. The choice to adopt is likely to be influenced more by social pressure than by media information. Laggards are also reluctant purchasers who are focused on the past. They may accept a product change only after their usual product has become unavailable. Both groups tend to be older and have less social status than other adopter categories.

Opinion leadership is most important in the early stages of the diffusion process. An example of opinion leaders being used to launch a product is the Tjapukai Aboriginal Dance Theatre.[31] The innovative dance theatre was created in the late 1980s in the tourist village of Kuranda in Queensland by Judy and Don Freeman. At the time of the launch, the population of Kuranda was 3000, tourism numbers were declining, and Australians showed little interest in shows featuring Aborigines. The Freemans were uncompromising about the quality of the show, but they still had the problem of creating awareness of it. One solution was to do overseas performances and to market the show to tour wholesalers. Satisfied customers in Europe spread information about the show through word-of-mouth, and tour wholesalers acted as gatekeepers (advisors) for their clients.

FACTORS AFFECTING THE DIFFUSION OF INNOVATIONS

The existence of opinion leaders is one factor that affects the diffusion process. The specific characteristics of the innovation also have an impact on the speed with which the product is adopted. Product characteristics that encourage adoption are:

1. **Relative advantage.** If the innovation is seen as meeting the consumer's needs better than existing alternatives, diffusion will be more rapid. This implies that the consumer must have felt a need for the product.

For example, the Newton MessagePad by Apple assists business people by providing a compact and portable system for recording daily schedules and sending faxes. The system has a distinct advantage over keeping schedule books and finding fax machines for sending important messages.

Figure 7.6: If the consumer perceives the Newton MessagePad to have relative advantage over other systems, diffusion will be more rapid.

2. **Comparability.** The more the innovation is consistent with the consumer's values, beliefs, and ways of acting, the more rapidly diffusion will occur. For example, sports drinks have become popular in Australia and New Zealand, and a large number of firms have been competing for market share in this area.[32] Sports drinks offer some advantages to active people and they do not require consumers to markedly change their usual behaviour. Therefore, their acceptance has been rapid, relative to more complicated and technical products.

3. **Simplicity.** The less complex the innovation, the more likely it is to be easily accepted. Conversely, the more difficult it is for the consumer to understand and use the innovation, the slower the diffusion process will be. For example, the computer is quite a complex innovation and its diffusion into the home market was relatively slow.[33]

4. **Observability.** The more that consumers are able to observe the positive effects of using the innovation, the more likely they are to adopt it. More visible innovations diffuse more rapidly than less visible ones.

5. **Trialability.** A new product is likely to be adopted more quickly if it is easy for the consumer to try the product without social or financial cost. Products that can be borrowed or that can be purchased in small amounts are likely to be more adoptable than products that must be purchased in total at one time.

6. **Perceived risk.** Products can have financial, physical, and social reasons risks for the consumer. There is risk in whether the product will perform as expected, in the consequences of the product's performance, and in the ability to reverse negative consequences. Risk may depend as much on the characteristics of the buyer as on the product itself. For example, a low-cost snack food product can be perceived as risky for consumers with certain health problems.

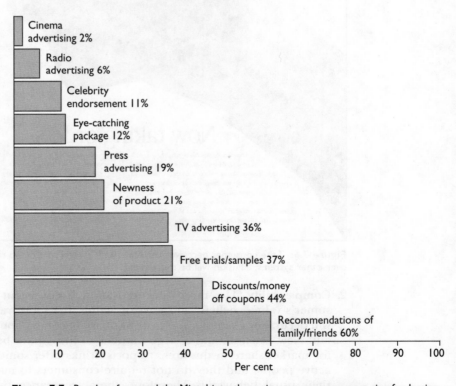

Figure 7.7: Results of research by Mintel into the major reason consumers give for buying new products or brands (*Source:* Adapted from *Marketing Globe,* Vol. 3, No. 7, 1993)

Other personal and marketing factors affecting the speed of diffusion of an innovative product include the target market, the type of decision that is involved, and the degree of marketing effort expended. Some groups are more accepting of new products than others. Products intended for elderly groups, for example, tend to diffuse more slowly than those intended for younger people. Similarly, diffusion is slower for products that demand collective decision making rather than individual decision making. In general, the more people that must agree on the decision, the more difficult the decision is to make. In addition, the amount and kind of marketing of the product is an important factor in building product awareness and gaining product acceptance. The research by Mintel (figure 7.7) shows that recommendation by family members and friends is important. It is therefore essential that consumers have positive experiences with the new product so that a positive recommendation will be made.

SUMMARY

A group consists of two or more individuals who have implicitly or explicitly defined relationships with one another. Groups can be classified on the basis of membership, amount of contact, organisation and attraction. Membership groups with frequent interpersonal contact exert the strongest influence and are known as primary groups. Those with less frequent contact are secondary groups. Groups may have a formal or an informal organisation. Attraction to the group ranges from positive to negative. Non-membership groups with positive attraction are known as aspirational groups.

All groups have norms, roles for members, and a status hierarchy. Norms are rules and standards of conduct. Roles are patterns of behaviour that have role parameters. A role-related cluster is a set of products that is needed by a group member in order to fulfil a role. Status refers to the position a person occupies in a group. The process of learning the group's norms and expectations is called consumer socialisation.

Groups exert power and influence. Informational influence is based on expert power. Normative influence is based on the power of the group to give rewards. Comparative influence occurs when the reference group serves as a basis for evaluating the consumer's self-image. The influence of the group varies with the knowledge and self-confidence of the consumer, the credibility and attractiveness of referents, and the solidarity of the group. The fact that groups exert pressure to conform can be used by marketers in sales situations. Group influence differs for products and brands. Two critical dimensions for determining group influence are the public/private dimension and the luxury/necessity dimension. Marketing strategies based on group influence include market segmentation, advertising strategies, and sales strategies.

Opinion leaders are people whose product-specific opinions are sought by less knowledgeable consumers. Opinion leaders tend to be more alert to mass media than other consumers, provide product information and are socially active. Except in the case of the market maven, opinion leadership is product specific. Celebrities are often used as public opinion leaders.

Diffusion is the process of adoption of innovations. Innovations can be classified as continuous, dynamically continuous, and discontinuous. Groups of individuals who adopt products at different times are innovators, early adopters, early majority, late majority and laggards. Product characteristics of relative advantage, simplicity, compatibility, trialability, and perceived risk affect the rate of adoption. Adoption is also influenced by the characteristics of the target market, by whether the decision is individual or collective, and by the degree of marketing effort. Opinion leaders are important in increasing the rate of adoption of new products.

Questions

1. What is a reference group? What kinds of features do reference groups have?

2. Differentiate between primary and secondary groups. Give examples of each.

3. Explain the concept of attraction. What is the attraction of dissociative and disclaimant membership groups? Can marketers use them successfully?

4. Describe the different forms of group influence. What power basis do each of the forms of influence have?

5. What are three different types of innovation? Identify three products that reflect these types of innovation. Describe the factors that would impede or facilitate adoption of each product.

6. What factors affect group influence? What determines the amount of influence a group can exert on the choice of products and brands?

7. How do celebrities act as opinion leaders? What are some of the problems with using celebrities as opinion leaders?

8. Describe cognitive dissonance and describe the purchase situations that are likely to lead to dissonance.

9. Explain the difference between formal and informal groups and discuss how each may impact on consumers' product class and brand choice.

10. Select three advertisements (print or television) that use group influence on purchase choice. What type of influence is being used? Explain why you think the advertisements do or do not work.

Case study questions

Read the article on pages 193–94, then answer the following questions.

1. A major factor in the success of Tupperware in the 1960s and 1970s was the group pressure to buy, exerted on people during Tupperware parties. Discuss what type of social influences would have been involved.

2. The move towards demonstration rather than group interaction creates different influences on the customer. What are they? Are they as effective?

3. **Project**: Trace the performance of Tupperware and other products that have changed from party to live demonstrations.
   (a) Determine their performance.
   (b) Determine whether or not the move from party to demonstration was a factor in their success/failure.

Case study

Tupperware Australia has a problem. The average age of its customers and the people who sell its products is falling. For most manufacturers, attracting younger buyers would be a boon. But for Tupperware, it means older customers are not coming to Tupperware parties. Worse, they are slipping into the category marketers fear most: lapsed customers.

Tupperware's sales growth is directly tied to the number of new direct sellers, or "demonstrators", it attracts each year. Last year, the number of Tupperware sellers grew 12% to 6000 and the company's retail sales jumped 15% to $80 million. The average sale from an in-home or in-office demonstration of Tupperware's plastic kitchenware and toys is $350. An average of seven or eight customers attend each party. No matter how many parties are staged each year, the number of people and sales at a Tupperware demonstration is constant.

Tupperware Australia wants to encourage increased spending by its existing customers and the return of lapsed Tupperware buyers. To achieve these aims, the company has launched the biggest marketing push since it arrived in Australia 30 years ago. New Tupperware products are being launched; a new magazine advertising campaign started in April; a tele-marketing bureau has been set up to process direct orders from customers; and in August, the company will launch its first television advertising.

Boosting Tupperware sales is a tall order. The company's products are found in 91% of Australia's homes: most possess four or five pieces of Tupperware. Ninety-seven per cent of Australians are aware of the Tupperware brand and annual per capita sales are higher in Australia than in any other country. Last year, 1.76 million adult Australian women attended Tupperware demonstrations.

Persuading existing customers to buy more products is Tupperware Australia's top priority. The average amount spent at a Tupperware party is $45. Ron Rawiller, managing director of Tupperware Australia, believes the addition of new products will encourage people to spend more.

"We see a big opportunity to increase our volume through new products, rather than by increasing our distribution," Rawiller says. In March, the company launched a new range of plastic storage containers for use in freezers. Another three new products will appear this year, designed by Tupperware's US parent company and made at its factory in the Melbourne suburb of Ferntree Gully.

Tupperware Australia sells 150 different products, 92% of which are kitchenware lines (for preparation, storage and serving) and 8% toys. All the products carry Tupperware's lifetime guarantee, which Rawiller says is one of the brand's key selling points. Toys are the company's fastest-growing product line, with some demonstrations staging toy-only parties.

Tupperware toys are imported from the US, while all Tupperware kitchenware is made at the Ferntree Gully factory, which supplies the Australian market and supplies Tupperware companies in Hong Kong, Singapore, Thailand, Malaysia and South Korea. The moulds used to make the kitchenware are produced by Melbourne company Diecraft, which was acquired by Tupperware Australia in the mid-1970s and is now the largest supplier of moulds to Tupperware worldwide. . .

Tupperware Australia sells its products to 30 distributors around the country, most of whom are husband-and-wife teams (the largest distributor turns over $5 million a year). The distributors in turn hire demonstrators, who stage parties, gather orders and collect products from the distributors. Tupperware Australia provides marketing support, staff training and accounting systems.

(continued)

Last year, Tupperware's network of 5600 demonstrators and 400 managers staged 220,000 demonstrations. Most of their customers are women, who attend an average of one to 1.5 Tupperware parties a year.

Direct-selling companies such as Avon and Nutri-Metics International have been hit by flat sales over the past decade, simply because their customer base has shrunk as more women have returned to the workforce. But Tupperware Australia's marketing manager, Brian Mottram, says Tupperware has not experienced the same problem.

"The times and venues of our demonstrations have changed to match women's changing lifestyles," he says. "Tupperware demonstrations are no longer two-hour parties held in people's homes on Saturday afternoons or on week nights. Now they are one-hour, or even 20-minute, demonstrations at somebody's home, office, club, barbecue or whatever. Our selling network is a lot more flexible than it was 20 years ago."

Although Tupperware has moved into new venues such as offices, Rawiller says it will never be sold through traditional outlets. "The product needs to be demonstrated to people because it is more expensive than rival plastic kitchenware products. We need to be able to point out its benefits, versatility, value-for-money and so on," he says. "Also, no ordinary retailer would ever stock all 150 Tupperware products."

The number of people signing on as Tupperware demonstrators grew at a steady 4–5% during the 1980s. Last year, it jumped to 12% . . .

Tupperware demonstrators are becoming younger: most are now aged between 18 and 40. That means they are selling Tupperware to their 18–40-year-old friends and cutting out older consumers. As a result, most women aged over 40 associate Tupperware with the plain, white or opaque storage containers sold in the 1960s and 1970s. "Few older people are aware of the range of new Tupperware products, colours and styles," Mottram says. "Our challenge is to win back those lapsed customers."

Late last year, Tupperware hired Samuelson Talbot & Partners as its new advertising agency (Mottram worked with Samuelson Talbot in his last job as marketing director of the toiletries maker Cussons Australia). An ad campaign started in women's magazines last month. In August, Tupperware will start running two-minute TV commercials in the Nine network's *Midday* program. Mottram says the ad campaign is designed to make consumers aware of the modern Tupperware range and new products.

The ad campaign features a 008 telephone number for consumers to request information and brochures, and place orders. The telephone orders are being channelled back to the demonstrators. "We are not planning to bypass the demonstrators and sell product direct to consumers from our factory," Rawiller says. "Obviously, that would undermine the demonstrator network, which is the backbone of our company."

Last year, Tupperware Australia started staging product displays in shopping centres. The staff working at the displays do not sell Tupperware: they demonstrate the products and take orders, which are sent to demonstrators.

New products will figure prominently in Tupperware's ad campaign. Traditionally Tupperware products melt when used in microwave ovens, but last year Tupperware's US parent launched its first range of kitchenware suitable for microwave ovens. Rawiller says the Australian company will redesign some of the US microwave products before launching them here.

The new ad campaign and products are expected to boost Tupperware Australia's sales by at least 10% this year. Rawiller is not sure how many new demonstrators will join the company's direct sellling network this year. "The 12% growth in demonstrator numbers last year surprised us," he says. "I really don't know how many new demonstrators we will attract this year."

Neil Shoebridge,
Business Review Weekly,
3 May 1991

SUGGESTED READING

M. Walker, D. Burnham and R. Borland, *Psychology*, 2nd edn, John Wiley and Sons, Brisbane, 1994, pp. 460–505.

C. H. Cooley, *Social Organisation*, Schoken, New York, 1990.

T. Shibutani, 'Reference Groups as Perspectives', *American Journal of Sociology*, Vol. 60, May 1955, pp. 562–69.

H. H. Kassarjian and T. Robertson (eds), *Perspectives in Consumer Behaviour*, Scott Foresman, Glenview, Ill., 1981.

R. B. Cialdini, *Influence: Science and Practice*, 2nd edn, William Morrow, New York, 1984.

ENDNOTES

1. 'Sports-mad Nation Sells Its Stars', *B&T*, 18 Feb. 1994, p. 13.

2. David Dressler and Donald Carns, *Sociology: The Study of Human Interaction*, Knopf, New York, 1973, p. 259.

3. This categorisation appears in Henry Assael, *Consumer Behaviour and Marketing Action*, PSW-Kent, Boston, Mass., 1984, p. 404.

4. William O. Bearden and Randal L. Rose, 'Attention to Social Comparison Information: An Individual Difference Factor Affecting Human Conformity', *Journal of Consumer Research*, 15, March 1989, pp. 473–81.

5. Scott Ward and Daniel B. Wackman, 'Children's Purchase Influence Attempts and Parental Yielding', *Journal of Marketing Research*, 9, Aug. 1972, pp. 316–19.

6. Peter H. Reingen et al., 'Brand Congruence in Interpersonal Relations: A Network Analysis', *Journal of Consumer Research*, 11, Dec. 1984, pp. 771–83.

7. Neil Shoebridge, 'Sports Stars Lift Bollés Outlook', *Business Review Weekly*, 4 April 1994, pp. 68–70.

8. This discussion is based upon Henry Assael, *Consumer Behaviour and Marketing Action*.

9. S. Alvin, C. Burns and Ellen Foxman, 'Role Overload and Its Consequences on Individual Consumer Behaviour', in Terence A. Shimp et al., *A.M.A. Educator's Proceedings*, American Marketing Association, Chicago, 1986. S. Onkvist and J. J. Shaw, 'Multiplicity of Roles, Role Conflict Resolution and Marketing Implications', in J. D. Lindquist (ed.), *Developments in Marketing Science VII*, Academy of Marketing Science, 1984, pp. 57–61.

10. Discussed in Assael, *Consumer Behaviour and Marketing Action*, p. 407.

11. This topic is discussed in Del Hawkins, Roger J. Best and Kenneth A. Coney, *Consumer Behaviour: Implications for Marketing Strategy*, Irwin, Boston, Mass., 1992, pp. 140–41.

12. Max Weber, in H. H. Gard and C. Wright Mills, *From Max Weber: Essays in Sociology*, 86, 1981, pp. 766–95.

13. George P. Moschis, 'The Role of Family Communication in Consumer Socialisation of Children and Adolescents', *Journal of Consumer Research*, Vol. 11, March 1985, pp. 898–913.

14. M. Deutsch and H. B. Gerard, 'Study of Normative and Informational Social Influences Upon Individual Judgement', *Journal of Abnormal and Social Psychology*, 51, 1955, pp. 624–36. Robert E. Burnkrant and Alain Cousineau, 'Informational and Normative Influence in Buyer Behaviour', *Journal of Consumer Research*, 2, Dec. 1975, pp. 206–15. John R. French and Bertram Raven, 'The Bases of Social Power', in D. Cartwright (ed.), *Studies in Social Power*, Institute of Social Research, Ann Arbor, Mich., 1959, pp. 150–57.

15. Neil Shoebridge, *Great Australian Advertising Campaigns*, McGraw-Hill, Sydney, 1992, pp. 69–82.

16. Sharon E. Beatty and Scott M. Smith, 'External Search Effort: An Investigation Across Several Product Categories', *Journal of Consumer Research*, 14, June 1987, pp. 83–95.

17. Neil Shoebridge, 'Weight Watchers on the Comeback Trail', *Business Review Weekly*, 8 Nov. 1991, pp. 88–90.

18. S. E. Asch, 'Effects of Group Pressure Upon the Modification and Distortion of Judgements', in Harold Geutzkow (ed.), *Groups, Leadership and Men*, Carnegie Press, Pittsburg, Penn., 1951.

19. S. Milgram, 'Behavioural Study of Obedience', *Journal of Abnormal and Social Psychology*, 67, pp. 371–78. S. Milgram, *Obedience to Authority: An Experimental View*, Harper and Row, New York, 1974.

20. F. S. Bourne, 'Group Influence in Marketing and Public Relations', in Rensis Likert and Samuel P. Hayes, Jr (eds), *Some Applications of Behavioural Research*, UNESCO, Paris, 1957.

21. William O. Bearden and M. J. Etzel, 'Reference Group Influence on Product and Brand Purchase Decisions', *Journal of Consumer Research*, 9, Sept. 1982, pp. 183–94. William O. Bearden, Richard G. Netemeyer, Jesse E. Teel, 'Measurement of Consumer Susceptibility to Interpersonal Influence', *Journal of Consumer Research*, 16, March 1990, pp. 461–71.

22. Neil Shoebridge, 'Health Becomes a Holistic Market', *Business Review Weekly*, 10 Dec. 1993, pp. 67–68.

23. Donald H. Gronbois, 'Improving the Study of Customer In-Store Behaviour', *Journal of Marketing*, 32, Oct. 1968, pp. 28–33.

24. Kenny K. Chan and Shekhar Misra, 'Characteristics of the Opinion Leader: A New Dimension', *Journal of Advertising*, 19, 3, 1990, pp. 53–60. James H. Myers and Thomas S. Robertson, 'Dimensions of Opinion Leadership', *Journal of Marketing Research*, 9, Feb. 1972, pp. 41–46. Thomas S. Robertson and James Meyers, 'Personality Correlates of Opinion Leadership and Innovative Buying Behaviour', *Journal of Marketing Research*, 6, May 1969, p. 168.

25. Lawrence F. Feick and Linda L. Price, 'The Market Maven: A Diffuser of Marketplace Information', *Journal of Marketing*, 51, Jan. 1987, pp. 83–97.

26. Neil Shoebridge, *Great Australian Advertising Campaigns*, McGraw-Hill, Sydney, 1992, pp. 59–68.

27. Paul F. Lazarsfeld, Bernard R. Berelson and Hazel Gaudet, *The People's Choice*, Columbia University Press, New York, 1948, p. 151.

28. Thomas S. Robertson, 'The Process of Innovation and the Diffusion of Innovation', *Journal of Marketing*, 31, Jan. 1967, pp. 14–19.

29. Everett M. Rogers, *Diffusion of Innovations*, The Free Press, New York, 1962. Everett M. Rogers and F. Floyd Shoemaker, *Communication of Innovations*, Free Press, New York, 1971.

30. Everett M. Rogers, ibid.

31. Tony Thomas, 'How a Boomerang Did the Trick', *Business Review Weekly*, 10 Sept. 1993, pp. 63–65.

32. Neil Shoebridge, 'Relentless Play in Sports Drinks', *Business Review Weekly*, 12 Nov. 1993, pp. 72–73.

33. Robert W. Shoemaker and F. Robert Shoaf, 'Behavioural Changes in the Trial of New Products', *Journal of Communication Research*, 2, Sept. 1975, pp. 104–9. Mary Dee Dickerson and James W. Gentry, 'Characteristics of Adopters and Nonadopters of Home Computers', *Journal of Consumer Research*, 10, Sept. 1983, pp. 225–35.

CHAPTER 8

Attitudes

OBJECTIVES

This chapter should help you to:
- understand the components of an attitude
- understand the impact that dissonance has on attitudes
- be able to list the functions of attitudes
- understand the role of feelings in attitudes
- be able to explain the differences between single component and multiattribute attitude models
- understand the predictive limitations of attitude models
- understand the differences between compensatory and noncompensatory models of attitudes.

INTRODUCTION

Many consumer behaviour studies are based on the assumption that people will make purchase decisions based upon their attitudes towards products or services. Many marketing activities, including segmentation, product development and positioning strategies, are based on the belief that creating the right attitude towards a brand is a critical factor in the success of that brand.[1] But there has been much disagreement over the years about the definition of an attitude and how attitudes influence behaviour. In this chapter we will examine the components of an attitude, how attitudes function to direct behaviour and how marketers measure and use attitudes in marketing strategy.

WHAT ARE ATTITUDES?

The most widely accepted, current view is that attitudes are 'global and relatively enduring evaluations of objects, issues or persons'.[2] These evaluations are generally seen as being comprised of affective, cognitive and behavioural information and experiences that guide responses. The affective component of an attitude is the consumer's emotional feelings towards the object. The cognitive component consists of the consumer's beliefs about an object. The behavioural, or conative, component is the consumer's tendency to act towards the object. Generally, a consumer's tendency to act would involve intention to buy and purchase behaviour.

The idea that an attitude consists of three components — sometimes referred to as the tricomponent model — suggests that the way in which a consumer feels (affective component), what he or she believes (cognitive component) and what he or she intends to do (behavioural component) will impact on the attitude formed towards an object, issue or person. The three components of an attitude can be assessed independently and may not be equally central to the overall attitude.[3] Some researchers believe that the emotional or affective component should be viewed separately from the evaluative (cognitive and behavioural) components of attitudes. For example, Cohen argues that remembering *feelings* may induce the same feeling or emotion (although to a lesser extent), whereas remembering *facts* involves a different type of retrieval process and does not necessarily induce feelings.[4] For a more detailed discussion of the affective component of attitudes, see Holbrook[5] and Hill and Gardner.[6]

 # NATURE OF ATTITUDES

While there may be some disagreement between theorists about which components of attitudes are more important, there is general agreement that:
1. attitudes are primarily learnt
2. attitudes tend to be consistent both internally and with each other
3. situations affect attitudes.

LEARNING ATTITUDES

Consumers develop attitudes through learning processes. Because information and experience are built up over time, attitudes may be either strengthened or weakened by new experiences and information. (Attitude change is discussed in more detail in chapter 9.) Information can be obtained from a wide range of sources including promotional material, experience of seeing or using the product and word of mouth. Family members have strong personal influences on consumer attitudes because of their early and long contact with the individual.[7] Peers also are an important source of information about products and services for the consumer and have a potent influence on consumer attitudes. According to Katz and Lazarsfeld, the influence of peers on attitude formation is greater than that of advertising.[8]

Personal experience with objects is the primary means by which attitudes are formed. Both classical and operant conditioning play a role in the formation of attitudes. Simple exposure to products over time may make a person more favourable to the product, if the product is at least neutral. This is often referred to as an 'exposure effect' and is based on familiarity with the product. Further, consumers will have favourable attitudes towards products that provide benefits because they have been reinforced by using the products, a case of operant conditioning.

Personality factors may also predispose consumers to develop positive attitudes towards some objects and not others. For example, the personality trait of extroversion is an early developing tendency to be outgoing and social that may have a biological basis. Extroverted persons are likely to find it easy to develop positive attitudes towards products and activities that are consistent with their personality characteristics. In contrast, more introverted persons may have negative attitudes towards the same products and activities.

ATTITUDE CONSISTENCY

One critical aspect of attitudes is their internal consistency. Internal consistency implies that, if the consumer has positive beliefs about an object, they will also have positive feelings towards the object and behave accordingly. For example, if the consumer believes that Australian-made products are high quality, he or she will feel positively about Australian-made products and will therefore tend to purchase them. This aspect of attitudes has important implications for attitude change, which are discussed in the next chapter.

In chapter 4, the role of memory was examined in relation to assimilation of new information. We saw in that chapter that new information is most likely to be integrated in a way that is consistent with original ways of thinking about the world. Similarly, attitudes towards related objects, people or issues tend to be consistent with each other.[9] For example, a consumer may believe that it is preferable to use recycled paper for writing and this attitude may be consistent with a positive attitude towards biodegradable detergents and pesticide-free fruit and vegetables. But it would be unlikely to be consistent with a positive attitude towards excessive amounts of product packaging. Attitudes may exist at a more general level (and therefore across product categories) or they may be product specific. Manufacturers who use the same brand across a range of different products are relying on the belief that if a consumer is familiar with one product within that range and has a positive attitude towards it, other products within the range will benefit from the same positive feelings.

Although it can generally be said that attitudes are consistent with other values and attitudes held by consumers, there are exceptions to this rule. These exceptions tend to produce a need to obtain consistency. For example, if a consumer believes that alcohol consumption leads to road accidents but also believes that it is important to drink alcohol to be accepted socially, he or she will need to find some way to reconcile these opposing attitudes. The theory that explains how consumers deal with these situations is called the 'theory of cognitive dissonance'.[10] The theory focuses on situations where two cognitive elements are inconsistent with each other and therefore create psychological discomfort. In the situation described above, a consumer may seek to reduce the level of felt dissonance by either:

1. stopping alcohol consumption when driving (eliminating one of the elements that is causing the dissonance)

2. remembering the number of times that he or she has driven while drunk and not had an accident (adding a piece of information to the attitude) or
3. questioning the link between the two events (for example, the person might say that accidents are more likely to be caused by poor road conditions or speeding).

Dissonance that occurs after the consumer has made an important purchase is known as post-purchase dissonance. Post-purchase dissonance is discussed more fully in chapter 15. Consumers who experience post-purchase dissonance will attempt to reassure themselves that they have made the correct product choice by seeking out information that supports their choice. A person who buys a car will be more likely to 'notice' similar cars on the road (reassuring the consumer that others have made a similar decision). And if the car is seen advertised at a lower price, the information is likely to be discounted — for example, the car has done more miles, been in an accident, or does not have the same warranty.[11]

SITUATIONAL INFLUENCES ON ATTITUDES

Situations may also affect attitudes, and it is not difficult to find instances in which this occurs. For example, you may have a favourable attitude towards using instant coffee for everyday occasions but prefer ground coffee for guests. Or you may prefer the flavour of imported chocolate over home brand varieties of chocolate but, in a tight budget situation, the attitude toward purchasing the home brand may become more favourable. Thus, repeated purchases of a product may not indicate brand loyalty or commitment to a product associated with strong positive attitudes, but may be situationally induced. The effect of situational factors is to make the prediction of behaviour from attitudes less straightforward than it may seem at first. The influence of situations on purchase behaviour is discussed further in chapter 16.

FUNCTIONS OF ATTITUDES

Katz described four different functions of attitudes.[12] According to Katz, consumers hold attitudes for utilitarian, value-expressive, ego-defensive and knowledge purposes. Figure 8.1 provides examples of advertising addressing each of the four attitudinal functions.

- **Utilitarian function** — Because consumers aim to satisfy particular needs, they are more likely to develop a positive attitude towards products that meet those needs.
- **Value-expressive function** — Attitudes may be seen as an expression of the 'self-concept' or values that are held by an individual.
- **Ego-defensive function** — Attitudes also protect an individual's ego from threats and anxiety. Advertisements for products such as hair colouring, pimple cream and aftershave often rely on the desires of consumers to be sexually attractive and socially acceptable to their peers.
- **Knowledge function** — Attitudes can also help consumers to assess products by highlighting important factors and giving consumers standards by which they can judge products.

(a)

(b)

(c)

(d)

Figure 8.1: Attitude functions illustrated in advertising: (a) utilitarian function; (b) value-expressive function; (c) ego-defensive function; (d) knowledge function

Advertising campaigns are designed to appeal to different functions of attitudes. The choice of function should depend on the importance of that function in relation to the product category and on the differential advantage offered by emphasising that function. For example, canned tuna has been traditionally advertised on the basis of the quality of the tuna in the can, but recent advertisements that emphasise the 'dolphin safe' fishing methods used to catch some tuna have changed the way in which some consumers compare different brands of tuna. This campaign would be classified under both the knowledge and the value-expressive functions, since it aims to change the criteria that a consumer uses to assess the product purchase.

 ## ATTITUDES AND CONSUMER DECISION MAKING

Attitudes can be subdivided according to the type of decision making involved in forming them. Consumer decision types and their associated hierarchies of effects in attitude formation are presented in table 8.1.

Table 8.1: Two hierarchies of effects in attitude formation

High involvement decision	Low involvement decision
Attitude based on cognitive processes	Attitude based on conditioning
Thinking	Thinking
Feeling	Doing
Doing	Feeling

HIGH INVOLVEMENT DECISIONS

In cases of high involvement decision making the consumer is likely to seek information, compare alternatives and carefully make a final decision (think, feel, do). The consumer's final attitude will be based mainly on the cognitive component of his or her attitude. This means that the consumer first develops beliefs about a brand based upon information search, then develops feelings about the brand and finally forms an intent to buy the brand.[13]

In high involvement decisions the buyer generally forms an attitude towards the product before purchasing it. For example, you are likely to decide carefully whether you like a house before you move into it. Your attitude towards the house forms before your behaviour, that is, you will develop an attitude and then move in. Of course, situational factors can still have an impact on your decision; for example, you may not like the house, but like the people that you will share it with, or it may be the best in a particular price range.

LOW INVOLVEMENT DECISIONS

When a product is classified as being less important, the hierarchy of effects differs from that of a more involved decision. The consumer is likely to collect only limited information before purchasing the product and will form feelings about the product after buying it (think, do, feel).

These feelings will be based on the experience with the product. For example, a consumer who believes that there are few differences between brands of toothpaste may buy toothpaste on the basis of price. If the product proves to be satisfactory, the consumer will probably continue to purchase the same product without feeling particularly committed to it. But if the product is disliked for some reason, the consumer is not likely to repurchase that brand but will consider other alternatives.[14]

EMOTION

Some product decisions, such as clothing choices, cannot be explained easily by adopting a logical framework to assess product choice. Some products are assessed in a positive way on the basis of very little information. Consumers talk of seeing a car or a house and 'falling in love with it'. While this reaction may be explained in terms of the product fitting into some subconscious set of criteria, it is often difficult for consumers to explain these types of decisions in a logical way. Some attitudes can therefore be seen to be based on 'gut reaction'. The consumer in this case has a positive feeling, acts on that feeling and then forms beliefs based on the action. This forms the basis of the consciousness–emotion–value (CEV) approach to understanding consumer purchase behaviour (discussed more fully in chapter 14).

MULTIATTRIBUTE MODELS OF ATTITUDES

Various models have been developed to describe attitudes and their relationship to behaviour. Some marketers believe that, although consumers may use different criteria to form judgements, it is the overall positive or negative rating of the product that is ultimately the most important factor.[15] This is described by the single component model. But this view has limitations. For example, two consumers may assess soft drinks on factors such as the amount of sugar, food colouring, artificial flavouring, taste, level of carbonation and type of container. They may both reach the same overall rating for the soft drink, but for different reasons. Consumer A may like the drink because of its taste, while Consumer B may like it primarily because it contains no artificial flavours or colours. Considering only the overall rating will not help a marketer to identify which characteristics are important for the market and why the product is the preferred choice.

Because of the problems associated with using a unitary measure of attitudes, multiattribute models have become widely used by market researchers. Multiattribute models assume that the evaluation of a product by a consumer will be a function of which attributes are important, whether the product is believed to have the attributes, and how important each attribute is in relation to other attributes (the weight).[16]

To understand the use of attributes by consumers, imagine that you are selecting a package of potato chips. The brands of potato chips differ in price, pack size, availability and flavour and each of these attributes may have some impact on your attitude towards individual brands and your purchase decision. As an individual consumer you may consider that flavour is the most important factor and that price and package size are secondary. Availability may not be an important factor at all because most stores carry the same brands. These assessments of importance are called weights. As a consumer, your attitude is likely to be most favourable towards the brand of potato chips that performs the best on the attributes that are important to you. Consumer assessments may be based on real comparisons but are also likely to be based partly on beliefs about the brand. These beliefs may be based on advertising or other promotional material or past experience.

Multiattribute models can also be called 'compensatory models' because a low score on one attribute can be compensated by a high score on another attribute. All of the attributes contribute to the overall rating of the brand or product but do so in different amounts. This focus on several attributes in forming an overall attitude towards a brand is most likely to occur when the decision is a high involvement one. It is well to recognise that, when a product requires only a low involvement decision, consumers tend to simplify the process.[17] Consumers may use only one or two major attributes and may automatically discard products or brands that do not display these attributes. (Compensatory decision models are discussed more fully in chapter 14.)

FISHBEIN'S MULTIATTRIBUTE MODEL

The most well known author in the area of modelling attitudes is Martin Fishbein who, with his associates, has developed a range of models over the past thirty years.[18] In the original Fishbein model, an attitude towards an object was believed to depend on two things:

1. the probability that the object has certain attributes
2. the value placed on those attributes.

For example, you are likely to develop a positive attitude towards a Mercedes Benz car if you believe that safety is very important in the choice of a vehicle and you believe that Mercedes Benz makes very safe cars.

The basic formula for the original model is as follows:

$$A_o = \sum_{i=1}^{n} b_i e_i$$

where:

A_o = attitude towards the object, o

b_i = strength of the belief that the object has attribute i

e_i = the evaluation of attribute i

n = the number of salient attributes.

To show how this model might work for the purchase of a car, let's suppose that we are trying to estimate which car a consumer is likely to hold the most favourable attitude towards. In table 8.2, the results for three brands of cars are calculated. At the bottom of each column are total scores for each brand. This score represents the summation of consumer beliefs about the brand's performance on each of the attributes weighted by the importance of the attribute. Comparison of the attitude scores for the three brands will reveal that consumers have the most favourable attitude towards brand A.

To calculate the scores, each attribute is calculated individually. For example, the calculation for the unleaded petrol score for brand A would be as follows:

$$A_o = \sum_{i=1}^{n} 5_i \times 5_i$$

$$A_o = 25$$

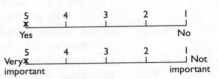

- The car runs on unleaded petrol.

- It is important that the car runs on unleaded petrol.

Table 8.2: Effect of brand attributes and attribute importance ranking on the brand evaluation of cars

Brand attribute (i)	Brand A	Brand B	Brand C
Fuel economy	25	15	10
Cassette player	5	1	5
Unleaded petrol	25	1	1
Low cost parts	25	15	10
Attitude score*	80	32	26

*Attitude scores are obtained by multiplying the score on each attribute by the importance ranking/weighting on that attribute.

FISHBEIN'S THEORY OF REASONED ACTION

One problem with the practical use of attitudes in marketing is that they are imperfectly linked to behaviour.[19] A consumer can hold a favourable attitude towards a product without intending to purchase the product. The marketer must not only understand the attitude that a consumer holds towards the product, but must also consider the likelihood of purchase. Later modifications of Fishbein's model incorporated the atttitude towards purchasing the product rather than simply the attitude towards the product. Thus, the extended Fishbein model focuses on the attitude towards the (purchase) behaviour rather than the attitude towards the product. This approach is called the 'theory of reasoned action'.[20]

A second major change in the extended Fishbein model is the inclusion of the influence of other persons on the consumer's attitude towards purchase. This influence is called a 'subjective norm'. It is the combination of a consumer's perception of what other people believe the consumer should do, and the consumer's motivation to comply with their wishes. Attitudes towards the purchase of some objects may be relatively immune to this influence. For example, a subjective norm is not likely to be an important influence on the purchase of laundry detergent. However, for other purchases involving highly visible products, the subjective norm may be very important in determining whether attitudes will result in behaviour.

The formula for the extended Fishbein model (also called the theory of reasoned action model) is stated below:

$$B \approx BI = w_1A + w_2SN$$

where:

B = actual behaviour
BI = intention to perform the behaviour
w_1 = beliefs and evaluations about the consequences of performing the behaviour
w_2 = beliefs about others' norms for the behaviour and the consumer's motivation to comply with those norms
A = attitude towards the behaviour
SN = social norms affecting the behaviour.

Although the extended Fishbein model looks complicated, it essentially states that a consumer's behavioural intention is a function of their own attitude towards performing the behaviour and the impact of social norms on performing the behaviour (see figure 8.2).

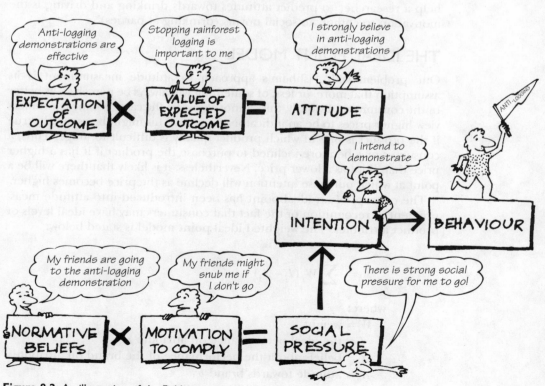

Figure 8.2: An illustration of the Fishbein model

In order to understand the extended Fishbein model more clearly, consider the previous example of purchasing a car. If we include factors such as friends' approval of the choice of car, and the consumer's need for approval from friends, the outcome of the equation could be quite different. If your friends thought that it would not be environmentally sound for you to drive a car with unleaded petrol and that the quality of the sound system was very important, the weighting of these factors would change and alter your decision. It is an advantage for marketers to be able to analyse both product attributes and the impact of social factors. Knowing how the consumer feels about actually purchasing the product (as well as product evaluation) is also important. The latter is an advantage because there is a better relationship between attitudes towards purchasing a brand and purchase behaviour than there is between attitudes towards an object and purchase behaviour.[21] For example, it is possible to have a negative attitude to toothpaste in general but, because teeth cleaning is necessary, the product must be bought. So it is the attitude towards the brand that is important.

The theory of reasoned action is particularly useful in predicting behaviour where cognitive dissonance may be a factor. If we return to the earlier drinking and driving example (pages 200–201), we may see that while an individual may believe that drinking and driving is not a good idea, strong social pressure to drink at parties may override the concern of the individual not to drink and drive. In this example, the major factor that may help a researcher to predict attitudes towards drinking and driving is the motivation to comply to social norms (drinking at parties).

THE IDEAL POINT MODEL

One problem with Fishbein's approach to attitude measurement is its assumption that more, or less, of something will always be perceived as better by the consumer. Obviously, this cannot always be the case.[22] Some consumers view higher prices to be an indicator of quality. This might be especially true if the product is one in which product quality is difficult to judge. Thus, a consumer may be more inclined to purchase the product if it has a higher price than if it has a lower price. Nevertheless, it is likely that there will be a point at which purchase intention will decline as the price becomes higher.

The concept of an ideal point has been introduced into attitude measurement in recognition of the fact that consumers may have ideal levels of product attributes. The weighted ideal point model is stated below:

$$A_b = \sum_{i=1}^{n} W_i (I_i - X_i)$$

where:

W_i = weight

I_i = the ideal performance on attribute i

X_i = beliefs about the performance of the brand on attribute i

A_b = attitude towards brand b

n = the number of salient attributes.

In order to predict what a consumer will do using the ideal point model, marketers ask consumers to rate the level of performance a brand has on a series of attributes. The consumers also provide information about the ideal performance on each attribute. Using this information, a difference score $(I_i - X_i)$ is computed.

A total attitude score for the brand can be computed by multiplying the weight given to each attribute by the difference score across the attributes. The resulting numbers are then summed to index the overall attitude towards the brand. In Fishbein's multiattribute model, higher scores denote preference. In the ideal point model, the lower score is the preferred brand. The best score a brand can receive under the ideal point model is zero, as the example in table 8.3 shows.

Table 8.3: Hypothetical ideal point multiattribute model for tea

Attributes	Importance (W_i)	Ideal point (I_i)	Beliefs (X_i) Brand A	Brand B
Tanin (1) Low to (7) High	4	5	4	2
Caffeine (1) Low to (7) High	4	6	4	3
Taste (1) Sweet to (7) Bitter	6	6	5	3
Total $\sum W_i (I_i - X_i)$			18	34

Worked example for Brand A:

$\sum W_i (I_i - X_i)$

$4 (5 - 4) = 4$
$4 (6 - 4) = 8$
$6 (6 - 5) = \underline{6}$
$ 18$

MARKETING USE OF MULTIATTRIBUTE MODELS

The Fishbein model and other multiattribute models are useful to marketers because they help with positioning, product development and target market strategies. Multiattribute models help marketers to:

1. **see how their brand or product is positioned in relation to the competition**. To do this, attitude scores for the company's brand and competing brands are computed using one of the multiattribute models previously discussed. The overall attitude score indicates the degree of favourability the brand enjoys. The contribution of components in producing the overall score shows similarity or dissimilarity of positioning among brands. The strength of the brand on some attributes may help marketers to position the brand in the most advantageous way.

2. **assess which attributes consumers use when they judge products and determine which ones are the most important**. Because products have many attributes upon which they can be evaluated, the same score can derive from different components and the weightings of

those components. The assessments that marketers make can indicate which aspects of the product are viewed as being weak, and thus provide input into future product development. For example, if consumers believe that car safety features are highly important, and the brand is weak in this area, the manufacturer may wish to invest funds in improving this aspect of their vehicle.

3. **decide whether different target markets have different attribute weightings**. For example, both parents and children may contribute to the decision about which breakfast cereal to buy. Children may favour the product with the best competitions; parents may favour the most nutritious product. Meeting the needs of both parties may increase the rating of the product, but may require two different advertising campaigns.

4. **develop new products**. Using attitude research, gaps may be identified in the market. Analysis of the attributes that are most highly favoured by consumers may reveal that no product currently meets these needs and that a new product could attract a significant part of the market.

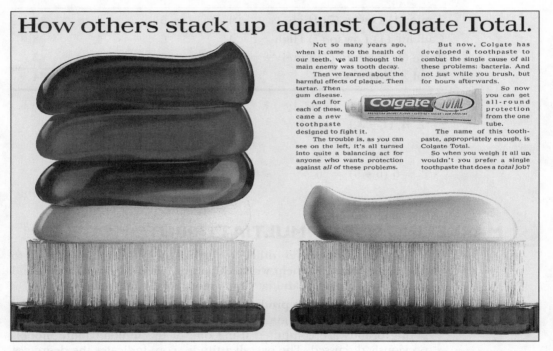

Figure 8.3: Colgate Total is designed to meet desired attributes in a toothpaste. The advertisement 'tells' the consumer that the new product will give all-round protection.

The multiattribute approach, like all models of human behaviour, makes assumptions about human behaviour and has limitations. Fishbein and other attitude reasearchers have generally assumed that behaviour is intentional and logical. But this is not always true. In the case of impulse purchasing and variety seeking, behaviour is often unplanned. In these cases, measurement of attitude towards a brand is less applicable.

PREDICTING BEHAVIOUR FROM ATTITUDES

As previously discussed, attitude models may help you to assess a consumer's attitude towards a product, but there may be a weak link between the attitude and the purchase (behaviour). For example, you may be able to predict that a friend is likely to buy you perfume or aftershave for your birthday but not which brand because there are too many factors that may influence the choice.

Some factors favour a relationship between attitudes and behaviour. Research has shown that there is a stronger relationship between attitudes formed on the basis of personal experience than between attitudes based on advertising.[23] This research suggests that when attitudes are formed on the basis of trial of the product they are easier to predict than attitudes acquired through advertising. Widespread trial of a product is more likely to result in strong attitudes to the product. Thus, marketers may encourage trials of products by offering free samples and gifts. Consumers who try the product because of the offer may develop a favourable attitude towards it, based upon experience.

Figure 8.4: Offers of free trials may result in the development of a favourable attitude to a product.

In contrast, there are some factors that limit the relationship between attitudes and behaviour,[24] such as personal and measurement factors. Personal factors that may limit the link between consumer attitudes and purchase intention are:

1. **lack of consumer involvement.** Attitudes towards low involvement products are likely to be weak. Under these conditions consumers are easily swayed by situational variations such as mood, attention fluctuation, price changes and other factors.

2. **lack of connection to consumer values.** Consumers may believe that a brand has certain characteristics, but may not perceive any benefit arising from those characteristics.

3. **lack of experience with the product.** As indicated previously, attitudes are stronger when they are based on product experience. Consumers who hold mildly favourable beliefs about a product are less likely to purchase than consumers who have used the product with satisfactory results.

4. **changes in the market.** Stockouts, price changes, appearance of new products, and reception of additional information may all cause the consumer to switch brands.

Attitude measurement can affect the connection between the assessed attitude and purchase behaviour in a number of ways. For example, the model used to examine brand attitudes will have an effect on the assumed strength of consumer attitudes for or against a product. It is essential that the *correct* consumer is asked about the *specific behaviour* of interest.

Asking the correct consumer involves obtaining a sample of respondents representative of the target market. Asking about the specific behaviour means that the attitude researcher must focus on an appropriate time frame and behaviour.[25] Thus, if the market researcher wants to know about the consumer's interest in purchasing a certain brand at a certain time or place, then the researcher must be careful to ask that specific question and not a more general one.

 ## APPLICATIONS OF ATTITUDE RESEARCH

Knowledge of attitudes can provide clues for improving sales and obtaining more market share. If a brand is assessed less positively than other brands, the marketer will want to improve the attitude towards that brand. Many of the approaches to improving attitudes focus on the cognitive component of attitudes.[26] The attitude models discussed earlier in this chapter suggest several options:

1. **Improve the rating of the product on key attributes**. For example, if a snack food is viewed as being too salty and this is a key selection criteria, reducing the salt level is likely to improve consumer perception of the brand.

2. **Increase the importance of a key attribute**. If the brand has good performance on a feature that consumers do not care very much about, it may be possible to change their evaluation of the attribute. For example, small cars such as Volkswagens were very efficient in terms of fuel consumption. However, many consumers viewed them as small, slow, ugly and uncomfortable. With the help of environmental changes such as rising petrol prices, marketers were able to convince consumers that the smaller cars were more efficient, which helped turn consumer attitudes in a more positive direction.

3. **Add an entirely new attribute to the consumer's alternative evaluation scheme**. Rather than try to outdo the competition on established attributes, add a new attribute that has been shown to be important to consumers. For example, consumers previously did not think much about cholesterol level as a variable in brand choice. Margarines and other food products that were low in cholesterol began to advertise this attribute after it became apparent that this attribute could be important to consumers.

4. **Decrease the importance of a weak attribute**. For example, in marketing a high-priced quality product faced with lower-priced competition, the marketer would emphasise the quality of the product. Advertising that stresses the worth of the better product suggests that price should not be the main criterion for purchase.

TRACKING ATTITUDE CHANGES

Consumer attitudes will change over time. Attitude change may take place as changes in information that allow the consumer to differentiate products. For example, consumers who are moving out of the parental home to set up a new home for the first time may initially buy products their parents used, but over time this practice might change as the consumers become more familiar with the different products that are available.

Social changes may also affect attitudes. For example, in the 1970s and 1980s, condoms were seen as less acceptable than the contraceptive pill. But with increased concerns about AIDS, condoms now fulfil more than a purely contraceptive function. Concerns about the environment may also change the criteria used to assess products as community awareness of these issues increases. Changes in values and value studies are discussed in greater detail in chapters 12, 13 and 17.

 ## SUMMARY

The study of attitudes forms a central part of any study of consumer behaviour. Attitudes can be defined as the 'global and relatively enduring evaluations of objects, issues or persons'. While this definition suggests that attitudes are relatively stable, they do change over time as the information available to the consumer changes.

There is general agreement that attitudes have three components: affective, cognitive and behavioural, although the importance given to each of these components varies among different theorists. This structure of attitudes is known as the tricomponent model of attitudes.

Attitudes are regarded as being learnt through a process of consumer socialisation, consistent with other beliefs and attitudes held and are affected by situations. Attitudes help consumers to satisfy particular needs (*utilitarian function*), express their self-concepts (*value-expressive function*), protect their ego (*ego-defensive function*) and organise the knowledge they have of the world (*knowledge function*).

The hierarchy of effects suggests that in high involvement decisions the consumer is more likely to develop an attitude before purchase, whereas in low involvement decisions the consumer is more likely to form an attitude based on experience with the product (post-purchase). Emotive decisions, based more on feelings, are likely to be a function of 'liking' a product and then developing the rationale for the decision post-purchase.

Different types of attitude models have been developed, ranging from single component models that consider the overall positive or negative rating of the product to more complex models that consider products on the basis of different attributes and how each of those attributes contributes to the ratings (multiattribute models). Fishbein's model of attitudes is a multiattribute model based on his theory of reasoned action, which proposes that attitudes are connected to intention to buy. The ideal point model proposes that attitudes are influenced by discrepancies between the consumer's ideal level of an attribute and the perceived performance of the brand on that attribute.

One of the major problems associated with the study of attitudes is the link between attitudes and behaviour. In all attribute studies, the marketers must be careful to include measures of likelihood of purchase. Research suggests that there is likely to be a closer link between attitudes and purchase when attitudes are based on experience (trial) of the product than attitudes based solely on advertising.

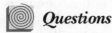

Questions

1. Select one product that you have learnt about through the socialisation you received as you grew up. Describe how your attitude has been shaped by learning processes.

2. Using coffee or tea as a specific example, describe the impact of social values on brand choice. What influence does situation have on the product and brand choice? Discuss your attitudes with students from different cultural backgrounds. Are their attitudes different and, if so, how do they differ? What are the implications of your findings for the marketing of coffee or tea in Australia?

3. What is meant by attitude consistency? Discuss the consistency of your attitudes to different product categories.

4. Discuss the impact that branding a new product with a familiar brand has on your assessment of that product. Consider both high involvement and low involvement products (for example, compare a new shampoo with a new stereo system).

5. Describe the theory of cognitive dissonance as it relates to attitudes. Can you find an example of cognitive dissonance that you personally have experienced?

6. Consider the four functions of attitudes and find advertising that appeals to each of these functions.

7. Discuss the tricomponent model of attitudes in relation to the marketing strategy for a high involvement product. (For example, look at the marketing strategy for computers: can you identify the affective, cognitive and behavioural components of the strategy?

8. Construct an example of a multiattribute model for a recent high involvement purchase decision. Does the attitude score reflect your final decision? Why or why not? Could this model have been used to predict your behaviour?

9. Describe the differences between the original Fishbein model, the extended Fishbein model and the ideal point model.

10. Discuss how you might use different types of models for different product categories and why. What does this information tell you about how research assumptions affect research outcomes?

11. What are the applications of multiattribute models of attitudes? Find examples of each of these applications.

12. Can marketers predict purchase behaviour from attitudes? Why or why not?

Case study question

Read the article on page 215 and discuss the situation described by Shoebridge in relation to Fishbein's theory of reasoned action.

Case study

BIG, traditional brand names are back in favor, right? Rocked by the recession, exhausted from the excesses of the 1980s and fearful that their lives are out of control, consumers are flocking back to the big brands they know and trust. They want the security and stability provided by old brands. It is a great time to be marketing Vegemite or Holden or Pears.

The revival of the big brand is a great theory. But wait. If big brands are enjoying a renaissance, why are sales of non-brands booming? Why are shoppers flocking to non-branded products such as bulk food-stuffs and non-branded retailers such as street markets? Why are sales of retailers' house-brand and generic lines climbing in many supermarket product categories? Why have house-brands managed to snatch sales in product categories dominated by well-established, trusted brand names?

The boom in sales of non-brands at a time when, according to researchers, people are seeking old, trusted brand names points to a significant change in consumerland. The gap between the way consumers think and the way they behave is widening. In the 1990s, do as I say, not as I do has been turned around: the message consumers are sending marketers is do as I do, not as I say.

The accepted theory among researchers is that attitudes follow behavior. People change the way they are behaving and then consciously change their attitudes. There is a lag between behavioral changes and changes in conscious attitudes (the word conscious is important: sub-conscious shifts in attitude will drive changes in behavior, but it is some time before people recognise and admit to their attitude shifts).

There are exceptions to the theory. One of the best examples of behavior following attitudes is the pro-sugar advertising campaign that ran from October 1983 to last November. Dramatic shifts in consumer attitudes towards sugar and its role in the diet drove significant changes in behavior. Absolute sales and Australians' consumption of sugar increased during the first seven years of the campaign's run.

There are several reasons for the widening gap between consumer attitudes and consumer behavior. One is the recession: people hold high ideals about the type of products they will and won't buy, but the recession is forcing them to behave differently. Another reason is that people will often tell a researcher they are doing one thing when they are actually doing the exact opposite.

People are looking for the reassurance offered by big brands, but they are abandoning brands in favor of cheaper non-brands. Researchers claim that as part of the swing back to old brands, people are unwilling to accept new brands. They are embracing their friends (old brands). But in the past two years there have been good sales of several new brands, including Holiday cigarettes, Fruche dairy dessert and Gold'n Canola margarine.

In theory, consumers' fears about the destruction of the environment is one of the key marketing trends of the 1990s. In reality, sales of most environment-friendly consumer products have been patchy. People are worried about the dangers of using laundry detergents and deodorants, but they are not willing to compromise on product price and performance for the sake of protecting the environment.

Researchers say the attitude of men towards their role in the family is changing. But the behavior of men — as manifested in activities such as caring for children — has changed little. The new man appears to be an invention of the research industry.

Sifting through the shades of grey that surround consumer attitudes and behavior is never easy. In the present marketing environment, recognising the gap between attitudes and behavior is critical.

Neil Shoebridge,
Business Review Weekly,
21 February 1992

SUGGESTED READING

B. S. Moore and A. Isen (eds), *Affect and Social Behaviour*, Cambridge University Press, New York, 1990.

I. Ajzen and M. Fishbein, *Understanding Attitudes and Predicting Social Behaviour*, Prentice-Hall, Englewood Cliffs, NJ, 1980.

ENDNOTES

1. D. A. Aaker, and J. G. Myers, *Advertising Management*, Prentice-Hall, Englewood Cliffs, NJ, 1987, p. 160.

2. I. Ajzen, 'Attitudes, Traits and Actions: Dispositional Prediction of Behaviour in Personality and Social Psychology', in I. Berkowitz (ed.), *'Advances in Experimental Social Psychology'*, Vol. 20, 1987, pp. 1–62. Gordon Allport, 'Attitudes', in C. A. Murchinson, (ed.), *A Handbook of Social Psychology*, Clark University Press, Worcester, Mass., 1935, pp. 798–844.

3. Y. Tsal, 'On the Relationship Between Cognitive and Affective Processes', *Journal of Consumer Research*, 12, 2, Dec. 1985, pp. 358–62. W. D. Wells, 'Attitudes and Behaviour', *Journal of Advertising Research,* 24, March 1985, pp. 40–44. R. B. Zajonic and H. Markus, 'Affective and Cognitive Factors in Preferences', *Journal of Consumer Research*, 9, Sept. 1982, pp. 123–31. Robert B. Zajonic, 'On the Primacy of Affect', *American Psychologist*, 39, Jan. 1984, pp. 117–23.

4. J. B. Cohen, 'Attitude, Affect and Consumer Behaviour', in B. S. Moore and A. M. Isen (eds), *Affect and Social Behaviour*, Cambridge University Press, New York, 1990, pp. 152–206.

5. M. B. Holbrook, 'Emotion in the Consumption Experience: Toward A New Model Of Human Consumer', in R. A. Peterson, W. D. Hoyer, and W. R. Wilson (eds), *The Role of Affect in Consumer Behaviour*, D. C. Heath, Lexington, Mass., 1986.

6. R. P. Hill and M. P. Gardner, 'The Buying Process: Effects Of and On Consumer Mood States', *Advances in Consumer Research*, 14, 1987, pp. 408–10.

7. Peter D. Bennet and Harold H. Kassarjian, *Consumer Behaviour*, Prentice-Hall, Englewood Cliffs, NJ, 1972.

8. Elihu Katz and Paul Lazarsfeld, *Personal Influence*, The Free Press, New York, 1955.

9. George S. Day, 'Theories of Attitude Structure and Change', in Scott Ward and Thomas Robertson (eds), *Consumer Behaviour: Theoretical Sources*, Prentice-Hall, Englewood Cliffs, NJ, 1973. Martin Fishbein and Jack Ajzen, *Belief, Attitude, and Intention*, Addison Wesley, Reading, Mass., 1975. Bobby J. Calder, 'Cognitive Consistency and Consumer Behaviour', in Harold Kassarjian and Thomas S. Robertson (eds), *Perspectives in Consumer Behaviour*, Scott Foresman, Glenview, Ill., 1981, pp. 258–70.

10. L. Festinger, *A Theory of Cognitive Dissonance*, Stanford University Press, Palo Alto, Calif., 1957.

11. R. E. Knox and J. A. Inkster, 'Post Decision Dissonance at Post Time', *Journal of Personality and Social Psychology*, 8, 1988, pp. 319–23.

12. D. Katz, 'The Functional Approach to the Study Of Attitudes', *Public Opinion Quarterly*, 24, Summer 1960, pp. 163–204.

13. Sharon E. Beatty and Lynn R. Kahle, 'Alternative Hierarchies of the Attitude–Behaviour Relationship: The Impact of Brand Commitment and Habit', *Journal of the Academy of Marketing Science*, 16, Summer 1988, pp. 1–10.

14. Michael L. Rothschild, 'Advertising Strategies for High and Low Involvement Situations', in J. C. Maloney and B. Silverman (eds), *Attitude Research Plays for High Stakes*, American Marketing Association, Chicago, 1979, pp. 74–93. Also see James L. Ginter, 'An Experimental Investigation of Attitude Change and Choice of a New Brand', *Journal of Marketing Research*, 11, Feb. 1974, pp. 30–40. Herbert E. Krugman, 'The Impact of Television Advertising: Learning Without Involvement', *Public Opinion Quarterly*, 29, Fall 1985, pp. 349–56.

15. Martin Fishbein and I. Ajzen, *Belief, Attitude, Intention and Behaviour: An Introduction to Theory and Research*, Addison Wesley, Reading, Mass., 1975.

16. For a review of the use of multiattribute models, see William W. Wilkie and Edgar A. Pessemier, 'Issues in Marketing's Use of Multiattribute Models', *Journal of Marketing Research*, 10, Nov. 1983, pp. 428–41.

17. M. Nakanishi and J. Bettman, 'Attitude Models Revisited: An Individual Level Analysis', *Journal of Consumer Research*, 1, 1974, pp. 16–21.

18. M. Fishbein, 'An Investigation of the Relationships Between Beliefs About an Object and the Attitude Toward that Object', *Human Relations*, 16, 1963, pp. 233–40.

19. M. D. Wells, 'Attitudes and Behaviour', *Journal of Marketing Research*, March 1985, pp. 40–44. M. G. Miller and A. Tessar, 'Attitudes and Behaviour', in M. E. Goldberg, G. Gorn and R. W. Pollay, *Advances in Consumer Research XVII*, Association for Consumer Research, Provo, Utah, 1990, pp. 86–90.

20. Martin Fishbein, 'Attitudes and the Prediction of Behaviour', in Martin Fishbein (ed.), *Readings in Attitude Theory and Measurement*, John Wiley and Sons, New York, 1967, pp. 477–82.

21. David H. Wilson, H. Lee Matthews and James W. Harvey, 'An Empirical Test of the Fishbein Behavioural Intention Model', *Journal of Consumer Research*, 1, March 1975, pp. 39–48.

22. The discussion in this section is based on Del I. Hawkins, Roger J. Best and Kenneth A. Cooney, *Consumer Behaviour: Implications for Marketing Action*, Irwin, Homewood, Ill., 1992, pp. 350–52.

23. R. H. Fazio, M. C. Powell and J. C. Williams, 'The Role of Attitude Accessibility in the Attitude to Behaviour Process', *Journal of Consumer Research*, 16, Dec. 1989, pp. 280–88.

24. R. E. Smith and W. R. Sinyard, 'Attitude–Behaviour Consistency: The Impact of Product Trial Versus Advertising', *Journal of Marketing Research*, Aug. 1983, pp. 257–67.

25. Y. Yi, 'The Indirect Effects of Advertisements Designed to Change Product Attribute Beliefs', *Psychology and Marketing*, Spring 1990, pp. 47–63.

26. James F. Engel, Roger D. Blackwell and Paul W. Miniard, *Consumer Behaviour*, Dryden Press, Chicago, Ill., pp. 308–9.

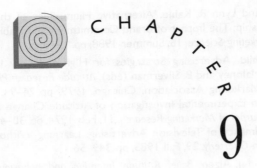

C H A P T E R

9

Attitude change and communication

This chapter should help you to:
- understand the importance of attitude change strategies to marketing activity
- explain the elaboration likelihood model
- understand and explain the communication process
- select the appropriate attitudinal strategy for different types of product decisions.

ROLE OF ATTITUDE CHANGE IN MARKETING STRATEGY DEVELOPMENT

A great deal of marketing activity is designed to change the way in which consumers think and feel about products. This activity is based on the belief that there is a strong link between the attitudes of consumers and their behaviour, or purchase intention. However, as the previous chapter showed, this link is not as well established as some theorists would suggest.[1] For example, as we saw with regard to drink-driving campaigns and other issues, a consumer may have a favourable attitude about the concept but may be more influenced by other factors, such as the cost — financial or social — of acting on the attitude. Alternatively, a consumer may have an unfavourable attitude towards the use of disposable nappies, but may live in a flat lacking the facilities to wash and dry cloth nappies easily, and may work long hours. The consumer may therefore decide that the benefits of using disposable nappies outweigh the costs. Thus, it is important to remember that communication strategies designed to change attitudes towards a product may not produce the desired behavioural change.

In times of economic recession, increased time constraints and changing social roles, factors other than attitudes may play an important role in which products are bought, when they are bought and why they are selected. Despite these limitations, attitudes form one part of the system consumers use to make decisions. It is from this perspective that we consider the role of attitude change in marketing strategy.

ELABORATION LIKELIHOOD MODEL OF ATTITUDE CHANGE

Attitudes and attitude change have been viewed from a number of theoretical perspectives. The multiattribute approach to attitudes, discussed in chapter 8, proposes that an attitude towards a brand is influenced by the consumer's beliefs about the brand and the consumer's feelings about those beliefs. The attitude towards the brand influences intention to buy and, ultimately, purchase behaviour. Several strategies for changing attitudes based on the multiattribute approach were suggested, such as improving the ratings on a key attribute, increasing the importance of a key attribute, adding a new attribute and decreasing the importance of a weak attribute.

Another approach to attitude change has been delineated by Petty and Cacioppo.[2] They conclude that although attitude theorists use many different models and variables, the theories can be classified as emphasising two distinct routes to persuasion to attitude change. Persuasion by a *central* route takes place through learning, evaluation and integration of information.[3] In contrast, persuasion through a *peripheral* route occurs without the consumer actively thinking about product-related information. Instead, it is a result of rewards, punishments and affective experiences that is associated with the product or the perceived expertise of the source of the message.[4]

Petty and Cacioppo believed that these two routes to persuasion formed an 'elaboration likelihood continuum'.[5] Their theory suggests that, when a person's motivation and interest in the product is high, the person will use learned information to evaluate different products. However, for lower involvement decisions, or when the consumer lacks the ability to differentiate between products, the consumer processes information through a peripheral route.

The elaboration likelihood model (ELM) is presented in figure 9.1. There are several assumptions underlying the model. One is that, as a consumer receives a message, he or she will begin to process it at some level. In an advertising context, the model assumes that when information depicted in an advertisement is important to the consumer (has personal relevance), that consumer will spend more time processing the information and will have more product-related thoughts.[6] In addition, the credibility of the claims is likely to affect the extent of information processing and the resulting attitude change.[7] If claims are credible and relevant, consumers generate thoughts that support the advertisement's arguments. If the claims are not credible, consumers may generate counterarguments. In contrast, when the personal relevance of the advertising is lower, attitudes may be more affected by other features such as the attractiveness of the pictures shown in the advertisement.[8]

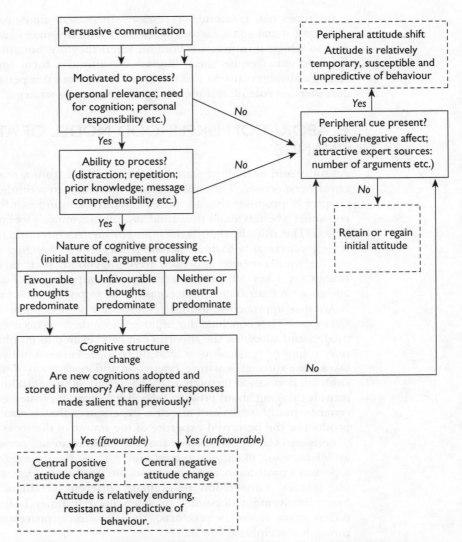

Figure 9.1: The elaboration likelihood model of persuasion (*Source:* Adapted from Petty 1977; Petty and Cacioppo 1981a, 1986)

The level of prior knowledge may also affect the persuasiveness of the information. If an individual has little prior knowledge of the product, providing more information may increase the likelihood of persuasion. But if the individual has a high level of knowledge, the persuasiveness of the message may be reduced unless the claims are credible.[9]

The strategies for attitude change in situations involving messages with high personal relevance differ from those used when the messages have low personal relevance. The willingness of the consumer to elaborate arguments in a high involvement condition suggests that the advertiser should concentrate on communicating product benefits (although marketers should be careful about overstating claims in order to discourage counterarguments). In contrast, low involvement conditions demand that the advertiser attend to the peripheral cues in the advertisement. These cues include the choice of spokesperson and the format of the advertisement.

SOCIAL JUDGEMENT AND ATTITUDE CHANGE

The elaboration likelihood model stresses the role of involvement in changing attitudes and its implications for promotional strategy. Sherif's 'theory of social judgement' has implications for ease of changing attitudes.[10] In brief, Sherif maintains that if a message is very different from the attitude held by a consumer, the message will fall into the consumer's 'latitude of rejection' and tend to be discounted. However, messages that propose only small changes in attitude will fall into the 'latitude of acceptance' and encounter less resistance.

Individual consumers have different latitudes of rejection and acceptance, which are related to their overall psychological flexibility and their involvement with the product category or brand. Sherif's theory suggests that promotional messages directed towards changing attitudes should not be too extreme. Moderate messages, proposing small changes in attitudes and presented at various time intervals, have a better chance of being accepted by the target audience.

LEARNING AND ATTITUDE CHANGE

As we saw in the previous chapter, a consumer's attitudes are learnt during the process of interaction with the environment. They may be acquired from cues picked up by observing the behaviour and attitudes of others, or through information received through more impersonal media channels, such as newspapers. Just as attitudes are formed through learning, they also can be altered through new information. However, this is not a simple process because information is only one component of attitudes.

One approach to changing attitudes that involves learning focuses on Katz's functional theory of attitudes, which was discussed in chapter 8 (pages 201–3). Katz believes that attitudes serve four functions: the utilitarian function, the value-expressive function, the ego-defensive function and the knowledge function. Advertising addresses a utilitarian function when it shows how the product will help the consumer achieve a previously unattainable goal. Other advertisements attempt to influence consumer values (value-expressive function). For example, anti-smoking campaigns attempt to change consumer values and alter behaviour by teaching the consumer that smoking is not glamorous or healthy. Of the various functions that can be addressed, this changing of values is perhaps the most difficult. Advertisements that teach the consumer about products that will help bolster the self-image address the ego-defensive function. Information contained in advertisements provides input for decision-making and attempts to change attitudes via the knowledge function.

DIFFICULTY OF ATTITUDE CHANGE: THE AUSTRALIAN MADE CAMPAIGN

To highlight how difficult it is to change some attitudes let us consider a topical situation. Many opinion polls cite unemployment and economic difficulties as among the major concerns of Australians. One factor that contributes to both these areas is the demise of manufacturing in Australia

because, as manufacturing declines, fewer job opportunities are available. This has far-reaching effects because Australian manufacturing is more likely to use Australian raw materials (such as fruit, vegetables, wheat and iron) and employ Australian workers to manufacture, transport, design and promote the products. There have been attempts in recent years to encourage consumers to buy more 'Australian made' products through a series of campaigns using, for example, such emotive slogans as 'Buy your kids a job'. Yet the campaigns have had marginal impact on the buying behaviour of Australians. While the fact that products are Australian made is important, it represents only one factor in the choice of a product. So if three products are of good quality, well designed and priced correctly, the fact that one is made in Australia could be an important criterion. If the Australian product is poor in quality, it will not be selected.

You may recall that the link between behaviour and a likely outcome is an important influence on whether attitude is associated with behaviour. For example, consider the likelihood that a consumer will purchase a particular perfume or car that is believed to improve the individual's sex appeal. If advertisers communicate a strong link between behaviour and outcome, this will reinforce the attitude.[11] If a consumer believes that buying Australian made products will directly affect the level of unemployment and economic health of Australia, the consumer is more likely to buy Australian made products. However, most consumers are aware that a range of economic policies have been unsuccessful in solving the deficit problem and are unlikely to believe that simply 'buying Australian' will have much impact. Thus, an individual consumer may not believe that a strong link exists between his or her behaviour and the likelihood of a favourable outcome. A strong belief in the ineffectiveness of a policy of buying Australian products would tend to make the arguments fall into the consumer's latitude of rejection.

The consumer's perception of the attributes of Australian products will also have an impact on the consumer's attitude and choice. Many attitudes towards Australian products may be based on outdated beliefs. Beliefs and feelings contribute significantly to the formation of attitudes. If the consumer believes that the products are more expensive and of lower quality and status, and that the purchase of them would probably not significantly improve the state of the economy, then they are unlikely to buy the products. Because this is an important and complex problem, the consumer is likely to generate counterarguments to the advertising message.

Figure 9.2: An advertisement for the Buy Australian campaign

Another difficulty that has hindered the success of Australian made products is the confusion that exists in some consumers' minds about whether 'Made in Australia' means what it says. Television programs such as 'The Investigators' have drawn attention to a number of products that could easily be assumed to be Australian because of their names or types (such as toy koalas), as well as products that are packaged but not made in Australia. Such revelations are likely to reduce the probability that consumers will feel that they can easily identify 'Australian made' products.

The familiar green triangle with the gold kangaroo provides a readily identifiable symbol that consumers can use as a shopping guide, but it is only effective if all Australian made products carry this symbol. Clearly identifying the product in this way will help to simplify the consumer's search process, but if an individual does not have a favourable attitude towards buying Australian made products, the search will not be undertaken in the first instance.

Table 9.1: AMR:Quantum survey of 'Australian made' licensees — percentage agreeing with the following statements, 1991 and 1994

	Percentage agreeing	
Statement	**1991**	**1994**
Australian made logo helps to sell product	66%	77%
Logo provides a competitive advantage	53%	63%
Having the gold kangaroo/green triangle symbol on products adds value	53%	64%

(*Source*: Extract from *Marketing*, March 1994, p. 8)

THE HIERARCHY OF EFFECTS AND ATTITUDE CHANGE

How could a marketer increase the probability of a consumer buying an Australian made product? The hierarchies of effects discussed in chapter 8 suggest that a number of different approaches could be considered:

1. For high involvement products such as cars or computers, information-based strategies that compare the product with imported products may prove the most effective. For example, statistics from motoring authorities and favourable articles in *Choice* magazine may influence car buyers to consider Australian made motor vehicles in a more favourable light.

2. For low involvement products such as tinned fruit or paper products, clearly showing the benefits of buying Australian is important. Reassuring consumers that their purchases will make a difference to the Australian economy and pricing products competitively will encourage trial. Figure 9.3 is an example of a low involvement product advertised with a reassurance appeal.

3. For the purchase of expressive products, such as fashion clothing or jewellery, suggesting that Australian made products have other qualities — for example, Australian diamonds are rare and exotic — may encourage consumers to develop a favourable attitude towards them. Showing aspirational groups, such as world class surfers, wearing Australian made clothes may also increase their appeal.

4. A fourth approach is to adopt the 'environmental strategy'. For example, when it became fashionable to buy environmentally friendly toilet paper, many supermarkets could not keep up with the demand. By showing consumers the long term benefits to Australia that are possible through small changes in their behaviour, and by appealing to the more altruistic consumers, shifts are more likely to occur.

"We felt the difference straight away"

Emily, Renee and Robert Di Donato Glenfield, Sydney

"Now that we drink CARO all the time, we've never felt better; we're healthier and certainly less stressed," said Robert

CARO is made from natural ingredients including barley and is completely caffeine free, so you can rest easy. That's why more people like the Di Donato's are drinking CARO everyday.

If you would like to share your CARO story, just drop us a line (and a photo if you like) to Anne Turner, PO Box 477, Bankstown, New South Wales 2200.

The natural difference

® Société des Produits NESTLE S.A. VEVEY, SWITZERLAND. Trade Mark Owners   FD 2758

Figure 9.3: In this advertisement, consumers are assured that Caro is an ideal substitute for coffee. As Italy is associated with quality coffee, the use of the Italian surname provides further positive assurance.

Wool industry puts a sock in it!

In an effort to reduce the wool stockpile, Pacific Dunlop's Holeproof division created 'Heroes', a line of men's socks in wool blends and pure wool. A million-dollar advertising and marketing campaign was designed and executed. It featured Narelle, a merino sheep, who romped across television screens around Australia, wearing her bright red socks. The message, spoken by a farmer in a weathered hat, was: 'If every Australian bought just two pairs of Holeproof Heroes, we could help save our wool industry and put this country back on its feet'.

The results were overwhelming. At the time of the campaign (1991), wool sock sales constituted 11 per cent of the Australian market, down from 30 per cent in 1980. By early 1993, sales had risen to 15 per cent of the total market. The Heroes range is now among Holeproof's top three sellers. Although Australians purchase 77 million pairs of socks each year (four to five pairs each) this effort has not significantly reduced the wool stockpile. However, the campaign's success was attributed to its appeal to the patriotic pride of Australians, with the emphasis on 'buying Australian'. Consumers want to feel that they are doing something to support the wool industry. At the same time, they are buying a stylish, reasonably priced product.

(*Source*: Compiled by Constance C. Adams from: S. MacLean, 'Holeproof Use Socks Appeal to Put Us Back on Our Feet', The *Age*, August 1991. D. Cameron, 'The Socking Truth About the Wool Pile', *Sydney Morning Herald*, 24 April 1993)

INFLUENCING ATTITUDE FORMATION

In order to consider how attitudes might be changed, it is necessary to remember the factors that influence them. Consumers collect the information upon which attitudes are based from a range of sources. These include the following:

1. **Experience with products and services**. Providing consumers with free samples, offers to purchase products at special introductory rates and coupons offering low prices or competition entry may encourage consumers to trial new products.

2. **Social influences**. Consumers may be indirectly influenced by the product choices of their social contacts. Shoes worn by other members of a sports team, products used by family members and music and other entertainment favoured by friends are all examples of informal factors that may influence attitudes towards products and services.

3. **Media influences**. Promotional activity undertaken through magazines, newspapers, billboards, radio and television may not only influence consumers' attitudes but also make them aware of the existence of products. A consumer who has a particular interest in, say, fishing, is more likely to be informed about products related to that interest — through fishing magazines and so on — than a person with little interest in the sport.

4. **Individual lifestyle factors**. Your lifestyle can influence your attitude to certain products and services. For example, the 'Life. Be in it' programs acknowledge that an individual's choice of recreational activity is related to their preferred lifestyle.

Figure 9.4: 'Life. Be in it' programs cover a broad range of interests, from reading to canoeing, walking to crafts, music to environmental interests. They aim to influence the attitudes of people of all lifestyles.

 ## THE COMMUNICATION MODEL

Attitudes are based on information received from the environment. The communication of information from various promotional sources is therefore a critical component in the formation of attitudes. In order to establish a framework within which the communication of information can be studied, researchers use the model shown in figure 9.5.[12]

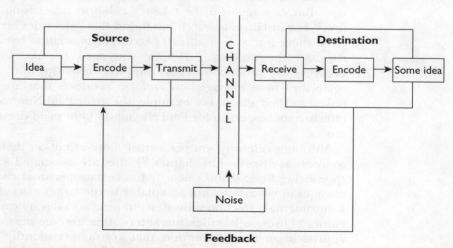

Figure 9.5: Communication model

SOURCE CHARACTERISTICS

In the communication model (see figure 9.5), the source of the message refers to the spokesperson used to communicate the message and to the firm that sponsors the message. The receiver of the communication evaluates the source of the message on the basis of three criteria: attractiveness, expertise and trustworthiness.[13] Similarly, firms are evaluated in terms of their past records of trustworthiness and expertise. Together these characteristics make up the 'source credibility'. Source credibility is an important factor in the ability of the message to change consumer attitudes.

Attractiveness

Attractiveness refers to the perceived social value of the spokesperson. It may refer to the physical appearance, social status, personality or similarity to the target market, and characters used in marketing strategies may possess one or more of these attributes. In particular, perceived similarity to the target market has been found to increase the attractiveness of the spokespersons in advertisements.[14] Physically attractive models are commonly used in advertising because in our culture a person's attractiveness is perceived to be linked with other positive characteristics, such as social skills and fashion awareness. This phenomenon is known as a 'halo effect', in which individuals who rate highly on one dimension are seen as also rating highly on other dimensions.[15]

Expertise

The perceived expertise of the spokesperson or the firm producing the product may also affect the credibility of the message.[16] For example, a well known hairdresser promoting shampoo or a sportsperson promoting sporting equipment is likely to be perceived as a reliable source of information. Celebrities are commonly used in advertising strategies, because they may be seen as knowledgeable and credible for some products. But care needs to be taken if celebrity advertising is to be effective.[17] For instance, research has found that celebrities are most credible when there is a real, or at least perceived, association between the celebrity and the product.[18] Despite the need to take the relationship between the product category and the celebrity into account, some celebrities have managed to endorse products that are not obviously linked to their status. For example, the actor Paul Newman has been an effective spokesperson for Paul Newman's Own salad dressings and pasta sauces.

Although celebrity sources attract more attention than non-celebrity sources (as discussed in chapter 7), they are associated with risk for the sponsoring firm. If the celebrity has certain personal characteristics or engages in behaviours not acceptable to the target market, this can have a detrimental effect on attitudes and product sales. Because of the difficulties of using celebrities, marketers often use 'the person in the street' approach on the assumption that consumers identify with ordinary people (for example, figure 7.2, page 174, and figure 13.5, page 334).

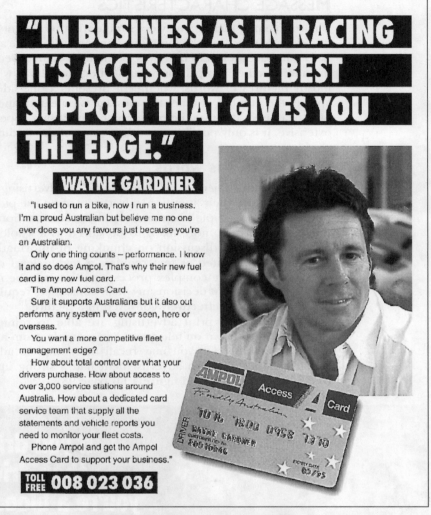

Figure 9.6: This advertisement succeeds in linking the product with a celebrity's achievements and his good business sense.

Trustworthiness

Although trustworthiness is related to expertise, the two do not necessarily go together. Trustworthiness also includes the ability of the message to appear sincere or objective. For example, if it is known that a sportsperson receives large amounts of money for endorsing a particular product, that person may be perceived as being unobjective or biased, even though he or she is an expert on the product category. And you may value the opinion of a friend who goes with you to buy clothing more than the opinion of a shop assistant, even though you may acknowledge the expertise of the shop assistant. This is because the friend is more likely to be objective and will not directly gain from your purchase.

MESSAGE CHARACTERISTICS

The source of a message may determine whether or not an advertisement is initially noticed, but the message contained within the advertisement also has an impact on its effectiveness. Some important aspects of the message include: whether it is primarily rational or emotional; whether it contains mostly pictures or words; whether it presents a one-sided or a two-sided appeal; the number of times the message is repeated; and the specific type of appeal used. Because the research on advertising appeals and formats is extensive, it is only possible to outline some of the findings in this text.

Pictures versus words

Consumers are subject to a large volume of advertising material and, in order to capture their attention, advertisers often use pictures rather than words to convey simple ideas and emotions. Information that is conveyed in pictorial form is more likely to be stored as a whole. (See chapter 4, page 86, for more discussion on chunking of information.) In contrast, information presented as text requires a higher level of interest by the consumer and more complex processing. Text may be more appropriate for high involvement decisions in which consumers require more information than could be effectively conveyed in a picture.[19]

Pictures used in print advertising are able to remind consumers of advertisements shown on television. For example, from a single frame of a television commercial, you may recall the complete advertisement, particularly if the television advertisement had a strong impact at the time (see figure 9.7 below, and figure 4.11, page 93).

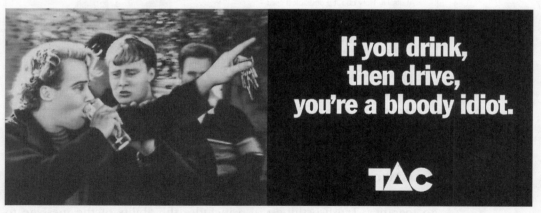

Figure 9.7: Exposure to this scene from a television commercial aids in recalling the whole commercial, allowing the message to be brought into active memory.

Emotional versus rational appeals

Using emotional appeals in advertising may be more effective for low involvement issues in which consumers believe that there is little difference between products in the same product class. An emotive advertisement may increase the level of involvement in the decision.[20] For example, the advertisement shown in figure 9.8 may increase the involvement of a consumer considering buying new tyres for a car. However, emotive advertising tends to contain little information on which to base a rational decision, and if the decision requires high involvement (and a consumer needs information with which to compare alternative products) a rational comparison may be more effective.

KEEP YOUR FAMILY SAFE. STICK WITH DUNLOP.

Available from Dunlop Super Dealers, Bob Jane T-Marts and Beaurepaires for tyres.

Figure 9.8: This advertisement uses fear and love to sell tyres by appealing to the need for children's safety.

One-sided versus two-sided appeals

A one-sided appeal presents a positive argument for the benefits of the sponsor's product. A two-sided appeal presents both positive and negative information. The two-sided argument might be either refutational or non-refutational. In a refutational argument, negative information about the product is discounted by the sponsor. In a non-refutational argument, the positive and negative aspects of the product are simply presented without any counterarguments.[21]

One might wonder why a sponsor would provide negative information about the firm's product to the consumer. The main reason for presenting a two-sided argument is that the appeal is seen as more credible by the target audience. Secondly, presenting the less positive aspects of the product tends to diffuse counterargumentation by the consumer, because the advertisement has already stated the counterarguments.[22] Thirdly, if the sponsor believes that the consumer has false beliefs about the product, the presentation of those beliefs allows the sponsor to correct them. Lastly, the product with minor negative characteristics can benefit from the comparison of the small negative aspects with the extensive positive aspects.

There is some evidence that the effectiveness of one- and two-sided appeals is mediated by the characteristics of the consumer.[23] If the consumer has a high level of education, is highly involved with the product, and disagrees with the company's position, a two-sided argument may be more effective. However, if the consumer has a lower level of education, less involvement with the product and believes the product to be satisfactory, the reverse is true.

Repetition

As you will recall from chapter 5, repetition plays an important part in the learning of information. For example, repetition of an advertisement may help the consumer to learn the information contained in the advertisement. Initial liking of the advertisement under low involvement conditions may enable the consumer to recall the advertisement. However, there is a danger that the advertisement will be seen as boring or annoying if the level of repetition is too high.[24] This is known as 'advertising wear out'. Marketers need to ensure that there is enough in the advertising content to maintain consumer interest.

Fear and humour appeals

Marketers often appeal to strong emotions to promote products. Fear appeals are most commonly used in campaigns such as road safety, AIDS awareness and anti-smoking, and in some insurance advertising. However, care needs to be taken to ensure that the level of fear aroused is only moderate, because research shows that if the advertisement is seen to be too frightening, consumers are more likely to 'switch off' and tune out the message.[25] Fear appeals are most effective when the consumer is provided with a solution to the problem, for example, by explaining how to handle friends who have had too much to drink before driving, rather than simply alerting consumers to the dangers associated with such behaviours.

Humorous advertising can be an effective way of gaining consumer attention.[26] In addition, humour can create a positive feeling towards the advertisement and the product. However, what one individual finds funny may be seen as silly or offensive by others. Humour may also divert the attention of the consumer from the content of the advertisement so that the advertisement itself may be recalled but not the brand of the product, thus defeating the purpose of the advertising.[27] In order to be effective, humour must have some connection with the product and should not belittle the target audience.

MEDIA CHARACTERISTICS

Advertising uses a number of different media to convey its message. The overriding decision for a marketer is which medium to choose to convey a message. The first consideration when selecting media should be the media habits of the target market. The second should be the level of product involvement of the consumer.

Earlier in this chapter, you learned that consumers process information about low involvement products via a peripheral route (pages 219–20). Under conditions that favour peripheral processing, broadcast media (radio and television) tend to be more effective transmission agents for low involvement products. For example, marketers use radio advertising to influence consumers as they drive to and from work, and this is advantageous mainly for low involvement products. Print media can also take advantage of driving time to convey limited information with frequent repetition. For example, on frequently and heavily travelled streets, billboards and other signs remind consumers of product alternatives. For high involvement products, print media have an advantage because they can carry extensive information.

All types of media have advantages and disadvantages because each one has a different geographic coverage, cost structure and audience. It is therefore important to assess the placement of advertising in relation to both the competition from other advertisements and sources and the use of different media by different target audiences. Magazines, newspapers, radio stations and, to a lesser extent, television stations all have distinct target audiences and can provide consumer profiles to help marketers make wise decisions about where to place advertising. For example, a large number of special interest magazines are available in Australia and New Zealand, which attract readers from specific segments of the market. These types of media provide information about readership that allows the marketer to be more efficient in reaching the target market and eliminate advertising waste. Television stations, while they may have very broad consumer profiles generally, can provide guidelines as to distinct consumer groups that are likely to watch specific types of programs. Where only a small number of television stations exist in a geographic area, the viewing population will be very diverse and communication with a specific audience may be more efficient using another medium.

RECEIVER CHARACTERISTICS

While it may be relatively simple to ensure that the content and delivery of a message meet the objectives of a marketing strategy, different people may intepret the information they receive in different ways. Each individual has different perceptual processing abilities and this will have an impact on the type of information received and how an individual reacts to it.

Factors such as the age, sex, socioeconomic status and cultural background of an individual obviously will affect the way in which the individual reacts to an advertisement. Other factors, such as the level of a consumer's self-esteem, may also impact on how easily the consumer is persuaded. People who have low levels of self-esteem are more likely to be persuaded by advertising than those with a strong feeling of self-worth. Intelligence also plays a part in how easily consumers can be persuaded to change their attitudes. Research suggests that more intelligent consumers are less likely to be persuaded by emotive advertising but are more susceptible to logical arguments.[28]

The intention of the consumer when he or she is exposed to information has an effect on the amount of information processed. Consumers who are seeking information for high involvement decisions are more likely to pay attention to advertising. However, since the majority of consumer decisions are low involvement ones, the ability to reach the consumer and break through the advertising clutter is critical.

ATTITUDE TOWARDS THE ADVERTISEMENT

Attitude towards the advertisement is the consumer's predisposition to respond favourably or unfavourably towards an advertisement on the basis of its characteristics rather than those of the product.[29] The consumer's feelings about the advertisement are important because they can influence feelings about the product. When consumers have positive feelings about an advertisement, they are more likely to have positive feelings about the brand and the sponsoring firm. Puto and Wells have referred to this phenomenon as a 'transformational effect'.[30] The transformational effect does not always occur, but when it does, the advertiser receives an added benefit from the advertising dollars.

Consumer involvement influences the degree to which liking an advertisement produces increased favourability towards the product. When the consumer is less involved, the attitude towards the advertisement seems to be more important. This is because consumers pay more attention to peripheral cues, such as the imagery and format, when they are not as concerned with product benefits. However, attitude towards the advertisement may have an effect on high involvement decisions as well.

Given that liking an advertisement is a factor that influences attitudes towards brands, it is sensible for advertisers to create likeable advertising. However, there are two qualifying findings that should be considered.

Firstly, advertising that is actively disliked sometimes produces excellent sales results. Disliked advertisements produce positive sales results when they increase the consumer's awareness of the product and influence memory. So, advertisements that are either positive or negative can be effective influencers of behaviour. Secondly, attitudes towards advertising are frequently quite weak. Therefore, product trial is often a stronger predictor of attitudes towards brand purchase.

ATTITUDE CHANGE AND PERSISTENCE OVER TIME

The three components of attitudes — knowledge, feelings and behaviour — have varying amounts of impact on the decision processes in different types of decisions. Knowing the type of decision process a consumer uses will enable the marketer to decide which of these components is most likely to elicit a change in attitude.

Early studies of the persistence of attitudinal change suggested that very few attitudinal changes lasted,[31] but more current research suggests some attitudes at least may be long-lasting.[32] Attitudes that are supported by a network of other, consistent attitudes and those that consumers are required to defend appear to be the most resistant to change. For example, holding political elections frequently may encourage consumers to discuss political ideas and hence become more committed to their views because they are required to defend them to their friends.

Similarly, consumers who are required to discuss or defend their product choice may be more likely to maintain that product choice. This suggests that encouraging consumers to display their brand loyalty may in fact increase that loyalty. Campaigns such as 'Ask me about my Toyota' may encourage buyers of Toyota motor vehicles to become more resistant to brand swapping, although the length of time between car purchases may moderate against this.

 S U M M A R Y

Marketing strategy is designed to change the way consumers think and feel about products. Multiattribute models of attitudes offer suggestions about how this might be done. The elaboration likelihood model suggests that attitude change can take place by a central route for high involvement decisions or by a peripheral route for low involvement decisions. These two routes to persuasion form an elaboration likelihood continuum. Sherif's theory of social judgement suggests that messages that are similar to the existing beliefs of the consumer are more likely to be accepted and therefore fall into the consumer's latitude of acceptance. Those that are very different will be contrasted and fall into the latitude of rejection. Katz maintains that attitudes can be changed by addressing the four functions of attitudes: the utilitarian function, the value-expressive function, the ego-defensive function, and the knowledge function. The hierarchy of effects model also has implications for attitude change.

Consumers collect information upon which to base attitudes from experience with products and services, social networks, and the media. The communication model, containing a source, a message, a medium of transmission, a receiver and feedback, provides a framework for considering the effectiveness of change processes. Source credibility depends upon perceived attractiveness, expertise and trustworthiness. Message characteristics include type of appeal (rational or emotional), the use of pictures or words, whether the argument is one-sided or two-sided, and the amount of repetition. Fear and humour are two specific types of appeals used in advertising. The most important considerations in choosing media are the media habits of the target market and the level of involvement of the consumer. Receiver characteristics interact with media and message characteristics to produce consumer responses. Age, sex, socioeconomic status and cultural background have an impact on how the consumer reacts to the message.

Besides having an attitude towards the product, consumers also have an attitude towards the advertisement. The attitude towards the advertisement can influence the consumer's memory for, and liking of, the advertised brand.

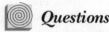

Questions

1. Consider your own behaviour with regard to buying Australian made products. Has it changed over time? If so, what factors have contributed to this change? Is your attitude similar to that of your friends and parents?

2. Spend 5 minutes writing down all of the advertising that you recall seeing in the past 24 hours. How many of these contained information with which you agree, and how many did not? Which type of advertisements were you more likely to recall? Can you explain why this occurred?

3. Collect some advertising material that uses people or cartoon characters. How does the type of person or character reflect the product? Which other people or characters could have been used? What impact would this have on the positioning and image of the product?

4. Compare different advertisements for the same product category — consider the differences between approaches used by competing brands. Look at the balances between pictures and text, differences in media selection and repetition of the same advertisement versus placement of slightly different versions of the same advertisement. Why do you think these differences exist? If an advertisement is used in both print and television, how has the advertisement been changed? Why do you think these changes were made?

5. Find copies of advertisements that you believe are funny. Compare your reaction to those of other members of your class and that of your lecturer. Can you explain the differences (if any) on the basis of age, sex or other different characteristics?

Case study question

Read the article on pages 237–238 and assess the advertising strategy used by Pfizer Inc. in relation to the formal research on attitude change and persuasive communication.

Case study

Advertising products that people like and want to buy is easy. In creating their marketing programs, manufacturers of chocolate, softdrink or beer start with the safe assumption that most consumers like their products. Advertising a product that people do not like, or that solves a problem most people do not want to discuss, is not easy.

During the past three years, the pharmaceutical company Pfizer Inc has found a way to advertise a product that treats a delicate, unpleasant and often embarrassing ailment: haemorrhoids. In 1988, the company started a low-key magazine advertising campaign for its Rectinol haemorrhoid treatment product. Since then, the campaign has moved on to radio and, earlier this year, television.

The ad campaign, which uses the cheeky theme, "Music to your rear", has turned Rectinol into one of the fastest-growing products in Australian pharmacies. When the campaign began, sales of all haemorrhoid treatments were stalled at $2.1 million a year. Last year, the market was worth $4.5 million, an increase of 114%. Rectinol's share of the category has marched from 30% to 54% since 1988 and awareness of the Rectinol brand name among haemorrhoid sufferers has more than doubled to 80%.

It was a different story in 1988. Rectinol was only available through the government-run pharmaceutical benefits scheme. It was one of the most frequently prescribed haemorrhoid treatments, but was an unprofitable brand for Pfizer. "It was losing money hand over fist," says Tim Templeman, Pfizer's marketing manager.

"It was a languishing brand," says David McLean, managing director of Pfizer's advertising agency, Sudler & Hennessey. "The Government holds down prices of products on the pharmaceutical benefits scheme and manufacturers have little room to manoeuvre in terms of pricing, packaging or product innovation. They also are reliant on doctors prescribing their product." Rectinol could be sold without a prescription, but few people had heard of the brand.

Three years ago, Pfizer decided to take Rectinol out of the pharmaceutical benefits scheme and relaunch it as an over-the-counter product. Rectinol's price was doubled, which Templeman says was the first price rise since 1986. Pfizer appointed Sudler & Hennessey — which already handled advertising for Pfizer's Combantrin worming tablets and Visine eye-drops — to create a consumer advertising campaign for the product.

"Pfizer took Rectinol out of the dispensary, put it in the front of pharmacies and exposed it to the risk of sale through advertising," McLean says. "The product responded and is now a profitable, growing brand."

It was the potential of the haemorrhoids market that encouraged Pfizer to push Rectinol into the over-the-counter medicine market. At least 10% of Australians suffer from haemorrhoids and an estimated 30% of people will develop haemorrhoids at some point in their lives. But the lack of aggressive marketing had squeezed the market's potential and relegated haemorrhoid treatments to the backroom of the pharmacy retail trade.

Taking Rectinol into open distribution and promoting it as a regular consumer product was risky. "Most people are reluctant to admit to having haemorrhoids," says Kurian Verghese, marketing director at Pfizer. "Asking a chemist for a haemorrhoid treatment is even worse than asking for condoms. Because of a typically Anglo-Saxon anxiety about the body, people were simply not willing to own up (to having haemorrhoids) in public. The advertising campaign had a more difficult task than just to sell the product: it had to legitimise the condition."

Pfizer and Sudler & Hennessey researched haemorrhoid sufferers during 1988. The research did not unearth any big surprises: consumers said the promise of quick relief from the pain and itching caused by haemorrhoids was the main selling point of a haemorrhoid treatment. But the research did give Sudler & Hennessey a guide to what to avoid in creating the ad campaign for Rectinol.

(continued)

"The research told us to not make fun of haemorrhoids in any way and that the tone of our advertising would be vital to its success," says Rob Pizzey, group account director at Sudler & Hennessey. "We had to be very careful about what we said in the advertising. We had to show respect for haemorrhoid sufferers."

Rival haemorrhoid treatment products such as Parke-Davis's Anusol and Haemorrex and Whitehall Laboratories' Preparation H were already being advertised in magazines aimed at pregnant women, and men aged 50-plus, who are the main sufferers of haemorrhoids. "Rectinol's rivals were all low-budget products, with small advertising exposure," McLean says.

The ad campaign for Rectinol started in 1988, with low-key ads in magazines such as *New Idea* and *Reader's Digest*. In 1989, the campaign became sassier, with a series of radio ads that talked about "bum deals" and "happy bottoms".

The radio ads introduced the "Music to your rear" theme and the use of string instruments to simulate the pain and discomfort felt by haemorrhoid sufferers. Sudler & Hennessey is experienced in creating advertising for "difficult" products, such as Pfizer's Combantrin worming tablets, and the period-pain treatment products Ponstan from Parke-Davis and Naprogesic from Syntex Australia. But Pizzey admits that finding a creative way to promote a haemorrhoid treatment was tough.

"We had to find a device that would make the product stand out and communicate the benefits of Rectinol, with a modest advertising budget. But we could not send up haemorrhoid sufferers or the ailment," he says. "The ad campaign had to generate quick sales to justify Pfizer's decision to move Rectinol into open distribution and justify further marketing expenditure to boost sales."

Sudler & Hennessey's associate creative director, Paul Paech, came up with the idea of using string instruments playing scratchy and discordant notes. The "Music to your rear" theme developed from there. "The use of sound effects gave us a way to solve the problem of how to communicate the problems of haemorrhoids and the benefits of Rectinol," Pizzey says.

The "Music to your rear" strategy was not researched extensively with consumers. "Our 1988 research gave us the parameters in which we could work," McLean says. "We did some conceptual research when the 'Music to your rear' theme was developed and knew the tone of our advertising would be correct." Pizzey says Pfizer's marketing executives were involved in every step of the campaign's development, so the "Music to your rear" strategy did not shock them.

In late 1990, Pfizer decided to advertise Rectinol on TV. Pizzey says the radio ad was "television-ed", with the creation of a 30-second commercial featuring a string quartet and the "Music to your rear" theme. The TV commercial began in February and will run, intermittently, throughout the year. Sudler & Hennessey also created new point-of-sale displays for pharmacies and a series of magazine ads aimed at pregnant women. The ads use the headline "Babies are a pain in the bum".

McLean says he "winced" when he first saw the magazine ads. "But we have managed to take a very difficult subject and cloak it in an element of whimsy and humor, without laughing at the patient or spending a fortune on advertising," he says. Pfizer's 1990–91 marketing budget for Rectinol is $500 000.

The 1988 price rise has contributed to Rectinol's increased market share among haemorrhoid treatments and, according to Pizzey, generated at least half of the market's growth during the past three years. Before the TV commercial began, Rectinol ranked 53rd on the list of top-selling over-the-counter medicines in pharmacies. It now ranks 22nd and McLean predicts it will land in the top 20 by the second half of this year.

McLean claims the Rectinol ad campaign has also reduced the embarrassment of asking a chemist for a haemorrhoid treatment. "It has given consumers a brand name, so they can buy a haemorrhoid treatment without discussing their ailment with the pharmacist or sales staff," he says.

Neil Shoebridge,
Business Review Weekly,
24 May 1991

SUGGESTED READING

R. Petty and J. T. Cacioppo, *Attitudes and Persuasion: Classic and Contemporary Approaches*, William C. Brown, Dubuque, Iowa, 1981.

Y. Wind, V. Mahjan and R. Cardozo (eds), *New Product Forecasting: Models and Applications*, Lexington Books, Lexington, Mass., 1981.

M. Schudson, *Advertising: The Uneasy Persuasion*, Basic Books, New York, 1984.

W. Leiss, S. Kline and S. Jhally, *Social Communications in Advertising: Persons, Products and Images of Well-Being*, Methuen, Toronto, 1986.

ENDNOTES

1. Martin Fishbein, 'Attitudes and the Prediction of Behaviour', in Martin Fishbein (ed.), *Readings in Attitude Theory and Measurement*, John Wiley and Sons, New York, 1967, pp. 477–92.

2. R. E. Petty and J. T. Cacioppo, *Attitudes and Persuasion: Classic and Contemporary Approaches*, William C. Brown, Dubuque, Iowa, 1981.

3. N. H. Anderson, *Foundations of Information Integration Theory*, Academic Press, New York, 1981.

4. S. Chaiken, 'Heuristic versus Systematic Information Processing and the Use of Source Versus Message Clues in Persuasion', *Journal of Personality and Social Psychology*, 39, 1981, pp. 752–66.

5. R. E. Petty and J. T. Cacioppo, 'The Elaboration Model of Persuasion', in L. Berkowitz (ed.), *Advances in Experimental Social Psychology*, Vol. 19, Academic Press, New York, 1986, pp. 123–205.

6. R. L. Celci and J. C. Olsen, 'The Role of Involvement in Attention and Comprehension Processes', *Journal of Consumer Research*, 15, 1988, pp. 210–44. Peter Wright, 'The Cognitive Processes Mediating the Acceptance of Advertising', *Journal of Marketing Research*, 10, Feb. 1973, pp. 53–62.

7. R. E. Burnkrant and H. R. Unnava, 'Self Referencing: A Strategy for Increasing Processing of Message Content', *Personality and Social Psychology Bulletin*, 15, 1989, pp. 628–38.

8. P. W. Miniard, S. Bhatla and R. L. Rose, 'On the Formation and Relationship of Ad and Brand Attitudes: An Experimental and Causal Analysis', *Working Paper Series*, College of Business, Ohio State University, Columbus, 1988. Martin R. Lautman and Larry Percy, 'Cognitive and Affective Responses in Attribute-Based Versus End-Benefit Oriented Advertising', in Thomas Kinnear (ed.), *Advances in Consumer Research*, 11, Association for Consumer Research, Provo, Utah, 1984, pp. 11–17.

9. J. W. Alba and H. Marmorstein, 'The Effects of Frequency Knowledge on Consumer Decision Making', *Journal of Consumer Research*, 13, 1987, pp. 14–25.

10. M. Sherif and C. E. Hovland, *Social Judgment*, Yale University Press, New Haven, 1964.

11. James McCullough, Douglas MacLachlan and Reza Moinpour, 'Impact of Information on Preference and Perception', in Andrew Mitchell (ed.), *Advances in Consumer Research*, 9, Association for Consumer Research, Ann Arbor, Mich., 1982, pp. 402–5.

12. Communication model adapted from W. Schromm and D. Roberts (eds), *The Process and Effects of Mass Communications*, University of Illinois, Cerbona, 1971.

13. For the seminal research on source credibility, see Carl J. Hovland, Irving Janis and Harold Kelley, *Communication and Persuasion*, Yale University Press, New Haven, Conn., 1953.

14. Timothy C. Brock, 'Communication–Recipient Similarity and Decision Change', *Journal of Personality and Social Psychology*, 1, June 1965, pp. 650–54.

15. K. Dion, 'What is Beautiful is Good', *Journal of Personality and Social Psychology*, 24, Dec. 1972, pp. 285–90.

16. P. M. Homer and L. R. Kahle, 'Source Expertise, Time of Source Identification and Involvement in Persuasion', *Journal of Advertising*, 8, 1990, pp. 30–39. M. E. Goldberg and J. Hartwick, 'The Effects of Advertiser Reputation and Extremity of Advertising Claim on Advertising Effectiveness', *Journal of Consumer Research*, 16, Sept. 1990, pp. 172–79.

17. T. R. King, 'Credibility Gap: More Consumers Find Celebrity Ads Unpersuasive', *Wall Street Journal*, 5 July 1989, p. 5. C. Atkin and M. Block, 'Effectiveness of Celebrity Endorsers', *Journal of Advertising Research*, March 1983, pp. 57–61. L. Kahle and P. Homer, 'Physical Attractiveness of the Celebrity Endorser', *Journal of Consumer Research*, 11, March 1985, pp. 954–61. G. McCracken, 'Who is the Celebrity Endorser: Cultural Foundations of the Endorsement Process', *Journal of Consumer Research*, 16, Dec. 1989, pp. 310–21.

18. M. A. Kamins, 'An Investigation into the "Match-up" Hypothesis of Celebrity Advertising', *Journal of Advertising*, 8, 1990, pp. 4–13. S. Misra and S. E. Beatty, 'Celebrity Spokesperson and Brand Congruence', *Journal of Business Research*, 21, Sept. 1990, pp. 159–73.

19. T. L. Childers and M. J. Houston, 'Conditions for a Picture Superiority Effect on Consumer Memory', *Journal of Consumer Research*, 11, Sept. 1984, pp. 643–54.

20. William J. McGuire, *The Effectiveness of Appeals in Advertising*, Advertising Research Foundation, New York, 1963. Michael L. Ray and Rajeev Batra, 'Emotion and Persuasion in Advertising: What We Do and Don't Know About Affect', in Richard P. Bagozzi and Alice M. Tybout (eds), *Advances in Consumer Research*, 10, Association for Consumer Research, Ann Arbor, Mich., 1983, pp. 543–48. E. Broadbent, 'The Hidden Preattentive Processes', *American Psychologist*, 32, 1977, pp. 109–18. A. J. Silk and T. G. Vavral, 'The Influence of Advertising's Affective Qualities on Consumer Response', in G. D. Hughes and M. L. Ray (eds), *Buyer/Consumer Information Processing*, University of North Carolina Press, Chapel Hill, N.C., 1974.

21. Discussed in Henry Assael, *Consumer Behaviour and Marketing Action*, PWS Kent, Boston, Mass., 1983, p. 599.

22. Michael Kamins and Henry Assael, 'Two-Sided Versus One-Sided Appeals: A Cognitive Perspective on Argumentation, Source Derogation, and the Effect of Disconfirming Trial on Belief Change', *Journal of Marketing Research*, Feb. 1987, pp. 29–39.

23. George M. Zinkhan and Claude R. Martin Jr, 'Message Characteristics and Audience Characteristics: Predictors of Advertising Response', in *Advances in Consumer Research*, Dec. 1987, pp. 404–20. Mark J. Alpert and Linda L. Golden, 'The Impact of Education on the Relative Effectiveness of One-Sided and Two-Sided Mass Communications in Advertising', in Bruce J. Walker et al. (eds), *Proceedings of the American Marketing Association Educators Conference*, Series No. 48, 1982, pp. 30–33.

24. H. Krugman, 'Why Three Exposures May Be Enough', *Journal of Advertising Research*, 12, Dec. 1972, pp. 11–14.

25. John R. Stuteville, 'Psychic Defense Against High Fear Appeals: A Key Marketing Variable', *Journal of Marketing*, 34, April 1970, pp. 39–45. S. W. McDaniel and V. A. Zeithaml, 'The Effect of Fear on Purchase Intentions', *Psychology and Marketing*, Fall/Winter 1984, pp. 72–83. M. S. LaTour and S. A. Zahra, 'Fear Appeals as Marketing Strategy', *Journal of Consumer Marketing*, Spring 1989, pp. 61–70. L. S. Unger and J. M. Stearns, 'The Use of Fear and Guilt Messages in Television Advertising', in P. E. Murphy et al. (eds), *Proceedings of the American Marketing Association*, American Marketing Association, Chicago, 1983, pp. 16–20. R. P. Hill, 'An Exploration of the Relationship Between AIDS Related Anxiety and the Evaluation of Condom Advertisements', *Journal of Advertising*, Vol. 4, 17, 1988, pp. 35–42.

26. T. J. Madden and M. G. Weinberger, 'Humour in Advertising', *Journal of Advertising Research*, Sept. 1984, pp. 23–29. B. D. Gelb and G. M. Zinkhan, 'Humor and Advertising Effectiveness After Repeated Exposures to a Radio Commercial', *Journal of Advertising*, 2, 1986, pp. 15–20. C. Scott, D. M. Klein and J. Bryant, 'Consumer Response to Humour in Advertising', *Journal of Consumer Research*, March 1990, pp. 498–501. A. Chattopadhyay and K. Basu, 'Humour in Advertising', *Journal of Marketing Research*, 27, Nov. 1990, pp. 466–76.

27. Calvin P. Duncan, James E. Nelson and Nancy T. Frontczak, 'The Effect of Humour on Advertising Comprehension', in Thomas Kinnear (ed.), *Advances in Consumer Research*, 11, Association for Consumer Research, Provo, Utah, 1984, pp. 432–37.

28. C. I. Hovland, I. L. Janis and H. H. Kelly, *Communication and Persuasion*, Yale University Press, 1953.

29. This discussion is based on Henry Assael, *Consumer Behaviour and Marketing Action*, pp. 236–38. Also see Julie A. Edell and Marian Chapman Burke, 'The Power of Feelings in Understanding Advertising Effects', *Journal of Consumer Research*, 14, Dec. 1987, pp. 421–33.

30. Christopher P. Puto and William D. Wells, 'Informational and Transformational Advertising: The Differential Effects of Time', in T. Kinnear, *Advances in Consumer Research*, 11, 1984, pp. 572–76.

31. T. D. Cook and B. R. Flay, 'The Persistence of Experimentally Induced Attitude Change', in L. Berkowitz (ed.), *Advances in Experimental Social Psychology*, 11, 1978, Academic Press, New York, pp. 1–57.

32. C. P. Haugtvedt, 'Persistence and Resistance of Communication Induced Attitude Changes', in D. Schumann (ed.), *Proceedings of the Society for Consumer Psychology*, Society for Consumer Psychology, Knoxville, Tenn., 1988.

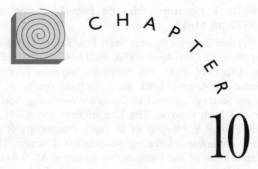

C H A P T E R

10

Families and households

OBJECTIVES

This chapter should help you understand:

- why the study of families and households is important to the understanding of buyer behaviour
- how families influence buying decisions
- different roles adopted by family members and how these roles impact on family decision making
- some of the changes that have occurred and how they have affected family decision making.

 ## CONSUMER SOCIALISATION

Families not only train future consumers — they are also the major consumption units within our society. Clusters of similar family types can form basic segments from which target markets for certain products can be selected. The household 'buys' as a unit, so purchase decisions for some products can involve a number of people. In order to develop products and create effective communication strategies, marketers need to monitor changes in family and household structures. They also need to know how families make purchase decisions.

We have considered the processes by which consumers learn about the world, how they process and remember information. Parents and other carers teach children the ways of behaving and thinking that the society considers good or acceptable. Although parents have the greatest influence on children, other adults, friends and the media also have considerable impact. This process of absorbing a society's values, customs and behaviours is called 'socialisation'. The goal is to have the child internalise the society's values so that disobeying them produces a sense of guilt. Children learn the expectations of the society both formally (through schools and other institutions) and informally by associating with and observing other people (see figure 10.1).

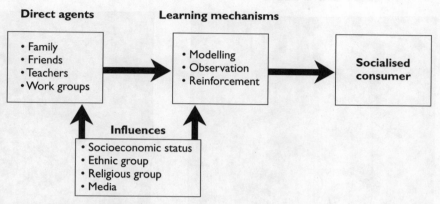

Figure 10.1: Consumer socialisation

Society teaches children marketplace behaviour. For most children, their earliest experience of shopping will be with other members of their family. From this activity they will learn a range of skills that form the basis of their future shopping behaviour: how to shop, where to shop, how to buy. They learn where to shop by observing how far mum or dad will travel to buy goods such as milk and bread (day-to-day commodity items). They learn that it is usual to go to the supermarket for most grocery items, and that it is acceptable to travel a distance to search for and buy specialist goods.

The evaluation of products purchased may also be influenced by families. Families with specific requirements such as those with food allergies or with special dietary needs, may 'teach' their members to read product labels carefully before purchase. They learn that some products are for family consumption but some are bought for special occasions; that some products are poisonous or should be used in specific ways, such as pharmaceutical products; that certain foods are nutritious and good to eat. Families with tight budgetary constraints may teach their members to compare product sizes and costs.

Children may also learn that shopping is a chore or that it is fun. They learn how to shop; what attributes of the store or product are important and even what brands should be bought. As children mature they learn about money and the different ways of paying for products.

Other people and the media have a significant impact on children, particularly television advertising. This is understandable when you consider that the average viewing time for children is over 18 hours a week and they will be exposed to 22 000 television commercials in any one year. In Australia, as in many countries, there is community concern about the impact of television advertising on children.[1] In response, the Australian Consumers Association conducted research and produced the book *I know what ads are*, to help children understand media messages (see figure 10.2).

What do I need?   What do I want?

Figure 10.2: Extracts from *I know what ads are* by Susan Churchman, for the Australian Consumers Association

Research into the effects of advertising on children is controversial with some identifying deleterious effects and others not.[2] In 1978, a select committee enquiry into children and television advertising reported that parental reaction to advertisements, their interaction with children and their socioeconomic groups had a direct impact on how children responded to advertisements.[3] More recent research carried out by the Australian Association of National Advertisers (AANA) shows that parents and friends have more influence on children's product choices.[4] This study reflects findings of overseas studies that show parental influence to be more powerful than television commercials.[5]

Commercials in Australia conform to the guidelines established by the International Chamber of Commerce, the Federation of Australian Commercial Television Stations and the Australian Broadcasting Tribunal. One guideline is that advertisements should not cause children to place demands on parents.[6] There are also guidelines as to the content of advertisements and what products should be advertised during children's programs.

While research shows that parents and friends have a stronger direct influence on children's responses to advertisements, the effect of television advertisements on parents and society in general continues to be the subject of debate.[7]

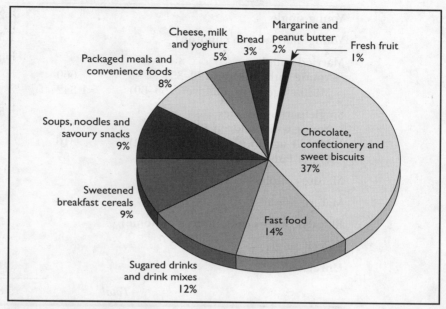

Figure 10.3: The proportions of advertising for different kinds of food shown in one week (Monday to Friday) between 3.30 and 6.00 p.m. (*Source: Choice* magazine, October 1990)

 # AUSTRALIAN HOUSEHOLDS

What is a family? The term 'family' technically means a group of two or more persons related by blood, marriage or adoption, not necessarily living in the same house. In Australia, there are two parent families, single parent families, blended families, extended families, childless families and many more types. There are also many people who live together but are not biologically related. From the point of view of marketing, the term 'household' is more useful than the term 'family' to describe a group of people living in one house. It is important, therefore, to consider not only the family as a unit of consumption, but also the composition of households within Australia, and their growth.

HOUSEHOLD COMPOSITION

There are approximately 5.8 million households in Australia. Table 10.1 gives details of their composition. It shows that approximately 70 per cent are married couple families (with or without children) and 35 per cent are two parent families with dependent children and adult children living at home.[8] Single parent families make up 9 per cent of all households. The most significant market segment, therefore, is made up of the households with two adults and at least two children.

Table 10.1: Household composition

		Total households (thousands)	%
Young single		240	4
Young married (no children)		1 326	23
Married couples		2002	35
Young with children (20–35)	660		
Middle aged with children (35–60)	1 342		
Single parent families		531	9
Young with children (20–35)	158		
Middle aged with children (36–64)	316		
Older families (65+)	57		
Mature couples		325	5.6
Mature single		433	7.4
Elderly couples (no children at home)		360	6
Elderly single		460	8
Unrelated		123	2
Total		5 800	

(*Source*: Compiled from 'Census Characteristics of Australia', *1991 Census of Population and Housing*, Australian Bureau of Statistics, Catalogue No. 2710.0, 1993)

The rate of household formation has continued to grow steadily, but the average household size has been steadily decreasing — from an average of 3.55 persons in 1961 to 2.5 persons in 1991. At the end of the 1970s and during the first four years of the 1980s there was an upturn in the birth rate. This has been termed the 'echo effect' — brought about by the children of the 'baby boomers' moving into adulthood. Since the mid-1980s, there has been a slowing-down of both household formation and birth rates. Around 20 per cent of households are made up of single people. Four per cent are 'young singles' and approximately 16 per cent are people over 36 living alone.[9]

THE CHANGING HOUSEHOLD

Over the last three decades, households in Australia have undergone significant changes that will continue to affect household composition into the next century. These changes are a function of four main factors:
- decline in marriage
- low birth rates
- increase in life expectancy
- increase in divorce rates.

Table 10.2: Registered marriages, divorces and births in Australia, 1987 to 1992 (crude rates per thousand of mean estimated resident population)

	Marriages	Divorces	Births
1987	7.0	2.4	15.0
1988	7.1	2.5	14.9
1989	7.0	2.5	14.9
1990	6.9	2.5	15.4
1991	6.6	2.6	14.9
1992	6.6	2.6	15.1

(*Source*: Compiled from 'Census Characteristics of Australia', *1991 Census of Population and Housing*, Australian Bureau of Statistics, Catalogue No. 2710.0, 1993. 'Population. Demographics and Trends', Australian Bureau of Statistics, 1992)

Single households

The fall in marriage rates means that the number of single households is likely to increase. An increasing number of people in Australia will remain unmarried all their lives. It has been estimated that as many as 20–25 per cent of women born in the early 1960s may never marry, compared with 4 per cent of those born in the 1930s.[10] Increasing divorce rates and increased life expectancy, particularly of women, means that many of the key decision makers in households will be female. Women generally live longer and are least likely to remarry after divorce.[11]

Single households are becoming a significant proportion of the Australian population. In 1990, the Australian Bureau of Statistics estimated that, by the year 2031, there will be 5.2 million Australians (20 per cent of the population) over the age of 65, compared with 1.9 million (11 per cent of the population) in 1990.

Smaller households

The number of children born in Australia per couple dropped from 3.51 in 1961 to 2.87 in 1971 and 1.91 in 1992. The decline is attributed to a number of factors. There has been a growth in the number of childless couples. A number of women are opting not to have children at all, for career and personal freedom reasons.[12] Many women have the view that the ideal number of children is two. More women are delaying childbirth until their thirties. The increase in de facto relationships is another contributing factor. Fertility rates in de facto relationships tend to be lower than those in marriage.

Studies in the USA[13] have shown that there are higher fertility rates among Asian migrants. As the number of Asian migrants to Australia increases, this may affect the country's overall fertility rate. The current trend, however, is towards smaller families.

More households

In the period 1971–1976, the rate of household formation was twice that of population growth, reflecting the fact that older members of the baby-boom generation were reaching the stage in their life cycles of separate household formation. The continued high rate of household formation during the second half of the 1970s and into the 1980s reflected the higher divorce and separation rates and the tendency for the young to leave the parental home at an earlier age. In the 1980s there was, however, a slight shift away from this. High youth unemployment, high retention rates in education and increased housing costs meant that young people remained at home longer.[14]

In summary, it would seem that the overall number of households in Australia will increase, but households will be smaller and more diverse.

AUSTRALIAN HOUSEHOLD CHARACTERISTICS

In the 1960s, the observation that families go through specific stages led to the introduction of the 'family life cycle' concept. The assumption was that, as a family moves through each stage of development, different products would be required and the volume of usage would vary. The idea developed of regarding the different stages as market segments. One of the earliest classifications of these stages was produced by William Wells and George Gubar (see table 10.3(a)). The classification system developed by Wells and Gubar makes certain assumptions about families, many of which have changed in the years since the model was developed. Two more modern approaches (see table 10.3(b) and (c)) attempt to overcome some of the problems associated with changes in society, such as divorce, the single lifestyle and childless couples. They are similar in that both are based on a flow chart of alternative life cycle paths; both use cutoffs of 35 years and 65 years. The Gilly–Ennis model treats any cohabiting couple as married and excludes households where dependent children are over 18.

Research by Charles Schaninger and William Danko found that these models have limitations, but that the Gilly–Ennis model produced better associations with products purchased. Their results prompted them to make the following observations about family life cycle models in general:[15]

1. Separation of full nest households by the presence of preschool-age versus school-age or older children is a particularly important determinant of family consumption patterns.
2. Retirement status (occupation of husbands at retirement for married couples) is superior to using age 65 to delineate attitude and consumption differences between middle aged and older households.
3. The Gilly–Ennis model could be improved by either combining delayed full nest and full nest I households or by identifying separate full nest I, II and III categories based on age 45.
4. None of the models does a very good job of identifying non-traditional or delayed progression family households or remarriages.
5. Divorced individuals without children at home have consumption patterns comparable with bachelors of similar age; thus positions within the current household, rather than sequential role complexes or extended parental roles determine their consumption pattern.

Table 10.3: Three versions of the family life cycle concept

(a) Wells and Gubar (1966) categories
Bachelor, young single
Newly married, young, no children
Full nest I, youngest child < 6
Full nest II, youngest child ≥ 6
Full nest III, older, dependent children
Empty nest I, older, no children, head in labour force
Empty nest II, older, no children, head retired
Solitary survivor I, older, widowed or divorced, in labour force
Solitary survivor II, older, widowed or divorced, retired
Other

(b) Murphy and Staples (1979) categories
Young single
Young married without children
Young married with children
Divorced
    Young without children
    Middle aged without children
    Middle aged without dependent children
Divorced
    Young with children
    Middle aged with children
Middle aged married without children
Middle aged married with children
Middle aged married without dependent children
Older married (no dependent children)
Older unmarried (no dependent children)
Other

(c) Gilly and Ennis (1982) categories
Bachelor I
Bachelor II
Newlywed
Single parent (young and middle aged)
Full nest I (child < 6)
Delayed full nest (child < 6)
Full nest II and III (youngest children > 6)
Childless couple (no children at home)
Older couple
Bachelor III
Other

(*Source*: Adapted from W. Wells and G. Gubar, 'The Life Cycle Concept', *Journal of Marketing Research*, Nov. 1966, pp. 355–63. Patrick Murphy and William Staples, 'A Modernised Family Life Cycle', *Journal of Consumer Research*, 6 June 1979. Mary Gilly and Ben Ennis, 'Recycling the Family Life Cycle: A Proposal for Redefinition', in Andrew A. Mitchell (ed.), *Advances in Consumer Research*, Vol. 9, Association for Consumer Research, Ann Arbor, Mich., 1982)

Taking these points into consideration, it may be more practical to classify Australian families into the following thirteen categories which could function as discrete market segments:

1. Young singles
2. Young childless couples
3. Young couples with children
4. Middle aged singles
5. Middle aged childless couples
6. Middle aged couples with children
7. Middle aged single parent
8. Mature aged singles
9. Mature aged childless couples
10. Mature aged couples with children (at home)
11. Mature aged couples with children (not at home)
12. Mature aged single parent with children (at home)
13. Mature aged single parent with children (not at home)

Although the stages of development do direct product category purchases, income can influence product form, brand choices and usage rate. Therefore, most marketers consider it necessary to identify income differences. For example, Roy Morgan Research uses the following categories and combines them with household income.

Stages of life cycle:
- Aged 34 or less, single, no children under 16 years in the home
- Aged 34 or less, single, with children under 16 years in the home
- Aged 34 or less, married, no children in the home
- Aged 34 or less, married, with children under 16 years in the home
- Aged 35+, married, with children under 16 years in the home
- Aged 35+, married, no children under 16 years in the home
- Aged 35+, single, with children under 16 years in the home
- Aged 35+, single, no children under 16 years in the home

Household life cycle:
- Young singles — head of household, single and under 45 with no children
- Young couples — couple with head of household under 45 and no children (under 16) present
- Young parents — head of household under 45, child(ren) present (also includes single parents)
- Mid-life families — head of household between ages 45 and 64, child(ren) present
- Mid-life households — head of household 45–64, no children present
- Other households — head of household aged 65 or older or retired

Age/children/household income:
- Under 35, no children and $50 000+
- Under 35, children and $50 000+
- Under 35, no children and <$50 000
- Under 35, children and <$50 000
- Over 35, no children and $50 000+
- Over 35, children and $50 000+
- Over 35, no children and <$50 000
- Over 35, children and <$50 000

What's happening to your market?

In a recent Radio 2BL interview, Hugh Mackay explained the changes in Australian society that are tearing apart the old certainties that many marketers still work by.

As Westpac has discovered, the social fabric has been torn permanently.

"We still indulge this myth that the average Australian house is home to a nuclear family," says Mr Mackay. But only about 26% of households are cosy and conventional.

"The other myth is that we're all comfortable, middle-class Australians," he says. "Whereas 15 years ago that was true for about 70% of our households, but now it's probably true for only about 40%."

"We've got a very big rich class and a very big poverty class in Australia. We're really a three-tiered society. Our households are divided by social class which is created by the dollar."

The other significant change is that households are fragmenting: 50% of Australian households contain only one or two people and 23% are single-person households, while 8%–9% are single-parent households.

"In Sydney and Melbourne in every third household tonight there will be an adult with no other adult to talk to," he says. The most significant implication is that loneliness is now a major social issue. "We are after all herd animals, and we are being increasingly cut off from the herd, suffering that psychological discomfort."

As a result, media consumption habits are changing. "Radio has stormed back into prominence. Among Australian adults the medium that we spend most time with now is not television but radio.

"Radio is the great antidote to loneliness. It creates the illusion of companionship for people who don't have sufficient real-life companionship. Talkback radio creates the illusion that we are in a kind of electronic neighbourhood where no such neighbourhood actually exists.

"It helps satisfy the psychological need for that kind of companionship."

The demographic changes also have impact on eating habits. "We still think of dinner as a formal family meal time with the family gathered around the table having chops and three veg. But we're becoming a society of snackers and grazers, eating what we can get, when we can get it, and eating at irregular times."

The microwave oven has had a dramatic impact. "Often the evening meal is something eaten in shifts, often by individuals. There is also much greater use of takeaway food, of eating out, and part-prepared food."

Why is the image of the ideal nuclear family still almost universally featured in advertisements? "The more urbanised we become, the more we harbour the dream of the rural life. And the more fragmented our households become, the stronger seems to be the appeal of the classic traditional nuclear family," he says.

"At the very moment when family values seem to be in disarray as evidenced by the demographic statistics, family values are back in fashion. So in advertising the portrayal of the happy nuclear family represents the dream — the rose-tinted mirror."

The fastest-growing household type in Australia is the non-kin household: people who have no sexual or blood connection.

Members of this group feel it is psychologically more comfortable to be part of a family-sized group. "So they rent a house together and pretend that they're a family. "The redefinition of the household leads to a redefinition of what the family is. We need the comfort, the security, the sense of identity that being part of a herd gives us.

"And if we haven't got a natural herd that has evolved in the traditional way we have to make one up."

Marketing, July 1991

TARGETING SPECIFIC HOUSEHOLD TYPES

If, as some writers suggest, 20 per cent of the population remain unmarried for their whole life, the proportion of single elderly people could be very high.[16] While it is tempting to see the 'singles' market as one group, it should be remembered that, just as there are different types of families, there are also different types of 'singles'. Single women are more likely than married women to be in the labour market and may make purchase decisions in ways that are different from each other as well as different from married women. Just as the 'younger singles' market should not be seen as one homogeneous group, nor should the 'older singles' market.

The diversity of needs and wants within the elderly singles group is likely to be just as great as the younger group. In the past, marketing to the older members of society has focused on a limited range of products but as this group increases in size, its impact on marketing activities will become more profound. As the over 65s enjoy a longer life span and possibly more financial security, marketers may apply the same sorts of segmentation strategies to the 'grey market' as have been applied in the past to the baby boomers.

The purchasing behaviours of some of the thirteen categories listed on page 250 are described in the box on page 253. It should be remembered that, just as families may differ in the ways in which they react towards each other, they also differ in wealth, social standing and lifestyles. The impact of these factors is considered elsewhere in this book, particularly chapters 11–13.

Using the family as a unit of analysis is appropriate for many products, especially those used by all or more than one family member. It is less useful for individual (personal) consumption situations.

Household changes, such as the trend towards single, smaller households and none or only two children, have implications for a range of products. Changes include:

- an overall increase in the consumption of houses, furnishings, appliances and white goods
- smaller houses and cars, different furniture, smaller fridges and washing machines
- an increase in the purchase of specialty clothes for children, toys, computers and sound equipment
- a decrease in the consumption of baby foods and baby care products
- decreased demand for child medical services and an increase in health care for the elderly
- an increased demand for travel and entertainment
- more service connection such as electricity and gas.

Family life cycle categories and their purchase behaviour

1. **Young singles**
   Clothes, records, entertainment, sports; cars; high use of personal care and fashion items; high media usage; prepared food products

2. **Young childless couples**
   Home purchase; furniture and furnishings; durables; leisure activities; sports; insurance; personal care and fashion items; high use of public entertainment

3. **Young couples with children**
   Baby needs; medical service and insurance; second car; labour saving appliances

4. **Middle aged singles**
   Travel; luxury goods; entertainment; home entertainment; hobbies and craft

5. **Middle aged childless couples**
   The same as singles but with higher discretionary incomes; travel; luxury goods; entertainment; home entertainment; hobbies; house services; home redecoration; refurnishing and replacement of durables; home maintenance products

6. **Middle aged with children**
   School fees; children's clothes and equipment; children's sports; hobbies; family holidays; financial services; medical services; home entertainment; possible replacement of furniture and durables; home maintenance products

7. **Middle aged single parents**
   Children's needs; medical services; home entertainment; labour saving devices; cash poor; fast foods; low cost entertainment

8. **Mature aged singles and childless couples**
   Reduced income; health care services; specialised housing; investment management; home care; some travel and low cost entertainment; high hobby and craft purchases

HOUSEHOLD DECISIONS

The realisation that many purchasing decisions are made jointly by several members of a household suggests that referring to a household decision unit may be as relevant as referring to an individual consumer. In a household, each member — whether it be a husband, wife or a child, makes a special contribution to purchase decisions. It cannot be assumed that one or another will necessarily make an independent decision because family structures may exert an influence, even though it may be a passive influence.

Before exploring how individual family members influence buying decisions, it is important to consider the family decision making process.

Family decision making is not one distinct act, but rather a combination of actions or tasks carried out by individual family members. There are at least five tasks that household members can carry out:

1. Information gathering
2. Influencing decisions
3. Deciding
4. Purchasing
5. Consuming (using).

All of these functions may be carried out by the same person, or different family members may have input to different parts of the decision process.

The 'information gatherer' is the person who 'collects' information about the product or service to be purchased. As this person can either disclose or not disclose information, they essentially act as gatekeepers. Their associated tasks may be looking through the advertising material delivered to the mailbox or actively seeking additional information from salespeople or from friends.

The 'influencers' are individuals who have the power to impact on any facet of the purchasing process. The 'decision maker' is the person who decides what will be bought. In the case of low involvement decisions, this may take place at the time of purchase such as choice of cake mix or brand of toothpaste at the supermarket. High involvement decisions may be made, or at least partly made, before purchase. For example, a particular store may be selected as the 'right' place to purchase a new stereo, and various brands may be evaluated prior to purchase by looking through information that has been collected by the information gatherer.

The 'purchaser' is the person who does the actual buying. The fifth element in this process is the 'consumer'. This could be the person who prepares meals or makes the clothes or it could be a family pet. Even a dog can influence a purchase decision by showing preferences for certain brands of dog food.

In most families, the majority of the purchase decisions related to the consumption of food, children's needs and cleaning products are still made by the female in the household. There are also, however, many men and teenagers who are responsible for the weekly grocery shopping and they may select brands and products which they prefer.

WHO INFLUENCES AND WHO DECIDES?

Until recently it was thought that males were the key influencers in the areas of the function and performance of products and how much money should be spent. Wives were thought to be more influential in the areas of style, design, colour and general aesthetics. Studies in the early 1970s supported the notion that the major influencers in family decision making processes are the husband and wife.[17] They also showed that their relative influence will generally vary depending on three major factors:

1. the type of product
2. the level of involvement
3. the stage in the decision making process.

One such study found that for some product categories the degree of influence was even, while for others either one was more dominant.[18]

Table 10.4: Sources of influence for purchases of certain product categories

Influence	Examples of products
Husband dominant influence	cars, insurance, lawnmowers
Wife dominant influence	food, clothing, household furnishings
Autonomous decision (either husband or wife equally likely to make decision)	petrol, personal gifts
Synchronous (joint decision by husband and wife)	houses, holidays, child's education

The influence of the husband and wife in buying decisions was found to vary according to the level of involvement in the product. For example, in a family with children and a non-working wife, the husband tended to have potential control over all major financial decisions. In areas where the wife had a high level of involvement, such as in kitchen appliances, sewing machines, washing machines and dryers, she usually had the most influence. When the buying decisions related to products for which both husband and wife had high levels of involvement, the influences of husband and wife were found to be more even. This was more likely when both husband and wife were working and control of the money was a joint decision.

Changing roles

Table 10.5 shows some interesting changes in decision making behaviour between 1955 and 1982. There has been a move away from role-specific purchasing patterns to more joint decisions across a range of product categories. Husbands still dominated the purchase of insurance and cars in 1982, but there was a trend towards joint decisions, especially in the area of cars. The move towards more joint and flexible spheres of influence has been a function of social changes, such as education, fewer children per family and more dual-career families.[19]

Participation by women in the workforce had increased from around 40 per cent in 1970 to 52 per cent by 1990. Currently 60 per cent of mothers in two parent families are in the paid workforce. Single mothers also increased their participation in the workforce from around 40 per cent to over 50 per cent during the 1980s. Watts and Rich[20] argue that economic necessity, the decline in average living standards since 1983 and the increasing number of single parent families have led to the growth in the employment of women in Australia.

More than 40 per cent of grocery shoppers are male, and an even higher proportion of convenience store shoppers are male.[21] These figures are important to note because they relate to low involvement purchases, suggesting that the purchaser is most probably the decision maker. Product decisions that have been traditionally made by men within families, such as for hardware or financial services, are also coming under the influence of more than one member of the family.

Table 10.5: Changes in purchase decision roles, 1955–1982

Decision area	1955 (%)	1973 (%)	1982 (%)
Life insurance			
Husband usually decides	43	66	40
Both husband and wife decide	42	30	57
Wife usually decides	15	4	3
Cars			
Husband usually decides	70	52	31
Both husband and wife decide	25	45	57
Wife usually decides	5	3	12
Holidays			
Husband usually decides	18	7	16
Both husband and wife decide	70	84	75
Wife usually decides	12	9	9
Houses or apartments			
Husband usually decides	18	12	13
Both husband and wife decide	58	77	80
Wife usually decides	24	11	7
Number of cases	727	248	204

(*Source*: Data for 1955 and 1973 from Isabella C. M. Cunningham and Robert T. Green, 'Purchasing Roles in the U.S. Family, 1955 and 1973', *Journal of Marketing*, 38, Oct. 1974, p. 63. Data formed from William J. Qualls, 'Changing Sex Roles: Its Impact Upon Family Decision Making', in Arnold Mitchell (ed.), *Advances in Consumer Research*, Vol. 9, Association of Consumer Research, Ann Arbor, Mich., 1982, pp. 267–70)

Observational research in the area of family purchases may indicate that a large number of purchases are still made by those traditionally linked to the person who will use the product. But observational research of purchases will not show *how* these decisions are made. For example, the purchase of paint for the family home may be made by a male within the family, yet colour cards may have been selected by a female and other family members may have been consulted as to the most appropriate colour. The final purchase may be dictated by the colour chosen rather than a preferred brand. This example oversimplifies the process, since some brands may be excluded before a colour choice is made. They may be excluded on the basis of cost (they could be regarded as 'too cheap' or 'too expensive'), availability (a paint store which only carries a limited range of brands may be consulted), or other factors, such as specialist applications related to climate or the type of material to be painted. Thus an apparently simple purchase may have been influenced by a combination of factors related to family roles, time availability and product features, over which the family has no control.

Figure 10.4: Research has shown that over 40 per cent of grocery shoppers are male, a fact which marketers nowadays need to take into account.

CHILDREN AND TEENAGERS

Today's children are the most informed generation of all time. They have access to and are able to use an enormous range of information technology. Because of this and because family units are smaller, today's children play an important role in family decision making for a wide range of products and in some cases may be sole decision makers.

Children's influences in buying decisions vary greatly according to their age and product category. Researchers recognise that younger children cannot obtain most products directly and must ask the mother or father. The mother or father will serve as the final decision maker and purchaser, especially for young children.

Scott Ward and Daniel Wackman[21] found that children's influence on buying decisions increased with age, to the point where they were able to make their own purchasing decisions in teenage life. It also differed across products. Ellen Foxman examined a collection of studies on children's influence in family decision making and concluded that children are likely to significantly influence decisions involving cereal, television, eating out, leisure activities, holidays, snack foods, confectionery and toys. Children generally tend to have more say in products that are less expensive and for their own use.[22] It should not be assumed, however, that parents do not have the final say in what is purchased.

Figure 10.5: By stressing the nutritional benefits of the product, this advertisement gives the parent good reasons for either acquiescing to the purchase or initiating purchase.

Where the importance of the product increases, children's influences tend to decrease, especially at a young age. When there is a conflict or disagreement between the husband and wife, children have the potential to influence family decisions by forming alliances with either husband or wife to produce a 'majority' decision.[23]

A study conducted among Sydney mothers indicated that children and teenagers have a powerful influence over what mum buys for the home.[24] Across 21 food items, the mothers indicated that their children (between 10 and 17 years) had influenced the purchase of the products as shown in table 10.6.

Table 10.6: Influence of children on products purchased

Product	Purchase influenced %	Specific brand %
Cereals	71	97
Soft drinks	60	95
Fast foods	60	98
Biscuits	58	93
Milk flavouring	55	96
Cheeses	52	92
Spreads	49	96
Candy bars	47	96

(*Source*: Peter Harrison, *'Teen Power': A Harrison Report on the Unique Potential of the 10–17-year-old Market,* Harrison Communications, Sydney, 1983)

According to the Harrison report, the 10–17 group influenced the brand of cereal purchased to the extent of $26.9 million; biscuits $11.4 million; and bread $17.7 million.

Kids hard to reach

Today's 16–18 year olds ignore television and don't buy newspapers according to a study by BBDO Europe in 20 European countries, but they are a marketer's dream because, without causes to rebel against or strong beliefs to hold onto, they define themselves through spending money. The report reveals that today's parents are more rebellious than their children. Broken marriages and the gloomy economy have combined to create 'middle-aged teenagers' who are obsessed with security, who see money as bringing spiritual values, buying them freedom and fulfilling their dreams. This generation adores and believes in advertising and likes to see humour, surprise and sex in ads, say the researchers. They do not, however, like ads with no relation to the product.

(*Source*: *Marketing Globe*, Vol. 3, No. 7, July 1993)

Other products for which teenagers influence the buying decision making process include: family holiday destinations (57 per cent); family cars (17 per cent); furniture and furnishings (41 per cent); banks (35 per cent).

Many teenagers, particularly girls, are now buying the family's grocery needs, and this tends to suggest that they may also be the decision makers with respect to brand choice. Older teenagers, with increasing purchasing power of their own, may be the primary decision makers for clothing, records, stereo equipment, hobbies, craft and reading material. The average weekly pocket money for the 10–17 age group is approximately $30 which translates into a buying power of $3 billion a year.

SINGLE PARENT HOUSEHOLDS

Currently there are 531 000 single parent households in Australia, and 80 per cent of these are headed by females. If current trends continue, this group is likely to increase. For these households, the family decision making models discussed previously are less than useful. As yet, no family decision making models have been developed to investigate how decisions within families headed by females differ. It could be hypothesised that the roles traditionally associated with the 'husband' have been assimilated by the female head of the household, or perhaps other male figures outside the family (or within an extended family) become major family influencers.

 # WHO SHOULD MARKETERS TARGET?

The changing structure of households and the variable task allocations among household members makes it difficult for marketers to target family decision makers. Product development, media selection and message strategies become more difficult to carry out. Different family members may act as the information gatherer for different types of purchases, or even on different occasions. And even though one individual may do the purchasing, he or she may have been subject to multiple influences that affect what is purchased. In contrast, not all purchases will be affected by other family members. Buying a birthday card for a friend is more likely to reflect what an individual believes the friend will like than whether other family members would think it appropriate. A family member is more likely to be affected by other members of the family when the product will be seen by other family members, or where the individual has a strong sense of family norms and standards.

Even the use of selection criteria based on whether the family is dual-career or not may be inadvisable. Research suggests that the level of cohesion in a family unit may have more influence on whether or not decisions are joint.[25] The study found that many consumption decisions will be influenced by family 'type'. When cohesion levels were high, the identification with the family was high. Family members who did most things together were more likely to choose the same brands, colours and types of products. At the other extreme, where high levels of autonomy were encouraged and family members had limited attachment or commitment to the family, there were many contradictory conclusions about family buying patterns.

If, as this study suggests, there are many different family types and therefore differing levels of family influence, using the family as a major influence on purchase decisions may have limited application. This will further complicate the 'who to target' problem in the future.

SUMMARY

Households are an important consumption unit. Not only do they account for the majority of purchases in the marketplace but family households also train children to be consumers. A household is considered to be a group of people living under one roof. Family households are those where there is a biological or kin relationship between the individuals in the household.

The number of separate households formed each year determines the number and type of products that are purchased in a community at any one time. The size of individual households determines the overall consumption levels of food and services such as electricity, gas and water.

The type of household formed will also determine product demand. Single households will require smaller washing machines and different styles of furniture. Households with children will require cots and toys and they have to fund the school and leisure activities of the children. Elderly consumers will require home security products, financial services and health care.

Social changes have led to more households being formed, with fewer individuals in each household. This leads to demands for different styles of housing, furniture, cars and durables. While it does not reduce the overall consumption level, it does impact on how households shop.

Changes in education, fewer children per family and dual career families have changed how families make decisions. It is now quite difficult to target decision makers and influencers in family purchases as the purchase roles have changed from gender based to time and skill based allocation.

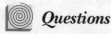 Questions

1. Consider the following case, then answer the questions that follow.

Jenny has always described herself as a careful shopper. She is concerned about the environment and the health of her family and considers both of these things when doing the weekly grocery shopping. She has always worked, although since the birth of her first child she has worked only part-time. She tries to buy products that she believes will have minimal impact on the environment and will produce 'good' nutritious meals for her family.

When she is rushed to hospital to give birth to her second child, her husband takes over the shopping for the first week, and then her mother-in-law moves in to take care of the family. Jenny comes home from hospital with the new baby to discover her kitchen cupboards filled with different products. She finds the freezer stocked with convenience food and red meat. Her pantry contains a new array of cleaning products.

(a) Describe how the buying pattern of this family may have been influenced:
  (i) by the husband
  (ii) by the grandmother.
(b) How might these changes be explained in terms of family learning and different buying influences?

2. Read this case, then answer the questions that follow.

> Robert and Jenny's children have started school but, in the intervening years, Rob and Jenny have divorced, although they remain friends. Jenny decides that it is time she bought a new car. She has a successful job as a product manager with a pharmaceutical company and wants a car that reflects that success. Rob meanwhile has taken up writing children's stories and, although he finds that money is very tight, he enjoys his new career.
>
> One Saturday, Jenny asks Rob if he will come and look at cars with her and the children. They drive to a local area that has a number of new car dealerships and begin looking at cars. The salesperson asks Rob what sort of car he is looking for. He says that they want a new car for Jenny. The salesperson looks at the family and suggests that a small, compact, economy car might be what they are looking for. He explains the fuel economy to Rob and tells Jenny about the colour range that is available, and then turns to Rob and asks what price range they are considering. Rob and Jenny leave the car yard and Jenny thanks Rob for his help, but decides that she will go back without him next week.

(a) What assumptions were made by the salesperson about this family's decision making?
(b) How might a marketer, who was more aware of the recent demographic changes to families, have approached the same situation?

3. Conduct an observational study into the supermarket behaviour of parents and children. Identify situations where the parents comply with a child's request and those where they do not. If you can observe both mother and father situations, note any differences in the way they respond to the child's demands.

4. Discuss the implications of combining the modernised family life cycle with a social economic model for market segmentation.

5. What role does the media play in shaping the consumption behaviour of parents and children?

6. Given that the decision roles in families are changing, can you suggest guidelines that would allow effective targeting of decision makers?

7. You have been asked for advice on the future design of household appliances. Given the changes in household structure, what changes would you recommend and why?

8. What products will be unaffected by the changes in household structure and changes to individual roles within the household?

9. Select three advertisements that are targeting specific individuals within a family unit. Who are they targeting? Do you think that the target is the right one for the product category being advertised?

10. Select some children's television commercials and examine the techniques used in relation to guidelines set by the Australian Broadcasting Tribunal.

Case study

The advertising of baby-food products is dominated by images of cute, chubby babies and happy, smiling mothers. But there is nothing cute about the baby-food market. It is fiercely competitive and increasingly unruly, with two rivals slugging it out for a share of the $70 million Australians spend on baby food each year.

The present baby-food battle started in March, when the American company Gerber Products relaunched its Gerber brand in Australia. This was the first time Gerber, the largest baby-food maker in the world, had directly handled the marketing of its products in Australia. Until last year, Gerber products were made and sold in Australia by the Edgell-Birds Eye division of Pacific Dunlop. The 34-year-old agreement between Edgell and Gerber ended on October 1. On the same day, Gerber opened its first Australian office and started planning the relaunch of its baby-food products.

Gerber captures 72% of baby-food sales in the United States, but its Australian market share has been 15–20% for more than a decade. H. J. Heinz dominates the Australian market, and last year it had 83.7% of baby-food sales, with Gerber taking the rest. Heinz is determined to thwart Gerber's expansion plans. It recently spent $2.4 million on a new baby-food production line at its Dandenong factory in Melbourne and is set to spend $2 million on new baby-food packaging. In December, Heinz launched seven new baby-food lines. In March, it began a $2-million marketing campaign for its baby-food products and is

pumping another $2 million into price-cutting and cooperative advertising campaigns with retailers.

Gerber is selling its products in jars, which account for 30% of the baby-food market. Edgell sold Gerber in cans and jars until late 1990, when it dropped the jars. Jars of baby-food traditionally sell for 50% more than cans, a big gap in a market as price-sensitive as baby food. Gerber's products are priced 10% below Heinz's jars. John Howell, the managing director of Gerber Australia, predicts Gerber's 16.3% share of Australian baby-food sales will increase to 25% in the next two years.

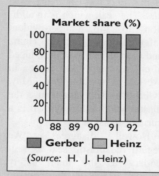

Market share (%)

(Source: H. J. Heinz)

Baby food accounts for 20% of Heinz sales in Australia, and the company generates wholesale sales of $50 million a year from its 104-product range. Heinz has already responded to Gerber's pricing strategy, cutting the price of its jars to a few cents above the Gerber products. "We had no option but to reduce our prices," says Ian Ellis, the Heinz director of marketing. "But we haven't matched Gerber's prices, because Gerber would have simply lowered its prices and

we would have followed each other down the price scale."

Heinz wants to avoid a repeat of the canned baked beans and spaghetti war of 1991–92, when Goodman Fielder launched the Wattie's brand in Australia and grabbed 10% of baked-bean and spaghetti sales, trimming Heinz's market share by four to five points. Before Wattie's arrived, retailers and manufacturers assumed the market had no growth potential. Thanks to Wattie's, the baked-bean and spaghetti market grew 14% last year. The market rivalry between Heinz and Wattie's has abated since October, when Goodman sold Wattie Foods to Heinz for $428 million.

Heinz is accustomed to fighting rivals in the baby-food business. It battled Edgell for more than 30 years and Nestle Australia for 20 years (Nestle quit the local baby-food market in 1986). Heinz knows that its dominance of the category leaves it open to predators. "Retailers do not like markets to be dominated by one supplier," Ellis says. "That is our Achilles' heel."

Ellis claims Heinz's steady product innovation and consistent advertising have boosted sales of baby-food (Heinz pioneered the baby-food market in Australia when it launched strained products in the early 1940s). The number of babies born in Australia climbed from 244 000 in 1988 to 257 000 last year, an increase of 5.3%. Sales of baby-food increased 19% in the same period. Last year, the number of births dipped 2.3%, but the baby-food market grew 6.2%.

(continued)

Gerber's John Howell tells a different story. He claims baby-food sales have been flat for the past 10 years and points out that Australia's per capita consumption of baby-food is low by world standards: 324 cans a year, compared with 456 cans in Britain and 624 in the United States.

When Pacific Dunlop bought Edgell in late 1991 it decided to concentrate on the Birds Eye and Edgell brands. Gerber was told its licensing agreement with Edgell would end in October last year. The company decided to continue selling its products here. Baby-food sales are flat in the US and Gerber, which operates in 68 countries, is relying on overseas markets to generate growth. "Gerber did not want to abandon the brand franchise it had built here," Howell says. "It also saw an opportunity to move beyond its traditional 15–20% share of the Australian market."

The relaunch of Gerber was originally planned for October, but it began in March, when Gerber products appeared in Queensland stores (they are now sold nationally). Gerber is importing jars from the US: none of its companies in the world produces canned baby-food and it could not find a can manufacturer in Australia.

Forty-five Gerber lines were presented to retailers, and most retail chains accepted 30 lines. Ellis says Gerber has already encountered supply problems, and the launch in New South Wales last month forced it to stop supplying some Queensland retailers.

Gerber products fall into four categories: first foods, for babies aged three to five months; second foods (five to seven months), third foods (seven to eight months) and toddler foods (eight months and older). Each type has different labelling and is sold in different sized jars, ranging from 71 grams to 170 grams. Heinz products are differentiated by colored labels: blue for strained products, red for "junior" food and green for toddler food. Since February 1991, Heinz has also sold Kids Cuisine, a range of dinners for children aged 18 to 36 months. Heinz has sold 6.6 million cans of Kids Cuisine, and Ellis says the products have expanded baby-food sales by 5.2%.

The Gerber products have been relaunched without the "tamper-evident" plastic seal Heinz uses on its baby-food jars. The seal, which is in addition to the tamper-evident safety-button used on Heinz and Gerber jars, was introduced after a tampering scare in Western Australia last May. "Gerber is silly not to use the plastic seal," Ellis says. "It is a curious decision."

Howell disagrees. "We regard the plastic seal as secondary to the main safety device, which is the pop-top button on the lid. We decided against a secondary device because it would divert some mothers' attention from the primary safety device."

The battle between Heinz and Gerber extends beyond the supermarket. Both companies are pushing their products through child-care and baby-health centres and hospitals. Gerber is running a direct-mail program, and Heinz is employing its five-year-old Heinz Baby Foods Advisory Service, which has seven nurses and two dietitians. "In the past, the service has extolled the generic benefits of processed baby-food," Ellis says. "Now it is becoming more Heinz-specific."

The Heinz baby-food marketing budget of $2 million this year ($1 million last year) includes a television and magazine advertising campaign, built on the theme "Every baby shines on Heinz". Gerber is not using TV advertising, relying instead on direct-mail and magazine advertising. "TV is an inefficient medium for a baby-food product," Howell says. "TV is a mass-market medium, but we are only talking to a small target market."

Later this month Heinz will launch a new range of baby-food products in jars. It is preparing to invest $2 million in new packaging facilities to enable it to match any product size Gerber launches in the future. Ellis thinks the Gerber relaunch, and the response by Heinz, will boost baby-food sales about 5% this year.

Howell believes Gerber has set a realistic market share target. "Two or three years ago, Gerber's share was in the low 20s, so we are simply aiming to get a bit above that level." He says Gerber Australia will be profitable when its market share reaches 25%. Heinz expects to lose some market share to Gerber, but Ellis says his company will hold Gerber's share to the combined level Gerber and Nestle had in the early 1980s — about 20%.

Neil Shoebridge,
Business Review Weekly,
7 May 1993

Case study questions

1. Having read the article on pages 263–64, which of the family life cycle categories used by Morgan (see page 250) do you think Gerber should target?

2. Do you think it is worth their while identifying and targeting market niches within this group? If so, what niches could you target? Would they be viable?

SUGGESTED READING

F. Furstenbert and G. B. Spanier, *Recycling the Family*, Sage Publications, Beverly Hills, 1984.

G. A. Carmichael, 'The Changing Structure of Australian Families', *Australian Quarterly*, Autumn/Winter 1985.

K. Funder, *Images of Australian Families: Approaches and Perceptions*, Australian Institute of Family Studies/Longman Cheshire, 1992.

M. Gilding, *The Making and Breaking of the Australian Family*, Allen and Unwin, Melbourne, 1991.

ENDNOTES

1. R. E. Hite and R. Eck, 'Advertising to Children', *Journal of Advertising Research*, Vol. 27, Nov. 1987, pp. 40–53. J. Esserman, *Television Advertising and Children: Issues and Research Findings*, Child Research Unit, McCallum Spealman, New York, 1983.

2. K. Atkin, 'The Effects of Television Advertising on Children', Report submitted to the Office of Child Development, Australian Government Publications, 1975. P. Palmer, *The Lively Audience: What Kids Do While Watching TV*, Allen and Unwin, Sydney, 1986.

3. J. Burke, *Children, Television Viewing and Food Nutrition*, Australian Broadcasting Tribunal Publications, Sydney, 1982.

4. M. O'Shannessy, *Children's Advertising and Nutrition*, AANA Publications, Sydney, 1994.

5. G. P. Moschis, 'The Role of Family Communication in Consumer Socialisation', *Journal of Consumer Research*, Vol. 11, March 1985, pp. 898–913. L. Carlson and S. Grossbart, 'Parental Style and Consumer Socialisation of Children', *Journal of Consumer Research*, Vol. 15, June 1988, pp. 77–94. T. L. Childers and R. R. Akshay, 'The Influence of Familial and Peer-based Reference Groups on Consumer Decisions', *Journal of Consumer Research*, Vol. 19, No. 2, Sept. 1992, pp. 198–211.

6. The Media Council of Australia, *Advertising Code of Ethics* (incorporating amendments), 30 April 1993. Australian Broadcasting Tribunal Reports, 1980–90.

7. J. Williamson, *Decoding Advertisements: Ideology and Meaning in Advertising*, Marion Boyars, London, 1978. T. Jagtenberg and P. D'Alton, *Four Dimensional Social Space*, Harper and Row, Sydney, 1990.

8. 'Census Characteristics of Australia', *1991 Census of Population and Housing*, Australian Bureau of Statistics, Catalogue No. 2710.0, 1993.

9. 'Census Characteristics of Australia', *1991 Census of Population and Housing*, Australian Bureau of Statistics, Catalogue No. 2710.0, 1993. P. Aries, 'Two Successive Motivations for Declining Birth Rates in the West', *Population and Development Review*, Vol. 6, No. 4, 1980, pp. 1–20.

10. G. A. Carmichael, 'The Changing Structure of Australian Families', *Australian Quarterly*, Autumn/Winter 1985. C. Isbister, 'The Family and Children of the Year 2000' and 'The Basic Unit of Society', *The Australian Family Quarterly*, for Australian Family Association, Vol. 11, No. 1, March 1990, pp. 6–16. P. McDonald, 'Family Trends and Structure in Australia', *Australian Family Briefings*, No. 3, Sept. 1993. L. J. Aspin, 'Structural and Role Changes within the Australian Family this Century', *Journal of the Home Economics Association of Australia*, Vol. 12, July 1980, pp. 2–13. A. Daly, 'Women in the Workforce and Family Structure in Australia', *Journal of Australian Population Association*, Vol. 7, No. 1, 1990, pp. 27-39.

11. G. A. Carmichael, op. cit. A. Meade, 'More Couples Say I Don't to Marriage', *Sydney Morning Herald*, 1 July 1992. C. Milburn, 'Recession Means More Couples Don't Say "I Do"', *Sydney Morning Herald*, 23 Dec. 1991. B. Zuel, 'The Power of One', *Sydney Morning Herald*, 25 May 1993. A. Horin, 'Living Together Gets Our Blessing', *Sydney Morning Herald*, 7 June 1991.

12. R. Rowland, 'An Exploratory Study of the Child Free Lifestyle', Paper presented to the 51st ANZAAS Congress, Brisbane, May 1981. L. Bloom, 'Childless Couples', *American Demographics*, Aug. 1988.

13. I. Bouvier, 'Immigration and Rising U. S. Fertility: A Prospect of Unending Population Growth', *Backgrounder*, Centre for Immigration Studies, No. 1–91, Jan. 1991.

14. D. Armstrong, 'The Displaced Parent Syndrome: How to Cope When the Children Won't Leave Home', *ITA*, April 1989.

15. C. M. Schaninger and W. D. Danko, 'A Conceptual and Empirical Comparison of Alternative Household Life Cycle Models', *Journal of Consumer Research*, Vol. 19, No. 4, March 1993, pp. 580–94.

16. G. A. Carmichael, op. cit. N. Shoebridge, 'Home Alone: A New Family of Buyers', *Business Review Weekly*, 5 Sept. 1994 , pp. 24–28.

17. H. L. Davis, 'Measurement of Husband–Wife Influence in Consumer Purchase Decisions', *Journal of Marketing Research*, 8, Aug. 1971, pp. 48–59.

18. H. L. Davis and B. P. Rigaux, 'Perception of Marital Roles in Decision Processes', *Journal of Consumer Research*, Vol. 1, June 1974, pp. 51–62. I. R. Foster and R. Wolshavsky, 'An Exploratory Study of Family Decision Making Using a New Taxonomy of Family Role Structure', and K. P. Corfman, 'Measures of Relative Influence in Couples', in T. Srull (ed.), *Advances in Consumer Research*, 15, Association for Consumer Research, Provo, Utah, 1989, pp. 665–70 and 659–64.

19. M. Watts and J. Rich, 'Equal Employment in Australia? The Role of Part-time Employment in Occupational Sex Segregation', *Australian Bulletin of Labour*, Vol. 17, No. 2, National Institute of Labour Studies, 1991, pp. 160–79, pp. 160–79.

20. C. Wright, 'Men Invade the Supermarket', *Australian Business*, 4 Feb. 1987.

21. S. Ward and D. B. Wackman, 'Children's Purchase Influence Attempts and Parental Yielding', *Journal of Market Research*, No. 9, Aug. 1972, pp. 316–19.

22. E. R. Foxman, P. S. Tansuhaj and K. M. Ekstrom, 'Family Members' Perceptions of Adolescents' Influence in Family Decision Making', *Journal of Consumer Research*, No. 15, March 1989, pp. 482–91.

23. P. Filiatrault and J. R. Richies, 'Joint Purchasing Decisions: A Comparison of Influence Structure in Family and Couple Decision-Making Units', *Journal of Consumer Research*, 6, Sept. 1980, pp. 131–40.

24. P. Harrison, 'Teen Power': A Harrison Report on the Unique Potential of the 10–17 year old Market, Harrison Communications, Sydney, 1983. G. Smith, 'Assessing Child and Youth Markets: Longitudinal Perspectives', *Research News*, Sept./Oct. 1989, pp. 16–26.

25. D. Olsen et al., *Families: What Makes Them Work?*, Sage Publications, Beverly Hills, 1983.

C H A P T E R

11

Social stratification

> OBJECTIVES
>
> This chapter should help you to:
> • understand the concepts of stratification and social class
> • appreciate the problems of measuring class
> • understand the nature of stratification and the class structures in Australia and New Zealand
> • know the problems and limitations of class based segmentation.

 ## SOCIAL CLASS

Social class is a form of social stratification, which is the ranking of people within a society into higher or lower social positions within the society. All societies practise some form of social stratification. In simple societies, individuals may be accorded high status because of individual characteristics such as wisdom, beauty or skills. In complex societies such as twentieth century Australia and New Zealand, we accord status to categories (groups) of individuals. These groups, or 'strata', regard the members of their group as equals, regard those in a lower stratum as inferior and regard those in any higher stratum as in some way superior. The usual outcome of social stratification is the unequal sharing of social rewards such as wealth, power and prestige.

In 1958, Pierre Martineau introduced the idea that social-class groups could be used as a basis for market segmentation.[1] Since then a considerable number of articles, both theoretical and applied, have been published on the use of class groups as market segments. Essentially, social-class segmentation is based on the assumption that as a result of constant inter-action with each other, the members of each stratum or class develop a shared way of thinking and behaving. This means that class membership determines such things as:

• lifestyle (values, interests and activities)
• resources (such as money and education)
• goods and services consumed.

While there is evidence that social-class clusters exist, their effective-ness as market segments is questionable. To date, direct use of class in marketing (segmentation and product positioning) has not occurred, although it is clearly an underlying variable for much marketplace behaviour.[2] To understand the difficulties of using social class as a means of identifying segments, we need to examine the concept of class.

STATUS SYSTEMS

Forms of stratification can vary from one society to another according to how 'closed' or 'open' they are. In closed systems such as feudal or caste systems, the boundaries between the strata are very clearly drawn and it is difficult for individuals to change their status. Membership is determined by birth and is lifelong. Because membership is prescribed, individuals have no free choice regarding their status. Caste systems are rare, the most widely known being that which exists in India. In an open or 'class' system, the boundaries between the strata are more flexible, there being no clear division between one class and the next. A feature of class-based systems is that individuals are able to move in and out of the class groups. This means that membership is achieved rather than prescribed. Social stratifi-cation systems in most Western societies, including Australia and New Zea-land, are class based.

Historically, in most Western cultures, class hierarchy is usually associ-ated with wealth. Because wealth has direct links to property ownership, this in turn leads to prestige (status) via the consumption of goods and services (including education and travel). The combination of income and property leads to power, in the form of political power or ownership of the means of production. The use of income as a basis for stratifica-tion in Western cultures goes back as far as ancient Rome, where, according to census records, six main income groups formed the social categories of the time. It is still an important element in class member-ship, but other factors such as education and occupation are also consid-ered effective indicators of status. According to the *Mackay Report on Class and Status in Australia*, while Australians think that a number of fac-tors contribute to a sense of class in Australia, actual class membership is almost entirely a matter of money, as money gives you some freedom of choice.[3]

Because in Western societies an individual's position is a function of wealth, there is some opportunity to change one's class by acquiring wealth and education. Initially, an individual's position in a class system is inherited, as children take on the social status of their family or kin group.

Achieved status is earned by an individual's action and performance and is commonly assigned during adult life. Apart from its 'open' nature, class-based stratification also exhibits the following characteristics.

- **Hierarchy**. The class groups are ranked from high to low status and individuals are allocated a group based on the membership criteria for each group.
- **Homogeneity**. People within a class are presumed to have similar behaviour patterns, attitudes and values. This means that they will be exposed to the same media and shopping areas and are likely to buy similar products and services. The homogeneity develops because members in each class group associate formally and informally with each other: they live in the same suburbs, have similar educational levels and join the same clubs.
- **Multi-dimensionality**. Class membership is usually determined by a number of interacting factors. The factors most often used are occupation, wealth (income), house type and location, educational credentials and behavioural standards, community participation, aspirations and recreational habits.[4]
- **Dynamism**. The status level of the individual factors affecting class membership may alter. For example, occupation classifications can have their accorded status either raised or lowered. In Australia, the status of accountants, for example, has been upgraded to professional status. Nursing is currently in transition.

Figure 11.1: Bedarra Island, near Cairns, is promoted as 'an oasis of pampered seclusion for the fortunate few'. The exclusive resort offers guests complete privacy and first-class facilities at a rate of around $530 per night.

⊚ SOCIAL CLASS AND SOCIOECONOMIC STATUS

To place individuals in class groups requires a classification system, and to be able to classify anything we need to establish characteristics that can be compared. Consequently, we must first understand what is meant by the term 'class'. Craig McGregor[5] writes that it provides the basic structure of all modern societies, including Australia, and that

> 66 It is central to political and economic power, the crucial determinant of who gets what, who is treated fairly, who is treated unfairly; in fact what chance you have of the 'good life'. 99

Other writers point out that in survey after survey over the past fifty years, the vast majority of Australians agree that there is such a thing as social class and most Australians are willing and able to place themselves in one class or another. But what are these classes? For most Australians, it seems that what you own and how much power you have determines your status. So money is a key factor, but so too is occupation. What work you do determines whether you are controlled by other people or you control others. Occupation can also determine how much money a person has and, more often than not, his or her education. There is a considerable difference in the prestige, control and money accorded to judges and bus drivers.[6]

The reasons for this are based on the social structure of Western industrialised societies, where five per cent of the population has ownership and control of manufacturing resources and other economic capital. The figure is slightly higher for the USA and Sweden, both with eight per cent. This means that 95 per cent of the population are workers and that wealth is generated by work-based income. Since work represents income, the amount of money your occupation pays and the level of skill required to do the job determines the status of your occupation.[7] Ann Daniel, in a 1983 synthesis of research into social stratification in Australia, concluded that the power and privilege that are given to occupations are best indicated by the level of prestige that members of the society accord them.[8]

MEASURING SOCIAL CLASS

There are two ways to identify social-class clusters. One approach is to have individuals place themselves in set categories. This is termed the subjective approach. Another is to establish independent criteria, rank them, and then identify individuals who meet the set criteria of each rank (irrespective of whether the individuals classify themselves in accordance with the ranking). This is termed the objective approach.

The subjective approach

In the subjective approach, there are three methods that can be adopted. These are reputational, sociometrical and self-allocation. These methods rely on individuals in the society knowing that classes exist, knowing what attributes are needed to be a member of each class and knowing whether they have them or not. In the reputational method, members of a society are asked to rank each other in terms of where they think the other person fits on the status hierarchy. The sociometric method is a form of network analysis in which the researcher identifies the social and professional interaction of the individuals in relation to each other. Both of these methods are costly in terms of time, labour and money. Because members must all know one another, this approach can only be used in small communities. For these reasons, they are rarely used by marketers and researchers in general.

In the self-allocation method, people are asked questions about what class they belong to or which class they identify with. Usually, people are given set class categories such as upper class, middle class, working class or lower class to choose from, with descriptors of each group provided. This is called a 'fixed-choice' option and is widely used by researchers. An alternative approach is not to provide people with set categories and, instead, to ask them to provide their own labels. This is called a 'free-choice' option. To do this, people must have formed a class identity so as to be able to classify themselves. Tables 11.1 and 11.2 show the different results obtained from each option in studies carried out between 1973 and 1984.[9]

Table 11.1: Class identity in Australia, 1973, 1984 (column percentages)

Class identity	1973 (free choice)	1973 (fixed choice)	1984 (fixed choice)
Upper	3	1	1
Middle	58	54	53
Working	21	41	43
Lower	7	4	3
Other	11	—	—
Total	100	100	100
(N)	(3239)	(4749)	(2939)

Table 11.2: Class identity in Australia over time (column percentages)

Class identity	1949[a]	1961[b]	1965[c]	1967[c]	1973[a]	1973[b]	1978[a]
Middle class	54	59	49	50	58	54	51
Working class	38	38	44	42	21	41	21
Other	8	3	7	9	21	4	29
Total	100	100	100	100	100	100	100
(N)	(129)		(1925)	(1668)	(3239)	(4749)	(184)

a Free-choice questions
b Fixed-choice questions
c Free-choice and fixed-choice questions

(*Source*: Adapted from J. Baxter, M. Emmison, J. Western and M. Western (eds), *Class Analysis and Contemporary Australia*, Macmillan, South Melbourne, 1991)

In table 11.1, the 1973 study used both free choice and fixed choice, but only fixed choice was used in 1984. In the 1973 study, there is a considerable difference in the number of people in the working class category. In the free choice, only 21 per cent put themselves into working class, yet with fixed choice 41 per cent selected working class. Since the total in the middle class does not vary significantly, it would appear that people are reluctant to volunteer a working-class identity. The study in 1984 which used fixed choice shows similar results to the one in 1973.

In table 11.2, which shows class membership over time in Australia, there is also a difference between the open-ended (free-choice) and fixed-choice questions. In 1949, in a free-choice situation, 38 per cent of individuals put themselves into the working class. Using the same method, only 21 per cent put themselves into the working class in 1973 and 1978.

Fixed-choice responses in 1973 resulted in 41 per cent being in the working class. It seems that when the characteristics of the group are described to them, more individuals put themselves into the working class, but unprompted, at least 21 per cent do not. It also demonstrates that changes in class size can vary depending on the type of method used. This means that the only valid comparisons that can be made in table 11.2 are between 1949a, 1973a and 1978a. Based on these three years, it seems that the number of people in Australia who thought of themselves as working class was declining.

The objective approach

This approach allocates class membership to individuals on the basis of a range of predetermined factors. A number of researchers in the United States have developed indices by which class groups can be ascertained. There are two particularly well-known indices, one being Lloyd Warner's Index of Status Characteristics which includes:
- occupation (weighting factor × 4)
- source of income (weighting factor × 3)
- house type (weighting factor × 3)
- dwelling area (weighting factor × 2).

The second well-known index is Richard Coleman's Index of Urban Status which includes:
- occupation
- source of income
- house type
- dwelling area
- education.

Coleman's Computerised Status Index uses an equal weighting system for all categories. For both Warner and Coleman, occupation is the key factor for class allocation.[10]

Since the 1960s, there has been a growing tendency in Australia among social researchers to use occupation as the main indicator of class membership. A number of occupational prestige scales have been developed in

Australia.[11] These scales are usually constructed by asking people to rank occupations according to their social desirability or prestige within the community. The most widely used scale was the Australian Standard Classification of Occupations (ASCO). This classification system was developed by asking people to rank the prestige of occupations by examining how factors such as gender, age, education, qualifications and work experience contributed to these evaluations. Similar results were found when the same exercise was conducted in New Zealand.[12] Market researchers such as Nielsen use the Australian Standard Classification of Occupations, which is described below.

Socioeconomic classification of current occupation

There are five socioeconomic groups of occupations defined by Nielsen based on ASCO (Australian Standard Classification of Occupations) which are broadly defined as follows:

A **Senior managers and administrators, doctors, lawyers**
e.g. government representatives, judges, magistrates, lawyers, general managers, medical practitioners, parliamentarians.

B **Professionals and specialist managers**
e.g. office managers, directors of nursing, education managers, specialist managers, farmers, shop managers, scientists, engineers, architects, surveyors, university teachers, social workers, journalists, practitioners.

C1 **Para-professionals, clerks, teachers, sales persons, personal service workers**
e.g. school teachers, technicians and associates, nurses, inspectors, marine engineers, ship pilots, sports persons, prison officers, telephonists, travel agents, salespersons, waiters and waitresses.

C2 **Tradespersons**
e.g. toolmakers, machinists, sheetmetal, metal, electrical, automotive electricians, building tradespersons, signwriters, carpenters, vehicle mechanics, food tradespersons, gardeners, hairdressers, sheep shearers.

D **Plant and machine operators, drivers, police**
e.g. police, bus/tram/car/truck and train drivers, plant operators, fire fighters, engine and boiler operators, machine operators.

E **Labourers and related workers**
e.g. industrial labourers, factory hands, forestry labourers, building and mining labourers, cleaners, porters, garbage collectors, housekeepers, quality controllers.

Janeen Baxter and others, using Goldthorpe's ten socioeconomic categories and the ASCO, found that 34 per cent of Australians could be classified as professionals (the upper group), approximately 40 per cent in the intermediate cluster, and 25 per cent in the working cluster.[13] (See table 11.3.)

Table 11.3: Socioeconomic groups in Australia

I	10.5%	Upper service, higher professional administrative and managerial, large proprietors
II	23.5%	Lower service, lower professional administrators, managers etc; higher grade technicians, supervisors of non-manual employees
IIIa	10.3%	Routine non-manual higher grade
IIIb	11.8%	Routine non-manual lower grade; personal service workers
IVa,b	8.9%	Small proprietors, own account workers, non-agricultural
IVc	1.6%	Farmers, smallholders
V	7.8%	Lower-grade technical, manual supervisory
VI	11.6%	Skilled manual workers
VIIa	13.3%	Semi-skilled and unskilled workers, non-agricultural
VIIb	0.7%	Agricultural workers

(*Source*: Adapted from J. Baxter, M. Emminson and J. Western, *Class Analysis and Contemporary Australia*, Macmillan, Melbourne, 1991)

SOCIAL CLASS AND EGALITARIANISM

Social class in Australia and New Zealand is a complex topic. The complexity stems from the fact that there is evidence of stratification in both societies while at the same time an egalitarian value system operates in both cultures. The cultural image of egalitarianism has been present in Australia since the nineteenth century, and has been fostered by both popular and academic literature. According to historians, in World War II, many youngsters who could have become officers chose to join the ranks and serve with their friends. This meant that the wealthy, the educated, the uneducated and the poor went into the ranks together. When they came into an atmosphere of class difference later in the war they resented it and rebelled. In 1978, Robert Ward[14] described the archetypal Australian as:

> **❝**... a practical man, rough and ready in his manners and quick to decry any appearance of any affectation in others. He not only believes that Jack is as good as his master but at least in principle probably a great deal better. He is a fiercely independent person who hates officiousness and authority — yet is very hospitable and, above all, will stick to his mates through thick and thin ...**❞**

This ideal has been supported by countless people including Donald Horne in 1964[15] and Craig McGregor in 1966,[16] who both stated that Australia was one of the most egalitarian of countries as it was without obvious class distinctions.

Egalitarianism has also been a pervasive theme in New Zealand culture. Historian Keith Sinclair observed that New Zealanders were willing to recognise that classes (in terms of rich and poor) existed, but that this did not translate into 'better than'. The aim was that all members of society should move towards a middle class standard of living so as to avoid the inequalities that are a part of English culture.[17] Other writers point out that, in reality, egalitarianism is a myth and that New Zealand is a society ruled by elites.[18] Certainly in 1949, people in Australia recognised that there were at least two class groups: middle and working class (see table 11.2, page 271). Many formal studies of class in Australia have found that no more than 10 per cent of Australians think that Australia is classless or egalitarian, nor that there is some inequality in Australia. Four fifths of Australians believe that social classes and inequality exist.

Sociological studies clearly show that class in fact provides the basic social structure of Australia and New Zealand.[19] Although McGregor wrote in 1966 that Australia did not have any obvious class distinctions, by 1987[20] he had changed his mind. He observed that in Australia, the class nature of society is disguised by a high standard of living, a subtle conservative hegemony and an admirable tradition of regarding class distinction as stupid. But the brute impact of class upon the life of every Australian is as inescapable here as anywhere else.

A less serious appraisal of the Australian class system appeared in the *Bulletin* in 1981. The author, Vicki Peterson, observed that few Australians will admit to being status conscious but that the 'ocker snob' is alive and well, and in Australia a good bank balance is worth more than Norman blood.[21]

Research by Hugh Mackay shows that Australians do not think they live in a classless society. They also think that money and material possessions are the main factors that determine class groups. If you are rich enough, you are upper class and if you are poor enough you are lower class. If you have 'some' money you are obviously somewhere in the middle. The interesting aspect is that while people used money to sort Australian society into class groups, money by itself does not accord status. Status was considered to be a function of such factors as education, speech and dress. Hence the need to use occupation as an indicator, because occupation influences both education and speech and, to a certain extent, dress.

There have been a number of studies designed to estimate class membership distribution in Australia. Unfortunately they use different parameters for allocation. When these are combined, the structure of social class in Australia and New Zealand takes the form of the reconstruction shown in table 11.4.[22] It can be seen that the class structure of both countries is almost identical.

Table 11.4: Class distribution in Australia and New Zealand

Class groups	Australia % pop.	New Zealand % pop.
Upper	4	4
Lower upper (professional/managerial)	9	10
Upper middle	6	8
Middle	37	44
Upper working	21	18
Working	16	14
Other	7	2

Two different worlds — within one city

AMANDA MEADE

This week's census has shown that the differences between the affluent municipality of Woollahra and the ethnically diverse city of Fairfield are deeper than the 25 kilometres that separates them would suggest.

Fairfield, in Sydney's southwest, covers more than 104 square kilometres and has some 25 suburbs. Woollahra, one of Sydney's oldest suburbs, includes Watson's Bay, Vaucluse and Double Bay, and the once working-class Paddington.

Mrs Margo Gelling-Goodman's sandstone house in Woollahra is older even than the eastern suburbs municipality in which it stands.

Built in 1856, it is a heritage-listed 10-room mansion, its grace overshadowed only by the woman who has occupied it for the past 50 years.

Mrs Gelling-Goodman discloses proudly that her home is the third oldest in the area, while most of the houses in Fairfield, where Frank and Vicki Fontana have also lived for half a century, are relatively new.

And the Italian-descended Fontanas will point proudly to those new houses on the hill behind their favourite haunt, the Marconi Club. Mr Fontana, 67, has had a long association with the Marconi Club and is now its senior vice-president and sports president.

The two basic community profiles released by the Australian Bureau of Statistics (ABS) this week show that in Fairfield only 36.9 per cent of the population speaks English exclusively at home. In Woollahra, the number of solely English-speaking homes is more than double that number, at 78.3 per cent.

And Vietnamese and Arabic languages are spoken more frequently in homes in today's Fairfield than Italian, traditionally the largest ethnic group in the city.

There are twice the number of Anglicans in Woollahra as there are in Fairfield, where the number of people who listed their religion as Judaism came in at zero. Conversely, 11.8 per cent of people in Woollahra said they were Jews.

More than a quarter of people from Woollahra listed their occupation as "professional", compared with just 5.6 per cent in Fairfield. The most common job in Fairfield was labouring.

The income ranges supplied by the ABS reflect these occupational differences vividly: in Fairfield fewer than 1 per cent earn more than $70 000 a year, while in Woollahra almost 10 per cent earn more than $70 000.

More than 7 per cent of Fairfield residents live in housing estates, compared with just 0.4 per cent in Woollahra.

But Mrs Gelling-Goodman insists the streets of Woollahra are not paved with gold: "Many elderly people here are on a fixed income," she said.

However, she did say that one could furnish an entire house in the best available materials without leaving Queen Street. "If you have the money, that is."

Sydney Morning Herald,
17 April 1993

SOCIAL MOBILITY

Social mobility is a feature of class systems. Because 95 per cent of the population in Australia and New Zealand are workers, and work status is dependent on occupational prestige, then by 'choosing' the right occupation an individual can climb the social ladder. Occupational mobility is high in Australia and New Zealand and much of the movement, although not all, is in an upward direction, irrespective of ethnicity.[23] Occupational mobility is made possible by access to education and by the relative prosperity of manual workers. However, even though there is a certain amount of social mobility from one generation to the next, the difference is not great. As table 11.5 shows, there is a slight shift towards the middle. This accounts for the increasing middle class and shrinking working class that is a feature of Australian society.[24]

Table 11.5: Percentage distribution of ever married working men aged 30–69 by class categories of fathers and sons (column percentages)

Class*	Fathers		Sons	
	Australia	New Zealand	Australia	New Zealand
I	9.1	10.7	13.7	16.7
II	5.7	9.6	13.5	18.5
III	5.2	3.1	7.9	6.3
IVa, b	16.0	16.2	12.6	13.0
IVc	19.0	20.2	7.4	10.3
V	6.3	7.6	9.6	9.3
VI	16.4	15.7	17.6	15.0
VIIa	17.4	13.9	16.1	9.9
VIIb	5.0	3.0	1.6	1.0
Ns (100%)	2294	699	2294	699

* See table 11.3 for description of classes.

(*Source*: Adapted from B. Consedine, 'Inequality and the Egalitarianism Myth', in D. Bedggood, *Rich and Poor in New Zealand*, George Allen and Unwin, Auckland, 1980)

Although there is a shift upwards in open systems, it is possible to move downwards. Two examples of these mobility patterns present in most Western cultures, including Australia and New Zealand, are the phenomena of the 'yuppie' and the 'underclass'.

What is a yuppie? A yuppie can be loosely defined as a Young Urban Mobile Professional Person. Essentially they are young, mainly professionals, but may also own small businesses. Their common feature is a high disposable income and a tendency to conspicuous consumption. McGregor describes them as:

> 66 ambitious upwardly mobile members of the Australian middle class who are in the process of using their education and their professional standing to push themselves to the very top of the class and even break the style, wealth and power barrier into the upper class. 99

Some yuppies are greedy: they have all the good taste, read the glossies, bleed the system for what it's worth, love the 'big' entrepreneurs. Yuppies are not unique to Australia, and their behaviour seems to be consistent wherever they develop (see page 278 for the traits of American yuppies).

A variation of the yuppie syndrome is the ultraconsumer. These are middle class and not necessarily wealthy, but they 'think rich'. They tend not to live in the more expensive suburbs and are inclined to buy 'labels'.[25]

Another emergent group in society is the underclass. This group is essentially the 'new' and potentially permanent poor of modern society. They are downwardly mobile urban people. They are people who have lost jobs, never had jobs, or whose jobs have been reclassified 'down'. These people may have come from 'good homes' but may be on welfare, and most certainly have minimal disposable income.[26]

If the polarisation of wealth in Australia continues, it may be that the middle class will diminish. Double-income professional people will gain more wealth in relation to the employed working class and the growing underclass.

Characteristics of American yuppies

- Yuppies are not overly concerned with their health.
- They attend the gym because they like to keep fit and socialise.
- They are concerned with financial success and products that display their success.
- Their needs are materialistic and preference is for fine foods, high tech products, sporty cars and a desire for convenience.
- They are interested in satisfying personal needs regardless of price. They do not rely on spiritualism or emotionalism for support.
- They take care of themselves through wise investments and careful money management.

(*Source*: J. Burnett and A. Bush, 'Profiling the Yuppies', *Journal of Advertising*, April/May 1986, pp. 27–35)

Figure 11.2: High unemployment rates have helped to create a new underclass in Australian society.

SOCIAL CLASS AND MARKETING

The assumption underlying class-based segmentation is that individuals in each class group identified would demonstrate similar marketplace behaviour patterns. In 1958, Martineau listed ten common differences between the middle and lower classes.[27] These differences, described in table 11.6, could have an impact on marketplace behaviour. Whether all of these differences would be relevant to Australians in the 1990s is questionable.

Table 11.6: Psychological differences between middle and lower classes

Lower class	Middle class
Is oriented towards the past	Oriented to the future
Lives and thinks in the short term	Plans for long term
More emotional	More rational
Less structured thinking	Structured thinking
Concrete thinking	Abstract thinking
Rural	Urban
Limited horizons	Expanded horizons
Limited sense of making choice	Greater sense of choice
See the world as revolving around the family	More concerned with national events
Concerned with security	Self-confident, willing to take risks

(*Source*: Adapted from Pierre Martineau, 'Social Classes and Spending Behaviour', *Journal of Marketing*, Oct. 1958, p. 129)

The few studies in Australia that have examined class-related behaviour show only minimal differences. Research carried out in the 1960s led Lois Bryson and Faith Thompson to conclude that working-class values tend to be more concerned with practical and material comfort concerns, whereas middle-class individuals are concerned with psychological well-being.[28] Other research has shown that working-class mothers are rigid in their sex role training programs: daughters were trained for female related tasks and sons for male related tasks.[29] Studies have also shown that working-class individuals were more rigid and less likely to move out of their localities for work.[30]

Australian lower middle-class and working-class fathers provide more help with children than they do with other domestic chores. Professional men, on the other hand, did a larger share of domestic labour and less childcare. In middle-class households in which mothers worked in full-time paid employment, fathers showed an increase in performance of household chores. However, the focus on child-related activity by working-class men may be a function of logistics and not attitude driven, as working-class fathers are generally home earlier and can help with bathing of children.[31]

McGregor observed that working-class people tend to use recreation as a form of escapism, favouring spectator sports, long hours in front of the television and pottering around the house.[32] Whether this description only describes the working class is debatable. Certainly, the lower-income groups have more health problems and eat poorer (although not necessarily cheaper) food.[33]

Assessing differences in behaviour across the class groups is becoming increasingly difficult. Although there has been some movement in class membership based on money, there has also been a blurring of boundaries between the class groups. This is a function of a range of separate but interacting features of Australian and New Zealand societies.[34]

In the case of Australia, it has been suggested that the influence of social and geographic mobility, rising living standards and the bureaucratisation of work helps to reduce homogeneity within and across the class groups. In addition, examination of occupations in ostensibly middle-class suburbs shows that judges and professors tend to live side by side with tradespeople and semi-professionals. As a result, some manual workers have adopted middle-class values and vice versa.

Work by Mark Western and Michael Emmison shows that a majority of Australians quite simply do not think of themselves or their lives in terms of class. They found that only 31 per cent think that their class group is an important source of their identity, while 69 per cent thought it important but would probably not use their class group to describe themselves.[35] In addition, both Australia and New Zealand are welfare-type communities that provide a relatively high degree of access to education and to education-related facilities. Across Australia, retention rates of students to Higher School Certificate level has increased to 75 per cent overall. Both societies have relatively high living standards and a high level of home ownership. Finally, when factors such as mass communication and smaller families are taken into consideration, it seems that while New Zealand and Australia may not be 'classless', class has no great cultural significance as a basis for social division.

An important aspect of Australian society is that while education, occupation and income have an effect on whether people think of themselves as middle class or working class, they do not generate entrenched or divisive value cleavages.

A study in France during the 1960s by Pierre Bourdieu reports differences across the classes in music, art and books. But there were no great differences in food items purchased. A similar study is being carried out in Australia and it will be interesting to see if any differences emerge.[36]

SOCIAL CLASS AND SEGMENTATION

Certainly, neither Australia nor New Zealand is a classless society in an objective sense, for there are quite distinct material consequences of income levels, and labour-market advantages. However, at present, considering the class structure in Australia and New Zealand, there are probably not many advantages in using class as a means of segmenting the market. The most fundamental problem is that, with the exception of the top socioeconomic cluster, the class clusters are too large for viable segmentation. At least 45 per cent of the population are in the middle group and over 30 per cent are in the working class.

In addition to the size factor, there are other issues that hinder the use of class in market segmentation. First, the classic measurements of social class are based on male occupation. Few measurements take into account the considerable impact of income-earning women in households, or the prestige level of the female's occupation. For this reason it may well be more useful to identify 'class households', taking into consideration such factors as the disposable income and education level of household members. This would provide a more realistic measure of income, but not necessarily how the income was spent. Other factors such as lifestyle and family life cycle would have to be included.

Moreover, Australians seem more prone than people in other countries to see themselves as middle class, irrespective of the techniques used to classify individuals. Since it is the sense of identification that allows behaviour patterns to emerge, this means that working-class individuals may well take on middle-class values and behaviours. Therefore, working-class households with two incomes may have the same tastes as a middle-class household and the means to satisfy them.

Of course, for products where a high level of income is necessary to purchase the product, occupation and income may provide the basis for useful segmentation. Many products are positioned as 'upper-class' products, and are associated with success and the good life. For example, some products such as Rolls Royce cars can only be purchased by the very rich, so the marketers of this product have a set target. This enables strategic decisions such as final price, products, distribution, and advertising to be more effective. However, occupation- or income-based segmentation is not useful for relatively low-cost products, such as Chivas Regal, which, although an expensive whisky, could be bought by at least 70 per cent of adults.

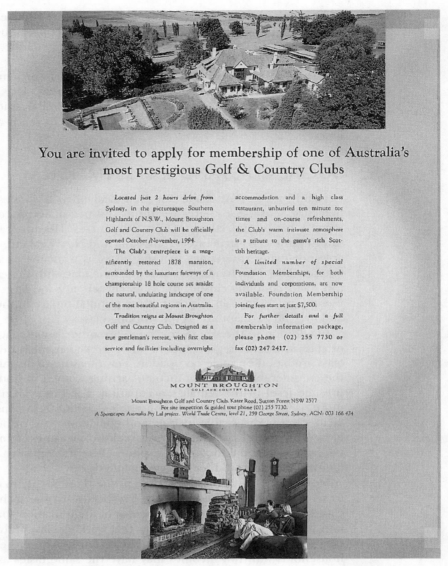

You are invited to apply for membership of one of Australia's most prestigious Golf & Country Clubs

Located just 2 hours drive from Sydney, in the picturesque Southern Highlands of N.S.W., Mount Broughton Golf and Country Club will be officially opened October /November, 1994.

The Club's centrepiece is a magnificently restored 1878 mansion, surrounded by the luxuriant fairways of a championship 18 hole course set amidst the natural, undulating landscape of one of the most beautiful regions in Australia.

Tradition reigns at Mount Broughton Golf and Country Club. Designed as a true gentleman's retreat, with first class service and facilities including overnight accommodation and a high class restaurant, unhurried ten minute tee times and on-course refreshments, the Club's warm intimate atmosphere is a tribute to the game's rich Scottish heritage.

A limited number of special Foundation Memberships, for both individuals and corporations, are now available. Foundation Membership joining fees start at just $7,500.

For further details and a full membership information package, please phone (02) 255 7730 or fax (02) 247 2417.

MOUNT BROUGHTON
GOLF AND COUNTRY CLUB

Mount Broughton Golf and Country Club. Kater Road, Sutton Forest NSW 2577
For site inspection & guided tour phone (02) 255 7730.
A Sportscapes Australia Pty Ltd project. World Trade Centre, level 21, 259 George Street, Sydney. ACN: 003 166 434

Figure 11.3: Prestigious clubs tend to attract the wealthier classes. Their advertising makes appeals to those with 'good taste' and who can afford high quality services.

Finally and most importantly, the class structure in both Australia and New Zealand is fluid and open and there is not enough homogeneity within the groups to justify market segmentation based on class. Education, mass communication and the increased potential for travelling locally and overseas (especially for young people) breaks down barriers. Psychological and behavioural boundaries are also becoming blurred. For example, a huge number of teenagers, no matter what class they belong to, wear Doc Marten shoes. Certainly the research by Mackay shows clearly that even middle-class individuals do not (except by way of money) know how to distinguish themselves clearly from working-class individuals, especially affluent working-class individuals, as the following quotes from interviewees show.[37]

> 66 There are no overt symbols of richness in Australian society except at the very peak.
>
> Pools are getting pretty average ... but an in-ground pool is still a bit better.
>
> Once it was a new car, now it's a European car. It's amazing the people who can afford a Volvo or a BMW.
>
> My sister in Rockdale [lower middle/working class suburb] with a Volvo considers herself better than the owner of a Datsun. 99

Mackay considers that Australian attitudes towards class and status are so contradictory and confused that marketing strategies using the concept need to be very carefully examined. Using occupation as a class indicator is useful for breaking down society into groups that may or may not have access to resources in the community and that have different perceptions of power and control. It does, however, result in groups that are much too big for viable segmentation. This means that they need to be broken down into smaller, more homogeneous groups, allowing the benefits of segmentation to occur.

Even though it is not directly useful as a segmenting variable, class groups do form the basic social structure in society. An individual's class forms the basis of his or her lifestyle and, consequently, of a lifestyle segment. These lifestyle segments allow for identification of smaller clusters within the large working-class and middle-class groups.

SUMMARY

In all societies, individuals are ranked by some criteria into status groups. In other words, all societies have a 'pecking order' for their members. These groups are then ranked in terms of their relative status, power and prestige, those having the most at the top and those having the least at the bottom.

Although all societies are stratified in some way, the methods and the criteria used to rank individuals can vary. Usually, the methods vary in terms of openness. 'Openness' is a term used to describe how easy it is to move in and out of specific groups. Most Western societies, including Australia and New Zealand, are fairly open societies whose members are ranked in terms of income and the related factors of education and occupation. The problem for most Western societies is that the use of these variables creates two large groups, whose sheer size makes it difficult to target them with a specific marketing strategy.

Also, the rising education standard, the incidence of double-income families, mass communication, ease of travel and the upgrading of many technical occupations has meant that psychological and behavioural differences between the groups are not sufficiently delineated for useful marketing strategies to be developed. These factors contribute to present doubts about the usefulness of class-based segmentation.

Questions

1. If you were given the task of assessing the viability of using a class-based segmentation for your specific product or brand, what recommendations would you make, and why?

2. Do you see yourself as a member of a specific class group? Why do you think you are a member? What is your experience of class-based influences on your life? Are you aware of them?

3. Discuss how the range of products you purchase is influenced by your class membership.

4. Social class groups are, for most people, reference groups. Discuss how people use them as reference groups.

5. The questionnaire below and on pages 285–86 is a measurement of social class. Discuss why it uses a range of socioeconomic factors to assess class groups.

6. Do you think that there is a range of product categories or brands that could benefit from class-based segmentation? If so, what are they? Why would class-based segmentation be viable?

7. Select two suburbs that you know are upper middle-class and working-class. Prepare a description of the types of shops in the area in terms of layout, design and merchandise.

8. Select four families of the same socioeconomic group and compare the amount they spend on food, the type of food they buy and the brands.

9. What are the different ways of measuring social class? Which one do you think is the most reliable measure? Why?

10. Select five advertisements that use status symbols to sell the products. Identify the status symbols and explain why they are being used.

QUESTIONNAIRE — WHAT'S YOUR CLASS?

CLASS in Australia is based on what you do for your living. Class is defined by the power you wield and the money you generate. And while many outsiders may judge your class by your lifestyle, the trappings of class are only superficial. The following questions have been designed to tell what class fits you best, what status you enjoy, what your chances are of upward or downward mobility. The questionnaire was devised by Dr Ann Daniel of the School of Sociology, University of NSW. Answer the questions in each of the three sections on Class, Lifestyle and Social Mobility by circling for each question the number next to the response most

appropriate for you. Add up these numbers to tally your score for each section. At the end of the questionnaire there are descriptions of what these scores mean in terms of your class, lifestyle and mobility.

Section 1 CLASS

Education, income, wealth, occupation and associations (networks) are factors important in the assessment of class.

Education

(1) What is the highest level of education you have reached? (Circle the relevant number)

Primary school only	1
Completed four years at high school	2
High school matriculation or trade certificate	3
Completed diploma at college or university	4
Completed a degree at university or college (CAE)	5
Completed a postgraduate or further degrees	6

(2) How would you describe the school you attended for the last years of your school-life?

Local State school	1
Low-fee-paying independent or religious school	2
Selective State high school	3
Private independent (GPS style) school	4

Income

(3) What is your own annual gross (before tax) income?

Below $8 000	1
$8 001 — 18 000	2
$18 001 — 28 000	3
$28 001 — 40 000	4
$40 001 — 55 000	5
$55 001 — 90 000	6
$90 001 — 200 000	7
More than $200 000	8

Wealth

(4) Do you or your spouse own the house in which you live?

No	1
Yes	3

(5) If you (or spouse) own your own home how much is it worth?

Less than $80 000	1
$80 001 — 160 000	2
$160 001 — 400 000	3
More than $400 000	4

(6) Do you (or spouse) have any other income-earning assets (e.g. shares, bonds, real estate, bank and other invested savings)?

No	1
Yes	2

(7) If you (or spouse) have such assets how much are they worth?

Less than $5 000	1
$5 001 — 20 000	2
$20 001 — 50 000	3
$50 001 — 200 000	4
$200 001 — 500 000	5
$500 001 — 2 million	6
More than $2 million	7

Occupation

This is the most widely used indicator of class. Australian occupations can be sorted into six categories according to the advantages they give in social and economic terms.
Note for scoring: If you are a student or retired, select the occupational grouping that relates to your previous or immediate future work.

(8) Which occupational category best describes you?

A. Senior executive (private or government), large land or business owners, high-level professionals (e.g. lawyers, architects, doctors) — 6
B. Middle managers and administrators, professionals (e.g. teachers, social workers, computer programmers), small business, farmers — 5
C. Clerks, representatives, agents, technicians, skilled trades — 4
D. Sales assistants, clerical assistants, communication and transport workers (e.g. drivers, telephonists, linesmen) — 3
E. Factory hands, semi-skilled and unskilled labourers, the temporarily unemployed — 2
F. Long-term unemployed, social security recipients — 1

(9) Which occupational category best describes your father or mother's job? (Pick the parent whose job was most important for the family income.)
A B C D E F. Score as above.

Associations

(10) Think of *two* of your closest friends who are in paid employment and tick the two categories that best fit the work of each.
A B C D E F. Score as above.

Section II LIFESTYLE FACTORS

These questions are about the way you live, and therefore indicate your social status.

(1) How would you describe the suburb in which you live?

Deprived and poor	1
Relatively inexpensive and ordinary	2
Middle range in price and status	3
Expensive and high status	4

(2) How would you describe your car (or company car)?

Battered and cheap	1
Mechanically sound and economy style	2
Cared-for, fairly recent and middle-price range	3
Thoroughly respectable (e.g. Volvo, Citroen, older BMW)	4
Prestige car (e.g. recent BMW, Mercedes, any Rolls Royce)	5

(3) Where did you spend your holidays?

At home, camping or caravanning	1
At a rented holiday unit	2
At an Australian resort hotel	3
At your own holiday cottage	4
Skiing in Australia or budget travel in the Pacific	5
Travelling overseas (Europe, America, Africa or Asia)	6

(4) What sport, if any, do you play most frequently?

Don't play any sport	1
Football, netball, hockey, ten-pin bowling, surfing	2
Lawn bowls, athletics, cycling	3
Cricket, rugby union, tennis, squash, swimming	4
Golf, horse-riding	5
Sailing, skiing	6

(5) In the past six months, how often have you eaten out with friends or had a formal meal at home?

Not at all	1
Occasionally (1 to 3 occasions)	2
Frequently (about once a month)	3
Regularly (once a week or more)	4

(6) Where do you usually buy your clothes?

At inexpensive chain stores (e.g. Target, Woolworths)	1
At good-quality department stores (e.g. Grace Bros)	2
At boutiques or designer sections of the 'best' stores	3

(7) What is the value for insurance of your household furniture?

Under $10 000	1
$10 001 to $30 000	2
$30 001 to $100 000	3
More than $100 000	4

(continued)

(8) What is the value for insurance of your own and your spouse's jewellery?

Under $10 000	1
$10 001 to $30 000	2
$30 001 to $100 000	3
More than $100 000	4

(9) If you were to have, or do have, children, what sort of high school would they attend?

Local State high school	1
Low-fee-paying independent or religious school	2
Selective State high school	3
Private independent (GPS style) school	4

(10) How would you describe your health?

Poor	1
Reasonable	2
First-rate	3

(11) How would you describe your body-weight?

Much too fat	1
Much too thin	2
Somewhat overweight	3
Correct weight for body-type and personality	4

(12) Do you do any of the following to care for your health? (You may tick more than one and score one point for each tick.)
— regular exercise
— sound moderate eating habits
— adequate relaxation
— not smoking
— low to moderate alcohol intake

(13) In the past six months have you been at least once to the following? (You may tick more than one; one point for each tick.)
— an art gallery or other visual art display
— the theatre for a play or musical
— a movie, rock concert or band
— the opera or ballet
— a symphony or classical concert

Section III MOBILITY

These questions are directed to the likelihood that you may move up or down the social class ladder.

(1) Do you enjoy your work?

No	1
Mostly	2
Yes	3

(2) Is your health good?

No	1
Usually	2
Yes	3

(3) Is your health likely to stay good for the next 10 years?

No	1
Probably	2
Yes	3

(4) How do you feel about your present job?

Content	1
Ambitious for promotion	3

(5) Are you engaged in further education, training or re-training in relation to employment?

No	1
Yes	3

(6) Do you invest the major part or your disposable income in money-earning concerns?

No	1
Yes	2

(7) What class do you think you belong to?

The upper class	6
The upper middle class	5
The middle class	4
The skilled working class	3
The traditional working class of 'battlers'	2
The most deprived class	1

(8) In the next 10 years are you likely to have moved up the social class ladder?

No — likely to lose present class position	1
Not likely to change	2
Probably move 'up' a bit	3
Probably move to more advantaged class	4

(9) Do you expect your children to move into a social position higher than yours?

No	1
Maybe	2
Yes	3

And finally

(10) Do you think that, in Australia, class makes any difference to how you live and what influence you have?

No	1
Yes	3

(11) Do you think class makes any such difference in other countries like England and the US?

No	1
Yes	3

Assess your own class, lifestyle and social mobility expectations as follows:

CLASS

9–13	very disadvantaged: the lowest class in this scheme
14–20	traditional, battling working class
21–30	skilled working class
31–38	definitely middle class
39–48	upper middle class
49–55	upper class

LIFESTYLE

9–12	very poor and of no interest to advertisers
13–17	still poor or frugal in habit
18–27	more comfortable, but nothing ostentatious
28–40	a very comfortable middle class lifestyle
41–51	decidedly expensive and cultivated tastes
52–57	extravagant, great fun, very conspicuous consumption

MOBILITY

11–15	content with your present position, or not interested in pushing yourself
16–24	ambitious, realistic and cautious
25–32	very eager, keen and driving towards achievement

Case study

Timing is an important element in the success or failure of any new product. When the Italian clothing manufacturer MaxMara opened its first Australian store nine months ago, the timing was unfortunate: the retail industry was still caught in the most severe downturn it had experienced since the 1940s. But MaxMara was convinced that Australian women could be coaxed into paying $1500 for a winter coat, $220 for a skirt, $270 for a pair of shoes and $450 for a handbag.

Despite its poor timing, MaxMara's move into Australia is succeeding. Sales figures are not available, but the monthly turnover of the MaxMara store in Melbourne's Collins Street is 25% above the optimistic pre-launch budget set by the company. MaxMara's offer of clothing and fashion accessories imported from Italy, and priced roughly the same as upmarket local fashion brands such as Trent Nathan and Carla Zampatti, is luring shoppers.

Encouraged by the response from Melburnians since the store opened in May last year, MaxMara and its local franchisee/wholesaler, the privately owned company Higgovale, are scouring Australia for more sites. Higgovale is also planning to boost MaxMara's presence in department stores. Five department stores carry MaxMara clothing and accessories: Daimaru in Melbourne, Aherns in Perth and David Jones in Brisbane, Sydney and Adelaide.

The negotiations that led to Daimaru's setting up a MaxMara department were handled by Bob Locke, a former divisional general manager of Coles Myer's Target discount store operation, who joined Daimaru's Australian operation early in 1989 as general manager of merchandise. During that time he dealt with several foreign suppliers with little or no presence in Australia. One of them was MaxMara.

Locke quit Daimaru Australia in February 1992 as part of a restructuring of the company's senior management and set up Higgovale. "I wanted to do something on my own," he says. "I felt MaxMara was the ideal brand to do that." Locke has worked full-time on MaxMara since leaving Daimaru. He was appointed MaxMara's master franchisee in Australia in 1992 and, working with the company's senior executives in Italy, devised a business plan for the Australian operation and selected a site and product range for the first store. This year Locke's company has taken responsibility for the wholesaling and distribution of MaxMara products to other retailers.

"MaxMara is very successful overseas, and has continued to expand despite the worldwide recession in retailing," Locke says. "We have a retailing formula and style that can weather an economic downturn." Another factor that encouraged Locke and MaxMara to set up shop here was the continuing reduction of tariffs on imported clothes, which makes them more affordable for local shoppers. Locke says people are showing a growing interest in international fashion brands.

MaxMara was established in 1951 by an Italian lawyer, Achille Maramotti, who still owns and runs the business. It operates 400 stores around the world. Two hundred of them trade under the MaxMara banner; the rest carry various retail names, including Max & Co, which is pitched at a younger market than the main MaxMara brand, and Marina Rinaldi, which specialises in large-size clothing. MaxMara clothes are produced at one factory, in Italy (MaxMara is one of the world's biggest buyers of Australian fine wool). Products are created by the company's own designers, plus a stream of "guest designers". Over the years, fashion gurus such as Karl Lagerfeld, Emmanuelle Khanh, Guy Paulin and Anna Marie Beretta have designed for MaxMara.

(continued)

Some of the upmarket foreign retailers that have arrived in Australia in recent years rely on tourists for the bulk of their sales, but Locke says that 98% of the Collins Street store's sales have been to local customers. "From the start, our aim was to sell MaxMara to Australians," he says. "We do not want MaxMara to be seen as a retailer for Japanese or American tourists."

Only products and brand names made and owned by MaxMara are sold in the company's stores. The Melbourne store stocks seven of the 15 product ranges that MaxMara sells in Europe and Asia. These include the core MaxMara range, which Locke describes as "contemporary classic with a subtle twist"; casual clothes under the Weekend label, which is 35% cheaper than the main MaxMara brand; Sportsmax, a range aimed at the under-40 market and 10–20% cheaper than MaxMara; and an evening-wear range called Pianoforte. MaxMara clothes are expensive, but Locke says they represent good value for money compared with rival foreign and local top-end fashion brands. "In terms of price, we have no direct rival among the fully imported foreign brands," he says. "Our prices are comparable to the top local designer labels."

So far, the marketing of the MaxMara brand and store has centred on advertising and editorial coverage in glossy women's fashion magazines such as *Vogue*, *Elle* and *Mode*, fashion shows for the store's customers, and promotions and other material in Melbourne daily newspapers. Locke has also started building a database of customers that will be used for direct-mail campaigns.

Finding sites for new stores is not easy. The Castlereagh Street district — which is home to upmarket retailers such as Louis Vuitton, Chanel and Hermes — is an obvious choice for the first MaxMara store in Sydney. Locke does not want consumers to put his retail chain in the same category as other high-priced, foreign fashion brands. "We deliberately avoid aligning MaxMara with the very top end of the fashion market," he says. "We want people to see MaxMara as a notch below the Chanels and Christian Diors.

"We want to lift the profile of the MaxMara brand in department stores, but we also must retain the uniqueness of the brand. We do not want it to be available everywhere."

Neil Shoebridge,
Business Review Weekly,
31 January 1994

Case study questions

1. Which socioeconomic group should Bob Locke target?

2. What factors could hinder the success of the MaxMara label?

3. Evaluate Bob Locke's choice of advertising medium.

SUGGESTED READING

T. Jagtenberg and P. D'Alton, *Four Dimensional Social Space*, Harper and Row Publishers, Sydney, 1989.

J. Baxter, M. Emminson and J. Western, *Class Analysis and Contemporary Australia*, Macmillan, Melbourne, 1991.

D. Bedggood, *Rich and Poor in New Zealand*, George Allen and Unwin, Auckland, 1980.

L. V. Domminquez and A. L. Page, 'Stratification in Consumer Behaviour Research: A Re-examination', *Academy of Marketing Science*, Vol. 9, No. 3, 1981, pp. 250–71.

ENDNOTES

1. P. D. Martineau, 'Social Class and Spending Behaviour', *Journal of Marketing*, Oct. 1958, pp. 121–41.

2. L. V. Dominquez and A. L. Page, 'Stratification in Consumer Behaviour Research: A Re-examination', *Academy of Marketing Science*, Vol. 9, No. 3, 1981, pp. 250–71. J. E. Fisher, 'Social Class and Consumer Behaviour: The Relevance of Class and Status', in M. Wallendorf and P. Anderson (eds), *Advances in Consumer Research*, Vol. 14, 1987.

3. H. Mackay, *The Mackay Report on Class and Status in Australian Society*, 1986.

4. R. P. Coleman, 'The Continuing Significance of Social Class to Marketing', *Journal of Consumer Research*, 10, Dec. 1983, pp. 265–80. L. W. Warner et al., *Social Class in America: A Manual of Procedure for the Measurement of Social Status*, Social Research Associates, Chicago, 1949.

5. C. McGregor, 'Class', *The Good Weekend*, 10 Oct. 1987.

6. J. Baxter, M. Emminson and J. Western, *Class Analysis and Contemporary Australia*, Macmillan, Melbourne, 1991.

7. B. Graetz and I. McAllister, *Dimensions of Australian Society*, Macmillan Educational Australia, 1988.

8. A. Daniel, *Power, Privilege and Prestige: Occupations in Australia*, Longman Cheshire, Sydney, 1983.

9. C. Chamberlain, *Class Consciousness in Australia*, Allen and Unwin, Sydney, 1983. B. Graetz, 'Structure and Class Consciousness: Facts, Fictions and Fantasies', *Australia and New Zealand Journal of Sociology*, 22, 1986, pp. 46–64.

10. R. P. Coleman and L. Warner, op. cit.

11. L. Broom and F. L. Jones, *Opportunity and Attainment in Australia*, Australia University Press, Canberra, 1976. L. Broom, F. L. Jones, P. McDonnell and T. Williams, *The Inheritance of Inequality*, Routledge and Kegan Paul, London, 1980. L. Broom, F. L. Jones and P. McDonnell, *Investigating Social Mobility*, Canberra: Monograph No. 1, Department of Sociology RSSS, ANU, Canberra, 1977.

12. F. L. Jones and P. Davis, *Models of Society: Class Stratification and Gender in Australia and New Zealand*, Croom Helm, Sydney, 1986.

13. Baxter et al., op. cit. (see note 6).

14. R. Ward, *The Australian Legend*, Oxford University Press, Melbourne, 1978. C. W. Bean, *Official History of Australia in the War of 1914–1918*, Vol. 1, Angus and Robertson, Sydney, 1937.

15. D. Horne, *The Lucky Country*, Penguin Books, Melbourne, 1964.

16. C. McGregor, *Profile of Australia*, Penguin, London, 1966.

17. K. Sinclair, *A History of New Zealand*, 4th edn, Penguin, 1973.

18. B. Willmott, *Culture and Identity in New Zealand*, G. P. Books, 1989. B. Consedine, 'Inequality and the Egalitarianism Myth', in D. Bedggood, *Rich and Poor in New Zealand*, George Allen and Unwin, Auckland, 1980.

19. F. L. Jones and P. Davis, op. cit. (see note 12).

20. C. McGregor, 'Class', in T. Jagtenberg and P. D'Alton (eds), *Four Dimensional Social Space*, Harper and Row, Sydney, 1989.

21. V. Peterson, 'The Anatomy of the Ocker Snob', The *Bulletin*, 8 Dec. 1981.

22. Table compiled from: E. O. Wright, in Baxter et al., *Case Analysis in Contemporary Australia*, Macmillan, Melbourne, 1991, p. 67; Australian Bureau of Statistics 1993; L. Broom, F. L. Jones, P. McDonnell and T. Williams, *The Inheritance of Inequality*, Routledge & Kegan Paul, London, 1980; F. L. Jones and P. Davis, *Models of Society: Class Stratification and Gender in Australia and New Zealand*, Croom Helm, Sydney, 1986; D. Bedggood, *Rich and Poor in New Zealand*, Allen and Unwin, Auckland, 1980; Institute of Family Studies.

23. Broom et al. (1980), op. cit., and Jones and Davis (1986), ibid.

24. L. Broom, F. L. Jones, P. McDonnell and T. Williams (1980), ibid. M. Western, 'Intergenerational Class Mobility Among Women and Men', Paper presented to TASA Conference, Macquarie University, Sydney, Dec. 1993. 'Learning Success', *Chapter*, April 1992.

25. C. McGregor, 'Class', *The Good Weekend*, 1987. 'Forget About the Yuppies, Now Meet the New Poor', *Business Review Weekly*, 14 Dec. 1990. 'The Nicer Nineties', *Australian Business Monthly*, Nov. 1991. R. Neill, 'After the Yuppie: The Ultra', The *Bulletin*, 3 May 1988. N. Shoebridge, 'The Baby Boomers are Seeking Higher, Kinder, Gentler Lives', *Business Review Weekly*, 5 July 1991.

26. Lindal Crisp, 'The Underclass', The *Bulletin*, April 1990. 'This is the other Australia', *Australian Business Monthly*, Aug. 1992.

27. P. Martineau, op. cit.

28. L. Bryson and F. Thompson, *An Australian Newtown*, Pelican Books, 1977.

29. B. Wearing, *The Ideology of Motherhood*, Allen and Unwin, Sydney, 1984.

30. F. Jones, op. cit.

31. J. Harper and L. Richards, *Mothers and Working Mothers*, Penguin, Melbourne, 1986.

32. C. McGregor (1987), op. cit.

33. M. Ragg, 'Health, Wealth and the Right Address', The *Bulletin*, 7 July 1992 (Comment on a Social Heath Atlas of Australia).

34. A. Graetz (1986), op. cit.

35. M. Emmison and M. Western, 'Social Class and Social Identity: A Comment on Marshall et al.', *Sociology*, Vol. 24, No. 2, 1990, pp. 241–53.

36. P. Bourdieu, *Distinction: A Social Critique of the Judgement of Taste*, Harvard University Press, 1984. A similar study is being undertaken by M. Emmison, 'The Australian Cultural Consumption Project: Preliminary Findings from the Brisbane Project', The Australian Sociological Association Conference, Macquarie University, Dec. 1993.

37. H. Mackay, op. cit.

CHAPTER

12

Consumer lifestyles

This chapter should help you to:
- understand lifestyle segmentation
- understand the interrelationship between lifestyle and psychographics
- appreciate the difficulties in lifestyle measurement
- know the current status of lifestyle research.

WHAT IS LIFESTYLE SEGMENTATION?

Although the term 'lifestyle' is easy to define, a precise interpretation of 'lifestyle segmentation' is not so easy. Lifestyle relates to how people live, how they spend their money and how they allocate their time. Three early marketing definitions of the terms are described in the box on page 292 and, although each definition is different, the idea of activities and opinions is evident in all three. The lifestyle concept is well known and widely accepted, particularly in the field of sociology, in which the study and comparison of the lifestyles of different class, ethnic and locality groups is a popular focus of study.[1] Your lifestyle choice is a function of many factors. It is influenced by the physical and social environment in which you develop; your personal capabilities, interests and values; and your access to the resources offered by your particular society.

In marketing, the underlying premise is that consumers' lifestyles will strongly influence their consumption behaviour. This being so, then consumers who have similar lifestyles are more likely to use similar products and services. This means that clusters of consumers — or segments — with similar lifestyles can be identified and the appropriate marketing mixes developed for each segment.

Some views of lifestyle

66Lifestyle reflects the overall manner in which people live and spend time and money.99

J. Wind, 'Lifestyle Analysis: A New Approach', *Journal of Marketing Research*, Vol. 6, No. 169, 1969, p. 302.

66Relevant activity (a manifest action) and attitude (a predisposition to act) variables that can quantitatively explore and explain the purchase and consumption of specific products, services or brands.99

T. P. Hustad and E. A. Pessemier, 'Segmenting Consumer Markets with Activity and Attitude Measures', (Working Paper), The Herman C. Krannert Graduate School of Industrial Administration, Purdue University, Indiana, 1971.

66A person's lifestyle is composed of his activities, how he spends his time at work and leisure; his interests — what he places importance on in his immediate surroundings; his opinions — where he stands on issues, society and himself; and some basic facts — his social class, stage in life cycle and his purchasing patterns.99

J. T. Plummer, 'The Concept and Application of Lifestyle Segmentation', *Journal of Marketing*, Vol. 38, 1974.

Applying the lifestyle concept to segmentation requires the marketer to identify lifestyle categories that can be measured. The most common approach has been to identify consumers who have the following factors in common, and then group them into lifestyle categories:

- shared interests
- similar activities
- similar opinions.

While this is a relatively straightforward notion, developing the concept into a viable segmentation tool has been complicated by two interacting factors:

- the influence of psychographic based segmentation
- the problems associated with the measurement of lifestyle segments.

To fully understand the complexity that surrounds lifestyle segmentation, the influence of each of these factors needs to be understood.

PSYCHOGRAPHIC BASED SEGMENTATION

The origin of psychographics as a segmentation measure is unclear. However, there is some agreement that it emerged in the 1960s as a means to extend the scope of demographic segmentation. The use of demographic profiles as a basis for market segmentation dominated the 1950s and 1960s. Its popularity is understandable. Age, income, education and occupation and other factual statistics are not only easy to measure, but also influence consumer behaviour. For example, elderly people have a greater need for health care products, children need toys, and families with babies require baby care products. But one thing that demographic information cannot do is capture what is going on in the consumer's mind.

Therefore, the reasons for buying a particular brand or choosing a specific product cannot be ascertained from demographic information. For example, you can use demographics to predict that a large family is more likely to purchase a station wagon or a van than a young single person, but you may not be able to ascertain which model or brand the family would choose.[2]

In the 1960s, because of the influence of motivation research, an understanding of consumers' personal needs and desires was seen as not only desirable but possible. It was thought that accurate assessment of personal needs and characteristics would allow marketers to predict consumers' product form and brand choices. Initially, attempts were made to identify clusters of consumers by using motivational and personality characteristics and matching these with their consumption behaviour. But as we saw in chapter 6, these attempts yield consistently low correlations when used to predict consumption behaviour.

Several researchers thought that it could be possible to obtain better correlations for consumption behaviour by combining demographic information, motives and personality into a new segmentation measure.[3] From this, they hoped that more viable and understandable segments would result. The new measure was given the label 'psychographics' which, literally translated from the Greek, would mean 'the measurement and mapping of consumers' motives and personalities'. Information is obtained from consumers through quantified, pre-coded questionnaires, which can be self-administered or administered by ordinary survey procedures. The pre-coding allows them to be analysed via one of the many component based, statistical, analytical techniques such as cluster or factor analysis.

PSYCHOGRAPHIC OR LIFESTYLE SEGMENTATION?

By the late 1960s, for reasons that are not clear, practitioners and academics had begun to include questions that were concerned with activities, interests and opinions (AIO statements) in their psychographic studies. This practice had become so prevalent by the 1970s that, in 1975, William Wells described psychographics as a segmentation approach that grouped individuals on the basis of activities, interests and opinions.[4] In the same article he also noted that there was considerable confusion about the demarcation between the two approaches. The outcome of this was that two different, but overlapping, segmentation approaches were given the same label. Instruments that showed only personality and motivation items were labelled psychographics, as were instruments with AIO statements. So, too, were the ranges of combinations that emerged during the 1970s and 1980s. The result of this is continuing confusion as to which factors differentiate lifestyle and psychographic segmentation, because both terms have been used to describe the following combinations:

- AIO statements alone
- AIO statements plus demographic items
- AIO statements plus personality and motivation items
- AIO statements plus personality, motivation and demographic items
- demographic items plus personality and motivation items.

Although the terms are used synonymously, the lifestyle label seems to be emerging as the dominant term. In part, this is a function of a gradual decline in the number of personality and motivation items included in questionnaires. However, there are exceptions to this labelling trend, as a study carried out in New Zealand in 1989 demonstrates. This study, which was described as an examination of the opinions and lifestyles of New Zealanders, was given the title 'A psychographic analysis of New Zealand consumers'.[5] The study covered approximately 480 questions, of which 35 were personality items and 24 concerned the respondents' views of themselves in relation to their families. Only 7 per cent of the items (12 per cent if you include the family items) were related to personality and motivation, yet the psychographic label was still used in the title. The results of the study are summarised below.

A psychographic analysis of New Zealand consumers

The following is a brief summary of the findings of the New Zealand lifestyle study, which identified six segments of New Zealand consumers.

Success driven extroverts (8.9%)
- Career and social players
- Living it up, socialising
- Excitement and pleasure focus
- Free enterprise ... self (me)
- Impressing people
- Money and modernity

Educated greens (12.4%)
- Societal reformers
- Supporting topical causes
- Intellect and education focus
- Modern naturalists
- Culture, fashion, sophistication
- Secure well-off future

Active family people (21.9%)
- Family life enthusiasm
- Active warm togetherness
- Children development focus
- Protective of family health, environment and heritage
- Family activities, outings

Traditional values family people (20.3%)
- Orderly family life
- Discipline and obedience
- Parental roles focus
- Traditional institutions
- Spiritual values ... trust
- Local community activities

Envious strivers (21.1%)
- 'Give me a break'
- Life's a struggle
- Achieving ambitions focus
- Cautious and conformist
- Wanting life's 'essentials'
- Escapist activities

Friendly quiet lifers (15.4%)
- Neighbourly chat enjoyment
- Familiar hassle-free life
- Friendly close-to-home focus
- Elderly and nostalgic
- Companionship
- Continued good health

MEASUREMENT OF LIFESTYLE SEGMENTS

The value of market segmentation for most products is unequivocal but, to be of practical use, the segments must be measurable, accessible and substantial. They must also be tangible, homogeneous clusters that can be clearly differentiated from each other. The differentiation aspect is important since it is this factor that allows a specific marketing mix to be developed for each segment. For a segmentation approach to yield truly differentiated segments, accurate measurement is crucial. Despite the many lifestyle/psychographic studies that have been carried out since the 1960s, controversy still surrounds the measurement techniques used to identify segments.

There are two approaches to lifestyle research — *general* and *specific*. In a general lifestyle study, the population in general is targeted, whereas in a specific lifestyle study product, users are targeted. General lifestyle studies are conducted through surveys of large, national samples of consumers. The data are then analysed using one of the multivariate statistical techniques such as cluster or factor analysis. The aim is to group together (cluster) individuals in a society who report similar activities, interests and opinions. Once the groups have been identified, the consumption behaviour of the individuals within the groups may be examined. The desired outcome is that the identified groups will display distinctly different marketplace behaviours. The interest in general lifestyle studies lies in their potential as 'antesegmentation' tools and monitors of change. This means that consumer segments can be identified prior to product use. Some questions that are often included in general lifestyle studies are shown below and on page 296.

Examples of general lifestyle study questions

How often do *you* engage in each of the following activities?

Indoor recreation and hobbies
a. Play a musical instrument
b. Listen to records and/or tapes
c. Paint, draw, or sculpt (art)
d. Write poetry/fiction/non-fiction for pleasure
e. Engage in crafts (ceramics, leather working, pottery, etc.)
f. Do woodworking or carpentry
g. Knit/crochet/do needlework
h. Design your own or others' clothes
i. Sew to make something
j. Sew to repair or mend something
k. Do repair or fix-up projects around the house
l. Go bowling
m. Exercise in a gym
n. Play pool or billiards
o. Play bridge or poker
p. Play chess
q. Play backgammon
r. Yoga or meditation at home

(continued)

Shopping and related activities
a. Purchase items through the mail
b. Purchase items by phone
c. Use trading stamps to purchase items
d. Use coupons in magazines or newspapers to purchase items
e. Return an unsatisfactory product
f. Shop in large discount stores (such as K-mart)
g. Shop in major department stores
h. Purchase a newspaper or a magazine at a newsstand
i. Shop in convenience food markets (such as the '7–11' chain)
j. Purchase drugs in discount drug stores
k. Shop at second-hand stores.

Eating, drinking and food preparation
a. Bake bread at home
b. Bake pastries at home
c. Cook outdoors (backyard, patio)
d. Preserve foods at home
e. Eat out at or bring food home from fast food restaurants
f. Give dinner parties.

Business travel
a. Travel by air for business purposes
b. Travel abroad for business purposes
c. Stay at hotels and/or motels during business travel
d. Use rental cars for business travel
e. Use a travel agency for business travel.

Vacation or pleasure travel
a. Travel by air for pleasure (vacation) purposes
b. Travel abroad for pleasure
c. Stay at hotels and/or motels while vacationing
d. Use rental cars for pleasure travel
e. Use a travel agency for pleasure trips
f. Take trips in a recreational vehicle (such as a motor home, travel trailer or camper).

Miscellaneous activities
a. Write letters to friends and relatives
b. Send or give greeting cards
c. Telephone friends or relatives locally
d. Telephone friends or relatives long distance
e. Telephone friends or relatives internationally
f. Borrow books and/or magazines from a local library
g. Use audio-visual materials at a local library
h. Work at a second job, including freelancing
i. Visit phone company offices
j. Type personal letters at home
k. Type at home to earn extra money
l. Work on your own car or other motor vehicle.

Writers have pointed out that general lifestyle studies can give insights into product category choices, but they do not necessarily provide insights into product form or brand choices.[6] Another problem is that the behaviour differences across a range of product categories can also be explained in terms of income and occupation.

For this reason, general lifestyle studies have limited application as segmenting tools. Lifestyle clusters are more useful if they are derived in conjunction with other segmentation variables, the most useful being product usage and benefits-sought segmentation.

Product-specific lifestyle studies are intended to build up a profile of the users of particular products. The users (or potential users) of a product are identified and then questioned about their lifestyles, product knowledge and perceptions. In essence, this is a combination of two segmenting approaches — lifestyle and behavioural. The survey instrument usually includes questions relating to product knowledge, usage and benefits sought, consumer demographics, media usage, and a battery of activities, interests and opinion statements. A classic example of this type of segmentation strategy is the study by Pernica, which examined the users of stomach remedies.[7]

In Australia, the earliest and most widely known specific lifestyle studies were those carried out in the 1970s by the *Age*. The main aim of these studies was to identify readership patterns and some general behaviour patterns of readers. The first study, entitled *The Different Australian*,[8] was carried out in 1975. Readers of the *Age* — the 'different' Australians — were compared with readers of 12 other Australian newspapers.

A second study, *The Age Lifestyle Study*,[9] was undertaken in 1982. Its aim was to identify and describe the characteristics of 'established readers' — those who purchased three or more issues per week and who had a definite affinity for the paper. The study identified fifteen population segments — seven male-based segments and eight female-based segments (see table 12.1). In the male-based segments, the 'family struggler' (24 per cent) was the largest group. In the female category, the 'pessimistic housewife' (21.2 per cent) and the 'older matron' (23.4 per cent) groups were dominant. Profiles of two segments are reproduced in figure 12.1, page 298.

Table 12.1: Lifestyle segments identified by *The Age Lifestyle Study*

	Segments	% of all males		Segments	% of all females
Male	Family struggler	24.0	*Female*	Older matron	23.4
	Aussie chauvinist	15.3		Pessimistic housewife	21.2
	Young free active	13.8		Independent Ms	11.4
	Experience seeker	13.8		Career mother	10.2
	Average successful dad	13.4		Frivolous Ms	9.8
	Urbane sophisticate	10.3		Family contributor	9.5
	Older traditionalist	9.5		Doting grandmother	7.4
				Sophisticated woman	7.1

(*Source*: *The Age Lifestyle Study*, 1982)

Male segment — Family Struggler (24 per cent of all males)

In contrast to the Average Successful Dad, Family Struggler has found that having children has significantly altered both his lifestyle and outlook. He now finds that he has to carefully manage his income in order to make ends meet.

He is concerned about inflation and its effect on prices and is more likely to have put off buying and doing things because of rising costs than other men he knows. He doesn't take much interest in other issues facing the country. His world revolves around his family, football and his mates (not necessarily in that order) and he leads a fairly straight-forward life.

He is a keen sports spectator ... [but] is less involved in the active participation of sports ... Caravanning, barbecues and picnics, going to the beach, driving and sight-seeing, gardening and playing cards, all are high on his list of activities.

He believes that governments know better than the average man and believes Australia needs a strong leader. He regards local news as more important than national affairs and he hardly notices international events. He shows little interest in overseas cultures and has no overseas travel ambitions.

Family Struggler is a great watcher of commercial television, enjoying quizzes, sport, news and talent shows. He prefers the *Sun* to the *Age* and buys the *Herald* with average frequency: 66 per cent read the *Sun*, 43 per cent read the *Herald*, 17 per cent read the *Age*.

He makes few purchasing decisions, leaving it to his wife. When he does shop, he prefers regional centres.

Female segment — Independent Ms (11.4 per cent of all females)

Independent Ms is young, generally in her early twenties, single or married, without children. Confident, ambitious and successful, she acts to maintain her liberated lifestyle. She does not believe that motherhood is the most important career for a woman.

Where not finishing off her studies, she is working full-time at an above-average income for her age and sex. She generally is happy with her education and training and regards her job as stimulating and important but finds it mentally tiring. She has a confident outlook about her future, believing she has the willpower to get ahead and has influence over her own life, that achieving success is important and that people can change the world around them if they want to.

This confidence carries over to her personal management because she can afford what she wants, does her own thinking and makes her own decisions. She has a wide range of interests including domestic and overseas travel, human behaviour, photography, conservation, architecture and building and computers.

Her social and leisure pursuits are very important to her. She frequently wines, dines, visits friends and goes to parties. Outgoing and adventurous, she likes to try different foods, vary her entertainment and meet new people. Her interest in clothes and fashion are an integral part of this social life. . .

Energetic and active, she is a keen participator in sport, particularly swimming, jogging and tennis, but she has less interest in being a spectator.

Politics and current affairs in Australia and around the world are followed with interest, presumably through her wide media intake. Some 37 per cent of Independent Ms read the *Age*, which is 1.85 times the average female level . . . She watches less television than other women but when she does, she prefers movies, news, documentaries, current affairs shows and comedies. She listens to FM radio frequently due to her interest in rock and pop music.

Figure 12.1: Sample profiles from *The Age Lifestyle Study*, 1982

VALIDITY AND RELIABILITY CONCERNS

It is difficult to estimate how many specific lifestyle studies have been carried out worldwide, but a conservative estimate would probably put the figure in the thousands. Most studies have been carried out by independent practitioners and few are publicised.

Lifestyle research is not without its critics. Anthony Adams pointed out that:

- there is a large gap between lifestyles and product or brand choice — lifestyles only explain 10 per cent of the variance in choice
- there is variance between brand behaviour — benefit segments do much better
- lifestyle research leads to over-segmentation
- lifestyle research tells you what you already know
- lifestyle research has limited actionability.[10]

The problems described by Adams in part stem from validity and reliability issues. A test is said to be valid if it measures what it intends to measure and that something said to be accurate and/or important really is important. The latter problem plagues most question/interview based research and is difficult to solve. To an extent, it is out of the control of the investigator, although skilled researchers can do much to mitigate the problem. The former issue — that the instrument measures what it purports to measure — is often a function of *content* and *construct validity* issues. Content validity refers to whether the questions measure what they say they are measuring and construct validity refers to whether the test instrument measures the theoretical constructs it claims to measure. This means that the design of the research is important. Because this design is in the hands of the investigator, the outcome is potentially controllable. Of the two validity issues, it is construct validity that has created the most problems for lifestyle researchers.

QUESTIONNAIRE CONSTRUCTION — THE ROLE OF THEORY IN LIFESTYLE RESEARCH

A consistent criticism of lifestyle research, particularly general lifestyle research, has been that its development has been haphazard in the sense that it has not been guided by any explicit theory of human behaviour.[11] Generally, an ad hoc collection of numerous AIO statements are prepared, administered and then analysed using multivariate statistical techniques. Such methods have been described as data reduction exercises and the resulting segments viewed as a product of the analytical techniques used — the implication being that the segments may not actually exist. For example, the 15 segments identified by the *Age* study may be a function of the questions asked and the analytical procedures used. This means that different questions would have produced 15 different segments.

Essentially, the role of theory in research is to provide an idea about the world that can be tested. For lifestyle research, this means direction as to which dimensions of individuals' lifestyles should be measured and how they should be measured. Items from hundreds of activity, interest, opinion and personal areas could be included in a survey instrument, so which ones do researchers include? For example, apart from the demographic questions, no specific selection criteria for the 481 items selected in the New Zealand study were described by the authors.[12] If researchers have an idea or theory that certain lifestyle groups, each with certain characteristics, exist in a society, then they could develop an instrument to test whether these segments actually exist. So, to be guided by theory requires that the researchers develop an idea of which lifestyle groups exist in a community and design an instrument to test whether these groups do, in fact, exist. This process is necessary if lifestyle segments are to be independent of product usage or other segmentation variables.

In lifestyle research, cluster analysis or factor analysis is used to group respondents according to their answers to largely ad hoc questions. If all the items are used in the grouping process (that is, no residuals) the resulting groups are too numerous and too small to be workable (actionable) segments. In order to decrease the number of groups, certain questions need to be weighted or discarded. Since there is no underlying theory to guide the selection of the key items, their selection becomes a function of data reduction techniques, that is, which variables result in the 'best' segments. This means that it is difficult to know whether the segments really exist or have been derived statistically. To ensure that such confusion does not occur, it is necessary to have some prior knowledge about which groups exist in a community, and the characteristics that individuals must have in order to be members of the group. Questions that would identify individuals with these characteristics can then be developed.[13]

In a specific lifestyle study, the segments are predetermined and the questions are used to give a clearer picture of the brand user. Even so, the researcher still needs some idea as to the type of lifestyle the user of the product might lead. Ideas can be obtained through unstructured interviews with product (or brand) users. The researchers can then use the identified range of activities, interests and opinions to develop questionnaires that can be administered to a larger sample of consumers and the results measured. Because the segments have been predetermined, product specific lifestyle research is not as dependent on theories of behaviour.

THE VALS PROGRAM — NINE AMERICAN LIFESTYLES

Although there have been a number of attempts to find a theoretical base for lifestyle research, the first attempt to systematically address the problem was the Values and Lifestyle Survey (VALS) developed by the Stanford Research Institute (SRI) International in the 1970s. The program was designed as an ongoing study into the changing values and lifestyles of Americans and is, perhaps, the most widely known general lifestyle study. The intent was that the information obtained would enable researchers to apply lifestyle and values information to marketing decisions. The main aim of the VALS program was to resolve the problems relating to the ad hoc selection of lifestyle items. According to Arnold Mitchell, nine segments were defined first, and then questions were designed to allocate people on the basis of their responses into a category, or segment.[14] The predetermined segments were derived by combining two theories of individual human development: Abraham Maslow's hierarchy of needs and David Riesman's social character theory (see pages 301–302).

Two theories of individual human development

Maslow's need hierarchy

Implicit in Maslow's theory (see page 19 for more information) is the notion that all individuals have inherent basic need states that must be satisfied if they are to evolve into fully functioning, healthy people. The basic (primary) needs are physical and are concerned with the survival of the individual as a living entity. When survival needs are met, the individual focuses on satisfying the psycho-social needs of belongingness, self-esteem and self-actualisation.

All individuals have the potential to go through each of the need stages, but the goals and behaviour required to satisfy the needs are functions of the individual and his or her environment.

Maslow cites Eleanor Roosevelt and Albert Schweitzer as having reached self-actualisation. Presumably these individuals satisfied all the need stages, but clearly their lifestyles were vastly different. Individuals may share a similar stage in the hierarchy but this does not necessarily mean that they share similar experiences or vice versa. According to VALS researchers, particular values arise out of these needs which in turn affect the individuals' lifestyles. This implies that in each need stage, individuals will share the same values which in turn determines their behaviour.

Riesman's social character theory

David Riesman's social character theory stipulates that societies go through different stages of development and, as they do, the individual members need to develop different 'social characteristics' to survive in the society. Societies move through traditional societies, outer-directed societies and inner-directed societies. In traditional societies, the rules that govern behaviour are externally controlled and enforced by mechanisms set by the ruling group. Formal punishments and sanctions are in place, so self-direction and monitoring is unnecessary. As societies evolve and become more complex and the members become more diverse in skills, talents and mobility (both geographically and socially), a different form of social control is required. This is especially true in situations in which members of one community explore, invade and colonise other communities. In these, often rugged and pioneer type communities, there is greater demand for initiative, self-control and self-direction in the individual. According to Riesman, 'the source of direction and control for the individual is "inner" in the sense that it is implanted early in life by the elders and directed towards generalised, but nonetheless inescapable, destined goals'. This means that the inner-directed types have internalised the rules of behaviour and will adhere to them even when the external controls are removed. As these pioneer type societies become more prosperous and bureaucratic, and their members become more interactive and sensitive to each other, different mechanisms for control are necessary.

(*continued*)

Increasingly, other people become the main focus instead of the physical environment. As people mix more widely and become more sensitive to each other, the need for inner-directedness decreases and this creates the need for the outer-directed type. This does not mean that the inner-directed types disappear altogether, but over successive generations they gradually recede. Riesman concludes that Americans are more shallow and more uncertain of themselves and their values. And because they are more demanding of approval, they represent a social character that depends on contemporaries — either people known to them or through the mass media — as a source of direction for appropriate behaviour and ways of thinking.

Researchers at SRI believed that all American adults could be assigned to one of the predetermined developmental stages. Essentially the stages are hierarchical (see figure 12.2). At the bottom of the hierarchy are the need driven groups — the **survivors** and the **sustainers**. These groups are the American poor and, at the time of the first VALS survey, represented 11 per cent of the population. The members of the survivor group are truly poor. They have poor health, little education and tend to be elderly. The sustainers are on the edge of poverty. They are young, still hopeful and struggling to get ahead. They tend to be angry, distrustful, anxious and often feel left out of things.

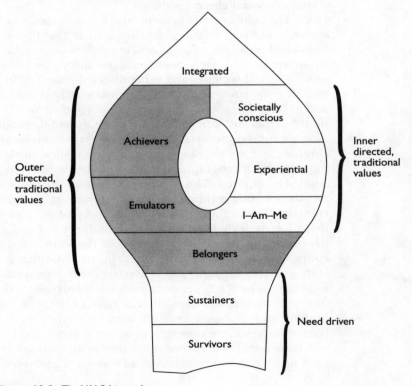

Figure 12.2: The VALS hierarchy

Members of the outer-directed groups have traditional values. They look to others for direction, are concerned with maintaining social standards of conduct and are very normative. They tend to focus on the 'visible, tangible and the material'. The three groups in this category are the belongers, the emulators and the achievers.

- **The belongers** are generally regarded as 'middle America'. They are more interested in fitting in with society than standing out. It is important for them to know their place and what is expected of them. They are traditional, conservative, conventional, nostalgic and unexperiential. The home is their domain.

- **The emulators** are psychologically more mature than the belongers because they demand more of themselves as they try to climb the social ladder. They are ambitious, upwardly mobile, status conscious and competitive. As a consequence, they tend to be in debt.

- **The achievers** are the leaders in business, professions and government. Efficiency, fame, status, the good life, comfort and materialism are the hallmarks of the achievers. These outer-directed individuals are affluent and able to respond to opportunity. They are very happy with their lifestyles and achievements and often indulge in luxuries.

The principal driving forces of the inner-directed groups are internal, not external. Emerging from the relative affluence of the 1950s and 1960s, these people seek something other than the intense materialism sought by the outer-directed groups. Personal priorities often take precedence over the wishes of others. The three groups in the inner-directed category are the I-am-me, the experientials and the societally conscious.

- **The I-am-me group** represents the transition stage from outer- to inner-directedness. Its members tend to be young, impulsive, well educated and predominantly male. Often, they are the children of achievers, and in many instances they are trend setters. Members remain in this group for a short time only as they move towards the experiential group.

- **The experientials** are interested in direct experience with life. They tend to be artistic, experimental and highly participating. Some find self-expression by becoming involved in social causes or activities such as rock climbing. They are independent, self-reliant, innovative people with moderate incomes.

- **The societally conscious** are concerned with the world at large. Their high sense of social responsibility leads them to support such causes as conservation and environmentalism. They wish to live lives that conserve, protest and heal.

The **integrated group** represented only 2 per cent of the population in the 1970s. The members of this group combine the best qualities of the inner- and outer-directed groups, resulting in unique and diverse lifestyles. They are fully mature in a psychological sense. The diversity and size (extremely small) of this group means that assessing product and media usage is both difficult and impractical.

Some general characteristics of these segments and their buying potential are shown in table 12.2. There have been numerous applications of VALS. One that has been publicly described was its implementation by the Beef Industry Council in the USA. In the 1970s the consumption level of beef declined — a trend that has continued. This decrease took place against a gradual increase in fish and poultry consumption. In order to understand these trends, the consumption patterns of meat and fish by the VALS segments were analysed (see table 12.3).[15] Respondents were asked if they had eaten any of the meat products in the last seven days. The average consumption rate was set at 100. So from the table it can be seen that survivors, for example, are below average consumers of turkey breast. This type of analysis alone does not show which groups are reducing beef consumption — to do this a longitudinal monitoring is required. But it does show that there are some differences (often slight) in consumption patterns among the groups. Consumption levels across all of the products (with the exception of fish by the sustainers) increased from the survivors category to the belongers category. Because income is a key element for membership in these groups, the cost of meat and fish may be a contributing factor. The beef industry targeted the achievers, the I-am-me group, the experientials and the societally conscious as these groups were increasing. The I-am-me group and the experientials tend to be health conscious and would not increase consumption, so the wisdom of this strategy choice is questionable, particularly in the light of the general trend across Western societies towards a fat-free lifestyle.

Table 12.2: Selected differences in AIOs among VALS (100 = Average rate of participation in activities)

Activities	Survivors	Sustainers	Belongers	Emulators	Achievers	I-am-me	Experiential	Societally conscious
Play golf	0	100	54	62	162	162	108	85
Go fishing	48	200	126	100	87	91	100	74
Go to museums	43	52	78	61	165	74	126	191
Watch TV game shows	233	225	158	108	42	17	42	50
Watch TV comedies	67	195	86	152	67	176	138	67
Read tabloids (e.g. *Enquirer*)	118	247	129	106	53	100	59	47
Read business magazines	36	64	100	36	186	100	114	157
Drink regular soft drinks	112	112	82	171	94	176	94	59
Drink diet soft drinks	50	50	80	90	110	120	150	170
Size of group	11M	6M	57M	16M	37M	8M	11M	14M
Median age	66	32	5	28	42	21	28	37
Median household income	<$5 000	$11 000	$17 500	$19 000	$30 000	$10 000	$22 000	$25 000

(*Source*: Adapted from T. C. Thomans and S. Crocker, *Values and Lifestyles — New Psychographics*, SRI, Menlo Park, Calif., 1981)

Table 12.3: VALS segments and meat consumption

	Beef	Lamb	Fresh fish	Fresh chicken	Turkey breast
Survivors	64	21	62	69	41
Sustainers	77	54	111	93	62
Belongers	98	96	90	97	75
Emulators	102	62	111	107	63
Achievers	115	125	108	107	155
I-am-me	90	174	119	90	110
Experiential	95	36	79	100	85
Societally conscious	109	160	121	108	154

(*Source*: Adapted from T. C. Thomans and S. Crocker, *Values and Lifestyles — New Psychographics*, SRI, Menlo Park, Calif., 1981)

VALS 2: ANSWERING THE CRITICS

The VALS program has received a number of criticisms regarding reliability and validity issues and thus the usefulness of the segments. The main issues concerned the value of using psychological developmental theories as a basis for segmentation. Writers such as Rebecca Holman[16] have argued that the hierarchical nature of the segments is a function of demographics such as income levels and is not necessarily related to an individual's psychological development. Holman also suggests that the program functions best as a social monitor, not a segmenting tool. John Rossiter points out that VALS is a hybrid of demographic and lifestyle segmentation.[17] However, a major problem is the lack of real differentiation between the segments — as the Beef Industry Council study demonstrates.

Whether such criticisms influenced SRI researchers or they were responding to changing lifestyles in America, SRI developed VALS 2 in the 1980s. VALS 2 places less importance on theories of psychological development and focuses more on the material resources, values and self-orientation of respondents. VALS 2 identified eight consumer segments (see figure 12.3). The main dimensions underlying the segments are resources and self-orientation. Resources encompass such aspects as income, material possessions and health. Self-orientation includes individuals' perceptions of themselves in society, their attitudes and activities. VALS researchers claim that there are three major self-orientations:

- **principle-oriented** consumers are guided by their beliefs (knowledge) about products rather than their feelings or from a need for approval from others
- **status-oriented** consumers are influenced by the opinions and behaviour of other people
- **action-oriented** consumers are motivated by the need for physical activity, novelty and change.[18]

VALS 2

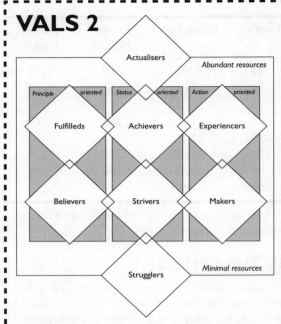

Actualisers
Enjoy the 'finer things'.
Receptive to new products, technologies, distribution.
Sceptical of advertising.
Frequent readers of a wide variety of publications.
Light TV viewers.
Value personal growth.
Wide intellectual interests.
Varied leisure activities.
Well informed, concerned with social issues.
Highly social.
Politically active.
Optimistic.
Self-confident.
Involved.
Outgoing.
Growth oriented.

Fulfilleds
Little interest in image or prestige.
Above-average consumers of products for the home.
Like educational and public affairs programming.
Read widely and often.
Moderately active in community and politics.
Leisure centres on home.
Value education and travel.
Health conscious.
Politically moderate and tolerant.
Mature.
Satisfied.
Reflective.
Open-minded.
Intrinsically motivated.

Achievers
Attracted to premium products.
Prime target for variety of products.
Average TV watchers.
Read business, news, and self-help publications.
Lives centre on career and family.
Have formal social relations.
Avoid excess change or stimulation.
May emphasise work at expense of recreation.
Politically conservative.
Moderate.
Goal oriented.
Conventional.
Deliberate.
In control.

Experiencers
Follow fashion and fads.
Spend much of disposable income on socialising.
Buy on impulse.
Attend to advertising.
Listen to rock music.
Like the new, offbeat and risky.
Like exercise, socialising, sports and outdoors.
Concerned about image.
Unconforming, but admire wealth, power and fame.
Politically apathetic.
Extroverted.
Unconventional.
Active.
Impetuous.
Energetic.

Believers
Respect rules and trust authority figures.
Enjoy settled, comfortable, predictable existence.
Socialise within family and established groups.
Politically conservative.
Reasonably well informed.
Buy American.
Slow to change habits.
Look for bargains.
Watch TV more than average.
Read retirement, home and garden and general interest magazines.
Traditional.
Conforming.
Cautious.
Moralistic.
Settled.

Strivers
Narrow interests.
Easily bored.
Somewhat isolated.
Look to peer group for motivation and approval.
Unconcerned about health or nutrition.
Politically apathetic.
Image conscious.
Limited discretionary income but carry credit balances.

Makers
Enjoy outdoors.
Prefer 'hands on' activities.
Spend leisure with family and close friends.
Avoid joining organisations, except unions.
Distrust politicians, foreigners and big business.
Shop for comfort, durability, value.
Unimpressed by luxuries.
Buy the basics.
Listen to radio.
Read auto, home mechanics, fishing, outdoor magazines.
Practical.
Self-sufficient.
Constructive.
Committed.
Satisfied.

Strugglers
Limited interests and activities.
Prime concerns are safety and security.
Burdened with health problems.
Conservative and traditional.
Rely on organised religion.
Brand loyal.
Use coupons and watch for sales.
Trust advertising.
Watch TV often.
Read tabloids and women's magazines.
Powerless.
Narrowly focused.
Risk averse.
Burdened.
Conservative.

Figure 12.3: The eight lifestyles identified by VALS 2

Instead of viewing the segments as hierarchical, the eight segments are depicted as a network (see the diagram in figure 12.3). The location of a segment on the network indicates a relationship. For example, the actualisers, fulfilleds, achievers and experiencers share similar resources. In the figure, the corners of each segment are overlapping in recognition of the fact that some segments may have elements in common.

To be useful to marketers, the segments should differ in their marketplace behaviours. From table 12.5, it appears that there are some differences in the purchase patterns of dishwashers and pick-up trucks, but differences in the other product categories are not as distinct. Therefore, for some products the segments are not useful. Also, it may well be that the high ownership of dishwashers by actualisers, fulfilleds and achievers is simply a function of income. And ownership of pick-up trucks by believers could be a function of occupation.

Table 12.4: A demographic profile of the VALS 2 categories

Categories	Percentage of population	% Male	Median age	Median income $	College education %	Occupation (white collar) %
Actualisers	8	59	43	58 000	95	68
Fulfilleds	11	47	48	38 000	81	50
Achievers	13	39	36	50 000	77	43
Experiencers	12	53	26	19 000	41	21
Believers	16	46	58	21 000	6	11
Strivers	13	41	34	25 000	23	19
Makers	13	61	30	23 000	24	19
Strugglers	14	37	61	9 000	3	2

Table 12.5: VALS 2 selected product ownership and activities (national average rate = 1.0)

Categories	Product ownership					Activities	
	Dishwasher	Fishing rod & reel	Colour TV	Pick-up truck	Do wood-working	Do kids' activities	Politics active
Actualisers	1.6[a]	0.9	1.1	0.7	1.2	1.5	3.1
Fulfilleds	1.4	0.9	1.1	1.0	1.0	1.3	1.4
Achievers	1.4	0.9	1.1	1.0	0.6	1.4	0.8
Experiencers	0.5	1.1	0.9	0.9	1.0	0.9	0.8
Believers	1.2	1.1	1.1	1.1	1.1	0.6	1.1
Strivers	0.9	0.8	1.0	1.0	0.5	1.1	0.6
Makers	0.8	1.4	1.0	1.5	2.0	1.2	0.6
Strugglers	0.4	0.9	0.9	0.5	0.5	0.4	0.5

[a]To be read: 'Actualisers own dishwashers at a much higher rate than the national average (1.6, or 60 per cent higher than the average). Fulfilleds (1.4), achievers (1.4), and believers (1.2) also have higher than average ownership of this appliance. Each of the other segments has a lower than average rate of ownership.'

(*Source*: SRI International, Menlo Park, Calif.)

LIFESTYLES IN AUSTRALIA AND NEW ZEALAND

Since the 1970s, a variety of lifestyle studies have been carried out by companies and research agencies. Some are general lifestyle studies, but the majority are product specific studies. In the late 1970s and early 1980s, VALS was introduced to Australia by the advertising agencies Young and Rubican (Australia) and Ogilvy and Mather.

Roy Morgan Research is currently operating its 'Omnibus' program, which is a weekly monitor of consumer opinions and trends. This is a similar program to the Standford study and has identified ten groups in Australian society:[19]

- **Basic needs**. This group is largely comprised of older people, generally over 50 years, with more women than men. This group includes older people who are retired workers and widows, many of whom are on fixed-income pensions. People in this group have a lower than average education, and hold traditional views, particularly on the family. They are competent, confident individuals who enjoy passive, spectator activities and are fairly satisfied with their lives.

- **A fairer deal**. This group, more likely than any other in Australia to describe themselves as working-class, tend to be under 40, on low incomes which make it essential to manage incomes to make ends meet. Full-time home duties for women and full-time employment for men reinforce traditional role definitions for family members in this group. Money worries, employment and insecurity create high levels of pessimism and cynicism within this group and many feel they are getting a raw deal out of life.

- **Traditional family life**. People in the traditional family life segment generally live in one or two adult homes, as few have children still at home. They still retain a strong commitment to traditional family roles and values. Many would be grandparents, and value the extended family links. Most are retired. They are very religious and consider that God has a very important place in their lives. They are somewhat more doubtful about the Devil and Hell than about Heaven and the positive aspects of Christianity. Education levels are generally lower than the Australian average, which is not surprising as they are mainly aged over 50 years. People in the traditional family life group consider themselves to be the most right wing politically. They are very cautious about new things and ideas. In terms of their lifestyle, they do not seek activity and excitement. They are concerned about their health, but have few real worries. They are satisfied with their home life, especially as most live in and own their home. Generally the traditional family life people are quite satisfied with their overall standard of living. They are above average viewers of commercial TV (VCR ownership is low) but listen to slightly less commercial radio than the average. 'Traditional family life' people are less likely to drink alcoholic and soft drinks than average, perhaps because they socialise less frequently.

- **Conventional family life**. This, the largest segment in the Australian population, is made up of people whose lives are centred around their families. It comprises slightly more women than men, generally over 30 years of age. On an average income, these people are seeking greater financial security, struggling to improve basic living standards and to give their children better opportunities than they have had in their lives. People in the conventional family life group are less ambitious than some of their more success-orientated counterparts, preferring to spend spare time with their families. They are generally seeking value for money in their basic purchases.

- **Visible achievement**. This group of over 30s are visible success stories who earn above average incomes but retain traditional values about home, work and society. They seek recognition of personal achievement, are confident and competent. They work for financial reward and job stimulation. They seek visible 'good living', travel, recreation and other evidence of success, and like to demonstrate that they are mature, successful, achievement-orientated individuals who hold traditional family-orientated values.

- **Look-at-me**. 'Look-at-me' refers to people who seek an exciting, prosperous life and who want to have more freedom from family commitments but a greater share of community resources. This is the youngest segment of the study. Unsophisticated, young, active people, the look-at-me people are primarily unmarried with no children to worry about. They are fashion and trend conscious, wishing to be seen as different from their families but similar to their peers. They are very active socially, wanting to escape the family home setting and enjoy both watching and taking part in sport and following healthy lifestyles. They are not politically active, nor are they concerned about social issues. Financially they do not tend to plan ahead or budget.

- **Something better**. These are the younger family types aged 20–39. People in the something better segment are likely to be well educated, have responsible jobs and be earning above average incomes. The something better person feels confident, ambitious and tends to be in secure full-time employment. Although somewhat traditional in social and political areas, the something better people see themselves as progressive and are less likely to hold traditional views of marriage. People in this group hold individualistic values, they believe there should be less government intervention in the lives of individuals; for example, smoking marijuana should be legal. People in this group also seek value for money — and recognise quality and convenience as important components of value.

- **Young optimism**. Young optimism refers to the student generation who are seeking to gain a place in society. This group is a little older than the look-at-me's and is at the core of the market that is interested in 'something new', different and experimental. They are active, well educated young singles or couples living together. For their age group, those who are working are on above-average personal incomes and are outgoing, ambitious and very career-orientated. They look forward to moving out of the family home and see themselves as upper middle class and very progressive. They have been called the 'young moderns', 'trendies' and, in the USA 'yuppies'.

• **Socially aware.** Socially aware refers to people who are community minded, politically and socially active and enjoy persuading others to their opinion. Although they tend to be more interested in community activities than business activities they believe that multi-national companies are a serious threat to Australia's independence. Young and middle age people with no real money worries, these make up the most educated, active segment of the community. The socially aware people tend to be higher income earners, who have overcome (or are yet to face) family commitments.

• **Real conservatism.** People in this group are cautious about new things and ideas, hold very traditional views on family life and tend to believe the government knows best. They have become observers of society rather than active participants and pride themselves on their tolerance and their understanding. This older post World War I group represents a very small proportion of the community.

The study was duplicated in a number of other countries and all the results were compared. As shown in table 12.6, each country in the study revealed similar size clusters.[20]

Table 12.6: Ten lifestyles in seven nations (*Base:* Respondents aged 18 years and over). The number of interviews conducted is shown in brackets under each country name.

	Australia (13 790) %	USA (1048) %	Canada (1038) %	England (992) %	Western Germany (1030) %	Japan (1430) %	New Zealand (1203) %
Basic needs	5	4	6	7	10	1	5
A fairer deal	6	7	6	10	2	2	6
Conventional family life	21	16	17	14	24	34	23
Traditional family life	23	21	17	24	22	21	22
Look-at-me	10	7	5	10	16	6	9
Something better	9	6	7	6	4	3	7
Real conservatism	4	**	3	7	1	2	2
Young optimism	6	7	9	5	1	6	4
Visible achievement	10	18	19	13	15	18	14
Socially aware	6	14	11	4	5	7	8
	100	100	100	100	100	100	100

** Less than 0.5%

(*Source*: Roy Morgan Research Centre. Used with permission.)

Another study was the 'True Who' study, produced by the Campaign Palace and carried out by Yann, Campbell, Hoare and Wheeler.[21] The methodology concentrated on attitude segmentation and was concerned with identifying consumer profiles based on cultural views. Four main social groups within Australia were identified: the Rosy Optimists, the Old Bronzed Aussies, the Browned-Offs and the True Blues, as described below.

True Who? An analysis of what today's Australian is really like

The 'True Blues' (15 per cent of Australia's adults)

Australia is the new frontier. We are an energetic, young country, making its way in the world. We have a secure future, with good opportunities for the young. These economic problems are only temporary. We are not culturally backward. We have no racial problems ... Aborigines definitely receive a fair deal. No, we haven't lost our compassion. We're a down-to-earth people and those who don't want to be like that should live somewhere else. This is the lucky country.

These are the attitudes which differentiate this cluster from all others. Yes, 'she'll be right mate' is the anthem of True Blue.

Interestingly, while this group is the most ready to agree that Australian society is structured in a way that everyone has the opportunity to make good, they are the least likely to accept that ours is a classless society.

Demographically, this small group in our population is marked by its youth, its blue collar socioeconomic status and its country-town origin. They identify strongly with the typical Australian image. They believe this 'True Blue' image is good for Australia and that it should be perpetuated. Predictably, 'typical Aussies' in TV commercials appeal to these people.

They are very proud Australians, and they disagree that we don't have a sense of national identity. They don't, however, identify with the image of Australians as it has been portrayed to date.

By way of general comment, this group in the population is also very important, not only because they, like the Old Bronzed Aussies, represent a large proportion of the population, but also because they are younger (baby boomers). They are the engine room for the future. They are, and will be in the immediate future, the opinion formers, the decision takers, the leaders in many ways.

These are Australians with a new set of values. They have a more worldly, cosmopolitan view on social, political and economic issues. They are not tied to the past, and are optimistic about the future.

The 'Browned-Offs' — the disenchanted immigrants and offspring (21 per cent of Australia's adult population)

66 ... xenophobia, a hatred and fear of foreigners, was just as much a part of the bush ethic as mateship and equality. 99
— Manning Clarke

Members of this segment of the Australian population are characterised by a belief that they don't belong in this country. It is not surprising, therefore, to find that they do not identify with what is seen as 'the typical Australian'.

They are less than flattering about Australia. They believe we have no real say in world affairs. They see us as tied to the past ... as a nation which still acts as if it was a part of England. They believe that Australians lack a sense of national identity.

This group is the only attitudinal segment which does not believe that Australia is a young, energetic country making its way in the world. They are undecided as to whether Australia is still the lucky country, and they disagree that Australia is 'the new frontier'.

(continued)

The 'Rosy Optimists' (30 per cent of Australia's adult population)

These people hold attitudes which are in stark contrast to those held by their Old Bronzed Aussie counterparts.

They do believe Australia has a secure future, with good opportunities for young people. They believe we have the best quality of life, that Australia is still the lucky country and that Australia can still offer people new experiences. They believe we are facing up to the difficulties of the future, and that we will get back on top. Australia isn't going downhill.

This group's approach to life and work, their values and attitudes, differs markedly to the more critical older generation, described earlier. They are more wordly, more contemporary, more balanced, more understanding. For example, they don't believe Australia won't get ahead while its people are enjoying the good life. They distinguish between the 'good life' and demanding 'more time off to relax', which they oppose. They don't believe we are too preoccupied with sport, that we are lazy and apathetic, nor that we are too relaxed to make any real progress.

They tend to strongly hold values which may be described as 'socially left'. They are adamant about the importance of preserving the natural environment. They are concerned that Aborigines don't receive 'a fair deal'. They believe Australia should have a new flag, one which is uniquely ours.

'Old Bronzed Aussies' — the conservative critics (34 per cent of Australia's adult population)

Members of this segment hold very strong traditional beliefs and opinions. They are very set in their ways and they doggedly cling to the past.

These Old Bronzed Aussies are differentiated on the basis of their belief that we need a stronger, tougher government who can deal with the troublemakers. They believe it important that the 'old fashioned' values be reinstated in order to put us 'on the right path again'. They are frustrated at the way in which Australia is heading and they are concerned that Australia no longer seems to be able to offer its people a secure future.

These older, conservative Australians are concerned about the prevailing work ethic in Australia. They believe that we are too relaxed to make real progress, and that we are too lazy and apathetic for our own good. They believe that we are not facing up to the difficulties of the future and, as a consequence, we are going downhill fast.

They see us as being 'all talk and no action'. They do not entirely blame the Australian psyche, per se, for this 'laziness', but, rather, they believe we have no incentive to work hard.

They are also critical about the cultural values we hold. They believe that we are preoccupied with sport, while being culturally backward.

They see Australia as 'a man's country'.

They are very patriotic, in the traditional sense. They see our present flag as an important reminder of our past, and they are totally opposed to the view that we should have a new flag, one which is uniquely ours. They consider the bicentennial to be an important landmark in our history and that everyone should get behind it to make it a success. They do not appreciate the trivialisation of this patriotism, however, and they hold that too many companies are jumping on the flag waving Aussie bandwagon.

They see Australians as down-to-earth people, and people who don't want to be like this, in their view, ought to live somewhere else.

This sector of the population is important if for no other reason than their sheer weight of numbers.

In general terms, they believe strongly and favourably in the Australian lifestyle — its relaxation and quality. Yet, they are intensely concerned for our future. They see us as lazy and undisciplined. To get back to being as good as we can be we need industry, more authority, the return of traditional values and better products; more commitment — more 'backbone'.

(Source: True Who? study, by R. Bryson, The Campaign Palace, and M. James, Yann Campbell Hoare Wheeler, Marketing Research Consultants, North Sydney)

A range of lifestyle programs, both specific and general, are currently being used in Australia and New Zealand. Even though there are still measurement difficulties, they provide considerable insights into the behaviour of consumers in the marketplace. One such insight is provided by the readership profile of Murdoch magazine readers (see table 12.7), which clearly shows that more socially aware and young optimists read *New Woman* than read the *Family Circle*. A clear understanding of these groups helps magazine publishers to target their articles and advertising more effectively.

Figure 12.4: Toyota — value for money. The 'something better' cluster could identify with this advertisement.

Table 12.7: Readership of Murdoch magazines by the ten segments

	Family Circle	Better Homes and Gardens	New Woman
1. Visible achievement	119	147	111
2. Something better	114	126	124
3. Basic needs	97	51	44
4. Real conservative	120	94	46
5. Traditional family life	102	88	21
6. Conventional family life	114	115	73
7. Young optimism	78	88	237
8. Socially aware	87	120	179
9. Look-at-me	71	70	183
10. A fairer deal	90	87	56

(*Source*: Roy Morgan Readership Survey, 1989)

 ## SUMMARY

Since the 1970s, there has been a growing interest in lifestyle by marketers. The reason for this interest lies in the unequivocal benefits that it provides. These benefits range from a broader understanding of consumers to the application of lifestyle research in market segmentation. However, the development of the lifestyle concept into a useful tool in segmentation strategy has been haphazard and disordered. The perceived benefits of lifestyle segmentation have motivated researchers and practitioners to continue the task of developing more reliable methods to identify lifestyle based segments. The ad hoc development of the knowledge base in lifestyle research and the conceptual and terminology confusion has ensured that this has not been an easy task. It is also a task that is by no means complete. However, there are a number of positive indicators that the current problems with lifestyle segmentation will be resolved. Researchers now accept that demographic components such as age, sex, education and access to resources are integral parts of lifestyle research because they have a fundamental effect on lifestyles. Certainly the lifestyle studies that have been carried out in Australia and New Zealand have provided marketers with useful descriptive profiles of clusters.

 ## Questions

1. Which do you think has the most influence on our lifestyles and personal characteristics, the social groups which we develop or our demographic profiles? Why have you reached this conclusion?

2. What factors have influenced the haphazard and confused development of lifestyle research? How do you think the confusion could have been avoided?

3. List the factors that accurately describe your own current lifestyle and those of your friends. Do you all belong to the same lifestyle segments? How similar are your consumption patterns? What are the key lifestyle factors that influence your consumption patterns?

4. Using the summary of the results of the New Zealand lifestyle study provided in the box on page 294, describe how you would develop a marketing mix strategy for the following products: video recorders, coffee, landcruisers.

5. Compare the New Zealand lifestyles described in the box on page 294 with the ten Australian lifestyles described on pages 308–10.

6. Discuss the relationship between social class and lifestyles.

7. What is the difference between a general lifestyle study and a specific lifestyle study?

8. Compare the American VALS 2 lifestyle segments (see page 306) with the ten Australian lifestyle segments described on pages 308–10.

9. Lifestyle segmentation can never be viable unless it has a sound theoretical base. Discuss.

 Case study

Is Hilton Hosiery crazy? On January 27, it launched a range of children's socks under the Zoo Feet brand. Retailers and consumers rushed to buy the socks. On April 24, Hilton dumped the brand. Ten days later, it launched new socks called Sea Feet. Same story. Sales are booming, but Hilton will axe the Sea Feet brand on July 31.

The company that devotes time, energy and money to launching a new brand, only to dump it three months later, is either brave or crazy. Hilton executives insist they are brave. The short life-cycle strategy is a key part of Hilton's plan to secure a share of the $70-million-a-year market for children's socks. Its quick-in, quick-out strategy is working. Australians bought 200 000 pairs of Zoo Feet socks in three months. Sales of Sea Feet are expected to pass the 200 000 mark. With its third and fourth sock brands for this year on the way, Hilton is confident it will sell more than one million pairs of children's socks by December.

Hilton, which was one of the textile companies acquired by Sara Lee Corporation from Linter Group last June, entered the socks market two years ago, launching a range of women's and children's products under the Razzamatazz, Kayser and Second Skin brands, its three top-selling brands in the hosiery market. The children's socks were sold under the Razzamatazz name. "The children's socks did not sell all that well," Hilton product manager Alisa Bennett says. "The colors and patterns were wrong." Late last year, Hilton ditched the Razzamatazz products and started looking for a new entrant in the children's sock market.

Last year, Australians shelled out $250 million to buy 72 million pairs of socks. Men's socks is the biggest sector of the market, representing 55% of sales, with children's socks accounting for 28% and women's socks 17%. Discount department stores such as K mart, Big W and Target are the biggest sellers of socks, capturing 44% of sales. Supermarkets account for 44% of sales, with department stores representing 12.5%. Pacific Dunlop dominates the market, snaring an estimated 40% of sales with brands such as Holeproof, Rio and Red Robin.

Australians buy between four and six pairs of socks each year, with sales growing only in line with population growth. Kevin Dutton, a director of Hilton's advertising agency, Badjar, attributes the lack of growth in the socks market to the absence of strong marketing campaigns by sock manufacturers. "Apart from Computer Socks (a Pacific Dunlop brand), nothing has happened in the socks market in terms of building strong brands," Dutton says. (His comment ignores the success of Holeproof Heroes, a brand launched by Pacific Dunlop last July. Consumers bought two million pairs of Heroes in five months.)

In looking for a new children's socks brand, Hilton identified supermarkets as the retail distribution channel that held the most potential. Bennett says most of the 24 million pairs of socks sold through supermarkets last year were low-priced imports, with little merchandising in stores and no branding of socks in supermarkets. "We were convinced there was a big opportunity to launch a strongly branded, well-merchandised product range in supermarkets," she says.

(continued)

To test its theory, Hilton conducted research among retailers and consumers. It discovered that socks are bought on impulse and few consumers go into supermarkets with the intention of buying socks. Consumers regarded most of the socks sold in supermarkets as dull, low-priced products, with no brand differentiation. Hilton decided to create a range of brightly colored socks that would catch the shopper's eye. It also developed the concept of introducing new sock designs every three months to tap impulse buying. Hilton set two target markets for its socks: the three-to-12-year-olds and mothers.

"If you look at product categories such as confectionery, shampoo and breakfast cereal, there is always an element of newsworthiness that captures the consumer's attention," Kevin Dutton says. "Socks did not have any newsworthiness." To encourage children and mothers to collect different socks, Hilton's designers created nine designs for the Zoo Feet range and another nine for Sea Feet.

Zoo Feet was launched under the umbrella Razzamatazz brand. Razzamatazz, which was launched in 1973 as the first hosiery brand sold in supermarkets, is Hilton's biggest brand and captures a quarter of the sheer hosiery market. Badjar conducted research to determine if consumers would accept a range of children's socks under the Razzamatazz name. "It wasn't a problem," Dutton says. "Razzamatazz is seen as a brand that represents value-for-money and a bit of fun. Also mothers, the main buyers of kids' socks, are very familiar with the Razzamatazz name."

The children's products are made at the Hilton hosiery and sock factory in the Melbourne suburb of Broadmeadows. The company employed a complicated production forecasting and planning scheme to organise the production of the sock brand with a short life-span. Hilton's marketing staff work with its production planners on a weekly basis, updating forecasts and increasing production of the best-selling sock designs. The factory works on a 48-hour turn-around, filling orders from retailers two days after they are placed.

Badjar created a 15-second animated television commercial to launch Zoo Feet and another 15-second ad to introduce Sea Feet. But Dutton says merchandising programs in stores, rather than TV advertising, has been the main driving force behind the success of Zoo Feet and Sea Feet. Hilton and Badjar created a big collection of display material for stores, including product bins, stickers and posters. The marketing budget for Zoo Feet and Sea Feet was $200 000–250 000 each.

Hilton's 150 sales representatives, who visit supermarkets once a week to restock hosiery displays and shelves, handled the distribution of the display material. "We could not have run such a big merchandising program without the sales force," Bennett says. "It is difficult for supermarket staff to cope with fast-changing product ranges."

Zoo Feet and Sea Feet sell for $3.50, or 40% more than the average price of socks sold through supermarkets. The Hilton products carry a 75% mark-up for retailers, compared with the 25–50% mark-up on basic socks. Coles Supermarkets and independent supermarket retailers carried the first two Feet ranges. Woolworths' supermarket division did not stock Zoo Feet or Sea Feet, a decision that Bennett claims Woolworths executives "admit was a mistake". Woolworths will carry the third Feet range, which will be launched in early August.

Hilton will present the third range to retailers during the next week and is developing a fourth range, which will be launched in late October or early November. Dutton says the new ranges will increase the "play value" of the socks. "The law of toy marketing dictates that the more you increase the play value of a product, the more kids like it," he says, "We are looking for ways to add play value to the socks, so kids will become more involved with the products."

The concept of selling a product range for just three months soon will be extended to the children's underwear market, with Hilton planning to launch products jointly with Kortex, the Melbourne-based underwear division of Sara Lee. Hilton also is planning to take the collectible concept into the women's and men's socks markets. In August, the company will launch Razzamatazz men's socks in supermarkets. The first range will cover plain socks, but Bennett believes the Zoo Feet and Sea Feet concept could be applied to the men's sock market.

Neil Shoebridge,
Business Review Weekly,
26 June 1992

Case study questions

1. In the article (pages 315–16), Neil Shoebridge comments that:

   66 A company that devotes time, energy and money to launching a new brand, only to dump it three months later, is either brave or crazy. **99**

   Hilton executives insist that they are brave. Are they brave or have they studied the market carefully? Identify and discuss the aspects of consumption behaviour that could have influenced Hilton's executives to adopt this strategy.

2. Can you suggest which lifestyle cluster(s) described in the text would be viable targets?

SUGGESTED READING

R. Pitts and A. Woodside, *Personal Values and Consumer Psychology*, Lexington Books, Lexington, Mass., 1984.

H. Mackay, *Reinventing Australia*, Angus and Robertson, Sydney, 1993.

R. Purto, *Beyond Mind Games: The Marketing Power of Psychographics*, American Demographic Books, Ithaca, NY, 1991.

ENDNOTES

1. There is a range of publications on Australian lifestyles such as: P. Hollingworth, *Australians in Poverty*, Nelson, Melbourne, 1980. A. F. Davies, S. Encel and M. J. Berry (eds), *Australian Society: A Sociological Introduction*, Cheshire, Melbourne, 1977. T. Jagtenberg and P. D'Alton, *Daily Life and Institutional Constraint: Four Dimensional Social Space*, Harper and Row, Sydney, 1989. H. Mackay, *Reinventing Australia*, Angus and Robertson, Sydney, 1993.

2. J. Atlas, 'Beyond Demographics', *The Atlantic Monthly*, Oct. 1984, pp. 49–58.

3. J. T. Plummer, 'The Concept and Application of Lifestyle Segmentation', *Journal of Marketing*, Vol. 38, 1974, pp. 33–37. R. Ziff, 'Psychographics for Market Segmentation', *Journal of Advertising Research*, Vol. 11, No. 2, 1971, pp. 12–24. F. Reynolds and W. Darden, 'Construing Lifestyle and Psychographics', in W. D. Wells (ed.), *Lifestyle and Psychographics*, American Marketing Association, Chicago, 1973. W. D. Wells and D. J. Tigert, *Activities, Interests and Opinions and Consumer Behaviour*, Foresman and Co., Glenview, Ill., 1973. Y. Wind, 'Lifestyle Analysis: A New Approach', *Journal of Marketing Research*, Vol. 6, 1969. T. P. Hustad and E. A. Pessemier, 'Segmenting Consumer Markets with Activity and Attitude Measures', Working Paper. The Herman C. Krannert Graduate School of Industrial Administration, Purdue University, Indiana, 1971.

4. W. D. Wells, 'Psychographics: A Critical Review', *Journal of Marketing Research*, Vol. 12, May 1975, pp. 196–213.

5. R. W. Lawson, Herman G. Mueller, A. Russell and B. Fiegler, 'A Psychographic Analysis of New Zealand Consumers', Australian Marketing Educators Conference, Elton Mayo School of Management, University of South Australia, Feb. 1991.

6. A. Sampson, 'Stake Through the Heart of Psychographics', *Rydges S & M*, Aug. 1986, pp. 86–88.

7. J. Pernica, 'The Second Generation of Market Segmentation Studies: An Audit of Buying Motivations', in W. D. Wells (ed.), *Lifestyle and Psychographics*, American Marketing Association, Chicago, 1973. M. E. Goldberg, 'Identifying Relevant Psychographics Segments: How Specifying Product Functions Can Help', *Journal of Consumer Research*, Vol. 3, Dec. 1977, pp. 163–69.

8. 'The Different Australian', the *Age* Reader: Probe Australian Social Barometer 1974/75.

9. *The Age Lifestyle Study*, the *Age* newspaper, Melbourne, 1982.

10. A. J. Adams, 'Five Reasons Why Lifestyle Research Rarely Works', Paper presented to the 11th Annual Convention, Market Research Society of Australia, Hobart, Sept. 1982. S. C. Cosmas, 'Lifestyles and Consumption Patterns', *Journal of Consumer Research*, Vol. 8, March 1982, pp. 453–55.

11. A. V. Bruno and E. A. Pessemier, 'An Empirical Investigation of the Validity of Selected Attitude and Activity Measures', in *Proceedings of Association of Consumer Research*, 1979. A. C. Burns and M. C. Harrison, 'A Test of the Reliability of Psychographics', *Journal of Marketing Research*, 16, 1979, pp. 32–38. D. R. Lehmann, and C. E. Britney, 'Determining an Approving Measure of the Reliability of Psychographic Measures', in B. A. Greenberg and D. N. Bellenger, *Contemporary Marketing Thought*, American Management Association, 1977. S. Mehotra and W. D. Wells, 'Psychographics and Buyer Behaviour: Theory and Recent Empirical Findings', in A. Woodside, J. N. Sheth and P. D. Bennett, *Consumer and Industrial Buying Behaviour*, North Holland, New York, 1979.

12. R. W. Lawson, et al. (1991), op. cit.

13. R. Holman, 'A Values and Lifestyle Perspective on Human Behaviour', in R. Pitts and A. Woodside (eds), *Personal Values and Consumer Psychology*, Lexington Books, Mass., 1984. J. Rossiter, 'Market Segmentation: A Review and Proposed Resolution', *Australian Marketing Researcher*, Vol. 11, No. 1, June 1987, pp. 36–58. S. E. Beatty, P. M. Homer and K. Kahle, 'Problems with VALS in International Research: An Example From an Application of the Empirical Mirror Technique', *Advances in Consumer Research*, Vol. 15, 1988, pp. 375–80. L. R. Kahle, 'Values Segmentation Debate Continues', *Marketing News*, 18, No. 4, 1984, p. 2. L. R. Kahle, 'The Nine Nations of North America', *Journal of Marketing*, Vol. 50, April 1986, pp. 37–47. S. Yuspeh, 'Slamming Syndicated Data', *Advertising Age*, 17 May 1984.

14. A. Mitchell, 'Nine American Lifestyles', Macmillan, New York, 1983. S. Mauk, 'How a Social Scientist Views Us', *Mainliner*, July 1980. David Riesman's social character theory can be studied further by reading his *The Lonely Crowd*, Yale University Press, New Haven, Conn., 1950.

15. *Meat Board Consumer Marketing Plan*, National Livestock and Meat Boards, U.S.A., 1985. T. C. Thomans and S. Crocker, *Values and Lifestyles — New Psychographics*, SRI, Menlo Park, Calif., 1981.

16. R. Holman, 'A Values and Lifestyle Perspective on Human Behaviour', in R. Pitts and A. Woodside (eds), *Personal Values and Consumer Psychology*, Lexington Books, Mass., 1984. J. Rossiter, 'Market Segmentation: A Review and Proposed Resolution', *Australian Marketing Researcher*, Vol. 11, No. 1, June 1987, pp. 36–58. M. Lees, 'VALS: Theoretical Review', Working Paper, Department of Management, University of Wollongong, NSW, 1986.

17. J. Rossiter, ibid. M. Lees, ibid.

18. SRI International, Menlo Park, Calif.

19. 'The Roy Morgan Value Segments: A Tool to Improve Management', *Marketing and Communications*, Melbourne, 1991.

20. G. C. Morgan and M. Levine, 'More Cost Effective TV Advertising Requires Understanding the Target Market and What the Target Watches', *Advertising — Making It Work*, 11R Conference, Sydney, 1992.

21. The Campaign Palace, 'True Who!' project. Yann, Campbell, Hoare and Wheeler, Sydney 1987. N. Shoebridge, 'Advertisers Discover "True Blue" Myth is Just That', *Business Review Weekly*, 22 Jan. 1988.

19 The Roy Morgan Value Segments, recorded interview with Michele Levine and communications, Melbourne, 8 Dec. 1997.

20 S. C. Hoyer and P. J. Leavitt, Cost-Effective Targeting: Making Resources Count, including the Target Audience and Where the Target Audience Is, Melbourne, 1997.

21 The Campaign Palace, 'So What?', project team: Campbell, Murdy, Andy Pauline, Sydney 1997, R. Shoebridge, 'Advertisers Discover This Idea', Perth is Just That, Business Review Weekly, 2 Jan. 1998.

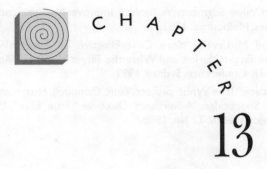

CHAPTER 13

Cultures and subcultures

OBJECTIVES

This chapter should help you to:
- know what is meant by culture and subcultures
- appreciate the difference between values, norms, customs and rituals
- understand how marketing is influenced by culture
- understand the elements that contribute to the cultural environment in which you live
- understand cultural change and how to monitor change
- appreciate cross-cultural differences and their impact on marketing strategy.

WHAT IS CULTURE?

A society's culture directs all aspects of the lives of its members, from the shape of buildings to the clothes people wear. It is the essence or substance of a society, made up of the shared ideas, meanings, values, morals and language, as well as the artefacts and services that are produced, used and valued by a group of people. The culture that surrounds us can be so familiar that, like the air we breathe, its influence goes unnoticed. Yet it is a powerful force affecting how we think about the world, our place in it and how we think of ourselves.[1] For example, each culture has ideas about what is beautiful and the influence of these ideas on people can be subtle. Few individuals would blame culture for their sense of discontent or contentment with their own attractiveness, but it is a function of their culture.

Cultural ideas, such as the image of the 'sun-bronzed Aussie', are supported in many subtle ways. Fashion magazines generally depict the ideal body as tanned and slim. Commercials for such products as soft drink and fast foods show beach scenes with scantily clad models having fun. The messages are subtle but consistent. Attractiveness becomes associated with a suntan and purchasing behaviour can be seen to reflect this goal.

Recent research has shown that Australians have one of the highest incidences of skin cancer in the world, yet to change their attitude to suntanned skin is difficult. Even though Australians have come to recognise the dangers of lying in the sun, the value of the bronzed look has persisted and has given rise to increased sales of artificial tanning products.

Because the culture of a society determines what products are offered in the marketplace and how they are distributed and paid for, it is essential for marketers to know their own culture[2] and understand the characteristics of any other cultures with which they do business.[3]

Subcultural groups can also be found in most societies. These are clusters of individuals who share values and behaviours that are different from the main culture and different from other groups in the same society. Often such groups form economically viable market segments or niches.

There are a number of ways to understand a culture. One is to study it from the evolutionary perspective, which is the view that cultures develop through stages of savagery, barbarism and eventually civilisation. Another is to collect historical information about the customs and characteristics of a given culture. The most widely used method of studying a culture is the systems approach in which specific aspects or elements are identified and their relationship to each other examined. Cultural systems, particularly modern ones, are not static. New ideas and practices continually replace old ones.[4] For example, in Western societies of the nineteenth century, tall, slim women with suntans would not have been considered attractive, whereas in the 1990s they are.

CULTURAL SYSTEMS

A cultural system consists of three functional elements.[5] These elements are totally interrelated in that they influence each other and they combine to shape and are shaped by each individual's cognition, behaviours, values and motivations (see figure 13.1).

1. **The physical environment** consists of the natural geography and human alterations to the culture's habitat. This dictates the economic base of the culture, which in turn shapes and is shaped by the social environment.

2. **The social environment** consists of the political, educational, class, family, legal and business structures which develop in response to the physical environment. For example, an agrarian culture will develop a class structure based on land ownership and an extended family structure. Children are more likely to be trained in land cultivation and animal husbandry.

3. **The training environment** consists of the formal and informal socialisation of individuals. Cultural values, norms, customs and rituals are learned through absorbing the ideas, modes of behaviour and aspirations that are acceptable to the group. Individuals are taught the world view or perspective of the culture. The process of learning about our own culture, i.e. the one we are born into, is called 'enculturation'. Learning about or borrowing from other cultures is called 'acculturation' and is usually a more difficult process for individuals. In Australia, many migrants face conflict between the cultural values taught at home and the values taught in schools. For example, girls may be taught to defer to men at home and to treat boys at school as equals.

Children learn the value of cooperation and competition through team sports and the grades achieved at school. Other values, such as the need to care for their health and the environment, can be taught through formalised educational programs in schools. Children also learn informally through movies, television and other entertainment that may have a moral or environmental message.

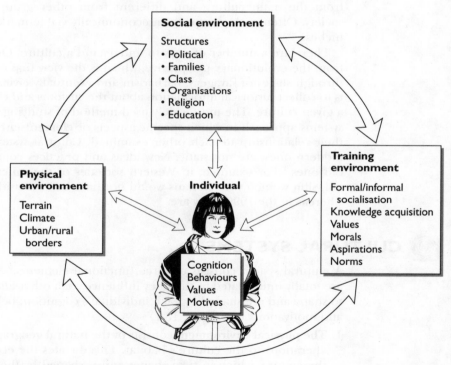

Figure 13.1: Culture's influence on the individual

Each culture develops its own values and social norms which form the basis of order in a society. Values delineate what is important, right and good, while the boundaries that a culture sets on behaviour are called norms. Values are the enduring beliefs regarding activities, relationships, feelings or goals that are important to the group's identity or well-being. Because they are often held unconsciously, or expressed as themes cutting across specific attitudes, the values of a society are not immediately apparent. They also represent the 'ideal' way in which life should be lived.[6] For example in Australia, equality is an important value but not all Australians are equal in power or in their access to resources. When financial success is dependent on having a job and unemployment is high, total equality is impossible.[7]

Generally values transcend specific objects and situations and serve as standards or criteria that tell us how to think and behave.[8] Some values are shared by many cultures such as wisdom, peace, nationalism, competitiveness and freedom. What distinguishes one culture from another is how they rank these values. This ranking constitutes the value system of a culture.

Cultural values are shared by the members of a society and are usually of two types — core values and peripheral values. Core values are the fundamental 'directives' of a culture. They tend to be limited in number, enduring and difficult to change. Peripheral values are more numerous and, although they are important to the culture, they are less resistant to change.

Social norms are rules that specify or prohibit certain behaviours in specific situations and are derived from cultural values. As such they are not behaviours but expectancies for behaviour. Norms guide behaviour on a day-to-day basis. For example, they determine what style of dress or gift is appropriate for a specific occasion, or how to use cutlery at a dinner table.

Some norms become customs through handing down from generation to generation, such as the custom in Australia of dressing boy babies in blue, girl babies in pink and brides in white. Gift-giving at weddings, birthdays and religious festivals such as Christmas are also customs.

Some norms are more important than others and these are known as 'mores'. Examples of social mores in a Western society include the prohibition of murder, incest and theft. Mores that are fundamental to a society are often controlled by law. Laws are norms which are reinforced by official legislation and incorporated into a written legal code. Punishment is usually the most severe for the breaking of laws and least severe for contravening the customs of a culture.

Rituals are standardised, recurring sequences of actions that can be either public or private.[9] If, every weekday, you get up at 7 a.m., have a cup of tea, shower, dress, clean your teeth and catch the five-to-eight bus to work, you are carrying out private ritualised behaviours.

 # CULTURE AND MARKETING

An important consideration for marketers is that a society's culture directs marketplace behaviour. It determines what goods are available for purchase, goods that are legal purchases and those that are socially acceptable. It also determines how marketers communicate information about their products, directs where goods are purchased and how they are paid for. The introduction of the abortion pill RU486 into Ireland, for example, would be difficult because of strong cultural values and legal sanctions associated with abortion.

CULTURE AND CONSUMPTION

Early this century, Thorstein Veblen introduced the idea of 'conspicuous consumption' — the view that we use 'things' to communicate to others who we are and our position in society.[10] This idea has prevailed and researchers such as Grant McCracken have argued that goods, particularly consumer goods, have cultural meaning. Not only do our possessions communicate to others who and what we are, they are intrinsically tied up with rituals.[11] According to McCracken the culture of a given society influences how a producer communicates to the marketplace and how individuals, through interaction, determine what goods are acceptable in relation to specific rituals.[12]

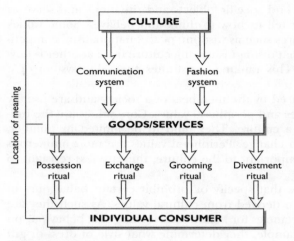

Figure 13.2: Cultural meaning and consumers (*Source:* Adapted from Grant McCracken, 'Culture and Consumption: A Theoretical Account of the Structure and Movement of the Cultural Meaning of Consumer Goods', *Journal of Consumer Research*, 13, June 1986)

If we take grooming rituals as an example, it is not acceptable for males in Australian society to wear make-up or use perfume, but deodorant and after-shave colognes are acceptable. Even though male perfumes are available, such as Joop for Men, the market is small. Thirty years ago, the acceptable dress for office workers was very formal. Women were not allowed to wear trousers and men had to wear suits and ties.

Now, trousers are acceptable dress for women in almost all situations, and men dress much more casually. However, older people are still expected to dress in a particular way or be labelled 'mutton dressed as lamb'. In general, products that are not within the accepted values and norms of a culture will not be adopted.

Figure 13.3: The history of swimwear — the influence of cultural change on dress

CULTURAL CHANGE

Australian society has undergone considerable change since the 1940s.[13] There is, however, a popular belief that the core values of Australians are still:

- egalitarianism
- hedonism
- the 'underdog'
- autonomy
- democracy
- family life

- humanitarianism
- mateship
- individualism
- informality
- freedom.

Many recent issues have demonstrated these values in Australia. The support for Compass Airlines in 1992, for example, as it battled its major creditors showed the importance Australians place on supporting the underdog. The family is also still a central feature of Australian life.[14] In 1978, a Clemenger report highlighted the dominance of the family in Australian life, and in 1989 most Australians thought that happiness was a good job and having children.[15]

Table 13.1: What kind of life do Australians want for themselves? Survey of attitudes to personal life goals

Personal goal in life that is most important	Total (2000) (%)	Male (992) (%)	Female (1008) (%)	Aged 18–20 (108) (%)	Aged 35–44 (357) (%)	Aged 60 and over (389) (%)	Uni. educated (207) (%)	Primary educated (235) (%)	Will vote ALP (794) (%)	Will vote Lib. (741) (%)	Will vote Aust. Dem. (178) (%)	Born in Aust. (1562) (%)	Born in UK (241) (%)	Born in South. Europe (44) (%)
A prosperous life (having a good income and being able to afford the good things in life)	8	12	5	18	7	9	8	11	10	6	10	8	7	13
An important life (a life of achievement that brings respect and recognition)	9	11	7	12	9	13	14	10	10	8	11	8	11	16
A secure life (making sure that all basic needs and expenses are provided for)	32	31	32	33	32	29	25	30	32	30	34	32	31	17
An exciting life (a stimulating active life)	5	7	4	16	3	2	15	1	5	4	9	5	5	5
A family life	46	40	51	21	49	48	36	47	42	51	36	46	48	51

Note: percentages rounded to nearest whole number.

(*Source*: *Sydney Morning Herald*, Saulwick Poll, 27 April 1989)

New Homelink™ 1800 from Telecom. Peace of mind for just ten cents more.

If your child needs to get hold of you on the phone, he can. And he won't need any money. He can do it with Homelink 1800.

Homelink 1800 from Telecom is like a reverse charge call he can dial himself.

And it gives you peace of mind for only 10 cents more than the standard* cost of the call. The total is simply charged to your account.

There's no connection charge for Homelink 1800. In fact, to get your number, all you have to do is **Freecall 1800 052 052.**

THIS IS AUSTRALIA CALLING.

Figure 13.4: Telecom Homelink 1800 — a product designed to respond to the high value placed on the family

The continued existence of a relatively stable social structure within Australia relies on the acceptance of social values. But this does not mean that values do not change. Changes within small parts of Australian society may take many years to be widely accepted, but as their acceptance grows the cultural values shift to accommodate them. In general, changes impact more easily on peripheral values. Where a core value comes under question, and if an increasing number of people cease to support it, the core value can shift to the peripheral level. If a peripheral value is supported by the majority of individuals over a long period then it will become a core value.

Technological change, economic insecurity, migration, the women's movement of the 1970s and increases in educational and workplace opportunities have had an impact on peripheral values such as optimism, health, environmentalism, marriage and the work ethic. Economic changes that give rise to consumer shifts towards gaining greater value from products and a greater concern for the environment may change consumer evaluations of products. Changes in our physical environment, such as technological innovations, sometimes force us to change our behaviours. Some changes occur slowly, but others can alter in the life of an individual. Consider, for example, the impact of computers, photocopiers and fax machines on our workplace behaviour.

Peripheral values that are developing or undergoing change include youthfulness, materialism, optimism, environmentalism and health. Society's attitude to marriage, divorce and de facto relationships has changed. Some writers suggest that the optimistic, 'she'll be right' attitude[16] is being replaced by a growing pessimism, following the economic troubles of the recession. They also report a developing interest in issues of morality and ethics and a renewed interest in spiritual matters — not the mass religion of the 1950s and 1960s but an interest in issues of morality and a concern for ethical business practices.[17]

Some say that an ageing population and concern for the environment have led to a devaluing of youth and materialism, while the importance of environment and health related values are increasing.[18]

 # TRACKING CULTURAL CHANGES

Marketers attempt to track cultural changes using mechanisms such as the VALS studies in America and Australia and social monitors, such as the Yankelovich Social Monitor from AMR:Quantum and the Dangar Research 'Indicator' social monitor. The 'Indicator' model has been developed in Australia and tailored to fit Australian values and attitudes. The social monitor studies differ from the VALS studies in that the VALS data track the size of predetermined segments (see chapter 12, page 300) while social monitors track the general direction of changes in the way consumers view their world.

Information from cultural change monitors is useful to marketers. It can be applied to such areas as:

- new product development
- positioning new brands
- re-evaluation of new brands in order to strengthen the current position, reposition brands and extend brand life cycles
- redefining target groups and market strategies
- decision making on brand advertising strategies with regard to target groups.

Behind the Monitor

The Australian Social Monitor, a rigorous survey conducted by AMR:Quantum, was adapted from the Yankelovich Social Monitor under licence from Yankelovich Clancy Shulman, the leading US market-research and public-opinion-polling company. The US version, in which a national sample of 2500 people aged 16 and over is interviewed, has been carried out annually for 22 years.

In this first Australian Social Monitor, 2000 people aged 16 and over were selected at random, interviewed in person for more than an hour, and asked to complete a lengthy questionnaire. Although participation in the Monitor took between three and five hours, 94 per cent of people in the sample returned their questionnaires, most of which were complete.

The survey covered a wide range of values, attitudes, beliefs and behaviour relevant to the social and marketing environment of Australia in the 1990s. It differs in scope and methodology from the tightly focused opinion polls which are a familiar aspect of party politics (both in its coverage by the media and in parties' assessment of their own performance).

To ensure that it covered the main issues relevant to Australians, the questionnaire used in the US Monitor was reviewed jointly with Australian social researcher Hugh Mackay. Items were revised and re-worded where necessary to make them more applicable to Australia, and items examining some new issues were introduced.

Interviews were conducted in every state and territory in a sample of towns and cities with populations of more than 5000. The results were weighted back to correspond to the Australian population distribution in terms of age group, sex and state or territory. Long as they were, the questionnaires were not able to cover all the issues. So for some issues, only a randomly chosen half of the sample was asked the questions. Where this was done, the results were also weighted back to match the general population distribution.

(*Source*: *The Bulletin*, 28 July 1992)

The underlying belief of these monitors is that, if marketers understand customer values and related attitudes, they will be better able to predict the behaviour of their consumers. There are a number of monitors and publications that describe current values and attitudes in Australia. Three well known studies are described on pages 329–35. They used different samples and different data collection techniques but have identified similar concerns and value shifts in Australian society. The Yankelovich Social Monitor and the *Readers Digest* study were based on quantified surveys and Mackay Research used non-directive group discussions and unstructured personal interviews, which are qualitative techniques.[19] The *Readers Digest* study surveyed subscribers whereas the Yankelovich Monitor used an Australia-wide sample.

STUDY 1: THE YANKELOVICH SOCIAL MONITOR

The first Australian Social Monitor was conducted by AMR:Quantum in April and May of 1992. This study, adapted from the American original, the Yankelovich Social Monitor, covers a wide range of values, attitudes, beliefs and behaviour relevant to the social environment in Australia in the 1990s. The major themes identified from this study were as follows:

1. Australians look to government regulators, consumer organisations and other owners and experts for guidance and protection when making purchases. They mistrust business. Australians in this study were more likely to be brand loyal and were cynical about the honesty and integrity of marketers.

2. Australian consumers, as were their American counterparts, were concerned about the level of control that they had over their own lives. They felt a need to be more in control of their own choices.

3. Australians value their work as a source of satisfaction and identity, not just a source of income.

4. Australians living in families believe in the sharing of tasks and decisions. Although there was general agreement that tasks should be shared, there was also agreement that, except for financial decisions, many tasks were still performed by the person traditionally responsible for them. For example, most men and women saw the responsibility for domestic tasks still being held by women.

5. Success for Australians is measured by the way they feel about their lives rather than money. Australians want money for the security and experiences it can buy.

6. Australians show considerable respect for the value of age and experience and felt that too much attention was often paid to the views of young people. This may be a function of the demographic changes affecting the baby boomers.

7. Australians are very concerned about a range of environmental issues but may not be likely to act on these concerns if prices for environmentally friendly products are more expensive or they are difficult to obtain.

8. Australians are concerned about immigration into Australia. There was a general feeling that migrants should adopt the 'Australian way of life' but there was also a strong feeling that migrants had the right to stay in touch with their traditions as long as they did not produce divisions within society.

9. There was considerable support for cutting or at least weakening the ties with Britain and America. This view was more strongly held by those under 35, but even in the older group only a minority saw the need to keep traditional ties strong.

10. The majority of Australians believed that life in Australia was a lot better than in most other countries and that their standard of living was better than that of their parents at the same age. But they were less confident that this standard of living would continue to be high.

The Yankelovich monitor concluded that consumers have changed radically since the early 1980s and that these changes have brought, amongst other things, an increase in the level of brand loyalty as consumers see well known brands as a short cut to evaluating quality and satisfaction levels.

Australian attitudes to shops, migrants, success and autonomy

In the shops

We are suspicious buyers who lack confidence in our ability to make good choices. And we are as angry about dishonesty in business as we are about dishonesty in government.

	% agree
I feel (moderately or strongly) the need for a better way of evaluating the quality and value of products and services.	83
Often I feel I don't know enough about the products I am buying to feel really in control of the purchase.	46

Doubting business, we look to government regulators, consumer watchdogs and other 'experts' for guidance and protection.

I really need people like *Choice* magazine [published by the Australian Consumers' Association] to prevent business taking advantage of the consumer.	87
Even well-known, long-established companies cannot be trusted to make safe, durable products without government setting industry standards.	76
Australian business is too concerned with making a profit and not concerned enough about its responsibilities to workers, consumers and the environment.	77

The quality of products and services is believed to be improving in some sectors and declining in others.

Quality has improved in:		But is worse in:	
Telephones	68	TV programs	48
Home appliances	57	Newspapers	32
Prepared foods	47	Clothing	32
Imported cars	46	Australian-made cars	30

Australian products in general have improved.	46

Despite the recession, most of us are seeking an elusive combination of reasonable quality and reliability for a reasonable price, rather than simply low prices. In the case of appliances, people were asked which characteristics had 'a strong influence on the decision to buy'.

	Influential in purchase of:	
Characteristic:	Large item	Small item
Known, trusted brand	56	49
Reasonable quality for price	63	63
Reliable, works like it should	80	81
Long-lasting, durable	79	72
Easy to fix or maintain	67	66
Easy to use	55	68
Low price	31	36

Corporate behaviour that makes us 'very angry' includes:

Companies selling information about me without my permission	78
People in positions of power saying one thing and meaning another	62
Companies saying things about their products just to sell them that may not be true	57

Whose hand on the lever?

% agree

Many Australians feel strongly that they need more control over their lives and the power to make their own choices.

It's very important for me to feel self-sufficient.	92
It's more important than ever for people to take control of their lives.	91
It's very important for me to feel in charge of every part of my life.	88
I'm looking for ways to get control over my life.	58

These concerns are particularly evident among younger respondents, especially those under 21; this may reflect their relative powerlessness and inexperience.

People tend to express dissatisfaction with aspects of life in which they are not as much in control as they would like to be.

Lately I find myself so involved in day-to-day practical matters that I feel I really don't have the opportunity to do things I really enjoy.	59
Often I feel I don't know enough about the products I buy to feel really in control of the purchase.	46
I feel I need to manage my time more efficiently.	82

Success matters

For Australians, success is measured not by money or material possessions but by the way we feel about our lives. Money is seen as a means to other ends we value rather than as a value in itself.

Symbols of success:	
Being satisfied with my life	81
Being in control of my life	74
Travelling for pleasure	52
Being able to afford things that are important to me	72
Having a successful investment strategy	41
Having enough money is very important to my happiness.	73
Our society should put less emphasis on money.	82
Doing enjoyable things and going to interesting places mean more to me than lots of possessions.	82
The only real measure of success is money. **(disagree)**	84

In short, we want more money for the security and experiences it can buy, as the means to an enjoyable, satisfying life, and not as a way of scoring or displaying our personal success.

Be different but be Australian

Migrants should adopt the Australian way of life.	86

Yet we agree that people should be diverse, and maintain and express their cultural traditions.

People should pass on to their children a sense of belonging to a particular religion, ethnic or national tradition.	66
I feel the need to demonstrate my own traditions.	52
(strongly agree)	25
I feel closer to people of the same religious, national or ethnic background.	38
Multiculturalism introduces barriers into Australian society.	57
Migration to Australia should be reduced.	71

We are evidently anxious about social divisions that arise when people form too tightly into subgroups that despise or remain aloof from the rest of the community. It is acceptable to be different as long as you are not 'too different'.

(*Source:* The Bulletin, 28 July 1992)

STUDY 2: 'AUSTRALIANS IN THE 1990s' — *READERS DIGEST*

A survey of *Readers Digest* subscribers suggests that 'middle Australia' can be clustered into three groups:

1. **Conservatives** (32%)

   This group was concerned with what other people thought. They sought familiarity and stability and were most comfortable with the sex roles of the past. This group was pessimistic about Australian society and the future and looked to others to take the lead. Discipline and punishment were an important part of the law for this group who saw obedience and respect as important virtues for children. The conservatives' 'escape' was watching aggressive entertainment rather than cultural pursuits and they preferred to watch rather than participate in sport.

2. **New traditionalists** (32%)

   This group was characterised as being self-confident, educated, eager to learn, interested in things from the past but receptive to new ideas. They were confident in their own beliefs and values, and confident in making decisions based on their own judgement. The new traditionalists tend to be early adopters of new products and new technology. They are more likely to be innovators and opinion leaders within their peer group. Leaders rather than followers, they are leading the resurgence of interest in a vast array of products — including fountain pens, oatmeal and traditionally brewed beer.[20]

3. **Shifters** (36%)

   This group occupied the psychological middle ground between the other two groups, sharing characteristics of both groups. They are described as 'good citizens'.

The subscribers surveyed showed only marginal differences in terms of age, occupation or education. The main differences were in attitudes and lifestyle and market behaviour.

STUDY 3: REINVENTING AUSTRALIA — MACKAY RESEARCH

In the second half of this century there has been unprecedented world-wide, social, cultural, political, economic and technological change. Everything from the roles of men and women, marriage and the family to the country's ethnic mix is being questioned and the Australian way of life is being radically redefined. This has caused a high level of angst and, according to Hugh Mackay, Australians are in the process of redefining who and what they are. The changes have not impacted on the core values of Australians to any significant degree. For example, the family is still important, but there is more acceptance of different types of families and of roles within the family.[21] This means that new norms are developing in response to questions of customs and manners, such as:

- What should children call step-parents and is it acceptable to call two people 'dad'?
- How do you introduce your de facto spouse?
- Should one shake hands when introduced to the opposite sex?
- Who should enter the lift first?

To cope with change, Mackay says that Australians are attempting to find their bearings by retreating into their 'domestic caves', escaping through drugs or adventure holidays, and by going 'back to basics'. There is also a refocusing on traditional values and lifestyles, particularly the outback. A range of behaviours associated with creating relationships, both at the individual level and the community level, have developed and the workplace and the neighbourhood have emerged as places of social contact.

Mackay explains the upsurge in the consumer's demand for quality customer service as a reflection of the need for human contact. Because so many Australians are battling loneliness and identify problems associated with fragmentation of families and neighbourhoods, all encounters with others (whether commercial or otherwise) are important.[22]

> **66**Faced with poor service, Australians feel affronted because, quite simply, they assume that when the retailer, the tradesman, the bank or the professional person has not paid enough attention to the personal component of the encounter, this means that it is not the person who has been valued, but only the person's money.**99**

The three studies outlined above represent different types of monitoring research, but they identify similar themes and cultural trends in Australia, trends not unlike those occurring in other countries. For example, they identified a 'retreat to the domestic cave' mentality which is similar to the 'cocooning in a new decade' trend in North America described by Faith Popcorn,[23] and changes in values and ideas that are occurring in most Western societies, described by Joseph Plummer (see table 13.2).[24] Both have identified escapism trends, 'eco' values and a refocus on traditional values.

Table 13.2: New ideas and values in Western cultures, identified by Plummer

Old ideas	New ideas
Self-denial ethic	Self-fulfilment ethic
Higher standard of living	Better quality of life
Traditional sex roles	Blurring of sex roles
Accepted definition of success	Individualised definition of success
Traditional family life	Alternative families
Faith in industry, institutions	Self-reliance
Live to work	Work to live
Hero worship	Love of ideas
Expansionism	Pluralism
Patriotism	Less nationalistic
Unparalleled growth	Growing sense of limits
Industrial growth	Information/service growth
Receptivity to technology	Technology orientation

(*Source*: Adapted from Joseph Plummer, 'Changing Values', *The Futurist*, Jan./Feb. 1989)

"Retirement planning? We didn't know what to do. But talks with the National cleared our thinking."

"It's confusing on your own".

"My Dad received a gold watch, some super and a pension," said Peter. "But approaching retirement today is like tip-toeing through a minefield. Not only is it financially complex, but the rules keep changing.

"I'm self-employed so we're not exactly novices with money. But the thought of juggling super, shares, property, allocated pensions, annuities etc. while trying to keep tax at a minimum and provide for adequate cashflow was keeping us awake at nights."

"That's when I suggested we talk to the National," said Pam.

"The National covered all our needs."

"Chris at our National branch introduced us to one of their specialists* in retirement planning, who took the time to understand our situation before tailoring a retirement plan especially for us.

"The service covered our changing day to day banking needs, investment planning (both National and non-National investments), and even helped us with our will. Nothing was overlooked," said Peter. "The bank provided and co-ordinated all these services free. We're satisfied that the National's planning will help us maintain the lifestyle we want. It certainly saved us sleepless nights," said Pam with a laugh.

To get your free copy of the National's 44 page booklet

©National Australia Bank Limited 1994. SS0103

which explains, in straight forward language, how to approach retirement with confidence, fill in the coupon below or call, **008 630 200.**

You can also arrange an appointment with one of our retirement advisers by calling this number. Begin tailoring your retirement now.

*Information is based on actual cases but the names and personal details have been changed. National Financial Planning Consultants are authorised representatives of National Australia Financial Planning Limited, a licensed dealer in securities and wholly-owned subsidiary of National Australia Financial Management Ltd. (NAFM) which, along with National Australia Trustees Ltd, is a wholly owned subsidiary of National Australia Bank Ltd. NAFM consultants may receive commission for business introduced to the National Australia Bank Group.

☐ Yes, I would like a free copy of "The time of your life."
☐ Yes, please call me to arrange an appointment.

Are you a National customer? Yes ☐ No ☐

Please complete and mail (No stamp required) to: Reply Paid 4343, National Australia Bank, GPO Box 4343, Melbourne Vic 3001.

Name: _____
            TITLE   GIVEN NAME   SURNAME

Occupation: _____

Address: _____

_____ Postcode: _____

Phone: BH:(___)_____ AH:(___)_____

★ National
Australia Bank

Tailoring banking to your needs.

JWT NSS 028

Figure 13.5: This advertisement is responding to the consumers of the 1990s who want security and good financial advice.

The three studies show that Australian consumers are becoming more vigilant and careful, expecting quality, fair prices and good service. The implication of these changes is that there will be a continuing and increased demand for:

- household products, such as entertainment units, computers, furniture, do-it-yourself and other home improvement products, gardening equipment
- health products, home exercise, vitamin and other supplements and products that enhance physical well-being, from cellulite creams to aromatherapy
- experiences to enhance self-development and fulfilment
- activities, such as interesting holidays and activities and education through both formal and informal sources
- environmentally sound products and packaging
- social shopping where the act of shopping becomes a central part of the product
- financial services that offer security rather than spectacular gains.

SUBCULTURES AND MARKETING

Within large, complex societies, small cohesive groups of people can be found. These groups are known as subcultures. A subculture has a specific set of values and norms that individuals must adhere to if they wish to remain members of the group. They rarely operate in a way which is entirely separate from their main society because they lack the size to support a separate community. For this reason, the members of these groups will adhere to most of the core values and norms, particularly the laws, of the 'umbrella society'. The groups may, however, be large enough to be viable market segments.[25]

A subculture has a general influence on attitudes and lifestyles and gives an individual a discernible identity. The influence of a subculture on an individual will depend on the strength of the association with that subculture. The more that a subculture is able to maintain a separate identity from the 'main' culture, the greater will be its potential influence. In the same way that segments can be defined by the individuals that are included in the subculture, they can also be defined by the mechanisms within that subculture which exclude 'outsiders'. The greater the ability of the subculture to exclude members, the greater its ability to influence individual members by isolating them from other groups.[26]

AGE AND SOCIAL CLASS AS SUBCULTURES

Whether age and class groups constitute true subcultures is the subject of much debate.[27] For these groups — for example, working, middle and upper class groups and distinct age clusters — to be accurately defined as subcultural groups, the individuals within each group should adhere to clearly identifiable values, attitudes and behaviours.

Apart from the upper class groups, identifying other class groups and associated values and behaviours in Australia is difficult (see chapter 11). It has been argued that there is a difference in behaviours, tastes and preferences across class groups but the differences are slight and often based on income, i.e. the resources to purchase products. High unemployment levels over the last decade have created a small 'underclass' of unemployed people.[28] It is still too early to know if the feelings of helplessness, loss of control and minimal access to possessions will impact on specific values such as autonomy, materialism or hedonism.

Yuppies

In the 1980s, marketers focused on the 'young upwardly mobile professional person' or 'yuppy', a product of the baby boomer or 'me-generation'.[29] Although an identifiable market segment, it is questionable whether this group constituted a subcultural group. During the 1980s, this affluent group epitomised the value of materialism and practised conspicuous consumption.[30] Many of this group from the middle and senior management levels are now feeling the impact of unemployment and those who retain jobs are concerned about their financial future. They have become, along with the rest of Australia, more conservative during the 1990s.

On the whole, yuppies feel that the future that they believed would be rosy is seriously threatened. Along with the rest of 'middle Australia', they long for a simpler and more 'authentic' lifestyle, because the rewards that they sought now seem unattainable or not worth the price that they paid. This group is also concerned about experiences and the quality of life rather than the short-term glamorous gains that propelled them forward in the 1980s. They are likely to be more interested in self-improvement courses and travel than in overt symbols of their success.[31]

Teenagers

Until the 1950s, teenagers were regarded as small versions of adults with limited rights. Then a large group of teenagers entered the market — the baby boomers, born between 1946 and 1964. This group became economically viable because of their numbers and the post-war years of economic prosperity meant that this group had money available to spend on consumer goods. At the same time, television entered the Australian marketplace and marketing developed at a rapid rate.

Today's teenagers are the children of the baby boomers. They grew up in a time of rapid technological change, mass communication and mass marketing. They are indulged by parents who bestow material possessions on them as symbols of love and security. As a group, however, their values and behaviours are similar to that of the adult population.[32] Some teenagers are more cynical and more concerned about the problems facing the world. Research by Harrison Communications in 1989 reported that some teenagers felt alienated. But they were also self-centred and materialistic. Some were also self-reliant, determined to carve out their own destinies and were more inclined to blame their peers, rather than society, for being unemployed.[33] Some research shows that the majority of teenagers are positive, optimistic and empowered. They have a much broader range of adult responsibilities due to the likelihood that either both parents are working or that they live in a household with a divorced parent.[34] Other research shows that there are teenagers who feel helpless and pessimistic. Many have opted to drop out of the system and there is an increase in teenage suicide and socially deviant behaviours.[35]

Brands that have been successful with this group, such as Coke and Levi, appeal to teenagers because, in a world over which teenagers have little control, they can at least select the brand of their choice. Brands which have been most successful contain strong rational appeals and clear benefits. Lifestyle advertising that is seen as contrived is quickly rejected by this street-wise group.

Coke speaks their language

NEIL SHOEBRIDGE

After a disappointing start, Coca-Cola South Pacific's 1992–93 advertising program has produced a winner. Late last year, it seemed the new crop of Coke ads would be dreary. The first offering for 1992–93 was a ho-hum affair featuring a group of teenagers dancing on roller-blades. But last month the soft-drink maker proved that it still has its finger on the pulse of the teenager market.

The new ad, which is called "City heat", features a group of teenagers dancing and drinking Coke during a hot night in an anonymous city. The star is a young rapper called Eric Sebastian, who declaims about himself, cola and the important things in life.

It is a world away from the fun-in-the-sun beach images that once dominated Coke advertising. At first glance, it seems similar to its roller-blading predecessor. The setting is the same (a street) and both casts appear the same (attractive teenagers). But "city heat" is stronger and more accurately targeted than its predecessor. It speaks the language of today's teenagers and puts its product back on the cutting edge of youth market advertising.

The move away from the beach has not happened over-night. Since the late 1980s, Coke has steadily introduced non-beach image into its adver-tising, setting its ads in rest-aurants, deserts and city streets. "City heat" continues this trend.

Teenagers are harsh critics. A research study conducted last year by the advertising agency Lintas (owned by the US com-pany Interpublic, which also owns Coke's agency, McCann-Erickson) showed that teens are extremely sceptical and cynical about advertising. They judge products' integrity by their advertising, but are also aware that ads exploit people's inse-curities and vulnerabilities. They appreciate clever ideas but dismiss lifestyle campaigns — which slot products into scenes of everyday life — as contrived and boring.

Teenagers are drawn to adver-tising campaigns and brand names that are "true to them-selves". They don't like "try-hard" brands — that is, those that try to be something they are not — or "me-too" products. They want brands and cam-paigns that are authentic and offer a clear benefit.

Coke is a powerful teen totem. It is more than their most popular softdrink; it is also a symbol of youth. According to Lintas's research, Coke and Levi's are two of the biggest brands among teenagers, who like their all-embracing, eclectic qualities. They are seen as "real", rather than "try-hard" or "me-too".

Marketing to the teenagers of 1993 is not easy. The high youth unemployment rate and issues such as AIDS and the destruc-tion of the environment have left many of them feeling anxious and powerless to exert control over their world. Their aim is simply to be happy. In the 1960s, teenagers wanted to change the world. In the 1970s, they wanted to trash the world. In the 1980s, they wanted to rule the world. Now, they want to create small islands of happi-ness. They believe that if they are content with themselves, their positive emotions will flow out to others.

The "City heat" commercial matches up well with Lintas's key findings on what teenagers are looking for in ad campaigns. Sebastian's rap includes lines such as, "Take me, I'm an orig-inal man", and exhortations to "get real". It also reprises some of the lyrics of the company's 1970s jingle, *I'd like to buy the world a Coke*.

The word "real" figures prominently in the new cam-paign, as part of a concerted effort to reinforce the brand's street credibility. Coke's pre-vious ads failed to come to grips with the key concerns of today's youth. "City heat" puts it squarely back on track.

Business Review Weekly,
19 February 1993

SUBCULTURES AS SEGMENTS

For subcultures to be economically viable market segments, they must be homogeneous and large enough to justify their use. Unless a product or message has direct relevance to the subculture, to the exclusion of other segments, then it may not be cost-effective to create a full or partial marketing mix for the segment.[36] In Australia, clearly identifiable subcultures are mainly those based on geographic clusters, religion or ethnicity (or race). Where people's occupations or their sexuality or particular interests provide a total context for everyday life, this can form the basis of a subculture. In military bases, for example, people live and work together and a subculture develops.

Homosexual groups have become more visible and identifiable within our society. Homosexuals may choose to live in particular areas, have their own venues for entertainment and have a different set of values that relate to their lifestyle. This group may also have different concerns, such as discrimination and health issues. Although small in terms of absolute numbers, this group has considerable spending power with an individual household income approximately 70 per cent higher than the national average.[37]

Homosexual males spend 50 per cent more on travel and 250 per cent more on grooming and fitness products than do heterosexual males. They also spend more on alcohol, homewares and entertainment. Apart from their spending power, this group are trendsetters in fashion and entertainment. For specific products, they constitute a valuable niche.

> **❝**There have been some stunning examples of the impact of gay tastes on the marketplace.
>
> Levi's jeans relaunched the classic '50s jeans, the 501, after their adoption by English gays began to make them popular with the mainstream again. Moving to take the initiative, Levi's advertised 501s with the deliciously ambiguous Levi's launderette ad, which shows a young man stripping down to his underpants in order to wash his Levi's without letting them out of his sight.
>
> To this list, Danny Vadasz [creative director of Bluestone Media] adds that the gay market has led the way to mineral water becoming a status beverage, running shoes becoming an indispensable fashion symbol and men wearing earrings. 'The gay community is very style and fashion conscious,' he says.**❞**
>
> (*Source*: *Marketing*, June 1992)

INTEREST OR ACTIVITY-BASED SUBCULTURES

Examples of activity-based subcultures are the 'computer kids', or skateboarders, for whom specific rituals, such as the wearing of Vison baggies, are expected. Both groups have their own media in the form of specialist magazines, and many develop their own jargon, which is difficult for those outside the group to understand.

Targeting of interest or activity-based subcultures can be economically viable, where there is a range of products that serve as key aspects of the group and where the group has its own media channels or direct mail is feasible. Often, activity-based subcultures cut across national boundaries and as such their economic viability is increased.

In Australia and New Zealand, two long-standing subcultural groups are the surfing (surfies) and lifesaving (clubbies) subcultures.[38] Even though these are similar activities, each has a unique pattern of attitudes and behaviours. Whether or not products, such as clothes, wetsuits, boards and accessories, are accepted is a function of 'group' acceptance. Brand labels accepted among surfies nowadays include Quicksilver, Rip Curl, Ocean & Earth, Rusty, Morey, Wave Rebel, Manta, Billabong, Kuta Lines and MCD.

Contrasts in clubbies and surfies

The following characteristics have been abstracted as being important in the descriptions both of lifesavers and of board riders in picturing the main characteristics of 'clubbies'.

- conservative, conformist, establishment types, extroverted
- prepared to accept discipline and formal authority
- make some sacrifice of leisure for patrol and rescue work
- interested in training and practice for competition and patrols
- particularly interested in competitive SLSA carnivals
- personal appearance is neat and tidy, with typically short hair, 'fit' looking as a result of training and competition
- wear speedos, terry towelling hats and zinc cream on beach and conventional dress away from beach
- enjoy the comradeship and social life associated with the club as well as the facilities it offers
- generally sociable and surf and mix in large groups
- variety of equipment used, much of which is kept in local surf life-saving club house and normally used in the vicinity of the club
- craft and gear frequently designed and built with surf lifesaving competition in view
- generally stick to one beach; may travel to other beaches for competition but do not travel from beach to beach in search of waves
- trained to handle a variety of different surf conditions and situations
- greater range of ages involved
- conventional attitudes towards drugs; are normally beer drinkers
- steady employment in regular 9 a.m. to 5 p.m. jobs.

(*continued*)

In a similar way there was much agreement among lifesavers and board riders as to the main characteristics of 'surfies'. The following characteristics have been abstracted as being important in these descriptions:

- individualist, independent, 'creative', unconventional
- hedonistic, self-centred (even 'selfish')
- casual, anti-establishment
- introverted
- opposed to discipline or control over individual freedoms
- dislike obligations or commitments
- slim physique — wear board shorts on beach, casual clothes, e.g. jeans and T-shirts, when away from beach
- unconventional attitudes towards drugs; smoke marijuana
- very mobile in their search for surf
- gather and surf in small groups
- prime object to 'have a good time' riding waves
- less conventional than 'clubbies' regarding jobs, hours of work, money, etc.

(*Source*: Kent Pearson, *Surfing Subcultures of Australia and New Zealand*, University of Queensland Press, 1979)

GEOGRAPHIC: URBAN VERSUS RURAL

Although there are some differences in marketplace behaviour across the states, the major difference in terms of lifestyle is the urban–rural division. The rural scene is often portrayed as the most significant aspect of Australian life, yet over 85 per cent of Australians live in cities. Distance and isolation have ensured that rural Australia is highly conservative, adhering to traditional values. Physical aspects of country living create specific demands for certain products, such as trucks, farm equipment, food storage equipment, clothes etc., but country values and lifestyle have had a strong impact on 'urbanites' of the 1990s.[39]

The angst of the 1990s has led to a growing obsession with the symbols of 'the country'.[40] Urban Australians are using 'country values' as a source of reassurance and comfort and as a way to lead less complicated lifestyles. The fantasy of having a place in the country and bringing up the children there is popular. For most urbanites this is not a reality but it does translate into a desire for country style furnishings, clothing (hence the value of the Country Road label), four-wheel drive vehicles and camping and a renewed interest in country and western music. The magazine *Australian Country Style* has a better circulation in cities than it does in the country.

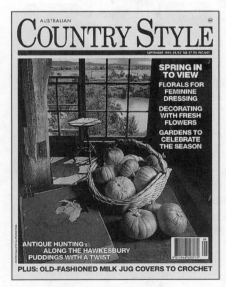

Figure 13.6: *Australian Country Style*, a magazine for the 1990s

Australian Country Style

Australian Country Style magazine went into production in 1988. Country living is the central theme of the magazine and it features articles on: people; homes and gardens; food and wine; fashion and accessories.

The target market is the age 35 plus females in the top three socioeconomic clusters. Circulation figures show it to be a popular theme for today's consumer.

Readership patterns (April 1993–March 1994)

Women	219 000
Men	83 000

Location

Urban	184 000
Country	117 000

Position in market	Audited circulation (period ended 30 Sept. 1993)
Australian Country Style	64 000
Country Looks	46 538
Interiors	48 550
Vogue Living	72 500
Belle	52 000

RELIGION

While Australia is predominantly a Christian country, in the 1991 census 2.6 per cent of the population identified themselves as adherents of a non-Christian religion and 13 per cent said they did not have any religious affiliations. (For 10.4 per cent of respondents, no religion was stated.) Seventy-four per cent of the population described themselves as Christian. The major non-Christian groups were Muslims (147 487), Buddhists (139 812), Jews (74 167) and Hindus (43 567). These groups are only a small percentage of the Australian population but, because of their unique sets of values and norms, they form groups that may provide marketers with very specific product opportunities. Many of these religious groups are likely to be more concentrated in particular suburbs or areas and have a great impact on the culture there. Specific religious practices may affect marketing activities such as the days and times that stores are open, the types of products that are acceptable and the language used to promote products.[41]

ETHNICITY

Over the last two hundred years, migrants to Australia have brought with them the cultural values of many countries. The Anglo-Celtic culture has been dominant since the eighteenth century. Currently, two-thirds of the Australian population are Anglo-Celtic in origin.

At June 1991, an estimated 23 per cent of the population was born overseas.[42] As table 13.3 shows, people who arrived in Australia prior to 1981 came mainly from the United Kingdom (36%), Italy (9.8%), Yugoslavia (5.5%) and Greece (5.2%). During the period 1990–91, however, immigrants mainly came from the United Kingdom (15.8%), New Zealand (8.5%), Vietnam (7.8%) and Hong Kong (5.4%).

Table 13.3: Birthplace by year of arrival (persons born overseas excluding overseas visitors)

Birthplace	Prior to 1981	1981– 1985	1986– 1987	1988– 1989	1990– 1991	Not stated	Total
Main English speaking countries:							
Canada	12 825	3 122	1 549	1 918	2 668	364	22 446
Ireland	33 456	4 414	3 921	5 952	2 756	1 232	51 731
New Zealand	117 027	47 306	31 484	42 917	19 156	6 169	264 059
South Africa	21 614	10 429	7 318	5 626	3 228	721	48 936
United Kingdom[(a)]	884 796	83 986	33 249	41 593	35 470	24 620	1 103 714
USA	21 808	6 047	3 161	4 725	7 088	861	43 690
Total	*1 091 526*	*155 304*	*80 682*	*102 731*	*70 366*	*33 967*	*1 534 576*
Other countries:							
China	22 274	10 056	9 214	22 818	11 977	1 566	77 905
Germany	94 901	8 472	2 122	2 273	2 119	2 005	111 892
Greece	126 431	2 643	1 374	1 160	845	3 422	135 875
Hong Kong	13 808	10 283	6 981	13 696	12 104	689	57 561
India	34 395	7 728	4 837	5 966	6 951	1 099	60 976
Italy	241 211	3 063	1 059	1 029	999	6 088	253 449
Lebanon	44 347	6 411	6 150	5 443	3 921	2 604	68 876
Malaysia	24 994	12 720	8 932	14 933	9 170	1 004	71 753
Malta	49 360	1 859	579	363	178	1 447	53 786
Netherlands	85 155	4 714	1 060	1 098	859	1 676	94 562
Philippines	13 260	16 327	14 317	17 025	10 539	1 507	72 975
Poland	43 396	13 655	3 366	3 794	2 662	1 677	68 550
Former USSR[(b)]	36 777	1 318	485	2 217	2 126	1 016	43 939
Vietnam	32 689	42 178	12 639	14 156	17 568	2 629	121 859
Yugoslavia	135 846	6 658	4 700	5 235	3 224	4 987	160 650
Other[(c)]	364 087	101 412	67 179	83 236	68 848	16 083	700 845
Total	*1 362 931*	*249 497*	*144 994*	*194 442*	*154 090*	*49 499*	*2 155 453*
Total	**2 454 457**	**404 801**	**225 676**	**297 173**	**224 456**	**83 466**	**3 690 029**

(a) Includes England, Scotland, Wales and Northern Ireland.
(b) Includes the Baltic States.
(c) Includes 'inadequately described', 'at sea' and 'not elsewhere classified'.

(*Source*: 'Census Characteristics of Australia', *1991 Census of Population and Housing*, Australian Bureau of Statistics, Cat. No. 2710)

Marketing needs ethnic balance

ANDY BIZIOREK

SYDNEY: Companies that can cross the cultural barriers of ethnic and racial groups in marketing their products will prosper in the 1990s, according to Indicator Australia chief executive Paul Leinberger.

Leinberger's statement was in response to the recent release of Census data, which indicated that in 1991, the largest age group was the 30 to 34 year segment. At the last Census, six years ago, the largest group was the 15 to 19 year sector.

The shift has been attributed to the increasing number of immigrants in the age group, as Australia's fertility rates continued to decline during the period. This has been verified to an extent by Bureau of Immigration Research figures, which exposed people aged 25 to 29 as the largest group of immigrants between 1983 and 1990.

Leinberger said the data confirmed that "fundamental shifts" were taking place in the Australian lifestyle. Australia was becoming an older, more diverse nation demographically, economically and culturally, he said.

"Such fundamental changes translate into market segments that will become increasingly narrow. As the 1990s evolve, Australia will become a land of particle markets. For example, expect to see more mature consumer clusters and fewer young family clusters in the next 10 years. And there will be a great number of racial and ethnic consumer clusters. For marketers, the opportunities are in the details," Leinberger said.

"Welcoming newcomers and native born minorities into the economic mainstream will be one of the biggest challenges marketers will face in the '90s. This means understanding lifestyle trends, shopping patterns, modes of transport and media preferences."

AMR:Quantum managing director Brian Fine said the age group was only marginally larger than others and that this fact had been overemphasised. It would be misguided of marketers to target only a five year age band.

"Other groups which are only marginally smaller include the 25 to 29 year group, the 35 to 39 and the 40 to 44. The difference between these groups equates to an athlete winning the 100 metres in a time of 9.9 seconds with second and third places at 9.95 seconds," Fine said.

"Marketers of most products and services should be looking at broader age groups such as 10 year bands. The two most significant in absolute size are the 25 to 34 and the 35 to 44 groups. In the exceptional situation there may be a niche product capable of being targeted in a narrower age range."

Fine said Australian Bureau of Statistics figures predict that by the year 2000, the 35 to 44 year group would be as significant in absolute numbers as the 25 to 34 group, followed closely by the 45 to 54 sector.

Chris Adams Research principal Chris Adams said: "Perhaps the greatest distinguishing feature of the 30 to 34 year old age group is that, on the life cycle continuum, they are positioned at the confluence of founding a family, cementing their friendships and consolidating their career."

"(They are) young enough to believe they can still have it all, mature enough to dedicate their efforts to that end. The thirty-something generation responds to products and services which expedite ... their busy and multi-faceted lifestyle. They are drawn to advertising which reflects their sense of confidence and control and which recognises that their behaviour is increasingly being governed by we, rather than I, centred concerns," she said.

B&T, 22 May 1992

The Anglo-Celts have shaped and continue to shape the present culture.[43] Within the remaining one-third, there are some sizeable ethnic clusters, in particular the Italian and Greek communities (Melbourne has the third largest Greek speaking population in the world). The predominantly Italian suburbs of Sydney are Ashfield, Burwood, Concord, Drummoyne and Fairfield. The predominantly Greek suburbs of Sydney are Marrickville, Canterbury, Randwick, Rockdale, Botany and South Sydney. Leichhardt has a mixture of both.

The immigration pattern since the 1950s has affected Australians' tastes in food. In the 1950s, the main household meal was likely to consist of 'meat and three veggies', with the potato as the main staple. Now it is often pasta or rice, and Australians at home and in restaurants enjoy Chinese, Italian, Thai, Indian, Japanese and Vietnamese dishes.[44]

Whether the ethnic clusters individually are viable segments, or even viable niches, has been the subject of considerable debate. One very successful use of ethnic subcultures was the OTC 'Memories' series of advertisements in the 1970s (see figure 5.5, page 109). The aim was to increase the use of the ISD overseas service by households. As the most likely users of such a service were people with family overseas, a series of commercials featuring a range of different national groups was devised, all with the same message — 'When you are thinking of home, go home on the telephone'.

In absolute terms, individual ethnic groups are small but they tend to cluster in specific localities. This means that locality based products such as retail outlets (food outlets in particular), banks, education and health services need to respond to the needs of the ethnic groups that they service.[45]

Immigration has had an impact on the 'greying' rate of the Australian population, as migrants tend to be of working age. So, when targeting the under 40s, even if it is not viable to target individual ethnic groups, the multicultural characteristics of the market should be acknowledged, particularly in distribution, packaging (product usage information) and marketing communication decisions. Even if specific media outlets such as ethnic newspapers are not used, advertisements in general should reflect the true ethnic balance in the community.

Figure 13.7: TeleItalia — media access to the Italian community

CROSS-CULTURAL MARKETING

With the small national market and the removal of tariffs, many Australian businesses both large and small have found it necessary to export. With the globalisation of markets, this is a trend that is likely to continue. Entering foreign markets is not easy as there are often many barriers to entry, such as regulations, political instability and tariffs. The type of product and type of entry strategy will influence the type of information and expertise required by the Australian firm. If there is direct involvement at the household consumption level, then extensive knowledge of household buying behaviour is necessary. Businesses should assess their own competency to manage an export program,[46] then create effective marketing strategies, based on such information as listed below.[47]

Information on foreign markets

Market characteristics
- Size of market — rate of growth
- Stage of development
- Stage of product life cycle, saturation levels
- Buyer behaviour characteristics
- Social/cultural factors
- Physical environment

Marketing institutions
- Distribution systems
- Communications media
- Marketing services (advertising, research, etc.)

Industry conditions
- Competitive size and practices
- Technical development

Legal environment
- Laws, regulations, codes, tariffs, taxes, etc.

Resources
- Manpower (availability, skill, potential, cost)
- Money (availability, cost)

Financial environment
- Balance of payments, foreign exchange rate, regulations, etc.

Political environment
- Current government policies and attitudes
- Long-range political environment

(*Source*: Adapted from Warren J. Keegan, 'A Conceptual Framework for Multinational Marketing', in S. Jain, L. R. Tucker (eds), *International Marketing*, 2nd edn, Kent Publishing Co., Boston, 1986)

Assessing buyer behaviour characteristics and identifying social/cultural factors can be difficult but necessary if marketing mistakes are to be avoided. Products may have to be altered to cater for differing tastes in the case of food and drink.[48] Many problems can occur in the area of packaging. The wrong colour or number can impact on sales — white in Japan signifies death; green represents danger or death in Malaysia; the number four is considered evil in Japan; two is considered unlucky in parts of Africa. Potential language problems should also be identified. Consider the impact of the following language errors.[49]

- On its initial entry into China, the symbols used for the name 'Coca-Cola' translated as 'a wax-flattened mare'.
- A shampoo called 'Evitol' was marketed in Brazil — the name translated as 'dandruff contraceptive'.
- A German chocolate-fruit product with the brand name 'Zit' was marketed in English speaking countries.

Even when countries have much in common, such as the United States and Australia, there are distinct cultural differences.[50] Some values are shared; others are not (see figure 13.8).[51]

AUSTRALIAN VALUES
Egalitarianism
Hedonism
Mateship
The 'underdog'
A 'fair go'
Disrespect for
  authority

AMERICAN VALUES
Equality
Progress
Activity
Achievement
Efficiency

SHARED VALUES
Nationalism
Materialism
Individualism
Youthfulness
Informality

Figure 13.8: Cultural differences between Australia and the US

American women place greater importance on their career, nationality, problem solving and convenience, whereas Australian women place more importance on dutifulness, egalitarianism, kin-group solidarity, home-making, mothering and cooking.[52] There are also differences in the way we use words, for example:

American —		*Australian* —	
	gas		petrol
	cookies		biscuits
	diapers		nappies
	jelly		jam
	sweater		jumper
	jumper		dress
	ketchup		sauce

Don Henderson and Reginald Smart identified a number of differences between Americans and Australians that marketers from both countries should be aware of (see table 13.4).[53]

Table 13.4: More cultural differences between Australia and the US

Americans	Australians
Americans are lifelong drifters.	Australians are more likely to settle down and 'stay-put', although they do travel overseas for holidays.
Americans trust people on the basis of performance and consistent behaviour and other people's view of the person.	Australians base their trust on the capacity for loyalty and commitment in a person and rely on their own judgement.
Americans think more about the future.	Their private life is more important to Australians and they expect satisfaction from all aspects of their life, not just their free time.
Americans like overtime and they work at a more intense pace.	Australians do not like to work overtime.
Americans say much.	Australians say little.
Americans overstate.	Australians understate.
Americans like people who agree with them as disagreement means rejection.	Australians like people who disagree with them as disagreement is not taken personally.
Americans accept authority within limitations.	Australians tend to denigrate authority and are uncomfortable with external controls.

Differences can also be seen in their approaches to certain marketing tactics, such as comparative advertising — Americans accept it, Australians reject it — and the American hard-sell approach which does not find favour in Australia.[54]

 SUMMARY

Culture has been defined as the essence or substance of a society consisting of the shared ideas, meanings, values and morals, as well as the language, artefacts and services produced, used and valued by a group of people. A society's culture shapes all behaviour, including marketplace behaviour. Products and communication messages that are outside the accepted parameters of a culture are high risk as they are likely to be rejected. It is therefore essential for marketers to understand their own culture and the other cultures of the places where they conduct business transactions.

Culture has been conceptualised as a system consisting of three functional interacting elements — the physical, the social and the training environment. These elements are totally interrelated in that they are influenced by each other and they combine to shape each individual's cognitions, behaviours, values and motivations.

Cultural values are enduring beliefs that certain ways of thinking and behaving are important. Norms are rules that describe acceptable and unacceptable behaviour. In order to understand a society, marketers need to understand its values and norms and monitor any changes. Cultures are not static and it is important to track changes in aspects of culture as these changes impact on marketplace behaviour.

Changes are occurring that are likely to increase demand for such items as:
- entertainment units, computers, furniture, do-it-yourself and other home improvement products and gardening equipment
- health products, interesting holidays and hobbies and education through both formal and informal sources
- environmentally sound products and packaging
- financial services that offer security rather than spectacular gains
- social shopping where the act of shopping becomes a central part of the product
- improved service quality.

Although most cultures have an 'umbrella' of core and peripheral values and norms there is also scope for subcultures to form. These subgroups adhere to the 'umbrella' culture but also form values and norms specific to their subgroup, which may be activity, ethnic or regional based. These groups can form the basis of economically viable market segments or niches. Although there are a number of ethnic subcultures in Australia, individually they are small and only viable for specific products, such as food and entertainment. There are, however, over five million individuals who are not Anglo-Celts. For this reason marketers need to acknowledge these individuals, particularly in product, packaging and communication decisions.

An emerging feature of business strategy is the globalisation of markets and the need to export. To be successful, organisations need to develop cross-cultural marketing skills.

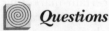

Questions

1. Advertising cannot change cultural values and norms, merely reflect them. Discuss this statement.
2. Discuss ethnicity and its relevance in marketing decisions.
3. Select at least three products that have failed in the marketplace because they did not comply with the current, acceptable social norms. Identify the norms breached. If the product or message was modified, could the product be relaunched? If modification is impossible, how easy would it be to change the social norms concerned?
4. Do you think understanding other cultures would help you to understand your own?
5. Australians who are not of Anglo-Celtic origin make up about one third of the population. Identify five individual ethnic groups and ascertain if there are any group-specific products. If you identify any such products, what factors would you build into the marketing mix?

6. Do you think that social class groups in Australia are subcultures? If so, discuss whether they would make viable market segments.

7. This chapter describes a number of changes that are occurring in Australia. Have you noticed these changes affecting you and your friends' behaviour? If so, which are having the most impact? Why do you think this is the case?

8. Identify and describe at least four activity/interest subcultures. Are they economically viable segments? Why or why not?

9. Cross-cultural differences between countries and subcultural differences within countries have different implications for marketing strategy. What are they?

10. Discuss the notion of products as symbols. Are there any products that are not cultural symbols? What are they and why are they not symbols?

 Case study

Is this a recipe for success? Take two of the world's biggest beverage makers, toss in two super-brands, add more than $100 million and mix well. The resulting products can be served hot or cold through vending machines, stacked in household refrigerators or heated at home in microwave ovens.

Beverage giants Nestle of Switzerland and Coca-Cola of the US think the recipe will work. Two months ago they announced plans to set up a joint-venture company to make ready-to-drink coffee and tea products in every country except Japan. Nestle will bring its expertise in the coffee and tea markets to the joint venture, plus its Nescafe coffee and Nestea tea brands. Coca-Cola will provide the marketing and distribution structure.

Talks to establish the joint-venture company, which will have an initial capitalisation of $US100 million, are taking place now and are expected to be finalised in the next three to four months. No timetable has been set for when the products will be launched, but US analysts think Nestle and Coca-Cola are keen to release their pre-mixed Nescafe and Nestea drinks before the end of this year.

Both companies are enthusiastic about the deal. Helmut Maucher, chairman and chief executive officer of Nestle, believes ready-to-drink coffee and tea products will be one of the fastest-growing segments of the world beverage market in the 1990s. "Through this joint venture, which combines the worldwide leadership position of Coca-Cola in beverage marketing and distribution with the strong global brands and technology of Nestle, we believe we can most effectively address the growing consumer demand for high-quality, ready-to-drink coffees and teas," Maucher says.

Executives from the Australian arms of Nestle and Coca-Cola say it is too early to comment on when the fruits of the joint venture will appear here. "There is still a lot of work to be done in the US before any products are launched," says a Nestle Australian spokesman. An executive of Coca-Cola's Australian bottling agent, Coca-Cola Amatil, says the development of the business in Australia is "some way off".

US analysts say the concentrates and beverage bases for the new coffee and tea drinks will be made by Nestle in the US and Europe and then slotted into Coca-Cola's 170-country distribution network. The partners will each pump $US50 million into the new joint venture during its first year.

When the new products are launched in Australia, local retailers will experience a sense of deja vu. Both Nestle and Coca-Cola have tried to crack the Australian tea and coffee markets, with a spectacular lack of success. Nestle launched four iced tea products in Australia between 1969 and 1984; all four failed. Coca-Cola test-marketed a hybrid softdrink-coffee product called Georgia Coffee in Adelaide during 1984–85 and quickly shelved it.

Although Georgia Coffee failed in Australia, its success in other markets, particularly Japan, is one of the key factors behind the launch of the joint venture between Coca-Cola and Nestle. Launched in Japan 16 years ago, Georgia Coffee, which is sold in cans through vending machines and supermarkets, is now a $US1.5-billion-a-year brand. It captures 34.3% of sales and the number one spot in Japan's $US4.4-billion ready-to-drink canned coffee market. Georgia Coffee is expected to appear in North America later this year.

(continued)

Canned coffees were launched in Japan in 1969 by a local coffee maker, Ueshima Coffee Co. The development of the sophisticated vending machines, with heating in winter and refrigeration in summer, spurred sales and turned ready-to-drink canned coffee into one of the fastest-growing segments of the Japanese beverage industry.

Sales have climbed from $US2.2 billion in 1986 to $US4.4 billion last year, with vending machines accounting for 78% of sales. The ready-to-drink canned tea market in Japan is smaller, with sales last year of $US500 million, up from $US91 million in 1985.

Georgia Coffee, which was launched by Coca-Cola's Japanese subsidiary in 1975, and named after the company's head office in Atlanta, Georgia, covers several flavors, including expresso, cappuccino, cafe au lait and basic black. Nestle entered the Japanese canned coffee market in September, in a joint venture with a division of Otsuka Pharmaceutical.

The success of canned coffee in Japan caught the eye of US beverage makers such as Kraft General Foods and Thomas J. Lipton (a Unilever division). Both launched canned coffee and tea products in their home market during 1989–90. Kraft General Foods is test-marketing brewed coffee sold in small cartons and a coffee-flavored liquid in bottles. Both products can be heated in a microwave oven or drunk cold. Nestle is also test-marketing a coffee-flavored drink, called Nescafe Mocha Cooler, in the US.

Georgia Coffee arrived in Australia in October 1984, when the local marketing company, Coca-Cola South Pacific,

launched it into an Adelaide test-market. Sold through vending machines only, the product could be bought hot in winter and cold in summer and was pitched at the take-away coffee drinker rather than buyers of traditional carbonated softdrinks.

A few months after Georgia Coffee's local debut, a Coca-Cola executive said the company had "no particular expectations" for it. "Because it was a totally new product, we really didn't know what to expect," the executive said. "We set out to discover the level of consumer interest in such a product."

The first phase of the Adelaide test-market ran from October to December 1984, with vending machines installed in 30 outlets, including colleges, petrol stations, staff canteens and a few corner stores. At that stage, the vending machines dispensed the coffee in cans and Tetra-paks. Few people bought the Tetra-paks, so the second stage of the test-market, which covered February to July 1985, used cans only.

The vending machines used in Adelaide were designed in Japan and needed elongated 240ml cans. Executives say the cost of producing special cans was one of the main reasons they decided against a national launch. But rival beverage marketers claim consumers rejected the idea of a pre-mixed coffee product. "Making a cup of coffee is not an arduous task," says one softdrink industry executive. "Why would people want to buy a pre-mixed coffee?" The test-market for Georgia Coffee was halted in July 1985.

One of the products Georgia Coffee competed against was

Nestle's Nescafe. One of the biggest individual brands sold in Australian supermarkets, Nescafe last year captured 40% of the $300-million-a-year instant coffee market, up from 37% in 1989, and outsold the number two brand, International Roast (also made by Nestle), by nearly 50%. Sales of Nescafe grew an estimated 8% last year.

Nestle has repeatedly failed to crack the tea category. Nestea iced tea is a big seller for Nestle in the US, but the company has been unable to persuade Australians to buy pre-mixed iced tea drinks. It launched four iced tea products between 1969 and 1985, with no success.

Nestle's last attempt to sell iced tea in Australia was in November 1984, when it launched a product called Tea Sling in a Queensland test-market. A lime-flavored tea drink available in two forms (ready-to-drink and powdered), Tea Sling was sold through supermarkets and milk bars. It was axed early in 1985. Three years ago, Nestle Australia's then managing director, Mike Garrett (now head of Nestle Japan), told *BRW* that the company had given up hope of selling iced tea in Australia.

"We've had four failures in 16 years," Garrett said. "We have abandoned the area." The joint venture between Coca-Cola and Nestle could give Nestle Australia a way to re-enter the tea market and provide Coca-Cola with products to compensate for the failure of Georgia Coffee.

Neil Shoebridge,
Business Review Weekly,
25 January 1991

Case study question

Read the article on pages 349–50. Using the checklist of information on foreign markets (page 345), identify the factors that contributed to the success of Georgia Coffee in Japan. Use the checklist to assess the potential success of Georgia Coffee in the Australian market.

SUGGESTED READING

T. Jagtenberg and P. D'Alton, *Four Dimensional Social Space*, Harper and Row Publishers, Sydney, 1989.

B. Graetz and I. McAllister, *Dimensions of Australian Society*, Macmillan Educational Australia, Sydney, 1988.

Stephen Knight, *The Selling of the Australian Mind*, Heinemann, 1990.

D. Storer, *Ethnic Family Values in Australia*, Prentice-Hall, Sydney, 1986.

R. Ward, *The Australian Legend*, Oxford University Press, Melbourne, 1978.

B. Willmott, *Culture and Identity in New Zealand*, G. P. Books, 1989.

H. Mackay, *Reinventing Australia*, Angus and Robertson, Sydney, 1993.

ENDNOTES

1. P. Worsley, *Modern Sociology*, Penguin, London, 1979. M. A. Coulson and D. S. Riddell, *Approaching Sociology: A Critical Approach*, Routledge and Kegan Paul, London, 1979. A. F. Davies, S. Encel and M. J. Berry (eds), *Australian Society: A Sociological Introduction*, Longman Cheshire, Melbourne, 1977. P. Berger and T. Luckman, *The Social Construction of Reality*, Penguin, Harmondsworth, 1971. T. Shibutani, 'Reference Groups as Perspectives', *American Journal of Sociology*, Vol. 60, May 1955, pp. 562–69. D. Edgar, *Introduction to Australian Society*, Prentice-Hall, Sydney, 1980. E. Hirschman, 'Cognitive Structure Across Consumer Ethnic Subcultures: A Comparative Analysis', *Advances in Consumer Research*, Vol. 10, 1983, pp. 679–90.

2. J. F. Sherry, 'The Cultural Perspective in Consumer Research', in R. J. Lutz (ed.), *Advances in Consumer Research*, No. 13, Association for Consumer Research, 1984, pp. 573–75. W. Henry, 'Cultural Values Do Correlate with Consumer Behaviour', *Journal of Marketing Research*, Vol. 13, May 1976, pp. 121–27.

3. L. Copeland, 'Foreign Markets: Not for the Amateur', *Business Marketing*, July 1984, p. 116. F. T. Haner and J. S. Ewing, *Country Risk Assessment*, Praeger, New York, 1985. S. Jain and L. R. Tucker, *International Marketing*, 2nd edn, Kent Publishing Co., Boston, 1986. V. Terpstra and R. Sarathy, *International Marketing*, 5th edn, The Dryden Press, Chicago, 1990.

4. C. Baldcock, *Australian Society and Social Change Theory*, Novak, Sydney, 1978. E. E. Edgar, *Social Change in Australia*, Cheshire, Melbourne, 1974.

5. P. Worsley, op. cit.

6. P. Worsley, op. cit. M. Sargent, *Sociology for Australians*, Longman Cheshire, Brisbane, 1983.

7. P. Hollingworth, *Australians in Poverty*, Nelson, Melbourne, 1980.

8. R. W. Connell, *Ruling Class, Ruling Culture*, Cambridge University Press, Cambridge, 1977. A. F. Davies, S. Encel and M. J. Berry (1977), op. cit. (see note 1). T. Jagtenberg and P. D'Alton, 'Four Dimensional Social Space', Harper and Row, Sydney, 1989. D. Edgar, *Introduction to Australian Society*, Prentice-Hall, Sydney, 1980. B. Graetz and I. McAllister, *Dimensions of Australian Society*, Macmillan Education Aust. Pty Ltd, 1988. T. Shibutani, op. cit. (see note 1).

9. D. W. Rook, 'The Ritual Dimension of Consumer Behaviour', *Journal of Consumer Research*, Dec. 1985, pp. 251–64.

10. T. Veblen, *The Theory of the Leisure Class*, Mentor Books, New American Library, New York, 1980 (1st published 1899).

11. D. W. Rook, op. cit.

12. G. McCracken, 'Culture and Consumption: A Theoretical Account of the Structure and Movement of the Cultural Meaning of Consumer Goods', *Journal of Consumer Research*, 13, June 1986, pp. 71–84.

13. T. Jagtenberg and P. D'Alton, op. cit. E. E. Edgar, *Social Change in Australia*, Cheshire, Melbourne, 1974. H. Mackay, *The Mackay Report: Contemporary Social Issues*, Mackay Research Pty Ltd, Sydney, 1986. H. Mackay, *The Mackay Report: Being Australian*, Mackay Research Pty Ltd, Sydney, 1988. L. Winton and L. West, *Survey of Consumer Opinion in Australia*, Australian Government Publishing Service, Canberra, 1987.

14. J. Clemenger, *Tomorrow's Parents — How Different Will They Be?*, John Clemenger NSW Pty Ltd, Sydney, 1978.

15. 'Happiness is a Good Job (and the Kids) — The Class of '72', *Sydney Morning Herald*, 27 April 1989, p. 17. 'Most Still Put Family First', *Sydney Morning Herald*, 17 March 1989, p. 6. 'A Return to Hearth and Hubby', *Sydney Morning Herald*, 10 Jan. 1989, p. 11.

16. B. Sweeny, 'She'll be Right No More', Brian Sweeney and Associates, Report commissioned by Mattingly and Partners, 1990.

17. 'The Caring, Sharing 90s', The *Age, Good Weekend*, 8 Aug. 1992.

18. H. Kendig and J. McCallum, *Greying Australia*, Australian Government Publishing Service, Canberra, 1986.

19. H. Mackay, *Reinventing Australia*, Angus and Robertson, Sydney, 1993.

20. 'Guess Which Brand is Back in the Whitegoods Market', *Business Review Weekly*, 22 Nov. 1992. 'How Parker Carved a Quality Niche', *Business Review Weekly*, 3 March 1989.

21. H. Mackay, *Reinventing Australia*, Angus and Robertson, Sydney, 1993.

22. H. Mackay, *Reinventing Australia*, Angus and Robertson, Sydney, 1993. H. Mackay, *The Mackay Report: Responding to the Consumer of the '90s*, Feb. 1991.

23. F. Popcorn, *The Popcorn Report*, Doubleday Currency, New York, 1991.

24. J. T. Plummer, 'Changing Values', *The Futurist*, Jan./Feb. 1989, pp. 22–24.

25. D. M. Stayman and R. Deshpande, 'Situational Ethnicity and Consumer Behaviour', *Journal of Consumer Research*, Vol. 16, No. 3, Dec. 1989, pp. 361–71. W. Henry, 'Cultural Values Do Correlate with Consumer Behaviour', *Journal of Marketing Research*, Vol. 13, May 1976, pp. 121–27. E. Hirschman, 'Cognitive Structure Across Consumer Ethnic Subcultures: A Comparative Analysis', *Advances in Consumer Research*, Vol. 10, 1983, pp. 679–90.

26. D. O. Arnold, *The Sociology of Subcultures*, Glendasary Press, Berkley, Calif., 1970.

27. R. T. Reynolds, B. Robey and C. Russell, 'Demographics of the 1980s', *American Demographics*, 2 Jan. 1980, pp. 11–19. R. W. Connell, *Ruling Class, Ruling Culture*, Cambridge University Press, Cambridge, 1977. A. F. Davies, S. Encel and M. J. Berry (1977), op. cit. (see note 1). T. Jagtenberg and P. D'Alton, *Four Dimensional Social Space*, Harper and Row, Sydney, 1989.

28. A. Giddens, *The Class Structure of the Advanced Societies*, Hutchinson, London, 1973. P. Hollingworth, *Australians in Poverty*, Nelson, Melbourne, 1980.

29. J. Burnett and A. Bush, 'Profiling the Yuppies', *Journal of Advertising Research*, April/May 1986, pp. 61–69.

30. J. Burnett and A. Bush, ibid.

31. 'Yuppie Spending Gets Serious', *Fortune*, 27 March 1989, p. 10. 'The Age of the Yuppie Draws to a Close', *Australian Financial Review*, 28 July 1988, p. 16. 'US Agency Ditches the Yuppie', *Sydney Morning Herald*, 10 March 1988, p. 3.

32. H. Mackay, 'The Mackay Report: Young Australians' in 'Teens Today', *The Bulletin*, 19 Dec. 1989. McCann Report, 'Young People in Australia', in 'Teens Today', *The Bulletin*, 19 Dec. 1989.

33. C. Gray, et al., *Literature Review of Studies of Youth Views and Attitudes*, Australian Government Publishing Service, Canberra, 1974. 'Today's Youth Value Independence', *Sydney Morning Herald*, 9 May 1989, p. 4.

34. N. Shoebridge, 'Wooing the Teens: The Old Rules No Longer Apply', *Business Review Weekly*, 10 July 1992, p. 81.

35. R. Eckersley, *Casualties of Change: The Predicament of Youth In Australia*, Australian Government Publishing Service, Canberra, 1988. J. Clemenger, 'Silent Majority is Australia's Greatest Worry — the Drug Menace', *Sydney Morning Herald*, 17 July 1989, p. 8.

36. W. Henry, 'Cultural Values do Correlate with Consumer Behaviour', *Journal of Marketing Research*, Vol. 13, May 1976. E. Hurschman, 'Cognitive Structure Across Consumer Ethnic Subcultures: A Comparative Analysis', *Advances in Consumer Behaviour*, Vol. 10, 1983. R. T. Reynolds, B. Robey and C. Russell, 'Demographics of the 1980s', *American Demographics*, 2 Jan. 1980, pp. 11–19.

37. 'Niche Marketing', *Marketing*, June 1992, pp. 16–19. A. O'Mally, 'The Gay Nineties', *The Marketer*, 1990, p. 12. V. Miller, 'Gays are Affluent but Often Overlooked Market', *Marketing News*, 24 Dec. 1990, No. 2, p. 2. R. Weekes, 'Gay Dollars', *American Demographics*, 10 Oct. 1989, pp. 10–12.

38. K. Pearson, *Surfing Subcultures of Australia and New Zealand*, University of Queensland Press, Brisbane, 1977.

39. H. Mackay, *Reinventing Australia*, Angus and Robertson, Sydney, 1993. H. Mackay, *The Mackay Report: Responding to the Consumer of the '90s*, Feb. 1991.

40. H. Mackay, ibid.

41. A. Borowski and J. Shu, *Australian Population Trends and Prospects*, Australian Government Publishing Service, Canberra, 1991. K. Edwards, 'All Ye Faithful', *Time Australia*, 25 Nov. 1991. Australian Bureau of Statistics, 'Census Characteristics of Australia', *1991 Census of Population and Housing*, ABS Catalogue No. 2710.

42. Australian Bureau of Statistics, 'Census Characteristics of Australia', *1991 Census of Population and Housing*, ABS Catalogue No. 2710.

43. R. W. Connell, *Ruling Class, Ruling Culture*, Cambridge University Press, Cambridge, 1977. A. F. Davies, S. Encels and M. J. Berry, 1977, op. cit. (see note 1). J. Jagtenberg and P. D'Alton, *Four Dimensional Social Space*, Harper and Row, Sydney, 1989. D. Edgar, *Introduction to Australian Society*, Prentice-Hall, Sydney, 1980. B. Graetz and I. McAllister, *Dimensions of Australian Society*, Macmillan Education Aust. Pty Ltd, 1988. R. Bennet, *Australian Society and Government*, M. M. and B. Book Company, Sydney, 1987.

44. G. Harrison, 'Marketing to a Multicultural Society', *Marketing*, June 1990, pp. 22–23. A. Grasby, 'The Facts Have Been Distorted and Australian Marketing Needs a New Brief', Rydges, in *Marketing*, Symposium No. 16, 1981. K. Tolhurst, 'Consign the Management to the Mists of Antiquity and Start All Over', Rydges, in *Marketing*, Symposium No. 16, Sept. 1981, pp. 20–29. P. Totaro, 'The Times are Right, We are Becoming a Gourmet Race', Rydges, in *Marketing*, Symposium No. 16, Sept. 1981, pp. 20–29.

45. D. Johns, 'New Markets Hidden in Ethnic Neighbourhoods', *Marketing*, Sept. 1990, pp. 7–9.

46. F. T. Haner and J. S. Ewing, *Country Risk Assessment*, Praeger, New York, 1985. S. Jain and L. R. Tucker, *International Marketing*, 2nd edn, Kent Publishing Co., Boston, 1986. V. Terpstra and R. Sarathy, *International Marketing*, 5th edn, The Dryden Press, Chicago, 1990.

47. W. J. Keegan, 'A Conceptual Framework for Multinational Marketing', in S. Jain and L. R. Tucker (eds), *International Marketing*, 2nd edn, Kent Publishing Co., Boston, 1986.

48. D. A. Ricks, 'How to Avoid Business Blunders Abroad', in S. Jain and L. R. Tucker (eds), *International Marketing*, 2nd edn, Kent Publishing Co., Boston, 1986. R. Hartley, *Marketing Mistakes*, 5th edn, John Wiley and Sons, 1993.

49. A. Stern, 'Making it in Japan', Adweek's *Marketing Week*, 12 Dec. 1988. D. A. Ricks, *Big Business Blunders*, Dow Jones–Irwin, Homewood, Ill., 1983.

50. P. Bell and R. Bell, *Implicated: The United States in Australia*, Oxford University Press, 1993.

51. P. Bell and R. Bell, *Implicated: The United States in Australia*, Oxford University Press, 1993. R. Bennett, *An Introduction to Australian Society*, Turton and Armstrong, Melbourne, 1977. D. Edgar, ibid. D. Henderson and R. Smart, 'A Fair Go for All Australians', *American/Australian Interactions*, 1991. 'The Australian — Happy, Sober and The Devil May Care', *Sydney Morning Herald*, 10 Aug. 1984, p. 3. 'One Step Back and to the Right', *Reak Research*, 1988. H. Mackay, *Being Australian*, Mackay Research, 1988. 'The New Conservatism', Lyndall Crisp, *The Bulletin*, 28 June 1988.

52. J. Carmen and R. March, 'How Important for Marketing are Cultural Differences Between Similar Nations', *Australian Marketing Researcher*, Vol. 3, 1979, pp. 5–20.

53. D. Henderson and R. Smart, 'A Fair Go for All Australians', *American/Australian Interactions*, 1991. 'Why American Culture Just Won't Translate', *B&T*, 23 Aug. 1991.

54. Neil Shoebridge, 'Why Advertisers Won't Name Names', *Business Review Weekly*, 9 Aug. 1991.

PART 3

CONSUMER
DECISION MAKING

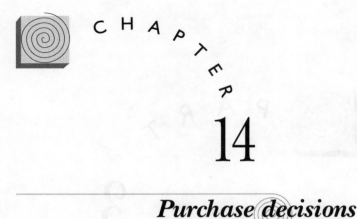

CHAPTER

14

Purchase decisions

OBJECTIVES

This chapter should help you to:

- understand some aspects of the decision process
- understand what causes problem recognition
- know what situations will cause consumers to engage in extensive search
- know how consumers evaluate information.

 PRODUCT ACQUISITION

There are many ways in which individuals can acquire goods and services. They can borrow, find or steal them; they can receive them as gifts. Within the area of consumer behaviour, the acquisition process has been studied from the perspective of marketplace transactions. In these transactions, goods and services are acquired through some form of payment, either directly or indirectly, as a service provided through taxes.

The purchase process starts when a consumer realises that he or she wants 'something'. This 'something' can be an object, service or experience, or a mixture of all three. The reasons that we as consumers want things are many and complex. Some explanations can be found in the fact that Australia, along with other Western nations, developed a 'culture of consumption' during the nineteenth century. Mass production and increased spending power provided the base for mass consumption, but consumption became an acceptable and valued activity because:[1]

> **"** People (or some very substantial segment of the population) began to consume at a level substantially above crude subsistence.
>
> People obtained goods and services for consumption through exchange rather than self-production.
>
> People tend to judge others and perhaps themselves in terms of their consuming lifestyles. **"**

According to Stanley Hollander and Kathleen Rassuli, historical records show that Neanderthals' possessions (such as tools, daggers, bracelets and rings) were buried with them.[2] Work by Mary Douglas and Baron Isherwood shows that ownership of goods (particularly those of adornment and status, such as hunting and cooking implements) was also prevalent in early societies.[3] Therefore, owning and using objects, either natural or manufactured, seems intrinsic to the human condition. As we saw in chapter six, humans have inherent needs that must be satisfied if the individual is to survive and develop into a fully functional person.[4] Obtaining food, medicine, housing, clothes, insurance and status goods is one way to satisfy these needs.

The realisation that he or she wants to buy something is the first step in what may be a simple or a complex series of decisions for the consumer. During a shopping trip, a person may see that a kiosk is selling Tangy Lime sorbet. She may, on impulse, decide to try the sorbet, so a purchase is made and the sorbet consumed. In this purchase situation, acquisition is fast and simple. But consider the purchase of a pair of spectacles. Even if the consumer already wears spectacles, he must usually visit his optician or ophthalmic surgeon to have his eyes tested and a prescription prepared. Frames then have to be selected and the glasses made. The manufacture can take two hours or two weeks depending on the prescription, and the purchaser has a product that he is likely to use for many years.

 THE PURCHASING PROCESS

Whether the purchasing process takes minutes or months, consumers make decisions about:
- what to buy
- when to buy
- where to buy
- how to buy.

What to buy is a key decision and unless it is made, the purchasing process stops. For example, the purchase of a car can only take place if the consumer decides to purchase a car. If there is a range of models to choose from, a suitable make and model must be decided on. Evaluating and deciding between the attributes of each model is complex, but must be done so that the 'what' to buy can be effectively decided.

Decisions as to where one purchases a product and how one pays for it must also be made. In most cases, distribution logistics will prescribe where the exchange takes place. Most consumer market products are bought through retail outlets, but services and industrial goods are obtained direct from the manufacturer or wholesaler. Moreover, an increasing number of consumer market goods are purchased direct from the manufacturer and home-based shopping is increasing.[5] In general, the medium of exchange in the Australian marketplace is money, although there are instances where barter occurs.[6] Money-based payment can be made in cash, by bank transfer, cheque or by credit card at the time of delivery or prior to delivery. The full price may be paid at point of transfer or partial payment can be made through a hire-purchase agreement or lay-by system.[7]

Often, payment terms can be used as an incentive to buy a product from a particular place. The offer of a delayed payment scheme to a consumer who wants a new lounge suite could influence the consumer to select a specific brand and style of lounge that he or she may not have purchased without the incentive.

How consumers arrive at and make these decisions is an important area of study in consumer behaviour and there is an extensive body of knowledge on the subject.[8] The most accepted way to regard the various aspects of purchase is as a series of decision phases.[9] The four key phases are:

- **Problem recognition**. This occurs when a consumer perceives that there is a difference between a desired state and an actual state. Unless this phase occurs, the consumer will not move through the subsequent phases.
- **Information search and evaluation**. Consumers can rely on stored information (internal search) or can gather additional information (external search) about products. If there are several alternative products, the consumers usually have to evaluate the options before making a choice.
- **Purchase**. The consumer decides on and acquires a product.
- **Post-purchase outcomes**. This is the behaviour that occurs after purchase, and includes satisfaction, dissatisfaction, product use and disposal.

The time between problem recognition and purchase can vary from seconds to years. Consumers can engage in limited or extensive information search and evaluation. The process can be interrupted and possibly stopped for a range of reasons. For example, a consumer could have decided that she wanted to buy a car, gathered information about all the models in her price range, compared the attributes of each car and made a selection. Just as she is about to make the purchase, a much sought-after overseas position is offered to her. The purchase process would halt while the offer is being considered and cease if the overseas position is accepted. The net effect of this is that the consumer has built up a knowledge base that will affect her next car purchase.

The diagram in figure 1.4 (page 13) shows the main factors that influence behaviour during purchase. Consumers bring to every purchase situation the sum total of their life experiences and their innate talents and capabilities. This is represented in the diagram by the psychological set. Consumers' psychological sets interact with their current or desired lifestyle and mood state, and drive purchase behaviour.

Some of these influences have been well researched, so the mechanics involved are known and understood. For example, situational factors such as store layout, merchandise displays and the behaviour of sales staff affect sales. Disinterested sales staff and stock-outs can cause consumers not to purchase or to buy another brand. But a pleasant atmosphere and point-of-sale promotions facilitate purchases and can cause consumers to make unplanned purchases.[10]

A consumer's affective state is a primary motivator of behaviour, and can have a direct and powerful influence on behaviour that is not captured by cognitive judgements.[11] 'Affect' is commonly defined as a subjective feeling that accompanies emotion and moods and the term is used to describe both emotion and mood states.[12] 'Emotion' is used to describe intense feelings that can generally be linked to a specific behaviour or event. Mood states are less intense and it is possible not to be consciously aware of one's mood and its effects. Mood may influence our attention level and behaviour, but only rarely will it interrupt the latter.[13]

Logic is only a small part in a buyer's decision to favour one product over another. In 1976, a study conducted at Harvard University showed that 80 per cent of managers' individual purchase decisions were determined by the right brain and only 20 per cent by the left brain.[14] Since the right brain is believed to house our creative, emotive facets, the implication is that emotions have a powerful impact on our choices. Morris Holbrook and others have pointed out that wants emerge and product choices are made through the interaction of reason (cognitions) and emotion (feelings). Reason and emotion interact continuously and are so closely interwoven that it seems foolish to even try and separate them.[15] Although emotions (mood states) affect consumers' responses to marketing activities such as advertising, search activities and product evaluation, how they do this is not well understood.

Essentially, consumer behaviour is a continuing activity. We are continually taking in and storing marketplace information. We use products constantly and in all facets of our lives. Few people do not purchase something in a single week and many consumers buy something daily. To understand how consumers purchase products, buying behaviour has been studied from the perspective of single transactions that are assumed to move through the four phases described above: problem recognition, information search and evaluation, choice and post-purchase outcomes. Movement through the phases can vary in terms of time and effort. In this chapter we examine the first three phases, purchase outcomes being covered in chapter 15.

PROBLEM RECOGNITION

Problem recognition occurs when a consumer perceives a difference between an actual and a desired state. Although the word 'problem' is widely used by writers, 'action' recognition is probably a better descriptor as the word 'problem' implies some difficulty or challenge. Many purchases are neither difficult nor challenging, but all require some action on the part of the consumer.

Problem recognition is triggered by the situation combined with the consumer's perception of the situation. Many situations can trigger a purchase, but the most common situations can be classified as:

- replacement, repair and maintenance
- changed circumstance
- marketing activities.

Replacement, repair and maintenance

Replacement is probably the most common trigger of all consumer purchases of goods. Consumption, damage, theft and wear will cause a consumer to purchase products. They may not, of course, purchase the same product, form or brand, but consumers will generally attempt to replace the product with one that has the same or similar features. Ensuring that something remains in a specific state may require the purchase of goods and services such as paint, hairdressers, plumbers, gardeners, house cleaners and the like.

Changed circumstances

Changes in lifestyle caused by events such as marriage, parenthood, illness or work will lead to new wants emerging. In fact, almost any alteration in our lives can activate the purchase process. Changes in our financial situation may cause us to reduce or increase spending. A decrease in finances may cause us to repair and maintain products and cut down on unnecessary purchases. An increase in finance can increase the possibility of wishes being met and a new range of wants emerging.

Buying certain products can trigger the purchase of other products. The purchase of a bed means that mattresses and sheets must be bought. The purchase of wall-to-wall carpet means that a vacuum cleaner will be required and the purchase of a computer means that software must also be purchased.

Because fashion, tastes and our preferences change, we will often become dissatisfied with some products even though there is no need to replace them. Products such as furniture, furnishings and clothes are particularly vulnerable. Consumers can become bored with products, causing them to stop buying the product category altogether.

Marketing efforts

Advertising, sales promotion, innovations and product modifications can change consumers' wants. Consumers' problems can be identified and they can be alerted to possible problems by advertising. If the product offers a solution, it will be considered and perhaps purchased.

Innovations and product modifications can create more efficient products, causing consumers to become dissatisfied with their current products. For example, computers have improved significantly since the 1970s, so that a 286sx processor is now outdated and many programs require 486sx processors.

The main task for management is to monitor any major developments that could create a demand for products that solve problems, as the lycra swimming vest helped solve the problem of cutting down exposure to the sun. Management should also try to identify the product attributes that satisfy consumers and those that do not.

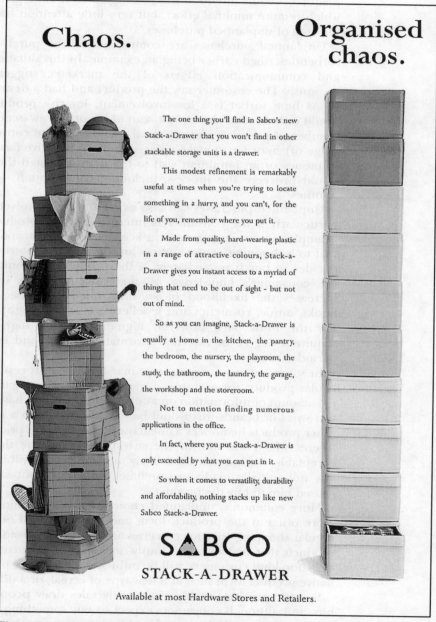

Chaos.

Organised chaos.

The one thing you'll find in Sabco's new Stack-a-Drawer that you won't find in other stackable storage units is a drawer.

This modest refinement is remarkably useful at times when you're trying to locate something in a hurry, and you can't, for the life of you, remember where you put it.

Made from quality, hard-wearing plastic in a range of attractive colours, Stack-a-Drawer gives you instant access to a myriad of things that need to be out of sight - but not out of mind.

So as you can imagine, Stack-a-Drawer is equally at home in the kitchen, the pantry, the bedroom, the nursery, the playroom, the study, the bathroom, the laundry, the garage, the workshop and the storeroom.

Not to mention finding numerous applications in the office.

In fact, where you put Stack-a-Drawer is only exceeded by what you can put in it.

So when it comes to versatility, durability and affordability, nothing stacks up like new Sabco Stack-a-Drawer.

SABCO

STACK-A-DRAWER

Available at most Hardware Stores and Retailers.

Figure 14.1: The message in this advertisement identifies the problem and describes how the product will help to solve it.

INFORMATION SEARCH, EVALUATION AND CHOICE

A major part of the decision process model is understanding how consumers gather and store information and how they use it to evaluate and select products. Much of the research in this area has focused on high-involvement or high-risk purchase situations where purchases are planned.[16] Some attention has been given to routine planned purchases, which require minimal effort, but very little attention has been given to the area of unplanned purchases.[17]

Unplanned purchases are commonplace, the purchase of the lime sorbet described earlier being an example. In this situation the exposure and communication efforts of the marketer triggered an instant response. The customer saw the product and had a desire to experience it. As lime sorbet is a low-involvement, low-risk product, a consumer would only need to do a quick scan of his or her awareness set (the total number of products and potential brands that the consumer has knowledge of) in order to make a decision. If no negative factors such as lack of money or an imminent visit to the dentist existed then the purchase would proceed; the process, including consumption, would take only minutes.

Unplanned purchases can also occur for high-involvement purchases, particularly if the consumer is interested in the product category. For example, a consumer may be a keen collector of teapots and during a visit to a shopping centre notices an unusual and interesting teapot and decides to buy it immediately. If the product is technically simple and the consumer's knowledge of alternative products is adequate, this increases the likelihood of an unplanned purchase. Clothes, shoes, books, music, cosmetics and jewellery are often bought in this manner. For the most part, however, high-involvement, high-risk goods will require a degree of external information search and evaluation over a period of time.

In some instances, a consumer may be in the process of buying a particular product, for example, a freezer. He may have gathered a substantial amount of information on available products and have selected one or two styles or brands that would be suitable. While on a shopping trip for other products he notices a one-day only, 50 per cent price reduction on a freezer which was one of the styles and brands he thought would be acceptable. At that point it is likely that a purchase will be made. His trip was not initially made to purchase the freezer but situational factors caused him to buy the product.

More commonly, unplanned choices occur in routine purchases and more often at the product, form and brand levels. Consumers on their regular shopping trips for groceries are exposed to in-store promotions or products that they were previously unaware of. Many consumers, particularly non-loyal customers, will be influenced to try new products, an alternative product form such as a new type of cereal, or a different brand.

Specific activities such as half-yearly sales draw people into stores to buy, and although consumers expect to buy something, they go for bargains and so rarely have a clear idea of what actual products they will buy.

Types of risk

The level of risk or uncertainty in a purchase perceived by a consumer is subjective. A consumer's perception of risk is related to the level of uncertainty associated with the purchase. There are several different types of risk a consumer may associate with a product. If all are experienced in any one purchase it is a high-risk purchase. The types of risk that can occur in a purchase situation include:

- **Functional risk**. The risk that the product will not perform as expected: will the gas heater really heat 12 cubic metres and will the electronic ignition still be working in five years time?
- **Physical risk**. The risk that the product will not cause harm. Will the automatic cut-out on the electric lawn-mower work?
- **Financial risk**. The risk of financial hardship if the product does not work or if it loses value. Now that I have bought the new house will the property market drop in value?
- **Social risk**. The risk that poor choice will cause embarrassment or loss of status, such as a committed environmentalist buying a Ford Falcon GT.
- **Psychological risk**. The risk that the product will damage the consumer's self-image, such as an inappropriate hairstyle or outfit.

According to Ted Roselius, consumers reduce risk by:
- Buying well-known major brands
- Brand-loyal behaviour
- Using consumer advisory and testing services, such as the Australian Consumer Association
- Buying the brand offering the best warranties and guarantees
- Buying the most expensive brand
- Using free trial options when offered.

(*Source*: Adapted from J. Jacoby and L. Kaplan, 'The Components of Perceived Risk', in M. Venkatesan (ed.), *Proceedings of the Third Annual Conference of the Association for Consumer Research*, Association for Consumer Research, Chicago, 1972. T. Roselius, 'Consumer Rankings of Risk Reduction Methods', *Journal of Marketing*, vol. 35, Jan. 1971)

How much effort a consumer is willing to expend on gathering and evaluating information is thought to be a function of a number of factors, but generally consumers will expend:

- **Maximum effort** in a high-involvement, high-risk, infrequent purchase, usually in the form of extensive, external information search and careful evaluation of alternative products.
- **Medium effort** when a purchase is low risk but important and intermittent, or the consumer has no knowledge or limited knowledge about the product. The consumer will gather some information about a small range of products.
- **No effort** or **minimal effort** in routine purchases (that may have varying levels of involvement) or low-risk products. In these situations, consumers usually rely on product information stored in their long-term memory system.

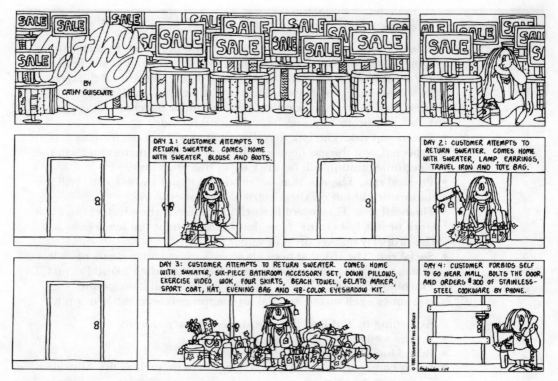

Figure 14.2: Sales are situational influences that can cause unplanned purchases.

Search

Consumers gain information about the marketplace and products in two ways: 'incidental' (ongoing) search and 'deliberate' (pre-purchase) search. All consumers engage in incidental search. Even when they are not planning a particular purchase they continually take in and store information about various aspects of the marketplace.

Figure 14.3: The act of browsing can provide consumers with a great deal of information.

Incidental search

Window shopping is a popular activity. Browsing through shopping centres and shops gives us a clear idea of what is on offer. So too does reading magazines, brochures and advertising material that comes through our letter boxes. After all, the key role of advertising is to provide consumers with information about products. This incidental search creates product awareness and knowledge and can be influential in creating an evoked set of products. An evoked set are those brands and products that consumers consider acceptable and which form the basis for choice.

Peter Bloch and his colleagues found that consumers who were interested in a product category engaged in ongoing, incidental search, and considered the activity fun. They were also heavy spenders within the product class.[18]

Because consumers talk about their purchases to their family and friends, other consumers are able to gather a considerable amount of product knowledge. This means that when consumers want to buy a similar product, not only is it possible for them to have stored product information, they also know 'who' has the relevant product knowledge.[19]

Direct search

All purchase situations involve direct search. Where the consumer is experienced (that is, has extensive product knowledge) and the purchase situation is routine and low risk, consumers are more likely to rely on stored information to make a choice. When consumers do not have enough information stored in their long-term memory, they will carry out an external search. External search is defined as the 'degree of attention, perception and effort directed towards obtaining environmental data or information related to the specific purchase under consideration'.[20]

There are several factors that will determine whether or not a consumer will engage in external search in a given purchase situation. These are listed in figure 14.4.[21]

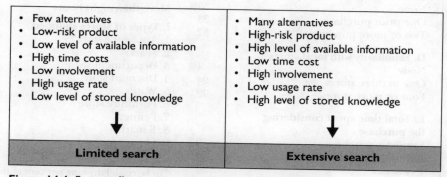

Figure 14.4: Factors affecting the extent of an external search

Consumers are more likely to compare alternatives if retail outlets are close to one another, and if travel between outlets and access by telephone is feasible. When consumers perceive a purchase has high risk factors they will engage in extensive search.[22] The common types of risk that consumers have to deal with were described on page 363. A purchase situation can involve some or all of these risk factors. The purchase of a dress or a suit, a hairstyle or a present for someone important will have high social and psychological risks but lower levels of technical, financial and safety risks. Consumers who are seeking a new hairdresser more often than not obtain recommendations from other customers, from experts such as beauticians and from articles in magazines.

How much search?

How much external search do consumers actually engage in? A study by Sharon Beatty and Scott Smith found that when purchasing a refrigerator, 42 per cent of respondents visited one store and 41 per cent considered one brand.[23] Jon Udell found that in the purchase of small appliances, 77 per cent of purchasers visited only one store.[24] A number of studies report similar behaviour, including Peter Dickson and William Wilkie's research, which shows some interesting findings, some of which are reproduced in table 14.1.[25]

Table 14.1: Summary of findings from the Dickson and Wilkie study of information search and shopping for durables

A. Purchase circumstances		F. Total number of stores visited	
Appliance failure	36%	One	37%
Replacement of working unit		Two	19
Needs some repair	24	Three	19
Working well	14	Four or more	25
Residential move	18	**G. Total number of brands considered**	
Other	8	One	32%
		Two	26
B. Who participated in the decision?		Three	26
Homemaker solely	29%	Four or more	16
Homemaker primarily	11		
Joint effort with spouse	52	**H. Total time spent shopping**	
Spouse primarily/solely	8	Less than two hours	45%
		Two to four hours	28
C. Previous purchase experience		Five to eight hours	14
None	35%	More than eight hours	14
One prior purchase	33		
Two or more purchases	32	**I. Types of stores shopped**	
		1. Appliance store[a]	59%
D. Familiarity with local stores		2. Sears	57
None	4%	3. Department store	27
One to three stores	24	4. Discount store	25
Four or more stores	72	5. Wards	18
		6. Furniture store	15
E. Total time spent considering the purchase		7. Penney	12
Same-day purchase	9%	8. K-mart	9
Within first week	24	9. Other type	13
1–4 weeks	33		
1–3 months	11		
3–6 months	11		
Over 6 months	13		

[a]To be read: Fifty-nine per cent of the purchasers shopped in at least one specialty appliance store during their decision process, while 57 per cent shopped at Sears, and so on.

J. Number of information sources used

1. Number of independent source types (friends and relatives, consumer reports):

Zero,	52%	Range	= 0 to 2 sources used
One,	37%	Mode	= 0 sources used
Two,	11%	Mean	= 0.58 sources used

2. Number of marketer source types (of the seven listed in part K, following):

Zero,	15%	Four,	6%	Range	= 0 to 7 sources used
One,	27%	Five,	5%	Mode	= 1 source used
Two,	25%	Six,	2%	Mean	= 2 sources used
Three,	19%	Seven,	—		

(*continued*)

K. Ratings of source usefulness

Information source	Buyers who consulted	Buyers who found source useful	Buyer's most used info source
1. Appliance salesperson[b]	59%	49%	41%
2. Newspaper ad	39	28	13
3. Friend or relative	38	31	13
4. Catalogue	35	28	9
5. Brochures/labels	28	25	9
6. Consumer reports	20	18	9
7. Appliance repairperson	14	10	5
8. Magazine ad	12	7	1
9. TV ad	10	5	1

[b]To be read: Fifty-nine per cent of the buyers reported having consulted a salesperson as an information source. Almost all of these people (49 per cent of the total sample) reported finding the salesperson to be a 'useful' source of information. When asked which source had been the 'most useful', 41 per cent of consumers reported that the salesperson had been.

L. Consumer's search interests

(Forced choice: pick one or the other) I was most interested in learning:

- As much as possible about the appliance. 69%
- vs.
- Just enough to make a choice. 31%

(Forced choice) I was most interested in:

- Enjoying the search ... because it was interesting. 32%
- vs.
- Spending as little time as possible. 68%

M. Consumer's search strategies

(Forced choice) During my decision process I primarily relied on:

- Past experience and knowledge. 69%
- vs.
- New information from search. 31%

(Forced choice) During my decision process I primarily relied on:

- Past experience and knowledge. 68%
- vs.
- Knowledgeable others' advice. 32%

N. Where purchased

Store type	Share of market	Bought on sale	Negotiated lower price	Bought at first store
Specialty appliance	37%	51%	28%	34%
Sears	30	89	4	46
Wards	9	92	8	22
Furniture	6	41	22	48
Discount	5	80	20	30
Department	4	69	13	38

O. Purchase behaviour

Bought at a special low price	76%
a. On sale	70%
b. Negotiated with salesperson	17%[c]
Brand loyalty	31%

P. Post-purchase satisfaction with new appliance

Very satisfied	71%
Satisfied	24
Neutral	3
Dissatisfied	2
Very dissatisfied	—

[c]Some consumers both bought on sale and negotiated a special low price; thus, the total exceeds 76 per cent.

(*Source*: W. Wilkie, *Consumer Behaviour*, John Wiley and Sons, NY, 1994. Adapted from P. Dickson and W. Wilkie, 'Consumer Information Search and Shopping Behaviour', in H. Kassargian and T. Robertson (eds), *Perspectives in Consumer Behaviour*, 4th edn, Prentice-Hall, Englewood Cliffs, NJ, 1991)

On the one hand, the majority of consumers report minimal use of information sources, yet 69 per cent stated that they relied on past experience and knowledge to make a choice. (The same percentage was interested in learning as much as possible about the appliance purchased.) Sixty-eight per cent did not want to waste time on the purchase and 76 per cent reported that they bought at a special low price. As brand loyalty (and this includes store loyalty) is a risk-reducing strategy used by consumers, it may be that the consumers in these studies bought during a sale period at 'trusted' outlets. An interesting aspect of this study is the number of respondents who relied on 'past experience and knowledge' yet report that they did not use external information sources. It may be that in these studies consumers are misreporting their behaviour. A study that observed actual behaviour found that consumers under-report the number of external sources used.[26] It is also possible that consumers are carrying out incidental searches, storing the knowledge and developing beliefs about a range of available products.

Factors such as experience, education, occupation, status and age have been found to influence search levels. Hans Thorelli and others,[27] in a cross-cultural study involving the United States, Norway and Germany, found that consumers who actively sought information were more likely to:

• have higher incomes
• be better educated
• be in professional occupations
• read more magazines and newspapers
• use consumer reports and independent agencies.

Other studies have found that:

• if consumers have only a few brands and limited information about all or some of the brands in the awareness set, then they are more likely to gather more information.
• as consumers become more knowledgeable about specific product categories then the amount of search decreases.
• as people grow older external search levels decrease.
• consumers with higher levels of education and in professional occupations expend the most effort, making use of independent assessors such as consumer reports.
• time constraints, transport, fatigue, boredom and information overload tend to reduce the amount of search carried out.[28]

Emotions and information search

A growing amount of research shows that emotions and mood states have a direct impact on how consumers obtain information and how much effort they are willing to make in order to gather and evaluate information. This is particularly so for non-technical, symbolic, intangible or aesthetic products.[29] Research has shown that:

• positive mood states help recall, create stronger belief formation and positive attitudes of both the product and the advertisement. Negative mood states have a negative effect on message product evaluation.[30]
• negative and positive feelings occur concurrently and both are important predictors of a message's effectiveness.[31]

- when compared to a sad program, a happy program created happier mood states which resulted in better understanding and recall. In general, commercials with a high emotional content are received more positively than informational commercials.[32]

According to David Zeitlin and Richard Westwood, emotions should be considered an integral and central aspect of a message.[33] They play three separate, interrelated roles.

- The emotion can be the benefit — a roller-coaster ride, rock concert, computer and video games.
- Emotional appeals can help to communicate the benefit — such as fun and excitement and the message 'things go better with Coke'.
- Emotions can influence attitudes to products. A positive emotional response to a message can create a positive attitude to a product.[34]

Consumers who are already in a positive mood state when they view advertisements are generally more receptive to the message, their recall being greater than that of consumers who were in a negative mood.[35] Although consumers' 'moods' are often affected by factors beyond a marketer's control, carefully crafted messages, friendly service and the general ambience of the sales environment can mitigate negative feelings and moods and maintain or increase positive feelings.

PRODUCT EVALUATION AND CHOICE

Consumers evaluate products even when there are no alternatives available in the marketplace. In the case of monopolies such as electricity, water and postal services, consumers may be unhappy with the product but, since there are no alternatives, must purchase them. Evaluation that directs choice can only occur when there are alternatives to choose from.

Most of the current knowledge and understanding of how consumers evaluate and choose products is based on the hierarchy of effects model.[36] This model assumes that consumers go through a series of stages when purchasing goods:

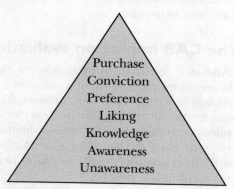

Purchase
Conviction
Preference
Liking
Knowledge
Awareness
Unawareness

Also known as the Cognitions-Affect-Behaviour (CAB) perspective, it is based on two assumptions. The first is that consumers develop cognitions (knowledge), which direct their affective responses (attitudes) to products, which in turn influence their behaviour. The second assumption is that the value consumers place on products is primarily functional. Functional, in this instance, is defined as the 'perceived benefit acquired from a product's capacity for utilitarian or physical performance'. The benefits are measured on a profile of product attributes such as reliability, durability, price and performance.[37]

The presumption is that consumers evaluate the functional attributes of products or brands on the basis of a number of choice criteria. To do this consumers must:

- establish the functional qualities they want from a particular product
- obtain information about the range of choices available
- select those products that have the desired qualities
- choose the product that provides the maximum benefit.

For example, someone buying a new phone may want to have portability within a certain distance, plus answering machine and memory capabilities. Telephones that have these characteristics and that are within the consumer's price range are selected for consideration. Other factors such as the number of messages on the tape, voice quality on the answer tape and on the phone will also be considered and compared before the consumer makes a choice.

Recently, the CAB perspective and particularly the assumption that consumers choose products only by evaluating their functional benefits have been questioned. These researchers suggest that a more useful understanding of why consumers choose specific products would be gained if a Consciousness-Emotion-Value (CEV) perspective was adopted and evaluative criteria expanded to include a range of non-functional values such as expressive, experiential and symbolic (social) values.[38]

The CAB perspective has had a profound influence on a range of marketing activities including product and communication strategy and planning; research topics, (attitude and multiattribute measurement); measurement techniques (multidimensional scaling and conjoint analysis) and choice modelling. For this reason an understanding of consumer evaluation strategies from this perspective is essential for students of consumer behaviour.

The CAB impact on evaluation and choice

CAB-based research shows that when faced with a range of products to choose from, the first thing a consumer does is create a cluster of brands (evoked set) that they can consider. The evoked set then becomes the basis for future choice. The process can either commence with consumers evaluating brands or with them evaluating attributes. Most decisions, however, are reached by processing attributes. Consumers who start with attribute evaluation usually switch to brand evaluation in the later stages of the evaluation process.[39]

When weighing up product attributes, consumers have been found to identify those criteria that are salient, as they will have a strong influence on choice. In some cases salient criteria may not feature as evaluative criteria. Safety is an important consideration in the purchase of non-prescription medicines or drugs, but because of the stringent testing by the Australian Standards Association, safety is assured and it would not feature as a differentiation factor. A criterion only becomes cognitively evaluative when it differs across products.

When an attribute is salient *and* differs across products consumers usually rank it as critical. Thus, in the purchase of a stove, critical attributes could be price, oven size and ease of cleaning; all the stoves considered will be judged on these base criteria.

The type and number of evaluative criteria can change over time and vary across products. A decade ago, key attributes of breakfast cereals would not have included low fat and sugar content. Low-involvement items such as grocery items, pantyhose and socks may have only two or three evaluative criteria, whereas high-risk products could have many. There is evidence that the number of attributes people normally evaluate is about six or seven.[40]

"No, not the food acid 260's, the anti-caking agent 551's"

Figure 14.5: Some consumers evaluate products on the basis of the additives they contain, i.e. they are key attributes in the evaluative process.

Decision rules

The CAB approach has influenced the study of how consumers make decisions. The assumption has been that consumers use specific strategies to reach decisions: these strategies are normally referred to as 'decision rules'. These decision rules, by creating some structure, can simplify the evaluation process. The two basic strategies that consumers can adopt are the compensatory and the non-compensatory approaches.

Compensatory approach

When consumers use the compensatory decision category, they evaluate each brand in terms of its attributes. Each attribute is valued or weighted in terms of its perceived importance. The attributes are then compared and trade-offs are made. A brand may be strong on three important attributes but weak on one, while another brand may be strong on three important attributes and weak on one — but not the same attributes.

Compensatory rules are commonly used when the number of brands is small and there is a large number of evaluative criteria. They are also used more often by highly educated people.[41]

The compensatory approach allows for favourable criteria to offset unfavourable criteria. If a brand is particularly strong on important attributes and weak on others, it will not matter. The brand is selected through an overall rating of attributes. Thus, in the purchase of a radio, where the weightings and evaluations are the same as those in table 14.2, Brand A will be the final selection.

Table 14.2: Compensatory approach: radio purchase

Criteria	Weighting (W)	Brand A Evaluation (E)	E × W	Brand B Evaluation (E)	E × W	Brand C Evaluation (E)	E × W
Price	3	10	30	8	24	5	15
Sound quality	3	8	24	9	27	9	27
Tape/CD attachment	2	4	8	6	12	7	14
Warranty	3	7	21	5	15	5	15
Style	2	7	14	7	14	7	14
			97		82		85

Weighting

1   2   3
Not important   Very important

Evaluation

10   9   8   7   6   5   4   3   2   1
Very good   Poor

Non-compensatory approach

The non-compensatory approach does not allow for weak attributes to be offset by strong ones. Food manufacturers know this. A key problem for Smiths when they attempted to launch their 'lite' crisps was the problem of taste. They wanted to produce a product that tasted like normal chips even though the salt and fat content were reduced.[42] It was important that any perceived change in taste would not be enough to negate the benefits of low salt and fat levels. Beer manufacturers had the same problem with the introduction of low alcohol beers in the 1970s.

There are at least three types of non-compensatory rules that consumers can adopt — the disjunctive, conjunctive and the lexicographic rules. The disjunctive and the conjunctive rules both use cut-offs to eliminate products from the evoked set. When consumers use the disjunctive rule they usually select the key aspects on the basis of the most important attributes, and eliminate the rest. The consumer also sets cut-off points. Consumers are thus setting minimum acceptable performance standards when they use the disjunctive rule. This is usually done on one or two attributes. In the purchase of a stove, if the 'sorting' was based on price and uprightness, Brand B would be selected as it is lower in price (table 14.3).

Table 14.3: Non-compensatory approach: kitchen stove purchase

	Brand A	Brand B	Brand C	Brand D	Acceptable level
Price	$1000	$650	$780	$900	$600–$800
Upright	Yes	Yes	Yes	Yes	Essential
Corian top	Yes	No	Yes	Yes	Essential
Good heat control	Yes	No	No	Yes	Desirable
Large oven	Yes	No	No	No	Desirable
Warranty	Yes	Yes	Yes	Yes	Minimum 1 year parts/labour
Warming drawer	Yes	No	Yes	No	Desirable
Colour/style	Yes	No	Yes	Yes	Black preferred

Level of importance of attributes

Price	1	Corian top	3	Large oven	5	Warming drawer	7
Upright	2	Good heat control	4	Warranty	6	Colour/style	8

The lexicographic rule operates as a series of eliminations. The brands are first compared across the main attribute and all the brands that meet the criteria are selected. The next important attribute is then compared and the brands which meet that criteria are selected, and so on until one brand remains. In our example of the cooker, on the first and second sorting Brand B and C would be selected, but on the third sorting Brand C would be selected because Brand B does not have a Corian top.

When consumers use the conjunctive rule they again use cut-offs. They do not identify key attributes but set cut-offs for each attribute, not just the most important ones. Therefore, the brand selected must meet all the cut-off points and this time Brand C in table 14.3 would be selected.

Information overload

Although consumers apply these decision rules either singly or in combination there is evidence that consumers do not use all the available information when forming decisions. Jacob Jacoby and his colleagues carried out an experiment to examine how consumers used nutrition information. The subjects were permitted to gather as much information about each brand of cereal, margarine and other food products as they liked. The information was easily accessible and included information on nutrition. The results showed that the subjects collected limited information over a small range of products and based their decisions on price, packet size and brand, ignoring the nutrition information.[43]

There are at least two possible reasons why the nutrition information was not used by the respondents. Either the information given was meaningless or too complex, or there was too much information provided. For example, consumers may not be able to understand what the following facts mean and therefore they do not use them to select a product.

Energy	455/108 cal
Protein	3.9 g
Fat	0.8 g
Carbohydrate	21.1 g
Sodium	720 mg

On the other hand, the following chart from a breakfast cereal pack is easy to understand. (See also an example of this on the 'Trim Soup' packet on page 211.)

High in complex carbohydrates	✓	Good source of vitamins	✓
Low in fat	✓	Good source of iron	✓
Low in salt	✓	High in fibre	✓
No cholesterol	✓	No artificial colours	✓
No preservatives	✓	No artificial flavours	✓

Other research shows that information overload can have a detrimental impact on a consumer's capacity to use information, particularly when consumers also perceive time constraints. In another study, Jacoby found that a moderate amount of information helps consumers make accurate choices, but that low and high levels of information had a negative impact on accuracy.[44] This means that marketers can help consumer decision making by providing clear, understandable, relevant information.

The CEV impact on evaluation and choice

The CEV perspective is an emerging area of thought and research that takes a broader view of consumer behaviour than the CAB approach. The emphasis is on consuming rather than on buying. As such, it represents a more holistic approach to the study of consumer behaviour, in that the purchase decision is only a 'small component in the constellation of events involved in the overall consumption experience'.[45] This perspective has had at least three significant effects on the conceptualisation and study of consumer decisions. One is the realisation that consumer evaluations of choices and of the benefits obtained from products continue after purchase. Another is the focus on the experiential aspects of purchase and consumption. This includes understanding what is being consumed during visits to art galleries and museums, or while listening to music and reading a book, as well as understanding the attachment and importance given to objects such as heirlooms and collectables. A third effect, and possibly the most important, is the realisation that consumers not only evaluate and choose products on the basis of their utilitarian benefits but also for their expressive and experiential benefits. Expressive benefits are those associated with the product's capacity to communicate aspects of the self (social image and personal values), group membership and status. Experiential benefits are benefits associated with the product's capacity to satisfy novelty, knowledge and creativity, and to create emotional arousal such as fun, excitement, joy and fear.

Jagdish Sheth, Bruce Newman and Barbara Gross have suggested five consumption values that form the basis of consumer preferences.

- **Functional value:** The perceived utility acquired from a product's capacity for functional, utilitarian and physical performance. A product acquires functional values through the possession of salient functional, utilitarian or physical attributes. Functional value is measured on a profile of choice attributes.
- **Social value:** The perceived utility acquired from a product's association with one or more specific social groups. A product acquires social value through association with positively or negatively stereotyped demographic, socioeconomic and cultural–ethnic groups. Social value is measured on a profile of choice imagery.
- **Emotional value:** The perceived utility acquired from a product's capacity to arouse feelings or mood states. A product acquires emotional value when associated with specific feelings or when precipitating or perpetuating those feelings. Emotional value is measured on a profile of feelings associated with the product.
- **Epistemic value:** The perceived utility acquired from a product's capacity to arouse curiosity, provide novelty and/or satisfy a desire for knowledge. Epistemic value is measured through direct questions about experiences.
- **Conditional value:** The perceived utility acquired through a product as the result of a specific situation or set of circumstances facing the choice maker. A product acquires conditional value in the presence of an antecedent physical or social contingency that enhances its functional or social value. Conditional value is measured on a profile of choice circumstances.[46]

These five consumption values can be condensed into three basic benefit categories:

- functional
- expressive (incorporating social and conditional values)
- experiential (incorporating epistemic and emotional values).

Although not directly associated with the CEV perspective, 'Means–End' theory could be viewed as an attempt to link expressive and experiential values to concrete product attributes. Jonathan Gutman sought to establish what consumers perceive to be a product's concrete attributes, trace the consequences that flow from these attributes and then build an understanding of which consequences are important in terms of the consumer's personal values. Using a laddering technique, he uncovered how consumers translate the attributes of a product into meaningful associations in terms of their underlying values. The product's attributes are the 'means' and the consequences derived from using the products are the 'ends'.[47]

In this way, values such as those by Lynn Kahle, listed below, may be achieved or maintained.

- Self-respect
- Security
- Sense of accomplishment
- Being well respected
- Warm relationships with others
- Self-fulfilment
- Sense of belonging
- Fun and enjoyment in life
- Excitement[48]

Since these values equate with the emotional, epistemic, and social consumption values described by Sheth, it may be that laddering and CEV are compatible.

According to Jonathan Gutman and Thomas Reynolds, marketers can more effectively differentiate their product from those of their competitors by conveying how the product's attributes can satisfy expressive and experiential values. The product can then be positioned to obtain optimum consumer motivation. This goal is not achieved by focusing on the product's attributes (the means) but by focusing on messages that allow the product to deliver the 'ends'.[49]

The CEV perspective has produced a considerable volume of speculative and sound theoretical discussion. There are, however, several issues, particularly those concerning the clarification of feelings, moods and emotions and their relationship with cognitions, that need to be resolved.[50]

JOINT DECISIONS AND MULTIPLE ROLES

In terms of absolute dollars and the volume of purchase transactions, purchases made by households and organisations are substantially more than those made by individuals. This means that the majority of purchase decisions are joint and involve more than one person. The purchase roles are listed on page 377. The first six are, in single decisions, carried out by an individual consumer; in households and organisations these roles are often carried out by different individuals.

Although households and organisations are different types of social units, much of their purchase behaviour is similar. The main differences between these purchasing units are listed below.

- The quantity of goods purchased. Organisations buy in large quantities.
- The type of goods purchased. Organisations buy more technical products, a limited variety of products and more customised products.
- Few suppliers. Organisations deal with few outlets, households with many.
- Interaction. Organisations are more likely to have direct, complex relationships that usually involve contractual agreements with their suppliers.
- Role allocation and management. Organisations are more likely to have formally allocated roles, often attached to a specific department — such as buyers and buying centres. Many organisations also have in place specific procedures for purchasing such as predetermined suppliers, set quantities and price.

Purchase roles

- **Initiator:** recognises that a problem situation exists and that a purchase must be made
- **Information gatherer:** brings together the information
- **Gatekeeper:** person who is able to control the information given to the evaluator or the decider, for example, a parent giving limited information to children
- **Evaluator:** sets the criteria for choice and examines the information about the product
- **Decider:** makes the final choice as to what, where and how the purchase is made
- **Purchaser:** carries out the actual transaction
- **User:** consumes or uses the product.

HOUSEHOLD PURCHASES

It is difficult to find out who makes decisions in households and how these decisions are reached. Family households, in particular, are not easy to study as they are private social groups. In addition, studying decision making is complex because researchers either have to carry out participant observation or rely on individual members' memory and perception of events. As we saw in chapter ten, families are very difficult to classify and we need to be aware that decisions in sole-parent families will differ from those made in two-parent households.

Within family households, certain members are often designated 'responsible' for certain roles and tasks but, equally, roles are often not fixed and may change from purchase to purchase. Grocery shopping is mainly carried out by adult females in a household although there is an increase in 'couples' and adult males shopping for groceries.[51] In 1978, Edward Bonfield found that husbands were more likely to search for information about lawn-mowers, household insurance and cars. Holidays were joint decisions and household groceries and furnishings were mainly the wife's responsibility.[52] Other studies carried out during the 1960s and 1970s in America tended to support these findings. Over the last two decades, the changes that have occurred in family structures — particularly the significant increase in dual-career families and the improved status of children, specifically teenagers — have affected these roles.[53]

A major reason for studying family decision making is to know who the product benefits and what benefits are expected. These are more easily identified in parent–child purchases where the child may want the fun of eating sweets, whereas the parent wants nutritious foods that will not damage teeth. Information about the taste, shape, colour and product-gifts (competitions, collectables and so on) is best directed at the child, while information about nutrition and price is best directed at the parent.

In the case of electronic equipment, furniture and other household durables, it can be difficult to identify which benefits appeal to which adult. Many advertisers adopt a policy of non-specific targeting. The advertisement in figure 14.6 shows two adults, but does not target any specific information to either. In general, this means that different marketing messages should be directed to different parts of the buying process. For example, products such as cereals are often purchased on a 'collective' basis. The child is often the initiator and user of the product, while the parent is the evaluator, decider and the purchaser.

How much luxury can you stand for less than $3.00 per week?

If you've always thought that running a spa pool would do permanent damage to your power bill, here's some great news from Hot Spring spas.

The cost of keeping a Hot Spring spa ready and waiting for you 24 hours a day, 7 days a week, is less than $3 a week!

SUPERIOR INSULATION

Not all spa pools are as cheap to run as Hot Spring spas, because other insulation systems simply aren't as effective.

The sides and base of a Hot Spring spa are totally encased in high density polyurethane foam. This means that even the plumbing pipes circulating the water are completely enclosed in insulation.

A Hot Spring spa needs only a small amount of energy to stay warm. It's ready when you are, and you'll enjoy your soak even more knowing how little you're spending.

LOW CHLORINE WATER TREATMENT

With a Hot Spring spa you won't have to sit in a haze of chlorine. New water treatment technology has reduced the need for chlorine by 50% and it's all thanks to ozone. Ozone is a powerful water purifier and is more effective than chlorine. A Hot Spring spa puts ozone to work, allowing you to enjoy clean, fresh water without any nasty fumes.

THE SAFETY FACTOR

Hot Spring Spas have just passed the new electrical safety standard set for Australia and New Zealand. They are the first and only spa pool manufacturer to have passed the new standard.

Every Hot Spring spa has a fully insulated, lockable cover. A key is required to open the cover so small children can't gain access.

THE ADVANTAGES OF PORTABILITY

Unlike the in-ground spas and hot tubs of the past, a Hot Spring spa is truly self-contained. It requires nothing more than a solid base to sit on and a 3-pin electrical socket to plug into.

The attractive redwood surrounds of a Hot Spring spa enclose all the plumbing, filtration equipment and insulation. With a little help from your friends, you can move a Hot Spring spa from a deck to a conservatory, or from one home to another.

A LUXURY YOU CAN AFFORD

In terms of initial outlay, Hot Spring spas aren't the cheapest spa pools on the market

but they are the best. In the long term, their low heating and maintenance costs make them particularly good value.

As you luxuriate in hot water with massage jets soothing and relaxing your tired muscles, you'll think that your Hot Spring spa is your best idea ever. Your family and friends will be certain to agree.

HotSpring *Portable Spas*

WHERE AUSTRALIA GOES TO RELAX

For further information, send this coupon to Hot Spring Spa Australasia Pty Ltd, 46 Nepean Highway, Mentone, Vic 3194, or phone toll free **008-677-877**

Name _____

Address _____

_____ Phone _____

AWW 4/94

Figure 14.6: This advertisement for HotSpring portable spas targets both adult decision makers.

Even though purchase roles vary across families, there are, however, generally two broad patterns of how decisions are made: consensual and accommodative. If the family members agree that they are going to build a swimming pool and agree that they would like an in-ground salt-water pool, then the decision pattern is consensual. If the family agree that they want to build a swimming pool but the mother wants a chlorine pool, the father does not want to have the expense of an in-ground pool and the two teenage children want a salt-water pool, then the pattern is likely to be an accommodative decision. This will create conflict that must be resolved if a purchase is to be made. To resolve conflict, family members can use persuasion or bargaining techniques to influence each other and thus made a decision.[54] Ultimately, agreement about what, how and when to purchase must be reached or the purchase will not take place.

ORGANISATIONAL DECISIONS

The term 'organisation' includes business, both private and public (such as Qantas); charities and other non-profit associations; and government organisations such as schools, hospitals, government offices and the military. Who makes what decision and how many individuals are involved depends on the type of purchase situation and what is being purchased.

A buying situation may be:

- Straight rebuy. These are routine and usually frequent purchases. As decision makers are familiar with the product and there may be a contractual agreement with suppliers, information search and evaluation would be minimal.
- Modified rebuy. Routine purchases where specifications and/or the suppliers are changed. Information search and evaluation levels would be higher than those of a straight rebuy.
- New buy. Since the item has not been published before, information search and evaluation will be extensive.[55]

The products purchased by organisations may be high or low risk, with functional, physical and financial risk being the most prevalent. Where the product is high risk, experts or specialists within the organisation may be given the task of collecting and evaluating information. If there are no experts inside the organisation, buying consultants may be employed. Some large organisations have buying centres where many of the day-to-day buying decisions are made. Smaller companies would normally allocate the task to a specific person.

Many organisations set up close relationships with their buyers and with their suppliers. The aim is to create relationships that go beyond single transactions, so that the purchaser, for example, obtains a range of other benefits that make it difficult to change to another seller. The outcome is that both parties would have high 'switching costs' if they were to leave the relationship and enter into marketplace exchanges with other organisations. The dynamics of the relationship, therefore, affect the buying decisions in each transaction, making it less likely that the purchaser will evaluate alternative sellers.[56]

SUMMARY

The acquisition process starts when consumers recognise that there is a discrepancy between their actual state and their desired state and decide to close the gap by buying a suitable product. Consumer decisions have been conceptualised as moving through four phases: problem recognition, information search and evaluation, choice, and outcomes. Different types of purchase situation affect the amount of effort customers will give to the purchase. Low-risk and/or low-involvement purchases usually require minimum effort while high-risk and/or high-involvement situations require considerable effort.

There are many factors that can cause consumers to move into a problem-recognition stage but the three most common situations are replacement, changed circumstances and the influence of marketing activities. The extent to which consumers will research other products and how carefully they will evaluate each product will depend on how they perceive the purchase situation. If the purchase is important to the consumer for reasons of risk and interest, he or she is more likely to engage in extensive search and in complex decision making. Complex decision making requires a consumer to create an initial list of possible brands. The consumer must also prepare a list of salient and desired attributes which are then matched against the attributes of each brand. By a series of matching and sorting techniques one brand is finally selected. During this process, consumers can use a compensatory or a non-compensatory approach. When consumers use a compensatory technique, they evaluate each brand in terms of its attributes and favourable criteria, which off-set unfavourable criteria. Each attribute is weighted and valued and the sum score of each brand is added to find the 'best' overall score. A non-compensatory approach uses a cut-off technique so that consumers are setting minimum acceptable performances on key attributes.

Until the 1980s consumer decision research and marketing strategy were almost wholly influenced by the Cognitions-Affect-Behaviour (CAB) perspective. This perspective assumes that consumers develop cognitions (knowledge) about products, which shape their affective response (attitude to the product) and ultimately direct their behaviour. It also assumes that the value customers place on products is primarily functional. To date most of the decision-making research, such as choice modelling, uses only physical, utilitarian attributes.

The CEV perspective is an emerging area of thought and research that focuses on the act of consuming, rather than on the purchase process. It thus represents a more holistic approach to the study of consumer behaviour, in that the purchase decision is only one part of the consumption process. This perspective, by legitimising the role of emotions on purchase decisions, has had a significant impact on how consumer decisions are conceptualised and studied. One such impact is the realisation that consumers not only evaluate and choose products on the basis of the product's utilitarian benefits but also for the product's expressive and experiential benefits. Expressive benefits are those that communicate aspects of the self (social image and personal values), group membership and status. Experiential benefits are those that satisfy novelty, knowledge, creativity and create emotional arousal such as fun, excitement, joy and fear.

The majority of purchase decisions involve more than one person. These are purchases made by households and organisations. Although there are similarities between household and organisation purchases, there are also differences. They are similar in that buying roles are allocated, some decisions are consensual, while others require individual members to accommodate the needs of others. Some differences are listed below.

- The quantity of goods purchased. Organisations buy in large quantities.
- The type of goods purchased. Organisations buy more technical products, a limited variety of products and more customised products.
- Few suppliers. Organisations deal with few outlets, households with many.
- Interaction. Organisations are more likely to have direct, complex relationships that usually involve contractual agreements with their suppliers.
- Role allocation and management. Organisations are more likely to have formally allocated roles.

A growing trend in organisational purchases is that they are forming 'close' relationships involving both contractual and informal agreements. The aim is to create 'switching' costs and to foster customer loyalty. An outcome of this tendency is that it will be more difficult for competitors to move in as purchasers are less likely to engage in external search.

 *Questions*

1. Select three products that you have recently purchased and identify the benefits, or values, that the products satisfy. Which values in each product were the most important? Why?

2. Monitor the routine purchases (products bought on a weekly or monthly basis) in your household for at least one month and identify the:
   - initiator
   - information gatherer
   - gatekeeper
   - evaluator
   - decider
   - purchaser
   - user.

   How were these roles determined? Do they ever change? Why do they change (or not change)?

3. Once you have identified the individuals who perform specific purchase roles in your household, find advertisements for a selection of the products and ascertain whether they reflect the roles accurately.

4. Discuss the limits of the CAB (Cognitions-Affect-Behaviour) perspective and the CEV (Consciousness-Emotion-Value) as approaches to the understanding of consumer purchasing behaviour.

5. Select a recent high-risk purchase or a current purchase (that is, you have not yet bought the product) and work out your selection using both the non-compensatory and compensatory approaches.

6. Discuss the differences between household and organisational purchases. Do you think the concept of relationship marketing is relevant to households?

7. There is some debate about whether information overload is a problem for marketers and consumers. Evaluate the pros and cons discussed in the literature.

8. Describe the means–end concept and discuss its relationship to the CEV approach to consumers' consumption behaviour.

9. Select three products that you would consider high-risk purchases and list the ways in which the marketer could help the consumer to reduce the risk level.

10. Discuss the concept of consumer involvement and show how marketers can
    (a) identify high involvement products
    (b) determine an appropriate communication message, that is, one that recognises involvement level and products purchased.

 Case study

Forget health and convenience. Taste will be the main theme in food marketing during the 1990s. After sacrificing taste and, at times, quality in the pursuit of healthy and convenient food during the 1980s, Australians are swinging back to taste. Health and convenience remain important ingredients for success in the food industry, but taste is king.

Food is the biggest and most volatile segment of the consumer goods industry. Food is Australia's biggest business, with the processed food industry turning over $30 billion a year, employing 16 per cent of the national workforce and generating 20 per cent of Australia's manufacturing sales. More new products are launched in the food industry each year than in any other industry. More advertising, research and promotional dollars are devoted to food than to any other product or service.

Food is also the most volatile sector of the marketing industry. Changes in the way Australians are thinking, feeling, shopping and consuming are first reflected in the food business.

Two of the most important social themes of the 1980s — the search for healthier lives and the "time bind" created by the increasingly frenetic pace of daily life and greater numbers of women entering the workforce — were clearly reflected in the food industry. Australians' search for healthy and convenient products during the 1980s fuelled strong sales of low-calorie food and beverages and fast-food products, and created new, robust markets such as muesli bars, frozen convenience meals and dried pasta-and-sauce mixtures. Low-calorie, low-salt, low-fat and low-sugar food dominated marketing in the late 1980s, while the rapid spread of microwave ovens boosted sales of food such as pre-prepared meals and frozen pizza.

Health and convenience remain important concerns for Australian food buyers, but they are no longer the main concern. "It would be suicidal to ignore health issues and the role of convenient products, but they are no longer at the cutting edge of food trends," says Ray Newell, regional planning director of the advertising agency Lintas, whose list of food clients includes EOI, Unifoods, Australian Pork Corporation and Streets Ice Cream. "These days, health is a given, a necessary part of being an acceptable food marketer in the 1990s. There is an element of boredom among consumers in terms of healthy food claims."

Last year, Newell spent two months studying food marketing trends in the US, working with various food researchers and groups such as the Food Marketing Institute in Chicago and New York's Centre for Advertising Studies, a worldwide information centre owned by Lintas's parent company, Interpublic. His findings have been interpreted for the Australian market in a report called *Food in the 1990s*. Newell's key conclusion is that taste is staging a dramatic comeback.

Newell predicts that herbs and spices, food flavourings, packet sauces and condiments will be the fastest-growing products in the food industry during the next few years. "People want to make healthy and convenient food more interesting. If manufacturers are unwilling to improve the taste of products, people will do it themselves," he says. "The practice of spicing up food will reach unprecedented heights during the 1990s."

Newell's findings are good news for companies such as Unilever, which sells a range of meal additives under the Continental brand name, and Mars Inc. Mars' MasterFoods herbs and spices division generated big sales in the 1980s with Dolmio and Kan-Tong sauces. Since the late 1980s, the company has expanded its product range, adding new lines such as Cuisine Essentials, a range of concentrated flavour bases, and Provincale, a spaghetti sauce that was test-marketed in Victoria and Tasmania and is being launched nationally this year.

Consumers' obsession with healthy foods has softened in recent years. Although fat contents remain a strong concern — fuelling strong sales of products such as Kraft Foods' Kraft Free salad dressing and Goodman Fielder Wattie's Gold'n Canola margarine — most of the fads of the 1980s have faded. People are interested in balanced diets and are increasingly sceptical about many of the health claims made for food products. The scepticism is a result of the claims and counter-claims made about the health benefits or dangers of foodstuffs such as sugar, red meat, bread and potatoes during the 1980s.

"People are reacting against the contradictory signals from food nutritionists and manufacturers," Newell says. "Australians have educated themselves about health issues and want balance. Their attitude is 'If I drink a can of Diet Coke, I can eat a chocolate biscuit'. It is all about trading off."

Business Review Weekly,
7 February 1992

Case study questions

1. Conduct a number of focus group interviews with your friends on the topic of food. Try to identify the functional, expressive and experiential values that they associate with:
   (a) food prepared and consumed at home
   (b) preprepared food purchased in supermarkets, butchers and delicatessens
   (c) restaurants, including fast-food outlets.

2. Record your results and discuss whether or not they accord with the observations and ideas described in the article above.

SUGGESTED READING

J. R. Bettman, *An Information Processing Theory of Consumer Choice*, Addison-Wesley, Reading, Mass. 1979.

H. Kassarjian and T. Robertson (eds), *Perspectives in Consumer Behaviour*, 4th edn, Prentice-Hall, Englewood Cliffs, NJ, 1991.

ENDNOTES

1. S. Hollander and K. Rassuli, 'Desire-induced, Innate, Insatiable: Historians' Views of Consumer Motivations and Behaviour in the 18th, 19th and 20th Centuries', Unpublished Working Paper, Department of Marketing and Transportation, Michigan State University, 1988.

2. Hollander and Rassuli, ibid.

3. M. Douglas and B. Isherwood, *The World of Goods*, Penguin Books Ltd, Harmondsworth, Middlesex, England, 1978.

4. A. H. Maslow, *Motivation and Personality*, 2nd ed., Harper and Row, New York, 1970.

5. N. Shoebridge, 'Shops of the Future', *Business Review Weekly*, 23 July 1993, pp. 36–39.

6. J. F. Sherry Jr, 'A Sociocultural Analysis of a Midwestern American Flea Market', *Journal of Consumer Research*, 17, June 1990. The barter system operates in Australia in the form of the Bartercard System. There is also a Barter Directory of Goods and Services.

7. In hire purchase, the customer pays a deposit and pays off an agreed price to the seller on a weekly or monthly basis. The consumer has immediate use of the goods. In the lay-by system, the seller holds the goods allowing the purchaser to pay the seller off gradually. The purchaser takes possession of the goods when the final payment is made.

8. F. Nicosia, *Consumer Decision Processes: Marketing and Advertising Implications*, Prentice-Hall, Englewood Cliffs, NJ, 1966. J. Howard and J. Sheth, *The Theory of Buyer Behaviour*, John Wiley and Sons, 1969.

9. D. Kollat and R. Blackwell, *Consumer Behaviour*, Holt, Rhinehart and Winston, New York, 1973. F. Hansen, *Consumer Choice Behaviour: A Cognitive Theory*, Free Press, New York, 1972. For a discussion on this process, see R. W. Olshavsky and D. H. Granbois, 'Consumer Decision Making — Fact or Fiction?', *Journal of Consumer Research*, Vol. 6, Sept. 1972, pp. 93–100.

10. P. Kotler, 'Atmospherics as a Marketing Tool', *Journal of Retailing*, 56, Winter 1974, pp. 48–63. R. Donovan and J. Rossiter, 'Store Atmosphere: An Environmental Psychology Approach', *Journal of Retailing*, 58, Spring 1982, pp. 34–57.

11. M. Holbrook, 'Emotions in the Consumer Experience', in R. A. Peterson et al. (eds), *The Role of Affect in Consumer Behaviour: Emerging Theories and Applications*, Heath, Lexington, Mass., 1986.

12. M. Gardner, 'Mood States and Consumer Behaviour: A Critical Review', *Journal of Consumer Research*, 12 Dec. 1985, pp. 281–300. P. Stout and J. D. Leckenby, 'The Nature of Emotional Response to Advertising: A Further Examination', *Journal of Advertising*, Vol. 17, 1988, pp. 53–57.

13. M. Clark and A. Isen, 'Toward Understanding the Relationship between Feeling States and Social Behaviour', in Leonard Berkowitz (ed.), *Cognitive Social Psychology*, Elsevier, North Holland, New York, 1982. A. Isen and B. Means, 'The Influence of Positive Affect on Decision Making Strategy', *Social Cognition*, 2, 1983, pp. 18–31. A. Isen and T. Shalker, 'The Effect of Feeling State on Evaluation of Positive, Neutral and Negative Stimuli', *Social Psychology Quarterly*, 45, 1982, pp. 58–63.

14. A. Konopacki, 'Emotionally Speaking Are You Selling to the Right Hemisphere', *Industrial Marketing*, Dec. 1982, pp. 14–17.

15. M. Holbrook, 'Emotions in the Consumer Experience', in R. A. Peterson et al. (eds), *The Role of Affect in Consumer Behaviour: Emerging Theories and Applications*, Heath, Lexington, Mass., 1986. M. Holbrook, J. O'Shaughnessy and S. Bell, 'Actions and Reactions in the Consumption Experience: The Complementary Roles of Reasons and Emotions in Consumer Behaviour', *Research in Consumer Behaviour*, Vol. 4, 1990, pp. 131–63. H. Mano, 'Emotional States and Decision Making', *Advances in Consumer Research*, 17, 1990, pp. 577–89. M. Clark and A. Isen, 1982, op. cit. (see note 13).

16. J. Mowen, 'Beyond Consumer Decision Making', *Journal of Consumer Marketing*, 5, 1988, pp. 15–25. R. Olshavsky and D. Granbois, 1979, ibid.

17. D. Rook, 'The Buying Impulse', *Journal of Consumer Research*, 14, Sept. 1987, pp. 189–99. J. Lastovicka, 'The Low Involvement Point of Purchase: A Case Study of Margarine Buyers', Paper presented to the Consumer Involvement Conference, No. 1, 1982. F. Piron, 'Defining Impulse Purchasing', in R. H. Holman and M. R. Solomon (eds), *Advances in Consumer Research*, Association for Consumer Research, Provo, Utah, 1982, pp. 509–14. C. J. Cobb and W. Hoyer, 'Planned Versus Impulse Purchase Behaviour', *Journal of Retailing*, Winter 1986, pp. 384–409.

18. P. Bloch and M. Richins, 'Shopping Without Purchase: An Investigation of Consumer Browsing Behaviour', in R. Bagozzi and A. Tybout (eds), *Advances in Consumer Research*, 10, Association for Consumer Research, Ann Arbor, Mich., 1983, pp. 389–93. P. Bloch, D. Sherrell and N. Ridgway, 'Consumer Search: An Extended Framework', *Journal of Consumer Research*, 13, June 1986, pp. 119–26.

19. A. Andreasen, 'Consumer Responses to Dissatisfaction in Loose Monopolies', *Journal of Consumer Research*, Vol. 12, Sept. 1985, pp. 122–35. Ralf L. Day, 'Research Perspectives on Consumer Complaining Behaviour', *Theoretical Developments in Marketing*, American Marketing Association, 1980. Ralph Day and S. B. Ash, *Consumer Responses to Dissatisfaction with Durable Products*, *Journal of Consumer Research*, Vol. 6, 1979. P. M. Herr, F. R. Kardes and J. Kim, 'Effects of Word of Mouth and Product Attribute Information on Persuasion: An Accessibility–Diagnosticity Perspective', *Journal of Consumer Research*, Vol. 17, March 1991, pp. 454–62. J. H. Holmes and J. D. Lett Jr, 'Product Sampling and Word of Mouth', *Journal of Advertising Research*, Vol. 17, 1977, pp. 35–40. M. Kiely, 'Word of Mouth Works', *Marketing Globe*, Vol. 3, No. 7, July 1993. M. Richins, 'Word of Mouth Communication as Negative Information', in Kinnear et al., *Advances in Consumer Research*, 1982, pp. 697–702. M. L. Richins, 'Negative Word of Mouth by Dissatisfied Customers: A Pilot Study', *Journal of Marketing*, Vol. 47, Winter 1983, pp. 68–78. TARP 1992: European Study of Consumer Complaints. TARP 1986: 'Consumer Complaint Handling in America: An Update Study', Office of Consumer Affairs, White House, Washington DC.

20. J. Engel, R. D. Blackwell and P. Miniard, *Consumer Behaviour*, 6th edn, Dryden, Chicago, 1990, pp. 513–14.

21. A. Goldman and J. Johansson, 'Determinants of Search for Lower Prices: An Empirical Assessment of the Economics of Information Theory', *Journal of Consumer Research*, 5, Dec. 1978, pp. 176–86. S. Beatty and S. Smith, 'External Search Effort: An Investigation Across Several Product Categories', *Journal of Consumer Research*, 14 June, 1987, p. 84.

22. K. Dedler, I. Gottschalk and K. G. Grunert, 'Perceived Risk as a Hint for Better Information and Better Products', in Kent Munroe (ed.), *Advances in Consumer Research*, 3, Association for Consumer Research, Ann Arbor, Mich., 1981, pp. 391–97.

23. S. Beatty and S. Smith, 'External Search Effort: An Investigation Across Several Product Categories', *Journal of Consumer Research*, 14, June 1987.

24. J. Udell, 'Prepurchase Behaviour of Buyers of Small Appliances', *Journal of Marketing*, 30, Oct. 1966, pp. 50–52.

25. P. Dickson and W. Wilkie, 'Consumer Information Search and Shopping Behaviour', in H. Kassargian and T. Robertson (eds), *Perspectives in Consumer Behaviour*, 4th edn, Prentice-Hall, Englewood Cliffs, NJ, 1991.

26. J. Newman and B. Lockeman, 'Measuring Prepurchase Information Seeking', *Journal of Consumer Research*, 2, 1975, pp. 216–22.

27. H. Thorelli, H. Becker and J. Engledow, *The Information Seekers*, Bollinger, Mass., 1975.

28. K. Dedler, I. Gottschalk and K. Grunert, 'Perceived Risk as a Hint for Better Information and Better Products', in K. Munroe (ed.), *Advances in Consumer Research*, 8, Association for Consumer Research, Ann Arbor, Mich., 1981, pp. 391–97.

29. M. Holbrook and R. Batra, 'Assessing the Role of Emotions as Mediators of Consumer Responses to Advertising', *Journal of Consumer Research*, 14, Dec. 1987, pp. 404–20. M. Gardner, 1985, op. cit. (see note 12). H. Mano, 1990, op. cit. (see note 15).

30. R. Batra and M. Ray, 'Affective Responses Mediating Acceptance of Advertising', *Journal of Consumer Research*, 13, 1986, pp. 234–49.

31. J. Edell and M. Burke, 'The Power of Feeling in Understanding Advertising Effects', *Journal of Consumer Research*, 14, Dec. 1987, pp. 421–33. P. Knowles, S. Grove and W. Burroughs, 'An Experimental Examination of Mood Effects on Retrieval and Evaluation of Advertisement and Brand Information', *Journal of the Academy of Marketing Science*, Vol. 21, 1993, pp. 42–50.

32. M. E. Goldberg and G. Gorn, 'Happy and Sad TV Programs: How They Affect Reactions to Commercials', *Journal of Consumer Research*, Vol. 14, Dec. 1987, pp. 387–403.

33. D. Zeitlin and R. Westwood, 'Measuring Emotional Responses', *Journal of Advertising Research*, 26, Oct./Nov. 1986, pp. 34–44.

34. M. Holbrook and R. Batra, 1987, op. cit. (see note 29).

35. M. Friestad and E. Thorson, 'Remembering Ads: Effects of Encoding Strategies, Retrieval Cues and Emotional Responses', *Journal of Consumer Psychology*, Vol. 2, 1993, pp. 21–29.

36. R. J. Lavidge and G. A. Steiner, 'A Model for Predictive Measurements of Advertising Effectiveness', *Journal of Marketing*, Vol. 25, 1961, pp. 59–62. T. E. Berry, 'The Development of the Hierarchy of Effects: An Historical Perspective', in J. Leigh and C. Martin (eds), *Current Issues and Research in Advertising*, Vol. 10, University of Michigan Press, Ann Arbor, Mich., 1987.

37. The majority of research measuring consumer decisions is based on functional, tangible attributes. For example, G. Punj, 'Presearch Decision Making in Consumer Durable Purchases', *Journal of Consumer Marketing*, 4, Winter 1987, pp. 71–82. J. Newman and B. Lockeman, 'Measuring Prepurchase Information Seeking', *Journal of Consumer Research*, 2, 1975, pp. 216–20. S. Beatty and S. Smith, 'External Search Effort: An Investigation Across Several Product Categories', *Journal of Consumer Research*, 14, June 1987, p. 84. J. Roberts and J. Lattin, 'Development and Testing of a Model of Consideration Set Composition', *Journal of Marketing Research*, Vol. 27, Nov. 1991, pp. 429–40.

38. M. Holbrook, 'Emotions in the Consumer Experience', in R. A. Peterson et al. (eds), *The Role of Affect in Consumer Behaviour: Emerging Theories and Applications*, Heath, Lexington, Mass., 1986. R. B. Zajonic and H. Markus, 'Affective and Cognitive Factors in Preferences', *Journal of Consumer Research*, Sept. 1982, pp. 121–31. M. Holbrook and E. Hirschman, 'The Experimental Aspects of Consumption: Consumer Fantasies, Feelings and Fun', *Journal of Consumer Research*,

Vol. 9, Sept. 1982, pp. 132–40. E. Hirschman, 'Innovativeness, Novelty Seeking and Consumer Creativity', *Journal of Consumer Research*, Vol. 7, 1980, pp. 132–40. W. T. Tucker, 'The Peach Faced Parrot', in W. Tucker (ed.), *Foundations for a Theory of Consumer Behaviour*, Holt, Rinehart and Winston, New York, 1957.

39. J. R. Bettman and C. W. Park, 'Effects of Prior Knowledge and Experience and Phase of the Choice Process on Consumer Decision Processes: A Protocol Analysis', *Journal of Consumer Research*, No. 7, 1980, pp. 234–37. W. D. Hoyer, 'An Examination of Consumer Decision Making for a Common Repeat Purchase Product', *Journal of Consumer Research*, 11, Dec. 1984. S. Beatty and S. Smith, 1987, op. cit. (see note 37).

40. J. R. Hauser and B. Wernerfelt, 'An Evaluation Cost Model of Consideration Sets', *Journal of Consumer Research*, 16, March 1990.

41. M. Rothschild, 'Advertising Strategies for High and Low Involvement Situations', in J. C. Maloney and B. Silverman (eds), *Attitude Research Plays for High Stakes*, American Marketing Association, Chicago, 1979. D. Lussier and R. Olshavsky, 'Task Complexity and Contingent Processing in Brand Choice', *Journal of Consumer Research*, 6, Sept. 1979.

42. 'Smiths on a Health Kick with New, Low Oil Crisps', *Business Review Weekly*, 7 June 1991.

43. J. Jacoby, 'Perspectives on Information Overload', *Journal of Consumer Research*, 10, March 1984, pp. 432–35.

44. J. Jacoby, D. E. Speller and C. Kohn, 'Brand Choice Behaviour as a Function of Information Overload', *Journal of Marketing Research*, 11, Feb. 1974, pp. 63–69. J. Jacoby, D. E. Speller and C. Kohn, 'Brand Choice Behaviour as a Function of Information Overload — Replications and Extension', *Journal of Consumer Research*, 1, June 1974, pp. 33–42. There is some debate as to how much information is 'too much to see'. J. E. Russo, 'More information is Better: A Re-evaluation of Jacoby, Speller and Kohn', *Journal of Consumer Research*, 1, Dec. 1974, pp. 68–72. J. Summers, 'Less Information is Better?' *Journal of Marketing Research*, 11, Nov. 1974, pp. 467–68. W. L. Wilkie, 'Analysis of Effects of Information Load', *Journal of Marketing Research*, 11, Nov. 1974, pp. 462–66. N. Malhotra, A. Jain and W. Lagakos, 'The Information Overload Controversy: An Alternative Viewpoint', *Journal of Marketing*, 46, Spring 1982, pp. 27–37. N. Malhotra, 'Information Load and Consumer Decision Making', *Journal of Consumer Research*, 8, March 1982, pp. 419–30.

45. M. Holbrook, 'Emotions in the Consumer Experience', in R. A. Peterson et al. (eds), *The Role of Affect in Consumer Behaviour: Emerging Theories and Applications*, Heath, Lexington, Mass., 1986. M. Holbrook, J. O'Shaughnessy and S. Bell, 'Actions and Reactions in the Consumption Experience: The Complementary Roles of Reasons and Emotions in Consumer Behaviour', *Research in Consumer Behaviour*, Vol. 4, 1990, pp. 131–63.

46. N. Sheth, B. I. Newman and B. L. Gross, 'Why We Buy What We Buy', *Journal of Business Research*, 22, 1991, pp. 159–70.

47. T. Reynolds and J. Gutman, 'Laddering Theory, Method Analysis and Interpretation', *Journal of Advertising Research*, Vol. 28, Feb./March 1988, pp. 11–31.

48. L. Kahle, S. Beatty and P. Horner, 'Alternative Measurement Approaches to Consumer Values: The List Values (LOV) and Values and Life Style (VALS)', *Journal of Consumer Research*, 13, Dec. 1986, pp. 405–409.

49. J. Gutman, 'A Means–End Chain Model Based on Consumer Categorization Process', *Journal of Marketing*, Vol. 46, Spring 1982, pp. 60–72. J. Gutman, 'Adding Meaning to Values by Directly Assessing Value–Benefit Relationships', *Journal of Business Research*, 20, 1990, pp. 153–60. T. Reynolds and J. P. Rochon, 'Means–End Based Advertising Research: Copy Testing is not Strategy Assessment', *Journal of Business Research*, 22, 1991, pp. 131–42.

50. J. F. Sherry Jr, 'Postmodernism Alternatives: The Interpretive Turn in Consumer Research', in T. Robertson and H. Kassarjian (eds), *Handbook of Consumer Theory and Research*, Prentice-Hall, Englewood Cliffs, NJ, 1991. E. Hirschman and M. Holbrook, 'Expanding the Ontology and Methodology of Research on the Consumption Experience', in R. A. Peterson (ed.), *The Role of Affect in Consumer Behaviour*, Heath, Lexington Mass., 1986.

51. C. Wright, 'Men Invade the Supermarket', *Australian Business*, 4 Feb. 1987.

52. E. Bonfield, 'Perception of Marital Roles in Decision Processes: Replication and Extension', *Advances in Consumer Research*, Vol. 5, 1978, pp. 300–307.

53. P. Harrison, '"Teen Power": A Harrison Report on the Unique Potential of the 10–17-year-old market', Harrison Communications, Sydney, 1983. H. H. Stipp, 'Children as Consumers', *American Demographics*, 22 Feb. 1988. E. R. Foxman, P. S. Tansuhaj and K. M. Ekstrom, 'Family Members' Perceptions of Adolescents' Influence in Family Decision Making', *Journal of Consumer Research*, No. 15, March 1989, pp. 482–91.

54. H. L. Davis and B. P. Rigaux, 'Perception of Marital Roles in Decision Processes', *Journal of Consumer Research*, Vol. 1, June 1974, pp. 51–62. W. Park, 'A Conflict Resolution Choice Model', *Journal of Consumer Research*, Vol. 5, 1978, pp. 124–35. R. Yelkur and L. M. Capella, 'Joint Adoptions Decisions by the Family: An Overview of Influencing Factors', in R. King (ed.), *Marketing Perspectives for the 1990s*, Southern Marketing Association, Richmond, VA., 1992, pp. 48–51. P. Filiatrault and J. R. Richies, 'Joint Purchasing Decisions: A Comparison of Influence Structure in Family and Couple Decision Making Units', *Journal of Consumer Research*, No. 7, Sept. 1980, pp. 131–40.

55. P. J. Robinson, C. Faris and Y. Wind, *Industrial Buying and Creative Marketing*, Allyn and Bacon, Boston, 1967.

56. C. Gronroos, 'Relationship Approach to Marketing in Service Contexts: The Marketing and Organisational Interface', *Journal of Business Research*, 20, 1990, pp. 3–11. C. Martin, A. Payne and D. Ballantyne, *Relationship Marketing: Bringing Quality, Customer Service and Marketing Together*, Butterworth Heinemann, Oxford, 1991. 'Philip Kotler Explores the New Marketing Paradigm', *Marketing Science Institute Review*, Vol. 1, Spring 1991, p. 1.

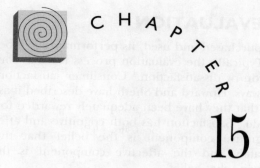

C H A P T E R

15

Post-purchase behaviour

After a product is purchased and used, it is evaluated
by the consumer. To analyse evaluation process it is
necessary to understand the consumer behaviour involved
in various ways. In the past, for a long time the consumer
behaviour scholars have been doing research in relation
to the various things they have been doing in relation.

OBJECTIVES

This chapter should help you to:
- understand the concept of post-purchase dissonance
- know the relationship between post-purchase evaluation and satisfaction/dissatisfaction
- know the role of consumer post-purchase evaluation in repeat purchasing and brand loyalty
- understand the role of marketing strategy in managing post-purchase evaluation.

INTRODUCTION

Product purchase is not the last stage in the consumer's decision making process. Whenever someone makes an important purchase, that consumer engages in post-purchase evaluation of the selection. The questions pondered will include whether the consumer made the best decision, whether the right attributes were used to determine the choice, and whether the decision could have been postponed to the consumer's benefit. The resolution of these questions has an important impact on the consumer's future purchase patterns.

In this chapter we consider the process of consumer post-purchase evaluation. Post-purchase dissonance is described and the factors leading to post-evaluative processes are outlined. The outcomes of satisfaction and dissatisfaction are considered in a framework of expectancy–disconfirmation theory. The effects of consumer decision making on complaining behaviour and repeat purchasing are considered. Finally, marketing strategies designed to manipulate post-purchase behaviours are outlined.

POST-PURCHASE EVALUATION

After a product is purchased and used, its performance will be evaluated by the consumer. Typically, the evaluation process leads to some level of consumer satisfaction or dissatisfaction.[1] Consumer satisfaction has been defined in various ways. Howard and Sheth have described it as being the customers' feeling that they have been adequately rewarded for the sacrifices they have made.[2] Satisfaction has both cognitive and affective components. The cognitive component is the belief that the product performed adequately and the affective component is the positive emotion accompanying that belief.

A general model of the post-purchase evaluation process appears in figure 15.1.[3] The model indicates that consumer expectations are confirmed or disconfirmed (the cognitive component). The gap between expectations and the actual performance of the product results in either satisfaction or dissatisfaction (the affective component). Post-purchase evaluation is an important stage in consumer decision processes because it provides information for future decision making. Evaluations are stored in memory and recalled in later situations, thus allowing the consumer to make rapid decisions about appropriate products. It also allows the consumer to assess personal knowledge of products and stores and form opinions about the consumer's adequacy in the marketplace.

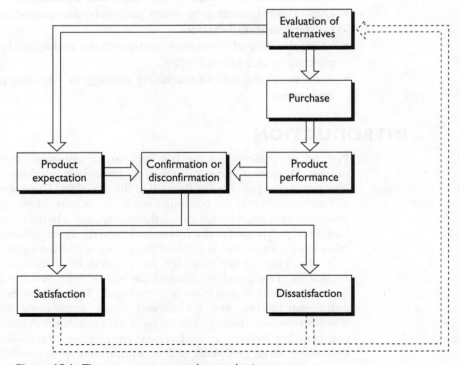

Figure 15.1: The consumer post-purchase evaluation process

Evaluation is conducted in the light of expectations the customer has for the product's performance in the particular situation in which it is used. The usage situation is an important factor in post-purchase evaluation because desirable product attributes in one usage situation may be quite different to those in another and, therefore, the basis of evaluation will be different.[4] For example, a consumer may have purchased a bottle of wine to drink alone, but may find it necessary to use it when entertaining friends and the 'choice' can be evaluated by others. Furthermore, the successful use of a product may require the purchaser to buy other, related products. For example, it is often necessary to buy batteries separately in order to use battery-operated goods. The way that these linked purchases fit into the consumer's consumption system will have an impact on satisfaction with the product.

Post-purchase evaluation may be conducted by both the user of the product and by the buyer who are not necessarily the same individual. However, because the user and the buyer are likely to interact with one another, the evaluations of the actual consumer are likely to be a critical factor in repeat purchases. For this reason, they are both of central concern in assessments of product quality.[5]

 # POST-PURCHASE DISSONANCE

Consumers often experience doubts about the wisdom of a decision they have previously made. For example, students often wonder if they made the right choice of university or university major, or whether they would have been better off at some other institution, studying another subject. This 'after the fact' reflection is known as **post-purchase dissonance**.[6] Post-purchase dissonance is a very common phenomenon that is likely to occur when the consumer has purchased a high involvement product or service.

Post-purchase dissonance occurs after the individual has made a relatively permanent commitment to a product or service. The choice will have involved an evaluation of several alternative choices which may have been equally attractive. And the consumer will have been required to give up one or more alternatives that may have been better than the one that was actually chosen. Dissonance is most likely to occur if the product choice involved complex decision making. Habitual or limited decision making is not likely to produce post-purchase dissonance because there is little evaluation of the attractive features of brands other than the chosen brand.

Purchase decisions that are followed by post-purchase dissonance have several typical characteristics. They include:

- **a high degree of commitment to the decision**. If the decision is irrevocable or very difficult to alter, consumers are likely to experience dissonance.
- **a high degree of importance to the consumer**. The more important the decision, the more dissonance the consumer is likely to feel. Products may be important because they are expensive, they have an impact on the consumer's self image, or they are risky for some other reason.

- **difficulty choosing between alternatives**. The more difficult the choice between alternatives, the more likely it is that the consumer will feel dissonance. Decision difficulty depends upon the number of alternatives available, the number of relevant attributes to be considered, and the number of 'trade-offs' between attributes offered by different brands.
- **voluntary choice**. Post-purchase dissonance is likely if the consumer is not compelled to choose a particular brand or product.
- **the personality of the consumer**. Some consumers are more likely to experience anxiety than others. If the consumer has a high tendency to experience anxiety, there will be a greater chance of post-purchase dissonance.

THEORIES OF POST-PURCHASE DISSONANCE

Post-purchase dissonance is a special case of *cognitive dissonance*, first discussed by Leon Festinger.[7] Festinger investigated the dissonance phenomenon by asking subjects to turn pegs in a pegboard over an extended period of time. Some of the subjects were paid $1 for participating in this highly boring task, whereas other subjects were paid $20. Festinger gave the subjects a questionnaire to evaluate their attitudes towards the experiment before and after participation. His findings were that subjects who had been paid $1 for participation, changed their attitudes towards the experiment in a more positive direction. Subjects who had been paid $20 remained negative towards it. Festinger concluded that the subjects, who were volunteers, needed to find justification for their participation. The higher-paid subjects could justify participation by receiving money, but this avenue was not open to the low-paid subjects. They could justify their participation only by re-evaluating the experiment and believing it to be a pleasurable experience.

Although Festinger's experiment has been criticised for methodological problems, it does show the importance of free choice in producing dissonance. If the subjects had not been volunteers, it would have been possible for the low-paid subjects to argue that they had been forced to participate. Thus their negative evaluations would not have been inconsistent with their actions, as they had a good reason to perform the task.

Some buyer situations will produce more conflict, and thus more dissonance, than other situations. Conflicts can be divided into three categories: *approach–approach conflicts*, *avoidance–avoidance conflicts*, and *approach–avoidance conflicts*.[8] In an approach–approach conflict the individual has two alternatives that are equally desirable. For example, if two films are equally attractive and showing at the same time, the consumer must make a choice about which one to watch. Approach–approach conflicts create little dissonance if both alternatives are equally good ones. In an avoidance–avoidance conflict, the individual has a choice between two undesirable alternatives and must pick the least undesirable of the two. For example, the consumer who finds that a favoured brand of a necessary product is out of stock may have to choose between unwanted alternatives. The final choice may be accompanied by feelings that the other choice may have been less odious.

Most consumer decisions, however, probably involve approach–avoidance conflict because brands differ in their desirable attributes. In an approach–avoidance conflict the alternatives possess some characteristics that make them desirable and some that make them undesirable. Consumers are attracted by the positive attributes and repelled by the negative attributes. If the decision is important, and the alternatives are relatively equal in their positive aspects, consumers will have a difficult time deciding on a brand. This difficulty, once the buyer is committed, is likely to lead to post-purchase dissonance.

Because post-purchase dissonance is an unpleasant psychological state, consumers tend to be strongly motivated to reduce it.[9] In order to do so, they are likely to follow one or more courses of action. Firstly, they may focus on the positive attributes of the brand they purchased, so that the brand becomes more desirable than at the time of purchase. Secondly, they will contrast the purchased brand to the brands not purchased by focusing on the negative aspects of those brands. At the same time, they may look for additional information from external sources that will confirm the brand choice. Thus, they may be particularly alert to media information that tells them about the positive aspects of their choice or the negative aspects of the alternatives they did not choose. The consumer is also likely to seek confirmation from friends and relatives about the correctness of the decision. If these efforts are not effective in reducing dissonance, the consumer may internally re-evaluate the decision so that its importance decreases.

MARKETING STRATEGIES FOR REDUCING POST-PURCHASE DISSONANCE

Reduction of post-purchase dissonance should be an important goal of marketers. The causes of dissonance described previously suggest strategies to produce more satisfaction with the choice. These strategies involve confirmation of the choice and reassurance of the consumer.

Advertising is a primary tool for achieving dissonance reduction. Advertising that tells the consumer that the recently purchased product was, in fact, the best choice confirms the consumer's decision. Such advertising often depicts satisfied users of the product. The provision of sufficient literature with the product helps ensure that the customer will be able to assemble and use the product. Firms provide extensive after-sales service and offer guarantees in order to circumvent dissonance. For example, Coles supermarkets guarantee Farmland meat. If the meat is not tender, customers can bring it back and receive a refund. Therefore, the risk of paying for an inadequate product is reduced. Finally, manufacturers and retailers often distribute post-purchase questionnaires and conduct telephone surveys of new buyers. These queries allow buyers to vent any frustration they have with the product, permit the seller to adjust the product to satisfy the buyer, and are effective means of reducing dissonance. Australian car manufacturers spend part of their promotion budgets on surveying customer satisfaction. The information they acquire allows them to monitor product quality and serves as a basis for designing future promotions. These communications reduce customer dissonance by showing the customer that the company is concerned about them after the sale.

Figure 15.2 contains examples of advertisements that illustrate dissonance reduction features. In the advertisement for Sunbeam toasters, the customer is offered a five year guarantee on the life of the toaster. The advertisement for Holden features an expert spokesperson — the Chairman and Managing Director of the company — who is proud to promote the firm's product. The advertisement tells the customer that Holden has reached new levels of safety and value in the family car market and offers a warranty on the performance of the car. Both advertisements state that the products are made in Australia, an attribute that some consumers may find reassuring.

Figure 15.2: Advertisements containing dissonance reduction features

As shown by Festinger (see page 392), individuals who are given large incentives for their actions tend to experience less attitude change than those who have small incentives. An implication of this finding for marketers is that offering too many incentives for a purchase may produce undesirable effects. If the incentive is excessive, the product may be devalued. Consider the purchase of a computer, with which the company is offering a printer plus two software packages. It is possible that the decision to purchase is based on the incentives and not the inherent attributes of the computer.

Organisations, as well as individual consumers, can be influenced by post-purchase dissonance. For example, the Australian issue of *Sports Illustrated* magazine advertises to media buyers in *Advertising Age* and other industry magazines. This serves not only to obtain new buyers but also to reassure organisations that habitually buy space in the magazine. The advertisement contains the caption, 'What does it feel like to find yourself in the right place at the right time?' and this, coupled with an image of a surfer hitting a wave, may suggest to advertisers targeting the 18–24 year-old sports-minded person that they have indeed chosen the right medium for their message. Similarly, Canon advertises its attitude towards service to organisational buyers (see figure 15.3). Copiers are necessary, rather complex business tools and they frequently need servicing. The advertisement attempts to reduce post-purchase dissonance by emphasising the availability of that service.

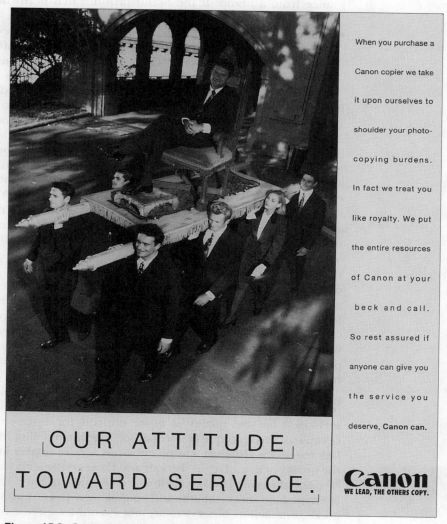

When you purchase a Canon copier we take it upon ourselves to shoulder your photo-copying burdens. In fact we treat you like royalty. We put the entire resources of Canon at your beck and call. So rest assured if anyone can give you the service you deserve, Canon can.

OUR ATTITUDE TOWARD SERVICE.

Canon
WE LEAD, THE OTHERS COPY.

Figure 15.3: Canon — service reassurance

SATISFACTION/DISSATISFACTION

When consumers purchase and use a particular brand, they expect it to perform in certain ways. The expected level of performance can vary from fairly low to very high, but the consumer will find a range of performances acceptable. According to Oliver's *expectancy disconfirmation model*,[10] satisfaction/dissatisfaction results from the comparison of the actual brand performance with the expected brand performance. Three types of expectations have been identified:

- **equitable performance**. If a brand offers equitable performance, the consumer obtains the performance he or she ought to receive given the various costs of purchasing and using the brand.
- **ideal performance**. Consumers hope for an optimum level of performance from a brand. If the brand provides that performance, the consumer has obtained an ideal performance level.
- **expected performance**. Expected performance is the level of performance that the consumer thinks the brand will actually offer. Most of the research on consumer satisfaction and dissatisfaction concerns the gap between expected and actual performance.

If the consumer has high expectations for the brand and the brand performs even better than expected, then satisfaction will result. In addition, an individual is likely to be happy with a purchase if it performs better than expected, even if the initial expectations were relatively low. In contrast, dissatisfaction is produced when a brand performs below expectations, even if the expectations were excessive. Dissatisfaction results in a negative attitude towards the brand, lower repeat purchasing, brand switching and complaining behaviour on the part of the consumer. When the brand simply performs as expected, the customer is in a state of non-satisfaction.

This view of satisfaction has some implications for product change. The manufacturer of a high quality product that decides to offer a lower cost, 'stripped-down' version of the product for the more cost-conscious market runs a risk of dissatisfaction with the cheaper brand. If, on the basis of observations of usage of the quality version, customers expect performance that is not forthcoming, they will experience some degree of dissatisfaction even though the financial cost of purchasing the product is lower. Conversely, a manufacturer whose products have improved over earlier versions will benefit from disconfirmation of expectations. Customers are pleasantly surprised with brand performance because they have received more than equitable performance.

A second model, *the gap model of service quality* (Servequal), has been proposed as a basis of examining the source of satisfaction/dissatisfaction with services.[11] Service quality is more difficult for researchers to measure because of three unique features of services: intangibility, inseparability and heterogeneity. However, customers assess service quality just as they assess the quality of manufactured goods and these assessments lead to satisfaction or dissatisfaction. The key attributes consumers use are: reliability, responsiveness, assurance, empathy and tangibleness. In contrast to assessments of goods, evaluations of services are not encounter-specific but represent the customers' global judgements across multiple service encounters. Such evaluations are similar to general attitudes towards the firm.[12] For services that are frequently used, confirmation/disconfirmation may lead to perceptions of service quality. For infrequently used services, such as legal or medical services, customers may not have a range of recent evaluations to help them assess quality. In this case, they may be more dependent on word-of-mouth or marketing communications than they are on experience.

THEORIES OF SATISFACTION/DISSATISFACTION

Various theorists have attempted to explain the basis of consumer satisfaction/dissatisfaction responses to product evaluation. In this section, we describe the assimilation–contrast theory, opponent process theory, and attribution theory and discuss their implications for consumer post-purchase evaluation.

Assimilation–contrast theory

According to the assimilation–contrast theory,[13] consumers may accept some level of deviance from their expectations. If the product is not very different from what the consumer expected, product performance will be assimilated and the product will be evaluated favourably. However, if the performance exceeds the consumer's zone of acceptance, the difference will be contrasted so that it appears even larger than it really is. Consumers would be expected to differ in their tolerance for deviations from expected performance, with some consumers being more tolerant than others. The implications of assimilation–contrast theory are that product claims must be moderate enough not to fall into the zone of rejection of the majority of the target market. The size of the rejection zone would, of course, vary with the strength of the individual's negative attitudes towards the brand.

Opponent process theory

The opponent process theory[14] attempts to explain why consumer experiences that were initially highly satisfying tend to be judged less satisfying at later occurrences. It is generally known that organisms tend to adapt to the stimuli in their environments so that stimulation wanes in intensity over time. For example, the perfume counter in the department store has an intense array of scents when you first arrive. However, the longer you spend in the presence of these odours, the weaker they appear to be, because adaptation is taking place. Adaptation is related to *homeostasis*, in which the body attempts to maintain a constant physiological state.[15]

The same homeostatic process may occur in emotional reactions to product performance. When positive or negative excitement threatens the consumer's psychological balance, a secondary process is triggered that returns the consumer to the original homeostatic state. The former process, the initial emotion, is known as a primary process and the latter, adaptive process, as an opponent process. Although the initial response is not likely to increase with repetitions, the opponent process becomes stronger so that the individual experiences less elation with subsequent experiences.

Repeat visits to a restaurant can illustrate that the state of extreme satisfaction is difficult to maintain. The consumer may have been extremely excited about the restaurant and its offering at first but, if back-to-back visits are made, the extremely positive evaluation tends to decay into non-satisfaction. Any reduction from the original level of quality of the restaurant, no matter how small, is likely to leave the customer with the feeling that 'the place is going downhill'. Furthermore, the customer is likely to contrast the original favourite with other restaurants and thus become vulnerable to brand switching. This implies that marketers must be very alert to deviations from quality and must build on alterations to brand characteristics in order to maintain high levels of customer satisfaction.

Attribution theory

People make attributions or guesses about the causes of their behaviour or the behaviour of others. Some research shows that these attributions may be central antecedents of consumer satisfaction and dissatisfaction.[16] Consumers can attribute the cause of any experience to their behaviour, the behaviour of some other person, or uncontrollable circumstances. When consumers have successful experiences, they are likely to attribute their satisfaction to some action or quality of their own, for example astuteness. However, when the experience has resulted in dissatisfaction, they are likely to place the blame elsewhere, for example, on the service personnel or on the producer of the product. Furthermore, dissatisfying experiences that are the result of product or service failure will be seen as much more unpleasant than those that result from the consumer's own behaviour, which are likely to be written off as beyond his or her control.

The obvious implication of this fundamental attribution error[17] is that maintenance of product quality is essential to the production of satisfaction. Furthermore, the tendency to engage in self-preserving cognitions suggests that attempts of manufacturers to avoid blame for product failure are likely to be met with resistance, even when they are not justified. Because retaining a customer should be of paramount importance, marketers need to monitor customer satisfaction continually.

INVOLVEMENT AND SATISFACTION/DISSATISFACTION

There is some evidence that the degree of involvement the customer has in the purchase situation influences the basis of satisfaction/dissatisfaction responses. Empirical work that has examined low involvement products indicates that the customer's prior expectations interact with the post-purchase experience to produce the level of satisfaction experienced by the customer. However, for high involvement products, pre-usage expectations may be a less important influence on the evaluation of the product than the actual product performance.[18] Patterson conducted a longitudinal examination of purchasers of slow combustion heaters, a relatively high involvement purchase for Australians living in the colder areas of New South Wales.[19] The products were relatively new on the market, few consumers had much experience with them, they were relatively expensive and the consumer could expect to use them over a period of time. The results indicated a direct link between performance and satisfaction when high involvement products are involved. This finding has important implications because it suggests that modification of expectations with point-of-sale material, advertising, sales promotions and educational materials may b less effective for high involvement products. Instead, it may be better for marketing managers to focus on perceptions of product performance. This focus could include functional and service aspects of the product. For example, major sources of customer disatisfaction in the study were poor initial installation and after-sales service. Improvement in these areas would be expected to improve the consumer's evaluation of the product. Attention to customer post-purchase evaluation is most important in the area of high involvement products because customers evaluate these products most intensely.[20]

WORD-OF-MOUTH AND COMPLAINING

When consumers are unhappy with a product or service, they are likely to look for ways to address their problem. Hirschman has proposed that there are three key options that face dissatisfied customers: to exit from the exchange relationship, to voice complaints, and to remain loyal.[21] Store and brand switching are exit behaviours. When a customer boycotts a product or retailer, he or she must search for new alternatives; therefore, exit behaviours are costly. Complaining also involves customer effort because the customer must locate appropriate recipients of the complaint and devote time and energy to explaining the complaint. Loyalty means that the customer continues the relationship and suffers in silence. The options chosen by the individual customer depend on the competitive nature of the industry (that is, whether substitutes are available) complaint channels, the personal characteristics of the consumer and the customer's beliefs about the nature of the problem. These beliefs include expectations, perceived worthiness of the complaint, the firm's perceived responsiveness to complaints and so on. Hirschman's conception of complaint behaviour is the basis for the model of complaint behaviour appearing in figure 15.4.[22]

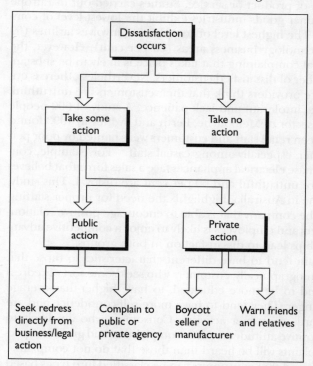

Figure 15.4: Classification of consumer complaint behaviour

Complaining behaviour can take the form of trying to obtain redress from a formal organisation such as the retailer, the manufacturer, and private or government groups organised to protect customers. Studies have shown that, of these sources, retailers receive more than 80 per cent of complaints and manufacturers receive less than 10 per cent.[23] In part, this is the result of the manufacturer being less immediately available to the consumer. Complaining to the Bureau of Consumer Affairs or making complaints known via television programs is relatively rare in Australia and New Zealand. The most frequent recipient of consumer complaints, however, are the friends and relatives of the consumer. Negative word-of-mouth is an important concern for marketers because research shows that consumers may tell twice as many people about a dissatisfying product experience than they would a satisfying one.[24] Some estimates show that negative word-of-mouth may be five times more influential than positive word-of-mouth.

Brand purchase can be strongly affected by negative word-of-mouth. One study of durable goods showed that 54 per cent of dissatisfied customers would not purchase the brand again and 45 per cent told friends not to purchase the brand.[25] This negative word-of-mouth can have very undesirable consequences on market demand for particular brands. For example, Australian-made cars gained a reputation for inferior quality through consumer complaints. This reputation opened the way for foreign competition and has been very difficult to overcome, despite rising quality.

The amount of consumer dissatisfaction with products and services varies depending on the type of product or service. Studies carried out in Europe indicate that the consumer goods industries exhibit the lowest level of complaints (22 per cent).[26] The highest level of complaining involves airlines (69 per cent) and high technology business areas (60 per cent). However, the actual amount of formal complaining that takes place is likely to be substantially less than the number of dissatisfied customers. Nevertheless, there is evidence that many service providers think that their customers are untruthful, disloyal, unappreciative, intolerant and lack patience. A study of 600 people employed in the retail sector of Melbourne, Perth and Sydney in 1993 found that relationships between retail staff and customers were tainted by poor perceptions of the customer, especially among casual staff.[27] For example, consumers seeking to purchase electrical appliances face a sales force that believes 43 per cent of them are untruthful and 60 per cent are disloyal. This study, the first of its kind done in Australia, highlights the need for proper staffing and training of staff. The company that is able to encourage positive relationships between customers and employees is likely to enjoy a competitive advantage, as poor relationships lead to dissatisfaction in both groups.

Persons who complain tend to have different characteristics to those that do not complain.[28] Demographically, customers who seek some sort of redress for their grievance tend to be more educated, to have higher-than-average income and to be younger. They tend to have more self-confidence and are relatively positive towards consumer activism. Consumers who are likely to complain have more positive attitudes towards complaining and greater expectations that their complaints will be heard than those that do not complain.

Some studies have found that consumers can be classified into types based on their propensity to complain and the kind of action taken. Singh divided consumers into four types on the basis of their consumer response styles.[29]

- **Passives** (14 per cent) took no action when they were disappointed by a product
- **Voices** (37 per cent) complained directly to the firm, but not to private or public groups

- **Irates** (21 per cent) took very little action but engaged in a lot of private complaining. They also complained to the firm responsible for providing the product.
- **Activists** (28 per cent) complained in every way possible: to their friends, to public agencies and consumer protection groups and to the manufacturers and retailers. They were especially noted for their degree of public complaining. Activists tended to be younger and to believe in the efficacy of complaining more than other groups.

Other factors that influence the willingness of a dissatisfied customer to complain include the importance of the decision, the knowledge and experience of the consumer, the difficulty of making the complaint and the possibilities of success.[30] Consumers are more likely to complain if the product was expensive, visible or time-consuming to choose. The consumers' previous complaining experience, their knowledge of how to lodge a complaint and the amount of time and trouble involved are important factors. Finally, if the manufacturer has promised satisfaction through a warranty or other mechanism, customers are more likely to insist on redress. If obscure clauses in the promise negate the manufacturer's responsibility, customers are likely to be particularly irate.

MARKETING RESPONSE TO CUSTOMER COMPLAINING

Marketers need to take complaints seriously and respond to them. Indeed, there is some evidence that they do so. Some research in the United States shows that manufacturers respond positively to complaints to least two thirds of the time.[31] Of these responses, 55 to 60 per cent are resolved to the customer's satisfaction. Successful handling of consumer complaints requires a positive attitude towards the consumer's situation. Firms with reputations for good customer service generally view complaints as warning signals and a source of vital information. Some simple precautions may help enhance customer retention and provide the firm with a competitive edge. These precautions are outlined below:[32]

- **Create realistic expectations**. Satisfaction is based on the gap between what customers expect to obtain and what they actually obtain. It is wise to base product claims on the real characteristics of the product rather than hoped-for characteristics because inflated claims are likely to be counterproductive. However, as simple as this concept might be, it is somewhat tricky to put into practice. Not only do most manufacturers want to emphasise the good features of their products, but consumers look for different features in products. Thus, good performance on one set of factors will not necessarily satisfy all customers.
- **Constantly monitor product/service quality**. The current interest in total quality management is based on the notion that the product received by the customer should have as few defects as possible. This can only be attained by continual evaluation and incremental product improvement. Firms need to be constantly vigilant and looking for ways to improve product quality.

Figure 15.5: Most companies recognise the importance of good customer service.

- **Provide the customer with adequate information.** Many products are complicated or difficult to use, increasing the chance that the customer may misuse the product and become dissatisfied as a result. Consumers may also need information about other, less complex products in order to determine whether the product is appropriate for their specific usage situation. Persons who purchase a product that does not meet their needs will either return it, will silently suffer or, in the worst case, complain to friends and relatives.

- **Offer realistic guarantees of satisfaction.** Post-purchase dissonance can be reduced if the customer is assured that there is an avenue of redress for product complaints. Guarantees should be offered in plain, understandable language so that the customer knows the limits of the guarantee.

- **Reward loyal customers.** Even satisfied customers may be tempted to try the competitor's brand, if only to make sure they still favour the original choice. Communications with loyal customers should stress that they are special and that the company is interested in them. Special deals for loyal customers can also reinforce brand purchase.

- **Develop a system for handling complaints.** Service personnel handle complaints more effectively if there is a pre-existing method for doing so established by the firm. No customer likes to be put on hold or told that 'it is not the company's policy'. Frequently, the best course of action will be an apology for the customer's inconvenience and responsible attempts to redress the grievance. Service personnel responsible for customer complaints should be carefully chosen and monitored, to ensure appropriate customer service. The system for handling complaints should also include a method of recording the nature of the complaint. This information can be useful in quality control and product improvement.

Specific techniques for collecting complaints include consumer hot lines and toll-free numbers. The original 800 number service was made free to callers in Australia in 1989. The alternative CustomNet One 3 is more recent, having been introduced in 1990. Besides being useful in facilitating reservations and orders, these toll-free numbers offer an excellent way for companies to collect customer complaints and suggestions.

REPEAT PURCHASING BEHAVIOUR

An important result of consumer satisfaction is the consumer's tendency to repurchase the product. Repeat purchases can come from habit or from continuing involvement with the brand.[33] Repeat purchases of high involvement products are often based on *brand loyalty*. Brand loyalty differs from habitual purchasing in that the customer is committed to the brand, believes it to be better than other brands and is resistant to purchasing other brands even when the favoured brand is unavailable. Brand loyalty is product specific. Customers that exhibit brand loyalty for one category of product may not exhibit it for other product categories. However, certain categories of products tend to have greater frequencies of brand loyalty. Largely, these are products that have a hedonistic component, such as cigarettes, some food items and automobiles. In addition, there may be a sliding scale of brand loyalty. That is, some customers are completely loyal to one brand, whereas others may be loyal to two or three brands. Other customers may show no loyalty to any brand and buy only according to price or availability.

Obtaining repeat purchases is a primary goal of most marketing strategies. Strategies designed to obtain repeat purchasing will differ depending on the number of habitual versus brand-loyal customers in the target market. Habitual purchasers may be influenced by price packages and discounts that would not motivate the brand-loyal customer to switch brands. Even if the brand-loyal buyer does try a new brand occasionally, the trial is often temporary. Studies of consumers conducted over the last 10 years show that satisfied customers who switch brands to take advantage of temporary price deals often switch back after the deal is over.[34] However, these loyal customers may stock up when their favoured brand has a promotional special.

Advertising that reassures the consumer that the brand still has the satisfying attributes it had in the past is aimed at the repeat purchaser. Other firms with competing products have a difficult time breaking the satisfaction–repurchase cycle. An example of advertising attempting to counteract repeat purchasing in the car industry was a television advertisement for Mitsubishi. The advertisement claimed that in the past Australian car buyers chose either Holden or Ford cars, but a new and better choice was now available for the Australian family — the Mitsubishi Magna.

 SUMMARY

Consumers re-evaluate their purchase decisions in the light of their particular usage situations. Post-purchase dissonance is an uncomfortable psychological state in which the consumer wonders if the best product has been chosen. Post-purchase dissonance is most likely to occur when the decision is highly important, irrevocable, difficult and freely made. Anxiety-prone individuals are most likely to experience post-purchase dissonance. Dissonance can be present in situations involving two positive alternatives (approach–approach conflict), two negative alternatives (avoidance–avoidance conflict), or both positive and negative characteristics (approach–avoidance conflict). Consumers try to reduce post-purchase dissonance by focusing on the positive attributes of the chosen brand, inflating the negative aspects of the non-chosen brand and looking for information confirming the choice. Strategies to reduce dissonance include advertising the positive qualities of the brand, providing after-sales service, and the use of post-purchase questionnaires.

Satisfaction and dissatisfaction are two results of post-purchase evaluation. The expectancy disconfirmation model proposes that these outcomes result from the discrepancy between expectations and actual performance. Three types of expectations are equitable performance, ideal performance, and expected performance. The Servequal model suggests that satisfaction or dissatisfaction with services is a global judgement across service encounters. Several theories have been used to explain aspects of satisfaction/dissatisfaction. Assimilation–contrast theory proposes that consumers have zones of acceptance of deviation from expectations. Opponent process theory suggests that consumers adapt their expectations so that initially pleasurable experiences become less so with repetition. Attribution theory indicates that, when consumers have a displeasing consumption experience, they are likely to blame the product or the service provider. Product involvement affects the intensity with which the consumer evaluates the product.

Dissatisfaction results in negative word-of-mouth and complaining. Consumers are most likely to complain to family and friends although they may also seek redress from retailers, manufacturers and other organisations. Consumers who complain are likely to be younger, more educated and more self-confident than non-complainers. The visibility of the product, cost of purchase, experience of the consumer and the existence of manufacturer's promises also influence complaining. Firms should respond to consumer complaints by creating realistic expectations, providing adequate information, offering realistic guarantees of satisfaction and rewarding customer loyalty.

Satisfaction can result in positive word-of-mouth and repeat purchasing. Customers engage in repeat purchases because of habit and brand loyalty. Brand loyalty differs from habit in that it implies an enduring involvement with the brand.

 Questions

1. Describe the process of post-purchase evaluation.

2. What is post-purchase dissonance? What conditions would encourage post-purchase dissonance?

3. Provide an example of approach–approach, avoidance–avoidance, and approach–avoidance conflicts from your own experience.

4. How do marketers try to reduce consumer dissonance?

5. What three types of expectations for product performance do consumers have? Which of these types of expectations produce the most consumer conflict and why?

6. Describe the expectancy–disconfirmation model.

7. What are the main propositions of the assimilation–contrast theory?

8. How does the opponent process theory explain declining consumer satisfaction with repeated purchases?

9. What is the fundamental attribution error and how can it contribute to consumer complaining behaviour?

10. When a consumer has a complaint about a product or service, what is he or she most likely to do?

11. What factors influence the willingness of a dissatisfied customer to complain about a purchase?

12. What strategies can marketers use to handle customer complaints? Why are these strategies likely to be effective?

13. What is the difference between brand loyalty and habitual purchasing?

14. How do advertisers attempt to foster repeat purchasing?

15. Describe the influence of word-of-mouth on repeat purchasing and brand rejection.

 ## *Case study*

Hypothetical scenario:

Mr Canning had been on a business trip to the United States and was returning to Sydney from Los Angeles. During the journey a number of unfortunate events occurred.

Approximately two hours flying-time before Sydney, the captain of the International Airline Service (IAS) informed the passengers, most of whom were American tourists, that there would be a two-hour delay due to bad weather in Sydney and that the flight may be diverted to Brisbane. About one hour out of Sydney the flight was diverted to Brisbane where Brisbane-bound passengers disembarked. After a delay of ninety minutes the flight with the remaining passengers took off for Sydney. The weather conditions meant that the plane had to circle Sydney's Mascot airport for 45 minutes after which it was decided to divert the flight to Melbourne.

All three hundred passengers disembarked at Melbourne's Tullamarine airport and were instructed to go to the transit lounge where airline staff would attend to them. The passengers were not told how to find the transit lounges and there were no airline crew in attendance.

A junior member of staff informed the passengers that because of the bad weather conditions they were unsure when a flight to Sydney could be arranged. Because the passengers had been travelling for over nineteen hours, they were tired and had either to make connecting flights in Sydney or had people waiting for them, the atmosphere in the transit lounge was tense.

The passengers were issued with a $4 food coupon which could be used in the airport cafeteria. Mr Canning went to the cafeteria and found that the coffee and sandwich that he had ordered cost $5.50. Not having any Australian money with him and as the cafeteria would not take American money, he was unable to 'top-up' the $4 coupon and was not able to buy the coffee and sandwich.

Another four hours passed and a senior staff member from IAS announced that the weather conditions in Sydney had improved and that the passengers would be put on the next flight to Sydney as the aircraft that they had arrived on was being serviced. Unfortunately there was only room for half of the stranded passengers on the next flight, and the airline announced that the remaining passengers would be transferred on the next plane.

Mr Canning, because he had by this time missed his connection at Sydney airport, decided to wait for the second plane rather than be caught up in the 'fight for seats' behaviour which developed. Finally, after being in transit for over 26 hours (thirteen hours overdue) Mr Canning boarded a plane for Sydney.

(*Source:* Case prepared by Associate Professor P. Patterson, University of Wollongong)

Case study questions

1. What action, if any, would you take if you were Mr Canning? What impact could these actions have on IAS?

2. How would this experience impact on any air travel decisions and choices made by Mr Canning?

3. If you were in a position to make decisions about how IAS should have acted in this situation, what actions would you have taken and why?

SUGGESTED READING

J. Singh 'Consumer Complaint Intentions and Behaviour: Definitions and Taxonomical Issues', *Journal of Marketing*, 52, January 1988, pp. 93–107.

S. Brown and R. Baltramini, 'Consumer Complaining and Word of Mouth Activities: Field Evidence', in T. Srull (ed.), *Advances in Consumer Research*, 16, Association for Consumer Research, Provo, Utah, 1989, pp. 9–16.

S. Steinberg, 'Customer Satisfaction — Where Are We Going? Where Have We Been?' American Marketing Association's Winter Educators Proceedings, 1993, pp. 362–69.

ENDNOTES

1. Richard N. Cardozo, 'An Experimental Study of Consumer Effort, Expectations, and Satisfaction', *Journal of Marketing Research*, 2, Aug. 1965, pp. 244–49. H. Keith Hunt, 'CS/D — Overview and Future Directions', in H. Keith Hunt (ed.), *Conceptualization and Measurement of Consumer Satisfaction and Dissatisfaction*, Marketing Science Institute, Cambridge, Mass., pp. 455–88.

2. John A. Howard and Jagdish Sheth, *The Theory of Buyer Behaviour*, John Wiley and Sons, New York, 1969.

3. Richard L. Oliver, 'Cognitive Model of the Antecedents of and Consequences of Satisfaction Decisions', *Journal of Marketing Research*, 17, Nov. 1980, pp. 460–69.

4. Harper W. Boyd Jr and Sidney J. Levy, 'New Dimensions in Consumer Analysis', *Harvard Business Review*, 41, Nov./Dec. 1963, pp. 129–40.

5. J. E. Swan, 'Consumer Satisfaction Research and Theory: Current Status and Future Directions', in H. K. Hunt and R. L. Day (eds), *Proceedings of the Seventh Annual Conference on Consumer Satisfaction — Dissatisfaction and Complaining Behaviour*, School of Business, Indiana University, Bloomington, Indiana, 1982, pp. 124–29.

6. This section is based on the discussion in James F. Engle, Roger D. Blackwell and Paul Miniard, *Consumer Behaviour*, Dryden Press, Chicago, 1990.

7. Leon Festinger, *A Theory of Cognitive Dissonance*, Stanford Tertiary Education Institution Press, Stanford, California, 1957.

8. The basic research in the area of conflict comes from Kurt Lewin, *A Dynamic Theory of Personality*, McGraw-Hill, New York, 1935.

9. W. H. Cummings and N. Venkatesan, 'Cognitive Dissonance and Consumer Behaviour: A Review of the Evidence', *Journal of Marketing Research*, 13, Aug. 1976, pp. 303–8.

10. R. L. Oliver and W. O. Bearden, 'Disconfirmation and Consumer Expectations in Product Usage', *Journal of Business Research*, 10, June 1985, pp. 235–46. E. R. Cadotte, R. B. Woodruff and R. L. Jenkins, 'Expectations and Norms in Models of Consumer Satisfaction', *Journal of Marketing Research*, 24, Aug. 1987, pp. 305–13.

11. A. Parasuraman, Valerie A. Zeithaml and Leonard Berry, 'A Conceptual Model of Service Quality and Its Implications for Future Research', *Journal of Marketing*, 49, Fall 1985, pp. 41–50.

12. Paul G. Patterson and Lester W. Johnson, 'Disconfirmation of Expectations and the Gap Model of Service Quality: An Integrated Paradigm', *Journal of Consumer Satisfaction, Dissatisfaction and Complaining Behavior*, 6, 1993, pp. 90–99.

13. Henry Assael, *Consumer Behaviour and Marketing Action*, PWS Kent, Boston, Mass., 1992.

14. Richard L. Oliver, 'What is Consumer Satisfaction', *Wharton Magazine*, Spring 1981, pp. 36–44.

15. Harry Helson, *Adaptation Level Theory*, Harper and Row, New York, 1964.

16. M. J. Bitner, 'Evaluating Service Encounters: The Effects of Physical Surroundings and Employee Responses', *Journal of Marketing*, 54, April 1990, pp. 69–82. F. Heider, 'Social Perception and Phenomenal Causality', *Psychological Review*, 51, pp. 358–74. H. H. Kelly and J. L. Michela, 'Attribution Theory and Research', *Annual Review of Psychology*, 31, 1980, pp. 457–501. Richard L. Oliver and John E. Swan, 'Consumer Perceptions of Interpersonal Equity and Satisfaction in Transactions: A Field Survey Approach', *Journal of Marketing*, 53, April, pp. 21–35.

17. E. E. Jones, 'The Rocky Road from Acts to Dispositions', *American Psychologist*, 34, pp. 107–17.

18. G. A. Churchill and C. Surprenant, 'An Investigation into the Determinants of Customer Satisfaction', *Journal of Marketing Research*, 19, Nov. 1982, pp. 491–501. R. L. Oliver and W. O. Bearden, 'The Role of Involvement in Satisfaction Processes', in R. P. Bagozzi and A. M. Tybout (eds), *Advances in Consumer Research*, 10, 1983, Association for Consumer Research, Ann Arbor, Mich., pp. 250–55.

19. Paul Patterson, 'Expectations and Product Performance as Determinants of Satisfaction for a High-Involvement Purchase', *Psychology and Marketing*, 10(5), Sept./Oct. 1993, pp. 449–62.

20. K. Gronhaug, 'Exploring Consumer Complaining Behaviour: A Model and Some Empirical Results', in W. D. Perrault (ed), *Advances in Consumer Research*, 4, 1977, Association for Consumer Research, Atlanta, GA, pp. 159–65.

21. Albert O. Hirschman, *Exit, Voice, and Loyalty: Responses to Decline in Firms, Organizations and States*, Harvard University Press, Cambridge, Mass., 1970.

22. This conceptualisation was first introduced by G. Day and E. L. Landon, 'A Model for Consumer Complaint Behaviour', in R. Day, *Consumer Satisfaction, Dissatisfaction and Complaining Behaviour*, School of Business, Indiana University, Bloomington, In., 1977. The current presentation is adapted from J. Singh, 'Consumer Complaint Intentions and Behaviour', *Journal of Marketing*, Jan. 1988, pp. 93–107.

23. S. P. Brown and R. F. Beltramini, 'Consumer Complaining and Word-of-Mouth Activities', in T. K. Srull (ed.), *Advances in Consumer Research, XVI*, Association for Consumer Research, Provo, Utah, 1989, pp. 9–11. J. E. Swan and R. L. Oliver, 'Postpurchase Communications by Consumers', *Journal of Retailing*, 65, Winter 1989, pp. 516–33.

24. P. M. Herr, F. R. Kardes and J. Kim, 'Effects of Word-of-Mouth and Product Attribute Information on Persuasion: An Accessibility Diagnosticity Perspective', *Journal of Consumer Research*, 17, 1991, pp. 454–62.

25. W. O. Bearden and J. E. Teel, 'An Investigation of Personal Influences on Consumer Complaining', *Journal of Retailing*, 57, Fall 1981, pp. 2–20. M. S. Moyer, 'Characteristics of Consumer Complaints', *Journal of Public Policy and Marketing*, 3, 1984, pp. 67–84. M. A. Morganosky and H. M. Buckley, 'Complaint Behavior', in M. Wallendorf and P. Anderson (eds), *Advances in Consumer Research, XVI*, Association for Consumer Research, Provo, Utah, 1987, pp. 223–26.

26. TARP, *European Study of Consumer Complaints*, 1992.

27. Barry Urquehart, 'It's War Between Staff and Customers', *Marketing*, Sept. 1993, p. 50.

28. J. E. Swan, 'Consumer Satisfaction Research and Theory: Current Status and Future Directions', in H. K. Hunt and R. L. Day (eds), *Proceedings of the Seventh Annual Conference on Consumer Satisfaction — Dissatisfaction and Complaining Behaviour*, School of Business, Indiana University, Bloomington, Indiana, pp. 124–29.

29. J. Singh, 'A Typology of Consumer Dissatisfaction Response Styles', *Journal of Retailing*, 66, Spring 1990, pp. 57–99.

30. Ralph L. Day, 'Modeling Choices among Alternative Responses to Dissatisfaction', in Thomas Kinnear (ed.), *Advances in Consumer Research*, Association for Consumer Research, Provo, Utah, 11, 1984, pp. 496–99.

31. A. J. Resnik and R. R. Harmon, 'Consumers Complaint and Managerial Response', *Journal of Marketing*, Winter 1983, 47, pp. 86–97.

32. This section is based on the discussion in J. F. Engle, R. Blackwell and P. Miniard, *Consumer Behaviour*, Dryden Press, Chicago, 1990.

33. N. Maddox, 'The Structure of Consumers' Satisfaction: Cross-Product Comparisons', *Journal of the Academy of Marketing Science*, Winter 1982, pp. 37–53. D. K. Tse and P. C. Wilton, 'Models of Consumer Satisfaction Formation', *Journal of Marketing Research*, 28, Jan. 1988, pp. 204–12. R. L. Oliver and W. S. DeSarbo, 'Response Determinants of Interpersonal Equity and Satisfaction in Transactions', *Journal of Marketing*, 52, April 1989, pp. 21–35. E. Swan and L. J. Combs, 'Product Performance and Consumer Satisfaction: A New Concept', *Journal of Marketing*, 40, April 1976, pp. 25–33.

34. T. Johnson, 'The Myth of Declining Brand Loyalty', *Journal of Advertising Research*, 16, March 1984, pp. 9–18.

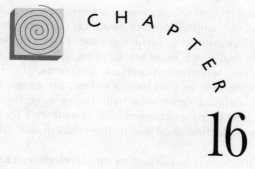

CHAPTER

16

Situational influences

This chapter should help you to:
- know what situational variables are
- understand the influence of situations on brand and product choice
- know the role of situational variables in models of consumer behaviour
- understand the impact of consumer situations on marketing strategies.

INTRODUCTION

Video companies, such as Melbourne-based Buena Vista Home Video, dream of the day when retailers see video tapes as regular product lines and when consumers collect videos just as they collect compact discs. That day may be dawning. Since August 1993, Buena Vista, a distribution division of the Walt Disney Company, has released 36 videos, and claims to have convinced retailers that videos are mainstream products. In an industry with a declining rental market, the for-sale category has shown solid growth.

Australians purchase or rent videos to suit specific consumption 'situations'. Children's videos, such as *Beauty and the Beast*, are the most popular, accounting for 38 per cent of sales. They are followed by feature films (30 per cent), music videos (7 per cent), sports videos (6 per cent), and fitness videos (3 per cent). Buena Vista gives customers limited time to buy Disney movies designated as classics. For example, *Beauty and the Beast* disappeared from retail shelves after six months. This strategy mirrors the cinema distribution strategy, keeps interest in old movies alive, introduces Disney movies to new generations of children, and creates a sense of urgency in the consumer purchase situation.[1]

The consumer's 'environment' consists of a series of situations in which consumers purchase, use, and dispose of products and brands. Situations contain particular 'circumstances' involving time, place, individual states and moods, and the influence of other persons, all of which bias consumer choice. In many consumer-purchase situations, the best choice depends upon the situation. In purchasing videos, for example, the consumer's choice will depend upon who will be viewing the video, the occasion for which it is being purchased, the consumer's feelings at the time of purchase, the selection available in the retail outlet, and a host of other variables.

The concept of situations is important to the development of marketing strategies because they have a direct impact on consumers' perception of brands, preferences for brands or product categories, purchasing behaviour, and post-purchase evaluation. Marketers need to understand how situations affect product purchase in order to be able to position products and effectively serve their target markets. This chapter deals with the effects of situation on consumer behaviour. In this chapter, we define 'situation' and discuss the nature and measurement of situational variables. The impact of situation on consumer-decision processes is described. Finally, the use of situational variables in developing marketing strategies is discussed.

 ## THE NATURE OF SITUATIONS

Situation has been variously conceived by marketers as part of the objective environment and as part of subjective or perceived environment. In this chapter, a situation refers to an instance of human interaction with the environment and involves behaviour, cognitive and affective responses, and environmental factors over a period of time.[2] Purchasing gifts at Christmas, visiting a restaurant, and going to a football game are all examples of situations.

There are several characteristics that must be present for a situation to exist. Situations must contain a person who interacts with a specific environment or set of environments. Situations must have a beginning and an end, although this time period can vary in length from very short (viewing a display in a shop window) to relatively long (negotiating for a house). Situations also have varying degrees of complexity. Complex situations may take place in multiple physical environments and involve many different behaviours and affects. For example, buying from a vending machine is a simple situation. A trip to the racetrack is a more complex situation that involves multiple decisions and feelings over the course of a day.

Situations are not always random. That is, consumers often select or construct the situations within which they place themselves. Consumers choose whether they will attend the opera or go to a football game, eat out at a restaurant or stay home and watch television alone, or go to movies with friends. Because many human preferences are relatively stable, situations tend to re-occur. When they do, consumers will often react similarly to the way they have learned to behave in the same situation in the past.

All aspects of consumer decision making are influenced by situations. Arousal, problem recognition and search processes are affected because situations elicit consumer needs and wants and offer cues on how those needs and wants might be fulfilled. Situations affect how important the different benefits of a product are to the consumer; therefore, they influence the evaluation of alternatives. Purchase decisions are altered by the particular constraints of the situation the consumer is in. Finally, postpurchase evaluations of products will alter with the situation because products are often suitable under some conditions and not others. Therefore, satisfaction, dissatisfaction and complaining are influenced by situations.

 # A MODEL OF SITUATIONAL INFLUENCE

According to Belk, the product and the situation are two factors that influence the consumer's decision making.[3] Figure 16.1 depicts this relationship. The model suggests that desirability of individual brand attributes may vary with the situation. In addition, the consumer can attribute product performance to the product, the situation or both. If the consumer attributes the successful performance of the product to the product itself, then attitudes towards it are likely to be much more positive than if performance is seen as situational. Therefore, it is in the marketer's interests to know when situations will be dominant over products.

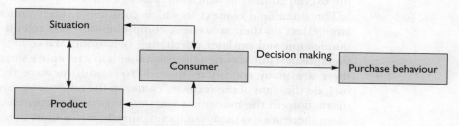

Figure 16.1: A revised stimulus-organism-response paradigm (*Source*: Adapted from Russell W. Belk, 'Situational Variables and Consumer Behaviour', *Journal of Consumer Research, 2*, Dec. 1975, p. 158)

Several factors have been found to influence the importance of situations versus products in determining brand choice. First, if the consumer is brand loyal or has enduring involvement with the product, the influence of the situation will be less. Second, the more the customer attributes the previous purchases to the characteristics of the product, the less the situation will make a difference. Therefore, if the consumer has carefully evaluated the product's attributes and feels that the best choice has been made, the same repurchase is likely to occur in a variety of situations. Third, situational factors are less powerful determinants when a product has multiple uses. Single-use situations are likely to exist for packaged goods and they tend to be purchased for consumption at specific times and places.

TYPES OF SITUATIONS

Understanding how product use varies across situations allows marketers to modify products if necessary, and use advertising messages to depict specific use situations. Therefore it is crucial that marketers understand the characteristics of situations. Consumers interact with environments in four basic types of situations: the communication situation; the purchase situation; the consumption, or usage, situation; and the disposition situation.[4] Each of these types of situation is described in detail below.

THE COMMUNICATION SITUATION

The communication situation is the setting in which the consumer is exposed to information about the product or brand. This information can come through personal or non-personal communication. Personal forms of communication involve conversations that consumers have with family, friends, relatives and salespeople. Non-personal communication consists of all forms of advertising, including billboards, direct mail, magazines and television commercials. The consumer's receptiveness to marketing communications varies with the internal and external conditions present when information is received. Internal conditions might include the consumer's mood at the time, his or her degree of interest in the product or service, and prior knowledge of the product or service. External conditions might include the consumer's shopping alone or in a group and the overall context in which the message was embedded.

The situational context in which consumers receive information has a large effect on their awareness, comprehension and retention of the communication and on later purchasing behaviour. Marketing messages have their greatest impact when the consumer is in a receptive situation. However, there are many conditions that interfere with message reception. These include the state of the receiver, clutter in the advertising environment and distractions in the immediate surroundings of the receiver.[5] Clutter occurs when there are too many competing messages in a short time or in a limited space. Consumers exposed to many advertising messages find it difficult to recall individual advertisements. If the consumer is watching television, the position of the advertisement within a string of commercials, the type of program being viewed, the involvement with the program and many other factors will influence the effectiveness of the message.

The issue of how consumer mood and involvement affects recall and evaluation is somewhat complex. Some research has shown that consumers process advertisements more thoroughly, are more positive about them and recall them better when they are embedded in a 'happy' program.[6] This has led many advertisers to avoid sponsorship on news programs and dramatic shows that have a negative tone. More recent studies have provided evidence for a consistency effect. Kamins and colleagues found that when consumers viewed happy advertisements embedded in happy programs they had more favourable attitudes to the advertisement and product purchase than when the same advertisement was embedded in a sad program.[7] The reverse was true of sad commercials. Program involvement, however, can have a detrimental effect on attitudes towards advertisements. People tend to view advertisements that appear during 'involving' television programs as intrusions and are less positive about the sponsor.[8]

THE PURCHASE SITUATION

The purchase situation is one in which a product is acquired. It can take place in a variety of environments such as supermarkets, department stores, restaurants and even flea markets. Within the retail environment, situational factors such as price changes, product availability, store layout, competitive deals and the helpfulness of salespeople become important to consumer choice and affect the distributor's channel and pricing strategies. In addition, the customer's shortage of time, the amount of crowding in the store, the presence of other people in the shopping environment, and even the weather may affect tendencies to purchase.

For example, suppose you are planning to give a very important dinner party for a large number of guests and you want to serve a special main course. What would you do under the following conditions?

- The supermarket does not have the item that you planned to serve as the main course. Do you go to another shop or buy a substitute?
- The price of the ingredients for the main course is much higher than expected. You believe that other outlets may have more reasonable prices.
- You have only 15 minutes for shopping, but the store is very crowded and there is a long queue at the checkout.
- The cut of meat you intended to serve does not look as good as you hoped. Other possible selections look fresher and better. However, they are more expensive and you will have to alter other parts of your menu if you change your mind.
- The weather has suddenly changed and become much cooler. The menu you had planned may not be as suitable on a cool day as on a warm one.
- You meet a friend in the supermarket who tells you that one of your guests dislikes or is unable to eat what you had intended to serve.

The above list reflects real conditions that may occur during a shopping trip and that would affect the actual choice the consumer makes in the retail environment. Consumers often face unanticipated purchase situations. These situations might involve a product or service failure, unexpected depletion of a product, stock-outs (product out of stock), or some change in the consumer's usual routine. Certainly, shopping conditions will affect the motives and intentions of the consumer in the particular situation.

An important part of the purchase situation is the amount and kind of information that is provided to the customer.[9] Consumers are unable to make reasoned choices if they do not have adequate information available to them. However, having too much information can result in 'information overload', so that consumers cannot separate relevant facts from those that are irrelevant. The issue of information overload is particularly important in the design of packaging, which must often contain a lot of detailed information. Other information factors, such as information format and form, can also affect the consumer's choice.

CONSUMPTION SITUATIONS

The consumption situation is one in which a product is consumed or used. Product selection depends on the situation in which the consumer anticipates using the product. To design effective marketing strategies, marketers must be able to identify the consumption or usage situations that relate to their particular product or service. Even within a narrow product range, consumption situations may vary. For example, there are several different situations where beverages are commonly consumed, and different beverages are chosen in different situations. Beer may be the desired beverage when watching football at home or relaxing with friends after a final exam. When one is out to dinner with a special friend, the chosen drink may be wine. In addition, the brand of beverage may vary with the situation. If friends have been invited for a special occasion, one is likely to purchase a more prestigious brand than one would buy for personal consumption. Manufacturers of non-alcoholic beers have capitalised on the impact of situation on consumption patterns by producing a beer that can be consumed without impairing driving ability.

The original Driza-Bone weatherproof coat has traditionally been made of heavyweight 100% cotton oilskin. Year after year it's protected against rain, sleet and snow.

But now that it's also made in a summer-weight version, a Driza-Bone comfortably keeps out the wet even when it's warm.

Call 008 773 800 for the name of your nearest Driza-Bone retailer.

The legend of the bush.

Driza-Bone Regular.

Driza-Bone Light.

Figure 16.2: There are now two types of Driza-Bone coats — suitable for cold and warm weather situations.

Figure 16.2 depicts an advertisement for Driza-Bone coats. Driza-Bone is a uniquely Australian garment designed for wet, cold weather. However, the weather in many parts of Australia is quite mild, even when it is rainy, which limits the number of situations where Driza-Bone can be worn. The new model of the coat, a summer-weight version, increases the number of consumption situations in which Driza-Bone can be worn.

Consumers usually know how the product will be consumed when they purchase it. For example, if a couple is inviting friends for dinner, they are likely to purchase special goods for that particular occasion. These purchases will be planned and will often involve extensive problem solving. However, as with purchase situations, consumption situations can sometimes be unexpected and necessitate emergency purchases. Emergencies cause consumers to buy quickly, without much reflection. As a result, they may pay more than they usually would, because they don't have time to shop around and compare prices. Unexpected situations often lead consumers to make extra shopping trips, to alter time spent shopping and may also result in consumer confusion, anxiety and less successful decision making.

For many services there is no difference between a purchase situation and a consumption situation, as consumers are purchasing and consuming simultaneously. As a result, situational factors become very important and may strongly affect post-purchase evaluation. For instance, many people find the ambiance of a restaurant to be as important as their enjoyment of the food. Restaurateurs must be alert to the effects of the restaurant's decoration, lighting, music, assortment of dishes, reservation policies, service and pricing structure. These factors are part of the consumption of the product or service and will affect the consumer's satisfaction with the restaurant.

DISPOSAL SITUATIONS

The least studied aspect of situational effects on consumer behaviour is what consumers do with goods once they have used them. Disposal situations are highly relevant to some businesses. Used car lots, auction facilities and services (such as for cars, real estate or fine art) and used clothing stores are obvious examples. Flea markets, rummage sales, and swap meets are industries that have grown up around the disposal of goods.[10] Disposal has implications for public policy as well, because many products are simply thrown away, thereby contributing to growing piles of rubbish. Many companies are experiencing strong societal pressure to alter their packaging strategies to reduce the environmental impact of excessive packaging when consumers throw it away. Further, in many countries, recycling has grown into an industry of substantial proportions.

The disposal of property may be accompanied by strong emotions that influence disposal strategies. Couples who divorce, for example, often find the division or sale of jointly owned goods to be an intensely emotional experience. McAlexander, Schouten and Roberts used interviews to examine how property is divided among divorcing partners.[11] They discovered four disposal situations which related to the motives and emotional states of the individuals involved. Some couples divided property as fairly as possible on the basis of economic value, personal identification with the articles, or need. In this case, disposal was relatively rational and involved a minimum of negative emotion. A second was for one of the partners to give up all the possessions to the former spouse. This situation was motivated by needs to assuage guilt, to make a clean break or to sever symbolic ties. Negative situations involved rivalry, punishment and clinging to power in the relationship. A spouse might lay claim to possessions that had value to the partner, or might violently destroy the property. Jettisoning or losing items that symbolised the marriage was also common among couples whose marriages were dissolving.

CHARACTERISTICS OF SITUATIONS

Many variables can be used to classify situations. In this book we use a classification scheme devised by Belk that uses objectively measured variables to describe situations. The system divides situations into those that are created by physical surroundings, social surroundings, temporal perspective, task definition and antecedent states.[12] These five classes of situational influence appear in table 16.1.

Table 16.1: Classification of situational influence

Physical surroundings	Tangible properties of the environment. Geographical and institutional location, decor, sounds, weather, crowding and other material surrounding a consumer.
Social surroundings	Interpersonal climate. The characteristics, roles and interactions of individuals. For example, the presence of guests or neighbours when purchasing a product in a department store.
Task definition	Intent or requirement to select, shop for or obtain information about a general or specific purchase.
Temporal perspective	Time of day, seasons of the year, orientation towards the past, present or the future.
Antecedent states	Momentary moods or conditions that occur before but in close temporal proximity to the current situation.

(*Source*: Russell W. Belk, 'An Exploratory Assessment of Situational Effects in Buyer Behaviour', *Journal of Marketing Research*, 11, May 1974)

PHYSICAL SURROUNDINGS

Physical surroundings are particularly important to retail outlets and service outlets such as restaurants, supermarkets and banks. Music, colour, merchandising and general layout of the store are some of the aspects of physical surroundings that affect shopper behaviour. For example, the pace of music in supermarkets affects the speed of shopping and this in turn affects sales volume. When slow music is played, sales in supermarkets tend to increase because shoppers slow their pace, linger in the store, and notice more brands.[13] Colour also has an impact on consumer shopping patterns.[14] Warm colours tend to attract customer attention but cool colours are more appropriate for places where complex products are sold and customers need to reflect on their choice.

The overall atmosphere of a retail setting has a number of effects on buyers.[15] In a restaurant, atmosphere will have an impact on the willingness of customers to linger over their meals and will also affect the amount they are willing to pay for the dinner. Therefore, more exclusive restaurants and shops support the quality of their offering and their price structures with a well-designed physical environment. Conversely, customers also use the physical surroundings of a retail establishment to connote low prices. They expect to have crowding, limited service and jumbled merchandise in discount stores. The use of the physical environment to create an appropriate mood is known as 'atmospherics'.

Physical surroundings can also have a negative impact on purchase behaviour. When retail environments are too crowded, consumers tend to limit their time in the store, reduce the purchases they make and change the way they use the information provided by the retailer.[16] Illogical traffic patterns, crowded racks and insufficient signage can create customer confusion and dissatisfaction with the shopping experience, which may translate into fewer purchases and a reluctance to return to the particular outlet. However, consumer choice also plays a role. Some research indicates that consumer reactions to crowded environments are moderated by perceptions of control. If the consumer has chosen to shop under crowded conditions and feels able to exit at will, reactions may be less negative and may even be positive.[17]

SOCIAL SURROUNDINGS

Consumption behaviour often takes place in the presence of other people. Other people can have a profound impact on buyer behaviour, because we tend to comply with the expectations of others. Examples of the social aspect of a situation are shopping with other people, consuming products with others and interacting with sales personnel.

The presence of other people in a shopping situation often encourages buying. Therefore, marketers often encourage group shopping by encouraging their customers to 'tell a friend' or 'bring a friend along'. Retailers that hold fashion shows for their patrons do so in part because people tend to treat the shows as entertainment and attend them with important others. Thus, the fashion show environment not only provides information about new lines of products but places the viewers in an exciting social atmosphere.

Sales personnel are, likewise, a very important part of the social surroundings of the retail environment.[18] Some salespeople are sought because they are knowledgeable in the customer's favourite product category, and their similarity to the customer encourages communication and repeat purchase behaviour. In addition, sales personnel who show a degree of deference to the customer can bolster the customer's self-image.

TEMPORAL PERSPECTIVE

The temporal aspect of a situation includes times of day such as morning, midday and evening, and seasons such as winter or spring. It includes the time between the purchase of a product and the expiration of its warranty. Having limited time will affect a consumer's purchase behaviour because such consumers tend to search less for information and may make unwise decisions.[19] The consumer's choice of retailers is also likely to be affected by the time dimension.[20] For example, Miller and McGinter found that family patronage of McDonald's restaurants was largely influenced by time of day.[21] Families were more likely to view the restaurant as more convenient for the evening meal than for meals at any other time. Similarly, the growth of convenience stores is based on people's tendency to look for convenient alternatives when time is short.

Figure 16.3: This advertisement for Grace Bros clothing anticipates the cooler months ahead.

Time also affects the kinds of products people shop for. Figure 16.3 contains an advertisement for Grace Bros that tells the customer that winter is on the way and they should prepare for cooler days by buying certain styles of winter clothing. In cold climates, people are often presented with the latest spring fashions when there is still snow on the ground, which may cause some dissatisfaction with the retail outlet.

The available time for making a choice also affects sensitivity to price. When the refrigerator breaks down, an emergency situation is created and consumers become less price sensitive. The replacement product may be purchased because it is conveniently available, rather than because it represents the best value for money.

TASK DEFINITION

How the consumer defines the task of buying is an important influence on the purchase approach. The task may be defined as buying for oneself, for the family or as a gift for some other person. The buyer may want a product that is the best possible or that just suffices. Sometimes buyers may desire the most expensive or high quality product because of its status value; at other times they may demand the least costly product.

Consumer behaviour researchers have recently become interested in gift-giving as a special purchase situation. Gifts account for at least 10 per cent of retail sales with the greatest percentage of gift-giving occurring just prior to Christmas, in the months of November and December. When one buys a gift, special motives and requirements, which do not exist when one buys for oneself, come into play.[22] Belk has developed a system, based on Heider's balance theory, which investigates the relationship between the giver's self-confidence, the giver's liking of the recipient, the giver's evaluation of the gift, and the giver's perception of how much the recipient will like the gift.[23] All variables were correlated with gift choice but the ideal self-concept of the giver was the most important variable.

Heider's balance theory

According to Heider, people view themselves as being involved in relationships with the objects, persons and ideas in their environment. These relationships can be positive, in that the individual has a favourable attitude towards the object, person or idea, or they can be negative. In addition, attitude objects have positive or negative relationships with each other. These relationships may or may not match the attitude of the individual. A person is in a balanced situation if he or she has positive attitudes towards two things that have positive attitudes towards each other. An unbalanced situation exists when (1) the individual has positive attitudes towards two things that are negatively related to each other; and (2) the individual holds positive and negative attitudes towards two things that are either positively or negatively related to each other.

A balanced situation would exist if the consumer had a positive image of the gift recipient, a positive image of the gift, and a belief that the recipient would also like the gift. An unbalanced situation would exist if the consumer had positive images of the recipient of a gift and of the gift itself, but a belief that the recipient did not like the gift.

People try to obtain consistency between their cognitions (beliefs) and their behaviour. Therefore, being in an unbalanced situation is uncomfortable and creates pressure for the individual to alter attitudes. To achieve balance in the situation above, the consumer could lower the evaluation of the gift recipient by believing them to be ungrateful or lacking in taste. They could lower their evaluation of the gift by blaming the manufacturer for misrepresenting the product. Alternatively they could revise their assessment of how much the gift recipient liked the gift.

Social risk is greater when one purchases a gift for someone else than when one buys a gift for oneself.[24] Consumers are usually willing to pay more for a gift than something for personal use because they want to ensure that the product or service carries the right symbolic message in terms of the type of gift and its prestige value. As a result, consumers are often willing to spend more time and money when shopping for gifts than when shopping for themselves. One marketing tool based on consumer need to reduce risk in a gift-giving situation is the issuing of gift vouchers, which enable recipients to purchase the gift they want. Gift vouchers eliminate the risk of making the wrong choice in gift-giving.

Gift-givers appear to shop differently for different kinds of recipients. Otnes, Lawrey and Kim categorised recipients of gifts into easy to please and difficult to please.[25] When they examined how consumers select gifts, they found an interaction between consumer type and the type of recipient. 'Pleasers' bought what the easy recipient wanted and gave the difficult recipient either what worked in the past or what they, the pleasers, personally liked. 'Providers' bought gifts throughout the year and had no particular strategies for difficult recipients. 'Compensators' gave fun gifts or multiple presents to easy-to-please recipients. They tended to negotiate with difficult recipients. 'Acknowledgers' had no strategy for easy recipients but had multiple strategies for hard-to-please people (for example, buy on impulse, buy an affirming gift, and buy group gifts). 'Socialisers' bought what they wanted the easy recipient to have. 'Avoiders' didn't have particular strategies and were somewhat averse to buying gifts.

Consumers also give gifts to themselves. These gifts are often seen as little indulgences that reward or console the consumer for some action previously performed. A example of an advertisement suggesting that a product is a self-gift appears in figure 16.4. The message provided by the advertisement is that the consumer deserves something special.

Figure 16.4: Baci chocolates — an example of a self-gift

ANTECEDENT STATES

While the four characteristics previously discussed are determined by the external environment, an antecedent state is the only characteristic which is internal to a consumer. An antecedent state can be regarded as a pre-existing psychological or physical condition that the buyer brings to the situation. One form of antecedent state is the momentary or temporary condition. For example, an individual experiences a momentary state when he finds himself short of money in the checkout line of the supermarket. This is a temporarily embarrassing condition that will affect purchases made during the current shopping trip but that can easily be remedied on subsequent trips. Frequent momentary conditions experienced by customers include being ill or tired, being distracted or alert, being hungry or full, being cold or warm, and having varying amounts of monetary resources.

Moods are transitory states that all consumers experience. They can both affect and be affected by the consumer's interaction with specific consumption situations.[26] Moods are related to emotions and are frequently described in emotional terms: happy, sad, depressed, angry and so on. Positive moods are associated with increased purchase behaviour on the part of consumers. However, negative moods can also be related to purchasing for some people under some conditions. Although it is difficult for marketers to manipulate moods, they often try to do so by means of store design, the use of music and colour and by advertising themes.

 ## SITUATIONAL INVENTORIES

It is useful for a marketer to know the kinds of situations in which a product is likely to be used because this knowledge can contribute to product design and promotion.[27] To try to understand how consumers purchase and use products, situational inventories are developed. Situational inventories are usually product-specific because of the great diversity of ways that individual products are used. For example, the situations affecting the choice of a soft drink are unlikely to be the same as the situations affecting the choice of perfume.

Situational inventories can be developed in various ways. One of the most popular ways is to use focus-group discussions, in which consumers engage in open-ended talks about the purchase or use of a specific product or service category. These discussions usually generate a large number of purchase and use situations which are reduced by rationally eliminating similar or relevant situations. To illustrate, it may not matter whether consumers use a food product as a snack in the afternoon or in the evening. Therefore, both these uses might be grouped together as a single-use situation involving snacking. The categorisation procedure is usually performed by expert judges, such as frequent consumers, manufacturers or researchers, who are familiar with that product or service category. The ultimate aim is to produce a list of situations that are closely related to brand choice and which can then be used to determine how various consumer segments differ in their choices across situations.

A list of situations in which snack-food items might be consumed appears on page 422. A study that used the inventory showed that the ten items could be grouped into four situational dimensions: planned purchasing situations, impulsive consumption situations, nutritive situations, and informal serving situations.[28] The study also revealed that consumers could be segmented according to their choices in different situations. For example, light salty snacks tended to be unplanned purchases for one segment and for use in informal serving and party situations by another segment. Substantial snacks were purchased across planned, nutritive and party situations by the nutrition-conscious segment. These results suggest that producers of light salty snacks should position their products primarily as party food. Producers of more substantial snacks, however, could position their products as appropriate to a wide variety of situations.

A situational inventory for snack foods

1. You are shopping for a snack that you and your family can eat while watching television in the evenings. (Planned situation.)

2. You are planning a party for a few close friends and are wondering what to have around to snack on. (Planned situation.)

3. Snacks at your house have become dull lately and you are wondering what you might pick up that would be better. (Impulsive situation.)

4. You are going on a long automobile trip and are thinking that you should bring some snacks to eat along the way. (Nutritive situation.)

5. You suddenly realise that you have invited a couple of friends over for the evening and you have nothing for them to snack on. (Informal situation.)

6. You are at the grocery store when you get an urge for a between-meal snack. (Impulsive situation.)

7. You are at the supermarket and notice the many available snack products; you wonder if you should pick something up in case friends drop by. (Informal situation.)

8. You are thinking about what type of snack to buy to keep around the house this weekend. (Informal situation.)

9. You are at the store to pick up some things for a picnic you are planning with friends and are trying to decide what kind of snack to buy. (Nutritive situation.)

10. You are thinking about a snack to have with lunch at noon. (Nutritive situation.)

(*Source*: Russell W. Belk, 'An Exploratory Assessment of Situational Effects in Buyer Behaviour', *Journal of Marketing Research, II,* 1974, p. 160)

Situational inventories can also be developed by using objective situational characteristics. The general procedure would be for the marketer to:

1. determine which situational characteristics are most relevant to the product or service category of interest

2. determine the number or level of importance of each characteristic

3. obtain an inventory of situations by exhausting all possible combinations of various levels of the situational characteristics

4. eliminate irrelevant situations.

A situational inventory developed by Kakkar uses two dimensions to describe situations in which beverages are consumed: importance and visibility.[29] The inventory appears in table 16.2. Importance refers to the consumer's involvement with the choice. Visibility is a social dimension which involves others seeing the product being consumed. Instead of being asked about the frequency with which each situation arises, consumers were asked to rate their feelings in each of the particular situations using the Mehrabian–Russell Emotional Mediators (Pleasure–Arousal–Dominance) Instrument (table 16.3).[30] This method allowed researchers to determine the consumer's emotional state in the period just prior to the use situation. Because consumers buy for emotional as well as rational reasons, the study has implications for devising advertising messages directed at particular situations.

Other inventories have used other dimensions to classify situations. For example, a frequent set of dimensions includes whether the user is buying the product as a personal product or as a gift and whether the product will be used in the presence of other people or alone.

Table 16.2: A two-dimensional situation inventory for beverages

Situation	Description
Low importance/ low visibility	You're home alone and have just turned on the TV to watch an afternoon movie. Before you settle down to watch it, you decide to get something to drink.
Low importance/ high visibility	You have just bought a new 23" colour TV. Several of your regular group are coming over to watch the game this weekend. You are deciding on what you should provide for the group to drink. From your past experience with the group, it does not matter too much what you have to drink on such occasions as long as there is plenty of it.
High importance/ low visibility	You have been living alone for a while, working most of the day, too tired to do anything in the evening. One weekend you suddenly decide that you are going to shake out of it and make yourself an absolutely perfect meal. You hunt for a recipe, shop for the exact groceries and spend a good deal of time getting everything ready. You are ready to lay it out in style, just for yourself, when you realise that you haven't planned on anything to drink with the meal. You wonder what beverage would best compliment the feast you have prepared.
High importance/ high visibility	You have just moved into a new neighbourhood and are anxious to meet your new neighbours. You enthusiastically accept an invitation to a potluck dinner next door and are particularly pleased to learn that your hosts are well known for their fancy dinners and large parties. You are asked to bring something to drink and you wonder what you should take to go along with the good food and new friends.

(*Source*: P. Kakkar, *Situational Influence on Emotional Response: Cognitive Structure and Cognitive Process.* Unpublished doctoral dissertation, University of California, Los Angeles, 1975, pp. 60–61)

Table 16.3: The Mehrabian–Russell emotional mediators instrument

Wide-awake	+4*	:___:___:___:___:___:___:___:___:	−4 Sleepy	A**
Controlled	+4	:___:___:___:___:___:___:___:___:	−4 Controlling	D
Melancholic	+4	:___:___:___:___:___:___:___:___:	−4 Contented	P
Aroused	+4	:___:___:___:___:___:___:___:___:	−4 Unaroused	A
Influential	+4	:___:___:___:___:___:___:___:___:	−4 Influenced	D
Awed	+4	:___:___:___:___:___:___:___:___:	−4 Important	D
Satisfied	+4	:___:___:___:___:___:___:___:___:	−4 Unsatisfied	P
Autonomous	+4	:___:___:___:___:___:___:___:___:	−4 Guided	D
Bored	+4	:___:___:___:___:___:___:___:___:	−4 Relaxed	P
Happy	+4	:___:___:___:___:___:___:___:___:	−4 Unhappy	P
Dominant	+4	:___:___:___:___:___:___:___:___:	−4 Submissive	D
Calm	+4	:___:___:___:___:___:___:___:___:	−4 Excited	A
Annoyed	+4	:___:___:___:___:___:___:___:___:	−4 Pleased	P
Hopeful	+4	:___:___:___:___:___:___:___:___:	−4 Despairing	P
Cared-for	+4	:___:___:___:___:___:___:___:___:	−4 In control	D
Relaxed	+4	:___:___:___:___:___:___:___:___:	−4 Stimulated	A
Dull	+4	:___:___:___:___:___:___:___:___:	−4 Jittery	A
Frenzied	+4	:___:___:___:___:___:___:___:___:	−4 Sluggish	A

* Numerical codes and identifying letters (P.A.D.) are not included on the original instrument.
** P represents Pleasure; A represents Arousal; and D represents Dominance. These are the three dimensions of psychological situations.

(*Source*: Adapted from A. Mehrabian and J. A. Russell, *An Approach to Environmental Psychology*, M.I.T. Press, Cambridge, 1974, pp. 216–17)

 ## STRATEGIC IMPLICATIONS OF SITUATIONS

Knowledge of situations can be helpful to marketers in developing marketing strategies. Situations affect market segmentation, product positioning, promotional mix, product development and distribution. A review of some of the uses of situation in strategic marketing is offered below.

MARKET SEGMENTATION

A disadvantage of situational inventories based upon objective listings of situational characteristics is that they are insensitive to people's variable reactions. Individuals often respond quite differently to identical situations, a tendency which is known as 'person–situation interaction'. A classic study showing an interaction between person and situation was conducted by Nisbett and Kanouse. They observed that most normal-weight consumers will make more purchases if they shop for groceries when they are hungry. In contrast, obese people made the same number of purchases regardless of how long it had been since they had eaten. Thus, the amount of purchasing depended not only on the situational variables in the store, but on the characteristics of the customer.[31]

There are many examples of interactions between situations and people. Australians, for instance, have been found to differ in their sensitivity to environmental issues. Although most favour improving the environment, only 25 per cent believe they can do much about it and fully a third believe they have no influence at all. It has been found that with regard to environmental issues, Australians can be segmented into 'dark green', 'pale green', 'grey', and 'black'.[32] These market segments differ in their willingness to pay more for environmentally friendly products. Thus, in a purchase situation involving a choice of brands that differ in price and ecological soundness, 'dark greens' will be responsive to environmental benefits of the product whereas 'black' customers, given the same choices, will tend to be influenced by price or some other factor.

The tendency for people to differ in their response to situational variables in the marketplace can be useful in market segmentation.[33] Because different consumers desire different product benefits, marketers can profit from using 'person–situation segmentation'. An example of this form of segmentation appears in table 16.4. In the table, consumers are categorised by the benefits they obtain from sunscreen. Each of these categories represents a different consumer segment.

Table 16.4: Consumer situation by benefits matrix for suntan lotion, aimed at the adult women segment

Situations	Consumer groups								Situation-specific benefits
	Young children		Teenagers		Adult women		Adult men		
	Fair skin	Dark skin	Fair skin	Dark skin	Fair skin	Dark skin	Fair skin	Dark skin	
Beach/ boat sunbathing					Summer perfume				a. Windburn protection b. Formula and container can stand heat c. Container floats and is distinctive (not easily lost)
Home-poolside sunbathing					Combined moisturizer				a. Large pump dispenser b. Won't stain wood, concrete, or furnishings
Sunlamp bathing					Combined moisturizer and massage oil				a. Designed specifically for type of lamp b. Artificial tanning ingredient
Snow skiing					Winter perfume				a. Special protection from special light rays and weather b. Antifreeze formula
Consumer-specific benefits	Special protection a. Protection critical b. Non-poisonous		Special protection a. Fit in jeans pocket b. Used by opinion leaders		Special protection Desirable scent for women		Special protection Desirable scent for men		

(*Source*: Adapted from Peter R. Dickson, 'Person–Situation: Segmentation's Missing Link', *Journal of Marketing*, 46, Fall 1982)

PRODUCT POSITIONING AND ADVERTISING

Products can be positioned for specific occasions or for a number of situations. For example, one study found that consumers thought of certain foods as appropriate to some meal time occasions and not for other occasions. Other foods, such as hamburgers, were viewed as appropriate for lunch and for evening tea.[34] Having one's product seen as acceptable across situations is an advantage as it tends to increase the volume of product sold. Therefore, some industries, such as the flower industry, have tried to position their products as appropriate to many uses and occasions.

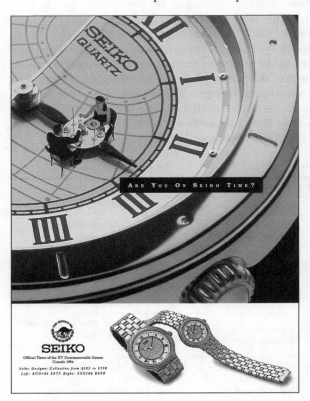

Figure 16.5: This advertisement positions the product for use in a specific situation.

The discovery of new usage situations can also be important for revitalising or repositioning products.[35] The producers of Napisan, originally known as a nappy soaker, discovered that their product was popular with lawn bowlers because it could remove grass and dirt stains from white uniforms. Furthermore, the product can be used on coloured items as well as white ones. These discoveries could open up new possibilities to position the product as a stain remover for coloured and white clothing.

Products are often advertised in a usage context. Therefore, the consumer's perceptions of how the product should be used influence the advertising theme, copy and layout decisions. The same product may be positioned for different situations. Alternatively, products may be positioned for specific situations. In figure 16.5, Seiko has positioned its designer collection watches for situations in which watches are worn as fashion items as well as for telling the time. Some have referred to this as 'framing' the product in a usage situation.

PRODUCT DEVELOPMENT

Products are developed not only for consumer types but also for specific situations. If there are usage situations that are not covered by existing products, there is an exploitable opportunity for the innovative marketer. Recently, Australians have become concerned with increases in ultraviolet radiation. They still want to use the beach in the middle of the day, but they don't want to be over-exposed to the sun's rays. A variety of new products have been developed, including special hats, cover-up swimwear and powerful sun blocks, to allow Australians to take advantage of outdoor life without suffering negative consequences.

Another recently developed product was created by Uncle Toby's, who made minor changes to existing products to come up with new cereals in the form of a bar.[36] The new breakfast-cereal bars, Lite Start, Sports Plus, and Sultanas 'n Wheat Bran, are targeted at Australians who are too busy to eat breakfast. According to *What Australia Eats*, a study conducted by the marketing consultancy Food Team, the number of people who eat nothing for breakfast is substantial, varying between 14 per cent and 31 per cent depending on the day of the week. The lack of easy, convenient breakfast substitutes coupled with a frequently occurring situation opens up opportunities for breakfast-on-the-go products.

Figure 16.6: An example of situational influence on product design. This cordless phone allows consumers to receive and make calls in situations where corded telephones cannot be used.

DISTRIBUTION

Distribution strategies can also be influenced by product purchase and usage situations. Products that are seen as convenience items, but which customers don't often think about, need to be widely available. Because customers don't often think about the product they tend to run out of it at inconvenient times and want to purchase it quickly.

Figure 16.7: Last minute purchases are often made at airports prior to travelling.

Examples of extensively distributed convenience products to be used in particular situations are sunscreen for the over-exposed beach-goer, mosquito spray for the traveller to Australia's top end, and pantyhose for the active business woman who may ladder her stockings at work. Even expensive items are sometimes conveniently distributed because people often fail to plan ahead. Duty-free shops at airports cater to the busy traveller who may not have had the opportunity to purchase gifts or personal essentials before arriving for the flight. The existence of retail outlets at the airport allows them to make last minute purchases. Conversely, important events often require the consumer to obtain special products. The distribution of these products can be more selective, because customers anticipate the event and are willing to exert effort to prepare for it.

Sale of items at special events represents a distribution response to consumer needs. When consumers attend rock concerts, football games and other events, they may not anticipate obtaining a souvenir. Once in the situation, however, a purchase of memorabilia may seem desirable. Furthermore, the use of these products may be linked to attending the specific event. Thus, audiences at rock concerts may wear shirts emblazoned with the name of their favourite rock band. Makers of licensed products take advantage of the effects of situation on consumer purchase patterns by producing items that are associated with specific events or clubs and by having products readily available at events or large club gatherings.[37]

SUMMARY

A situation is an instance of human interaction with the environment that involves behaviour, cognitive and affective responses, and environmental factors over a period of time. Situations have beginnings and ends and vary in degrees of complexity. They affect consumer behaviour by eliciting needs and wants, offering cues, influencing the importance of benefits, and altering the basis of post-purchase evaluation. Factors that influence the importance of situation in product purchase and evaluation are the degree of brand loyalty of the consumer, the involvement status of the consumer and the number of uses the product has.

The four basic types of situation are the communication situation, the purchase situation, the consumption situation and the disposition situation. Aspects of situational influence include physical surroundings, social surroundings, task definition, temporal perspective and the antecedent state of the consumer. Physical surroundings are the tangible properties of the environment. Social surroundings include the presence of other people, their characteristics, and the roles that each person plays. Task definition is the reason for the person being in the situation. Temporal perspective includes the time of day or year, and the person's orientation to past, present or future. Antecedent states include moods and all conditions occurring before the current situation.

Situational inventories have been constructed to measure the effect of situation on purchasing behaviour. Inventories can be developed by using focus-group information or by examining objective situational characteristics. Person–situation matrices describe the benefits that different market segments seek in different situations.

Knowledge of situations helps marketers segment markets, position products, devise promotion strategies, develop new products, and distribute products appropriately.

Questions

1. What is a situation? Why is it important for marketing managers to understand the concept of a situation?

2. What factors determine whether the consumer's choice will be influenced more by the characteristics of the product or by the nature of the situation?

3. What kinds of situations exist? Give examples of each type of situation.

4. What kinds of variables would be classified as part of the physical surroundings?

5. What kinds of variables would be classified as part of the social surroundings?

6. Describe a particular buying situation and list the temporal variables that might affect that situation.

7. Choose a product category and show how one's task definition might change the particular product purchased.

8. What is meant by the term 'antecedent conditions'?

9. How does the process of buying a gift differ from purchasing for one's self?

10. How could one construct an inventory to measure the effects of situation?

11. What is a person–situation interaction? How does it affect buyer behaviour?

12. How is the concept of situation used in marketing strategy?

Case study

IKEA is an unusual retailer. The sales staff in its brightly lit, barn-like stores are almost invisible. They never approach shoppers, but wait until the customer asks for help. The retailer sells furniture, but it never delivers. Its products are sold unassembled in flat cartons, which shoppers collect from shelves at the back of the store or from a loading dock.

Ikea's soft-sell, do-it-yourself retailing formula is a hit with shoppers. Although furniture sales have been depressed since 1989, Ikea claims to have lifted sales 15 per cent over the past 12 months. This year, the opening of a new store in Sydney and growth from Ikea's existing stores along the east coast are expected to boost sales by 20 per cent.

Executives at Ikea Australia will not discuss their company's sales or profits. But rival furniture retailers estimate that the five company-owned Ikea stores in Sydney, Brisbane and Melbourne, plus a franchised store in Perth, turned over $15 million in 1990–91, up from $13 million in 1989–90. The new store scheduled to open in the Sydney suburb of Moore Park on July 18 is expected to turn over $2 million during its first year.

Mikael Bartroff, Ikea Australia's managing director, refuses to talk about sales figures, but he is more than willing to explain why the furniture and homewares retailer, which was set up in Sweden in 1947 and is now run by senior executives based in Sweden and Denmark, is thriving. "Shoppers see Ikea as a value-for-money retailer," Bartroff says.

"In the current environment, that is what people are looking for."

That value-for-money image has not been easy to achieve. Six years ago, the Swedish krona was devalued by 30 per cent and, because all the buying is done through a central office in Sweden, prices in Ikea's Australian stores jumped 25 per cent. Overnight, Australian shoppers categorised Ikea as an expensive retailer. "We have spent the past six years fighting that perception," Bartroff says. He claims that by holding price increases to less than 2 per cent a year since 1986, Ikea has won the fight. "People now think Ikea offers value for money," he says.

Ikea's 15 per cent growth during the past year has been driven by new customers, rather than increased spending by its existing customers. But its marketing manager, Michael Flynn, admits that consumer awareness of the Ikea name is low. In February, Ikea hired a new advertising agency, John Bevins, which has since launched a television and newspaper ad campaign built around the theme: 'Where quality is not a matter of chance. It's a choice'. Bartroff says: "People who know Ikea are very loyal to it. The trick is to get them to our stores in the first place."

Ikea arrived in Australia in 1975, 28 years after it was established in Sweden as a mail-order furniture and homewares business . . . The first Australian Ikea store was opened in the Sydney suburb of St Leonards by Jerd Kastengreen, a Swede who had been transferred to Australia

with the Swedish trade commission . . .

Late in 1989, Ikea bought back the franchises in NSW, Victoria and Queensland. "The franchisees had different opinions on how the business should be run and a lot of time was spent agreeing to disagree," Bartroff says. "Also, some of the stores were losing money. The franchisees wanted to sell, so we bought."

A new management team for Ikea Australia was hired, headed by Bartroff, a Dane who had spent six years working for Ikea Greece. The Perth store is still franchised and Bartroff says Ikea Australia is unlikely to buy out the Perth franchisee.

Ikea Australia employs the retailing formula used by Ikea around the world. Products are either grouped in mock room settings or stand alone, so shoppers can see them in isolation or as part of a room. People are encouraged to browse, checking prices, gathering information and making buying decisions without help from sales assistants. No Ikea customer is confronted with a salesman asking "Can I help?"

The retailer's key selling tool is the Ikea catalogue, which is distributed once a year through letterboxes and stacked in piles at the entrance to the store. Ikea distributed 50 million catalogues, designed, produced and printed in Europe, around the world in 1990. The catalogue used in Australia every September is also used in Iceland, Hong Kong, Dubai, Singapore, Saudi Arabia and the Canary Islands. Ikea Australia sent out two million catalogues last year.

This year's 168-page catalogue includes prices and specifications for 7000 products, including a $995 sofa, $125 swivel chair, $2960 kitchen and $6 picture frame. Once shoppers have selected a product, they go to the back of the store and collect it — packed unassembled in a flat carton — put it on a trolley and wheel it through the checkout and collect the product from the store's loading dock.

The Ikea stores include a playroom for toddlers, video room for older children and a snack bar. Its Moorabbin store also offers a car-washing service for customers. "Our aim is to make an Ikea store friendly and entertaining," Flynn says. It also tries to keep shoppers in the store for as long as possible: Flynn claims customers spend, on average, four hours in an Ikea shop. Ikea stores do not deliver, but will arrange delivery through outside contractors.

By selling products unassembled, employing few sales staff and not delivering, Ikea keeps its warehousing, distribution and product-handling costs low. Bartroff says the money saved on staff and warehousing is pumped into store design and fit-out. "But our cost structure is a lot different to many conventional retailers," he says.

Except for the glassware, crockery, linen and knick-knacks sold in its Market Hall section, all Ikea products are sold unassembled. Customers put them together at home using a tool that comes with each product. Flynn claims the home assembly is part of Ikea's appeal. "It gives people a sense of involvement and achievement," he says. "It also contributes to our value-for-money image."

All the products Ikea sells are designed by the retailer and made under contract by 1500 suppliers around the world. Furniture accounts for 70 per cent of the Australian company's sales and its top-sellers are kitchen kits and sofas. The Australian stores, which range in size from 4000 to 6000 square metres, carry 60 per cent of the stock found in Ikea's larger European and US stores; 10–15 per cent of products sold here come from Australian manufacturers.

Ikea Australia's expansion plans are modest. Bartroff says the Sydney market can support only five Ikea stores while the maximum number in Melbourne is three and in Brisbane two.

The retailer is developing its mail order division, which accounts for only 4 per cent of sales at present, but Bartroff says mail-order will never dominate Ikea. "Part of the Ikea sales philosophy involves getting people to browse through our stores and take the products home with them," he says. "So there is a limit to how far we would want mail-order selling to grow."

Neil Shoebridge, *Business Review Weekly*, 28 June 1991

Case study questions

1. Ikea is a 'store-based' distributor, even though it would be possible for Ikea to adopt a mail-order approach. As such it has given importance to store atmosphere and customer service. What are the characteristics of their merchandise and their target market that makes this a viable strategy?

2. Do you think the availability of multi-media technology will have an impact on their strategy? If so, what would be the impact and why would it occur?

SUGGESTED READING

R. Belk, 'Situational Variables and Consumer Behaviour', *Journal of Consumer Research*, 2, December 1975, pp. 157–164.

G. N. Pungi and D. W. Stewart, 'An Interaction Framework for Consumer Decision Making, *Journal of Consumer Research*, 10, September 1983, pp. 181–196.

P. Dickson, 'Person–Situation: Segmentation's Missing Link', *Journal of Marketing*, 6, Fall 1982, pp. 56–64.

ENDNOTES

1. Neil Shoebridge, 'Videotape Sales Slow to Move on to Fast Forward', *Business Review Weekly*, 1 Oct. 1993, pp. 76–77, 79.

2. J. Paul Peter and Jerry C. Olson, *Consumer Behaviour and Marketing Strategy*, Irwin, Homewood, Ill., 1990, p. 315.

3. Russell W. Belk, 'Situational Variables and Consumer Behaviour', *Journal of Consumer Research*, 2, Dec. 1975, pp. 157–64.

4. Fleming Hanson, *Consumer Choice Behaviour: A Cognitive Theory*, Free Press, New York, 1972.

5. Peter H. Webb, 'Consumer Initial Processing in a Difficult Media Environment', *Journal of Consumer Research*, 6, Dec. 1979, pp. 225–26.

6. Marvin E. Goldberg and Gerald H. Gorn, 'Happy and Sad TV Programs: How They Affect Reactions to Commercials', *Journal of Consumer Research*, 14, Dec. 1987, pp. 387–403.

7. Michael A. Kamins, Lawrence J. Marks and Deborah Skinner, 'Television Commercial Evaluation in the Context of Program Induced Mood: Congruency Versus Consistency Effects', *Journal of Advertising*, 20, June 1991, pp. 1–14.

8. Gary F. Soldow and Victor Principe, 'Response to Commercials as a Function of Program Context', *Journal of Advertising Research*, 21, April 1981, pp. 59–65. C. Whan Park and Gordon W. McClung, 'The Effect of TV Program Involvement on Involvement With Commercials', in Richard J. Lutz (ed.), *Advances in Consumer Research*, Vol. 13, Association for Consumer Research, Provo, Utah, 1986, pp. 544–48.

9. The discussion of informational influence in purchase situations is based on James F. Engle, Roger D. Blackwell and Paul W. Miniard, *Consumer Behaviour*, Dryden Press, Chicago, Ill., pp. 209–10. Also Jacob Jacoby, Donald Speller and Carol Kohn, 'Brand Choice as a Function of Information Overload', and James A. Bettman and Michael A. Zins, 'Information Format and Choice Task Effects in Decision Making', *Journal of Consumer Research*, 6, Sept. 1979, pp. 141–53.

10. Russell W. Belk, John Sherry and Melanie Wallendorf, 'A Naturalistic Enquiry Into Buyer and Seller Behaviour at a Swap Meet', *Journal of Consumer Research*, 14, March 1988, pp. 449–70.

11. James H. McAlexander, John W. Shouten and Scott D. Roberts, 'Consumer Behaviour and Divorce', *Research in Consumer Behaviour*, 6, 1993, pp. 153–84.

12. Belk, Dec. 1975, pp. 157–64.

13. G. C. Bruner II, 'Music, Mood and Marketing', *Journal of Marketing*, Oct. 1990, pp. 62–82.

14. J. Bellizzi, A. Crawley and R. Hasty, 'The Effects of Colour in Store Design', *Journal of Retailing*, Spring 1983, pp. 21–45.

15. J. Donovan and J. R. Rossiter, 'Store Atmosphere: An Environmental Psychology Approach', *Journal of Retailing*, Spring 1982, pp. 34–57.

16. G. Harrell, M. Hutt and J. Anderson, 'Path Analysis of Buyer Behaviour Under Conditions of Crowding', *Journal of Marketing Research*, Feb. 1980, pp. 45–51. S. Eroglu and G. D. Harrell, 'Retail Crowding', *Journal of Retailing*, Winter 1986, pp. 346–63.

17. Michael K. Hui and John G. Bateson, 'Perceived Control and the Effects of Crowding and Consumer Choice on the Service Experience', *Journal of Consumer Research*, 18, Sept. 1991, pp. 174–84.

18. M. J. Bitner, 'Evaluation Service Encounters', *Journal of Marketing*, April 1990, pp. 69–82.

19. E. Mattson and A. J. Dobinsky, 'Shopping Patterns', *Psychology and Marketing*, Spring 1987, pp. 46–58.

20. B. E. Mattson, 'Situational Influences on Store Choice', *Journal of Retailing*, Fall 1982, pp. 46–58.

21. Kenneth E. Miller and James L. Ginter, 'An Investigation of Situational Variation in Brand Choice Behaviour and Attitude', *Journal of Marketing Research*, 16, Feb. 1979, pp. 111–23.

22. S. K. Banks, 'Gift-Giving: A Review and an Interactive Paradigm', *Advances in Consumer Research*, Vol. 6, 1979, pp. 319–24. J. F. Sherry, 'Gift-Giving in an Anthropological Perspective', *Journal of Consumer Research*, 10(2), pp. 157–68.

23. R. W. Belk, 'It's the Thought That Counts: A Signed Digraph Analysis of Gift-Giving', *Journal of Consumer Research*, 3, Dec. 1976, pp. 155–62. R. W. Belk, 'Gift-Giving Behaviour', *Research in Marketing*, Vol. 2, 1979, pp. 95–126.

24. M. Vincent and W. Zikmund, 'An Experimental Study of Situational Effects on Risk Perception', in M. J. Schlinger (ed.), *Advances in Consumer Research*, Association for Consumer Research, Chicago, Ill., 1975.

25. Cele Otnes, Tina M. Lowry and Young Chan Kin, 'Gift Selection for Easy and Difficult Recipients: A Social Roles Interpretation', *Journal of Consumer Research*, 20, Sept. 1993, pp. 229–44.

26. M. P. Gardner and R. P. Hull, 'Consumers' Mood States', *Psychology and Marketing*, Summer 1988, pp. 169–82. R. Lawson, 'The Effects of Mood on Retrieving Product Information', in M. Wallendorf and P. Anderson, *Advances in Consumer Research*, Vol. 12, Association for Consumer Research, Provo, Utah, 1987, pp. 404–7.

27. The discussion in this section is based on Henry Assael, *Consumer Behaviour and Marketing Action*, pp. 531–33. Russell W. Belk, 'An Exploratory Assessment of Situational Effects in Buyer Behaviour', *Journal of Marketing Research*, 11, May 1974, p. 160.

28. Russell W. Belk, 'An Exploratory Assessment of Situational Effects in Buyer Behaviour', *Journal of Marketing Research*, 11, May 1974, p. 160.

29. P. Kakker, *Situational Influence on Emotional Response, Cognitive Structure and Cognitive Process*, Ph.D. Dissertation, University of California, Los Angeles, 1975, pp. 60–61.

30. A. Mehrabian and J. A. Russell, *An Approach to Environmental Psychology*, M.I.T. Press, Cambridge, 1974, pp. 216–17.

31. R. E. Nisbett and D. E. Kanouse, 'Obesity, Food Deprivation and Supermarket Shopping Behaviour', *Journal of Personality and Social Psychology*, 12, Aug. 1969, pp. 289–94.

32. George Camarkaris, 'How Green Was My Market', in Peter Graham (ed.), *Australian Marketing: Critical Essays, Readings and Cases*, Prentice-Hall, New York, 1993, pp. 64–66.

33. Peter R. Dickson, 'Person–Situation: Segmentation's Missing Link', *Journal of Marketing*, 6, Fall 1982, pp. 56–64.

34. 'Catalyst Measurement Mapping Method Identifies Competition, Defines Markets', *Marketing News*, 14 May, 1982.

35. Jagdish Sheth and Glenn Morrison, 'Winning Against the Marketplace: Nine Strategies for Revitalising Mature Products', *Journal of Consumer Marketing*, 1, 1984, pp. 17–28.

36. Neil Shoebridge, 'Uncle Toby's Baits a Hook for Breakfast-On-The-Run Brigade', *Business Review Weekly*, 12 Nov. 1993, pp. 70–72.

37. Neil Shoebridge, 'Acme's Guns and Roses Bonanza Taps Black-Shirt Brigade', *Business Review Weekly*, 5 March 1993, pp. 89–90. (Article reproduced in this book as case study on pp. 162–63.)

PART

4

MACRO
CONCERNS

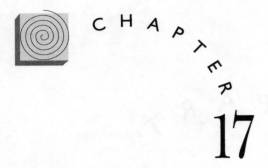

C H A P T E R

17

Monitoring the environment

OBJECTIVES

This chapter should help you to:

- know why it is important for marketers to understand the environment
- know why it is necessary to understand change
- know what factors are more likely to cause change
- become familiar with key aspects of the present environment
- identify some key areas of change.

 ## INTRODUCTION

Unless a business has a clear understanding of the society of which it is a part, it will not be able to operate efficiently or effectively. Not only must it understand current behaviours, it must also be alert to the impact of change. Changes in consumer values and behaviour, technology, economic conditions and politics (at both the local and global level) can all affect product demand, how products are distributed and how they are bought and consumed. Managers need to be able to identify any changes in the environment that will affect the business and develop appropriate coping strategies.

There have been many books and articles written that identify the forces of change and provide advice on coping strategies.[1] This is understandable when you consider that the development of the transistor and microchip has not only changed how all technically based products are made, but also came close to destroying the whole economy of Switzerland. Until the 1960s, the Swiss produced high quality mechanical products such as watches, clocks and sewing machines. The use of electronic components instead of electric motors meant that most factories had to re-tool. The development of computers and word processing packages has made typewriters all but obsolete and compact disc technology has not only destroyed the vinyl record industry but also all the associated industries, such as needle and turntable manufacturers.

In the past twenty years, the Australian community has been disrupted by an unusually large number of social, cultural and technical changes. These changes came from a range of sources such as population changes, technological developments, new ideas and changes in the physical environment. Changes from these sources, singly and combined, impact on people and marketplace behaviour. For example, technological and chemical advances in health care since the 1950s have led to a reduction in infant mortality rates and a massive increase in life expectancy.[2] Increased life expectancy and nutrition education that started in the 1970s altered consumer demands. By the 1980s consumers wanted, among other things, gyms, fitness centres and food products that were high in fibre and low in salt, fat and sugar. A number of industries, particularly the sugar industry, were casualties of this change (see the box on page 438).

Figure 17.1: In the 1980s, consumers were made aware of the dangers of eating too much fat and sugar, and a range of products was soon developed to meet the new demands.

One factor in the management of change is how well an organisation monitors its environment. Monitoring involves not only identifying where change occurs but also correctly assessing consumer response. Assessing consumer response is crucial, as the launch and failure of Molly

McButter demonstrated. Since the 1980s, many consumers have become obsessed about their fat intake, and manufacturers are generating big sales with no-fat or low-fat products. The launch of Molly McButter in 1990 was designed to capitalise on this attitude/value change. Alberto Culver (Australia) described the product as an alternative to butter for people who did not want to use butter because of the fat content. The product was made of flakes of corn starch sprayed with butter or cheese, and was designed to be sprinkled over hot food. Unfortunately, the flakes did not melt as butter would. So, despite the fact that it was responding to the healthy lifestyle perspective being adopted by consumers, the product failed. This was because even though consumers have developed an attitude change to fat, they have not necessarily changed their attitudes towards butter. Consumers wanted a product that looked and tasted like butter, but without the fat. It is understandable then, that a more realistic butter substitute — Gold'n Canola margarine— was more successful.[3]

Sugar — an industry at war

In the 1980s, consumers became health conscious and particularly concerned with their consumption of sugar and fat. The sugar industry was suddenly under threat and is still fighting for survival. Domestic consumption fell from 75 200 tonnes in 1980 to 70 200 tonnes in 1983. Raw sugar export prices also declined from US65c per pound in 1975 to US4c per pound in 1985. During this period, 80 per cent of sugar produced in Australia was sold overseas. The outcome was financial ruin for many farmers.

In 1985, to counter the growth in the use of artificial sweeteners, the sugar industry embarked on a major advertising program. They warned consumers not to be misled by advertising and labels on sweeteners. This, coupled with the 'Sugar, a natural part of life' campaign started in 1983, has been partly responsible for creating more positive attitudes towards sugar.

The war against the artificial sweeteners has been costly. The 'Sugar, a natural part of life' campaign cost $32.5 million and the 1985 campaign over $2 million. Although the former campaign was dropped in 1991, its successor, the 'Short and Sweet' campaign which stressed the superior taste of sugar, has helped to maintain positive attitudes.

Sugar consumption has, however, remained low. In 1990–91, Australians each consumed 46 kilograms of sugar either directly or in food and drink, which was a 1 per cent decrease from 1989–90.

(*Source*: Compiled from Tim Allerton, 'Sugar Industry Goes Sour on Health Foods', *Weekend Australian*, 6–7 April 1985; Neil Shoebridge, 'CSR Makes Do With a Little Less Sweet-talking', *Business Review Weekly*, 6 October 1991. See also the case study in this book on pages 75–6.)

MONITORING CHANGE

There are certain areas in which changes, if they occur, affect marketplace behaviour so marketers should monitor them carefully. These areas include demographics, technological and scientific development, socio-economic conditions, values and ideas and political systems. In this section we will discuss some of these areas and their relevance to consumer behaviour.

DEMOGRAPHICS

Demographics is the study and description of individuals and groups of people in a community in terms of size, distribution and composition. The factors that are usually measured are population size and distribution, age, ethnic mix and household structure. Monitoring and predicting demographic changes requires the collection and interpretation of information about past and present trends. In general, demographic information is easy to obtain as most governments collect and publish demographic data.

Population size and spread determine the absolute size of potential markets and where the greatest concentration of people is. Currently, the total population of Australia is 17 million and, by the year 2011, it is expected to be over 20 million. The population of New Zealand is 3.5 million. In both countries there has been a marked decline in the rural population since the 1970s, a trend that is continuing.[4] Australians, for example, prefer to live on the coast and in the capital cities. And half of the population of New Zealand lives in Auckland.

Table 17.1: Population of each state and capital city in Australia

State	Population (million)	City	Population (million)	Percentage of state population living in capital city
New South Wales	6.0	Sydney	3.6	62.8
Victoria	4.5	Melbourne	3.0	70.3
Queensland	3.0	Brisbane	1.3	44.9
Western Australia	1.5	Perth	1.2	72.6
South Australia	1.5	Adelaide	1.0	72.8
Tasmania and Northern Territory	0.5	Darwin/Hobart	0.3	41.3

(*Source*: ABS Census Characteristics of Australia — 1991 Census of Population and Housing)

Australia is a fairly homogeneous nation, but there are some differences across the states. The growth rate in each state has been uneven since the 1970s. Between 1976 and 1986, Queensland and Western Australia grew at twice the rate of the other states, and continue to do so even though the overall growth has slowed. This means that demands for housing and related products are much higher in these states. Although the birth rate per population is highest in the Northern Territory, a greater population density in the eastern states means that more children are born and live in these eastern states.[5]

Table 17.2: Rate of population growth in the Australian states (1976–1989)

Year	Queensland	New South Wales	Victoria	South Australia	Western Australia
1976	11.51	4.72	7.64	5.80	10.57
1981	10.78	5.26	3.55	3.39	9.36
1986	10.64	5.36	5.08	4.61	10.89
1987	1.95	1.44	1.14	0.83	2.76
1988	2.44	1.57	1.24	1.00	2.87
1989	3.19	1.22	1.38	1.15	3.13

(*Source*: Australian Bureau of Statistics, *1991 Year Book*)

Income levels are similar across the states with New South Wales having the highest average weekly earnings of approximately $608 and Queensland having the lowest at $594. However, spending patterns are different in the capital cities (see table 17.3). The noticeable differences are Sydney and Perth for housing, Melbourne for fuel and power and clothing and footwear and Adelaide for medical care. Other statistics reveal that Adelaide also has the highest sales of bottled water. And Victoria and Tasmania have the highest purchase rates for winter clothes.[6]

Table 17.3: Percentages of total expenditure in the capital cities — market estimates at June 1986

	Brisbane	Sydney	Melbourne	Adelaide	Perth
Housing costs	9.50	11.46	9.73	9.21	10.86
Fuel and power	1.62	1.81	2.18	1.70	1.85
Food	17.00	16.72	16.98	16.62	17.07
Alcohol and tobacco	3.39	4.68	4.71	4.30	4.49
Clothing and footwear	5.78	6.41	7.40	6.78	6.09
Household equipment	7.59	6.48	6.78	7.20	7.52
Medical care	5.62	5.64	5.79	6.96	5.69
Transport	14.56	15.39	14.75	15.43	15.20

(*Source*: States year books, 1991)

Government statistics reveal that television viewing is similar across states, with a national average of 21.6 hours per week; Sydney has the highest percentage of radio listeners. Newspaper readership is fairly evenly spread, but people in Melbourne and Adelaide read them the least.[7]

Table 17.4: Newspaper reach in the capital cities (14+ years)

	Sunday (%)	Saturday afternoon (%)	Weekday morning (%)	Weekday afternoon (%)
Brisbane	89	15	64	40
Sydney	73	—	45	53
Melbourne	21	39	72	40
Adelaide	70	—	63	52
Perth	84	30	75	44

(*Source*: Morgan survey 1986)

Age clusters

The median age of the Australian population is 33 and, if the current trend continues, it will be 38 by the year 2021. The net effect of this is that by 2011, approximately 2.6 million Australians will be over 65.

Table 17.5: Projected number of Australians aged over 60, 1981–2001

Age group	Population (000)				Percentage increase		
	1981	1991	2001	2011	1981–91	1991–2001	2001–2011
60–64	613.9	718.8	768.2	1 145.2	17.1	6.9	49.1
65–69	535.8	654.5	629.8	853.0	22.2	−3.8	35.4
70–74	401.2	502.9	590.6	636.2	25.3	17.4	7.7
75–79	261.1	384.4	475.5	453.2	47.2	23.7	−2.6
80–84	154.6	234.1	302.4	359.4	51.4	29.2	18.9
85+	102.5	162.5	256.8	348.1	58.5	58.0	35.6
65+	1 455.3	1 938.4	2 255.3	2 659.9	33.2	16.4	17.9
Total population	14 926.8	17 008.6	18 916.7	20 557.1	14.0	11.2	9.7

(*Source*: ABS Statistics)

The expected increase in the number of people aged over 65 in the twenty-first century is due to the ageing 'baby boomers'. Currently the baby boomers are aged between 35 and 50 with the main cluster being between 38 and 45. This represents an unusually large age cluster. Because of its sheer size, this group drives marketplace demand. By 2011, the oldest of the baby boomers will turn 65. For this reason, it will be increasingly important to understand the behaviour of people in their 'third age'.

Although current marketing efforts are focused on the over-35 age group, marketers are beginning to focus on the over-50 group as the first of the baby boomers will turn 50 in the 1990s. When the baby boomers turn 50 they will be the largest group of 50 year olds this century. They will also be healthy, affluent, educated, sophisticated and careful.

Grown up, cashed up, and ready to spend

LEA WRIGHT — marketing writer

Forget tales of the future being dominated by free-spending "superannuants" because it will be the maturing baby boomers that lead the spending spree — once the recession is over.

A study produced by advertising agency Doorley Buchanan called the Challenge of Change says that from 1986 to the year 2000, the 35 to 54 age group will increase by 44 per cent; the 55 to 64 will steady and the over 65s will rise 35 per cent.

"What we have been talking about in the past is an aging of the population based on percentage figures rather than real numbers. The real major increase will be among the 35- to 54-year-old age group," agency chief executive Mr Malcolm Rankin said.

The study was prepared from report material from ABS statistics, IBIS, ABARE, Australian Taxation Office, newspapers and other sources.

Key to the findings is that the 35- to 54-year-old consumers of the late 1990s will be among the most wealthy and best educated.

The study predicts this group may unleash a spending explosion on the Australian market in the middle to the late part of this decade.

"At 45, people reach their peak earning period and there is decreased importance on the mortgage. They have extra real spending power. Wives will be back at work, they will be coming into inheritances, and people who have never saved will start to," Mr Rankin said.

The study says the 35 to 54s will be more individualistic and not so easily reached through mass marketing techniques.

These people will be highly motivated and look for a high quality of life — and will be prepared to pay for quality goods and services.

They will be sophisticated, having grown up with media and marketing; looking for experiences and participation in activities; convenience orientated; and will value leisure time and be health conscious.

"Key words will be healthy versus health, style versus fashion, value versus cheap and natural versus artificial."

As people seek greater choice, the market leaders of early 1990s with 40 per cent shares could see them whittled away to maybe a 20 per cent stake in the late 90s, Mr Rankin added.

For marketers, opportunities will lie with quality niche products. Consumers will be turned off by superficial advertising or a hard sell that is too trite or overt. Product life cycles are also likely to be shorter.

The study points out that behind the rise of the 35- to 54-year-old spenders are key changes to the economy, environment, technology and society.

Economically, the study noted the vice-like squeeze on the middle class.

In 1986, about 33 per cent of all households earned more than 50 per cent of all income. By 1996, 38 per cent of households are expected to control 70 per cent of all income — as such polarising the rich and the poor, or the spenders and the subsisters.

The family home will also be increasingly used as an equity source for loans, and will increase the spending power and disposable income of homeowners.

The report notes the environment will remain a strong issue but people will not want to suffer inferior products to support the environment.

In the home, men are expected to participate more in household chores, including shopping. For marketers this necessitates a major change from the present assumption that women are the prime household grocery shoppers.

Outside the home, the consumer mood is changing and it is becoming less fashionable in the late 90s to have showy wealth, and that the community — church, dinner parties and barbecues — will become more important.

Sydney Morning Herald,
11 April 1991

Research indicates that the older consumer will be predominantly female and of European descent. One feature of our older generation is that women live on average eight years longer than men. In the over-65 category, the ratio of women to men is 1 to 0.7, but by the time people reach the over-85 category the ratio is 2 to 1. Currently, people of European descent dominate the over-65 group, but this will gradually change due to an increase in migrants from Asia. In the 1950s only 1.3 per cent of the population were originally from Asia but now over 20 per cent of migrants are from Asian countries.[8]

One way to estimate some of the demands of the elderly in the next century is to examine the research relating to consumers who are currently over 60. Studies show that, provided health and income remain the same, the type of activities that the aged engage in do not dramatically change.[9] Only a competence developed by middle age continues to be an activity into old age. Skills in new, complex tasks and the development of new interests tend not to emerge.[10] Other research demonstrates that people maintain growth in creativity and conceptual and other faculties throughout their sixties and into their seventies. Certainly, participation in sports requiring high levels of physical activity and stamina decline with age. But if a person has an active interest in sport, this is likely to be maintained and substituted with other, less strenuous sporting activities such as golf, bowls and walking.

In essence, what people do in middle age will shape their lifestyles in old age. To understand the activities of the over-65 group in 2011, we need to look at the lifestyle of the current baby boomers, and understand the needs of the current elderly as these needs will also be applicable to the 'third age' boomers.[11]

The main needs of today's elderly are:[12]
- to render some socially useful service
- to be considered part of the community
- to enjoy normal companionship
- to be recognised as individuals
- to have the opportunity for self-expression and a sense of achievement
- to have health protection and care
- to be stimulated mentally
- to have suitable living arrangements and family relationships
- to enjoy spiritual satisfaction.

The barriers to achieving these needs can be lack of:
- physical ability
- companionship
- time
- transportation
- finance.

Any business that can provide products to satisfy these needs will benefit. Many universities currently offer 'University of the third age' courses and the demand for these is likely to increase. An important aspect of the elderly consumer that will continue, and become more important, is the 'age' issue. Most middle-aged and elderly people think of themselves as 10–15 years younger than they are. Because the current baby boomers are preoccupied with youth, 'age' will need to be featured carefully in the next century.[13]

Figure 17.2: The joy of looking younger (© Ella Baché)

Recent research in Australia shows that:[14]

- people in the 50-and-older age group are highly individualistic. This means that elderly consumers do not constitute a homogeneous market, but they can be differentiated on demographic and lifestyle dimensions
- the needs of the over 50 group are not being met, particularly in the area of financial services
- most mature age people are vital, healthy and active
- many mature consumers adapt well to change, particularly technological change, but extreme age is a barrier. The adoption of automated teller machine (ATM) cards is quite high in the 50–65 group, but negligible in the over-85 group. Adopters in the 50–65 group are more likely to be married, to have been professional or white collar workers, to be better educated, to be in a higher income bracket and to be female. However, one technological advance that has had some effect on elderly consumers is the use of bar codes. Because the price is not displayed on the item, customers need to remember the shelf price and many elderly consumers have difficulties, particularly when goods are on special offer.[15]
- people do not view retirement as an end to a career and a life, but as a third stage in life in which new experiences can be learned.

The potential of the current elderly consumer is not being adequately developed.[16] Some organisations offer the elderly challenging activities but many of the clubs currently catering for senior citizens offer limited activities. The 'oldies' of the twenty-first century will be much more powerful and more demanding. They will require a broader range of leisure activities. With increased longevity, better health and early retirement, more older age groups than ever before are now participating in leisure activities. According to statistics, people aged over 60 spend one third of their time on purely leisure pursuits. For people in other age groups who are employed in paid work, only one fifth of their time is leisure time.[17]

Figure 17.3: Older people of the 1990s tend to remain active and healthy after retirement.

The elderly of the future will, on the whole, be highly motivated and seek a high quality of life and be prepared to pay for quality products. They will be looking for experiences and participation in activities, be convenience-oriented, value leisure time and be health conscious. The key words will be healthy versus health, style versus fashion, value versus cheap and natural versus artificial.[18]

In essence then, the elderly will require a broader range of leisure activities, including social clubs, relevant entertainment venues and television and radio programs. They will also require suitable clothes, shoes and cosmetics, and health, transport and financial institutions will have to meet their special needs.

Ethnic clusters

The ethnic and religious patterns in Australia have changed over the last three decades. As we saw in chapter 13 (see page 342), the number of migrants from the Middle East and Asia has significantly increased. The expectation is that by the year 2010, 16 per cent of the population will be of Asian descent. Much of the current impact is in Sydney.[19] According to a Monash University study, Sydney's foreign-born population increased from 31.5 per cent in 1986 to 35.7 per cent in 1992. Overseas immigration was responsible for 78 per cent of Sydney's urban growth. Approximately 73 per cent of Australia's Lebanese migrants live in Sydney, as do half of its migrants born in China, Hong Kong and the Philippines.[20]

Single ethnic groups are not large enough to target specifically for a range of products. But service providers such as Telecom, Optus, Australia Post and the health services do need to ensure that the needs of specific ethnic clusters are met, particularly their language needs. As ethnic groups tend to cluster in specific localities, product assortment in supermarkets, specific banking services and health services can be more effectively targeted. Certainly, businesses should be alert to the various ethnic communication outlets, such as newspapers.

SBS

The best way to reach all Australians

Figure 17.4: The major strength of SBS is that it can 'reach all Australians'.

TECHNOLOGICAL AND SCIENTIFIC CHANGES

Since the 1920s, the rate of technological and scientific discoveries and inventions has been astronomical. Although in the 1960s Alvin Tofler argued that people would not be able to cope psychologically and socially with the rate of change,[21] this does not appear to be the case. Consumers have willingly purchased and used much of the new technology but they have been selective. For example, they did not adopt the Balans chair and they took twenty-five years to adopt the microwave oven, but they took just six years to adopt VCRs.

New technology has had a profound effect on all aspects of our lives. Just consider the impact of the contraceptive pill, microsurgery, genetic engineering, lasers and, of course, the ubiquitous computer. Of major importance for organisations is the impact of technology on the way they interact with their customers.

VCRs now in 73 per cent of Australian homes

RICHARD BASIL-JONES and A. C. NIELSEN

Almost three-quarters of Australian households (73 per cent) have a VCR, according to the latest figures reported by A. C. Nielsen which operates the peoplemeter TV ratings service.

Statistics show the trend in VCR penetration in Australia and the United States.

It is interesting to note the higher penetration levels in Australia from 1984 to 1986, which are now on a par with the US.

With television viewing being recorded by peoplemeters, additional information, such as the level of VCR recording, can be monitored.

About 8 per cent of TV usage is for the purpose of recording a TV program, that is, 5 out of every 60 minutes.

The level varies slightly by city. Sydney and Perth lead the way in the 6 a.m. to midnight period, with 9 per cent of televisions being used for recording,

with Melbourne having the lowest level at 6 per cent.

As might be expected, the highest level of VCR recording is on the weekends with Sunday the most popular day.

Most recording is carried out in the evening, in particular the 8.30 to 10.30 p.m. period. Up to 16 per cent of televisions are being used for recording during these times.

Sydney Morning Herald,
5 September 1991

Shopping towards 2000

A recent impact of the new technology has been to change the way in which consumers buy goods. This change came in the form of the bar code. Bar codes are strips of coded information on a product (or its packaging). These codes not only trigger the price, they also trigger inventories and a range of accounts automatically. The main drawback of bar codes for consumers is that the price is displayed only on the supermarket shelf and not on the packet.[22] Stores that have adopted bar codes — mainly the big supermarket chains such as Woolworths, Coles, Jewel, Bi-Lo and Franklins — are able to record stock and accounting data immediately, which is a considerable benefit. And although the absence of a price on the product prevents consumers from checking the price charged at the checkout, supermarket managers point out that the docket provided gives out a written description of each product purchased and its price. This means that it is easier for the consumer to identify the product and assess the charges made. The Supermarket Association has acknowledged the difficulty that some customers are experiencing. Since it is in its interests for the bar codes to be adopted, it has established the regulation that if there is a price discrepancy between the shelf price and the price produced by the bar code, the customer is entitled to have the product free of charge.

More recent advances in technology have had an even more profound effect on our shopping behaviour. For organisations, it has meant fundamental changes in the way they organise the distribution of products and how they communicate with customers. Plastic cards, computer linkages and telecommunications allow producers to be in direct contact with their customers. For example, consider the effect that ATMs and electronic funds transfer systems have had on how we obtain cash from our bank accounts and how we pay for the products we purchase. It is no longer necessary to wait in queues in the bank. And you don't need to go to a shop to purchase an item — you can simply buy it over the telephone with your card. Technology, and consumers' adoption of it, is changing how we shop now and how we will shop in the future. We no longer need to carry large amounts of cash as the 'cashless' society has emerged. Soon consumers will be able to use individual scanners in supermarkets. The scanners will keep a running tally of how much they have spent. The amount may be charged to an account, or if the customer wishes to tender cash they will be given a special card that replaces coins. Supermarkets like the idea of scanners because they allow shoppers to accumulate credit points for special discount, encouraging them to return.[23]

Home shopping is here already. A number of companies are able to organise phone purchases and deliver the product direct. We can book theatre tickets, pay bills, donate money to charity and send flowers with only a phone and a plastic card. Coles–Myer set up its Myer Direct mail order division in 1989 to test the home shopping market. Myer now sends 10 catalogues a year to 500 000 customers and generates annual sales of $70 million. Myer management predict that sales will soar to $300 million in the next four to five years. Home shopping not only applies to goods. Australia's first direct-only financial institution has 30 000 customers across Australia, all managed by one branch in Adelaide. All contact is through the telephone and the physical and electronic mail system.[24]

This means that shop owners will have to look carefully at the goods they stock. More attention will need to be given to the experiential aspects of shopping. For example, the Melbourne based Lost Forests is a chain of franchise retail stores, with eight stores in Australia, one in New Zealand and three in the United States. The stores sell soft toys and are designed to be 'fairy-tale' experiences. Children (and adults) go to the shop to 'buy' the experience as much as the toys.[25]

The latest innovation is the 'smart card'. These are cards with magnetic strips containing coded messages that allow transactions to be recorded. Purchaser information then transfers to company computers. Simple examples are phone cards and transport cards. One documented use of the smart card is the Vision Value Club which established the first frequent shopper smart card. This is a promotion delivery system, in which consumers can accumulate points for items purchased in specific stores. Each member is issued with a card containing personal data, which also includes cash linkages to that member's accounts. Even though the customer obtains points and discounts from specific stores, the card can be used in all stores with Visa facilities. The specified stores are equipped with a terminal dedicated to the Vision system. The terminal includes a computer, colour touch screen, keypad, smart card reader and printer. Arby's restaurants, an American fast food chain, are currently testing a frequent diner club. Customers receive a free membership card. When they use the card, they can win instant prizes and gain points towards food prizes, car repairs and movie tickets.[26]

Used this way, the smart card operates a two-way communication system. The companies obtain information about the purchasing habits of each customer, and customers can, through the terminals, obtain information on promotional deals. This means that companies do not have to print special brochures, advertisements and labels. The information is recorded on a laser video disc and delivered to the customer whenever the smart card is used.

Although plastic cards and direct access technology have numerous advantages, they also have disadvantages.[27] The main advantages, which are linked to the card payment systems, are:

- reduced cheque cost
- reduction of the cost of handling cash
- improved record maintenance
- guaranteed payment by customers
- automatic records.

The main disadvantages to the consumer are theft and misuse. Most financial institutions and retail organisations have set up mechanisms for dealing with credit card fraud. However, consumers are at risk unless they take precautions. Customers should:

- keep PIN numbers and cards separate
- not pre-sign invoices
- formally request that their names and addresses are not included on data sheets.

Currently, legal agencies and government committees such as the New South Wales Privacy Committee monitor credit card activity.

Targeted communication

Developments in audiovisual systems, particularly laser discs, cable television and interactive terminals have created the possibility of targeting consumers more directly. For example, the Doctors' Television Network (DTN) is available in 1210 medical centres. The 'network' is played on televisions in doctors' waiting rooms and carries programs and advertisements aimed at patients.[28] DTN's main audience is young mothers who visit the doctor on average 16.3 times per year, compared with 8 times per year for the average Australian. Its secondary audience is people aged over 50.

Once multimedia systems are operating in Australian homes, it will be possible for consumers to scan for product information, identify available promotions, pay bills, order products and even design or alter customised products without even leaving home.

SOCIOECONOMIC CHANGES

Technological developments have influenced our health and well-being, the way we work and play, how we manage our household chores, how we are educated and how we interact with each other. They have also indirectly influenced gender roles. In fact, they have affected all aspects of our lives. Changes in the economic state of society impacts on work and the amount of money consumers can spend in the marketplace.

The recession of the 1980s has created a more careful, more astute shopper and was a major factor in the emergence of the 'adversarial shopper'. Adversarial shoppers are suspicious about prices, brands, marketing strategies and companies. They believe that they deserve value for their money and are determined to secure low prices and good value.[29] A study conducted by Grey Advertising in 1992 found that impulse buying has dropped sharply, that 42 per cent of consumers make a list before going shopping and stick to what is written on the list and that more than half set limits on how much they are prepared to spend.[30]

The workplace

The workplace has changed over the last 30 years. Technological advancements have changed the way we work, there has been an increase in the number of women (both married and single) in the work force, the emergence of part-time work and early retirement. In 1954, only 13 per cent of married women with dependent children were in paid work. By 1993, 67 per cent of married women aged between 25–54 were in the work force. Twenty-four per cent of paid work is part-time and although women dominate this bracket, men are also entering part-time work in increasing numbers. The number of women entering the professions is also increasing, and 'flexi-days' and hourly patterns are changing.[31]

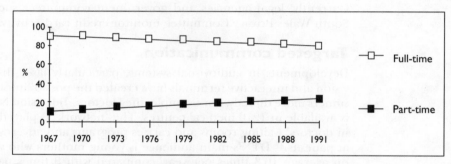

Figure 17.5: Growth in part-time/casual employment

Table 17.6: Numbers of people in full-time employment (figures in thousands)

	1970 (000)	1992 (000)	Increase (%)
Males	3508	3967	13
Females	1239	1839	49
Total	4747	5806	22

(*Source*: Australian Bureau of Statistics, 1970 and 1992)

There has been a steady decline in marriage rates since the early 1980s, an increase in de facto relationships and more people are staying single. Couples who do marry are postponing childbirth and having fewer children. Statistics show that the number of women having their first child after the age of 40 has increased at the rate of 60 per cent in the last five years.[32]

These changes have a number of implications for consumer lifestyles and marketplace behaviour. Dual incomes and fewer children mean that households are richer but smaller and more joint decision making is occurring. One outcome of this is that families with dual incomes have more discretionary income. This has created a demand for clothes, leisure activities and material goods such as toys, computers and home entertainment systems. Increased income levels and leisure time has led to an increase in tourism and travel and the use of restaurants and other entertainment services. Also, the roles of males and females have changed. Car and financial services advertisements are now targeted at both men and women. There has been a merging of roles, which accounts for the success of magazines such as *HQ*.

Figure 17.6: *HQ* magazine targets its articles, features and advertisements at both sexes.

Women today have less free time and more money and are more willing to spend money on clothes, make-up, child care, home services, semi-prepared meals and frozen foods. There is, and will continue to be, an increased demand for commercial teams of workers in the areas of house cleaning and maintenance, pet care and cooking.[33]

Even though women have higher incomes they have less free time, which means they have less exposure to the media and less time to shop, a role that is being increasingly carried out by men.[34] Advertising media and messages will need to be carefully selected and constructed to reflect these factors. For example, men are being and will continue to be shown as purchasers and users of a range of household products. To cater for the increasing number of people in full-time work, supermarkets have now extended shopping hours and Coles–Myer is trialing 24-hour trading.[35]

Trends, values and behaviour

As we saw in chapter 13, cultural values and behaviours of people in a society are not static. They evolve and develop, shape and are shaped by the society. Fads, such as the 'pet rock' craze of the 1980s, come and go but some changes are fundamental and enduring. The changes in values and behaviours that Australians have undergone over the last twenty years have been profound and to a large extent destabilising. Australians are more cautious about the marketplace and relationships than ever before.

Recent research in Melbourne and Sydney shows that Australians are confident about the future and that they believe they have better lives than their parents. The major concerns are unemployment, especially for young people, and money. Most Australians prefer to holiday in Australia and the US.[36]

According to Hugh Mackay, the cry of the 1990s in Australia is 'back to the basics'.[37] Mackay sees this cry as an attempt to introduce some stability and a sense of purpose into what has become a destabilised and direction-less society. This is reflected in the quest for traditional values. His research shows that the words of the 1990s are:

• responsibility	• loyalty	• integrity
• restraint	• domesticity	• safety
• moderation	• morality	• discipline
• heritage	• balance	• simplicity
• conservation	• decency	• purity
• nature	• family	• motherhood.

The 'caring sharing' 1990s[38] have had an impact on spending. For example, spending on luxuries has decreased. Spending on:
• imported leather shoes has decreased by 15 per cent
• marble tiles has decreased by one third
• occupancy in five star hotels has decreased by 14 per cent
• French champagne has decreased by 40 per cent.
Parker Bros. report that there has been a 20 per cent increase in the purchase of board games, which may indicate that families are spending more time together.

A key feature of today's consumer is the need to know. The Australians of the 1990s are better educated than previous generations and more cosmopolitan. Retention rates to senior school level are high, at approximately 75 per cent. The numbers of university students have increased from 50 per thousand in 1950 to 180 per thousand in 1990. At the end of 1995, one in ten Australians will have a degree.[39] Better educated consumers want to know about the products they buy. This allows them to make better choices in increasingly complex purchase situations. An outcome will be the continued demand for product information on packages, more information content in advertisements and an increase in the use of advice agencies such as the Australian Consumers Association.

Australians are also concerned with the physical environment, as the article below shows. Consumer concern has created a demand for environmentally friendly business practices and products. This means that businesses will have to respond to these concerns by changing how they produce and package goods.[40]

The consumer is not a fool

MICHAEL KIELY

Which topics are most popular with newspaper readers, do you think? Sex scandals? Crime stories? Disaster reports? World crises?

No — the hot topics with readers are the environment and pollution!

Quadrant Research's Starch study for the Newspaper Advertising Bureau found that the environment and pollution achieved the highest "noted" score of 82% followed by legal/court cases (78%), accidents and disasters (77%) and world events (76%). Items "noted" by around two-thirds of all readers were political and government policy and crime and drugs (both 69%) with major local events scoring 65%.

Other high-interest topics were business/finance and industrial relations stories (62%), editorials (61%), shopping and retailing (59%), sport (58%), and entertainment (57%).

Sports items were "noted" by 66% of males while shopping and retail editorials were recalled by 64% of females, confirming the old sexual stereotypes that many commentators would have us believe no longer existed.

The study measured readership levels of 351 editorial items that appeared in metropolitan and regional dailies, Sunday and national newspapers.

NABSCAN, the Bureau's computer database, has analysed over 6000 nationwide interviews.

One in every three newspaper readers surveyed (34%) was able to recall having read over half of the copy in the selected items and more than half (54%) could remember noticing them first time around.

Reg Mowat, the Bureau's director, said high "noted" (being able to remember the item) and "read most" (having read more than half of the item) scores confirm that newspaper readers are hungry for information.

The figures also show that readers are not easily fooled. Travel — which is exclusively advertorial and puffery — scored very low in interest, with only 43% noted and 24% read most.

Earlier NABA figures show the popular advertorial approach can damage an advertiser's efforts. While simple-minded marketers who insist that their editorial appears on the same page or near their advertisement are shooting themselves in the foot. Such placement turns readers off.

If there is related editorial on the same page, only 19% of readers note the advertisement and only 13% read it. If there is unrelated editorial, the "noted" figure jumps to 31% with 23% reading most of the copy.

Similarly, if related editorial appears on the opposite page, the advertisement scores 26% with only 19% reading the copy. But advertisements appearing with no support at all score 44% "noted" and 35% read most.

Newspaper readership patterns can give you a valuable window on the mind of the consumer.

Marketing, October 1992

The rise and fall of ECA

Environmental Choice Australia (ECA) was launched in October 1991 by the commonwealth, state and territory governments, meeting as the Australian and New Zealand Environment Council (ANZEC). The role of the ECA panel was to verify, through independent testing, environmental claims made by manufacturers in order to 'crack down' on false and misleading claims. The aim was to reduce confusion caused by the variety of so-called 'green' claims made by manufacturers. Manufacturers could apply to ECA voluntarily for approval of claims about their products and packaging. Once approved, the company had to agree to work by the code of ethics developed by ECA. The company would then be able to place the ECA logo on their product and packaging. Under the program, products had to be resubmitted for analysis by an independent scientific committee every two years. Samuel Taylor was one of the first manufacturers of 'environmentally friendly' products to be endorsed by ECA.

However, the ECA program was closed on the 1 May 1994 for a number of reasons. The Trade Practices Commission started to enforce the Trade Practices Act. Although the Act does not specifically address the issue of 'green claims', such claims are covered by the bans on unfair trading (an example of the TPC's guidelines appears on page 477). Other factors were the lack of support from manufacturers and the difficulty of establishing suitable assessment criteria to determine what constitutes 'environmentally friendly'.

A more recent approach to the issue of 'green marketing' has been made by Reckitt and Colman Products. With assistance from CSIRO, they have formulated the 'life cycle analysis' model, which measures the environmental impact of products such as their Down to Earth brand in five ways:

1. Reducing water-borne waste through biodegradable formulation
2. Minimising landfill through the very high recyclable content of the packaging
3. Reducing greenhouse gas emissions and airborne pollutants through recycled plastic which requires less energy to produce
4. Reducing reliance on finite resources through the use of 'regrowable' resources
5. Reducing total energy requirements through the elimination of unnecessary ingredients.

(*Source*: Reckitt & Colman, 1994)

CONVENIENCE
Consumer must find it easy to do business with you.

DISCOUNTING
Price cutting will become even more of a problem as marketers try to find a quick way to the consumer's heart.

CHOICE
More options and customised solutions to consumer problems.

SPEED
Consumers want to make better use of thier limited time so they don't want to wait in line.

VALUE-ADDING
The alternative to price cutting – giving the consumer something extra.

QUALITY
Getting the best for your business will win you more devoted consumers.

CUSTOMER SERVICE
Demands for service are steadily rising as customers come to realise how pleasant it can be.

LIFESTYLE
Products need to fit the consumer's hectic lifestyle while meeting an increasing demand for quality.

AGE WAVES
Companies need to respond to the major demographic groups – the aged and the baby boomers.

TECHNO-EDGE
Using technology to its fullest to improve your product is a must in a world where technological advancement is growing fast.

Figure 17.7: The ten trends that will affect business in the 1990s (*Source: Sydney Morning Herald*, 7 July 1991. From *Managing the Future* by Robert B. Tucker. Compiled by David McCaughan, McCann Erickson)

Downshifting in Australia

A report by Grey Advertising and Brian Sweeney and associates describes six key trends in consumer behaviour that will dominate the 1990s. These are:

- downward experimentation — buying lower-priced and generic products
- standards of quality — low prices and good quality. Eighty-two per cent of consumers believe that expensive brands do not guarantee quality
- purchase justification — people will only buy if they need the product
- price consciousness — limits on spending
- mission-based buying — consumers know what they are looking for and how much they are prepared to pay. They gather information and check prices before they buy
- value for money — value is judged in terms of what a product is worth in personal terms. Products perceived to be of equal quality will be chosen on the basis of emotional and financial needs.

LIFESTYLES OF THE FUTURE

Lifestyles of the future will be more sophisticated yet more simple. Concern with the environment will be maintained and the use of recyclable containers, chemically safe cleaners and natural, organically grown produce will continue. The focus will be on being 'natural' and many companies are already responding to this, such as Holeproof's new natural range of 'eco-sound' underwear. At the same time people will start using multimedia information and entertainment systems, play virtual reality games[41] and expect cures for the major illnesses such as cancer.

Consumers will continue to be interested in managing their 'well-being' and will continue to take responsibility for their health. It has been suggested that governments may adopt a regulatory role to channel people's energies in positive directions to promote a healthier and more vital community.[42] But regulation may be unnecessary as the consumers of the future will be more focused on issues relating to their own health and the health of the community.

LEISURE IN THE 1990S AND BEYOND

Changes in the work force and new values of the 1990s will impact on a range of consumer activities, but one of the key areas will be leisure. Changes in work patterns, early retirement, longevity and a healthier elderly population have created changes in both our attitudes to leisure and the number of individuals enjoying leisure pursuits. The population as a whole is interested in participating in more leisure activities.[43]

Leisure is the primary activity for over one fifth of Australians, with 58 per cent of all leisure time devoted to passive activities such as television. Retired people spend one third of the day involved in leisure.[44] As the baby boomer bulge moves towards retirement, more and more activities will be leisure related.

Data collected during household expenditure surveys show that spending on recreational activities has remained stable at around 12 per cent of the weekly wage. A time pilot study carried out by the Australian bureau of statistics found that, on average, men spent 21 per cent of their day in labour force activity while women spent 10 per cent.[45] Recreational activity for the aged is shown in table 17.7.

Table 17.7: Leisure activities for the aged

Leisure activity	Leisure time for the aged (%)
Volunteer, community work	1.4
Social life, entertainment	5.3
Active leisure	4.2
Passive leisure	20.1

(*Source*: A. Boag, Recreation participation survey activities done away from home. Ideas for Australian recreation, AGPS, Canberra, 1989)

A survey by the Australian Institute of Family Studies shows that going to the movies, concerts, eating out, bushwalking and picnicking are the activities Australians want to do more. Half of the respondents said that they were restricted by the lack of money and women were more restricted if they had children. About one third of the adults regularly garden and read books, although it is mainly the men who garden and the women who read books. Teenagers wanted more involvement in outdoor activities such as bushwalking, sailing and surfing. The study also found that 87 per cent of teenagers watch television and videos. Although most respondents want to participate in sporting activities, most said that it was either too expensive, they did not have transport or they did not have time to play sport.[46]

The two factors that will shape leisure activities in the future are the new focus on the family and money constraints. The tendency of the 1990s is a renewed interest in domesticity. This means that consumers will take greater pride in their homes and be more nostalgic. Home improvement products will be in demand as will gardening, music and a range of craft and hobby products.

The focus will be on establishing and maintaining a small circle of friends rather than having many acquaintances. This, coupled with a renewed interest in domesticity, means that consumers will entertain more at home. The focus on the home for entertainment will lead to an increased demand for home computers, optic fibre-linked entertainment networks, wrap round sound systems, virtual reality and high definition television.[47] For the affluent, this may also lead to the purchase of air-conditioning systems, security intercoms and a range of home benefits operated by touch buttons.[48]

The focus on health and youth will force the elderly groups to engage in more active sports and join clubs and associations. They will take more holidays and the demand for organised holidays, perhaps with specific themes such as the 'wine and dine' tours conducted in the Barossa Valley, will increase. Self-education and continuing education will also be in high demand.[49]

People with money will attend more cultural activities that are already well supported. But for some people, lack of money will prevent them participating in many leisure activities.[50] Lack of sufficient money is a key factor in the participation of leisure activities by the elderly. This may also be an issue for a sizeable proportion of the baby boomers in the twenty-first century. They will move into low cost leisure activities such as walking and pinoche as well as home-based activities. This could translate into the demands of a large segment, which will be a viable target for budget tours and inexpensive entertainment.

SUMMARY

This chapter explains why it is important to understand both the current ideas and behaviours and the future trends in our environment. The changes that have come from technical and scientific research, the knowledge explosion and changing social roles over the last thirty years have detribalised and fragmented the Australian community. Although technical and scientific advances have made life easier and healthier for consumers, they have also made consumers' choices more complex.

Consumers of the future will be able to shop in many different ways, and have access to an incredible range of products. Consumers of the future will also be older and more sophisticated and will demand value for money. Younger consumers are more likely to be single or living in de facto relationships. Families will continue to be small, with both parents working. Male–female roles will blend and for some products, particularly household products, both men and women will have to be targeted. There will be fewer children in relation to adults and, as families will be wealthier, more money will be spent on children. This will affect education, toys, clothes, entertainment and games.

A key feature of present and future consumers is the need to be better informed, which means there will be an increased demand for product information in advertisements. They will continue to manage their health and the focus will be on maintaining a state of 'well-being'. Family and friends and the family home will become more important and consumers will spend time and energy creating comfortable environments.

Questions

1. The emergence of the adversarial shopper means that producers and retailers will have to compete on price. Discuss.

2. What impact would the development of a viable electric car have on the automotive industry? What impact would it have on consumers?

3. Women in dual-career families buy the same products as non-working women. Discuss.

4. Identify two products that have recently come onto the market and assess their potential success.

5. Interview some elderly people to find out where they get information about the products they buy. What implications do your findings have for marketing communication planning for products aimed at the elderly consumer?

6. Interview some people from different age groups to find out how they respond to Hugh Mackay's words — do they want to 'go back to basics'?

7. Pick two recent inventions that could be commercialised within the next few years and assess the impact they will have on business and consumers.

8. What are the implications of the 'caring sharing 1990s' for exclusive clothing manufacturers?

9. Identify a product that is under threat from a change in the environment. Prepare a report advising the company that produces the product how to manage the situation.

10. To give a product 'environmentally safe' status requires the creation of set criteria by which the status can be determined. What factors do you think could make the creation of set criteria a difficult task?

Case study

One of the key marketing trends of the 1980s was the emergence of the New Woman. As the number of women in the workforce climbed and male-female roles blurred, marketers, researchers and advertising agencies belatedly recognised the New Woman's arrival and devised strategies to reach her. Convinced they now have the New Woman well covered, marketers are moving on to the New Man.

That is a mistake. The acceptance of the New Woman label by marketers has obscured the fact that the New Woman is not a neat, homogeneous group of consumers. In accepting the New Woman tag and then focusing on its logical extension, the New Man, marketers and agencies have made two errors: they have assumed the New Woman exists as a single target for advertising and have pigeonholed her before they fully understand her.

Marketers know the statistics: just under 60 per cent of all women aged over 18 are in the workforce, 51 per cent of married women work, 43 per cent of women in the workforce have children, 45 per cent of women with children under the age of five work. But many companies wrongly assume they can toss all working women into a neat package and label it the New Woman. New Women, rather than New Woman, is a more accurate description of the consumers that have appeared in recent years.

Pigeonholing any group of consumers is dangerous but often necessary in a market as small as Australia. The US market is large enough for companies to be able to prosper by targeting only 1–2 per cent of the population. Australia's population of 17 million dictates that most marketing campaigns must be mass-marketing campaigns. But even in such a small market, the New Woman designation is too broad.

Smart researchers point out that the conflicts currently raging between the various types of New Women are more bitterly fought than the traditional male-female conflicts. Take the stay-at-home new mothers. They are divided into two groups: new mothers who have no intention of returning to the workforce and new mothers who have decided to stay at home for five or six years and then resume their careers. The needs, attitudes and self-images of both groups are very different and they respond to different marketing messages.

A more obvious conflict exists between stay-at-home women and working women. Researchers say the conflict is one-sided: the stay-at-homers dislike the women who return to work after having children, while the working women have no strong feelings about the stay-at-homers. To succeed in marketing to these women, they must be treated as very different groups.

US researchers describe the stay-at-homers as "the nurturers": they will respond to advertising pitches that place value on the nurturing jobs they do. The working women, particularly working new mothers, are "the realistics": juggling work and domestic duties, they want no-nonsense sales pitches that do not glorify either activity.

The throwaway line that the New Woman "wants it all" ignores the cold reality that, in most cases, she is forced to do it all. If he exists at all, the New Man is in a minority. Women are still the keepers of the family dinner, still do most of the housework and still take on most child-raising duties.

That is why laundry detergent advertising, for example, is still dominated by images of women; no matter what the New Man says in research groups, the New Woman is still washing the clothes. Meadow Lea's long-running 'You oughta be congratulated' campaign works in the 1990s because it offers a measure of comfort to frazzled women. Yes, cooking a batch of scones deserves recognition.

New Women are not only working women or stay-at-home new mothers. The values and attitudes held by women in their forties and fifties have changed in recent years and those changes have earned them the New Woman sobriquet. For most of the 1980s, advertisers ignored older consumers; the few ads aimed at people over 45 were directed at men, promoting "male" products such as superannuation. As the business world finally realises that the over-45 group will be the most affluent group of consumers in the 1990s, marketers are struggling to develop strategies to reach this group of wise, experienced shoppers. The over-45 group, particularly women, want advertising that glorifies their age and includes them in mainstream life, not advertising or products that dwell on age and its limitations.

Neil Shoebridge, *Business Review Weekly*, 1990

Case study questions

What impact will the change in values described by Hugh Mackay (see page 452) have on the New Woman discussed in Neil Shoebridge's article? Will they be different from the influences on the New Man? How will they impact on the current conflict between the traditional woman and the New Woman?

SUGGESTED READING

T. Jagtenberg and P. D'Alton, *Four Dimensional Social Space*, Harper and Row Publishers, Sydney, 1989.

S. Goldberg and F. Smith, *Australian Cultural History*, Cambridge Uni. Press, 1988.

Alvin Tofler, *Power Shift*, Bantam Transworld Pub., 1990.

ENDNOTES

1. I. Ansoff, *Corporate Strategy*, McGraw-Hill, New York, 1965. M. Porter, 'Competitive Strategy: Techniques for Analysing Industries and Competitors', Free Press, New York, 1980. D. Katz and R. L. Khan, *The Social Psychology of Organisation*, John Wiley and Sons, New York, 1966. R. Estes, 'Consumerism and Business', *California Management Review*, Vol. 14, No. 2, 1971. W. H. Hegarty, 'Strategic Planning in the 1980s — Coping with Complex External Forces', *Planning Review*, Vol. 9, No. 5, 1981.

2. B. Jones, *The Impact of Technological Change in Australia*, School of Graduate Studies, Monash University, 1989. B. Jones, *Australia as a Post-industrial Society*, Occasional Paper No. 2, Dec. 1985. A. Tofler, *Power Shift*, Bantam Books, New York, 1990. J. Naisbitt, *Megatrends*, Warner Books, New York, 1982. 'The Ruthven Report', *Rydges*, Oct. 1984.

3. 'Who Read the Consumers' Minds: Hits and Misses of 1991', *Business Review Weekly*, 20 Dec. 1991.

4. Australian Bureau of Statistics, 'Census Characteristics of Australia', *1991 Census of Population and Housing*, published 1993.

5. Australian Bureau of Statistics, 1993, ibid.

6. Australian Bureau of Statistics, *1991 Year Book*.

7. Australian Bureau of Statistics, *1991 Year Book*.

8. Australian Bureau of Statistics, 'Census Characteristics of Australia', *1991 Census of Population and Housing*, published 1993.

9. D. B. Oliver, 'Career and Leisure Patterns of Middle Aged Metropolitan Out Migrants', *Gerontologist*, 12, 1989.

10. M. Lambing, 'Leisure Time Pursuits Among Retired Black by Social Status', *Gerontologist*, 12, 1990.

11. P. Laslett, *A Fresh Map of Life: The Emergence of the Third Age*, Weidenfeld and Nicholson, London, 1989. DDB Needham Study, *The Over 45s*, DDB Needham, Sydney, 1987.

12. M. Puner, *To the Good Life: What We Know About Growing Old*, Macmillan, London, 1974.

13. L. Underhill and F. Caldwell, 'What Age Do You Feel? Age Perception Study', *Journal of Consumer Marketing*, Summer 1983. G. Smith, 'Avon is Now Calling on Women at Work and Geriatrics', *Business Review Weekly*, May 1993.

14. 'Oldies Under the Microscope', *Marketing*, June 1992. Overview of research carried out by St. George TAFE in Sydney, Report, 'Marketing to the Mature Australian'.

15. M. Puner, *To the Good Life: What We Know About Growing Old*, Macmillan, London, 1974.

16. P. Selby and M. Schechter, *Aging 2000 — A Challenge for Society*, MTP Press, Boston, 1982.

17. L. Earle, 'Recreation Patterns Among Older Australian Adults', *Australian Journal on Ageing*, Vol. 3, Aug. 1988. V. Wright, 'Leisure: Be In It — Or Else: How to Handle the Shock', *The Weekend Australian*, 24–25 April 1982. Commonwealth Department of the Arts, Sport, the Environment, Tourism and Territories, *Recreation Participation Studies*, Australian Government Publishing Service, Canberra, 1987. D. Mercer, 'Australians' Time Use in Work, Housework and Leisure: Changing Profiles', *Australian and New Zealand Journal of Sociology*, 212, No. 3, 1985.

18. P. Selby and M. Schechter, *Aging 2000 — A Challenge for Society*, MTP Press, Boston, 1982. J. D. Teaff, 'Leisure Services with the Elderly', *St. Louis Times Mirror*, Mosby College, 1985. E. Palmore, 'Total Change of Institutionalisation Among the Aged', in *Gerontologist*, 16, 1976. B. Kaplan, *Leisure: Lifestyle and Lifespan*, W. B. Saunders and Co., Philadelphia, 1979. J. R. Murphy, *Recreation and Leisure Service*, Lea and Febiger, Philadelphia, Pa., 1975. L. H. McAvoy, 'The Leisure Preferences, Problems and Needs of the Elderly', *Journal of Leisure Research*, 1979. R. Rapoport, *Leisure and the Family Lifecycle*, Routledge and Kegan Paul, 1975. Carol Davis & Assoc. Pty Ltd., 'Winning the 35 plus Consumer: The Baby Boomers and Beyond', Sydney, April 1993. J. Waldrape, 'The Baby Boomer Turns 45', *American Demographics*, Vol. 13, Jan. 1991, pp. 12–16.

19. Australian Bureau of Statistics, 'Census Characteristics of Australia', *1991 Census of Population and Housing*, published 1993.

20. 'Australia's Changing Face', *Sydney Morning Herald*, 16 June 1993. Bureau of Immigration Research, *Australian Population Trends and Prospects*, AGPS, 1991.

21. A. Tofler, *Power Shift*, Bantam Books, New York, 1990.

22. B. R. Garland and D. E. McGuinness, 'Study of Price Accuracy in the New Zealand Supermarket Industry, Asia Pacific International', *Journal of Marketing*, Vol. 4, No. 3, 1992.

23. 'Electronic Shopping Boom', *Sydney Morning Herald*, 24 April 1994.

24. N. Shoebridge, 'Shops of the Future', *Business Review Weekly*, 23 July 1993.

25. 'Lost Forests Take Root in Far-off Lands', *Australian Professional Marketing*, Dec./Jan. 1992/93.

26. 'Smart Card Electronic Marketing: Merchandising for Tomorrow', in 'Computers in Marketing', *Marketing*, April 1991. S. Rapp, 'Playing Footsies with the Future', *B&T*, Feb. 1994.

27. 'Trouble at the Hole in the Wall', *Business Review Weekly*, July 1989. 'Bar Codes and Beyond', *Business Review Weekly*, May 1990.

28. 'Waiting Rooms a Network Paradise', *Business Review Weekly*, 3 May 1991. 'Can a Computer Disk Sell a Truck?', Paula George Marketing, June 1992.

29. 'Advertisers Must Switch On to Cynical Spenders', *Business Review Weekly*, Dec. 1992. 'The Cut-Price Commandos', *Business Review Weekly*, 5 March 1993. H. Mackay, 'The Anxious Eighties: The Impact of Social Change on Australian Community Attitudes and Values', *Australian Psychologist*, 23, 81, 1988.

30. *Downshifting in Australia*, Grey Advertising and Brian Sweeny and Associates, 1992.

31. ABS, *Working Life*, Canberra, 1992. D. Mercer 1985, op. cit. (see note 17).

32. Australian Bureau of Statistics, 'Census Characteristics of Australia', *1991 Census of Population and Housing*, published 1993.

33. H. Mackay, 'Responding to the Consumer of the 1990s', *The Mackay Report*, 1991. J. Beaumont, 'The 1960s: A Stupid Decade', *Sunday Telegraph*, 19 Aug. 1990. T. W. Beed and W. L. Walker, 'Men's Attitudes Towards Women', Marketing Services Department, Australian Consolidated Press, NSW, 1987. J. Sinclair, *Images Incorporated: Advertising As Industry and Ideology*, Croom Helm, Sydney, 1989. H. Glezer, 'Changes in Marriage and Sex Role Attitudes Among Young Married Women', *IFS*, Vol. 3, 1983.

34. C. Wright, 'Men Invade the Supermarket', *Australian Business*, 4 Feb. 1987. M. D. Reilly, 'Working Wives and Convenience Consumption', *Journal of Consumer Research*, March 1982. 'The Men Who Man the Shopping Carts', Shopper Behaviour Kit, *Progressive Grocer*, 1979. H. F. Ezell and W. H. Motes, 'Differentiating Between the Sexes', *Journal of Consumer Marketing*, Spring 1985. 'The Year 2000: A Demographic Profile of the Consumer Market', *Marketing News*, May 1984.

35. K. Lyons, 'Opening the Doors to New Customers', *Australian Professional Marketing*, Sept. 1992.

36. Reported in Peter Cotton, 'Here's Looking at Us', *The Good Weekend*, 8 October 1994.

37. H. Mackay, *The Mind and Mood of Australia in the 90s*, Angus and Robertson, Sydney, 1992. L. Crisp, 'You in the 90s', *The Bulletin*, 19 Sept. 1990.

38. D. Macken, 'The Caring Sharing Nineties', *The Good Weekend*, 8 August 1992. See F. Popcorn, *The Popcorn Report*, Doubleday, 1991.

39. Australian Bureau of Statistics, *1990 Year Book*, No. 73, Canberra.

40. H. Mackay, 'Environmentalism: The New Pantheism', A Clemenger Report, Clemenger Agency, 1990. I. W. McNair (ed.), *Australian Public Opinion Polls*, Quadrant Research Services, NSW, 1988. N. Shoebridge, 'Business Seeks a Way to Board the Green Bandwagon', *Business Review Weekly*, 27 April 1990. S. White, 'Green is Good', A Clemenger Report, Clemenger Agency, 1990.

41. D. Smith, 'Sex and Drugs in Cyberspace', *Sydney Morning Herald*, 7 Sept. 1991.

42. J. Brown, *Sport and Recreation: Australia on the Move*, AGPS, Canberra, 1983. R. Castle, et al., *Work, Leisure and Technology*, Longman Cheshire, Melbourne, 1990. A. Boag, 'Recreation Participation Survey: Activities Done Away from Home', *Ideas for Australian Recreation*, Australian Bureau of Statistics, Canberra, 1989.

43. T. Blamey, 'Leisure Time Increase Is So Good …', *Marketing World*, Vol. 2, No. 1, Dec. 1984. B. Stoddart, *The Tyranny of Australian Leisure: 1884–1984*, National Leisure Seminar Discussion Papers, AGPS, Victoria, 1984. S. Parker and R. Paddick, *Leisure in Australia — Themes and Issues*, Longman Cheshire, 1990. G. Lawrence and D. Rose, *Sport and Leisure Trends in Australian Popular Culture*, Harcourt Brace and Jovanovich, Toronto, 1990. L. Smith, 'Leisure Futures — The Impact of Demographic, Societal, Economic and Technological Trends in the Pattern of Leisure in the 1980s', *The Australian Accountant*, Vol. 51, Nov. 1981.

44. A. Boag, 1989, op. cit. (see note 42).

45. S. Winocur, L. Rosenman and A. Cross, 'Women and Retirement: Some Key Factors Affecting the Decision Making Process', Paper presented to the Social Policy Research Centre Conference, University of NSW, July 1991. *Juggling Time*, Monograph from the Office of the Status of Women, Department of the Prime Minister and Cabinet, 1991.

46. Australian Introduction Family Studes, *Leisure Patterns of Australian Families*, 1993.

47. P. Hughes, 'Australia 2000', Youth Studies, Feb. 1991. 'In Remote Control', *Vogue Living*, Dec. 1993. E. Corcoran, 'Why Kids Love Computer Nets', *Fortune*, Dec. 1993. R. Guillatt, 'Perfect Marriage of Voice Video and Text', *Business Review Weekly*, 4 June 1993.

48. L. Sandercock, 'Work and Play', *Australian Society*, Sept. 1983. J. Brahaut, *Leisure Education for Age 45 and Over*, Transactions of the Menzies Foundation, Vol. 8, 1985.

49. L. Sandercock, ibid.

50. J. Casimir, 'No Pay No Play', *Sydney Morning Herald, Spectrum*, 18 Sept. 1993.

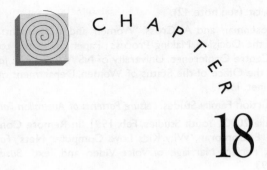

C H A P T E R

18

The regulatory environment

O B J E C T I V E S

This chapter should help you to:

- understand the reasons for consumer protection
- understand why regulation is important
- have a broad overview of the organisations that influence and design legislation
- be familiar with the laws that affect marketers
- know some of the concerns that consumers have with the marketplace.

 CONSUMER PROTECTION

All marketplace exchanges have inherent responsibilities. Consumers should obtain as much knowledge about products as possible and the agreements they enter into.[1] Marketers should conduct their transactions within the ethics and laws of the social system of which they are a part. If a business adopts a marketing perspective, and it values its customers, then fair and efficient transactions should occur.[2]

For the most part, our day-to-day marketplace transactions are carried out to the satisfaction of the parties involved. But marketplace exchanges can be accompanied by acts of deceit, swindle and quackery. Written evidence from 1500 BC shows that for over three thousand years societies have found it necessary to develop some form of marketplace code to protect both consumers and business. Business needs protection because consumers shoplift, make fraudulent claims and misuse products.[3] Behaviours such as those described, for example, in the Annual Reports of the New South Wales

Government's Analytical Laboratories, demonstrate the continued need for regulation. In the report for 1988/89, the laboratories found:

- Eleven per cent of samples failed to meet the requirements of the *NSW Pure Food Act*, with 38 food samples containing the preservatives not permitted in those particular foods and four containing horic acid, which is not permitted in food generally.
- A survey of 138 Australian wines found sorbitol, a sugar alcohol used to improve inferior wines, in 10 wines from the same company. Another company in the Griffith area was adulterating wine with apple juice.
- Only 6 per cent of the 411 meat samples tested contained meat less than what was listed on the label compared with 9 per cent of the previous year's samples.

Most modern societies provide consumer protection through the legal system and government legislation. In Australia additional protection is also provided by industry self-regulation. Apart from formal regulation, Australia also has a substantial number of active consumer groups and government authorities that monitor marketplace practices and offer support to consumers.

Until the twentieth century, the idea of *caveat emptor* (which means 'buyer beware')[4] dominated marketplace transactions in Australia, New Zealand and in many other countries such as the United States and Britain. Purchasers had to be able to judge accurately the quality of products and the fairness of each transaction. When buying goods and services, accurate judgement often depends on specialised technical and legal knowledge which few consumers possess. This inequity caused consumers to put pressure on business and government to create and maintain fairness in the marketplace. The current level of protection offered to today's consumers was not easily obtained.

CONSUMER ACTIVISM

In Australia during the nineteenth century, there were strikes, petitions and public meetings organised by consumer activists that often led to the government forming select committees and royal commissions to investigate serious misbehaviour. For example, in New South Wales in 1879, petitions and public meetings forced a select committee enquiry into conditions in and management of abattoirs. But it was not until 1902 when the New South Wales government introduced the *Cattle Slaughtering and Diseased Animals and Meat Act* that formal controls were introduced.[5]

The first organised community groups that gave some attention to consumer concerns in Australia were the National Council of Women, formed in Victoria in 1896, the Housewives Association of Australia and the Country Women's Association formed in 1917 and 1922 respectively. While these organisations were not formed to deal specifically with marketplace issues, they occasionally lobbied industry and government on issues relating to the price and quality of food and commodities.

The campaign for consumer rights gradually gained strength early this century and focused consumer interest at a global level. This was due in part to the publication and global availability of books by protesters, such as *The Jungle* by Upton Sinclair, published in 1906, which exposed the unsanitary conditions of the meat-packing works in America, and Rachael Carson's *Silent Spring*. Improved communications made it easier to form community and lobby groups. Although consumer activism had gained ground in most Western industrial nations by the 1950s, it was publications such as Vance Packard's *The Hidden Persuaders* and the efforts of consumer activists such as Ralph Nader in the United States that polarised international action.[6] The outcome was a more intense and organised consumer activism at a global level during the 1960s, which has been labelled the Consumer Movement by many writers.[7]

A key feature of the 1960s was the formation of the International Organisation of Consumers Unions (IOCU) in the Netherlands. The IOCU's role is to represent consumers on all sorts of subjects from food standards to monopolies, safety standards to environmental concerns.

The cause for consumer rights gained impetus through the US presidential campaign of John F. Kennedy in the 1960s. A key part of his election platform was a consumer Bill of Rights, summarised below. The essence of this Bill is that consumers and producers should have equal power.[8] Kennedy's Bill of Rights influenced activism in Australia, New Zealand, some European countries and Asian countries such as Singapore, Hong Kong and Taiwan.

In the 1980s, additional rights were added, such as:[9]
- the right to a clean and healthy environment
- the rights of minorities
- anti-discrimination
- the right to privacy
- the right to consumer education.

The Consumer Bill of Rights

Right to safety
Consumers have the right to be protected against goods or marketing practices that are harmful to health or life.

Right to be informed
Consumers have the right to be protected against false and misleading information and be able to obtain sufficient information to make wise purchase decisions.

Right to choose
Consumers have the right to have access to a variety of products and services at a competitive price.

Right to be heard
Consumers' interests should receive full and sympathetic consideration in formation of marketplace policy and should have access to redress.

(*Source*: Adapted from 'Message from the President of the United States Relative to Consumers' Protection and Interest Program', Doc. No. 364, House of Representatives, 87th Congress, March 1962)

CONSUMER GROUPS IN AUSTRALIA

Consumer groups wield considerable power in the marketplace and businesses need to take their views into account when developing marketing strategies.[10] In 1959 the first consumer organisation, the Australian Consumers Association (ACA), was formed in New South Wales. Since then many consumer groups have been formed in all states to support consumers. Those formed before 1980 are summarised in table 18.1.

Table 18.1: Consumer groups in Australia formed before 1980

Organisation	Formation date
Housewives Association	1917
Country Women's Association	1922
Standards Association of Australia	1929
Union of Australian Women	1950
Australian Consumers Association	1959
Home Economics Association of New South Wales	1962
Consumer Association of Victoria	1962
Canberra Consumers Group	1963
Northern Region Consumers Association (Tasmania)	1963
Brisbane Consumers Group	1964
Knox Parks Group, Victoria	1964
North Central Victoria Consumer Group	1964
Organisation of Queensland Consumers	1967
Law Consumers Association	1969
Consumers Against Rising Prices (CARP)	1970
Association of Consumer Education	1970
Hobart Consumers Group	1971
Central Queensland Consumers Association	1973
Queensland Consumers Association	1975
Consumer Association of Western Australia	1975
Medical Consumers Association	1976
Consumers Law Reform Association	1977
Consumers Association of South Australia	1977

Most of the consumer organisations in Australia are members of the Australian Federation of Consumer Organizations (AFCO) which was formed in 1974. Currently there are 71 consumer organisations affiliated with AFCO. Its stated philosophy (see page 468) is based on the same consumer Bill of Rights drafted by the Kennedy government in the 1960s, in that it is committed to the achievement of eight consumer rights.[11]

The Australian Consumers Association was established to support consumers in the following areas:[12]

1. Improve the quality of goods and services by means of tests and research as well as publishing the results in its magazine *Choice*.
2. Provide help and advice to consumers on all aspects of consumer issues.
3. Strengthen consumer legal protection areas through lobbying government to pass laws to protect the interest of consumers.

About AFCO

The Australian Federation of Consumer Organizations Inc. (AFCO) was founded in 1974 as the peak body for consumer organisations in Australia. It is a non-government organisation, with no party political affiliations. As a Federation, AFCO is composed of full and associate member groups. In 1993, it had 71 member groups in all states and territories. There is no individual membership of AFCO, although individuals may subscribe to the newsletter, and receive other AFCO publications.

Philosophically, AFCO is committed to the achievement of eight consumer rights:

1. **The right to satisfaction of basic needs**
2. **The right to safety**
3. **The right to be informed**
4. **The right to choose**
5. **The right to be heard**
6. **The right to redress**
7. **The right to consumer education**
8. **The right to a healthy environment**

Together, these eight rights form the basis for the ongoing work of the International Organization of Consumer Unions (IOCU), and its consumer group members, including AFCO, worldwide.

'Consumers, by definition, include us all', said John F. Kennedy in his 15 March 1962 declaration to the US Congress announcing the first four consumer rights. 'They are the largest economic group, affecting and affected by almost every public and private economic decision. Yet they are the only important group whose views are often not heard.'

As a peak body for consumer groups, it is AFCO's primary task to ensure that the views of its member groups are heard. AFCO's structure ensures that all member groups have the opportunity to have input into AFCO's policies and programs.

AFCO member groups elect a Council of up to thirteen people which meets several times a year. The Council elects a five person Executive, which meets more frequently, and includes the Chair, Treasurer and Secretary. The Executive and Council are responsible for appointing a Director, who is responsible for the management of a small Secretariat based in Canberra. In 1993, there were four full-time and three part-time AFCO employees, one of whom was based in Perth.

AFCO member groups meet together at General Meetings, which provide a forum for a new Council to be elected biennially and for policy discussion to occur on an annual basis. Over the first nineteen years of its operation AFCO has put the views of its member bodies and the interests of consumers generally, to government and industry. AFCO has ensured that the public is made aware of these views through the media. AFCO has lobbied ministers and other Members of Parliament, discussed consumer positions with industry, and organised consumer representation on a wide variety of committees. AFCO has facilitated information flow between member groups, and maintained a watching brief on international issues through its membership of IOCU.

(*Source*: Australian Federation of Consumer Organizations Inc. (AFCO), 1994)

Food advertising and the ACA

NEIL SHOEBRIDGE

Food manufacturers were warned. For a decade, advertising industry lobbyists have predicted that government health officials and consumer bodies will start agitating for restrictions on food advertising. That time has come. If food companies fail to move quickly and decisively, they could easily find themselves in the same tightly regulated advertising boat as cigarette makers.

For many years, restriction-happy consumer groups have had food on their hit-list of products that should be restricted in terms of how, when and where they are marketed. Now that they have suffocated the advertising options of the cigarette industry — and are aggressively pushing for tighter restrictions on liquor advertising — bodies such as the Australian Consumers Association (ACA) and the Australian Federation of Consumer Organisations (AFCO) are training their guns on the food industry.

Consumer groups have convinced governments to introduce tough food labelling and packaging laws in recent years. Some wild proposals, including one that calls for all ingredients to be listed on screen during a food product's TV commercial, have been floated. Such extreme proposals mask a more serious objective: the launch of government-regulated food advertising standards.

The ACA and AFCO are smart, powerful groups with close links to government health departments. Their first targets in the food industry are confectionery, snack-food products such as Smith's Crisps and Twisties and fast-food restaurants. If they succeed in pushing through restrictions on the advertising of these products, they will move on to other food categories.

The ACA is leading the charge. To launch its attack on food advertising, it has chosen a highly emotive subject: the promotion of what it claims are "unhealthy" food products to children. It is a smart strategy. Most people wrongly assume that kids are unsophisticated, gullible consumers who sit in front of the TV set and blithely accept everything they see and hear. They forget or ignore the fact that today's kids are extremely advertising and marketing literate.

But consumer groups know that whipping up concern about advertising directed at children is child's play, in the same way that cigarette ads were an easy mark. A recent report in the ACA's *Choice* magazine claims that 75% of food advertising aimed at kids sells products high in fat, kilojoules, sugar and salt and low in fibre. It maintains that only 10% of food advertising promotes healthy foodstuffs such as fruit, vegetables and unsweetened cereal products.

The ACA makes some extraordinary claims about food advertising. It alleges that studies prove that children see TV as an important source of information about nutrition. It also claims that food advertising aimed at kids skews their knowledge about what is good to eat towards food products high in fat, kilojoules, sugar and salt, and promotes over-consumption of "unhealthy" foodstuffs.

Executives from the food and advertising industries have their own studies that they claim prove that advertising does not warp children's eating habits. They also criticise the ACA's role as a self-appointed food industry watchdog.

The battle over food advertising restrictions will degenerate into a rambling and confusing parade of claims and counter-claims. Food companies will point out that advertising does not force people to buy products (the old freedom-of-choice argument that failed to save cigarette ads). Consumer groups will claim that the effect of advertising on Australians' eating habits is too important to be left to industry self-regulation.

In 1989, food was the largest individual category in the advertising industry, with total media advertising spending of just under $320 million. The ACA has put forward a set of proposed changes to food advertising standards that is breath-taking in its audacity. The ACA wants food industry-funded TV commercials that promote better nutrition, stricter monitoring of industry self-regulation and tax incentives for the makers of high-nutrition foodstuffs who cannot afford advertising.

Food advertisers and their ad agencies are only now starting to fight back. They are calling for reason in the debate over food advertising and pointing out flaws in the ACA's arguments. But the food and advertising industries need to match the tough, street-wise tactics of their opponents. If they don't, they will slowly see their advertising options disappear.

Business Review Weekly

The article on page 469 indicates the role that the ACA played in the food advertising debate. Since its inception the ACA has become a major political force through the formulation and lobbying of social issues. It has been a major force in:

- the introduction of a national recall code for dangerous products
- the drafting of class action legislation
- *Freedom of Information Act*
- standard of design quality and service for all goods
- upgrading of consumer education in Australian schools.

Its current interests span genetic engineering, food irradiation and environmental issues. In October 1992 the ACA launched a campaign to achieve 'truth in labelling', in collaboration with twenty-four industry and community groups. The aim of the campaign was to have the 'Made in Australia' labelling changed. An outcome was a paper produced by the federal government that proposed, among other things, the labels 'Made in Australia' for manufactured goods and 'Produce of Australia' for raw materials. Apart from its power as a consumer lobby group, the ACA has considerable influence in the marketplace. Its independent analysis and reporting of product tests have had an impact on the sale of many products. For example, a report in ACA's *Choice* magazine stating that most brands of paté had high levels of bacteria caused a massive slump in sales overnight.[13]

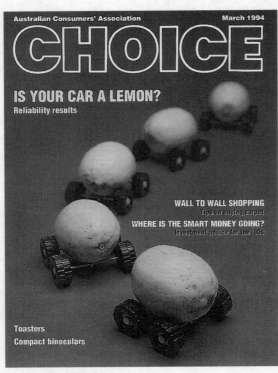

Figure 18.1: *Choice* magazine

A major concern of consumer groups is to educate the consumer, to improve their decisions and protect them against fraudulent behaviour. It does this by providing training courses for schoolchildren, by independent testing, through the publication of the consumer information magazines *Choice*, *Consumer Interests* and *Advancing Consumer Interest*, and by performing a watchdog role. In this capacity it gives public warnings about products, such as the following notice on insect bombs:

❝ ACA warning on insect bombs
The Australian Consumers' Association magazine, *Choice* has warned that insect bombs, those small aerosol cans containing insecticide and a propellant, have been linked to at least five fires since November 1991. Insect bombs release a stream of insecticide in rooms with serious flea and cockroach infestations. The propellant — the gas that forces the insecticide gas out of the can — is highly flammable, and can ignite and explode if it contacts a naked flame or spark. ❞

CONSUMER PROTECTION LEGISLATION

In addition to consumer organisations, there is a variety of legislation at both state and federal levels designed to protect consumers. The legislation has developed in parallel with marketing activity and can be seen to reflect the changes in marketing activities over the past fifty years. In this sense the law has evolved as marketing activities, and the social climate in which marketers operate, have changed.

According to Peter Dunstan, the current legislation in Australia is expected to achieve five goals:[14]

1. to achieve a balance of bargaining equality between buyer and seller
2. to rectify the imbalance in economic power between the individual and collective interest
3. to reduce the incidence of purchase-related losses and injuries
4. to ensure an equitable distribution of such losses and injuries
5. to relieve some of the problems of poorer consumers.

For these goals to be achieved there needs to be:
- set standards for products
- effective mechanisms to receive and act on consumer complaints
- regulation of agreements between buyers and sellers
- provision of information about products and consumer rights in marketplace transactions.[15]

While the current legislation in Australia is not complete, it does go some way towards implementing these mechanisms so that the goals may be achieved. All of the states have consumer affairs departments or bureaus that provide information and initiate consumer-related legislation. They are:

NSW Department of Consumer Affairs
ACT Consumer Affairs Bureau
Queensland Consumer Affairs Bureau
WA Department of Consumer Affairs
Victorian Department of Consumer Affairs
Northern Territory Office of Consumer Affairs
Tasmanian Department of Justice, Consumer Affairs Division
South Australian Department of Consumer Affairs
Federal Bureau of Consumer Affairs

The current government departments evolved out of consumer protection councils established in the 1960s and early 1970s. These are:

Consumer Protection Council of Victoria, formed 1964
Consumer Affairs Council of New South Wales, formed 1969
Northern Territory Consumer Protection Council, formed 1969
Consumer Protection Council of Tasmania, formed 1970
Consumer Affairs Council of Queensland, formed 1971
Commission for Consumer Affairs, South Australia, formed 1971.

Apart from Ministries of Consumer Affairs at both state and federal levels, there is a range of government bodies and agencies at both the state and federal levels that manage marketplace transactions. These include:

Trade Practices Commission
Prices Surveillance Authority
NSW Prices Commission
Australian Standards Association
Register of Encumbered Vehicles (NSW)
Rental Advisory Board.

The central authorities are the Federal Bureau of Consumer Affairs and the Federal Trade Practices Commission. The Federal Bureau of Consumer Affairs is responsible for:
• the development of policy issues relating to consumer affairs
• the development of legislative proposals
• the development and enforcement of product safety and product information provisions of the *Trade Practices Act.*

The Trade Practices Commission is responsible for administering the competition and consumer protection provisions of the *Trade Practices Act.* In consumer protection it is responsible for the law covering such matters as misleading and deceptive conduct, unconscionable conduct and prohibited sales techniques.

Historically the volume of legislation designed to protect consumers is high. Since 1833 in New South Wales, there have been over 200 pieces of legislation related to consumer protection. The nature of the legislation has been varied and for the most part issue-specific, as can be seen from the following sample of New South Wales Acts.[16]

1901 Dairy Supervision Act
1902 Public Health Act
1912 Factories and Shops Act
1915 Weights and Measures Act
1927 Marketing and Primary Products Act
1941 Auctioneers and Agents Act
1943 Lay-by Sales Act
1948 Landlord and Tenant Act (amendment)
1954 Textile Products Labelling Act
1957 Credit Sales Agreement Act
1960 Hire Purchase Act
1974 Motor Traders Act
1977 Landlord and Tenant (Rent Bonds) Act
1981 Consumer Protection Act
1984 Credit Act and Cognate Act
1987 Fair-trading Act
1987 Consumer Claims Tribunal Act
1989 Trade Measurement Act

With each state creating separate Acts, the current volume of legislation is high. In Victoria alone there are more than 22 current Acts relating to consumer protection.

Consumer legislation, both state and federal, is designed to protect consumers across a number of areas, including:

- unfair practices and codes of conduct
- public information
- dispute resolution
- standards and hazardous products
- prices
- advertising.

UNFAIR PRACTICES AND CODES OF CONDUCT

There is legislation in Australia at both state and federal level that relates to the establishment of codes of conduct and unfair practices. Appropriate standards of conduct are developed through legislation designed to create certainty, equity and consistency in commercial dealings. The role

of legislation in this area is threefold. First, the legislation has codified or summarised a large body of court-made law (common law). Second, the legislation rectifies various laws, developed over time, which are perceived as inequitable or inappropriate for modern day marketing practices. In this way the law has moved away from the earlier 'buyer beware' approach to an approach that more directly protects the consumer from unscrupulous activities of marketers. For example, current legislation provides a 'cooling off' period for contracts signed so that consumers are not pressured into signing agreements with high pressure salespeople. Third, the legislation provides a mechanism for the ongoing process of legislative evaluation and reform.

Each Australian state has created its own legislation to protect consumers. This means that there is no comprehensive system of legislation. The key state legislation includes:

The Sale of Goods/Fair Trading Acts 1958 (Victoria)

The Sale of Goods Act 1923 (NSW)

Sale of Goods Act 1896 (Queensland)

Sale of Goods Act 1895 (South Australia)

Sale of Goods Act 1895 (Western Australia)

Sale of Goods Act 1896 (Tasmania)

Sale of Goods Ordinance Act 1954 (ACT)

Sale of Goods Act 1972 (Northern Territory).

These acts cover a range of concerns, such as: the formation of contracts; the transfer of property and title of goods; implied conditions and warranties in contracts; the rights of the unpaid seller; remedies for breach of contract; and fraud and undue influence.

In 1974, the *Trade Practices Act* was introduced by the federal government. The Act deals with restrictive trade practices and consumer protection. The restrictive practices provisions control, among other things, anti-competitive agreements, exclusive dealing, price discrimination, resale price maintenance, secondary boycotts and abuse of power by firms having a substantial degree of power in a market.[17] This indirectly protects the consumer from excessive prices and to some degree unscrupulous behaviour by imposing substantial fines on individuals and corporations involved in restrictive practices. The Act covers a wide range of prohibited conduct, such as pyramid selling, and regulates misleading and deceptive conduct. Remedies available in the consumer protection area include penalties, damages, corrective advertising orders and orders for rectification.[18] The following is a hypothetical example of a corrective advertisement as it would be published in a newspaper.

CORRECTIVE ADVERTISEMENT

Best-Buy Travel Company wishes to inform that the recent advertisements for its Skiing Package to New Zealand did not make it clear that the cost stated did not include ski hire, lessons and chair-lift tickets.

The management of Best-Buy Travel regrets that readers may have been misled by the advertisement and advises that future advertisements showing prices for holiday packages will clearly state all inclusions and exclusions.

I. M. Best
Best-Buy Travel Company

The federal legislation applies to the sale of goods between states or territories and between Australia and other countries. Because of the limited application of the legislation to transactions within states, each state has adopted uniform fair trading legislation which incorporates the unfair practices provisions of the federal *Trade Practices Act*.[19] Perhaps from this some form of all-encompassing guideline may emerge.

Some of the relevant unfair practices provisions which are common to both the *Trade Practices Act* and state legislation provide that a person in trade or commerce shall:

(a) not engage in conduct which is misleading or deceptive
(b) not engage in conduct which is in all circumstances unconscionable
(c) in connection with the supply of goods or their promotion, not make a false representation as to the matters specified in the provisions
(d) not engage in conduct liable to mislead the public as to the nature of the manufacturing process, character, suitability for purpose, or the quality of any goods.

In addition to the federal legislation, the states individually have mechanisms for dealing with unfair practices, such as the Office of Fair Trading in Victoria. When the Ministry is satisfied that a case exists, it is empowered by legislation to develop options for the eradication of such practices.

Knowledge of unfair practices can be brought to the notice of the Ministry or Department either by customers directly, by industry groups or by community based organisations. The number of inquiries and complaints received and pursued by the Trade Practices Commission between 1991 and 1993 was: consumer protection — 3472; restrictive trade practices — 1645. A total of 112 318 complaints and inquiries were not pursued.[20]

PUBLIC INFORMATION

Legislation empowers the various ministries of consumer affairs to provide advice and information to the public as preventative measures. For example, they can provide advice on the necessary skills to avoid or resolve disputes. The ministries provide facilities for telephone and counter inquiries, extensive networks of community advice services, forums and educational programs. They also produce pamphlets such as the one reproduced in figure 18.2. The Federal Bureau of Consumer Affairs produces *Minder*, a newsletter providing information to consumers. Consumer checklists are also available from the Trade Practices Commission. (An example is shown in figure 18.3.) The checklists give information on a range of consumer issues and rights, such as the right to safe goods, how to buy jewellery, interpreting marketing claims and the rules for consumer refunds.[21]

DISPUTE RESOLUTION

As well as the system of civil jurisdiction in the courts, consumer protection legislation provides consumers with an informal and inexpensive means of dispute resolution, through tribunals and conciliation functions. The tribunals aim to provide an accessible, quick, cost-effective and informal method for resolving disputes. Referees who reside over the tribunals are legally qualified. They are appointed by the governor in council and are independent of the ministry. Their decisions are legally binding.

Before actions reach the tribunals, conciliation staff of the ministries usually negotiate with the parties in an effort to reach common ground.[22]

A Fair Go For Consumers

Contracts

Whenever you agree to buy goods or services you enter a contract. A contract cannot easily be cancelled — so you need to know what you are agreeing to.

Most sellers look after their customers. But some may mislead or deceive you or try to use their stronger position to get you to enter a contract that is not in your best interests. A seller who does this may be breaking the law. You may be able to do something about it.

How the law protects you

Under the Fair Trading Act, conduct which is misleading or deceptive, or likely to mislead or deceive, is prohibited. Unconscionable conduct by a seller is also prohibited.

Conduct which is misleading or deceptive or likely to mislead or deceive is conduct which conveys a meaning which is inconsistent with the truth. Conduct which merely creates confusion in the minds of customers is not misleading or deceptive.

EXAMPLE — Misleading advertising

Advertisements which make claims about products must be accurate. Claims which cannot be supported by evidence may be misleading.

Unconscionable conduct is where one party to a transaction takes advantage of another party who is at a serious disadvantage.

EXAMPLE — High pressure sales tactics

Watch out for the door-to-door salesman who:
- will not leave until you sign on the dotted line
- does not explain clearly what you are signing or what it will cost you
- misleads you about what you are buying

- does not tell you that there is a 'cooling off' period in which you can change your mind if you buy on credit
- uses one of your friends or relatives to influence you.

EXAMPLE — Unclear contracts

You might find it hard to understand the contract the seller wants you to sign. This sometimes happens if:
- you do not read well
- English is hard for you to understand
- you have a disability — like being hard of hearing
- you are sick
- the language is complicated or the layout is hard to follow
- there are conditions in 'fine print'.

Some firms use standard contracts with the terms already set out. These are often useful and time-saving. But you do not have to accept them on a 'take-it-or-leave-it' basis.

You have the right to negotiate terms that suit you.

And you have a right to be told exactly what you are letting yourself in for.

EXAMPLE — One-sided contracts

Watch out for one-sided contracts that:
- are not clear about your legal rights
- are so tough that you cannot help breaking the contract
- make false statements about what you agreed to, or how much debt you are taking on
- make it easy for the seller to get out of the deal.

A seller who does not tell you about harsh terms may be breaking the law.

A seller using any of these tactics may be guilty of 'unconscionable conduct'.

When are you covered by this law?

You are covered when you buy goods or services for yourself or your family, or to use around the home.

What can you do if you do not get a fair go?

Make sure you have all the facts about the deal. Make sure that your facts are right.

It is important to keep copies of contracts and other documents.

Then get advice.

You can ask Consumer Affairs to assist. The telephone numbers are on the back of this leaflet.

There might be laws that cover your case.

You can also ask at the nearest office of the Trade Practices Commission.

Depending on the advice you get, you may also want to get legal advice.

If you go to court

If the court finds you have been the victim of unconscionable conduct, it can help you in several ways.

For example, it can:
- order the seller to pay compensation for loss or damage
- cancel or change the contract
- order the seller to give you a refund
- order the seller to provide some service for you.

How can Consumer Affairs help you?

Consumer Affairs can also go straight to the seller to persuade them to change their practices.

It can ask the court to order the seller to stop the conduct, or to pay compensation.

The Department itself can take legal action against sellers. It might do this to help prevent other consumers being caught.

Always attempt to solve the problem yourself first. If you are not satisfied with the response, don't forget that Consumer Affairs may be able to help.

Consumer Affairs
Head Office
1 Fitzwilliam Street
Parramatta NSW 2150
PO Box 972 Parramatta NSW 2124
Telephone: (02) 895 0111
Fax: (02) 895 0222

Consumer Affairs is a New South Wales Government department.

Figure 18.2: Reproduced with permission from Consumer Affairs, New South Wales

CONSUMER CHECKLIST

GREEN MARKETING CLAIMS — WHAT DO THEY MEAN?

(The following checklist was taken from a Trade Practices Commission leaflet.)

Claims like 'environmentally friendly', 'ozone safe' and 'dolphin safe' abound on products as diverse as shaving cream and tuna. As Australians have become more conscious of the environment, marketers have developed new products and changed existing ones. They have also put new labels on products claiming various environmental benefits. Some of their claims may be confusing. Others may even be misleading. There are a lot of grey areas in 'green' marketing.

The Trade Practices Commission has issued a guideline warning manufacturers, importers and marketers to take care with such claims. The guideline will help to ensure that consumers and ethical marketers are not disadvantaged by false or misleading claims about the environmental impact of products.

What do the claims really mean?

As a concerned consumer, you can play a role. Before you choose or pay more for a product that is claimed to be good for the environment, ask yourself 'What do the claims really mean?' This checklist will help you make the best choice.

Vague terms

Some products are promoted with vague terms like 'environmentally safe', 'environmentally friendly' or 'green'. Almost all products have *some* adverse impact on the environment either in their manufacture, packaging, use or disposal. Look for details, for example, a list of ingredients or specific claims about environmental benefits when deciding what to buy.

Graphics

Some packages have pictures of forests, the earth, or endangered species without any explanation. Ask yourself if these images mean anything. Is the product any better for the environment than competing brands? Look for something which explains *why* the image is there.

Explanations

Is there a clear explanation of what exactly is environmentally good about the product? All claims should be spelled out in language you can understand. For example, a claim that a detergent is 'phosphate-free' should explain the possible bad effect of phosphate, for example, it promotes the growth of algae which can clog up rivers.

Linked claims

Are the environmental claims linked to some feature of the product, for example, extraction, transportation, manufacture, use, packaging or disposal of the product? A product with some good environmental features might still be harmful. For example, a disposable nappy might be made of wool fibre that is not chlorine bleached — but it could be difficult to dispose of its plastic liner and packet.

Who says it's good?

Can the manufacturer back up any claims made about environmental benefits?

Biodegradability

'Biodegradability' is beneficial only if a product breaks down in a reasonable time and into residues that do not harm the environment. What consumers need to know is — how long does it take and what's left? Ask yourself whether claims about biodegradability really tell you anything about this.

Is it a real benefit?

Are the claims made in an appropriate context or setting? For example, it would be misleading to claim that a product was 'not tested on animals' if neither it nor others like it had ever been.

Endorsements

Some products carry endorsements by either government or private schemes. Check to see that claims include: the grounds on which the endorsement was given; how the products will help the environment; and the nature of the scheme itself.

What the Trade Practices Act says

The Trade Practices Act prohibits conduct that is misleading or deceptive or is likely to mislead or deceive. It is an offence for a firm to falsely represent that goods are of a particular standard, quality, value, grade, composition, style or model or have had a particular history or previous use. It is also an offence to indicate that goods or services have approval or sponsorship that they do not have. If you have doubts about environmental claims on a product, write to the manufacturer for clarification.

For further information or to lodge a complaint, contact your local office of The Trade Practices Commission.

Many manufacturers making environmental claims publish a toll-free information number on their packaging. Try ringing these numbers to check out the claims.

Figure 18.3: Trade Practices Commission leaflet, July 1994

STANDARDS AND HAZARDOUS PRODUCTS

All states have legislation that establishes specific standards, weights and measures although most of the Acts are product-specific, as the following sample of New South Wales legislation since the nineteenth century shows:

The Pharmacy Act 1897
The Real Property Act 1900
The Bread Act 1901
The Pawnbrokers Act 1902
The White Phosphorous Marches Prohibition Act 1915
The Milk Act 1931
The Hire Purchase Act 1941
The Motor Dealers Act 1974.

The *Trade Practices Act* and various state based legislation empowers ministers and commissions to develop compliance programs aimed at ensuring that standards established by legislation are maintained. Authorities such as the Australian Standards Association set and monitor standards. They are empowered to test the measurement of retail instruments (for example supermarket scales), packaged goods and trade instruments. The regulation of repair and service, the provision of advice and attention to consumer complaints and queries are also within the power of the authorities.[23] The National Food Authority attends to such matters as food irradiation, genetically modified organisms in food, and health and nutrient claims made by manufacturers.

Also within the power of the authorities is the ability to create legislation prohibiting certain claims about products.[24] An example of this is the recent review of the Food Standards Code. In 1992, the National Food Authority reviewed its Foods Standards Code. In conjunction with government bodies such as the Better Health Commission and the Food and Nutrition Policy Development Steering Committee, the legislation governing the health claims made by food manufacturers was changed. In 1993, new regulations came into force for health messages and nutrient claims, such as those used to promote low-fat and cholesterol-reducing foods and sports energy foods such as Sustagen and Lucozade. The new regulations restrict food marketers to precise ingredient claims and will outlaw the use of generic terms such as 'fresh' and 'natural'. This means that many companies will have to change their marketing strategies, particularly their communication strategies.[25]

Energy labels on electrical appliances record the level of energy required to operate the product. As these are of concern to the regulatory bodies, labels are closely monitored by the National Electrical Appliances Energy Labelling Advisory Panel and the Australian Water Resources Commission (Appliance and Plumbing section). The ACA also provides independent check testing for the regulatory agencies to assist them in verifying manufacturers' energy label claims.

In 1991, the federal government tightened the requirements for the terms used and the claims made in relation to products that were positioned as environmentally sound. Some states such as Victoria followed suit (see the article on page 479).

'Green' labels under scrutiny

LEITH YOUNG

A wide range of so-called "green" product labels are likely to be banned or modified under a national scheme being considered by state and federal environment ministers.

The proposal, strongly supported by Victoria's Environment Minister, Mr Crabb, would set out a voluntary code by which manufacturers would stop making meaningless, misplaced or loosely defined claims.

If this failed to stop the confusion around promoting green products, it would be backed by law, in Victoria by changes in the Fair Trading Act.

Mr Crabb will seek agreement on details of the scheme at a meeting of state and federal ministers next month. It is expected to gain broad support and come into practice later this year.

For years, the Victorian Government, retailers and many manufacturers have wanted quality control over companies that see the public's interest in the environment as a golden marketing opportunity.

Draft documents for this scheme list, in four categories, the claims made in the name of green selling.

One category is meaningless statements, such as "No nasties", "Biocycle safe", "Ozone friendly", "Environmentally friendly", "Harmonious with nature" and "Non-polluting".

Another lists misplaced or illusory claims, such as "CFC-free" or "Phosphate-free" when chlorofluorocarbons and phosphates were not normally found in the product. One example could be a brand of bath soap

MISPLACED OR MISLEADING CLAIMS (Claims which could not be used on unrelated products)	MEANINGLESS STATEMENT (Claims which could only be used with qualification)
TO BE CONTROLLED BY CODE OF PRACTICE	WOULD BE CONTROLLED BY FAIR TRADING ACT
CFC free (when not normally used in products) Phosphate free (when not normally used in product) Solvent free (when not normally used in product) Use of Symbol (e.g. Dolphin) with no obvious connection to product, its use, or disposal Petrochemical free (when not normally used in product)	Biocycle Safe Contains no pollutants Energy Saver Environmentally Friendly Environmentally Safe Natural Fragrance Natural Herbal Additives No dangerous Chemicals No Hard Chemicals Non-polluting Non-Residual Organic Ozone Friendly Petrochemical Free Synthetic Ingredients Uses only carefully selected herbs, minerals etc.

labelled "No CFCs" and "Free of dioxin and harmful preservatives".

This category would also prohibit the use of symbols like dolphins or koalas where there was no obvious connection with the product, its use or disposal.

A third group concerns claims that require clear and uniform definition, such as "Fully biodegradable", "Made from recycled plastic" and "Recyclable".

The last lists claims that must be verifiable by independent testing, like "Aluminium free", "Vegetable-based surfactants", and "Made without solvents".

Some legal control can already be exercised under trade practices law. But Mr Crabb said these powers would, if necessary, be extended by regulations defining exactly what is

meant by such terms and when they can be used.

The scheme is a two-level approach, using voluntary compliance with the code of ethics, and laws.

Mr Crabb said he expected that market pressure, such as bad publicity from flouting the code, would make most companies comply.

An early concept of a Government-approved "green spot" product label has been overtaken by green ticks, stripes, trees, animals and other symbols decorating supermarket shelves.

But under this scheme, manufacturers who agreed to have their products tested by a technical committee to verify their claims could, if they wanted, display a sign or logo yet to be designed.

The Age, 14 June 1991

Compliance is managed by the enforcement of penalties, such as having the company or individual's licence to trade revoked, and by administrative action. Fines for misconduct may be imposed, such as the $52 000 fine imposed on Coles Myer for mislabelling children's nightdresses (see the article below). The minister may seek written undertakings from offenders to alter their conduct, enlisting industry cooperation to change behaviours as well as issuing warnings to individual traders.

Coles Myer fined over nightie labels

PETER GREGORY

The retailer Coles Myer Ltd was fined a record $52 000 in the Federal Court yesterday for selling and mislabelling 6000 children's nightdresses in 1990.

Coles Myer pleaded guilty to 10 charges of contravening the Trade Practices Act over the nightdresses which were given the wrong "fire danger" labels.

The federal Minister for Consumer Affairs, Mrs McHugh, said the fine was the highest imposed for breaches of a consumer product safety standard.

Mrs McHugh said children were put at real risk of severe burns or death if nightwear was not properly labelled and parents did not know the real risk of them catching alight.

"The message to all clothing suppliers — retailers, manufacturers and importers — is clear. They have a duty to protect the public and ensure that safety standards are met. If they fail to do so for whatever reasons, they face prosecution," she said.

In his published judgment, Mr Justice Keely said that the nightdresses, instead of bearing a red label with a fire danger symbol and the words "Warning High Fire Danger Keep Away From Fire", had a label that read "Styled To Reduce Fire Danger".

He said the nightdresses were distributed and sold in each of K-mart's 137 stores throughout Australia from February 1990. Federal Bureau of Consumer Affairs officers bought some of the nightdresses in June and July 1990.

Mr Justice Keely said Coles Myer, in its defence, said it had never been charged before with mislabelling garments. It said the offences were not deliberate, that it had cooperated with the prosecution and that there was no reason to believe that any child had been injured as a result of the mislabelled nightdresses.

He said it was not known how many of the nightdresses had been returned or how many were still in the community. He

said Coles Myer had also shown that a number of steps had been taken to ensure that members of the public were made aware of the mislabelling.

He said Coles Myer made three mistakes before the offences were committed. A buyer's assistant marked the wrong category for the nightdresses; an inspection report of a carton of the nightdresses wrongly said that they had been correctly marked, and pressure of work prevented quality-control staff from undertaking their usual store visit.

Mr Justice Keely said the offences were serious. He said Coles Myer did not use enough foresight before the initial offences occurred. After receiving notice of the offences, it failed to take effective and quick action to ensure that the nightdresses were removed from sale.

The Age,
9 December 1992

Today's consumer is faced with a large variety of products and must not only make decisions based on quality and price, but also must consider safety aspects of the product. In many cases the possible hazards associated with the use of particular products are quite obvious, but some products have inherent dangers that may not be obvious to the average consumer. In 1986 the product safety provisions in Division 1A of Part V of the federal *Trade Practices Act* came into effect. This makes the *Trade Practices Act* the principal federal legislation regulating product safety to stop the supply of unsafe goods and/or remove unsafe products from the marketplace.

KILL IT BEFORE IT KILLS YOU.

If you own one of these early model Mistral fans, destroy it immediately. Several people have already been killed in fires caused by the fans. If you keep using it, it WILL catch fire. DO NOT THROW IT OUT, DESTROY IT. For more information call 03 691 4462 (Please have your fans with you when you call.)

FAULTY MODELS: Model GA 12–10, all styles;
Model GA 16–70, all styles;
Model GA 16–40, all styles.

CFA   Office of Fair Trading   SEC

Figure 18.4: This advertisement was developed in conjunction with an advertising agency by the then State Electricity Commission of Victoria and with the support of the Office of Fair Trading. It was published in several editions of Melbourne's two daily newspapers during January 1993, at the start of the summer hot period. The advertisement was in fact an adaptation of one published 12 months before, shortly after a coronial inquiry concluded that the deaths of two children had resulted from a fire caused by this cooling fan.

A feature of the amendment is that it allows the Minister for Consumer Affairs to provide public warnings, recalls, bans and product information standards or safety standards.[26] Bans are issued publicly through notices such as those shown on page 483. Most of the product recalls monitored by the minister are voluntary recalls, where a company or industry informs the minister of defects or problems. In 1993–94, a total of 222 voluntary recalls were monitored,[27] comprising:

- 87 medical
- 35 motor vehicle
- 6 toys
- 14 electrical
- 32 food
- 48 other.

Statutory authorities can initiate public warnings, such as the action taken by the State Electricity Commission of Victoria, in conjunction with the Office of Fair Trading, to warn consumers of a potentially dangerous product (see figure 18.4).

There is a body of recently enacted legislation dealing with liabilities for defective or unsafe products. Until recently in Australia the liability was 'fault based', which meant that the injured party had to prove that the damage was caused by some defect or unsafe feature of the product. In July 1992, Australia adopted a strict product liability regime in line with overseas trends. Provided that it can be shown that there was a defect in the product and that damage occurred because of the defect, the manufacturer would be held liable. This will hold even if the manufacturer has taken all possible care and although the defect may not have been discoverable. In essence the burden of proof has shifted to the manufacturer.

PRICES

Legislation plays a role in determining excessive prices in the marketplace. The federal *Prices Surveillance Act 1983* provides for the surveillance of and the holding of inquiries into prices charged for certain goods and services. The Prices Surveillance Authority, established under the Act, has general power to inquire into specific matters with the approval of the minister. Under the legislation, certain goods and services can be subject to price assessment. Recently the Prices Surveillance Authority responded to concerns about the 70 per cent discounts offered by Goldmark Jewellers. Consumers thought that the pre-markdown price was too high. The Authority hired independent jewellers to value a sample of the retail chain's stock. They concluded that the pre-markdown price was reflective of the actual market value of the stock and the reason for the high markdown was that Goldmark was able to buy jewellery cheaper than its competitors, because of their established relationship with overseas suppliers.[28]

The Authority can increase, decrease or even suggest that a public inquiry be held into the price increases. Various state and territory laws also provide for the fixing of prices at which specific goods or services may be sold.

PRODUCT BANS AND RECALLS

WATER SKI DEVICE BANNED

The Minister for Justice and Consumer Affairs has announced a ban on the supply of a water ski line release system marketed under the name of 'Quickie Line Release'.

The ban follows investigations into the safety of the product by the Federal Bureau of Consumer Affairs.

A number of serious injuries have resulted from the failure of the product, and both the Victorian and New South Wales Consumer Affairs Ministers have banned it.

'However, it is not clear how many units may still be available for retail sale in those States and Territories which have not introduced the ban,' the Minister said.

A spokesman for the Bureau said the major fault with the device appeared to be in the design of the release mechanism, where an unacceptably high amount of force was needed to trigger the release mechanism under normal operating conditions.

NEW LABELLING REQUIREMENTS FOR SUNGLASSES

The Minister for Justice and Consumer Affairs has announced changes to the Australian standard for sunglasses and fashion spectacles that would require some suppliers to label their products 'Not suitable for driving' and 'Not suitable for people with defective colour vision'.

'The Federal Bureau of Consumer Affairs has advised me that some sunglasses and fashion spectacles can alter the wearer's perception of colour. This could create difficulties for some drivers negotiating traffic lights and road signs, and with this in mind I have moved to advise consumers of the possible danger of wearing some glasses while driving,' the Minister said.

He said the vast majority of glasses on the market would not require any labelling changes, but those that were found to alter the wearer's colour perception would be subject to the new requirements.

EXERCISE BIKE WARNING

The Minister for Justice and Consumer Affairs has warned consumers to be careful when using exercise cycles around young children.

The Minister issued the warning after figures released by the National Injury Surveillance Unit (NISU) revealed 41 cases of injury to children caused by exercise cycles. The injuries occurred when fingers or limbs were caught in the spokes and sprockets of exercise bikes not fitted with safety guards.

'Recently manufactured exercise cycles have safety features built in, but in the past, many have been supplied without wheel and sprocket guards.

'The Federal Bureau of Consumer Affairs will survey new exercise bikes to see if there are safety problems with those currently available. And in the future, suppliers may be required to ensure exercise bikes are fitted with approved safety guards on wheels, chains and sprockets,' the Minister said.

BANNED CANDLES ON SALE IN MELBOURNE

The Minister for Justice and Consumer Affairs has warned consumers of the dangers of self-relighting candles after officers of the Federal Bureau of Consumer Affairs (FBCA) found several brands on sale throughout Melbourne.

'Self-relighting candles are dangerous. They were banned from sale in 1977 after fire authorities warned of the risk of burns to children. Anyone who has recently purchased self-relighting candles should dispose of them as soon as possible,' he said.

He said the novelty candles which re-light after they are blown out, should be immersed in water before being placed in the rubbish bin.

The Minister warned that anyone selling self-relighting candles was committing an offence under the Trade Practices Act and risked a fine of up to $100 000 for corporations and $20 000 for individuals.

FBCA officers discovered two types of relighting candles in Melbourne. *Magic Relighting Candles* look like normal birthday candles and are sold in a flat yellow packet. The thinner *(Super) Sparkling Candles* have no visible wick, are red, blue, green, pink and fluoro colours, are 170 mm long and come in a flat black package.

Figure 18.5: Examples of bans and recalls from *Minder*, issued by the Federal Bureau of Consumer Affairs

THE IMPORTANCE OF REGULATION

The basis of much of the legislation that protects consumers and marketers is concerned with the concept of fairness and equity. Even though it may cause problems for the community and marketers in terms of compliance, enforcements and consumer confidence, it is necessary. There are unscrupulous consumers and marketers and, although moral and ethical behaviours are normal practice, regulation is a necessary safety net. Only strict regulations can protect consumers from monopolies and strict regulations regarding testing in industries, such as the drug and chemical industry, can help prevent repeats of such tragic incidents as the thalidomide disaster in the 1960s.

The thalidomide tragedy

Thalidomide was developed as a sedative and used as a sleeping pill. It was tested on animals and then released to the marketplace. It became popular and pregnant women found it useful for controlling the nausea of early pregnancy and for curing sleeplessness. All the indications were that the drug had no side effects. It was not until a Sydney doctor, William McBride, linked the drug to an increase in the number of deformed babies that the alarm was raised. Well over 20 000 deformities were linked to the product.[29]

There are situations where the forces of the marketplace may not result in the best solution for both the customer and the organisation. A good example of this is the case of safety information. If a product hazard is small and not widely known, such as the adverse side effects that can on rare occasions occur with vaccinations, a seller may be reluctant to advertise a safety improvement as this could raise consumer concerns unduly. The producer must balance the additional sales that may be gained from rivals by convincing consumers that the product is safer, against the sales that it may lose by disclosing to customers the fact that the product contains hazards of which they may not have been aware. If the advertising and marketing of safety improvements is discouraged, the incentive to adopt such improvement is reduced.

But if the producer is liable for the consequences of a hazardous product, no question of advertising safety improvements to the consumer will arise. A producer will adopt cost-justified precautions, not to divert sales from competitors but to minimise liability to injured consumers. In this way it can be seen that regulations actively encourage producers to be more customer-focused.

Another factor is the cost of regulation. The costs of regulation, particularly testing, are enormous. Sick people can die while stringent testing is conducted on new life-saving drugs. In this instance, the issue is striking the right balance between testing, costs and risks associated with delaying the drug's availability due to testing rules.

HOW MUCH REGULATION IS NECESSARY?

Given the need for regulation the question is how much regulation is necessary. This is the subject of much debate.[30] Essentially there are two different viewpoints — those who support strict product liability and those against it.

The proponents of strict product liability consider it necessary for the following reasons:

1. Manufacturers have a moral responsibility for the safety of their products.
2. It protects people from themselves, and prevents people from taking voluntary risks (hard drugs).
3. Modern methods of production and distribution impose an unfair burden on injured persons by requiring them to prove negligence against a manufacturer.
4. It is cheaper to allow the consumer to have direct action against the manufacturer and thereby avoid the possibility of a multiplicity of actions by internalising the cost to the manufacturer. An incentive may be created for the manufacturer to prevent accidents and to implement more effective quality control measures.
5. It is reasonable that individuals should not bear the risk of loss caused by defective products. Usually an individual will not have insured against the risk of personal injury. The cost of insurance can easily be obtained by the manufacturer with the result that the cost of the insurance will be passed on to the consumer in the price of the product. In Australia such costs are not built into the price of the products.[31]

Those against product liability legislation argue that it is unnecessary and in fact counterproductive for the following reasons:

1. With strict liability a manufacturer is liable for the design and marketing defects. A design defect can occur in a product which, although manufactured in accordance with specifications and quality control standards, is still defective in the sense that it fails to provide the perquisite degree of safety generally expected of it.

   Marketing defects may not be related to the product itself, but from inadequate information, instructions or warnings supplied with the product when it is distributed or advertised in the market. To hold a manufacturer liable for marketing defects which are clearly no fault of the manufacturer is unfair. This illustrates the difficulties involved in arguing on the basis of 'fairness' and 'equity'. What may be fair to one party of the transaction (the consumer) may be unfair to the other party (the manufacturer).

2. Legislation may encourage consumers to ignore warnings and disregard manufacturers' limitations (e.g. use by dates). Producers could unreasonably be held liable for losses that are at least in part the fault of the consumer, or for defects that they could not have foreseen. It is argued that if liability exists, even though defects in the product were not discoverable under the scientific and technical knowledge at the time the product was produced, the incentive to innovate will be curtailed. This means that strict product liability may inhibit the development of new products to the ultimate disadvantage of the whole community.

3. A significant rise in the number of product liability cases in the courts will increase manufacturing costs, which will be passed on to the consumer.[32] Freer access to the law does not necessarily mean that those people who are in the greatest need of protection will gain it.
4. The impossibility of assessing the likely amount of claims could render the cost of adequate insurance prohibitive. Manufacturers may resort to self-insurance. The price of some products may be raised to the detriment of consumers in general. It has been argued that this could result in Australian products becoming less competitive in the international marketplace.

It can be seen from these arguments that there is no simple answer to the problems of legislation to protect consumers from product defects. However, a lack of product standards can also influence the demand for products. Stringent standards for products can in fact make products more attractive in international markets and lead to economic success. While product liability laws may slow the rate of product innovation, they may also be the key to long-term success in the marketplace.[33]

SELF-REGULATION

For the most part, those who are opposed to excessive regulation prefer the notion of self-regulation. Many industry groups argue that rather than impose more legislation on industry, industries should be encouraged to maintain good marketplace practices and if necessary form their own regulatory bodies. Many industries prefer to keep the consumers informed about product defects. There is also the view that competition will maintain equity in the marketplace, for example, in the control of prices.

NUTTELEX HEALTH MARGARINE:

WE ARE NOW BEING INUNDATED WITH TELEPHONE ENQUIRIES, REGARDING INCREASED PRICES NOW BEING CHARGED IN THE SUPERMARKETS.

OUR WHOLESALE PRICES HAVE NOT BEEN RAISED AND WE DO NOT PROPOSE DOING SO.

WE ASK ALL NUTTELEX CONSUMERS TO JOIN US IN RESISTING ANY UNNECESSARY INCREASE IN THE RECOMMENDED RETAIL PRICE (METROP. AREAS) OF $1.66 PER 500 GRAM TUB.

NUTTELEX FOOD PRODUCTS P/L.
594-600 CHURCH STREET
RICHMOND VIC. 3121
TEL: (03) 428 3585

"AUSTRALIAN OWNED — AUSTRALIAN MADE."

Figure 18.6: The background to this advertisement is explained in the article on page 487.

Margarine price falls after public tipped off

ALEX MESSINA — consumer affairs reporter

A small margarine maker has shocked the supermarket giants, Coles and Safeway, into reversing a price rise of 20 cents on a brand of margarine.

In what is thought to be an unprecedented tactic, Nuttelex Food Products yesterday placed a newspaper advertisement urging consumers to resist price rises for Nuttelex margarine.

The managing director of Nuttelex, Mr Gordon McNally, recommended that if Safeway and Coles did not reverse the price rise consumers should buy Nuttelex from Franklins and Jewel supermarkets, whose prices had not risen.

The tactic forced a quick about-face. Safeway and Coles immediately reverted to the lower price.

Coles admitted that the rise was unjustified. It said its low-price policy could mean increasing a price if a big competitor did so. Safeway was first to raise the Nuttelex price.

On Coles' price policy, Mr McNally said: "Are they going to tell the true story? Here is a case where they put up the price for a tub (of Nuttelex) and there's not one iota of difference (in the wholesale price) we were charging 18 months ago."

The general manager of Safeway, Mr Trevor Herd, was "infuriated". "I have never seen a manufacturer take an ad out recommending the price at which we should sell." He said the Nuttelex price was increased because Safeway made no money from it.

Other margarine makers raised their wholesale prices recently by seven cents. Mr McNally said that was no reason to increase the Nuttelex price, and certainly not by 20 cents. "In our book it's a rip off ... The supermarkets (Coles and Safeway) are taking the public for a ride."

His advertisement urged consumers to resist paying more than $1.66 for a 500-gram tub.

Since Monday last week, Coles had sold Nuttelex for $1.86, after Safeway increased its price to $1.85. This morning the prices revert to $1.66 and $1.65. Franklins and Jewel prices remain at $1.63.

Mr McNally said his recommended price gave retailers an ample margin of about 17.5 per cent on a wholesale price of about $1.41. Victorians buy about 100 000 tubs of Nuttelex a week.

A spokeswoman for Coles, Ms Veronica McGowan, said of the price increase: "I think we are at a bit of a loss to explain it. When very senior management were alerted, they thought it was an unjustified increase ... Quite frankly, it was too much too quickly."

The Age, 27 February 1992

Many industries have established their own regulatory bodies, particularly professional services such as medical, legal and accounting groups. For marketing an important regulatory body is the Media Council of Australia, of which the Advertising Standards Council is a part.[34]

The Media Council of Australia is an unincorporated voluntary association of twelve media associations consisting of:

Australian Newspaper Council
Australian Accreditation Bureau
News Limited Group
Regional Dailies of Australia Limited
Australian Magazine Publishers
The Outdoor Advertising Association
Australian Suburban Newspapers Associations Pty Ltd
Associated Rural Press
Australian Cinema Advertising Council
Federation of Australian Radio Broadcasters
Federation of Australian Commercial Television

The main function of the Media Council is to control the accreditation of advertising agencies throughout Australia so as to formulate and apply common rules across advertising. The Media Council has developed a number of advertising codes to cover the advertising of specific products, and advertising generally (see chapter one, page 3). The Advertising Code of Ethics applies to all forms of advertising and all marketers should be aware of it.[35] The Australian Marketing Institute also has in place a Code of Professional Conduct, with which all marketers should be familiar (see figure 18.7).

Australian Marketing Institute
Code of Professional Conduct

1 *Members shall conduct their professional activities with respect for the public interest.*

2 *Members shall at all times act with integrity in dealings with clients or employers, past and present, with their fellow members and with the general public.*

3 *Members shall not intentionally disseminate false or misleading information, whether written, spoken or implied, nor conceal any relevant fact. They have a duty to maintain truth, accuracy and good taste in advertising, sales promotion and all other aspects of marketing.*

4 *Members shall not represent conflicting or competing interests except with the express consent of those concerned given only after full disclosure of the facts to all interested parties.*

5 *Members in performing services for a client or employer, shall not accept fees, commissions or any other valuable consideration in connection with those services from anyone other than their client or employer except with the consent (express or implied) of both.*

6 *Members shall refrain from knowingly associating with any enterprise which uses improper or illegal methods in obtaining business.*

7 *Members shall not intentionally injure the professional reputation or practice of another member.*

8 *If a member has evidence that another member has been guilty of unethical practices it shall be their duty to inform the Institute.*

9 *Members have a responsibility to continue the acquisition of professional skills in marketing and to encourage the development of these skills in those who are desirous of entry into, or continuing in, the profession of marketing management.*

10 *Members shall help to improve the body of knowledge of the profession by exchanging information and experience with fellow members and by applying their special skill and training for the benefit of others.*

11 *Members shall refrain from using their relationship with the Institute in such a manner as to state or imply an official accreditation or approval beyond the scope of membership of the Institute and its aims, rules and policies.*

12 *The use of the Institute's distinguishing letters must be confined to Institute activities, or the statement of name and business address on a card, letterhead and published articles.*

13 *Members shall co-operate with fellow members in upholding and enforcing this Code.*

Figure 18.7: Australian Marketing Institute, Code of Professional Conduct

In 1992, the Media Council received 691 individual complaints,[36] compared with: 638 in 1991; 1000 in 1990; 956 in 1989; 507 in 1988. Most of the complaints in 1992[37] (see table 18.2) related to ethical standards, sexism and those that infringed taste and decency, such as the use of fear appeals by several of the private health funds.

Table 18.2: Complaints by area of concern

Complaint	Received	Current	Upheld	Not upheld	Outside charter	Otherwise settled
Ethics	438	15	151	259	12	1
Alcohol	9	0	1	7	1	0
Cigarette	2	0	0	1	1	0
Therapeutic	25	0	4	17	4	0
Slimming	6	1	4	1	0	0
Sexism	83	2	9	72	0	0
Taste and decency	65	3	7	54	1	0
Discrimination	23	2	5	16	0	0
Safety	37	0	18	18	1	0
Breach law	1	1	0	0	0	0
Children	2	0	0	2	0	0
Other	0	0	0	0	0	0
Total	691	24	199	447	20	1

(*Source*: Compiled from Media Council Reports 1988–92)

As table 18.3 indicates, most complaints were related to the television and print media. A key concern for consumers was the number of television commercials screened. The majority of the complaints came from individual women and women's organisations. The portrayal of women in advertisements is still a sensitive issue and is carefully monitored by women's organisations.[38]

Table 18.3: Complaints by media type

Media type	Received	Current	Upheld	Not upheld	Outside charter	Otherwise settled
Cinema	3	0	2	1	0	0
Print	251	9	94	134	14	0
Television	395	14	99	277	4	1
Radio	10	0	2	7	1	0
Outdoor	32	1	2	28	1	0
Other	0	0	0	0	0	0
Total	691	24	199	447	20	1

(*Source*: Compiled From Media Council Reports, 1988–92)

Uproar over mother-to-be in Toyota ad

CAROLINE MILBURN — community affairs reporter

The image of a headless, naked pregnant woman in an advertisement to promote Toyota's new family car sparked outrage yesterday from Government senators and women's groups.

The advertisement appeared in daily newspapers throughout Australia under the heading: "There's nowhere more comfortable than inside a wide body."

More than 100 people telephoned Toyota's head offices in Melbourne and Sydney to complain about the advertisement.

A large number of telephone complaints were also received by the Advertising Standards Council, according to a spokesman.

Senator Rosemary Crowley said the headless image was offensive because it reduced a woman's body to a mechanical device such as a car.

She said the ad breached voluntary industry standards on the portrayal of women in advertising established by a joint Government and community committee last year. Senator Crowley said complaints about the advertisement would be discussed at the next caucus committee meeting on the status of women.

Senator Margaret Reynolds urged Toyota to withdraw the advertisement. She said her Townsville office was deluged with callers complaining that the advertisement insulted women by comparing them with the interior space available in a car.

A group representing more than 500 businesswomen also branded the advertisement as sexist. Ms Attracta Lagan, the executive officer of the NSW-based Women and Management, said women were tired of advertisers asking women to take their clothes off to sell products.

She said the industry constantly offended women by dissecting their bodies in advertisements and using them as objects. But Ms Lagan said last year's semi-naked image of the pregnant actor Demi Moore, which appeared on the cover of the US magazine "Vanity Fair", was not offensive. "The photograph was not demeaning because the full-figured image of Ms Moore was relevant to the magazine article in which she was interviewed about her pregnancy and its effect on her life," she said.

The Coalition Against Sexual Violence Propaganda, which represents 400 community groups nationwide, also called on Toyota to withdraw the advertisement. A spokeswoman for the coalition, Ms Liz Conor, said women were angry about the advertisement's "smug, lewd message".

However, a spokeswoman for the Australian Psychological Society, Dr Sandra Neil, rejected such criticism. Dr Neil, a clinical psychologist, said the advertisement's subliminal message was one of comfort and beauty.

"The message is that it's comfortable in the womb and so I thought it must be a comfortable car," Dr Neil said. "I just thought that it was a lovely rounded, full-term tummy."

Mr Simon Lloyd, a spokesman for Saatchi and Saatchi, the agency that devised the advertisement, rejected the criticism. He said the image of a pregnant woman's stomach was used because it was a universal metaphor for the safe carriage of children.

Management officials at Toyota's Sydney office did not return calls from "The Age" yesterday. However, the company later released a faxed statement, which said the advertisement was designed to appear once in national and metropolitan newspapers to announce the launch of the new model Camry car.

The Age,
16 March 1993

Self-regulation may seem an attractive avenue to keep consumer regulations up to date, since it does not require the same lengthy procedure that legislation requires for its enactment. The major difficulty with self-regulation lies in the inability to provide meaningful deterrents to those who do not conform to the regulations. Self-regulation has also been criticised because, unlike legislation, those forming the regulations come from within the industry and so may not have a realistic view of the community standards or wishes.

CONSUMER CONCERNS

Since the 1960s, the number of consumer organisations, government departments and other regulatory agencies has grown. The last ten years have seen further developments in legislation and the number of regulatory bodies. Although there is considerable protection for consumers and some key problem areas have been remedied, new concerns continually emerge.

In 1986, the Trade Practices Commission conducted a survey of consumer opinions.[39] The main finding of the study was that two thirds of all respondents could not spontaneously recall a consumer problem. Of the one third that could, the key areas were poor quality of goods, price (overpriced or hidden costs) and delays or unavailability of products. The survey found that there was a high degree of general satisfaction among consumers about the products they buy. The group reporting the most concerns were individuals who had tertiary education and were professionals.

The product categories where the main problems occurred were:
* real estate (purchase and rental). The majority of concerns related to inadequate property descriptions, poor service quality, high costs and delays.
* government services (housing, local government and Telecom) point of sale, staff courtesy and incompetence.
* motor vehicles, mechanical, electrical and structural faults, service and repair problems.
* the repair of recreational electronic goods, TV, videos and general household appliances. The inadequacy of information on products (product use instructions).

Industry legislation, government authorities and consumer organisations have considerably reduced the level of consumer concerns in specific areas. But consumer concerns are a continuing factor in the marketplace. As the environment changes so do the issues that concern consumers. Computer databases have created concerns about privacy; environmental dangers have changed the way consumers think about packaging; increased consumer education has changed the way consumers use information; and industry improvements have increased consumer expectations.

Consumers are concerned with issues such as irradiation of food, genetically modified products and the use of organochlorines and toxins. Some ongoing concerns are environmental issues, including recycling of packages, unsatisfactory service, such as in repairs to household items and service from government departments, and misleading labelling.[40] Even in today's tightly monitored marketplace, companies are still mislabelling their products and making misleading statements.

The summary of complaints received by the NSW Department of Consumer Affairs between 1983 and 1992 (see table 18.4) shows that complaints about product quality have remained consistently high.

Table 18.4: Complaints relating to practice received by the NSW Department of Consumer Affairs (by percentage of total complaints received)

Practice category	1983 NSW %	1984 NSW %	1985 NSW %	1986 NSW %	1988 NSW %	1990 NSW %	1991 NSW %	1992 NSW %
Advertising and representation	7.1	7.6	5.7	4	7	7	8	8
Sales methods	4.1	4.1	6.3	7	4	5	3	3
Packaging/labelling	1.5	1.6	1.0	1	0.05	1	1	2
Charges	5.8	4.9	4.9	7	7	7	8	8
Product quality	44.6	46.6	42.9	45	52	45	44	46
Credit practices	8.1	5.8	4.7	3	4	4	6	5
Contracts	16.9	17.7	23.0	23	15	12	16	17
Guarantees/warranties	8.2	7.8	8.1	7	14	14	10	8
Offers of redress	3.8	3.9	3.4	3	5	5	4	3

(*Source*: Adapted from the NSW Department of Consumer Affairs Annual Reports, 1983–1992)

Tasmanian tigers yanked out of the brewing wilderness

ANDREW DARBY

HOBART: Captain Jablonski, fresh off the nuclear submarine USS Topeka, found something he liked at a cocktail party in Hobart this month. "Give me some more of that Two Dog," he drawled.

The Two Dog that passed the American sailor's taste test is better known to Australians as Cascade Premium Lager, the brew with a pair of Tasmanian Tigers on the label.

It was sold yesterday to Carlton and United Breweries as part of a $27 million joint venture with the Cascade group. The deal will provide what the CUB managing director, Mr Pat Stone, describes as the corporate "horsepower" needed to put Premium before more drinkers, both nationally and internationally, like Captain Jablonski.

After five years Cascade Premium holds a 7.5 per cent share of Australia's premium-beer sales, a matter of pride to the small Tasmanian brewery that claims to be Australia's oldest manufacturer.

But the sale of the Premium label, the Hobart brewery and other linked assets to Cascade's long-time Melbourne rival has raised concerns in Hobart.

Mr Stone said the deal allowed other CUB products to be brewed in Tasmania and that, in future, Cascade Premium might be brewed outside the island. He said: "It's not sold in Queensland as Tasmanian beer, it's sold as Cascade beer."

However, some print advertisements say the lager is "pure beer out of the Tasmanian wilderness".

The Federal Justice Minister, Senator Tate, who lives in Hobart when not in Canberra, said marketing and promotion of Premium Lager was based on an image of a pure Tasmanian product. "To maintain that image the brew must be produced in Tasmania. CUB ... must be warned not to fall foul of the provisions of the act which prohibit misleading and false advertising."

The Trade Practices Commission confirmed that it was examining the deal, but focusing on the powerful market position it would give CUB in Tasmania.

The Age,
19 January 1993

A 1993 survey by the *Financial Review*[41] showed that the television industry is one of the worst performers in consumer satisfaction stakes, ranking with banks and used-car dealers. The most consumer friendly industries included supermarkets, video stores, travel and telephone service. The survey found that 64 per cent were more aware of quality in customer service than they were five years ago.

According to consumer organisations and government authorities, the three key areas of consumer concern that are likely to dominate the 1990s are:[42]
- banking services
- privacy issues
- superannuation and life insurance.

The banking industry in Australia was deregulated in the 1970s, and is now one of the most deregulated banking systems in the world.[43] During the 1980s and into the 1990s consumer complaints have continued to rise.[44] Complaints received by the Australian Consumer Association and the ABC television program *The Investigators* indicate banking services, transactions and bank charges are the main concerns.[45] The volume of complaints forced an inquiry into the banking industry.[46] The recommendations of relevance to consumers are that:[47]
- a code of banking practice be developed
- banks develop efficient mechanisms for handling complaints
- banks disclose all fees, charges and interest rates across all products
- banks set mechanisms for recovering actual costs due to early loan repayments rather than setting penalties
- customers have access to all personal information concerning them contained in bank records.

In 1993, a major issue in retail banking was privacy.[48] Bank customers are concerned with:
- collection, storage and security of data
- access by individuals to their personal records
- accuracy of records
- use of personal information
- disclosure to third parties.

Privacy issues are of concern to consumers across a range of industries. Of major concern is the amount of stored information that relates to individual consumers. Computers and sophisticated database programs have made it possible for organisations to store a considerable amount of information about people. A fact that disturbs consumers is that this information can be given and sold across organisations. When the federal government tried to introduce the Australia Card in 1987, there was massive public objection. According to Tom Dixon 'it is clear the debate over privacy rights goes to the heart of the status of the consumer in the information society of the 21st century'.[49] In New South Wales, concern with privacy issues led to the formation of the Privacy Committee in 1975 and the introduction of the *Privacy Act 1988*. The key components of the *Privacy Act* are the setting of parameters for the operation of the consumer credit reporting industry and the provision of enforceable rights for individuals regarding information which relates to their personal credit worthiness.

In its 1991 Annual Report, the Privacy Committee noted that in New South Wales, in stark contrast to the hundreds of millions of dollars invested each year in information technology, there is virtually no financial commitment to the protection of privacy. It observed that the people have paid dearly for 'privacy on the cheap'. The majority of complaints received by the Privacy Commission were related to mailing lists (direct marketing) and credit lists.[50]

Table 18.5: Nature of complaints received by the Privacy Commission (as percentage of total complaints)

Direct marketing	20%
Third party access to personal data	13%
Adoption	5%
Debt collection methods	5%
Media	3%
Medical	3%
Insurance (AIDS)	2%
Tenancy	2%
Credit related	17%
Employment	8%
Banks	5%
Police methods — criminal records	5%
Prisons	3%
Surveys and research	3%
Surveillance	2%
Roads and Traffic Authority	1%

The survey of complaints shows that the major areas of concern are direct marketing, credit disclosures and third party access to personal data. An observation is that some companies are in breach of the *Privacy Act*. A concern of the committee is the non-concensus disclosure of information by organisations for direct marketing purposes. Committee policy is that, in general, information collected for one purpose should not be used for another purpose without the consent of the information subject.[51]

The focus of consumer complaints in the life insurance industry is on the penalty charges that the early surrender of policies incurs. A consequence of this is that the value of the pay-out can be lower than the accumulated premiums and interest. Consumer groups doubt that this practice is appropriate. The problems with superannuation are similar. Consumers are concerned about the charges associated with 'super' funds, with the first years of interest going in entry and exit fees and policy charges.[52] The concerns with life insurance and superannuation funds led to government intervention in the form of a Senate inquiry and legislation. It is too early to know whether the measures taken will alleviate consumer concerns.

Privacy issue threatens all database marketers

VICTOR ROSS

Victor Ross fought the anti-direct marketing regulators in Europe and came to Australia to sound the alarm!

What can you learn from the British experience about the privacy issue?

The short answer is to stay in Australia and count your blessings. Also to keep your powder dry: you will need it before long.

Privacy has become an issue partly because of legitimate concerns of people perplexed by the society they live in, partly because the issue has been high-jacked for political ends, just as green issues have.

Australian direct marketers have opted for self-regulation and you are probably right, given the pressures bearing upon you. But self-regulation is not an easy option — it demands a degree of industry discipline and co-operation that we, in Britain, have found difficult to achieve.

What are the pressures that have persuaded you that you cannot just maintain the status quo?

1. Public Opinion: the most important of them all — the views of your customers, potential customers, and those who purport to speak for them.

You do not have the image problems our industry has in the UK and in some other countries. But my guess is that the figures of "discontenteds" are likely to go up rather than down.

You'd be well advised to do comparable research at regular intervals to take the public's temperature and measure the effect of remedial action you are taking.

2. The Pressure of Indirect Legislation: all the legislation that is taking place elsewhere, or in your own country at the Commonwealth level which does not affect you directly creates a climate that makes global warming seem positively benign.

This sort of legislation can be traced back to the Declaration of Human Rights with its own progeny such as the International Covenant on Civil & Political Rights to which Australia is a party; the OECD Guidelines which create new concepts of the right of access to personal data, the right to correction, and the right to compensation for certain kinds of abuse; closer to home, there is your Human Rights & Equal Opportunity Commission Act 1986 which embodies the Articles derived from the International Covenant; then there is the 1975 Privacy Committee Act which is so far confined to NSW.

Finally, there is the Privacy Act of 1988, a Federal Act establishing 11 Information Privacy Principles which apply to the Commonwealth public sector only, but are a model for future state legislation and a good imitation of the Council of Europe (CoE) Data Protection Principles which underpin the Convention to which most Europe countries including Britain now adhere.

3. Rival media: newspapers, magazines, radio, and television stations are naturally among your detractors — trumpeting in mock horror about junk mail in order to under-mine an efficient competitor eating into their revenues.

4. International users: the toughest pressure for data protection could come from data users in your own country who want to engage in trans-border data transfer and are afraid that, if Australia does not have legislation that matches standards obtaining elsewhere, they will be able neither to import data nor export services and thus suffer competitive disadvantage.

It was an unholy alliance of bleeding hearts and business interest in trans-border data flows that speeded the ratification of the CoE Convention for "The Protection of Individuals with regard to Automatic Processing of Personal Data" in the UK.

It was this same Convention that spawned the most detailed discussion of the application of Data Protection Principles to direct marketing ever held anywhere, with the involvement of such heavyweights as the International Chamber of Commerce, the British Home Office, the Reader's Digest, and an assortment of continental hawks and hawkettes.

That discussion resulted in the famous Recommendation (85) 20 for the Protection of Personal Data used in Direct Marketing. It shows what happens when lawgivers try to penetrate an area that is the proper preserve of self regulators. The Recommendation runs to four pages; but explaining what the four pages mean takes 10 pages.

(continued)

It is my experience as a negotiator that if one is going to engage in a dialogue of the kind ADMA has started with the Privacy Committee of NSW, one must have a very clear idea where the sticking points are — where you are prepared to say: so far no further.

This requires agreement within the industry on what I call the direct marketing minima — the conditions in the absence of which a healthy industry cannot operate. There are three:

1. Unhindered access to public lists such as the electoral roll, telephone directories, trade and professional registers, share registers — anything published and universally available must by definition be available to a data collector and user going about legitimate business;

2. Every data collector must be free to use personal data acquired in the course of customer relations, i.e. data supplied by the data subject or arising naturally in the course of commercial transactions;

3. Third, data collectors must be free to acquire similar data from, and disclose them to, third parties.

If this is too sweeping, you might consider a voluntary curb on those freedoms which we have negotiated in the UK and which forms the basis of our self-regulatory Code of Data Protection. This says in effect:

1. There is no restriction at all on the use of publicly available data.

2. On the other hand, where either personal data are being disclosed to a third party for direct marketing purposes, or where data are being used by the data collector for a purpose substantially different from that for which they were collected *and* which the data subjects could not reasonably have foreseen at the time of collection *and* to which it is probable that they would have objected if they had known ... in those cases, our UK code requires data users to notify data subjects early enough for data subjects to object to such use of their names and for data users to act upon such objections.

The UK Code voluntarily provides a way for the data subject to avoid being sucked into the direct marketing maelstrom if he doesn't like it, and a means of exiting once he is in it.

These are important safeguards that take account of concerns felt by some individuals about the receipt of unsolicited postal advertising. But it is essential that the *voluntary* nature of providing an escape route be never compromised, that your industry never bow to a statutory limitation on the sending of commercial communications.

By all means offer self-restraint and show understanding for public anxieties about unsolicited postal advertising. But make sure this is seen as an offering from the goodness of your heart or more likely a commercial calculation motivated by enlightened self-interest — but never an admission that the freedom of commercial expression is subject to limitations other than those applying to any other form of expression, such as the laws of libel.

There is a revealing passage in the Privacy Committee's discussion paper, Recommendation C on page 32, which reads: "All reasonable care shall be taken to deliver unsolicited advertising in a manner which does not cause litter or jeopardise the delivery of regular mail."

There are only two things wrong with this Recommendation: one, it has nothing to do with Privacy or data protection and, two, it makes a totally unwarranted, unacceptable, and unrealistic distinction between advertising mail and regular mail.

Advertising mail *is* regular mail. Once you allow such a spurious distinction to gain a foothold, you are halfway down the slippery slope.

The way in which litter, a highly emotive environmental issue, is slipped into the debate should show you how much you have to be on your guard.

There is only one way to reconcile the vociferous regulators with the pursuit of legitimate commercial interests, to reconcile public anxieties with business freedoms, and to show you are caring citizens — self-regulation.

It has many detractors here in Australia. They thrive in continental Europe where self regulation is branded as British perfidy designed to undermine the rule of the law.

The very opposite is the truth: it is the way to complement the law, to make good laws work better, to safeguard interests that the law cannot protect, to uphold respect for the law which might otherwise fall into disrepute by trying to legislate for trivial purposes and finding itself openly flouted.

Marketing,
October 1990

SUMMARY

Marketplace regulation is necessary to protect both consumers and marketers from undesirable behaviour. The activity of consumers in the twentieth century has resulted in modern consumers having considerable equity and protection in the marketplace. The legislation and regulations that relate to consumer protection in Australia form a large body of information that must be familiar to those undertaking any marketing activity.

This chapter provided a broad overview of the consumer organisations and the legislation relevant to consumer protection. It focused on key aspects of the *Trade Practices Act* and discussed self-regulation as it relates to the media industry. The regulatory environment must be studied and understood in relation to the development of marketing strategies.

Questions

1. In order to ensure that self-regulation will operate, how should industries manage self-regulation?

2. Why is it that men do not appear to be concerned with sexist advertising involving men?

3. The regulation/deregulation debate is an important issue for marketers. Interview two marketing practitioners and two consumers about the topic. What opinions do they share? Where do they differ? Do you think any differences could be resolved?

4. Do you think consumer organisations will continue to play a central role in consumer protection? Do you think their role will change in the future?

5. Prepare a report on the issues surrounding the 'Made in Australia' label.

6. The proliferation of mailing lists and ease of storing and obtaining consumer information is a matter of concern for consumers. Find out the current views and recommendations of federal and state Departments of Consumer Affairs and the Australian Consumers Association.

7. Obtain a copy of the *Trade Practices Act* (there should be one in your library) and examine the sections dealing with false and misleading advertising. Can you find any advertisements that are in breach of any part of this section?

8. Discuss the problems of regulation in the services industry.

9. A customer purchases a solar-powered garden lamp which turns out to be faulty. The manufacturer claims that the customer did not read the instructions carefully. The customer denies this. What avenues of redress are open to the customer?

10. Consumer concerns with nutrition have implications for product development, packaging and advertising. Prepare a report on these concerns and examine the proposals of the Australian Federation of Consumer Organisations. The report should focus on identifying those aspects to which the government has made a positive response and those to which it has not, and should explain the government response.

Case study — a patient's story

Scenario:

A 40 year old woman was a gynaecological patient. The patient was required to stay overnight at a private hospital, nominated by the specialist. The patient had not stayed in a hospital for 15 years. She had private hospital insurance, top cover, with choice of own doctor.

Patient experience:

After having experienced a recurring medical problem for some time without receiving a satisfactory diagnosis from my doctor, I telephoned his office to seek further advice. In the first instance, I spoke to his nurse about the matter. The nurse said that she would speak to the doctor and suggested that I telephone her later in the day to receive his advice. When I telephoned again, she said that the doctor suggested that I might consider routine, exploratory surgery. Because I was uncertain about proceeding with the surgery, I asked to speak to the doctor instead of receiving his advice through his nurse. When I spoke to the doctor, he said that although the operation was not absolutely necessary, he suggested that it was advisable in order to put my mind at ease. For this reason, I agreed to have the operation. At that time, I spoke to his nurse again to find out what I needed to do before entering hospital a few days later. She told me to collect the necessary forms from the surgery and to take them to the admitting hospital.

After getting the forms, I went to the hospital. Upon entering the reception area, I spoke to the clerk on duty who gave me additional forms to complete. My first impression of the hospital was positive. The clerk was polite and helpful. Upon completing the forms, I waited a short time before seeing the admitting officer in her office. I was told that I would need to arrive at the hospital by 11.30 a.m. on the day of the operation and was instructed not to have anything to eat or drink after 7 a.m. When I asked her about the operation, she said that it was routine surgery that required one night in hospital. Since I had the top private hospital insurance, I asked that I be given a private room or a shared room with two beds. The admissions officer assured me that every attempt would be made to comply with my wishes.

On the day of the operation, I arrived at the hospital at the appointed time. After a short wait in the reception area, I was taken to a room with 4 beds rather than being given a private room or a room with 2 beds as I had requested. Also, there was no attempt made by the hospital staff to explain why my request was unable to be met.

Shortly after I arrived in my hospital room, I was told by one of the nurses that my doctor had 5 operations that day and that I was the fifth operation. Since I was not expected to go into the operating theatre until later in the afternoon, I read a book and talked to the other patients for the next four hours. Because we all had the same doctor and were having the same operation, we discussed the operation among ourselves. It soon became apparent, however, that none of the women, including myself, had been given any information by the doctor about the surgical procedure or what to expect after the operation. When one of the nurses asked me if the doctor had explained the operation to me, I told her that he had only said that it was routine surgery and that I would be sore for about 48 hours afterwards. The nurse said that I should have been given more information by the doctor and that I could request further information since there were always some risks associated with this type of surgery. If I had not been preparing to go into surgery shortly thereafter, I would have wanted to know more details about the operation. But, because I was becoming increasingly nervous, I was afraid to ask any questions that might cause me additional distress. Thus, I told the nurse that the doctor had indicated that it was a minor operation and that I was satisfied with his explanation.

During the day, a number of nurses came into the hospital room to take further details about each of the patients. Also, the anaesthetist spoke to each of us in order to obtain pertinent information, such as whether we smoked cigarettes, drank alcohol or were allergic to any anaesthesia. Later in the day, a nurse asked each of us if we wanted a pre-op shot before going into the operating theatre. We all agreed to have a shot for sedation purposes except for one woman. About 3.30 p.m., I received the shot. But, since I was not scheduled to go into the operating theatre until 6.30 p.m., the shot was no longer effective by the time I was ready for the operation.

When I returned to my room after the operation and recovery period, it was almost 9 p.m. I found the other three women sitting up in their beds, eating their dinners. Even though I had a drip and did not feel like eating anything at that time, I was not told by the nurses that I could not have dinner. When I realised that the other women did not have a drip and did not seem to be experiencing the same amount of pain, I asked the nurses why I was having a drip and feeling so badly. All that the nurses were able to tell me was that there had been some complications during my operation which the doctor would explain the next day. During the night, I woke up and felt a bit sick in the stomach. Thinking that crackers and tea might help the condition, I called for the night nurse who offered me sandwiches. Because I believed that sandwiches might not be appropriate, she gladly agreed to give me several packets of crackers and a cup of tea with milk.

The following morning at around 7 a.m., the doctor came to see me. After drawing the curtains, he asked me how I was feeling. I told him that I was sore and he said that he expected me to be very sore. Then he explained that the operation had revealed that there was nothing medically wrong with me. Even so, the original surgical procedure had not been successful and, therefore, an alternative procedure had been required in which a larger incision into my abdomen was necessary. The doctor advised me that during the original surgical procedure, my bowel had possibly been pierced which necessitated my remaining in the hospital a few more days to have fluids and rest my bowel. When I told the doctor that a nurse had already given me solid food during the night, he became very upset and told the accompanying nurse to make certain that this situation did not happen again. I then noticed that there was a large sign above my bed, indicating fluids only.

Since I was in a great deal of discomfort and needed to rest, I asked that my curtains be kept drawn. But, each time that a nurse entered the room, my curtains would be re-opened without the nurse first asking if I wanted them to be pulled back. Thus, I had to keep asking for the curtains to be closed throughout my hospitalisation. For this reason, I felt that the nurses showed a general lack of sensitivity to my needs. In fact, during the entire time that I was in hospital, I found most of the nursing staff to be abrupt and uncooperative. Since I was not able to get out of bed without assistance, I had to ring frequently for a nurse to accompany me to the toilet which was located across the corridor. There was often a long wait before a nurse arrived at my bed and an even longer wait before a nurse returned to the toilet to help me back to my bed. Instead of wanting to make me feel comfortable, the nurses never voluntarily adjusted my bed. I had to ask them to do so. The nurses also continually encouraged me to have shots administered to ease the pain. Although the initial pain killers may have been necessary, the subsequent shots seemed entirely unnecessary. In fact, I suspected that these shots were mainly administered for the convenience of the nursing staff rather than to alleviate my pain. That is, as long as I was kept sedated, I was not an inconvenience to the nursing staff. This suspicion was further reinforced when one of the nurses told me that each ward was given five nurses regardless of how many patients were on the ward. Thus, my ward had approximately 50 patients or 1 nurse for every 10 patients whereas the maternity ward had only 5 patients or 1 nurse for every patient. Instead of the nurses on the maternity ward making an effort to help the busier nurses on my ward, I was told that they preferred to read magazines.

When I was told that I could go home, it was difficult to find a nurse available to sign me out of the hospital. Fortunately, a trainee nurse, who had been the most helpful of all the nurses during my stay, found a nurse in the lounge room who agreed to come out and sign the necessary papers so that I could leave. As you can appreciate, I had an overall negative reaction towards the surgeon, nurses, and general hospital staff. Interestingly enough, it was not until I returned to the doctor's surgery a week later to have my stitches removed that the doctor gave me a piece of paper that described this type of surgery and explained what to expect afterwards. Of course, this information was irrelevant since the doctor waited to give it to me after my operation had already occurred!

(*Source*: Case prepared by Dr Constance Hill, Department of Management, University of Wollongong)

Case study questions

1. What avenues of redress are open to the consumer whose experiences are described on pages 498–99? Could the Department of Consumer Affairs intercede on the consumer's behalf?

2. The Australian Medical Association is a self-regulatory body for medical practitioners. Assess whether or not this situation is in breach of its Code of Practice.

3. Do you think that the Australian Medical Association's Code of Professional Conduct responds to the consumer rights described on pages 466 and 468?

SUGGESTED READING

F. Zumbo, G. d'Arville and S. Leaver, *The Marketers Compliance Manual*, CCH Australia, 1993.

ENDNOTES

1. H. B. Thorelli, 'Consumer Information as Consumer Protection', in J. Cady (ed.), *Marketing and the Public Interest*, Marketing Science Institute, Cambridge, Mass., 1978, pp. 269–90. H. B. Thorelli, 'Consumer Rights and Consumer Policy: Setting the Stage', *Journal of Contemporary Business*, Autumn 1978, pp. 3–16. H. B. Thorelli, 'Co-determination for Consumers', *Business Horizons*, Vol. 23, No. 4, Aug. 1980, pp. 269–90. H. B. Thorelli, 'The Future for Consumer Information Systems', in J. Olsen et al., *Advances in Consumer Research*, 8, Association for Consumer Research, Ann Arbor, Mich., 1980, p. 222.

2. P. Murphy and G. Laczniak, 'Marketing Ethics: A Review with Implications for Managers, Educators and Researchers', in B. Enis and K. J. Roering (eds), *Review of Marketing*, American Marketing Association, Chicago, 1981. 'AMA Adopts New Code of Ethics', *Marketing Educator*, Fall 1987, pp. 251–66.

3. J. Farrel, 'Cracking Down on Coupon Fraud', *Marketing Week*, 12 June 1989. R. E. Wilkes, 'Fraudulent Consumer Behaviour', *Journal of Marketing*, Vol. 42, 1978, pp. 67–75. R. Dewolf, 'Consumers Aren't All Angels Either', *DuPont Context*, Nov. 1973, pp. 9–10. N. Zabriskie, 'Fraud by Consumers', *Journal of Retailing*, Vol. 48, 1972, pp. 22–27. A. D. Cox, D. Cox and G. P. Moschis, 'When Consumer Behaviour Goes Bad: An Investigation of Adolescent Shoplifting', *Journal of Consumer Research*, Vol. 17, 1990, pp. 526–30. M. A. Jolson, 'Consumers as Offenders', *Journal of Business Research*, Vol. 2, 1974, pp. 89–98.

4. W. G. Magnuson and J. Carper, 'Caveat Emptor', in D. A. Aaker and G. Day (eds), *Consumerism — Search for the Consumer Interest*, The Free Press, New York, 1982, pp. 267–78.

5. D. H. Borchardt, 'Check-List of Royal Commissions, Select Committees and Boards of Enquiry', La Trobe University Library, Bundara, 1975.

6. J. C. Boland, 'The Nader Crusade: The Anti-Business Lobby is Alive and Kicking', *Barron's*, Vol. 61, No. 41, 1981. R. Nader, 'The Price of Liberty is Eternal Vigilance', *Association Management*, Vol. 34, No. 10, 1982.

7. D. A. Aaker and G. Day (eds), *Consumerism — Search for the Consumer Interest*, The Free Press, New York, 1982. R. O'Herrmann, 'Consumerism: Its Goals, Organisations, and Future', *Journal of Marketing*, Oct. 1970, pp. 55–60. L. Berry,

'Marketing Challenges in the Age of the People', *MSU Business Topics*, Vol. 20, No. 1, Winter 1972. G. Borrie, 'Consumerism — The Final Word', *Marketing* (UK), Jan. 1978. R. M. Gaedeke and W. W. Etcheson, *Consumerism*, Canfield Press, San Francisco, 1972. D. Jobber, 'Consumerism: The Public's Awareness of their Rights', *European Journal of Marketing*, Vol. 13, No. 3, 1979. R. Layton and G. Holmes, 'Consumerism — A Passing Malaise or a Continuing Expression of Social Concern', *The Australian Quarterly*, Vol. 46, No. 2, June 1974, pp. 12–19.

8. 'Message from the President of the United States Relative to Consumers' Protection and Interest Program', Doc. No. 364, House of Representatives, 87th Congress, March 1962. 'Coming a Rush of New Consumer Safety Rules', *U.S. News and World Report*, July 1977.

9. J. Saee, 'Consumerism: Its Implications for Marketing in the 1990s', *Journal of the Home Economic Association of Australia*, Vol. 23, March 1991, pp. 7–9.

10. J. Box, 'The Power of Consumer Organisations', *European Journal of Marketing*, Vol. 16, No. 6, 1982, pp. 24–35. P. Kotler, 'Megamarketing' *Marketing*, The Duskin Publishing Group, Annual Edition, No. 4, 1989, pp. 23–29. 'Many Consumers Trust Activists More Than They Do Business People', Sentry Insurance Co. Study, *Marketing News*, Vol. 11, No. 2, 1977, p. 10.

11. Australian Federation of Consumer Organisations, *Strategic Plan 1992–1995*, 1993.

12. 'Consumers' Choice' — 25 Years of the Australian Consumers Association, 1984. Australian Consumers Association Annual Reports 1982–1984. *Consumer Protection in NSW: Its Development and Directions*, Department of Consumer Affairs, 1993.

13. M. Ragg, 'Paté Sales Spread Thinly in Slump', *The Australian*, 2 Nov. 1987.

14. P. Dunstan, 'Industry Needs to Communicate Better', *Australian Financial Review*, 22 Oct. 1985.

15. J. Goldring et al., *Consumer Protection Law in Australia*, Butterworth, Melbourne, 1987.

16. T. Wicks, *The Subject Index to the Acts and Regulations of N.S.W.*, The Law Book Company, Sydney, 1984.

17. *Trade Practices Act*: Part IV Sections 45 to 51; Part VI Sections 75b to 87; Part VI Sections 80 and 80a.

18. *Trade Practices Act*: Part VI Section 82; Part V Sections 52 to 72a.

19. The Consumer Affairs Bureau in Queensland introduced legislation in 1989 to amalgamate the *Consumer Affairs Act 1979–89, Door to Door (Sales) Act 1966–1973, Unordered Goods and Services Act 1973–1989, Mock Auctions Act 1973*.

20. Trade Practices Commission, *Annual Report*, 1992–93, Appendix 3, p. 131, Inquiries and Complaints Statistics, AGPS, Canberra, 1993.

21. The Ministry of Consumer Affairs in Victoria has a consumer support program and publications such as the *Fairplay Magazine*, *Price Action* quarterly newsletter, the *Renting Right Kit*, the Bottom Line Radio News Service and various other services. The Prices Surveillance Authority publishes a quarterly magazine called *Price Probe* and is engaged in considerable media work. There is also a range of independent publications such as the *Mackay Reports* published by Mackay Research: *Value for Money*, Sept. 1991, *Greater Customer Loyalty*, June 1992.

22. Negotiations may become a more important feature in the future. Elizabeth Jurman notes that applications to the Consumer Claims Tribunals have dropped by 36 per cent since the fees were increased from $10 to $40. E. Jurman, 'Consumer Gripes Fall as Tribunal Fees Rise', *Financial Review*, 27 Feb. 1993.

23. Australian Standards Association, Annual Reports 1987–1992.

24. See the *Trade Practices Act*, Sections 62 and 63. There are also numerous provisions in each of the states and territories providing for the declaration of product standards and in particular for the declaration of standards in relation to the wholesomeness and purity of foods and drugs. For example, the NSW *Sale of Goods Act 1923*, the South Australian *Manufacturers Warranties Act 1974*, the Queensland *Consumer Affairs Act 1970* and the *Weights and Measures Act 1951–1983* (A.C.T.), the *Law Reform (Manufacturers Warranties) Ordinance 1977* and the Victorian *Consumer Affairs Act 1972*.

25. 'Further Flak for Environmental Choice', *Australian Professional Marketing*, Sept. 1992.

26. *Trade Practices Act (Amendment Act) 1986*.

27. Federal Bureau of Consumer Affairs, *Annual Report 1993–94*.

28. 'Goldmark Buys Proud's', *Australian Financial Review*, 22 Sept. 1989. 'Goldmark have Good Potential for Providing Cash Flow', *Australian Financial Review*, 7 Sept. 1981.

29. H. B. Taussig, 'The Thalidomide Syndrome', *Scientific American*, Aug. 1962.

30. V. Royster, 'Regulation Isn't a Dirty Word', *Wall Street Journal*, 9 Sept. 1987. A. R. Andreasen, 'Consumer Behaviour Research and Social Policy', in T. Robertson and H. Kassarjian (eds), *Handbook of Consumer Behaviour*, Prentice-Hall, New York, 1991. M. Gardiner-Jones, 'The Consumer Interest: The Role of Public Policy', *California Management Review*, Vol. 26, Fall 1973. J. Pfeffer and G. R. Salancik, *The External Control of Organisations*, Harper and Row, New York, 1978. M. Shanks, 'The Consumer as Stakeholder and the Implications for Consumer Organisations', *Journal of Consumer Policy*, No. 6, 1983. C. Haney, 'Public Rights and Corporate Social Responsibility: A Profitable Marriage', *Retail Control*, Vol. 48, No. 7, March 1980. M. Williams, 'Environmentally Safe Can Enhance Sales' *Advertising Age*, Vol. 63, June 1992, p. 3. L. Freeman and J. Dagnoli, 'Green Concerns Influence Buying', Survey in *Advertising Age*, Vol. 61, 1990. Lori Kelsor, 'Steak Companies Welcome Consumer's Grilling', *Advertising Age*, Oct. 1985.

31. J. Goldring et al., 'Consumer Protection Law in Australia', Butterworth, Melbourne, 1987.

32. W. Frew, 'Judge Underlines the Burdens of Litigation', *Financial Review*, 15 Oct. 1992.

33. See R. McKean, 'Product Liability: Trends and Implications', *The University of Chicago Law Review*, 1989, pp. 3–63.

34. *About the Advertising Council*, The Media Council, 1993.

35. The Media Council of Australia, *Advertising Code of Ethics (incorporating amendments)*, 30 April 1993.

36. The Media Council Reports, 1988–1992.

37. The Media Council Reports, 1988–1992.

38. D. Anthony, 'What Do Women Want?', *Marketing*, Nov. 1993. C. Lumby, 'Sexist or Sexy?', *The Independent Monthly*, Nov. 1993.

39. *Survey of Consumer Opinion in Australia*, 1987, Watson Ferguson and Co.

40. *Survey of Consumer Opinion in Australia*, ibid.

41. L. Boylen, 'Thumbs Down for TV', *Financial Review*, 23 March 1993.

42. Federal Bureau of Consumer Affairs, *Annual Report 1992*.

43. D. Mercer, 'The Future of Banking', *Banking*, Spring, 1993.

44. R. J. White, 'Banking in the 1990s: Back to Basics', *The Australian Banker*, Oct. 1991. T. J. Valentine, 'Critical Issues Arising Out of the Martin Enquiry', *The Australian Banker*, Feb. 1991, p. 17. 'Banking: The State of Play', *The Australian Banker*, Dec. 1991. M. Ullmer et al., 'Australian Banking — That Was the Year That Was', *The Australian Banker*, Feb. 1992, p. 15. T. L. Valentine, 'Banking: The State of Play', *The Australian Banker*, Feb. 1992, p. 51. W. S. Weerasooria, 'You and Your Bank', *The Australian Banker*, Dec. 1991, p. 329.

45. Banking problems were reported in *Choice* in: September 1990; April 1991; September 1992; November 1992; February 1993.

46. The Australian Banking Ombudsman's Annual Report, 1992–1993.

47. The House of Representatives Standing Committee on Finance and Public Administration, *A Pocket Full of Change*, Australian Government Publishing Service, Canberra, 1991.

48. K. O'Connor, 'Privacy and the Retail Banking Customer', *The Australian Banker*, June 1993, p. 126.

49. Tim Dixon, 'Private Lives', *Consuming Choice*, July 1993, p. 4. 'Privacy Issue Threatens All Database Marketers', *Marketing*, Oct. 1990, p. 34 (see pages 495–96 of this book).

50. Privacy Committee Annual Reports 1990, 1991, 1992, 1993. See also the ICAC Report (Privacy Committee Annual Report, 1991, p. 3).

51. Privacy Committee Annual Reports 1990, 1991, 1992, 1993.

52. See the Rice Kacher Report on Life Industry, June 1993, and The Trade Practice Commission, The National Consumer Affairs Council and The Senate Select Committee on Superannuation 1993.

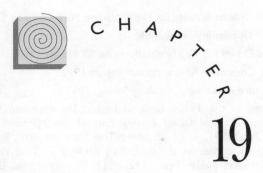

C H A P T E R

19

Concluding issues in consumer behaviour

INTRODUCTION

Since the 1950s, consumer behaviour has developed a substantial body of knowledge and is now a significant area of study within marketing. During this period, two managerial needs have directed consumer research: to identify consumer segments and to develop viable marketing mix strategies. As a result there is a considerable amount of accumulated information about consumer demographics and other statistics, media and shopping behaviour, attitudes and purchase decisions.[1]

The decision model that emerged in the 1970s conceptualised purchasing as a process consisting of five specific phases:[2]

- problem recognition
- information search
- evaluation
- choice
- outcome.

This is still the dominant paradigm in consumer research. Its success can be attributed to the many practical benefits it gives managers, such as perceptual mapping, product positioning and development, message construction, media selection and sales-incentive planning. The substantial developments in cognitive psychology, particularly in relation to memory and data processing, resulted in a more sophisticated understanding of how consumers process information. One outcome has been the continuing popularity of the consumer decision paradigm.

In recent years a number of events have led to the view that the decision paradigm is too narrow to effectively study the full range of behaviours associated with consumer behaviour. The main reasons for the development of this view are:

- the emergence of post-modernism
- global markets
- relationship marketing
- consumer power.

POST-MODERNISM

Post-modernism is a research approach that studies consumer behaviour from a consumption, as opposed to a buying, perspective. This means that the subject matter of research encompasses not only the buying process but also the way in which people use products in everyday life. As such, researchers can study what products mean to people and their role in shaping and expressing the 'culture' of a society.[3]

Because its focus is on the meaning of products, post-modernism extends the current research perspectives in at least two ways:

- it extends consumer research beyond the purchase act and its immediate outcomes (satisfaction/dissatisfaction) into the realms of product use and consumption
- it forces the acknowledgment that consumers choose products for reasons other than utilitarian ones.

Although there are a number of reasons for the emergence of post-modernism, two shortcomings of the consumer decision paradigm are key contributors. These shortcomings are the preoccupation with conscious knowledge as a driver of behaviour to the exclusion of emotions (the CAB approach), and a presumption that the purchase act is all that constitutes the domain of consumer behaviour. Post-modernists argue that a preoccupation with the belief that 'rational' consumers make choices based on the functional performance (utility factors) of products has created a limited understanding of the purchase act itself and consequently a narrow understanding of consumer behaviour.[4]

CONSUMPTION VERSUS PURCHASE

Marketers know that what consumers do with products (that is, how products are consumed) can impact on future choices. For example, many consumers misuse non-stick cookware. This has a teflon coating which, once scratched, will rust so that the non-stick feature is lost. Instead of using plastic or wooden implements, consumers use metal implements that damage the coating. The outcome is a negative view of the products. The problem for the manufacturer is that there is nothing wrong with the product, but they need to 'train' the user. Also, consumers' attitudes and behaviours in relation to the disposal of products can shape packaging decisions and recycling options for products — for example, you can now trade-in old phones and spectacles as well as cars. These are behaviours which are reasonably easy to identify and to which it is possible to develop appropriate strategic and tactical responses. It is not so easy to identify the symbolic meaning and use of products as, often, consumers are not consciously aware that they use products as symbols.

Consumers can, for example, use products as expressions of their personalities and as memories of significant 'others' and events in their lives such as owning a grandfather's watch. People become attached to products, and children often personalise products such as dolls and stuffed toys — they name them, regard them as friends and keep them as lifelong companions. Understanding how consumers relate to products during use can impact on message content and after-purchase care.

Figure 19.1: The personalisation of a product

According to Meryl Gardner:[5]

> 66 the traditional information processing paradigm enriched our understanding of the cognitive mediators of consumer behaviour and is able to explain much buyer behaviour which takes place. Conventional research, however has neglected the experiential aspects of consumption. 99

Gardner points out that while abandonment of the information processing approach would be self-defeating, supplementing it with a knowledge of consumer emotions would be beneficial. An important task for theorists is the incorporation of the experiential dimension into the information processing paradigm.

Consumer behaviour theory and research techniques are already being influenced by the post-modernists because an increasing number of studies seek to clarify the impact of emotions on decision making. An important task for researchers will be the clarification and classification of emotions. For example, a distinction needs to be made between emotions as antecedent states and emotions produced by the purchase and use of products. The former has implications for understanding how consumers interact with messages and the choices they make.

 # GLOBALISATION

International markets have been a reality for many Australian businesses for some time. This movement towards internationalisation is a global phenomenon. Currently, and in the future, most companies will have to compete globally in order to survive. Michael Porter listed several reasons why businesses will increasingly become global.[6] These are:

- the increasing similarity of countries in terms of communication, distribution and financial channels
- financial markets are becoming more global, with large amounts of money moving across nations
- technological changes in production, communication and distribution have reshaped competition

- reduction in trade barriers has opened up more nations, and therefore, local business, to global competition.

In Australia, the majority of global business activities have taken place at the organisational level, at which businesses sell to businesses, but there is an increasing trend for Australian businesses to enter foreign consumer markets.

Apart from an increased focus on internationalisation (in which firms target a range of countries and develop specific marketing mix strategies for each country), there is an increasing trend towards globalisation. When a company offers a specific marketing mix to all of the countries in which it operates, then the label 'global' marketing is applied. Underpinning global market strategies is the notion that there are 'global consumers' — a group of consumers that transcend national boundaries. In theory, this allows a business to offer a standardised global marketing mix.[7] Whether this is possible in practice has been debated since the early 1980s, but it does seem impossible to completely standardise a marketing mix at the tactical level (implementation). Local factors such as price constraints, differing distribution facilities and regulations and, of course, cultural differences have an impact even though the consumer may be considered to be a global consumer. There is also growing speculation about the existence of a completely homogenised global consumer. Even in the case of global products — such as computers, video recorders and sound equipment — differing customs and regulations will create a need for some localisation of products, packaging, pricing and advertising tactics. For this reason the 'thinking global but acting local' has become a preferred option for most businesses.[8]

GLOBAL ADVERTISING

One issue that has been the focus of discussion and research is that of global versus standardised advertising. Common advertising themes and advertisements have been used by various multinational organisations such as Esso and Coca-Cola. According to Theodore Levitt, the rapid growth of international trade, technology and rising living standards means that basic appeals in messages will work. Commonality of products plus the notion that many consumer motives are the same — for example, the desire to be beautiful, free of pain, healthy and successful — work towards the success of global advertising.[9] In countries where cultures are similar — such as the United States, Canada, Britain, Australia and New Zealand — the viability of global advertising increases.)

Figure 19.2: An example of successful global advertising ('Coca-Cola', 'Coke', the Dynamic Ribbon device, 'Always' and the 'Always' logo are trademarks of the Coca-Cola Company.)

Global advertising is of importance to the Australian advertising industry. Since the deregulation of the advertising environment in 1992, the number of American made advertisements in particular has been increasing steadily.

How this trend will affect marketplace behaviour and what impact it will have on Australian culture is as yet unknown. While it may be cost effective for global organisations to create global advertisements, their messages may not be effective, that is, they may not be producing the correct consumer response.[10]

Made in America

NEIL SHOEBRIDGE

When the rules that cover the screening of foreign television commercials in Australia were changed last year, local television producers howled that our screens would be flooded with imported ads. The flood has not eventuated. What has eventuated is a steady stream of awful ads from the United States, ads that are at best irrelevant and at worst insulting to Australians.

Before the new rules were introduced, only 20% of an individual television commercial's content could be sourced overseas; the rest had to be made locally. Under the new rules, 20% of all ads put to air each year can be imported. In theory, one in five television commercials can be made overseas. At the moment, foreign ads account for about 11% of total television advertising and a much higher percentage of bad television advertising.

Consider the toy marketer Hasbro Inc. Since the rules were changed, Hasbro has introduced a collection of irritating, American-made ads for various toys and games. Most of the ads have been imported complete with American accents. In some cases, Hasbro has changed a jingle or a phrase for the Australian market, with often disastrous results. An ad for the game Yahtzee features a group of people wearing Texan cowboy hats, while the voiceover sings how people in Australia love

playing Yahtzee. Other Hasbro ads feature people with the broadest American accents ever heard on Australian television.

Since last year, the commercial breaks on Australian television screens have been dotted with American accents, phrases and the strangely plastic models favored by American ad agencies. For examples of ads starring models made from American plastic, check out recent commercials for Coca-Cola, Hanes, Pert Plus, McDonald's and Plenitude. Yes, they do look different from Australian models and they are easy to spot.

It is hard to imagine Australian television viewers warming to an ad that is clearly designed to play in Milwaukee rather than Melbourne. Commericals for running shoes that feature obscure, black American rap singers or basketball players appear out of context on Australian screens. Everything about the ads Pizza Hut is running for its new Bigfoot pizza is American: American accent, American lounge room, American teenager, American policeman. The present ad from rival pizza maker Domino's features a white, rap-singing teenager who looks and sounds as if he comes from California. Puhleeze.

There is a clear reason why some marketers are using imported ads: to save money. Toyota, for example, saved

thousands of dollars earlier this year by importing ads for the Lexus car from Los Angeles rather than making the ads here. Several companies that had not used television advertising before the rules changed jumped at the chance to appear on the box: witness the rush of ads promoting new perfume brands such as Joop, L'Egoiste, Obsession and White Diamonds.

Many of the companies that have grabbed ads from overseas appear to have forgotten they are selling to consumers in Australia, not Arkansas. Sticking an Australian voice on an American ad to disguise its origins does not work. In some cases, the scenery and cast of the ad are so glaringly American that the use of an Australian voice-over simply underlines the fact that it is an import.

Imported ads stand out, but for once standing out from the crush of commercials that goes to air every night is not an advantage. Increasingly, Australians are searching for products that are made in Australia. If a local product and an import deliver the same quality, convenience and price, the local product is getting the nod from a growing number of people. How do these consumers react when they see a commercial that is clearly made in America? Not very well.

Business Review Weekly,
1 October 1993

The increasing emphasis on global consumers and consumer markets means that consumer behaviour research will need to focus more on cross-cultural consumption behaviours. Of particular importance will be studies of the differences (and similarities) in the symbolic aspects of products and how exposure to global marketing impacts on existing culturally based differences in consumption.

 # REGULATION AND ETHICS

Increased access to education, training and communication networks has created a more sophisticated consumer; a consumer who is more knowledgeable and more willing to participate in community and special interest group activities. Although there are significant differences across nations, since the 1960s consumers have increased their power in the marketplace. One outcome has been a continuing trend towards marketplace regulation. Another has been an increase in the number of industries that have adopted self-regulation and codes of practice.

In an environment in which consumers are able to influence governments and organisations to adopt both ethical and socially responsible behaviours, how and when consumers do so needs to be understood. This broadens the scope of consumer research into consumer politics, ethics and the pro-active and reactive responses of organisations. Such research is difficult but necessary because this type of consumer behaviour can, and does, affect a company's 'bottom line', a fact recognised by many marketers. Some of the difficulties stem from the nebulous nature of concepts such as 'ethical' and 'socially responsible behaviour'. For example, people have differing ideas of what constitutes ethical behaviour.

Probably the most basic and most common conceptualisation of ethics is the notion of reciprocal rights that is expressed in the term 'do unto others as you would have them do unto you'. This theme has formed the basis of many philosophies and religions for centuries. Essentially, it means that the rights of others are at least equal to your own.[11]

If this perspective is adopted, and expressed in our behaviours, then the issue of unethical behaviour does not arise. But what if your action towards one person damages or disadvantages another? For example, the creation of new roads that leads to the demolition of people's houses. The road will benefit many people but disadvantage a few. In this instance, the 'do unto others' rule has problems. For this reason we often adopt a utilitarian perspective towards ethical behaviour which has as its base the notion of 'the greatest good for the greatest number'. Ethicalness, or moral rightness, is determined by the consequences of the act. The consequences are determined by whether or not there is a net increase of benefits in the society and whether the best means possible have been used to accomplish the act. Some people argue that ethics are determined by the society and that there can be no universal standard. Each culture sets its own ideas of acceptable behaviour that are reflected in individual behaviour.[12]

Understanding the nature of ethical and socially responsible behaviour in our own and different cultures is an old problem, but one that is likely to be the issue for the twenty-first century. So, if a full understanding of the nature of consumer behaviour is to be achieved, consumer researchers will need to study the political and ethical dimensions of consumers in relation to the consumption of goods and services.

 # RELATIONSHIP MARKETING

Relationship marketing refers to the move away from an emphasis on single buyer–seller transactions to a focus on the creation and maintenance of on-going relationships as the key aim of marketing activity. During the 1980s, marketing researchers observed that companies in the industrial and services markets were developing networks of buyer–seller relationships and strategic alliances with each other. The aim of these relationships was not to seek a temporary increase in sales, but to create involvement and product loyalty by building a lasting bond with a customer. This is achieved through the management of the interaction between the individuals involved in the exchange process, rather than the manipulation of the marketing mix variables alone.[13]

In consumer markets there has been a growth of services, an increase in niche markets for certain products and an increased use of direct communication — such as mailing lists — in consumer markets. These factors have led to a focus on the management of the actual relationship between buyer and seller. This means that although product and distribution decisions need to be made so that each transaction is valued, after-purchase communication links with consumers also need to be maintained. This alters the nature of post-purchase behaviour research because it expands the focus beyond the satisfaction/dissatisfaction dimension.

Another factor in the growing relevance of buyer–seller relationship management is the notion that the differences between consumer marketing and industrial marketing may not be all that great. Traditionally, consumer and industrial markets have been considered different. Some of the factors that exist in industrial markets that differentiated them from consumer markets are listed below:

The products:
- are bought less frequently
- are more technically complex
- are bought in bulk
- have a higher service component.

The buyer–seller interactions involve:
- direct communication
- negotiation
- contractual agreements
- direct delivery (and thus fewer 'middlemen').

But today, some of these factors apply equally to certain consumer purchases, such as houses, cars and household durables.[14] With the development of consumer databases and improved telecommunications, direct access to individuals in consumer markets is not only feasible but practised, particularly in the area of services.

RESEARCH METHODOLOGY ISSUES

Essentially, these developments will continue to have an impact not only on consumer behaviour, but also on how information is gathered. In a recent paper, William Wells[15] listed five guidelines to ensure that consumer behaviour as a discipline moves into the future from a position of strength:

1. **Leave home** — consumer behaviour starts with the antecedents of decisions and ends with ecological effects. Consumer choices range from life-altering options (such as houses) to low-level options (such as brands of gum). In the past, too much effort has been spent on researching low-level decisions relating to brand choice. Future research should focus on life-altering decisions such as education, a new home or a new child and on post-purchase choices, that is, what consumers do with products after the purchase and how this use impacts on future decisions. By engaging in this type of research, the study of consumer behaviour will become more valuable to the society as a whole.

2. **Forsake 'mythodology'** — five methodological myths are believed to impede progress. These myths are that:
   - students represent consumers — they do not and they should not be used as respondents
   - the laboratory represents the environment — it does not
   - statistical significance confers real significance
   - suitable disguised correlation becomes causation
   - once confessed, research limitations simply go away.

   These myths do more harm than good. Researchers who forsake them will do more valid work.

3. **Reach out** — business government and foundations and adjacent academic disciplines command data, constructs, methods and perspectives that can enrich our work. Consumer researchers who participate in these resources gain sophistication, range and depth.

4. **Start small and stay real** — the search for abstract, universal theories has not increased our understanding of consumer behaviour. Consumer researchers who ask, 'so what?' about the outcome of every investigation will fulfil the promise that authenticates the field.

5. **Research backwards** — the surest route to an important discovery is to start with a definite objective and work backwards. Researchers who work backwards conserve resources, maintain motivation and produce valuable results.

If researchers rise to the challenges portrayed in these guidelines, not only will the scope and subject of consumer behaviour and research increase, but interesting (and hopefully more accurate and viable) research will eventuate.

SUMMARY

The last three decades have seen a number of developments in consumer behaviour theory and research, which have come about for a number of reasons. We have discussed some of these reasons in this chapter. From within the discipline, the emergence of post-modernist ideas have and will continue to shape how we understand the factors that impact on consumers' purchase behaviour. These ideas have enriched our understanding of consumer behaviour, mainly by expanding our understanding of product usage and by developing product usage research beyond the functional dimension.

An adjunct to post-modernism is a recognition of the totality of each consumer's life, particularly the capacity to influence and control marketplace behaviours that are outside the purchase situation. Understanding how and why consumers, in their roles as citizens, can actively influence governments and other social groups will be an increasingly important area of study for consumer researchers. The increasing focus on the dynamics of the relationship between buyer and seller means that the interaction before and after purchase may lead to interesting research. It is certain that all of these developments will ensure that consumer behaviour will continue to be an interesting and dynamic subject.

Questions

1. Although this chapter describes the similarities between industrial and consumer marketing, can you describe any differences between these two markets?

2. In what circumstances could a 'global' advertisement work in Australia?

3. Discuss the role of consumer education in developing and supporting consumer sovereignty.

4. Identify at least three American advertisements shown on Australian television. State whether you think they would appeal (or not appeal) to Australian viewers. Why?

5. Do you think that a focus on the interaction between buyers and sellers will impact on how well they treat each other?

6. Do you think it is possible for an industry to effectively self-regulate its members? What are some of the practical difficulties of self-regulation? Do you think they can be overcome?

SUGGESTED READING

J. F. Sherry Jr, 'Postmodernism Alternatives: The Interpretive Turn in Consumer Research', in T. Robertson and H. Kassarjian (eds), *Handbook of Consumer Theory and Research*, Prentice-Hall, Englewood Cliffs, NJ, 1991.

G. R. Laczniak and P. Murphy, *Ethical Marketing Decisions: The Higher Road*, Allyn and Bacon, Needham Heights, Mass, 1993.

ENDNOTES

1. M. Wallendorf and G. Zaltman, *Readings in Consumer Behaviour*, (Section One), John Wiley and Sons, New York, 1979. J. G. Helgeson, E. Kluge, J. Mager and C. Taylor, 'Trends in Consumer Behaviour Literature: A Content Analysis', *Journal of Consumer Research*, Vol. 10, 1984.

2. J. Mowen, 'Beyond Decision Making', *Journal of Consumer Marketing*, No. 5, Winter, 1988, pp. 15–25. R. Olshavsky and D. Granbois, 'Consumer Decision Making — Fact or Fiction', *Journal of Consumer Research*, 6, Sept. 1979, p. 98.

3. E. C. Hirschman and M. Holbrook, *Postmodern Consumer Research*, Sage, New-bury Park, Calif., 1992. E. C. Hirschman and P. LaBarbera, 'Dimensions of Possession Importance', *Psychology and Marketing*, 7, Fall, 1990, pp. 215–33. J. F. Sherry, 'Postmodernism Alternatives: The Interpretive Turn in Consumer Research', in Thomas Robertson and H. Kassarjian (eds), *Handbook of Consumer Theory and Research*, Prentice-Hall, Englewood Cliffs, NJ, 1991.

4. C. J. Thompson, W. B. Locander and H. R. Pollio, 'Putting Consumer Experience Back into Consumer Research: The Philosophy and Method of Existential-Phenomenology', *Journal of Consumer Research*, Vol. 16, Sept. 1989, pp. 133–46.

5. M. Gardener, 'Mood States and Consumer Behaviour: A Critical Review', *Journal of Consumer Research*, No. 12, 1985, pp. 113–15.

6. M. Porter, *Competitive Strategy Techniques for Analysing Industries and Competitors*, Free Press, New York, 1982.

7. T. Levitt, 'The Globalization of Markets', *Harvard Business Review*, May/June 1983, pp. 92–102. A. R. Andreasen, 'Cultural Interpenetration: A Critical Consumer Research Issue for the 1990s', *Advances in Consumer Research*, Vol. 17, 1990, pp. 148–60. J. J. Boddewyn, R. Soehl and J. Picard, 'Standardization in International Marketing: Is Ted Levitt in Fact Right?', *Business Horizons*, Nov./Dec. 1986, pp. 69–75. J. A. Costa, 'Toward an Understanding of Social and World Systemic Process in the Spread of Consumer Culture', *Advances in Consumer Research*, Vol. 17, 1990, pp. 168–76. P. Kotler, 'And the Walls Came Down', *Journal of Marketing*, Feb. 1991, pp. 10–19. R. D. Buzzell, 'Can You Standarise Multinational Marketing?', *Harvard Business Review*, Nov./Dec. 1968, pp. 102–13. J. M. Carmen and M. M. March, 'How Important for Marketing are Cultural Differences Between Similar Nations?', *Australian Marketing Researcher*, Vol. 3, Summer, 1978–79, pp. 5–20. J. Whitelock and D. Chung, 'Cross Cultural Advertising: An Empirical Study', *International Journal of Advertising*, No. 8, 1989, pp. 291–309.

8. N. Shoebridge, 'The New Guard of Marketing Prepares to Sweep In', *Business Review Weekly*, 17 May 1991, pp. 156–60.

9. T. Levitt, op. cit. (see note 7).

10. A. C. Fatt, 'The Danger of Local "International Advertising"', *Journal of Marketing*, 31, 1967, pp. 60–62. A. T. Shao, L. P. Shao and D. H. Shao, 'Are Global Markets with Standardised Advertising Campaigns Feasible?', *Journal of International Marketing*, No. 4, 1992, pp. 32–39.

11. M. Valasques, *Business Ethics: Concepts and Cases*, Prentice-Hall, Englewood Cliffs, NJ, 1982. G. J. Warnock, *Contemporary Moral Philosophy*, Macmillan, London, 1967. M. Warnock, *Ethics Since 1900*, Oxford University Press, London, 1966.

12. N. Gifford, *When in Rome: An Introduction to Relativism and Knowledge*, Albany Press, New York, 1983.

13. M. Christopher, A. Payne and D. Ballantyne, *Relationship Marketing: Bringing Quality Consumer Service and Marketing Together*, Butterworth Heinemann, Oxford, 1991.

14. E. Fern and J. Brown, 'The Industrial/Consumer Marketing Dichotomy: A Case of Insufficient Justification', *Journal of Marketing*, Vol. 48, Spring 1984, pp. 68–77.

15. W. Wells, 'Discovery-oriented Consumer Research', *Journal of Consumer Research*, Vol. 19, March 1973, pp. 489–504.

Index